Data Entry and Validation with C# and VB .NET Windows Forms

NICK SYMMONDS

Apress™

Data Entry and Validation with C# and VB .NET Windows Forms

Copyright © 2003 by Nick Symmonds

ISBN (pbk): 1-59059-108-9

Printed and bound in the United States of America 12345678910

Technical Reviewer: Adriano Baglioni

Editorial Board: Dan Appleman, Craig Berry, Gary Cornell, Tony Davis, Steven Rycroft, Julian Skinner, Martin Streicher, Jim Sumser, Karen Watterson, Gavin Wright, John Zukowski

Assistant Publisher: Grace Wong

Project Manager: Beth Christmas

Copy Editor: Nicole LeClerc

Production Manager: Kari Brooks

Proofreader: Linda Siefert

Compositor: Susan Glinert Stevens

Indexer: Rebecca Plunkett

Artist: April Milne

Cover Designer: Kurt Krames

Manufacturing Manager: Tom Debolski

Distributed to the book trade in the United States by Springer-Verlag New York, Inc., 175 Fifth Avenue, New York, NY, 10010 and outside the United States by Springer-Verlag GmbH & Co. KG, Tiergartenstr. 17, 69112 Heidelberg, Germany.

In the United States: phone 1-800-SPRINGER, email orders@springer-ny.com, or visit http://www.springer-ny.com. Outside the United States: fax +49 6221 345229, email orders@springer.de, or visit http://www.springer.de.

For information on translations, please contact Apress directly at 2560 Ninth Street, Suite 219, Berkeley, CA 94710. Phone 510-549-5930, fax 510-549-5939, email info@apress.com, or visit http://www.apress.com.

The source code for this book is available to readers at http://www.apress.com in the Downloads section.

For Celeste. You are the love of my life.

Contents at a Glance

Contents

About the Author

Nick Symmonds started out his professional life as an electronics technician. While getting his bachelor's degree in electrical engineering from the University of Hartford, he started to gravitate toward programming. Nick has spent quite a few years programming in assembly, C, C++, and VB. Recently, he has latched onto .NET like a lamprey and loves digging into the .NET core. Nick has written several articles on programming and has two books currently out: *Internationalization and Localization Using Microsoft .NET* (Apress, 2002) and *GDI+ Programming in C# and VB .NET* (Apress, 2002). He works for the Security and Safety Solutions division of Ingersoll-Rand, developing and integrating security software.

Nick lives with his family in the northwest hills of Connecticut and enjoys golfing, biking, and exploring the hills on his motorcycle.

About the Technical Reviewer

Adriano Baglioni got his first taste of computers as a freshman in high school, using BASIC on a PDP-11/70. He pursued his interest in computers at Rensselaer Polytechnic Institute (RPI), where he graduated with a bachelor's degree in computer and systems engineering. He followed that up with a master's degree in computer science, also from RPI. He has worked in the computer industry for 20 years, programming mostly in C and C++. His experience runs the gamut from embedded programming on 8051s to scientific programming on mainframes. He currently works at Veeder-Root Co., developing software for environmental monitoring equipment.

When it's time to take a break from the computer, Adriano enjoys hiking, biking, and camping with his wife, Carol.

Acknowledgments

THIS IS MY THIRD BOOK for Apress. Each time it becomes more enjoyable. The level of professionalism within this company is unparalleled. Thanks to Beth Christmas for keeping me on track as my project manager. Nicole LeClerc did a wonderful job again as copy editor. I can't believe how fast you do what you do. Thanks to all those at Apress who helped and advised me on this book.

Special thanks go out to Adriano Baglioni. Without his technical review comments, this book would not be nearly as good as it is. It was a pleasure working with you again.

Introduction

ANYONE WHO HAS EVER worked with a computer has had to enter data into it somehow. Anyone who has done any Windows programming (or DOS programming, if you go back far enough) has had to write data entry screens. What is data entry without some kind of validation?

Then again, what is validation? *Validation* is the process of the receiving data (via the keyboard, the mouse, voice, serial connections, and so on) and making sure that the data meets the specifications you have laid out. For instance, if you are looking for a number but receive a character, your validation code would ignore that character.

I wrote this book because it encompasses pretty much what most Windows programmers do on a day-to-day basis. As programmers, we all work with data. We collect it, massage it, store it, retrieve it, and present results back to the user. As a matter of fact, data entry and validation are likely such constant themes throughout your programming day that I bet you don't even realize you're doing them.

When most new programmers think of data entry, they think "Booooring!" What often comes to mind are endless screens of text-based data entry fields for insurance companies. Where is the fun in that? After all, there is no chance for any creativity and after a few weeks of this kind of work, life becomes dull. It seems like assembly-line programming at its worst.

Data Entry Code Can Be Interesting

Is data entry and validation really this simple and dull? I think not. If it were, I would have changed professions long ago.

Data entry involves two aspects. One is to collect data and the other is to make sure the data makes sense. The fun part is how you go about programming it.

If you think that writing screen after screen of data entry fields is boring, how do you think end users feel using these screens? I would say they feel even more bored. Your job as a programmer here is twofold. First, you need to make the data entry screens not so boring to use, and second, you need to make the screens not so boring to program. An additional task is to make the screens sensible. The only thing worse to a user than an uninteresting program is a frustrating one. How many times have you used a program and had to hunt down certain data fields in screens where they don't belong? You tend to wonder, what were they thinking?! Perhaps you have received some feedback like this about your own program.

Who Should Read This Book

This book is for intermediate and well-seasoned programmers who are already writing in .NET or want to change over to .NET. I assume a level of programming knowledge commensurate with a basic understanding of .NET and a good understanding of programming in general. Readers should know some object-oriented and general programming techniques such as the following:

- Function overloading

- Inheritance

- Class design and instantiation

- Use of threads and the advantages (and pitfalls) of threading

- Exception handling

Readers should also be familiar with some of the .NET-specific topics such as the following:

- Garbage collection

- JIT compiler

- Organization of the .NET namespaces

Why You Should Read This Book

Take a look through your friendly local bookstore's computer book section. You will find quite a few books about .NET. They all seem to fall somewhere in the following categories:

- Books on everything you could possibly know about C# in 1,500 pages (ditto for Visual Basic .NET [VB .NET])

- Books outlining how to do a specific task within .NET, such as writing an ASP page

- All kinds of books about the .NET Framework and the philosophy behind it

- Books for all the "idiots" and "dummies" who write the majority of our computer programs

Basically what you will see are "task" books. Rarely will you see a book devoted to a programming specialty that requires knowledge of quite a few tasks along with interesting uses of the .NET Framework and good general practices. Some examples of task book topics that I have seen are as follows:

- Programming games in .NET

- Writing scientific programs in .NET

- Writing a scalable client/server program in .NET

If you think about some specialties, you may need several books just to get all the information you need to accomplish what you do every day. This book isn't a task book; it's a programming specialty book. In it you will find information on subjects such as

- Programming graphics

- Programming Windows Forms

- Using localization

- Using XML

- Building user controls

I cover quite a few other topics as well. You see, by including these few subjects in this book, I've saved you from buying five other books. Granted, I don't go into great depth on any of these items, but by the time you finish reading this book, you'll be familiar with them and know how to use them. Isn't that what you're really interested in, anyway?

What Makes This Book Unique

Visual Studio .NET is not new anymore. Since the product's release in early 2002, Microsoft has been evangelizing the advantages of .NET, Web services, and just moving ahead in the programming game in general.

You probably already have a couple of books on .NET.[1] Perhaps you have written a program or two just to try things out and kick the tires a little. My local

---

1. Perhaps you have one of my previous books on .NET: *GDI+ Programming in C# and VB .NET* or *Internationalization and Localization Using Microsoft .NET*.

bookstore has multiple shelves filled with books on .NET. What distinguishes this book from the others is the application-oriented aspect. As I have stated, I present an end result here that you may not see in other books.

You will see quite a few techniques in this book that you can surely find elsewhere. However, instead of showing you how to program mouse events, for example, I show you how to program mouse events within the context of the all-important data entry screen.

You might consider this book a consolidation of best practices for getting the most out of the .NET Framework with an eye toward the user interface and data validation. Knowing a technique is not the same as knowing how to apply it. This book teaches you how to better apply what you probably do on a daily basis, but within the context of .NET.

What You Will Get Out of This Book

As with my last two books, I decided to include all examples in both C# and VB .NET. I like to do this because it appeals to a wider audience, and it also lets you see what the differences are between C# and VB when you are programming the same task. You will also see how C# and VB .NET really do use the same underlying framework to accomplish the same tasks. As a developer, I feel that this is one of the most awesome advantages to come out of .NET as a whole.

As far as the Framework goes, you will see quite a bit of it in the chapters ahead. Think about all the things necessary for a good data entry screen. Here is some of what you will see:

- Determining which controls to use and when

- Writing a world-ready program

- Creating graphics using the GDI+ namespaces

- Threading

- Using collection classes

- Understanding accessibility issues

- Deciding which type of document interface to use

- Performing everyday data validation

- Extending controls

- Creating custom data validation controls

- Using error handling

- Understanding XML and hardware I/O

Being able to create friendly and usable data entry screens is not really taught in schools or even treated as a subject in most books. This book tries to remedy that situation and get you on the road to writing an effective program.

A Word About the Examples

I encourage you to enter at least some of the examples by hand in both languages. I feel it is good to be familiar with the two flagship languages of .NET: VB .NET and C#. You will see some cases where VB is better than C# and some cases where C# is better for a particular task than VB.

For those of you who want to run the examples without the pain of writing them, you can download all the code from the Downloads section of the Apress Web site (http://www.apress.com).

All the examples in this book have gone through a thorough review process. They are not professional-level, robust products, but they should work as intended. I take responsibility for all programming errors in this book. If you find an error, please let me know about it and I will post the corrected code on the Apress Web site. You can reach me at nicksymmonds@attbi.com.

Some Points About the Code

The code that I wrote for the examples follows some simple guidelines. I describe those guidelines here so you will know what to expect and where to find certain code sections.

Designating Events

I like to know what is happening in my code and I also like to be able to control it. There is quite a bit of functionality in the IDE that allows you to automatically handle events or assign event handlers using the IDE. As far as VB .NET goes, you can get an event handler for a certain control by double-clicking the control. The IDE will generate the event shell for you similar to VB 6.0. This consists of the event handler procedure name followed by the event it handles. It looks like this:

```
Private Sub cmdClose_Click(ByVal sender As System.Object, _
                        ByVal e As System.EventArgs) Handles cmdClose.Click
```

The C# IDE does much the same thing, except that it creates a delegate for you and assigns the delegate within the "Windows Form Designer generated code" section.

I do not use this method of programming for events for the following reasons:

- The IDE will choose the name of my event handler. I can change it later, but in the case of C# I need to dig through the "Windows Form Designer generated code" section to find the delegate assignment.

- Using VB, you cannot remove or change the event handler assignment at runtime.

You are also able to assign event handlers for C# using the IDE directly. You can do this by assigning handler names in the Properties screen of the IDE, as shown in Figure 1.

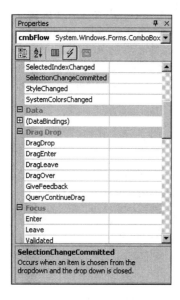

Figure 1. Assigning event handlers via the Properties screen

Although this is all well and good, it has two problems:

- The delegate assignment is done in the "Windows Forms Designer generated code" section.

- If you delete the control, the event handler code still remains.

Here is what I prefer to do. If I know at design time what I need, I assign all my event handlers in the constructor. This puts them all in one place, one right after the other.

For VB code, I use the AddHandler command to assign delegates to events. This allows me to assign multiple events to one handler, and it also allows me to use RemoveHandler later in the code to remove a delegate from handling an event.

Compartmentalizing Code

I like to use regions. I use a section at the top of each class to hold all the class local variables. I put all the mouse handling events in their own region. I like to put all class properties in their own region.

Using regions is a great way to partition your code and see only the section of code that you are working on.

Included Code

When I provide code in this book, I usually do not include the "Windows Form Designer generated code" region. I instead put a marker to note where this section belongs.

This section contains all the stuff the IDE puts in your code that concerns the controls on your form. It also has the Dispose method for both C# and VB. The constructor for VB is in this section as well, but the C# constructor is not.

Anyway, if you are typing in the project as I describe, the IDE will fill in this code for you. Including it is a waste of paper.

It is time to turn the page and start programming. I hope that you will find this book interesting and gain some insights that help you in your career.

CHAPTER 1

The .NET Data Entry Controls

THIS CHAPTER COVERS the controls that most of you are familiar with. In fact, I am willing to bet that you work with many of these controls on a daily basis. Perhaps you did not know this. For instance, did you know that the TextBox, ComboBox, Button, and so forth all have the built-in capability to let you validate what the user is doing at a given moment? In fact, many controls allow you to tailor what data the user can enter so you do not even have to validate. This chapter covers many of these controls.

When I first started programming in Visual Basic (VB) as a young lad, I used the TextBox for just about every type of user input. However, I did not set up the TextBox to do much of the validation work for me. I relied on my own code to do this. This chapter shows you how to use the TextBox and other controls to do much of the validation for you.

If you have done any user interface programming at all, I am sure you are familiar with many of these controls. If you are a VB 6.0 veteran and are just starting out in .NET, you will find that many of the familiar controls now have some pretty interesting additional functionality. Much of this functionality has to do with how the user enters data and how you validate it.

Validation Defined

I should first explain what I mean by "validation" when it comes to the basic controls. There are quite a few things you need to keep in mind when setting up fields in a form. Here are some considerations to make when you use TextBoxes and other free-form data entry controls:

- Is the user allowed in this field?

- Should the field be numeric or alpha, or both?

- If the field is numeric, what are the bounds?

- Is there a minimum length to the field?

- Is there a maximum length to the field?

- Should control characters be allowed?

- Are there any other characters that are not allowed?

- Should the field be validated on a character-by-character basis or when the user leaves the field?

- Will there be multiple lines to this field?

Believe it or not, .NET provides controls that actually allow you to set up many of these parameters as control properties without your even writing any validation code. Let's look at some of the validation events. In the following sections, I outline some of the most commonly used controls.

Every visible control that can be written to can let you know when it is time to perform any validation. Two events are raised concerning validation:

- *Validating:* This occurs when the control tells you it needs validation.

- *Validated:* This occurs when the control thinks you are finished validating.

There is also a Boolean property called CausesValidation that, if set to false, suppresses these two events.

The validation events are considered *focus events*. The focus events occur when a control either gets the focus of attention on a form or loses it. These events occur in a certain order that lets you determine when you want to validate. The order is as follows:

- *Enter:* The cursor has entered the control.

- *Focus:* The control has gained focus of the keyboard and mouse.

- *Leave:* The input focus is leaving the control.

- *Validating:* The control is currently validating.

- *Validated:* The control is done validating.

- *Lost Focus:* The control has completely lost focus.

If you capture the Validating event, your delegate can either let the subsequent events go on or suppress them. You would suppress subsequent events if your validation code indicated a failure.

I cover validation events in more detail later in this chapter.

The Simple Data Entry Controls

In this section, I start with the most basic property of any of the controls derived from the Control base class, the Text property. If you are familiar with .NET, you know that everything is derived from some object and its lineage can be traced back to the original System.Object base class. This includes all the data entry controls.

For you VB 6.0 programmers who are new to .NET, this may seem a little daunting. After all, the TextBox is just there. The same is true for the Label and ComboBox. You probably never knew—or considered—that these controls derived from anything. VB 6.0 hides quite a bit of the plumbing from the programmer.

 NOTE   The VB 6.0 label text field is the Caption property. The VB 6.0 text box text field is the Text property. The fact that these two are named differently yet serve the same purpose may lead you to believe that in VB 6.0 they are not the same control with slightly different behaviors (as in .NET). The TextBox and Label controls in .NET both have the same Text property. This is because they derive from the same base class.

The Base Control

The .NET Framework has a particular base class called System.Windows.Forms.Control. This class is responsible for quite a bit of the functionality of the following derived controls:

- Button
- DataGrid
- GroupBox
- ListView
- ListControl
- TreeView
- Label

- TextBox
- DateTimePicker
- MonthCalendar
- ScrollableControl

These are just a few of the controls that derive from the base control. I cover some of the other controls, such as the PictureBox and Splitter controls, in Chapter 5.

What these controls give you that VB 6.0 does not is a sense of continuity and behavioral predictability. After all, they share many of the same properties, methods, and events.

So, now you know how the major controls are derived from a base control and how the Text property (and many others) is the same for all of these. If you scan the .NET help files on some of these controls, you will find properties that are inherited from the Control base class and some that are peculiar to the control itself. I encourage you to look at the help for a particular control. If you pick a property that is derived from a parent class, you will be able to trace the control through its lineage back to the Control class. You can go back further even to the base Object class.

If you are not familiar with inheritance and such, you will find this quite eye-opening. You may even wonder if you can make your own TextBox or Button controls. This is a good thing to wonder about because the answer is yes. As a matter of fact, I take you through how to extend one of these controls to make your own application-specific control in Chapter 8.

So far I have mentioned what I think simple data validation is. Pretty soon I present a small example that shows how to use some simple validation rules. In the next section, however, I want to touch on data entry.

Simple Data Entry

When most people think of data entry, they think again of the TextBox. This is probably the most used control on a form. In fact, if you want to really make the user work at it, you could make the TextBox the only data entry control on a form. There are a few other controls, though, that you may not think of right away as data entry controls. I have already mentioned some of them in the list of controls derived from the Control class (see the sidebar "The Base Control").

For instance, how about the GroupBox? How can you use this control for data entry? It doesn't do anything, right? Well, it can do two things. It can group controls together so that the user sees controls with common functionality in one place. It also does another important thing regarding RadioButtons.

Normally, RadioButtons are mutually exclusive controls with respect to each other. What do I mean by this? Suppose you have four RadioButtons on a form. Anytime one of the RadioButtons is clicked, its Checked property is set to true. When this happens, all the other RadioButtons on the form are automatically unchecked. Only one RadioButton can be checked at a time.

Putting a RadioButton in a GroupBox separates it programmatically from RadioButtons that are outside of the GroupBox. A RadioButton that is inside a GroupBox can be checked at the same time that a RadioButton outside the GroupBox is checked. Figure 1-1 shows how this looks.

Figure 1-1. A form showing how RadioButtons can be grouped

While I'm on the subject of GroupBoxes and RadioButtons, the RadioButton is a great data entry control. You may not think of it in those terms, but judicious use of RadioButtons allows you to give valid choices to users that they can't screw up. As far as validation goes, this is the perfect control. The user can only choose what you want him or her to.

You will normally use the RadioButton when you know the data that the user will need to choose during design time. Its practicality is also limited to only a few choices on a page, really. Hundreds of RadioButtons on a single page can be rather overwhelming. I once tried out some software where the programmer was obviously enamored with the VB RadioButton. It was a terminal emulation program. Figure 1-2 shows what part of the modem configuration screen looked like.

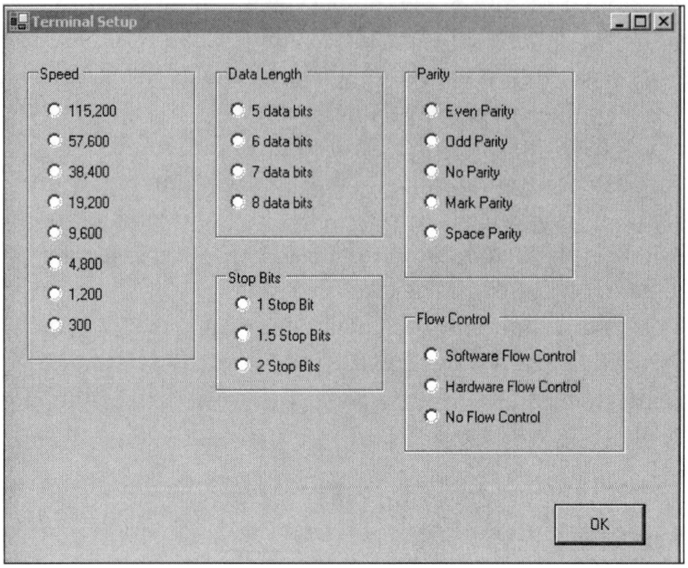

Figure 1-2. A busy RadioButton screen

Figure 1-2 shows a partial screen as I remember it. Anyway, my point here is that this screen is overloaded with RadioButtons. The screen may be foolproof, but the number of choices seems daunting and it is difficult to tell at a glance just what the communications port is set for.

There is another problem with using RadioButtons in this manner. Can you guess what it is? The screen is hard-coded for only these values. Suppose, as a programmer, you wanted to use a serial port that was capable of speeds of 28.8Kbps. You would need to change the screen and recompile the program.

A better way to present these particular choices is via ComboBoxes. Figure 1-3 shows this same port configuration screen using ComboBoxes.

This is a much better way to present the various choices to the user. The screen is succinct and these controls do not allow the user to make strange choices.[1] When the user clicks the OK button, you can run some code that determines if the values the user chose make sense.

Now suppose your serial port was tweaked to provide greater speed than your choices allow. If you filled each ComboBox with entries from an external file such as an .ini file, there would be no screen changes necessary to add an entry to or delete an entry from one of these ComboBoxes. If you plan ahead and think about how each screen of your program works, you can usually make things easier for yourself down the line from a maintenance perspective.

---

1. Well, yes they can, but this is where data validation comes into play.

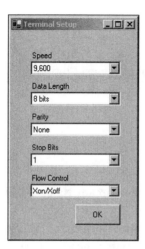

Figure 1-3. An alternate terminal setup

NOTE Be careful about how many items you have in your ComboBox. The .NET help file states that the maximum is 100. If you allow a user to type in new values, you will get an exception if the number of values exceeds the maximum. Granted, most users would not do this, but I guarantee that your friendly test engineer will.

Simple Validation

So now you have your two terminal setup screens and the user has made his or her choices and has clicked the OK button. What now?

Let's start with the RadioButton screen. There is really no on-the-fly validation that you can effectively use for this screen. In the click event handler for the OK button, you will need to write some code to see if the choices the user made are correct. Usually this entails plenty of if-then blocks and various sanity checks. If something is wrong, you need to pop up an error message that tells the user what is wrong and how to fix it.

The problem with this approach is that you could go back and forth, with the user making changes and you rejecting them. Wouldn't it be better to force the user to choose only those values that make sense?

This is where the second form comes in. What you can do here is on-the-fly validation that is easy for you and unobtrusive to the user. Here are the basic steps:

1. Disable all the ComboBoxes except for the first one. Also disable the OK button.

2. When the user makes a choice, fill in the values for the next ComboBox and enable it.

3. Repeat step 2 until all the choices are made.

4. Enable the OK button.

By the time the user gets to click the OK button, you have already validated all the choices and there is probably no need to point out any errors to the user.

The best way to demonstrate this is to create an example. The example in this section is fairly simple, but it serves to explain how you can steer the user toward certain data choices. Once the choices are made, you can be sure they are correct and there is no need to validate them.

This example includes the coded screen shown in Figure 1-3. To make the process a little easier, I limit the scope of finished serial port setup choices to the following. They are shown here as speed, data length, parity, and stop bits.

- 9600, 7, odd, 1

- 9600, 7 even, 2

- 9600, 8, none, 1

- 4800, 6, mark, 1

- 4800, 7, space, 1

- 4800, 7, space, 2

- 2400, 5, odd, 1

- 2400, 5, even, 1

- 2400, 5, even, 1.5

- 2400, 6, odd, 1

In reality there are many more choices, but limiting this program to these choices serves the example's purposes.

A Simple Validation Example

First of all, start a new C# or VB program project and call it "SerialPort." Follow these steps to create the form:

1. Add a Label and change its text to **Speed**.

2. Add a ComboBox below the Label and name it **cmbSpeed**.

3. Add a Label below the ComboBox and change its text to **Data Length**.

4. Add a ComboBox below the preceding Label and name it **cmbLen**.

5. Add a Label below the preceding ComboBox and change its text to **Parity**.

6. Add a ComboBox below the preceding Label and name it **cmbParity**.

7. Add a Label below the preceding ComboBox and change its text to **StopBits**.

8. Add a ComboBox below the preceding Label and name it **cmbStop**.

9. Add a Label below the preceding ComboBox and change its text to **Flow Control**.

10. Add a ComboBox below the preceding Label and name it **cmbFlow**.

11. Add a Button to the bottom of the form and call it **cmdClose**. Change its text to **Close**.

12. Set the form's start-up position to Center Screen.

Figure 1-3 shows what this form looks like. Listings 1-1a and 1-1b contain the code for this terminal setup program.

NOTE   I usually do not show the Windows Form Designer–generated code for the C# examples. There is nothing extraordinary in this code. The VB examples show only the constructor and dispose methods contained in the "Windows Form Designer generated code" section of the code. The missing code is noted by ellipses on three consecutive lines.

Listing 1-1a. C# Code for the Terminal Setup Program

```csharp
using System;
using System.Drawing;
using System.Collections;
using System.ComponentModel;
using System.Windows.Forms;
using System.Data;

namespace SerialPort
{
  /// <summary>
  /// For example purposes this is the list of possibilities.
  /// 9600,7,o,1
  /// 9600,7,e,2
  /// 9600,8,n,1
  /// 4800,6,m,1
  /// 4800,7,s,1
  /// 4800,7,s,2
  /// 2400,5,o,1
  /// 2400,5,e,1
  /// 2400,5,e,1.5
  /// 2400,6,o,1
  /// Any type of flow control
  /// </summary>

  public class Form1 : System.Windows.Forms.Form
  {
    private System.Windows.Forms.Label label1;
    private System.Windows.Forms.ComboBox cmbSpeed;
    private System.Windows.Forms.ComboBox cmbLen;
    private System.Windows.Forms.Label label2;
    private System.Windows.Forms.ComboBox cmbParity;
    private System.Windows.Forms.Label label3;
    private System.Windows.Forms.ComboBox cmbStop;
    private System.Windows.Forms.Label label4;
    private System.Windows.Forms.ComboBox cmbFlow;
    private System.Windows.Forms.Label label5;
    private System.Windows.Forms.Button cmdClose;

    private System.ComponentModel.Container components = null;
```

```csharp
public Form1()
{

  InitializeComponent();

  this.StartPosition = FormStartPosition.CenterScreen;

  //Handle the click events for each combo box
  cmbSpeed.SelectedIndexChanged  += new EventHandler(this.Speed);
  cmbLen.SelectedIndexChanged    += new EventHandler(this.DataLen);
  cmbParity.SelectedIndexChanged += new EventHandler(this.Parity);
  cmdClose.Click                      += new EventHandler(this.CloseMe);

  cmbSpeed.DropDownStyle = ComboBoxStyle.DropDownList;
  cmbSpeed.Items.Add("9,600");
  cmbSpeed.Items.Add("4,800");
  cmbSpeed.Items.Add("2,400");
  cmbSpeed.SelectedIndex=0;

  cmbFlow.DropDownStyle = ComboBoxStyle.DropDownList;
  cmbFlow.Items.Add("NONE");
  cmbFlow.Items.Add("XON/XOFF");
  cmbFlow.Items.Add("HARDWARE");
  cmbFlow.SelectedIndex = 0;

}

protected override void Dispose( bool disposing )
{
  if( disposing )
  {
    if (components != null)
    {
      components.Dispose();
    }
  }
  base.Dispose( disposing );
}

#region Windows Form Designer generated code
...
...
...
#endregion
```

```
[STAThread]
static void Main()
{
  Application.Run(new Form1());
}

private void Form1_Load(object sender, System.EventArgs e)
{
}

#region Click events

private void Speed(object sender, EventArgs e)
{
  switch (cmbSpeed.Text)
  {
    case "9,600":
      cmbLen.Items.Clear();
      cmbLen.Items.Add("7 Bits");
      cmbLen.Items.Add("8 Bits");
      break;
    case "4,800":
      cmbLen.Items.Clear();
      cmbLen.Items.Add("6 Bits");
      cmbLen.Items.Add("7 Bits");
      break;
    case "2,400":
      cmbLen.Items.Clear();
      cmbLen.Items.Add("5 Bits");
      cmbLen.Items.Add("6 Bits");
      break;
    case "1,200":
      cmbLen.Items.Clear();
      cmbLen.Items.Add("8 Bits");
      break;
  }
  cmbLen.SelectedIndex = 0;
}

private void DataLen(object sender, EventArgs e)
{
  switch (cmbLen.Text)
  {
    case "5 Bits":
```

```
      if (cmbSpeed.Text == "2,400")
      {
        cmbParity.Items.Clear();
        cmbParity.Items.Add("ODD");
        cmbParity.Items.Add("EVEN");
      }
      break;
    case "6 Bits":
      if (cmbSpeed.Text == "4,800")
      {
        cmbParity.Items.Clear();
        cmbParity.Items.Add("MARK");
      }
      if (cmbSpeed.Text == "2,400")
      {
        cmbParity.Items.Clear();
        cmbParity.Items.Add("ODD");
      }
      break;
    case "7 Bits":
      if (cmbSpeed.Text == "9,600")
      {
        cmbParity.Items.Clear();
        cmbParity.Items.Add("ODD");
        cmbParity.Items.Add("EVEN");
      }
      if (cmbSpeed.Text == "4,800")
      {
        cmbParity.Items.Clear();
        cmbParity.Items.Add("SPACE");
      }
      break;
    case "8 Bits":
      if (cmbSpeed.Text == "9,600")
      {
        cmbParity.Items.Clear();
        cmbParity.Items.Add("NONE");
      }
      break;
  }
  cmbParity.SelectedIndex = 0;
}
```

```csharp
private void Parity(object sender, EventArgs e)
{
  switch (cmbParity.Text)
  {
    case "NONE":
      if (cmbLen.Text == "8 Bits")
      {
        cmbStop.Items.Clear();
        cmbStop.Items.Add("1");
      }
      break;
    case "ODD":
      if (cmbLen.Text == "5 Bits")
      {
        cmbStop.Items.Clear();
        cmbStop.Items.Add("1");
      }
      if (cmbLen.Text == "6 Bits")
      {
        cmbStop.Items.Clear();
        cmbStop.Items.Add("1");
      }
      if (cmbLen.Text == "7 Bits")
      {
        cmbStop.Items.Clear();
        cmbStop.Items.Add("1");
      }
      break;
    case "EVEN":
      if (cmbLen.Text == "5 Bits")
      {
        cmbStop.Items.Clear();
        cmbStop.Items.Add("1");
        cmbStop.Items.Add("1.5");
      }
      if (cmbLen.Text == "7 Bits")
      {
        cmbStop.Items.Clear();
        cmbStop.Items.Add("2");
      }
      break;
```

```
        case "SPACE":
          if (cmbLen.Text == "7 Bits")
          {
            cmbStop.Items.Clear();
            cmbStop.Items.Add("1");
            cmbStop.Items.Add("2");
          }
          break;
        case "MARK":
          if (cmbLen.Text == "6 Bits")
          {
            cmbStop.Items.Clear();
            cmbStop.Items.Add("1");
          }
          break;
      }
      cmbStop.SelectedIndex = 0;
    }

    private void CloseMe(object sender, EventArgs e)
    {
      this.Close();
    }

    #endregion
  }
}
```

Listing 1-1b. VB Code for the Terminal Setup Program

```
'/// For example purposes this is the list of possibilities.
'/// 9600,7,o,1
'/// 9600,7,e,2
'/// 9600,8,n,1
'/// 4800,6,m,1
'/// 4800,7,s,1
'/// 4800,7,s,2
'/// 2400,5,o,1
'/// 2400,5,e,1
'/// 2400,5,e,1.5
'/// 2400,6,o,1
'/// Any type of flow control
```

```vbnet
Public Class Form1
  Inherits System.Windows.Forms.Form

#Region " Windows Form Designer generated code "

  Public Sub New()
    MyBase.New()

    'This call is required by the Windows Form Designer.
    InitializeComponent()

    Me.StartPosition = FormStartPosition.CenterScreen

    'Handle the click events for each combo box
    AddHandler cmbSpeed.SelectedIndexChanged, AddressOf Speed
    AddHandler cmbLen.SelectedIndexChanged, AddressOf DataLen
    AddHandler cmbParity.SelectedIndexChanged, AddressOf Parity
    AddHandler cmdClose.Click, AddressOf CloseMe

    cmbSpeed.DropDownStyle = ComboBoxStyle.DropDownList
    cmbSpeed.Items.Add("9,600")
    cmbSpeed.Items.Add("4,800")
    cmbSpeed.Items.Add("2,400")
    cmbSpeed.SelectedIndex = 0

    cmbFlow.DropDownStyle = ComboBoxStyle.DropDownList
    cmbFlow.Items.Add("NONE")
    cmbFlow.Items.Add("XON/XOFF")
    cmbFlow.Items.Add("HARDWARE")
    cmbFlow.SelectedIndex = 0


  End Sub

  'Form overrides dispose to clean up the component list.
  Protected Overloads Overrides Sub Dispose(ByVal disposing As Boolean)
    If disposing Then
      If Not (components Is Nothing) Then
        components.Dispose()
      End If
    End If
    MyBase.Dispose(disposing)
  End Sub
```

...
...
...
```vb
#End Region

  Private Sub Form1_Load(ByVal sender As System.Object, _
                          ByVal e As System.EventArgs) Handles MyBase.Load
  End Sub

  Private Sub Speed(ByVal Sender As Object, ByVal e As EventArgs)

    Select Case (cmbSpeed.Text)
      Case "9,600"
        cmbLen.Items.Clear()
        cmbLen.Items.Add("7 Bits")
        cmbLen.Items.Add("8 Bits")
      Case "4,800"
        cmbLen.Items.Clear()
        cmbLen.Items.Add("6 Bits")
        cmbLen.Items.Add("7 Bits")
      Case "2,400"
        cmbLen.Items.Clear()
        cmbLen.Items.Add("5 Bits")
        cmbLen.Items.Add("6 Bits")
      Case "1,200"
        cmbLen.Items.Clear()
        cmbLen.Items.Add("8 Bits")
    End Select
    cmbLen.SelectedIndex = 0

  End Sub

  Private Sub DataLen(ByVal Sender As Object, ByVal e As EventArgs)

    Select Case (cmbLen.Text)

      Case "5 Bits"
        If cmbSpeed.Text = "2,400" Then
          cmbParity.Items.Clear()
          cmbParity.Items.Add("ODD")
          cmbParity.Items.Add("EVEN")
        End If
```

```
          Case "6 Bits"
            If cmbSpeed.Text = "4,800" Then
              cmbParity.Items.Clear()
              cmbParity.Items.Add("MARK")
            End If
            If cmbSpeed.Text = "2,400" Then
              cmbParity.Items.Clear()
              cmbParity.Items.Add("ODD")
            End If
          Case "7 Bits"
            If cmbSpeed.Text = "9,600" Then
              cmbParity.Items.Clear()
              cmbParity.Items.Add("ODD")
              cmbParity.Items.Add("EVEN")
            End If
            If cmbSpeed.Text = "4,800" Then
              cmbParity.Items.Clear()
              cmbParity.Items.Add("SPACE")
            End If
          Case "8 Bits"
            If cmbSpeed.Text = "9,600" Then
              cmbParity.Items.Clear()
              cmbParity.Items.Add("NONE")
            End If
        End Select
        cmbParity.SelectedIndex = 0

    End Sub

    Private Sub Parity(ByVal Sender As Object, ByVal e As EventArgs)

        Select Case (cmbParity.Text)
          Case "NONE"
            If cmbLen.Text = "8 Bits" Then
              cmbStop.Items.Clear()
              cmbStop.Items.Add("1")
            End If
          Case "ODD"
            If cmbLen.Text = "5 Bits" Then
              cmbStop.Items.Clear()
              cmbStop.Items.Add("1")
            End If
```

```
        If cmbLen.Text = "6 Bits" Then
            cmbStop.Items.Clear()
            cmbStop.Items.Add("1")
        End If
        If cmbLen.Text = "7 Bits" Then
            cmbStop.Items.Clear()
            cmbStop.Items.Add("1")
        End If
      Case "EVEN"
        If cmbLen.Text = "5 Bits" Then
            cmbStop.Items.Clear()
            cmbStop.Items.Add("1")
            cmbStop.Items.Add("1.5")
        End If
        If cmbLen.Text = "7 Bits" Then
            cmbStop.Items.Clear()
            cmbStop.Items.Add("2")
        End If
      Case "SPACE"
        If cmbLen.Text = "7 Bits" Then
            cmbStop.Items.Clear()
            cmbStop.Items.Add("1")
            cmbStop.Items.Add("2")
        End If
      Case "MARK"
        If cmbLen.Text = "6 Bits" Then
            cmbStop.Items.Clear()
            cmbStop.Items.Add("1")
        End If
    End Select
    cmbStop.SelectedIndex = 0

  End Sub

  Private Sub CloseMe(ByVal Sender As Object, ByVal e As EventArgs)

    Me.Close()

  End Sub
End Class
```

You can see from the code that I set up the form such that the user can choose any type of flow control he or she wants. It is a different story, however, when it comes to the other choices.

Starting with the chosen speed, I fill in the other drop-down boxes according to only what is allowed considering the other values. This is a great way to handle both data input and data validation at the same time. When the user finishes making his or her choices and clicks the Close button, I already know that the user's choices are valid. There is no need for any error messages or corrections by the user because he or she is allowed to choose only what I allow.

Be careful when you create a form that is validated on the fly in this manner. If you have more than a few ComboBoxes and quite a large choice matrix, you will soon enter programmers' hell.

The Lowly TextBox

At the start of this chapter I wrote that the TextBox is a control that I use very often for data input. I imagine that you have also used it for all kinds of data input tasks. Here are a few things I can think of that I have used the TextBox for:

- Alpha input only

- Numeric input only

- Alphanumeric input with some restrictions

- Date input

- Copy/paste input from the Clipboard

Fortunately, the TextBox control has quite a few properties that you can use to set up data validation as the user is typing in values. For instance, you can limit the length of the string that this box will hold. This validation property is an easy one and requires no length validation by you. Another easy one is AcceptsReturn.

Now this AcceptsReturn property is one that I wish were in the VB 6.0 TextBox control. What this allows you to do is tell the TextBox to accept the Enter key as a valid character (in a MultiLine TextBox) or activate the default button on the form. Many times in VB 6.0 I have written code to automatically click the OK button on a form if the user presses the Enter key while typing in a TextBox. The AcceptsReturn property in the .NET TextBox means I do not have to write any code anymore to do this.

NOTE   The AcceptsReturn property *only* works with a MultiLine TextBox, *only* when you set the AcceptButton property of the form to a valid Button, and *only* when the AcceptsReturn property of the MultiLine TextBox is set to false. If these three conditions are not true, then pressing the Enter button in a MultiLine TextBox will create a new line. If the form does not have an AcceptButton assigned, pressing Enter in any single-line TextBox does nothing. Assigning an AcceptButton to the form automatically activates the AcceptButton you assigned whenever you press the Enter key in any single-line TextBox.

Here is a list of properties that you can assign to a TextBox to help in data entry and validation:

- AcceptsReturn

- AcceptsTab

- AllowDrop

- CanFocus

- CharacterCasing

- MaxLength

- MultiLine

- PasswordChar

- TextAlign

- WordWrap

Now these are just values you can set that frame the TextBox for your particular use. You can take advantage of quite a few other properties, methods, and events for data entry restriction purposes. Before I get into using the TextBox events for data entry restriction and validation, I want to demonstrate some simple things you can do with a TextBox to encourage or force data entry restrictions on the user.

Listings 1-2a and 1-2b show a form with several TextBoxes, a ComboBox, and a Button. The only thing I do as far as the code is concerned is change some properties of the TextBoxes to alter their behavior a little. This example shows how easy .NET makes this type of task.

First, create a new C# or VB project. Mine is called "TextBox_c" for C# users and "TextBox_VB" for VB users. You should note that using a keyword as a namespace can wreak havoc with your program. Be careful what you call your programs. Add the following controls:

1. Add a Label and change its text to **Max Text Length**.

2. Add a ComboBox below the Label and name it **cmbMaxLen**.

3. Add a Label and change its text to **Upper Case**.

4. Add a TextBox and call it **txtUpper**.

5. Add a Label and change its text to **Password**.

6. Add a TextBox and call it **txtPassword**.

7. Add a Label and change its text to **Centered**.

8. Add a TextBox and call it **txtCentered**.

9. Add a Label and change its text to **Multi Line**.

10. Add a TextBox and call it **txtMultiLine**. Set its MultiLine parameter to true and make it big enough to handle a few lines of text.

11. Add a Button and call it **cmdClose**. Change its text to **Close**.

Your form should look like the one shown in Figure 1-4.

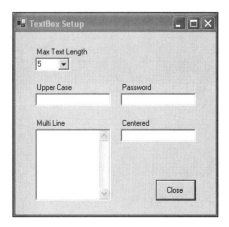

Figure 1-4. The form setup for the TextBox example

Listings 1-2a and 1-2b show the code for this example. The only thing I make note of during the running of the program is the text length. You are able to choose the text length and it will be applied to all the TextBoxes except for the MultiLine TextBox.

Listing 1-2a. C# Code for the TextBox Setup Example

```csharp
using System;
using System.Drawing;
using System.Collections;
using System.ComponentModel;
using System.Windows.Forms;
using System.Data;

namespace TextBox_c
{
  /// <summary>
  /// This project shows how to set up the TextBox to perform some elementary
  /// text entry validation
  /// </summary>
  public class Form1 : System.Windows.Forms.Form
  {
    private System.Windows.Forms.Label label1;
    private System.Windows.Forms.ComboBox cmbMaxLen;
    private System.Windows.Forms.Button cmdClose;
    private System.Windows.Forms.Label label5;
    private System.Windows.Forms.Label label6;
    private System.Windows.Forms.Label label7;
    private System.Windows.Forms.TextBox txtUpper;
```

```csharp
    private System.Windows.Forms.TextBox txtPassword;
    private System.Windows.Forms.TextBox txtCentered;
    private System.Windows.Forms.Label label8;
    private System.Windows.Forms.TextBox txtMultiLine;

    private System.ComponentModel.Container components = null;


    public Form1()
    {
      InitializeComponent();

      cmbMaxLen.Items.Clear();
      cmbMaxLen.Items.Add("5");
      cmbMaxLen.Items.Add("10");
      cmbMaxLen.Items.Add("15");
      cmbMaxLen.Items.Add("20");
      cmbMaxLen.SelectedIndexChanged += new EventHandler(this.ChangeLen);
      cmbMaxLen.SelectedIndex = 0;

      txtUpper.CharacterCasing = CharacterCasing.Upper;
      txtPassword.PasswordChar = '*';
      txtCentered.TextAlign = HorizontalAlignment.Center;
      txtMultiLine.Multiline = true;
      txtMultiLine.ScrollBars = ScrollBars.Vertical;
      txtMultiLine.WordWrap = true;
      txtMultiLine.AcceptsReturn = true;
      txtMultiLine.AcceptsTab = true;

      this.AcceptButton = cmdClose;
      cmdClose.Click += new EventHandler(this.CloseMe);

    }

  protected override void Dispose( bool disposing )
  {
    if( disposing )
    {
      if (components != null)
      {
        components.Dispose();
      }
    }
```

```
    base.Dispose( disposing );
  }

#region Windows Form Designer generated code
...
...
...
#endregion

    [STAThread]
    static void Main()
    {
      Application.Run(new Form1());
    }

    private void Form1_Load(object sender, System.EventArgs e)
    {
    }

    #region control events

    private void ChangeLen(object sender, EventArgs e)
    {
      txtUpper.MaxLength = Convert.ToInt32(cmbMaxLen.Text);
      txtPassword.MaxLength = txtUpper.MaxLength;
      txtCentered.MaxLength = txtUpper.MaxLength;
    }

    private void CloseMe(object sender, EventArgs e)
    {
      this.Close();
    }

    #endregion

  }
}
```

Listing 1-2b. VB Code for the TextBox Setup Example

```
Public Class Form1
    Inherits System.Windows.Forms.Form
```

```
#Region " Windows Form Designer generated code "

    Public Sub New()
    MyBase.New()

    'This call is required by the Windows Form Designer.
    InitializeComponent()

    cmbMaxLen.Items.Clear()
    cmbMaxLen.Items.Add("5")
    cmbMaxLen.Items.Add("10")
    cmbMaxLen.Items.Add("15")
    cmbMaxLen.Items.Add("20")
    AddHandler cmbMaxLen.SelectedIndexChanged, AddressOf Me.ChangeLen
    cmbMaxLen.SelectedIndex = 0

    txtUpper.CharacterCasing = CharacterCasing.Upper
    txtPassword.PasswordChar = "*"c
    txtCentered.TextAlign = HorizontalAlignment.Center
    txtMultiLine.Multiline = True
    txtMultiLine.ScrollBars = ScrollBars.Vertical
    txtMultiLine.WordWrap = True
    txtMultiLine.AcceptsReturn = True
    txtMultiLine.AcceptsTab = True

    Me.AcceptButton = cmdClose
    AddHandler cmdClose.Click, AddressOf Me.CloseMe

    End Sub

#End Region

  Private Sub Form1_Load(ByVal sender As System.Object, _
                         ByVal e As System.EventArgs) Handles MyBase.Load
  End Sub

#Region "control events"

  Private Sub ChangeLen(ByVal sender As Object, ByVal e As EventArgs)
    txtUpper.MaxLength = Convert.ToInt32(cmbMaxLen.Text)
    txtPassword.MaxLength = txtUpper.MaxLength
    txtCentered.MaxLength = txtUpper.MaxLength
  End Sub
```

```
Private Sub CloseMe(ByVal sender As Object, ByVal e As EventArgs)
    Me.Close()
End Sub

#End Region

End Class
```

Start fooling around with the fields in this form and you will see that certain restrictions have been placed on data entry. Click in the Centered TextBox and then press the Enter key. You will see that the form unloads. This is because I made the form's default AcceptButton the Close button. Each TextBox has its AcceptsReturn value set to false except for the MultiLine TextBox. I set this TextBox in the constructor to accept the Enter key. Normally in VB 6.0, I would have had to write code to do this.

NOTE   By the way, did you try tabbing through the controls? You should because this is a very common way to get from one control to another without using the mouse. Why allow for no mouse? After all, we are in the twenty-first century here and Windows programs have been out for many years now. The answer is speed. Anyone who uses a program for any length of time tends to find the easiest way to enter data. It is your job to facilitate that. Correct tab order of controls is one way to do this.

When I tab through my program, I go from one control to another, but not in the order I want. Add the following code to the constructor of your program.

C#

```
cmbMaxLen.TabIndex = 0;
txtUpper.TabIndex = 1;
txtPassword.TabIndex = 2;
txtMultiLine.TabStop = false;
txtCentered.TabIndex = 3;
cmdClose.TabIndex = 4;
```

VB

```
cmbMaxLen.TabIndex = 0
txtUpper.TabIndex = 1
txtPassword.TabIndex = 2
txtMultiLine.TabStop = False
txtCentered.TabIndex = 3
cmdClose.TabIndex = 4
```

Note that I turned off the tab stop for the MultiLine control. This is because I want the tab to be used as a real tab in this TextBox. Because it would be impossible to tab out of it, there is no reason to tab into it.

Another Level of Complexity

OK, that was admittedly easy. What you will do now is enhance the form with validation code that is contained in event handlers. This lets you extend the data entry restrictions on the fly. You can prevent the user from typing in just about anything you want while he or she is typing. This takes a little more know-how and also a little more thought.

Add a few more controls to your TextBox project form:

1. Add a Label and change its text to **Alpha**.

2. Add a TextBox and call it **txtAlpha**.

3. Add a Label and change its text to **Number**.

4. Add a TextBox and call it **txtNumber**.

5. Add a Label and change its text to **Mixed**.

6. Add a TextBox and call it **txtMixed**.

Your newly redecorated form should look like Figure 1-5.

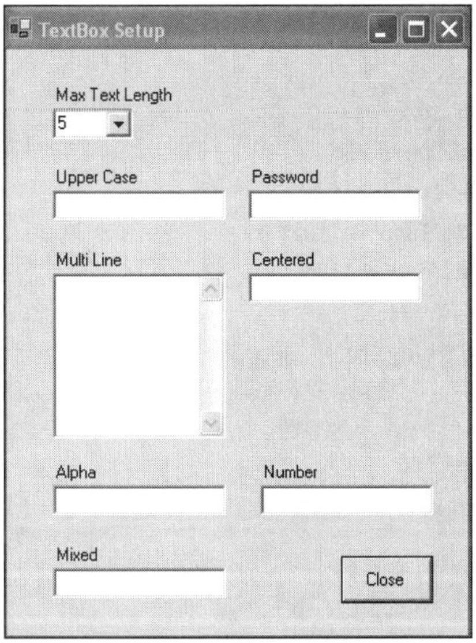

Figure 1-5. New controls on the TextBox form

As you can probably guess, you are allowing only letters (uppercase) in the Alpha box and only numbers in the Number box. The Mixed box will contain the following:

A–F

0–9

<

>

=

The way to do this is to capture the KeyPress event of the TextBox. You can also do this with the KeyDown event if you want. In your constructor, add the following lines of code.

C#

```
//Event based input restricted controls
txtAlpha.CharacterCasing = CharacterCasing.Lower;
txtMixed.CharacterCasing = CharacterCasing.Upper;
txtAlpha.KeyPress  += new KeyPressEventHandler(this.InputValidator);
txtNumber.KeyPress += new KeyPressEventHandler(this.InputValidator);
txtMixed.KeyPress  += new KeyPressEventHandler(this.InputValidator);
```

VB

```vb
'Event based input restricted controls
txtAlpha.CharacterCasing = CharacterCasing.Lower
txtMixed.CharacterCasing = CharacterCasing.Upper
AddHandler txtAlpha.KeyPress, AddressOf Me.InputValidator
AddHandler txtNumber.KeyPress, AddressOf Me.InputValidator
AddHandler txtMixed.KeyPress, AddressOf Me.InputValidator
```

Add the following code to the ChangeLen delegate.

C#

```csharp
txtAlpha.MaxLength = txtUpper.MaxLength;
txtNumber.MaxLength = txtUpper.MaxLength;
txtMixed.MaxLength = txtUpper.MaxLength;
```

VB

```vb
txtMixed.MaxLength = txtUpper.MaxLength
txtNumber.MaxLength = txtUpper.MaxLength
txtAlpha.MaxLength = txtUpper.MaxLength
```

Now add the following event handler to the bottom of your form's code.

C#

```csharp
private void InputValidator(object sender, KeyPressEventArgs e)
{
  TextBox t;
  if(sender is TextBox)
  {
    t = (TextBox)sender;
    if (t.Name == txtAlpha.Name)
    {
      //If it is not a letter then disallow the character
      if(!Char.IsLetter(e.KeyChar) && e.KeyChar != (char)8 )
        e.Handled = true;
    }
    if (t.Name == txtNumber.Name)
    {
```

```csharp
        //If it is not a letter then disallow the character
        if(!Char.IsNumber(e.KeyChar) && e.KeyChar != (char)8 )
          e.Handled = true;
      }
      if (t.Name == txtMixed.Name)
      {
        //Allow only 0-9,A-F,<>?=
        if(Char.IsNumber(e.KeyChar))
          e.Handled = false;
        else if(Char.ToUpper(e.KeyChar)>='A' && Char.ToUpper(e.KeyChar)<='F' )
          e.Handled = false;
        else if(e.KeyChar=='<' || e.KeyChar=='>' ||
         e.KeyChar=='?' || e.KeyChar=='=')
          e.Handled = false;
        else
          e.Handled = true;
      }
    }
  }
```

VB

```vb
  Private Sub InputValidator(ByVal sender As Object, _
                             ByVal e As KeyPressEventArgs)
    Dim t As TextBox
    If sender.GetType() Is GetType(TextBox) Then
      t = CType(sender, TextBox)
      If t.Name = txtAlpha.Name Then
        'If it is not a letter then disallow the character
        If (Not Char.IsLetter(e.KeyChar) And _
              e.KeyChar <> Microsoft.VisualBasic.ChrW(8)) Then
          e.Handled = True
        End If
      End If
      If t.Name = txtNumber.Name Then
        'If it is not a letter then disallow the character
        If (Not Char.IsNumber(e.KeyChar) And _
              e.KeyChar <> Microsoft.VisualBasic.ChrW(8)) Then
          e.Handled = True
        End If
      End If
```

```
    If t.Name = txtMixed.Name Then
      'Allow only 0-9,A-F,<>?=
      If (Char.IsNumber(e.KeyChar)) Then
        e.Handled = False
      ElseIf (Char.ToUpper(e.KeyChar) >= "A"c And _
              Char.ToUpper(e.KeyChar) <= "F"c) Then
        e.Handled = False
      ElseIf (e.KeyChar = "<"c Or e.KeyChar = ">"c Or _
              e.KeyChar = "?" Or e.KeyChar = "="c) Then
        e.Handled = False
      Else
        e.Handled = True
      End If
    End If
  End If
End Sub
```

You can see that you are allowing only uppercase letters in the mixed TextBoxes. You can also see that you are assigning the same delegate to handle each control's KeyPress events.

 TIP You can handle events from many different sources with one delegate. That is why the delegate definition includes the Sender object. You use this object as I have to find out who sent the event.

If you read the code carefully, you will find what seems to be redundant code. Do you see it?

You are setting the CharacterCasing for the Mixed control to uppercase. However, in the delegate you are converting the character to uppercase before you test to see if it is between "A" and "F" inclusive. Why should you change case twice? The answer is because you are handling the key press before Windows is. The .NET control has not had a chance to change the case of the key press to uppercase yet, so you need to. Setting the Handled property of the KeyPressEventArgs object to true tells .NET not to bother with this key press. In essence, it throws it away. VB 6.0 had this same type of functionality by setting its KeyAscii value in the KeyPress event to 0.

I think that you will see as I do that restricting data entry is often the best way to actually validate user input. No error checking or error messages are needed.

NOTE   I want to switch gears here for a second and talk about the syntax for the InputValidator code you just entered.

Those of you coming from a C or C++ background may find the VB code a little overblown. It seems as if you need to do a bit more coding in VB to achieve the same result as in C#. Having written in extensively in all four languages, I can say that in general this is true. Those of you coming from a VB 6.0 background may see the C# code as a little on the terse and confusing side. If you think this is true, try C++ with all its pointers.

Anyway, if you look a little deeper into both routines, you will see that they are essentially the same. They do not just perform the same functionality, but they use many of the same commands. With very few exceptions, you can do the exact same things in VB as you can in C#. This is the beauty of the .NET Framework. This, I think, is what truly distinguishes .NET from other development platforms. You can leverage all the disparate language talents of your programming team on the same project.

A Look at Other Data Entry Controls

So far you have been introduced to the ComboBox and TextBox controls. You have seen how to control input specifications from one control by what is chosen in another. You have also been introduced to some of the TextBox properties and events to control what the user inputs.

You may be thinking that this is all you need. Although you could obviously make some simple data entry screens with just these two controls, you would be missing out on providing a much richer user experience by using other data entry controls.

I think an introduction to the other controls is in order here.

The Button Control

You see this control all the time. Usually, it is relegated to calling up help, canceling a process, or completing a process. So what are its data entry uses?

- You can put a picture on a Button and use it as a way to let the user jump to another data screen. An example would be a zip code lookup table.

- You can use a Button as an intermediate acceptance device. If the user clicks the Button, some fields may become disabled or enabled depending on the value in another field.

- Often you have very complicated validation rules that preclude on-the-fly validation. You can use a Button to start the validation process.

Though the Button can be a multipurpose control, you may want the user to see some visual cues when he or she clicks it. The folks at Microsoft took a good look at the CheckBox and RadioButton and saw that these two controls are really buttons with some fancier display properties. If you look at the MSDN help, you will see that both the CheckBox and the RadioButton derive from the Button class.

The CheckBox Control

You can use this control in a list to allow the user to choose values within that list. CheckBoxes are not mutually exclusive within the same parent control.

Suppose you have a set of nicely segregated data entry screens in a program. If the program is fairly complex, you will probably want to allow some users to have access to some screens and other users to have access to other screens. You could easily use CheckBoxes to allow an administrator to check off which screens are allowed for which users.

You can also use a CheckBox to indicate a binary property. Such a property would be true/false, yes/no, default/unique, and so on. Using a CheckBox in this manner allows you to use a single control for two states of a property. This is not the case for the RadioButton, however.

The RadioButton Control

This control is very similar to a CheckBox in that it provides a visual cue to the user as to just what he or she has chosen. The similarities end there, though. The RadioButton is a mutually exclusive device within the same parent control.

Remember Figure 1-1, where I showed a grouping of controls? I placed several RadioButtons on the form. Some of them, however, are within a GroupBox. The RadioButtons that are outside the GroupBox are mutually exclusive with each other but not with those contained in the GroupBox. The same is true for the RadioButtons within the GroupBox.

RadioButtons should always come in multiples. This is because clicking a RadioButton always sets its value to true. You can never turn it off by clicking it again. The only way to do this is to choose another RadioButton.

Although you can use two RadioButtons to indicate a binary choice, this is a waste of a control. You are better off using a CheckBox.

The DateTimePicker and MonthCalendar Controls

These two controls go hand in hand. Many times you will need to ask for a date from a user. Perhaps you will need a way to activate and deactivate an alarm system using a PC program.

The MonthCalendar control is actually pretty cool. You can change its look to suit your needs, and you can personalize it to display certain dates in bold. The main reason for using the MonthCalendar is to allow the user to visually select a date or range of dates. Of course, selecting a range of dates can be somewhat problematic because it requires quite a bit more validation. For those times when you need the user to select only a single date, the DateTimePicker is a better choice.

You can configure the DateTimePicker to show either time or date, or some custom format. If you configure it as a date control, you can have a drop-down calendar appear for the user to select from. If you configure it as a time control, you can have the user click an integrated spin button to choose the time. Of course, the user can also type in the date or time if he or she wants.

One thing to note about the calendar controls is that they are locale sensitive. This means that if you have the current thread's culture set to Russian, then your calendar will show dates in Russian also. This is pretty cool. Figure 1-6 shows what these controls look like to the user.

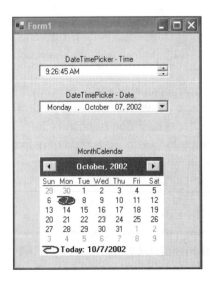

Figure 1-6. Date and time controls

The ToolBar and Menu Controls

These controls are what the user uses as his or her first attempt at navigating your program. These controls also represent the user's first shot at trying to find out how to do something. A good portion of your design process should be involved with setting up the menu and toolbar (if you have them).

If you are a VB 6.0 veteran, you know how frustrating menu design can be. There is no chance to create a menu at runtime, and right-click pop-up menus (context menus) are a real pain to work with in multiple-document interface (MDI) forms. .NET has a really nice menu system that you can add to, delete from, and change at runtime. Also, the context menu system is a breath of fresh air for VB programmers.

To my mind, all good programs include at least a basic toolbar. The toolbar takes the most common tasks a user will perform and assigns them to buttons. These buttons have pictures on them so the user can see at a glance what each button does.

I expand on the menu and toolbar issue in a later chapter on user interface design. I do want to say this, though: If you are writing a Windows program, your menu system should follow the Windows generic menu layout as much as possible. The person who uses your program will expect to find certain functionality in certain areas in the menu. For instance, if you were to put the top-level Help menu choice at the far left of the screen and the top-level File menu choice at the far right of the screen, you would confuse and anger more than a few people.

The TreeView and ListView Controls

These are some of my favorite data entry controls. I know what you are thinking: These controls are just a neat way to display data and they are not good for much else, right? Wrong.

Let's take the TreeView. Used wisely, this control can show an enormous amount of information in a very compact space. It shows data in a hierarchical manner that helps you easily see relationships between different objects. For instance, suppose you want to show a list of streets in a town. You could have five drop-down boxes starting with country, then state, then county, then town, and then street. You could do this easily on a form, but switching between locations is not so intuitive.

Now think about showing this information in a hierarchical fashion using a TreeView control. What the user sees is pretty much the whole database of streets on one screen. Traversing the tree to a different street is very intuitive. Figure 1-7 shows two ways to view streets.

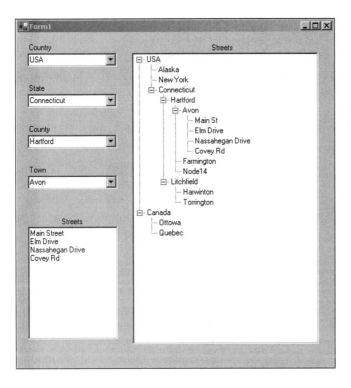

Figure 1-7. Viewing data via a TreeView versus viewing data via ComboBoxes

You can use the ListView control to show data in one of several formats. You can show data via icons (large or small), in single-line record format, or in table format. Just like in Windows Explorer, where you can change the data display format, the ListView allows you to change its format at runtime.

Now so far I have explained the TreeView and ListView controls from a data display point of view. However, they also make excellent data entry devices. Suppose Figure 1-7 showed names of people who lived in a certain town instead of streets in a town. Using the left side of the screen, how would you move someone's name from one town to another? I can tell you it would not be intuitive and it might involve another control.

Using the TreeView, I can drag a person's name from one town to another very easily, and all the while I can still see the whole picture. Drag and drop is a powerful data entry tool. It is even easy to do drop validation on the fly while the user drags his or her mouse over certain nodes.

I go into much more detail on ListViews, TreeViews, and drag and drop in Chapter 10.

The Data-Bound Controls

The DataGrid control displays tables that are accessed via ADO.NET directly into a grid format. VB programmers should be quite familiar with this. The DataGrid control is certainly a powerful data access tool.

Other types of data binding are included with many of the other controls that I have already mentioned in this chapter. You are able to bind a property of a control to a property of an object. The word "object" is important here. You can bind a property of a control to a field in a data set, for example. A data set is an object. Another type of object is a control. You can bind a property of one control to another. For instance, you can bind the Text property of a TextBox to the Text property of a ComboBox. No code is necessary to explicitly transfer data from one object to another whenever that data changes. This is way cool!

So where would you use data binding from a property of one control to the property of another? Well, suppose you have a series of tabs with a bunch of fields that you need to fill in or choose values from. Next to this tab section, you have a summary section. This summary section includes several TextBoxes (or other controls) whose Text property is bound to the Text property of some important controls within the tabs. You could make this a sort of running total.

Perhaps a small example is needed here to graphically explain how this would work. I have a passion for wines, and I want to make a wine stock program. First of all, I create a new C# or VB project called "DataBound."

This project contains one screen with quite a few controls. I use a TabControl, a Button, and several Label and TextBox controls. There are two tabs on the tab control. The first one is shown in Figure 1-8.

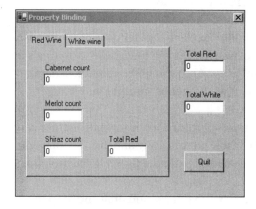

Figure 1-8. The Red Wine tab for the DataBound project

As you can see in Figure 1-8, you will need two tab pages on the tab control. You will also need to name the TextBoxes on the Red Wine tab as follows:

1. Name the Cabernet count **txtCab**.

2. Name the Merlot count **txtMerlot**.

3. Name the Shiraz count **txtShiraz**.

4. Name the Total Red **txtRed**.

Name the Total Red TextBox that is on the form itself **txtTotRed**. Name the Total White TextBox that is on the form itself **txtTotWhite**. Name the Button **cmdQuit**.

Now click over to the White wine tab, and you should add the controls shown in Figure 1-9.

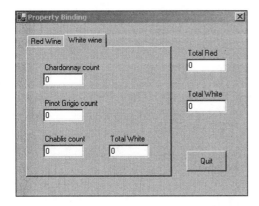

Figure 1-9. The White wine tab for the DataBound project

Name the TextBoxes on the White wine tab as follows:

1. Name the Chardonnay count **txtChardonnay**.

2. Name the Pinot Grigio count **txtPino**.

3. Name the Chablis count **txtChablis**.

Can you guess what I am trying to accomplish here?

As I put numbers in each of the wine count boxes, I want the total to add up automatically and transfer over to the totals section off the tab control. This totals section gives me a running summary of the important values on each tab without having to refer back to the tab all the time. The summation of all the wine totals is done using the validating events, and the transfer of data from each tab to the totals section is done via property data binding.

Not only do I want the addition and data transfer to happen automatically, but I also want to limit the input TextBoxes to numbers only. You already know how to restrict the input of the TextBoxes. I add to that knowledge with simple validating events and data transfer.

Listings 1-3a and 1-3b show the code for this project. It is not very difficult to understand, but I explain the important bits after the code listings.

Listing 1-3a. C# Code for the DataBound Project

```csharp
using System;
using System.Drawing;
using System.Collections;
using System.ComponentModel;
using System.Windows.Forms;
using System.Data;

namespace DataBound_c
{
    /// <summary>
    /// Summary description for Form1.
    /// </summary>
    public class Form1 : System.Windows.Forms.Form
    {
        private System.Windows.Forms.TabControl tc;
        private System.Windows.Forms.TabPage t1;
        private System.Windows.Forms.TabPage t2;
        private System.Windows.Forms.Label label1;
        private System.Windows.Forms.TextBox txtCab;
        private System.Windows.Forms.Label label2;
        private System.Windows.Forms.Label label3;
        private System.Windows.Forms.Label label4;
        private System.Windows.Forms.Label label5;
        private System.Windows.Forms.Label label6;
        private System.Windows.Forms.Label label7;
        private System.Windows.Forms.Label label8;
        private System.Windows.Forms.Label label9;
        private System.Windows.Forms.Label label10;
```

```
private System.Windows.Forms.Button cmdQuit;
private System.Windows.Forms.TextBox txtRed;
private System.Windows.Forms.TextBox txtTotRed;
private System.Windows.Forms.TextBox txtWhite;
private System.Windows.Forms.TextBox txtChablis;
private System.Windows.Forms.TextBox txtPino;
private System.Windows.Forms.TextBox txtChardonnay;
private System.Windows.Forms.TextBox txtTotWhite;
private System.Windows.Forms.TextBox txtShiraz;
private System.Windows.Forms.TextBox txtMerlot;

private System.ComponentModel.Container components = null;

public Form1()
{
  InitializeComponent();

  cmdQuit.Click += new EventHandler(this.CloseMe);

  //This is the tab for the red wines
  txtCab.CausesValidation = true;
  txtCab.Validating += new CancelEventHandler(this.ValidateRed);
  txtCab.KeyPress   += new KeyPressEventHandler(this.InputValidator);

  txtMerlot.CausesValidation = true;
  txtMerlot.Validating += new CancelEventHandler(this.ValidateRed);
  txtMerlot.KeyPress   += new KeyPressEventHandler(this.InputValidator);

  txtShiraz.CausesValidation = true;
  txtShiraz.Validating += new CancelEventHandler(this.ValidateRed);
  txtShiraz.KeyPress   += new KeyPressEventHandler(this.InputValidator);

  txtCab.Text = "0";
  txtMerlot.Text = "0";
  txtShiraz.Text = "0";

  //This is the tab for the white wines
  //This is the tab for the white wines
  txtChardonnay.CausesValidation = true;
  txtChardonnay.Validating += new CancelEventHandler(this.ValidateWhite);
  txtChardonnay.KeyPress   += new KeyPressEventHandler(this.InputValidator);
```

```csharp
            txtPino.CausesValidation = true;
            txtPino.Validating    += new CancelEventHandler(this.ValidateWhite);
            txtPino.KeyPress += new KeyPressEventHandler(this.InputValidator);

            txtChablis.CausesValidation = true;
            txtChablis.Validating += new CancelEventHandler(this.ValidateWhite);
            txtChablis.KeyPress += new KeyPressEventHandler(this.InputValidator);

            txtChardonnay.Text = "0";
            txtPino.Text = "0";
            txtChablis.Text = "0";

            //Do the data binding summaries
            txtTotRed.DataBindings.Add("Text",txtRed,"Text");
            txtTotWhite.DataBindings.Add("Text",txtWhite,"Text");

            //Call the delegate to start totals
            ValidateRed(new object(), new CancelEventArgs());
            ValidateWhite(new object(), new CancelEventArgs());

        }

        protected override void Dispose( bool disposing )
        {
            if( disposing )
            {
                if (components != null)
                {
                    components.Dispose();
                }
            }
            base.Dispose( disposing );
        }

        #region Windows Form Designer generated code
        ...
        ...
        ...

        #endregion
```

```
[STAThread]
static void Main()
{
  Application.Run(new Form1());
}

private void Form1_Load(object sender, System.EventArgs e)
{
}

#region events

private void CloseMe(object sender, EventArgs e)
{
  this.Close();
}

private void ValidateRed(object sender, CancelEventArgs e)
{
  int     reds = 0;
  TextBox t;
  string  msg;

  //Remember we call this once with a generic object
  if(sender is TextBox)
  {
    t = (TextBox)sender;
    msg = t.Name + " Needs a number.";
  }
  else
    msg = "Wine count cannot be blank";

  if(txtCab.Text == "" ||
    txtMerlot.Text == "" ||
    txtShiraz.Text == "")
  {
    MessageBox.Show(msg);
    e.Cancel = true;
    return;
  }
```

```csharp
        reds =  Convert.ToInt32(txtCab.Text);
        reds += Convert.ToInt32(txtMerlot.Text);
        reds += Convert.ToInt32(txtShiraz.Text);

        txtRed.Text = reds.ToString();
    }

    private void ValidateWhite(object sender, CancelEventArgs e)
    {
      int whites = 0;

      if(txtChardonnay.Text == "" ||
         txtPino.Text == "" ||
         txtChablis.Text == "")
      {
        e.Cancel = true;
        return;
      }

      whites =  Convert.ToInt32(txtChardonnay.Text);
      whites += Convert.ToInt32(txtPino.Text);
      whites += Convert.ToInt32(txtChablis.Text);

      txtWhite.Text = whites.ToString();
    }

    private void InputValidator(object sender, KeyPressEventArgs e)
    {
      if(!Char.IsNumber(e.KeyChar) && e.KeyChar != (char)8 )
        e.Handled = true;
    }

    #endregion
  }
}
```

Listing 1-3b. VB Code for the DataBound Project

```vb
Public Class Form1
    Inherits System.Windows.Forms.Form


#Region " Windows Form Designer generated code "
```

```vb
Public Sub New()
    MyBase.New()

    'This call is required by the Windows Form Designer.
    InitializeComponent()


AddHandler cmdQuit.Click, AddressOf Me.CloseMe

'This is the tab for the red wines
txtCab.CausesValidation = True
AddHandler txtCab.Validating, AddressOf Me.ValidateRed
AddHandler txtCab.KeyPress, AddressOf Me.InputValidator

txtMerlot.CausesValidation = True
AddHandler txtMerlot.Validating, AddressOf Me.ValidateRed
AddHandler txtMerlot.KeyPress, AddressOf Me.InputValidator

txtShiraz.CausesValidation = True
AddHandler txtShiraz.Validating, AddressOf Me.ValidateRed
AddHandler txtShiraz.KeyPress, AddressOf Me.InputValidator

txtCab.Text = "0"
txtMerlot.Text = "0"
txtShiraz.Text = "0"

'This is the tab for the white wines
txtChardonnay.CausesValidation = True
AddHandler txtChardonnay.Validating, AddressOf Me.ValidateWhite
AddHandler txtChardonnay.KeyPress, AddressOf Me.InputValidator

txtPino.CausesValidation = True
AddHandler txtPino.Validating, AddressOf Me.ValidateWhite
AddHandler txtPino.KeyPress, AddressOf Me.InputValidator

txtChablis.CausesValidation = True
AddHandler txtChablis.Validating, AddressOf Me.ValidateWhite
AddHandler txtChablis.KeyPress, AddressOf Me.InputValidator

txtChardonnay.Text = "0"
txtPino.Text = "0"
txtChablis.Text = "0"
```

```vbnet
                'Do the data binding summaries
                txtTotRed.DataBindings.Add("Text", txtRed, "Text")
                txtTotWhite.DataBindings.Add("Text", txtWhite, "Text")

                'Call the delegate to start totals
                ValidateRed(New Object(), New System.ComponentModel.CancelEventArgs())
                ValidateWhite(New Object(), New System.ComponentModel.CancelEventArgs())

            End Sub


        ...
        ...
        ...


    #End Region

        Private Sub Form1_Load(ByVal sender As System.Object, _
                                ByVal e As System.EventArgs) Handles MyBase.Load
        End Sub

    #Region "events"

        Private Sub CloseMe(ByVal sender As Object, ByVal e As EventArgs)
          Me.Close()
        End Sub

        Private Sub ValidateRed(ByVal sender As Object, _
                                ByVal e As System.ComponentModel.CancelEventArgs)
          Dim reds As Int32 = 0
          Dim t As TextBox
          Dim msg As String

          'Remember we call this once with a generic object
          If (sender.GetType() Is GetType(TextBox)) Then
            t = CType(sender, TextBox)
            msg = t.Name + " Needs a number."
          Else
            msg = "Wine count cannot be blank"
          End If
```

```vbnet
    If (txtCab.Text = "" Or _
       txtMerlot.Text = "" Or _
       txtShiraz.Text = "") Then
      MessageBox.Show(msg)
      e.Cancel = True
      Return
    End If


    reds = Convert.ToInt32(txtCab.Text)
    reds += Convert.ToInt32(txtMerlot.Text)
    reds += Convert.ToInt32(txtShiraz.Text)

    txtRed.Text = reds.ToString()
  End Sub

  Private Sub ValidateWhite(ByVal sender As Object, _
                            ByVal e As System.ComponentModel.CancelEventArgs)
    Dim whites As Int32 = 0

    If (txtChardonnay.Text = "" Or _
       txtPino.Text = "" Or _
       txtChablis.Text = "") Then

      e.Cancel = True
      Return
    End If

    whites = Convert.ToInt32(txtChardonnay.Text)
    whites += Convert.ToInt32(txtPino.Text)
    whites += Convert.ToInt32(txtChablis.Text)

    txtWhite.Text = whites.ToString()
  End Sub

  Private Sub InputValidator(ByVal sender As Object, ByVal e As KeyPressEventArgs)
    If (Not Char.IsNumber(e.KeyChar) And e.KeyChar <> "8"c) Then
      e.Handled = True
    End If
  End Sub

#End Region
End Class
```

Compile and run the program. Enter some values in the count fields and then move to different fields. You will notice that as you try to move to another field, the validating events for these various TextBoxes are being invoked and are adding up totals. As soon as the total field in each tab is filled in, the data is immediately transferred to the summation fields outside the tab control. Let's look at some of the code.

```
txtCab.CausesValidation = true;
txtCab.Validating += new CancelEventHandler(this.ValidateRed);
txtCab.KeyPress  += new KeyPressEventHandler(this.InputValidator);
```

In the preceding code, I assign a delegate to the Validating event that is of type CancelEventHandler. The CancelEvent object contains a Cancel argument that if set to true stops the control from losing focus. The ValidateRed delegate is shown here:

```
private void ValidateRed(object sender, CancelEventArgs e)
{
  int     reds = 0;
  TextBox t;
  string  msg;

  //Remember we call this once with a generic object
  if(sender is TextBox)
  {
    t = (TextBox)sender;
    msg = t.Name + " Needs a number.";
  }
  else
    msg = "Wine count cannot be blank";

  if(txtCab.Text == "" ||
     txtMerlot.Text == "" ||
     txtShiraz.Text == "")
  {
    MessageBox.Show(msg);
    e.Cancel = true;
    return;
  }

  reds =  Convert.ToInt32(txtCab.Text);
  reds += Convert.ToInt32(txtMerlot.Text);
  reds += Convert.ToInt32(txtShiraz.Text);

  txtRed.Text = reds.ToString();
}
```

My error checking consists of seeing if the TextBox has a value. If it is blank, I do not let the user go on. Notice that I have a different error message if I know who sent the event than if I did not. You should always show the most explicit error messages that you can.[2]

You will see that at the end of the constructor I call each of the validation routines with a blank Sender object and an empty CancelEventArgs object. This is to get the ball rolling at start-up.

The code that does the data transfer is as follows:

```
//Do the data binding summaries
txtTotRed.DataBindings.Add("Text",txtRed,"Text");
txtTotWhite.DataBindings.Add("Text",txtWhite,"Text");
```

All I do is tell the DataBinding property of the control which field to bind to which field of the source control. It is that easy, and as you can see from running the program, it is that cool.

 TIP   Study the MSDN help for the .NET controls carefully. You'll often find programming gems there that you can take advantage of. This is so different from VB 6.0.

What's Missing

So what is not in this code? It seems like you have everything you need, right? Well, for one thing, I have virtually no error checking, just validation code. If I did not restrict the input TextBoxes to numbers, I could easily crash the program. As now it is not too hard to crash it. In addition, the way I handle the validation events is very simple. Chapter 7 goes into much more detail on this topic.

You will also notice that I have structured the example to be simple enough that each Validation event depends on only one control. Add a few more tabs and a few dozen more interdependent input fields and you can have a mess that is not so easily handled. I cover this in much more detail in Chapter 7.

---

2.   Do not go overboard here. I have seen error messages in the form of paragraphs.

What About Cut and Paste?

Try to enter anything other than numbers in the input fields of the previous program and the validation code stops you. Or does it? Want to crash this program? Copy some text to the Clipboard and paste it into one of the input fields. Now leave that field and your program falls over. Bang! Big hole in the validation code here.

Cut and paste is something that I am always on the lookout for because I have been caught before with that trick. Of course, a good test engineer will catch it before a customer ever does, but still, you do not want that kind of bug to escape. What to do?

Try setting the AllowDrop property of one of the input TextBoxes to false. This does nothing. The AllowDrop property is for actual drag-and-drop operations. What you have to do here is catch another event. After all, the control must know this is happening. You just have to let it tell you.

There is an event called TextChanged that you can hook into to detect and correct this type of thing. Try this with the txtCab control. I show this in C# only, as it is easy enough to convert to VB. Enter the following code in the constructor:

```
txtCab.TextChanged += new EventHandler(this.Pastings);
```

Now enter the following method at the bottom of your form code:

```
private void Pastings(object sender, EventArgs e)
{
  TextBox t;
  if(sender is TextBox)
  {
    t = (TextBox)sender;
    if (t.Name == txtCab.Name)
    {
      for (int x =0; x<txtCab.TextLength; x++)
      {
        if (!char.IsNumber(txtCab.Text,x))
        {
          txtCab.Text = "";
          break;
        }
      }
    }
  }
}
```

What happens here is that I catch the pasting operation and clear the TextBox if I detect a nonnumeric character.

There are a few different ways to handle this situation, but the example I present here shows you the easiest. If you want to be more sophisticated, you could save the text in a separate variable while you are typing. Then when the user pastes something illegal into the control, you can delete the existing text and replace it with known good text from your variable. This is what I would do in a real program. I would also notify the user via an error message with something to the effect of "Don't do that!"

Selecting Text

Quite a few times when you enter data, you will need to go back and edit existing fields. To facilitate editing of fields in which you have already edited data, you can highlight the text that is already in that field. Of course, this applies to controls with an editable text property.

What does this do for a user? Well, if the user wants to completely replace the information in a TextBox, it saves him or her a few keystrokes. If the text is not selected, the user must use the mouse to select it. This can be a pain, especially if the text runs beyond the visible scope of the TextBox. It certainly slows down editing and navigation.

It is interesting to note what the TextBox does for you during navigation. Open up a new C# project and put several TextBoxes on the screen. Run the program and tab through each control. You will notice that the text in each control is selected automatically. Now click your mouse in one of the controls. The text in this control should not be selected anymore. Start tabbing again and all the controls will have their text selected except for the control you visited with the mouse before.

I think this is a neat little feature of the .NET TextBox control. You may want to expand this functionality. As you have seen, once you visit a control with the mouse, the text deselects and does not get automatically selected again for you. However, you can do this yourself.

This next quick example is the last one in this chapter. It shows not only how to programmatically select text in a TextBox, but also how to connect and disconnect events and their delegates. Perhaps the user does not want to have all previous visited fields selected. It would be nice to provide the user with a way to turn this off. This is a usability issue that you should be aware of. When you create a fairly complicated program, it is fine to have defaults for certain things, but they should be considered just that: defaults. If you can, you should provide for some kind of configuration screen that allows the user to override these defaults.

Start a new C# or VB program. Mine is called "SelectText." Add the following controls:

1. Add a Label and change its text to **Unlimited Text**.

2. Add a TextBox below the Unlimited Text Label and call it **t1**. Add **The quick brown fox jumps over the lazy dog** as its text.

3. Add a Label and change its text to **10 characters**.

4. Add a TextBox and call it **t2**. Change its text to **1-10**.

5. Add a Label and change its text to **10 characters**.

6. Add a TextBox and call it **t3**. Change its text to **1-10**.

7. Add a CheckBox called **chkSelect**. Change its text to **Select**.

8. Add a Button called **cmdQuit**. Change its text to **Quit**.

Make the form appear in the center of the screen upon start-up. Your screen should look like the one shown in Figure 1-10. By the way, because this is a small program, I allow you to go ahead and double-click the Quit button to have .NET create the delegate for you. I allow it just this once, though—don't make it a habit!

Figure 1-10. The SelectText program form

You can see from Figure 1-10 that the text in the first box overruns the length of the box. If this text were not selected upon entry, it would take some seconds for you to overwrite this text with a single word. A few seconds may not seem like much, but it can add up not only in time but also in frustration.

Listings 1-4a and 1-4b show the code for this small program. The code is fairly easy, but if you think about it, it is also very powerful.

Listing 1-4a. C# Code for the SelectText Program

```csharp
using System;
using System.Drawing;
using System.Collections;
using System.ComponentModel;
using System.Windows.Forms;
using System.Data;

namespace SelectText_c
{
  /// <summary>
  /// This project shows how to connect/disconnect delegates and events.
  /// It also shows how to programmatically select text
  /// </summary>
  public class Form1 : System.Windows.Forms.Form
  {
    private System.Windows.Forms.Label label1;
    private System.Windows.Forms.Label label2;
    private System.Windows.Forms.Label label3;
    private System.Windows.Forms.Button cmdQuit;
    private System.Windows.Forms.TextBox t1;
    private System.Windows.Forms.TextBox t2;
    private System.Windows.Forms.TextBox t3;
    private System.Windows.Forms.CheckBox chkSelect;

    private System.ComponentModel.Container components = null;

    public Form1()
    {
    InitializeComponent();

      chkSelect.CheckedChanged += new EventHandler(this.FlipSelect);

    }

    protected override void Dispose( bool disposing )
    {
      if( disposing )
      {
        if (components != null)
        {
          components.Dispose();
        }
      }
```

```
      base.Dispose( disposing );
   }

   #region Windows Form Designer generated code
…

…

…

   #endregion

   [STAThread]
   static void Main()
   {
     Application.Run(new Form1());
   }

   private void cmdQuit_Click(object sender, System.EventArgs e)
   {
     this.Close();
   }

   private void Form1_Load(object sender, System.EventArgs e)
   {
   }

   #region events

   private void FlipSelect(object sender, EventArgs e)
   {
     if (chkSelect.Checked)
     {
       t1.GotFocus += new EventHandler(this.SelectMe);
       t2.GotFocus += new EventHandler(this.SelectMe);
       t3.GotFocus += new EventHandler(this.SelectMe);
     }
     else
     {
       t1.GotFocus -= new EventHandler(this.SelectMe);
       t2.GotFocus -= new EventHandler(this.SelectMe);
       t3.GotFocus -= new EventHandler(this.SelectMe);
     }

   }
```

```
      private void SelectMe(object sender, EventArgs e)
      {
        t1.Select(0,t1.TextLength);
        t2.Select(0,t2.TextLength);
        t3.Select(0,t3.TextLength);
      }

      #endregion
   }
}
```

Listing 1-4b. VB Code for the SelectText Program

```
Public Class Form1
    Inherits System.Windows.Forms.Form

#Region " Windows Form Designer generated code "

  Public Sub New()
    MyBase.New()

    'This call is required by the Windows Form Designer.
    InitializeComponent()

    AddHandler chkSelect.CheckedChanged, AddressOf FlipSelect



  End Sub

  'Form overrides dispose to clean up the component list.
  Protected Overloads Overrides Sub Dispose(ByVal disposing As Boolean)
    If disposing Then
      If Not (components Is Nothing) Then
        components.Dispose()
      End If
    End If
    MyBase.Dispose(disposing)
  End Sub

  ...
  ...
  ...

  ...
```

```
#End Region

  Private Sub Form1_Load(ByVal sender As System.Object, _
                          ByVal e As System.EventArgs) Handles MyBase.Load

  End Sub

#Region "events"

  Private Sub FlipSelect(ByVal sender As Object, ByVal e As EventArgs)
    If chkSelect.Checked Then
      AddHandler t1.GotFocus, AddressOf Me.SelectMe
      AddHandler t2.GotFocus, AddressOf Me.SelectMe
      AddHandler t3.GotFocus, AddressOf Me.SelectMe
    Else
      RemoveHandler t1.GotFocus, AddressOf Me.SelectMe
      RemoveHandler t2.GotFocus, AddressOf Me.SelectMe
      RemoveHandler t3.GotFocus, AddressOf Me.SelectMe
    End If

  End Sub

  Private Sub SelectMe(ByVal sender As Object, ByVal e As EventArgs)
    t1.Select(0, t1.TextLength)
    t2.Select(0, t2.TextLength)
    t3.Select(0, t3.TextLength)
  End Sub

#End Region

  Private Sub cmdQuit_Click(ByVal sender As System.Object, _
                          ByVal e As System.EventArgs) Handles cmdQuit.Click
    Me.Close()
  End Sub
End Class
```

Remember back in the Introduction when I said that I prefer to roll my own delegates instead of letting .NET create them for me? Well, this is the main reason. Notice that the VB delegate for the Quit button uses the Handles keyword after the argument list. I cannot programmatically unhandle this delegate. However, the delegates that I assigned using the AddHandler method can be unhandled. And I do just that in this program with the delegate that selects text.

What is really neat about removing the connection between the event and the delegate is that there is no code in the delegate that tests to see if I need to select the text according to the CheckBox value. If I need to select text, I connect the delegate; if not, I disconnect the delegate. This can make for far less code in a complicated scenario. Less code means fewer potential bugs.

Summary

In this chapter you learned the basics of data entry and validation. I demonstrated some of the more common data entry controls. I also showed you how to do some simple validation. When you work with data entry controls, it is always best to use properties of the control itself to do as much validation for you as possible.

Also in this chapter, I showed you a new way to do data binding by connecting the text value of one control to another. This makes for no-code data entry. At the end of the chapter, I showed you how the cut-and-paste functionality of Windows can bypass some of your validation code and cause problems. Sometimes these common helpful functions require workarounds that you may not have thought of.

Chapter 2 deals with designing user interface data entry screens. Validation will take a back seat to presentation in the next chapter.

UI Design Considerations for Data Entry

IN CHAPTER 1, I introduced you to some of the controls that you will commonly use in data entry forms. Because data entry and validation go hand in hand, I also introduced you to some fairly simple data validation techniques. Of course, because no self-respecting chapter on data entry controls would be seen without examples, I included a few to whet your appetite. Though some of these examples included hints for designing screens, I did not intend to really go into that subject at the time.

This chapter covers user interface (UI) design with an eye toward data entry. Now you may think that what you saw as examples in Chapter 1 was enough to get you started on designing data input screens. You would be incorrect—it is not nearly enough. I cover the following topics in this chapter:

- Using the integrated development environment (IDE) to make UI design easier

- Deciding what controls to use and when

- Using OLE custom controls (OCXs) in .NET programs

- Presenting egregious examples of data entry screens

- Employing current field–based data entry screen design

- Using the menu system and toolbar

- Navigating fields

- Understanding ambient properties

- Adjusting screen resolution and resizing screens

As I write this list I can think of about 80 other things to add. As I come across them, I will mention other topics as well. First things first, however: Let's start with what the user sees.

Screen Consistency

I have been around long enough to have used hundreds of programs to accomplish a certain task. I have even written a few of them myself. I have also been a longtime Windows user.

What I see in Windows programs from Microsoft is consistency in navigation and use. What I see in most programs from vendors other than Microsoft is the same type of consistency. However, sometimes I come across a program whose screen layout defies description. Not only is the layout different and unintuitive, but the help is usually obscure as well.

I will generalize here and say that most people's frustration level at a computer program increases in direct proportion to how much they paid for it. I know this is true for me. What do I mean here? If I am paying tens or hundreds of dollars for a program, I expect it to work intelligently and be relatively bug-free. I expect the help to be comprehensive and I expect the program to work as advertised. If this type of program is unusable, I get frustrated easily.

If I get shareware for $5.00 or freeware, I have no such expectations. Instead, I consider these types of programs to be disposable and I pretty much use them only for the task at hand. If this type of program is difficult to use, I do not get all twisted; I figure I got what I paid for.

What kind of program do you want to write? Whenever I write a program that I put any kind of time into, I prefer to make it intuitive for other users. I do this no matter how much I sell it for. I think you should too. The user should already know how to use your program (somewhat) before he or she ever unwraps it.

A Good Screen Layout Example

The first step in creating a program with consistency is screen layout. You need to try to lay out your screens so that navigation is easy. You also need to make sure the information the user needs about your program is readily available. Figure 2-1 shows a screen shot of a simple auto parts entry program. This screen is meant to be used by someone who enters information in the database for use by the auto parts shop's front counter staff later.

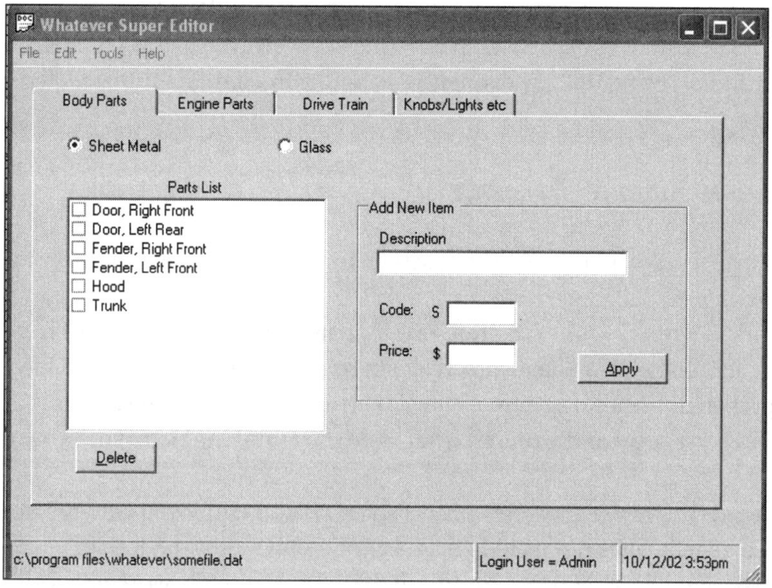

Figure 2-1. An example of effective screen layout

Anyone who has used a Windows PC before will pretty much know how to run this program. There are some exceptions, but they can be learned pretty quickly. For instance, look at the menu. It is pretty standard. Before I even click a menu item, I already know what the subchoices will be for the most common things. I know that loading and saving a database will be under the File menu. I also know this is where the Exit choice is.

The Tab control segregates the different categories of car parts in a logical manner. Radio buttons are kept at a minimum and are used as navigation tools in this case.

The screen is set up for maximum usability. I know just by looking at it that I will be able to check off some items in the list and click the Delete key to remove them. If the program is written well, I have a good idea that clicking the Apply button will make the new part immediately show up in the parts list. This is instant feedback.

Look at the status bar at the bottom of the screen. I know who is using the system, what file is being edited and, of course, the time and date.

Notice that the two buttons, Delete and Apply, have their first letters underlined. This means that I can press Alt-D to invoke the Delete key. I can press Alt-A to apply a new part to the database. These hot keys are very important to data entry screens. You will find that as a person uses a program often, he or she will try to find the fastest way to use it. If you help the user out with hot keys and other shortcuts, your program will be more successful.

By the way, what is the most common shortcut key in all the Windows programs ever made? The F1 key, of course. Users know this key will always bring up help. These days, it should bring up context-sensitive help. More on this subject later.

A Bad Screen Layout Example

OK, I showed you a pretty good data input screen in the previous section. Now for a little contrast.

I have worked with a number of programs that are rather bizarre to use. I have seen data that should be connected spread all out over several different tabs. I have seen incomprehensible menu systems. I have seen all kinds of strange things that make me scratch my head and wonder, what were they thinking? I am sure you have as well.

Figures 2-2, 2-3, and 2-4 show a mythical screen for an employee data record. Although the screen itself is not used in any program that I know of, it does represent the design of a screen for a program that I have actually worked with.[1]

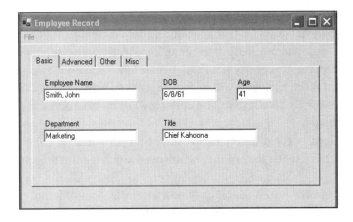

Figure 2-2. Example of bad screen design, part 1

So let me first list the things that are wrong with this screen and this tab. First, the menu has only one top-level entry. This tells me that everything is bunched under one entry. In fact, here are the entries in the order in which they appear:

---

1. Needless to say, this program was not well received and has been revamped.

- Exit

- Load

- Help

- Save

This is bad. This menu has entries that are in the wrong order, and it also has entries that do not belong under the File heading. The Load menu item actually loads a new employee screen for data input. This is not very intuitive at all.

In addition, the tabs are labeled incorrectly. The Basic and Advanced data tabs are OK, but the other two tabs, to me, mean the same thing. What is the difference between Other and Misc?

Next, the first tab, Basic, uses all TextBoxes for data entry fields. This is prone to error, especially when users enter the date. If a user enters a date in a plain old TextBox, you need quite a bit of validation code to make sure the entry is correct. Not only that, the dates must be shown according to the culture setting of the computer. In other words, the date shown here must read "8/6/61" in places other than the United States.

Now look at the Employee Name field. There is only one field for both first and last names. I have seen this method of entering names in several different programs. I can see all kinds of errors being introduced here. For instance, suppose a user enters the name **Kenneth James**? Which is the first name and which is the last name? It could be either.

The DOB and Age fields bring up something that I have seen before. Why ask for a birth date then ask for an age? Hello! This is a computer we are working with here. Just because Age is a field in the database does not mean a user has to enter an age manually if his or her birth date is known. Entering the age here is not only a waste of time, but it's also a drain on my older brain cells.

The Department and Title fields are OK here.[2]

Figure 2-3 shows the next tab in this screen.

---

2. You know how marketing people are. They all have big sounding titles.

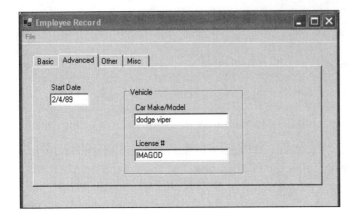

Figure 2-3. Example of bad screen design, part 2

This tab is typical of a screen that I have worked with. Somehow this type of information is not "advanced" in my mind. Also note that a TextBox is again used for a date field.

So how about the tabs, Other and Misc? Figure 2-4 shows an example of what I found in such a tab.

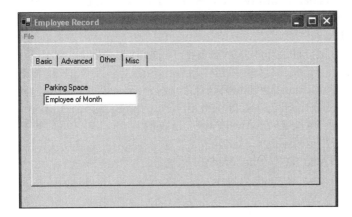

Figure 2-4. Example of bad screen design, part 3

As you can see, the parking space for the employee is noted on a completely different tab than the rest of the car information.

You can tell from the design of this screen that some of these tabs were added at a later date to provide for extra fields. The person designing the software must have thought that keeping the existing screen layout was more important than keeping consistent data.

One last thing to note about this screen: Once you get past the first tab, you no longer have any idea which employee's data you are editing. Unnecessary flipping back and forth between screens is a very bad thing.

Now I have obviously left off quite a few of the data fields in these tabs for demonstration purposes. But think about this. If there were, say, 20 other fields per tab and the flow was as bad as these few data fields, how much time would it take to learn this program? How much frustration would it cause?

 TIP   I once saw this quote about software programs: "Writing software is about relieving pain." I have no idea where the quote came from, but it always stuck with me. If you can relieve some of the pain of doing a task by using software, then that software is successful. If your software is painful to use, you have failed.

Keeping Information Flow Simple

This is probably the most important aspect of designing data entry screens. The goal here is to present information in such a way that the data flow makes sense. For instance, you saw from the last section on inconsistent screens that some of the employee's car information was on one page and some was on another page. This does not make sense.

Along with data flow comes navigation flow, which consists of the following:

- How many screens should the program have?

- How should the user get from one field to another?

- How is the data structured? Is it hierarchical or disparate?

- Does it make sense to use a menu or toolbar?

- What are the ease-of-use issues?

- What are the usability issues?

These last two points are very important indeed. How easy the program is to use plays to the casual and unsophisticated user. How usable the program is plays to the power user and people who are very computer literate. Although it may seem as if these two points are diametrically opposed, they are not. In fact, the best programs have all aspects of both.

Here is a list of items that enhance ease of use:

- Menus

- Toolbars

- Simple layout

- Context-sensitive help

- Preselected fields based upon already selected entries

- Visual cues such as icons and pictures

- Explicit error messages and verbose directions

- Autocompletion of data

The power user looks for features such as the following:

- Easy tabbing between fields

- Hot keys

- Speed keys

- Consistency between screens

- Context menus

- Macro capability

Of course, the power user looks for all the items in the preceding list as additions to the basic ease-of-use items.

To see how ease of use and usability can go hand in hand, you will set up a simple single screen that has aspects of both. This program will detail how to use the following controls:

- Menu control

- Context menu

- ListView

- Toolbar

- Hot keys

- Speed keys

- DateTimePicker

- Elementary graphics

The following data editing example is fairly complicated in its setup. What I try to show you is how to set the stage for data entry. You will find no validation code here, as this program does not really do anything. All the values are canned.

What you will find are controls that make navigation easy. You will find an intuitive interface with related data fields all in the same place. You will also find ways to improve navigation speed. I have included keyboard shortcuts that greatly enhance the experience for the power user.

This is a fairly long example, so you may want to download the code from the Downloads section of the Apress Web site if you get tired of entering in the code by hand.

TIP Whenever possible, you should try to enter code by hand. Making mistakes is half the process of learning. Whenever I read a computer book, I always try to enter all the code myself. I gain a lot of insight that way.

The Data Editing Example

This example is a rewrite of the employee record form. Start a new project in C# or VB. Mine is called "PowerUser." There are two forms in this project. Here is what you need to do to set up the first form:

1. Add a TabControl and call it **tc1**.

2. Using the Properties window of the TabControl, add the following three tab pages: tp1 with the text **Basic Data**; tp2 with the text **Position**; and tp3 with the text **Personal**.

3. Add an ImageList control to the form and call it **imgToolBar**.

4. Add a Button to the form called **cmdOK**. Change the text to **OK**.

5. Add a Button to the form called **cmdCancel**. Change the text to **Cancel**.

6. Add a Button to the form called **cmdHelp**. Change the text to **Help**.

7. Add a Button to the form called **cmdEdit**. Change the text to **Edit**.

8. Add a StatusBar to the form and call it **sb1**.

9. Add a Button to the form called **cmdListByEmp**. Make the text blank.

10. Add a Button to the form called **cmdListByNum**. Make the text blank.

11. Add a Label to the form and change its text to **Employee Name.**

12. Add a TextBox to the form called **txtEmp**.

13. Add a Label to the form and change its text to **Clock Number**.

14. Add a TextBox to the form called **txtNum**.

Your screen should look like the one shown in Figure 2-5.

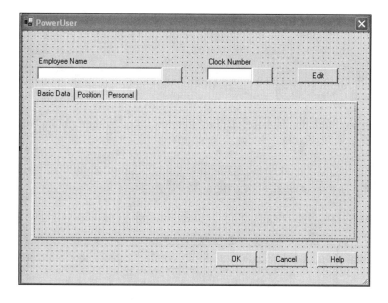

Figure 2-5. Form controls for the PowerUser project

Now it is time to put some controls on the tab pages. Perform the following steps in the controls on this (Basic Data) page:

1. Add a Label whose text reads **Last Name**.

2. Add a TextBox called **txtLast**.

3. Add a Label whose text reads **First Name**.

4. Add a TextBox called **txtFirst**.

5. Add a Label whose text reads **M.I.**

6. Add a TextBox called **txtMI**.

7. Add a Label whose text reads **Title**.

8. Add a TextBox called **txtTitle**.

9. Add a Label whose text reads **Department**.

10. Add a TextBox called **txtDept**.

11. Add a Label whose text reads **Years With Company**.

12. Add a Label called **lblYears**. Change its border style to Fixed3D.

13. Add a Label whose text reads **Date of Hire**.

14. Add a DateTimePicker control called **dtHire**.

Your form should now look like the one shown in Figure 2-6.

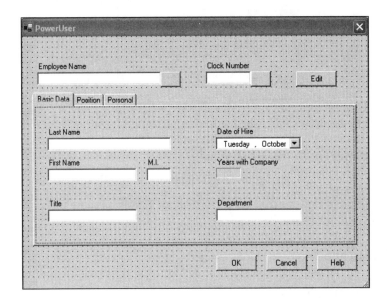

Figure 2-6. The first tab of the PowerUser project

Now add the following controls to the second tab. This is the Position tab.

1. Add a GroupBox whose text reads **Employee Type**.

2. Add a Label inside the GroupBox whose text reads **Code**.

3. Add a ComboBox inside the GroupBox called **cmbPay**.

4. Add a CheckBox inside the GroupBox called **chkManager**. Its text should read **Manager**.

5. Add a RadioButton inside the GroupBox called **optHourly**. Its text should read **Hourly**.

6. Add a RadioButton inside the GroupBox called **optSalary**. Its text should read **Salary**.

7. Add a Label to the tab page whose text reads **Reporting Staff**.

8. Add a ListView to the tab page called **lstEmps**.

The second page of the tab should look like Figure 2-7.

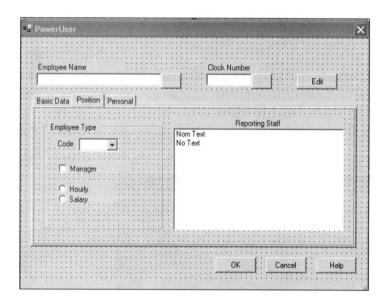

Figure 2-7. The second tab of the PowerUser project

Now for the third and final tab. Add the following controls to the Personal tab:

1. Add a Label whose text reads **Birthday.**

2. Add a DateTimePicker control called **dtBirthday.**

3. Add a PictureBox called **pic.**

4. Add a GroupBox whose text reads **Automobile.**

5. Add a Label inside the GroupBox whose text reads **Car 1.**

6. Add a TextBox inside the GroupBox called **txtCar1.**

7. Add a Label inside the GroupBox whose text reads **Car 2**.

8. Add a TextBox inside the GroupBox called **txtCar2**.

9. Add a Label inside the GroupBox whose text reads **License**.

10. Add a TextBox inside the GroupBox called **txtLic1**.

11. Add a Label inside the GroupBox whose text reads **License**.

12. Add a TextBox inside the GroupBox called **txtLic2**.

13. Add a Label inside the GroupBox whose text reads **Parking Space**.

14. Add a ComboBox inside the GroupBox called **cmbParking**.

The third tab page should look like Figure 2-8.

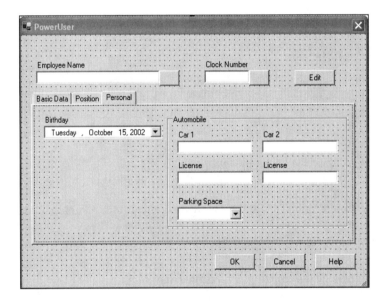

Figure 2-8. The third tab page of the PowerUser project

Whew! Now that you have that out of the way, it is time to add the code. You will add the second form later.

Code for the Data Entering Example

The code for this form has several main sections. They are the form's constructor, the form's Load event handler, and several delegates that handle various events.

Enter the form's code and put the following variable declarations just above the constructor.

C#

```
#region Class Local Variables

ToolBar    tb1;
MainMenu   mnu;

#endregion
```

VB

```
#Region "Class Local Variables"

  Dim tb1 As ToolBar
  Dim mnu As MainMenu

#End Region
```

As you can see here, I have a ToolBar and a Menu as an internal variable. Later, I will add these two controls to the form. I could have decided to add them in the form designer itself, but I wanted to show you that it is not always necessary to do that.

In fact, you can use some of these controls to your advantage in some unusual situations. Suppose you want to have a data structure that holds a list of people's names and their photographs. You also want this list to be in sorted order regardless of the order in which you add people's names. You could make a class or a structure to do this for you, but you could also use a control to handle this.

You can declare a ListView as an internal variable and add people's names to it in any order you want. You can set the ListView control up to hold its list in an ascending sort order. Using a control this way gives you the capabilities of the control without your ever having to add it to any other visible controls list. Although there are ready-made collections for this sort of thing in .NET, there may be a specialized data structure you need that you can realize using a normally visible control. Anyway, it is something to think about.

Listings 2-1a and 2-1b show the code for the constructor of this form.

Listing 2-1a. C# Constructor Code for the PowerUser Main Form

```csharp
public Form1()
{
  InitializeComponent();

  //Close the program when OK/Cancel/Help buttons are clicked
  cmdOK.Text      = "&OK";
  cmdOK.Enabled   = false;
  cmdOK.Click     += new EventHandler(this.ApplyChanges);
  cmdCancel.Text  = "&Cancel";
  cmdCancel.Enabled = false;
  cmdCancel.Click += new EventHandler(this.ApplyChanges);
  cmdHelp.Text    = "&Help";
  cmdEdit.Text    = "&Edit";
  cmdEdit.Click   += new EventHandler(this.EditFields);

  //Do the menu
  mnu = new MainMenu();
  this.Menu = mnu;
  MenuItem Top = new MenuItem("&File");
  mnu.MenuItems.Add(Top);
  MenuItem Next = new MenuItem("&New", new EventHandler(this.MenuHandler));
  Next.Shortcut = Shortcut.F5;
  Top.MenuItems.Add(Next);
  Next = new MenuItem("&Save", new EventHandler(this.MenuHandler));
  Next.Shortcut = Shortcut.F6;
  Top.MenuItems.Add(Next);
  Next = new MenuItem("-");
  Top.MenuItems.Add(Next);
  Next = new MenuItem("E&xit", new EventHandler(this.MenuHandler));
  Next.Shortcut = Shortcut.F12;
  Top.MenuItems.Add(Next);

  Top = new MenuItem("&Record");
  mnu.MenuItems.Add(Top);
  Next = new MenuItem("&Previous", new EventHandler(this.MenuHandler));
  Next.Shortcut = Shortcut.F7;
  Top.MenuItems.Add(Next);
  Next = new MenuItem("N&ext", new EventHandler(this.MenuHandler));
  Next.Shortcut = Shortcut.F8;
  Top.MenuItems.Add(Next);
```

```
Top = new MenuItem("&Help");
mnu.MenuItems.Add(Top);
Next = new MenuItem("&Help", new EventHandler(this.MenuHandler));
Next.Shortcut = Shortcut.F1;
Top.MenuItems.Add(Next);
Next = new MenuItem("&About", new EventHandler(this.MenuHandler));
Top.MenuItems.Add(Next);

//Do the images for the toolbar and buttons
imgToolBar.Images.Clear();
imgToolBar.Images.Add(Image.FromFile("new.ico"));
imgToolBar.Images.Add(Image.FromFile("save.ico"));
imgToolBar.Images.Add(Image.FromFile("delete.ico"));
imgToolBar.Images.Add(Image.FromFile("prev.ico"));
imgToolBar.Images.Add(Image.FromFile("next.ico"));
imgToolBar.Images.Add(Image.FromFile("help.ico"));
imgToolBar.Images.Add(Image.FromFile("search.ico"));

//Do the toolbar
tb1 = new ToolBar();
this.Controls.Add(tb1);
tb1.ImageList = imgToolBar;
tb1.Appearance = ToolBarAppearance.Flat;
tb1.ButtonClick += new ToolBarButtonClickEventHandler(this.ToolBarHandler);

//Make a space that we can add when we want to
ToolBarButton btnSpacer = new ToolBarButton();
btnSpacer.Style = ToolBarButtonStyle.Separator;

ToolBarButton btn  = new ToolBarButton();
btn.ImageIndex = 0;
btn.ToolTipText = "New Employee";
btn.Tag = 'N';
tb1.Buttons.Add(btn);

btn = new ToolBarButton();
btn.ImageIndex = 1;
btn.ToolTipText = "Save Record";
btn.Tag = 'S';
tb1.Buttons.Add(btn);
```

```
            btn  = new ToolBarButton();
            btn.ImageIndex = 2;
            btn.ToolTipText = "Delete Employee";
            btn.Tag = 'D';
            tb1.Buttons.Add(btn);
            tb1.Buttons.Add(btnSpacer);

            btn = new ToolBarButton();
            btn.ImageIndex = 3;
            btn.ToolTipText = "Previous Record";
            btn.Tag = 'P';
            tb1.Buttons.Add(btn);

            btn = new ToolBarButton();
            btn.ImageIndex = 4;
            btn.ToolTipText = "Next Record";
            btn.Tag = 'E';
            tb1.Buttons.Add(btn);
            tb1.Buttons.Add(btnSpacer);

            btn = new ToolBarButton();
            btn.ImageIndex = 5;
            btn.ToolTipText = "Help";
            btn.Tag = 'H';
            tb1.Buttons.Add(btn);

            //Set up the list view of employees
            lstEmps.SmallImageList = imgToolBar;
            lstEmps.View = View.List;

            //Do the buttons
            cmdListByEmp.FlatStyle = FlatStyle.Popup;
            cmdListByEmp.Height = txtEmp.Height;
            cmdListByEmp.Top = txtEmp.Top;
            cmdListByEmp.ImageList = imgToolBar;
            cmdListByEmp.ImageIndex = 6;
            cmdListByEmp.ImageAlign = ContentAlignment.MiddleCenter;
            cmdListByEmp.Tag = true;
            cmdListByEmp.Click += new EventHandler(this.CallEmployees);

            cmdListByNum.FlatStyle = FlatStyle.Popup;
            cmdListByNum.Height = txtNum.Height;
            cmdListByNum.Top = txtNum.Top;
            cmdListByNum.ImageList = imgToolBar;
```

```
    cmdListByNum.ImageIndex = 6;
    cmdListByNum.ImageAlign = ContentAlignment.MiddleCenter;
    cmdListByNum.Tag = false;
    cmdListByNum.Click += new EventHandler(this.CallEmployees);

    //Do the status bar
    StatusBarPanel sb = new StatusBarPanel();
    sb.AutoSize = StatusBarPanelAutoSize.Spring;
    sb.BorderStyle = StatusBarPanelBorderStyle.Sunken;
    sb.Text = "Employee:";
    sb1.Panels.Add(sb);

    sb = new StatusBarPanel();
    sb.AutoSize = StatusBarPanelAutoSize.Contents;
    sb.Text = DateTime.Today.ToLongDateString();
    sb1.Panels.Add(sb);
    sb1.ShowPanels = true;

    txtEmp.ReadOnly = true;
    txtNum.ReadOnly = true;

    dtHire.Format = DateTimePickerFormat.Short;
    dtHire.MaxDate = DateTime.Today;
    dtHire.ValueChanged += new EventHandler(this.CalcTime);

//Do the tabindexes on the form itself
txtEmp.TabIndex = 0;
cmdListByEmp.TabIndex = 1;
txtNum.TabIndex = 2;
cmdListByNum.TabIndex = 3;
cmdEdit.TabIndex = 4;
tc1.TabIndex = 5;     //Doing this starts the tabbing on the tab page
cmdOK.TabIndex = 6;
cmdCancel.TabIndex = 7;
cmdHelp.TabIndex = 8;
//Do the tabindexes on the first tab page
txtLast.TabIndex = 0;
txtFirst.TabIndex = 1;
txtMI.TabIndex = 2;
dtHire.TabIndex = 3;
txtDept.TabIndex = 4;
//Do the tabindexes on the second tab page
cmbPay.TabIndex = 0;
chkManager.TabIndex = 1;
```

```
optHourly.TabIndex = 2;
optSalary.TabIndex = 3;
lstEmps.TabIndex = 4;
//Do the tabindexes on the third tab page
dtBirthday.TabIndex = 0;
txtCar1.TabIndex = 1;
txtLic1.TabIndex = 2;
txtCar2.TabIndex = 3;
txtLic2.TabIndex = 4;
cmbParking.TabIndex = 5;

}
```

Listing 2-1b. VB Constructor Code for the PowerUser Main Form

```
Public Sub New()
  MyBase.New()

  'This call is required by the Windows Form Designer.
  InitializeComponent()

  'Close the program when OK/Cancel/Help buttons are clicked
  cmdOK.Text = "&OK"
  cmdOK.Enabled = False
  AddHandler cmdOK.Click, AddressOf ApplyChanges
  cmdCancel.Text = "&Cancel"
  cmdCancel.Enabled = False
  AddHandler cmdCancel.Click, AddressOf ApplyChanges
  cmdHelp.Text = "&Help"
  cmdEdit.Text = "&Edit"
  AddHandler cmdEdit.Click, AddressOf EditFields

  'Do the menu
  mnu = New MainMenu()
  Me.Menu = mnu
  Dim Top As MenuItem = New MenuItem("&File")
  mnu.MenuItems.Add(Top)
  Dim Nxt As MenuItem = New MenuItem("&New", _
                        New EventHandler(AddressOf MenuHandler))
  Nxt.Shortcut = Shortcut.F5
  Top.MenuItems.Add(Nxt)
  Nxt = New MenuItem("&Save", New EventHandler(AddressOf MenuHandler))
  Nxt.Shortcut = Shortcut.F6
  Top.MenuItems.Add(Nxt)
```

```vbnet
Nxt = New MenuItem("-")
Top.MenuItems.Add(Nxt)
Nxt = New MenuItem("E&xit", New EventHandler(AddressOf MenuHandler))
Nxt.Shortcut = Shortcut.F12
Top.MenuItems.Add(Nxt)

Top = New MenuItem("&Record")
mnu.MenuItems.Add(Top)
Nxt = New MenuItem("&Previous", New EventHandler(AddressOf MenuHandler))
Nxt.Shortcut = Shortcut.F7
Top.MenuItems.Add(Nxt)
Nxt = New MenuItem("N&ext", New EventHandler(AddressOf MenuHandler))
Nxt.Shortcut = Shortcut.F8
Top.MenuItems.Add(Nxt)

Top = New MenuItem("&Help")
mnu.MenuItems.Add(Top)
Nxt = New MenuItem("&Help", New EventHandler(AddressOf MenuHandler))
Nxt.Shortcut = Shortcut.F1
Top.MenuItems.Add(Nxt)
Nxt = New MenuItem("&About", New EventHandler(AddressOf MenuHandler))
Top.MenuItems.Add(Nxt)

'Do the images for the toolbar and buttons
imgToolBar.Images.Clear()
imgToolBar.Images.Add(Image.FromFile("new.ico"))
imgToolBar.Images.Add(Image.FromFile("save.ico"))
imgToolBar.Images.Add(Image.FromFile("delete.ico"))
imgToolBar.Images.Add(Image.FromFile("prev.ico"))
imgToolBar.Images.Add(Image.FromFile("next.ico"))
imgToolBar.Images.Add(Image.FromFile("help.ico"))
imgToolBar.Images.Add(Image.FromFile("search.ico"))

'Do the toolbar
tb1 = New ToolBar()
Me.Controls.Add(tb1)
tb1.ImageList = imgToolBar
tb1.Appearance = ToolBarAppearance.Flat
AddHandler tb1.ButtonClick, AddressOf ToolBarHandler

'Make a space that we can add when we want to
Dim btnSpacer As ToolBarButton = New ToolBarButton()
btnSpacer.Style = ToolBarButtonStyle.Separator
```

```
Dim btn As ToolBarButton = New ToolBarButton()
btn.ImageIndex = 0
btn.ToolTipText = "New Employee"
btn.Tag = "N"c
tb1.Buttons.Add(btn)

btn = New ToolBarButton()
btn.ImageIndex = 1
btn.ToolTipText = "Save Record"
btn.Tag = "S"c
tb1.Buttons.Add(btn)

btn = New ToolBarButton()
btn.ImageIndex = 2
btn.ToolTipText = "Delete Employee"
btn.Tag = "D"c
tb1.Buttons.Add(btn)
tb1.Buttons.Add(btnSpacer)

btn = New ToolBarButton()
btn.ImageIndex = 3
btn.ToolTipText = "Previous Record"
btn.Tag = "P"c
tb1.Buttons.Add(btn)

btn = New ToolBarButton()
btn.ImageIndex = 4
btn.ToolTipText = "Next Record"
btn.Tag = "E"c
tb1.Buttons.Add(btn)
tb1.Buttons.Add(btnSpacer)

btn = New ToolBarButton()
btn.ImageIndex = 5
btn.ToolTipText = "Help"
btn.Tag = "H"c
tb1.Buttons.Add(btn)

'Set up the list view of employees
lstEmps.SmallImageList = imgToolBar
lstEmps.View = View.List
```

```
'Do the buttons
cmdListByEmp.FlatStyle = FlatStyle.Popup
cmdListByEmp.Height = txtEmp.Height
cmdListByEmp.Top = txtEmp.Top
cmdListByEmp.ImageList = imgToolBar
cmdListByEmp.ImageIndex = 6
cmdListByEmp.ImageAlign = ContentAlignment.MiddleCenter
cmdListByEmp.Tag = True
AddHandler cmdListByEmp.Click, AddressOf CallEmployees

cmdListByNum.FlatStyle = FlatStyle.Popup
cmdListByNum.Height = txtNum.Height
cmdListByNum.Top = txtNum.Top
cmdListByNum.ImageList = imgToolBar
cmdListByNum.ImageIndex = 6
cmdListByNum.ImageAlign = ContentAlignment.MiddleCenter
cmdListByNum.Tag = False
AddHandler cmdListByNum.Click, AddressOf CallEmployees

'Do the status bar
Dim sb As StatusBarPanel = New StatusBarPanel()
sb.AutoSize = StatusBarPanelAutoSize.Spring
sb.BorderStyle = StatusBarPanelBorderStyle.Sunken
sb.Text = "Employee:"
sb1.Panels.Add(sb)

sb = New StatusBarPanel()
sb.AutoSize = StatusBarPanelAutoSize.Contents
sb.Text = DateTime.Today.ToLongDateString()
sb1.Panels.Add(sb)
sb1.ShowPanels = True

txtEmp.ReadOnly = True
txtNum.ReadOnly = True

dtHire.Format = DateTimePickerFormat.Short
dtHire.MaxDate = DateTime.Today
AddHandler dtHire.ValueChanged, AddressOf CalcTime

'Do the tabindexes on the form itself
txtEmp.TabIndex = 0
cmdListByEmp.TabIndex = 1
txtNum.TabIndex = 2
cmdListByNum.TabIndex = 3
```

```
        cmdEdit.TabIndex = 4
        tc1.TabIndex = 5      'Doing this starts the tabbing on the tab page
        cmdOK.TabIndex = 6
        cmdCancel.TabIndex = 7
        cmdHelp.TabIndex = 8
        'Do the tabindexes on the first tab page
        txtLast.TabIndex = 0
        txtFirst.TabIndex = 1
        txtMI.TabIndex = 2
        dtHire.TabIndex = 3
        txtDept.TabIndex = 4
        'Do the tabindexes on the second tab page
        cmbPay.TabIndex = 0
        chkManager.TabIndex = 1
        optHourly.TabIndex - 2
        optSalary.TabIndex = 3
        lstEmps.TabIndex = 4
        'Do the tabindexes on the third tab page
        dtBirthday.TabIndex = 0
        txtCar1.TabIndex = 1
        txtLic1.TabIndex = 2
        txtCar2.TabIndex = 3
        txtLic2.TabIndex = 4
        cmbParking.TabIndex = 5
    End Sub
```

There is quite a bit of code in this constructor. In fact, much of this code could have been dispensed with by setting the properties of the controls at design time. Often that is just what I do for small programs.

I must say this, though, about using the design-time property pages: When working in a team situation, I have found it is best to set up as many of the properties programmatically as I can. It is very easy for one person to screw up a nice setup by resetting some property in code that you have previously set via the property page. By the same token, anyone who accidentally sets a property using a property page will have the control set up the way it should be via code.

Anyway, regardless of how you decide to set up controls, if all your coding team members use the same design philosophy regarding the UI, you should be OK.

So, back at the ranch, our coding hero is busy entering in setup parameters for this small project. Let's discuss some of what's going on here. First of all, I get the code for the Buttons out of the way. I assign a delegate to each Button's click events. I also assign the text to the Buttons. I am doing this in code here to show you how the hot key system works.

Menus, ToolBars, and So On

The *hot key* system gives you the ability to underline a single letter in a word. This single letter then becomes the hot key, and when the user presses the Alt key plus this underlined letter the default action for that control will occur. This means that for a Button, it will be clicked; for a Tab page, that page will get the focus; for a menu item, the code for that choice will be invoked; and so on.

Look at any decent program and you will see hot keys for all the menu choices and all the buttons on the screen. This is vital to speeding up the user interface. The average user who uses your program once in a while will probably not use the hot keys, but someone who is proficient in your program will.

The next thing I do in the constructor is set up the menu system. Notice that I assign hot key–based text to the menu and I also assign delegates to handle the menu choices. I could assign a different delegate for each choice, but a single one is all that is needed. The delegate signature includes a sender object that I can use to figure out which menu item was clicked. These hot keys are called *access keys* in .NET parlance.

By the way, for you VB programmers new to .NET, notice that each menu choice is an object. This is very important to realize. In VB 6.0, each menu choice is just that: a choice. It is impossible using native VB 6.0 commands to add or delete menu items programmatically. In .NET, when the delegate is called, the object that is defined as the sender is the MenuItem object. In VB 6.0, each menu choice has its own click event. In .NET, you can combine all the click events into one delegate.

Because I add the menu to the project via code rather than adding it at design time, I need a way to add it to the list of controls that the form knows about. Usually, adding the control object to the control's collections of the form does that. The menu is different. You need to tell the form explicitly which menu to use. You can do so with the following bit of code.

C#

```
mnu = new MainMenu();
this.Menu = mnu;
```

VB

```
Dim mnu as MainMenu = new MainMenu()
me.Menu = mnu
```

One reason to add the menu in this way is that it makes it easy to change menus midstream. Suppose you have two levels of administrative users. One level is the superuser and the other level is the everyday user. You could have a complete menu system for each. One line of code is all it takes to show the superuser menu as opposed to the normal menu. I am using this feature in a program I am writing for work right now.

One more thing about the menu system for this project: I use speed keys to enhance the menu. A *speed key* is similar to a hot key in that you can invoke code by pressing it. However, it is not necessary for a speed key to be visible, whereas a hot key is visible.

I have assigned a hot key of Alt-X to the Exit menu choice. The user cannot press Alt-X any time to exit the program—the Exit menu choice must be visible on the screen first. I have assigned the speed key F12 to the same Exit menu choice. I can now press F12 at any time in this program and it will exit immediately. You can also assign speed keys to a menu and an accessibility object. I cover accessibility in Chapter 3. Speed keys are called *shortcuts* in .NET.

 CAUTION   Be careful that you do not assign the same hot key to multiple visible controls. You will not get the functionality you expect. Also, do not assign multiple hot keys within the same text. If I had done "E&x&it" instead of "E&xit", the letter *i* would be underlined, but Alt-X would be the trigger. This would definitely be undesirable.

Once the menu is done, I set up the ToolBar. This is interesting in that the ToolBar needs two objects to work properly. The first is the ToolBar itself (not too hard to figure that one out), and the second is an ImageList object. This ImageList holds all the icons I will use for the ToolBar. Using an ImageList does two things:

- An ImageList is fast because the images are stored in one place in memory in a binary format.

- An ImageList is necessary for localization. You can have several ImageLists, where each one contains images appropriate for a particular culture. You would then assign the proper ImageList to the ToolBar according to the culture setting.

The ImageList is assigned to the ToolBar so that you can reference the number of the image with the ToolBar rather than load a specific picture. No ToolBar code changes are necessary to change the picture shown to the user.

The ToolBar I set up is similar to the menu. I set each button's ToolTip text and assign a delegate to handle the click events. Notice that I assign a letter to each ToolBar button's Tag property. This letter corresponds with the hot key letter I assigned to each MenuItem. Doing this makes it easy for me to identify which Button was clicked, and because the Button Tag is the same as the Menu mnemonic, I can use the same code for the Button as the Menu.

There is one thing wrong with assigning a letter to the ToolBarButton Tag. This assignment is hard-coded, which makes it virtually impossible for me to localize both the menu and the ToolBar and still use the same parsing code for both. After all, the text for Exit in German does not contain an *x*, so the MenuItem mnemonic would be different. I would need to change the tag for each ToolBarButton for each culture I need.

 CROSS-REFERENCE   I cover localization concerns in Chapter 3. I show you a better way to synchronize the ToolBar and Menu code that is independent of text.

Adding the ToolBar to the form is simply a matter of adding to the form's controls collection as follows.

C#

```
tb1 = new ToolBar();
this.Controls.Add(tb1);
```

VB

```
tb1 = new ToolBar()
me.Controls.Add(tb1)
```

The last thing I would like to talk about in this section of code is the tab order. Now in VB 6.0, tab order is sometimes a tricky thing. If you have a situation like this project, with controls that are hidden inside tab pages, you can really get screwed up. In VB 6.0, each control on a form must have a unique tab index. This means that while you are tabbing through the controls on the first tab page, you could suddenly be taken to a control that is on another page but is invisible to the user at the moment. Suppose that control is a button that reformats your hard drive and the user pressed the Enter key. Your system would be toast!

The .NET controls work differently with regard to tab order. Each control can have the same tab index. The control that is in focus is determined by both the tab order index and the z-order. This allows me to give the controls that are the first page of the tab the same tab indexes as those on any other page. Because the controls on the current page have higher z-order that those on the other pages, the tab order works as I intended it to.

This is a great step forward in the history of tab orderdom. In VB 6.0, I would need to constantly turn on and off each control's TabStop property depending on if the control was visible at that moment or not. It is a pain in the neck and subject to bugs. Coding tab order in .NET is comparatively easy.

Now that you are done with this constructor code, let's move on to the next order of business.

Setup via the Form Load Event

Listings 2-2a and 2-2b show the code for the form's Load event handler and a helper function. First double-click the form, and then put the helper function below the Load event handler.

Listing 2-2a. C# Code for the Load Event Handler and Helper Function for the PowerUser Project

```csharp
private void Form1_Load(object sender, System.EventArgs e)
{
  FillList();

  foreach (TabPage p in tc1.TabPages)
  {
    foreach (Control c in p.Controls)
    {
      c.Enabled = false;
    }
  }
}

private void FillList()
{
  txtEmp.Text = "John Smith";
  txtNum.Text = "504";
  txtLast.Text = "Smith";
  txtFirst.Text = "John";
  txtMI.Text = "Q";
  txtTitle.Text = "Marketing Manager";
  txtDept.Text = "Marketing";
  dtHire.Value = DateTime.Parse("6/23/97");

  cmbPay.Items.Clear();
  cmbPay.Items.Add("W01");
  cmbPay.Items.Add("W02");
  cmbPay.Items.Add("W03");
  cmbPay.Items.Add("W04");
  cmbPay.Items.Add("B01");
  cmbPay.SelectedIndex = 0;
```

```
    lstEmps.Items.Clear();
    lstEmps.Items.Add("Grunt 1", 0);
    lstEmps.Items.Add("Grunt 2", 0);
    lstEmps.Items.Add("Grunt 3", 0);

    txtCar1.Text = "Pickup Truck";
    txtLic1.Text = "NOBUGS";

    cmbParking.Items.Clear();
    cmbParking.Items.Add("A1");
    cmbParking.Items.Add("A2");
    cmbParking.Items.Add("A3");
    cmbParking.Items.Add("A4");
    cmbParking.Items.Add("B1");
    cmbParking.Items.Add("B2");
    cmbParking.Items.Add("B3");
    cmbParking.Items.Add("B4");
    cmbParking.Items.Add("-NA-");
    cmbParking.SelectedIndex = 0;

    chkManager.Checked = true;
    optSalary.Checked = true;

    pic.SizeMode = PictureBoxSizeMode.StretchImage;
    pic.Image = Image.FromFile("nick symmonds.jpg");

}
```

Listing 2-2b. VB Code for the Load Event Handler and Helper Function for the PowerUser Project

```
Private Sub Form1_Load(ByVal sender As System.Object, _
                    ByVal e As System.EventArgs) Handles MyBase.Load
  Dim p As TabPage
  Dim c As Control

  FillList()

  For Each p In tc1.TabPages
    For Each c In p.Controls
      c.Enabled = False
    Next
  Next


End Sub
```

```
Private Sub FillList()
  txtEmp.Text = "John Smith"
  txtNum.Text = "504"
  txtLast.Text = "Smith"
  txtFirst.Text = "John"
  txtMI.Text = "Q"
  txtTitle.Text = "Marketing Manager"
  txtDept.Text = "Marketing"
  dtHire.Value = DateTime.Parse("6/23/97")

  cmbPay.Items.Clear()
  cmbPay.Items.Add("W01")
  cmbPay.Items.Add("W02")
  cmbPay.Items.Add("W03")
  cmbPay.Items.Add("W04")
  cmbPay.Items.Add("B01")
  cmbPay.SelectedIndex = 0

  lstEmps.Items.Clear()
  lstEmps.Items.Add("Grunt 1", 0)
  lstEmps.Items.Add("Grunt 2", 0)
  lstEmps.Items.Add("Grunt 3", 0)

  txtCar1.Text = "Pickup Truck"
  txtLic1.Text = "NOBUGS"

  cmbParking.Items.Clear()
  cmbParking.Items.Add("A1")
  cmbParking.Items.Add("A2")
  cmbParking.Items.Add("A3")
  cmbParking.Items.Add("A4")
  cmbParking.Items.Add("B1")
  cmbParking.Items.Add("B2")
  cmbParking.Items.Add("B3")
  cmbParking.Items.Add("B4")
  cmbParking.Items.Add("-NA-")
  cmbParking.SelectedIndex = 0

  chkManager.Checked = True
  optSalary.Checked = True

  pic.SizeMode = PictureBoxSizeMode.StretchImage
  pic.Image = Image.FromFile("nick symmonds.jpg")

End Sub
```

There is not much to talk about here except to say that because this is an example, I need to stuff some fake entries in some of the controls. One thing to note here is the use of the DateTime structure. If you are wondering why I do not create an instance of this structure (you should be wondering this), it is because this structure has several static methods. One of these is the Parse method that I use here.

TIP .NET has quite a few classes and structures with static methods. You should know by now what static methods are and how to use them. Making your own static classes and methods can be very useful.

Handling Events in the Form

The next section of code deals with the event handlers for this form. Listings 2-3a and 2-3b show the code for the various delegates that handle the events I am interested in.

Listing 2-3a. C# Code for Event Delegates

```
#region Events

private void CalcTime(object sender, EventArgs e)
{
  lblYears.Text = (DateTime.Today.Year - dtHire.Value.Year).ToString();
}

private void CallEmployees(object sender, EventArgs e)
{
}

private void ApplyChanges(object sender, EventArgs e)
{
  foreach (TabPage p in tc1.TabPages)
  {
    foreach (Control c in p.Controls)
    {
      c.Enabled = false;
    }
  }
}
```

```csharp
    cmdEdit.Enabled   = true;
    cmdOK.Enabled     = false;
    cmdCancel.Enabled = false;
}

private void EditFields(object sender, EventArgs e)
{
  foreach (TabPage p in tc1.TabPages)
  {
    foreach (Control c in p.Controls)
    {
      c.Enabled = true;
    }
  }
  cmdEdit.Enabled   = false;
  cmdOK.Enabled     = true;
  cmdCancel.Enabled = true;
}

private void ToolBarHandler(object sender, ToolBarButtonClickEventArgs e)
{
  switch ((char)e.Button.Tag)
  {
    case 'N':   //New
      //Your code here.
      break;
    case 'S':   //Save
      //Your code here.
      break;
    case 'D':   //Delete
      //Your code here.
      break;
    case 'X':   //Exit
      this.Close();
      break;
    case 'P':   //Previous
      //Your code here.
      break;
    case 'E':   //Next
      //Your code here.
      break;
    case 'H':   //Help
      //Your code here.
      break;
```

```
      case 'A':    //About
        //Your code here.
        break;
    }

}

private void MenuHandler(object sender, EventArgs e)
{
  MenuItem m;
  if(sender is MenuItem)
    m = (MenuItem)sender;
  else
    return;

  switch (m.Mnemonic)
  {
    case 'N':    //New
      //Your code here.
      break;
    case 'S':    //Save
      //Your code here.
      break;
    case 'D':    //Delete
      //Your code here.
      break;
    case 'X':    //Exit
      this.Close();
      break;
    case 'P':    //Previous
      //Your code here.
      break;
    case 'E':    //Next
      //Your code here.
      break;
    case 'H':    //Help
      //Your code here.
      break;
    case 'A':    //About
      //Your code here.
      break;
    }
}
#endregion
```

Listing 2-3b. VB Code for Event Delegates

```vb
#Region "Events"

  Private Sub CalcTime(ByVal sender As Object, ByVal e As EventArgs)
    lblYears.Text = (DateTime.Today.Year - dtHire.Value.Year).ToString()
  End Sub


  Private Sub CallEmployees(ByVal sender As Object, ByVal e As EventArgs)
  End Sub


  Private Sub ApplyChanges(ByVal sender As Object, ByVal e As EventArgs)
    Dim p As TabPage
    Dim c As Control

    For Each p In tc1.TabPages
      For Each c In p.Controls
        c.Enabled = False
      Next
    Next
    cmdEdit.Enabled = True
    cmdOK.Enabled = False
    cmdCancel.Enabled = False
  End Sub


  Private Sub EditFields(ByVal sender As Object, ByVal e As EventArgs)
    Dim p As TabPage
    Dim c As Control

    For Each p In tc1.TabPages
      For Each c In p.Controls
        c.Enabled = True
      Next
    Next
    cmdEdit.Enabled = False
    cmdOK.Enabled = True
    cmdCancel.Enabled = True
  End Sub


  Private Sub ToolBarHandler(ByVal sender As Object, _
                             ByVal e As ToolBarButtonClickEventArgs)
    Select Case (CType(e.Button.Tag, Char))
      Case "N"c 'New
        'Your code here.
      Case "S"c    'Save
```

```vb
        'Your code here.
      Case "D"    'Delete
        'Your code here.
      Case "X"    'Exit
        Me.Close()
      Case "P"    'Previous
        'Your code here.
      Case "E"    'Next
        'Your code here.
      Case "H"    'Help
        'Your code here.
      Case "A"    'About
        'Your code here.
    End Select

End Sub

Private Sub MenuHandler(ByVal sender As Object, ByVal e As EventArgs)
  Dim m As MenuItem
  If (sender.GetType Is GetType(MenuItem)) Then
    m = CType(sender, MenuItem)
  Else
    Return
  End If

  Select Case m.Mnemonic
    Case "N"    'New
      'Your code here.
    Case "S    'Save"
      'Your code here.
    Case "D"    'Delete
      'Your code here.
    Case "X"    'Exit
      Me.Close()
    Case "P"    'Previous
      'Your code here.
    Case "E"    'Next
      'Your code here.
    Case "H"    'Help
      'Your code here.
    Case "A"    'About
      'Your code here.
  End Select

  End Sub
#End Region
```

Let's look at the menu delegate. This is the only one where I test to see if a MenuItem actually called it. Note that the C# code is more straightforward for this task than the VB code.

C#

```
MenuItem m;
if(sender is MenuItem)
  m = (MenuItem)sender;
else
  return;
```

VB

```
Dim m As MenuItem

If (sender.GetType Is GetType(MenuItem)) Then
  m = CType(sender, MenuItem)
Else
  Return
End If
```

The C# code is easy to read in that it just asks the system: "Is the sender a MenuItem?" The VB code needs to explicitly check object types by using a method of one object and a .NET native method to get the type of a built-in object. Also note the type change. If I am to work with the methods and properties of an object, .NET must know what that object is. Changing type in C# is (to my mind) easier than in VB.

Steering the User

There are two delegates in this section that change the state of the Edit, OK, and Cancel buttons. Perhaps I should explain why you need to enable or disable these buttons at all. Basically it is to prevent the user from doing anything he or she should not be able to do.

At start-up, all the controls on the tab pages are disabled. This means that the user cannot make any changes. Because the user cannot make changes, there is no point in allowing the user to click OK or Cancel. This eliminates any sanity-checking code in the delegates that determine if the user should even be here. This has advantages to you in that potential bugs are fewer. It also has advantages for the user in that the user knows he or she cannot click OK or Cancel because those options are grayed-out. This is called "leading the user by the nose."

The user must click the Edit button to enable the controls for editing. Doing this also enables the Cancel and OK buttons, and at the same time disables the Edit button. After all, the user knows he or she is editing the record; there is no reason to allow the user to click it twice in the same session. Again, this eliminates potential bugs and state variables. Once the user clicks the OK or Cancel button, the screen reverts to its normal view-only mode.

This kind of user interface programming is quite common in database applications. Opening a database as read-only is much easier and faster than opening it up as read/write. Also, read/write involves record locking which, if not necessary, can cause program slowdowns.

It is always best to make sure that the user explicitly knows what he or she is doing. By clicking the Edit button, the user knows he or she is editing the record. The user is not allowed to leave the record until the edit is complete, either by clicking OK or Cancel.

Now, can you find the bug in these two routines? It is actually a problem of omission. I do not disable the buttons that allow the user to change records. These buttons, menu choices, and toolbar buttons relating to changing the record should all be disabled while the record is being edited. Either that or you should include code that notifies the user of unsaved changes when a record is changed without explicitly saving it.

Here is another point about the difference between C# and VB syntax. Consider the following lines of code.

C#

```csharp
foreach (TabPage p in tc1.TabPages)
{
  foreach (Control c in p.Controls)
  {
    c.Enabled = true;
  }
}
```

VB

```vb
Dim p As TabPage
Dim c As Control

For Each p In tc1.TabPages
  For Each c In p.Controls
    c.Enabled = False
  Next
Next
```

Notice the similarities. Both code snippets do the same thing using the same .NET constructs. However, the C# code is a little more compact in that you are able to (in fact, you must) declare and use a variable within the foreach clause. VB does not allow this; the variable must be declared on a separate line before use.

The Completed Data Entry Form

Notice that the CallEmployees delegate is empty. This delegate is used to call up the Employees form. You will fill this in later when I go over the second form.

Try compiling and running this project. Your initial form when running should look like the one shown in Figure 2-9.

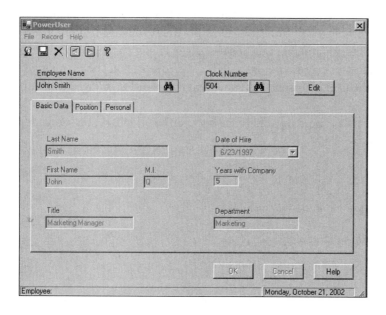

Figure 2-9. Running employee form

Select each tab and you will see all the controls are disabled. Now click the Edit button and your form should look like Figure 2-10.

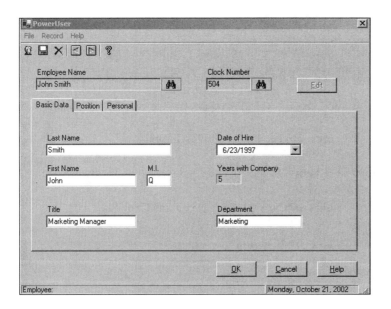

Figure 2-10. The form in edit mode

Notice that all the editable controls are enabled. Also notice that the OK and Cancel buttons are enabled, but the Edit button is not.

Start tabbing through the form as it is and the tab order will make sense. Even though many of the controls on the tab control have the same tab order index, only those at the top of the z-order (in this case, the first tab page) are being tabbed through. You now have a working employee record editing form. There is one last thing to add to this project, though: a shortcut to editing any record you want. You can do this via the search buttons next to the Employee Name and Clock Number fields.

Adding Quick Access to Employees

Now it is time to add a second form. This new form will be called up when the user clicks the cmdListByEmp and cmdListByNum buttons. These two buttons are used as a speedy way to call up a particular employee either by name or clock number. To set up the employee list form, follow these steps:

1. Add a new form called **EmpList**.

2. Make this form a fixed dialog box with no minimize or maximize buttons showing. Also make it start in the center of the screen.

3. Add a label to this screen whose text is centered and reads **Employees**.

4. Add a ListView control to the form called **lstEmps**.

5. Add a Button called **cmdOK** whose text reads **OK**.

6. Add a Button called **cmdCancel** whose text reads **Cancel**.

That's it for this form. It is pretty simple, as you can see from Figure 2-11.

Figure 2-11. The employee list form

Now it is time to add code to this form. The code is short enough to show here in its entirety. Listings 2-4a and 2-4b show the complete code for the EmpList form.

Listing 2-4a. C# Code for the EmpList Form

```csharp
using System;
using System.Drawing;
using System.Collections;
using System.ComponentModel;
using System.Windows.Forms;

namespace PowerUser_c
{
```

```csharp
public class EmpList : System.Windows.Forms.Form
{
  private System.Windows.Forms.Button cmdOK;
  private System.Windows.Forms.Label label1;
  private System.Windows.Forms.Button cmdCancel;
  private System.Windows.Forms.ListView lstEmps;

  private System.ComponentModel.Container components = null;

  #region class local variables

  string[,] Employees = new string[,] {{"Person A", "500"},
                                        {"Person B", "502"},
                                        {"Person C", "501"},
                                        {"Person D", "503"}};

  #endregion

  public EmpList( bool ByEmployee )
  {
    InitializeComponent();

    cmdOK.Click     += new EventHandler(this.UnloadMe);
    cmdCancel.Click += new EventHandler(this.UnloadMe);

    lstEmps.Items.Clear();
    lstEmps.View = View.Details;
    lstEmps.GridLines = true;
    lstEmps.FullRowSelect = true;
    lstEmps.Sorting = SortOrder.Ascending;
    lstEmps.Scrollable = true;

    //Add column headers
    lstEmps.Columns.Add(ByEmployee ? "Name" : "Clock #", -2,
                        HorizontalAlignment.Center);
    lstEmps.Columns.Add(ByEmployee ? "Clock #" : "Name", -2,
                        HorizontalAlignment.Center);

    //Add some people
    for(int k=0; k<Employees.GetLength(0); k++)
    {
      ListViewItem main = new ListViewItem(Employees[k, ByEmployee ? 0 : 1]);
      main.SubItems.Add(Employees[k, ByEmployee ? 1 : 0]);
      lstEmps.Items.Add(main);
    }
```

```
            lstEmps.ColumnClick += new ColumnClickEventHandler(this.ChangeSortOrder);
        }

        protected override void Dispose( bool disposing )
        {
          if( disposing )
          {
            if(components != null)
            {
              components.Dispose();
            }
          }
          base.Dispose( disposing );
        }

        #region Windows Form Designer generated code
...
...
...

        #endregion

        private void EmpList_Load(object sender, System.EventArgs e)
        {
        }

        private void UnloadMe(object sender, EventArgs e)
        {
          this.Close();
        }

        private void ChangeSortOrder(object sender, ColumnClickEventArgs e)
        {
          if(lstEmps.Sorting == SortOrder.Ascending)
            lstEmps.Sorting = SortOrder.Descending;
          else
            lstEmps.Sorting = SortOrder.Ascending;

        }
      }
    }
```

Listing 2-4b. VB Code for the EmpList Form

```vb
Public Class EmpList
    Inherits System.Windows.Forms.Form

#Region "class local variables"

    dim Employees(,) as string = new string(,) {{"Person A", "500"}, _
                                 {"Person B", "502"}, _
                                 {"Person C", "501"}, _
                                 {"Person D", "503"}}

#End Region

#Region " Windows Form Designer generated code "

  Public Sub New(ByVal ByEmployee As Boolean)
    MyBase.New()

    InitializeComponent()

    AddHandler cmdOK.Click, AddressOf UnloadMe
    AddHandler cmdCancel.Click, AddressOf UnloadMe

    lstEmps.Items.Clear()
    lstEmps.View = View.Details
    lstEmps.GridLines = True
    lstEmps.FullRowSelect = True
    lstEmps.Sorting = SortOrder.Ascending
    lstEmps.Scrollable = True

    'Add column headers
    lstEmps.Columns.Add(IIf(ByEmployee, "Name", "Clock #"), -2, _
                        HorizontalAlignment.Center)
    lstEmps.Columns.Add(IIf(ByEmployee, "Clock #", "Name"), -2, _
                        HorizontalAlignment.Center)

    'Add some people
    Dim k As Int32
    For k = 0 To Employees.GetLength(0) - 1
      Dim main As ListViewItem = _
              New ListViewItem(Employees(k, IIf(ByEmployee, 0, 1)))
      main.SubItems.Add(Employees(k, IIf(ByEmployee, 1, 0)))
      lstEmps.Items.Add(main)
    Next
```

```
      AddHandler lstEmps.ColumnClick, AddressOf ChangeSortOrder

    End Sub

  …

  …

  …

#End Region

  Private Sub EmpList_Load(ByVal sender As System.Object, _
                        ByVal e As System.EventArgs) Handles MyBase.Load

  End Sub

  Private Sub UnloadMe(ByVal sender As Object, ByVal e As EventArgs)
    Me.Close()
  End Sub

  Private Sub ChangeSortOrder(ByVal sender As Object,
                        ByVal e As ColumnClickEventArgs)
    If (lstEmps.Sorting = SortOrder.Ascending) Then
      lstEmps.Sorting = SortOrder.Descending
    Else
      lstEmps.Sorting = SortOrder.Ascending
    End If
  End Sub

End Class
```

Now that you have entered this code, you will need to go back to the main form and fill in the CallEmployees function.

C#

```csharp
private void CallEmployees(object sender, EventArgs e)
{
  Button b = (Button)sender;

  EmpList frm = new EmpList((bool)b.Tag);
  frm.ShowDialog();
}
```

VB

```
Private Sub CallEmployees(ByVal sender As Object, ByVal e As EventArgs)
  Dim b As Button = CType(sender, Button)

  Dim frm As EmpList = New EmpList(CType(b.Tag, Boolean))
  frm.ShowDialog()
End Sub
```

How the Employee Form Works

I use the same form when the user clicks either of the two search buttons located on the first form. What I want to do is to allow sorting of the employee list either by name or by clock number. I could use two forms but that is a waste. An object-oriented approach would be better.

Programmers who work in C++ have always had access to overloaded methods. VB programmers have not. I am betting, though, that even though the majority of VB programmers may not know about overloading, they wish they had it.

In short, *overloading* methods means that you can have more than one function with the same name but with different arguments. The classic example here is adding two numbers. In VB 6.0, if you wanted to add two longs and also add two singles, you would need two functions. One would be called AddLong with long integer arguments. The other would be called AddSingle with single type arguments.

Wouldn't it be better to have a single method called Add that took either type of argument? Overloading allows you to do that. You can have a method called Add that takes longs, and another method called Add that takes floats. This is called *polymorphism,* and it's a big part of object-oriented programming.

VB 6.0 programmers, rejoice! You can now overload functions.

One of the methods in a class that you can overload is the *constructor.* In C# the constructor is defined as having the same name as the class. In VB .NET the constructor is defined as having the name "New". Because constructors can be overloaded, this means that they can take arguments. This is very important in .NET. Look at the help for the Bitmap class. It has 12 overloaded constructors. I dare say that most of the classes in .NET have more than one constructor. And, hey, if they can do it, why shouldn't you?

This form has a single constructor, but it does have arguments. The argument denotes how the form should appear and how the sorting should happen. If the user clicks the button next to the employee's name, then the list is shown and sorted by employee. If the user clicks the button next to the clock number, then the list is shown and sorted by clock number.

Changing the Sort Order

Notice that I have a delegate assigned to the column header click event. This allows me to change the sort order every time the user clicks the column header. It does not matter which header is clicked, I still sort according to the first column. There is nothing explicit that says this is what will happen, and the novice user will probably not know this is available. The power user, however, will have seen this trick in another program and will expect it here.

It is very important to include as many common power-user tricks as possible in your data entry program. I have said it before, but these little things that allow the user to speed his or her way through your program will make the program a success.

So how would you improve this form? I can think of a few things that I would add to a professional program:

- Allow the user to move columns.

- Make the first column the sort column. If another column is moved here, then the list is re-sorted according to that column.

- Allow the user to print a quick columnar report based on the column setup and sort order the user created in this form.

You can implement these improvements fairly easily. The .NET help is pretty comprehensive and is much better than previous versions.

There are a whole host of things that you can add to this example to make it a real program. But, of course, I leave the coding up to you.

A Different Data Entry Screen: Console Applications

People who are old like me cut our teeth in the world of DOS. It is often something we all wish never evolved into Windows. DOS was very easy to work in. It was also very limiting.

Anyway, enough nostalgia. How many of you have written small utility programs? I know I have written a whole host of them. I often like to write small programs without a Windows interface. It makes the program smaller and consequently faster.

Back when I started out programming, writing windowless programs was called a living. Now they are called *console applications*. Few people can make a living these days writing just console applications. These applications do have their uses, though, and you should be aware of how to write them.

C and C++ programmers have always enjoyed the ability of writing console applications. VB programmers never could. The most common use for console applications these days is as debugging screens for a program. Often console applications are meant to be used only by those who wrote them or those with a great deal of technical knowledge about what they are doing.

The following example transfers the employee list screen from the last example to a console program. This program is tiny and has only one function, but it gives you an idea of how to get data from a user, validate it, and display some results. This is all easy in a Windows program, but you need a slightly different plan of attack when you write a console program.

First, start a new VB or C# console project. Mine is called "Console." Listings 2-5a and 2-5b show the code for this program.

Listing 2-5a. C# Code for the Console Program

```csharp
using System;
using System.Collections;

namespace Console_c
{
  /// <summary>
  /// Console application for simple data entry
  /// </summary>
  class Class1
  {

    [STAThread]
    static void Main(string[] args)
    {
      bool ByEmp = false;
      SortedList Emps = new SortedList();

      Emps.Add("500", "Person A");
      Emps.Add("502", "Person B");
      Emps.Add("501", "Person C");
      Emps.Add("503", "Person D");

      Console.WriteLine("Welcome to the Console Application for Data Entry.\n");
```

```
while(true)
{
  Console.WriteLine("Enter the sort key for employees.");
  Console.WriteLine("\n'N' for Sort by name, " +
                    "'C' for Sort by clock #, 'X' to exit program.");
  string SortOrder = Console.ReadLine();
  if(SortOrder.ToUpper() == "N" )
  {
    ByEmp = true;
    break;
  }
  else if(SortOrder.ToUpper() == "C" )
  {
    ByEmp = false;
    break;
  }
  else if(SortOrder.ToUpper() == "X" )
    return;
  else
  {
    Console.WriteLine("Only 'N' for Sort by name, " +
                      "'C' for Sort by clock # is allowed." +
                      " ('X' to exit program)");
    Console.WriteLine("\n\n");
  }
}

SortedList PrintEmp = new SortedList();
string Header = ByEmp ? "\tNames\t   Clock #" : "\tClock #\t   Names";


for(int k=0; k<Emps.Count; k++)
{
  if(ByEmp)
    PrintEmp.Add(Emps.GetByIndex(k), Emps.GetKey(k));
  else
    PrintEmp.Add(Emps.GetKey(k), Emps.GetByIndex(k));
}

Console.WriteLine("\n{0}", Header);
Console.WriteLine("\t--------------------");
for(int k=0; k<PrintEmp.Count; k++)
```

```
      {
        Console.WriteLine("\t{0}\t{1}", PrintEmp.GetKey(k),
                                    PrintEmp.GetByIndex(k));
      }

      Console.ReadLine();
    }
  }
}
```

Listing 2-5b. VB Code for the Console Program

```
Module Module1

    Sub Main()
    Dim ByEmp As Boolean = False
    Dim Emps As SortedList = New SortedList()

    Emps.Add("500", "Person A")
    Emps.Add("502", "Person B")
    Emps.Add("501", "Person C")
    Emps.Add("503", "Person D")

    Console.WriteLine("Welcome to the Console Application for Data Entry.\n")

    While (True)
      Console.WriteLine("Enter the sort key for employees.")
        Console.WriteLine("\n'N' for Sort by name, " + _
                        "'C' for Sort by clock #, 'X' to exit program.")
      Dim SortOrder As String = Console.ReadLine()
      If (SortOrder.ToUpper() = "N") Then
        ByEmp = True
        Exit While
      ElseIf (SortOrder.ToUpper() = "C") Then
        ByEmp = False
        Exit While
      ElseIf (SortOrder.ToUpper() = "X") Then
        Return
      Else
        Console.WriteLine("Only 'N' for Sort by name, " + _
                        "'C' for Sort by clock # is allowed." + _
                        " ('X' to exit program)")
        Console.WriteLine("\n\n")
      End If
    End While
```

```
Dim PrintEmp As SortedList = New SortedList()
Dim Header As String = _
            IIf(ByEmp, "\tNames\t   Clock #", "\tClock #\t   Names")

Dim k As Int32
For k = 0 To Emps.Count - 1
  If (ByEmp) Then
    PrintEmp.Add(Emps.GetByIndex(k), Emps.GetKey(k))
  Else
    PrintEmp.Add(Emps.GetKey(k), Emps.GetByIndex(k))
  End If
Next

Console.WriteLine("\n{0}", Header)
Console.WriteLine("\t--------------------")
For k = 0 To PrintEmp.Count - 1
  Console.WriteLine("\t{0}\t{1}", PrintEmp.GetKey(k), _
                                 PrintEmp.GetByIndex(k))
Next

Console.ReadLine()

  End Sub

End Module
```

As you can see from the program, I am in an infinite loop waiting for a key press from the user. This key press needs to be followed by a carriage return before the ReadLine() function returns. I then decide how to format the output based on what the user pressed.

One of the common things I see new programmers doing when testing for a character or string is either testing only for one case or testing for both upper- and lowercase. What I do here is convert the character to uppercase and only test for that. It uses less code and is not as subject to error.

One other thing I would like to bring your attention to is the type of collection I use. I use a SortedList to hold both the original information and to hold the displayable information.

The .NET Framework has a wide selection of collection classes. I suggest strongly that you become familiar with them. I use a specialized collection class in this example because it removes a lot of the work I would normally need to do.

I could have used a simple multidimensional array like I did in the Windows version of this program. The reason I chose the SortedList is because it holds a key-value pair and it automatically sorts on the key. I used the simple array in the

Windows version because for display purposes I put the information in a ListView control, which did the sorting for me.

Remember a while back when I said that I like defining some controls directly in code rather than placing them on the form itself? One of the reasons for this is that I can use some capability of the control that I would otherwise have to program myself.

It is not a hard stretch to rewrite this console application so that I use a ListView control as the vehicle to hold the sorted information. I could then go back to using a simple multidimensional array for the original employee list. I would use the ListView control to sort the information for me, and then I could extract the information as I printed it on the screen. The user never sees this invisible control.

Like anything else in .NET, however, the ListView control inherits quite a bit of functionality from parent classes and also includes a specialized collection. Why go overboard with all the features of the ListView control when you can implement a standard specialized collection, as I do in this example?

By the way, VB 6.0 programmers should definitely be at home with collections and the foreach construct. Although the collections provided in C# are not in the same form (more methods and properties) as the VB collection, they serve the same purpose. If you are a VB 6.0 programmer and you want to use the VB 6.0 type of collection, you can. VB .NET has a collection object that is identical to the VB 6.0 collection object. If you are a VB 6.0 programmer and you want to transfer over to C#, you will need to write a collection class that wraps up a SortedList and exposes the familiar four properties of a VB 6.0 collection:

- Add

- Remove

- Count

- Item (you will need to implement an iterator for this)

Screen Size, Control Manipulation, and Other Screen Management Options

OK, so now you know how to use some controls for data input in a Windows program. This section explores some other UI issues such as screen size, manipulation of controls, and so on.

You can do several things in your program to make for a better user experience. These things are not specific to data entry programs; they are useful for any Windows program that you make using .NET.

Most good software these days takes into consideration the limitations of the computer it is running on. This is especially true for the video monitor, as I describe in the next section.

Resolution Considerations

I am currently writing this text using a 21-inch monitor at a resolution of 1280×1024 pixels. This is a big monitor with a high resolution. I can fit all kinds of stuff on the screen. However, I also write and program on a laptop with a resolution of only 1024×768 pixels. Consequently, some things get more cramped and the software I use that is common to both machines needs to take this into consideration.

When you write your software, you will also need to take into consideration the resolution of the user's screen. It could be as low as 800×600 or as high as 1600×1200 (or even higher). Video Graphics Adapter (VGA) started out at 640×480, but for the most part you can discount that these days.

If you write your program on your 1600×1200 work monitor, and you design the form so it's maximized and designed to show all the information on the screen at once, you'll be unpleasantly surprised when you test it on a 800×600 screen. (Um . . . you will test it, won't you?)

How do you make your program work on any screen from 800×600 on up? The best way to accomplish this is by using features of .NET Windows forms that allow for automatic resizing of controls.

As you can probably guess, I have been writing extensively in VB 6.0. When I need to program a form in VB 6.0 I use a third-party control that I bought that allows me to resize the controls. Although it is possible to do control resizing using VB code, it is not pretty. In fact, if I wanted to write my own resizing code for VB 6.0, I would really need to use a subclasser to accomplish anything effective.

Anyway, back to .NET. You can do two things to make sure that your form works well on just about any computer:

- Size the form to be 800×600 fixed size.

- Size the form to be 800×600 and use the resizing capability of the controls.

The first option is easy. Create a new project and make the default form 800×600. Now alter the following properties in the Properties page:

1. Set the FormBorderStyle to FixedSingle.

2. Set the StartPosition to CenterScreen. (This or CenterParent is what I use most of the time.)

3. Set the MaximizeBox to false.

4. Set the MinimizeBox to false.

Now run your program. You will not be able to change the size of the form or even minimize it. If you like, you can put back the minimize button and now you can have the form either minimized on the task bar or normal size on the screen.

If you want to be really nasty, you can set the Locked property, which prevents the user from even moving the form. I once worked with a programmer who overlaid one form from one executable on top of another from a different executable and prevented the forms from being moved. This was his way of simulating multi-threading in VB 5.0. Not good.

Enabling Form Resizing

This type of form setup is very effective but also totally inelegant. It may be OK for quick-and-dirty projects and dialog box–style forms, but not for a nice program. What you need is to provide the user with the ability to size the form to any size he or she wants and still have all the controls look nice and in proportion. You will do this next.

Start a new VB or C# project. Mine is called "Resizable." Make the form size 536×432 and add the following controls:

1. Add a Label whose text reads **ComboBox**. Center the text within the Label.

2. Add a ComboBox below the Label.

3. Add a Label below the ComboBox whose text reads **Some List**. Center the text within the Label.

4. Add a ListView below the Label.

5. Add a Label whose text reads **TreeView**. Center the text within the Label.

6. Add a TreeView below the Label.

7. Add three buttons at the bottom of the form labeled **OK**, **Cancel**, and **Help**.

Figure 2-12 shows how the form should look.

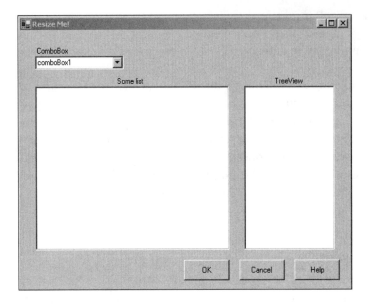

Figure 2-12. A resizable form

Now run the program. Resize the form and you can see that the controls do not move; instead, they disappear. You can see this happen in Figure 2-13.

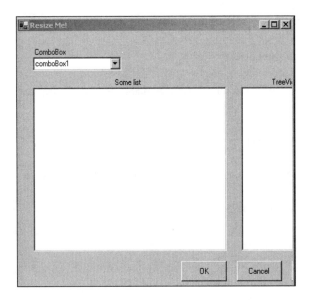

Figure 2-13. Disappearing controls

I guess the fastest way to fix this is to add scroll bars to the form itself. Try it. Change the form's AutoScroll property to true. Now run the form again. Instead of the controls totally disappearing, you will be able to scroll to them. This is shown in Figure 2-14.

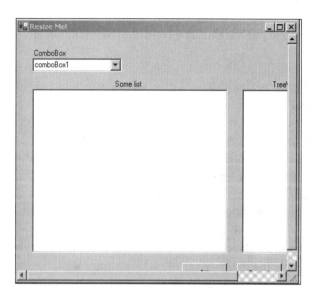

Figure 2-14. A form with scroll bars

Allowing the Controls to Resize

I suppose this is better than before, but still I would not like to work with a form that looks like this when maximized on my low-resolution screen. The best thing you can do here is to use the Anchor property of each control. You should also make sure that the user can't make the form smaller than a minimum size. Anchoring the controls without a minimum size can make for tiny controls, which makes your form look silly.

Change the following properties on the form and the controls:

1. Change the MinimumSize property on the form to be the current size, 536×432.

2. Change the Anchor property of the three buttons to be Bottom, Right.

3. Change the Anchor property of the TreeView control to be Top, Bottom, Right.

4. Change the Anchor property of the TreeView Label to be Top, Right.

5. Change the Anchor property of the ComboBox Label and the ComboBox to be Top, Left, Right.

6. Change the Anchor property of the Some List Label to be Top, Left, Right.

7. Change the Anchor property of the ListView control to be anchored at all sides.

Now compile and run the program. As you resize the control, you will see that you cannot make it smaller than the original size. Also, note that I am keeping the width of the TreeView control static while enlarging the ListView control to take up the space. You may want to do something like this when one control holds all the information you need in its default size. If there were a list with long strings in the ListView, expanding the form would let me see them better.

I also like to keep the standard buttons in the same place all the time. There is no need to alter the size or placement of these buttons.

So, after playing around with the Anchor property, I bet you are wondering what the Docking property is all about. Docking allows a control to be "pinned" to another control. If you dock one of the major controls on this form, such as the TreeView, to the bottom of the form, you will see it takes up all the room at the bottom of the form. Now any control that is docked to the bottom of the form after the TreeView will sit on top of the TreeView. Try this out and see what uses you can come up with for the Docking property.

Ambient Properties

The last thing I want to talk about in this chapter is the ambient properties. Did you even know these existed? There is no such property as "Ambient" on any control that you will find.

Try this. Increase the font size on the last form you made. You should see the font size on all the form's controls also increases. The Font property is an ambient property.

Most controls take some of their properties from the parent control. Here is what happens with ambient properties. If certain properties on a control are not explicitly set, that control will try to get its value for that property from the parent control. Once the property has been set, you can change the parent property and the control's property will not change. Try this:

1. Change the font on one of the buttons to be bold.

2. Set this Font property back to normal on the button.

3. Change the Font property on the form to be bold.

All the controls on the form change to bold except the button you just worked with. This is because you have already explicitly set this property on this control.

If the control has no parent, then it tries to set the property via the Site property. In other words, it tries to find some other control to ask what it should do.

I said that there was no such property as "Ambient" on a control. There is, however, an AmbientProperties class. This class defines the following properties as ambient:

- Cursor

- Font

- ForeColor

- BackColor

So why include this class in the Framework? You will want to inherit from this class if you make your own control. Just like writing a program that behaves according to a preconceived set of rules, your control will also be "expected" to have these ambient properties. Perhaps you should even add more.

Summary

This chapter introduced you to basics of UI design with regard to data entry programs. You used the following controls, among others:

- Menu

- ToolBar

- StatusBar

- Tab

Using these controls, you learned how to set up a simple data entry form and steer the user to enter values that were valid to begin with. You also saw how to prevent the user from doing certain things based upon the current data entry situation.

In the PowerUser project, you used certain Buttons to enable and disable some controls as well as other Buttons. This is desirable so you don't have to constantly check if the user is supposed to click a certain button while the program is in a certain state.

The last part of the chapter dealt with resizing controls and ambient properties. Both of these things will gain importance as you move on through the book.

The next chapter deals with more advanced data validation, including the use of some new controls.

CHAPTER 3

Data Presentation Screen Issues

IN CHAPTERS 1 AND 2 you dealt with only a portion of the data entry program; you stuck pretty much to designing the data entry screen itself. But what about the program as a whole? You will need to give some thought to how you want your program to work in its entirety.

This chapter deals with more of the predesign, if you will, of the data entry program you are writing. I cover in detail how to write multiple-document interface (MDI) and single-document interface (SDI) applications. Each of these design philosophies has advantages and disadvantages.

While I am on the subject of program design, I think it is prudent to cover some other, often forgotten aspects of program design: localization and accessibility. I cover these topics at the end of the chapter.

NOTE   I wrote a book on localizing software using .NET called *Internationalization and Localization Using Microsoft .NET* (Apress, 2002).[1] My discussion about localization in this chapter is nowhere near as thorough as in my previous book. It is intended here as an introduction.

The Single-Document Interface

This is the simplest interface you can present to the user. In a complicated program, however, it can also be the most confusing.

In Chapter 2 I showed you an employee editing form. It was a single-screen program where all data was entered on just one screen. Suppose this Employee screen was part of a bigger HR program that also included screens for training, payroll, and scheduling. An SDI program requires that you close one screen before

---

1. Shameless plug, I know, but I have to be my own marketing person when I can.

opening another. There would be no way to just flip back and forth between screens. This is the classic definition of an SDI program. Here are some common examples:

- *Notepad:* You must close one document before editing another.

- *WordPad:* You must close one document before editing another.

- *Calculator:* You can use only one calculator at a time.

In a classic SDI program such as Notepad, if you want to edit two documents at once you need to run two instances of the program. Neither instance of Notepad knows the other exists, and they do not interact. Figure 3-1 shows what a classic SDI HR application that includes an Employee screen might look like.

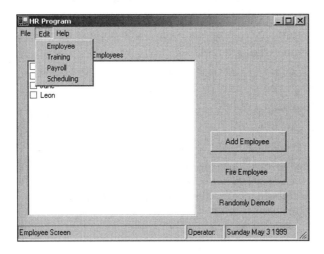

Figure 3-1. SDI example

The Employee screen in Figure 3-1 is rather simplistic. In order for the user to go to the training screen, the program would have to replace the Employee screen you see here. Although this works, it is limiting.

Another Type of SDI Program

Another type of SDI program is common these days. I call it the *scatter effect* program. In the case of the hypothetical HR program shown in Figure 3-1, if the user chose the Training module while in the Employee screen, the program would not replace the Employee screen. It would instead bring up another form on the desktop, which would look like a separate program altogether. However, it is not. The different screens can interact with each other and exchange information.

In this scenario, the user can have four forms open on the desktop, one for each module (Employee, Training, Payroll, and Scheduling). Can you imagine a program that could have a dozen or more forms open on the desktop at once? To me, this is chaos, but I bet you have already used a program that does this.

VB 6.0 has an option to work in an SDI environment or an MDI environment. The default is MDI, and this keeps things organized. I have a coworker, though, who likes the SDI environment. This means that each window is a separate screen, including all the forms, classes, and modules he has open. I frequently see him with a few dozen forms scattered all over his desktop.

If you come from the MSVC++ world or you have not programmed yet, you may not have seen this effect in VB 6.0. However, you do see it in Microsoft Word. Word used to have an MDI interface. It used to be that you could open up Word and then open as many documents as you wanted inside Word. Word is arguably the most ubiquitous program in the world, and I bet many people like to edit many documents at once. Word is now an SDI application, which means that each document is in a separate window. In my opinion, all this does is clutter up the taskbar.

The Multiform SDI Example

This next example shows you quite a bit about how SDI programs work. It includes five screens. There is a main screen that lets you choose to edit different parts of an HR program. I will be working from the example shown in Figure 3-1.

Before you attack the coding of an SDI program, you need to come up with a plan for how it will work. My plan for this one is based loosely on how Microsoft Word works:

- The program has a main form with a menu.

- The menu allows the user to choose different parts of the HR program to work on.

- Each part of the HR program is a new form that appears on the desktop in a random place.

- The main form has a Window menu option that shows all the HR screens the user has open.

- The Window option has a submenu item called "Close All Windows" that closes all the currently open windows.

- The Window menu option of the main screen denotes with a check mark the child form that is currently in focus.

- If the user chooses one of the forms listed under the Window menu option, that form gains focus.

- Only one instance of any of the HR forms can be running at a time.

- If the user chooses to edit a form that exists on the desktop, that form will gain focus.

- If the user closes an existing form, that form is deleted from the Window menu option.

- If the user closes the main form, the open windows automatically shut down.

This list does not even include any data entry or validation requirements. This example is just to show you what is involved in keeping track of SDI child forms in an SDI environment.

NOTE   Because I write examples in this book in both VB and C#, I append my example names with either –vb or –c. You do not have to do this, of course.

Start a new C# or VB Windows project. Mine is called "SDISample." You will need to follow these steps before you add any code:

1. Add a MainMenu to the form.

2. Type **File** in the MainMenu item and call it **mnuFile**.

3. Below mnuFile, type in **Close** and call this item **mnuClose**.

4. Next to mnuFile, type in **Edit** and call this item **mnuEdit**.

5. Below mnuEdit, type in **Employee** and call this item **mnuEmp**.

6. Below mnuEmp, type in **Training** and call this item **mnuTrain**.

7. Below mnuTrain, type in **Payroll** and call this item **mnuPayRoll**.

8. Below mnuPayRoll, type in **Scheduling** and call this item **mnuSked**.

9. Next to mnuEdit, type in **Window** and call this item **mnuWindow**.

10. Next to mnuWindow, type in **Help** and call this item **mnuHelp**.

11. Add a status bar to the form.

12. Add a Panel to the Panels collection in the status bar and make it read **Employee Screen**. Change the AutoSize property to Spring.

13. Add a Panel to the Panels collection in the status bar and make it read **Operator:**. Change the AutoSize property to Contents.

14. Add a Panel to the Panels collection in the status bar and type in the date. Change the AutoSize property to Contents.

15. Set the ShowPanels property to true.

16. Make the form start in the center of the screen.

Your form should look like the one shown in Figure 3-2.

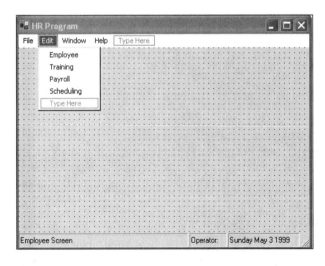

Figure 3-2. The main form for the SDI example

OK, you have this form—now for the others. First up is the Employee form. This one looks just like the form shown in Figure 3-1. Follow these steps:

1. Add a Label whose text reads **Employees**. Center the text.

2. Add a CheckedListBox with several items in the Items collection.

3. Add a Button whose text reads **Add Employee**.

4. Add a Button whose text reads **Fire Employee**.

5. Add a Button whose text reads **Randomly Demote**.

6. Add a Button whose text reads **OK**.

7. Add a Button whose text reads **Cancel**.

That's it for this form; you will not add any code to this form. The form should look like the one shown in Figure 3-3.

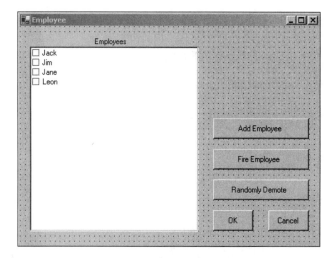

Figure 3-3. The Employee screen for the SDI project

The other three forms are really easy to create. They do not include any controls. Although it may seem boring, this example is meant to show an SDI project as a whole. Besides, as you will see, a form without any controls behaves slightly differently from one with controls.

Perform the following steps to finish the form setup for this project:

1. Add a Windows form called Payroll and change the text to **Payroll**.

2. Add a Windows form called Training and change the text to **Training**.

3. Add a Windows form called Scheduling and change the text to **Scheduling**.

That's it. Now it's time to add the code.

There are a few ways you can accomplish the objectives set out for this SDI project. For instance, you can give each child form a reference to the main form whenever it is called. This way, you can communicate back and forth to see what the state of the child form is. The states you are interested in are as follows:

- Is the child form active?

- Is the child form in focus?

- Is the parent form active?

It would not be too hard to have the child form tell the main form about its state. There is a better way, though. It is possible for the main form to keep track of everything about the child form without having to write any code at all in the child form. You do this using delegates.

Before I get into the code, I want you to look in the online help for the Form class. Look at all the events that can occur when just about anything happens to the form. Decide which events you can use and see if you come up with the same list as I have.

 NOTE It is very important that you understand how delegates work. You will see me adding new event handlers to events that happen in the child forms. You must understand that I am *not* replacing the event handler for these forms with my own delegates. I am *extending* the list of delegates that get called when this event happens. The base event handler for any event always occurs first, and you can override this if you want to.

There is something else I would like to point out before I start with the code. Usually you will see delegates being assigned as part of the initialization of a form. Most of the time, a programmer knows which delegates need to be assigned to which events at compile time.

I have done things a little differently in this project. The delegates get assigned to events dynamically. Because the main form can call up any child form at any time, this program needs to be a bit more reactive.

Anyway, here is the code. Get into the code pane of the main form. You will need to assign some class local variables, and you will put this section just above the form's constructor. The code for this follows.

C#

```
#region Class Local Variables

Payroll     PayForm;
Employee    EmpForm;
Scheduling  SkedForm;
Training    TrainForm;

#endregion
```

VB

```
#Region "Class Local Variables"

  Dim PayForm As Payroll
  Dim EmpForm As Employee
  Dim SkedForm As Scheduling
  Dim TrainForm As Training

#End Region
```

As you can see, you are keeping track of the forms via these variables. Basically, if the variable is null, the form does not exist—yet.

Before you code the constructor, you will need to add the delegates. Listings 3-1a and 3-1b show the delegate code for this project.

Listing 3-1a. C# Code for Event Delegates

```
#region Menu delegates

private void CloseMe(object sender, EventArgs e)
{
  this.Close();
}

private void OpenWindow(object sender, EventArgs e)
{
  MenuItem m;
```

```
if(sender is MenuItem)
  m = (MenuItem)sender;
else
  return;

if(m == mnuEmp)
{
  if(EmpForm == null)
  {
    EmpForm = new Employee();
    EmpForm.Load      += new EventHandler(this.ListWindows);
    EmpForm.GotFocus  += new EventHandler(this.ListWindows);
    EmpForm.Disposed  += new EventHandler(this.ByByWindow);
    EmpForm.Show();
  }
  else
    EmpForm.Focus();
}

if(m == mnuTrain)
{
  if(TrainForm == null)
  {
    TrainForm = new Training();
    TrainForm.Load      += new EventHandler(this.ListWindows);
    TrainForm.GotFocus  += new EventHandler(this.ListWindows);
    TrainForm.Disposed  += new EventHandler(this.ByByWindow);
    TrainForm.Show();
  }
  else
    TrainForm.Focus();
}

if(m == mnuPayroll)
{
  if(PayForm == null)
  {
    PayForm = new Payroll();
    PayForm.Load      += new EventHandler(this.ListWindows);
    PayForm.GotFocus  += new EventHandler(this.ListWindows);
    PayForm.Disposed  += new EventHandler(this.ByByWindow);
    PayForm.Show();
  }
```

```
      else
        PayForm.Focus();
    }

    if(m == mnuSked)
    {
      if(SkedForm == null)
      {
        SkedForm = new Scheduling();
        SkedForm.Load      += new EventHandler(this.ListWindows);
        SkedForm.GotFocus  += new EventHandler(this.ListWindows);
        SkedForm.Disposed  += new EventHandler(this.ByByWindow);
        SkedForm.Show();
      }
      else
        SkedForm.Focus();
    }
}

private void ListWindows(object sender, EventArgs e)
{
  mnuWindow.MenuItems.Clear();

  mnuWindow.MenuItems.Add("Close All",
                          new EventHandler(this.CloseAllWindows));
  mnuWindow.MenuItems.Add("-");
  if(EmpForm != null)
    mnuWindow.MenuItems.Add(EmpForm.Text,
                            new EventHandler(this.FocusForm));
  if(PayForm != null)
    mnuWindow.MenuItems.Add(PayForm.Text,
                            new EventHandler(this.FocusForm));
  if(TrainForm != null)
    mnuWindow.MenuItems.Add(TrainForm.Text,
                            new EventHandler(this.FocusForm));
  if(SkedForm != null)
    mnuWindow.MenuItems.Add(SkedForm.Text,
                            new EventHandler(this.FocusForm));
```

```
  foreach(MenuItem mnu in mnuWindow.MenuItems)
  {
    if(EmpForm != null && sender == EmpForm &&
       mnu.Text == EmpForm.Text)
    {
      mnu.Checked = true;
      break;
    }
    if(PayForm != null && sender == PayForm &&
       mnu.Text == PayForm.Text)
    {
      mnu.Checked = true;
      break;
    }
    if(TrainForm != null && sender == TrainForm &&
       mnu.Text == TrainForm.Text)
    {
      mnu.Checked = true;
      break;
    }
    if(SkedForm != null && sender == SkedForm &&
       mnu.Text == SkedForm.Text)
    {
      mnu.Checked = true;
      break;
    }
  }
}

private void FocusForm(object sender, EventArgs e)
{
  MenuItem m;

  if(sender is MenuItem)
    m = (MenuItem)sender;
  else
    return;

  foreach(MenuItem mnu in mnuWindow.MenuItems)
    mnu.Checked = false;
```

```csharp
            if(EmpForm != null && m.Text == EmpForm.Text)
              EmpForm.Focus();


            if(PayForm != null && m.Text == PayForm.Text)
              PayForm.Focus();


            if(TrainForm != null && m.Text == TrainForm.Text)
              TrainForm.Focus();


            if(SkedForm != null && m.Text == SkedForm.Text)
              SkedForm.Focus();


          m.Checked = true;
        }

        private void CloseAllWindows(object sender, EventArgs e)
        {
          if(EmpForm != null)
            EmpForm.Dispose();
          if(PayForm != null)
            PayForm.Dispose();
          if(TrainForm != null)
            TrainForm.Dispose();
          if(SkedForm != null)
            SkedForm.Dispose();

        }

        private void ByByWindow(object sender, EventArgs e)
        {

          if(sender == EmpForm)
            EmpForm = null;
          if(sender == PayForm)
            PayForm = null;
          if(sender == TrainForm)
            TrainForm = null;
          if(sender == SkedForm)
            SkedForm = null;

          ListWindows(null, null);
        }

        #endregion
```

Listing 3-1b. VB Code for Event Delegates

```vb
#Region "Menu delegates"

  Private Sub CloseMe(ByVal sender As Object, ByVal e As EventArgs)
    Me.Close()
  End Sub

  Private Sub OpenWindow(ByVal sender As Object, ByVal e As EventArgs)
    Dim m As MenuItem

    If sender.GetType() Is GetType(MenuItem) Then
      m = CType(sender, MenuItem)
    Else
      Return
    End If

    If m Is mnuEmp Then
      If EmpForm Is Nothing Then
        EmpForm = New Employee()
        AddHandler EmpForm.Load, AddressOf Me.ListWindows
        'AddHandler EmpForm.GotFocus, AddressOf Me.ListWindows
        AddHandler EmpForm.Click, AddressOf Me.ListWindows
        AddHandler EmpForm.Disposed, AddressOf Me.ByByWindow
        EmpForm.Show()
      Else
        EmpForm.Focus()
      End If
    End If

    If m Is mnuTrain Then
      If TrainForm Is Nothing Then
        TrainForm = New Training()
        AddHandler TrainForm.Load, AddressOf Me.ListWindows
        'AddHandler TrainForm.GotFocus, AddressOf Me.ListWindows
        AddHandler TrainForm.Click, AddressOf Me.ListWindows
        AddHandler TrainForm.Disposed, AddressOf Me.ByByWindow
        TrainForm.Show()
      Else
        TrainForm.Focus()
      End If
    End If
```

```
    If m Is mnuPayroll Then
      If PayForm Is Nothing Then
        PayForm = New Payroll()
        AddHandler PayForm.Load, AddressOf Me.ListWindows
        'AddHandler PayForm.GotFocus, AddressOf Me.ListWindows
        AddHandler PayForm.Click, AddressOf Me.ListWindows
        AddHandler PayForm.Disposed, AddressOf Me.ByByWindow
        PayForm.Show()
      Else
        PayForm.Focus()
      End If
    End If


    If m Is mnuSked Then
      If SkedForm Is Nothing Then
        SkedForm = New Scheduling()
        AddHandler SkedForm.Load, AddressOf Me.ListWindows
        'AddHandler SkedForm.GotFocus, AddressOf Me.ListWindows
        AddHandler SkedForm.Click, AddressOf Me.ListWindows
        AddHandler SkedForm.Disposed, AddressOf Me.ByByWindow
        SkedForm.Show()
      Else
        SkedForm.Focus()
      End If
    End If


End Sub


Private Sub ListWindows(ByVal sender As Object, ByVal e As EventArgs)
  Dim mnu As MenuItem

  mnuWindow.MenuItems.Clear()

  mnuWindow.MenuItems.Add("Close All", _
                          New EventHandler(AddressOf Me.CloseAllWindows))
  mnuWindow.MenuItems.Add("-")
  If Not EmpForm Is Nothing Then
    mnuWindow.MenuItems.Add(EmpForm.Text, _
                          New EventHandler(AddressOf Me.FocusForm))
  End If
  If Not PayForm Is Nothing Then
    mnuWindow.MenuItems.Add(PayForm.Text, _
                          New EventHandler(AddressOf Me.FocusForm))
  End If
```

```
    If Not TrainForm Is Nothing Then
      mnuWindow.MenuItems.Add(TrainForm.Text, _
                              New EventHandler(AddressOf Me.FocusForm))
    End If
    If Not SkedForm Is Nothing Then
      mnuWindow.MenuItems.Add(SkedForm.Text, _
                              New EventHandler(AddressOf Me.FocusForm))
    End If


    For Each mnu In mnuWindow.MenuItems
      If Not EmpForm Is Nothing And sender Is EmpForm AndAlso _
        mnu.Text = EmpForm.Text Then
        mnu.Checked = True
        Exit For
      End If
      If Not PayForm Is Nothing And sender Is PayForm AndAlso _
        mnu.Text = PayForm.Text Then
        mnu.Checked = True
        Exit For
      End If
      If Not TrainForm Is Nothing And sender Is TrainForm AndAlso _
        mnu.Text = TrainForm.Text Then
        mnu.Checked = True
        Exit For
      End If
      If Not SkedForm Is Nothing And sender Is SkedForm AndAlso _
        mnu.Text = SkedForm.Text Then
        mnu.Checked = True
        Exit For
      End If
    Next
End Sub

Private Sub FocusForm(ByVal sender As Object, ByVal e As EventArgs)
  Dim m As MenuItem
  Dim mnu As MenuItem

  If sender.GetType() Is GetType(MenuItem) Then
    m = CType(sender, MenuItem)
  Else
    Return
  End If
```

```
    For Each mnu In mnuWindow.MenuItems
      mnu.Checked = False
    Next

    If Not EmpForm Is Nothing AndAlso m.Text = EmpForm.Text Then
      EmpForm.Focus()
    End If

    If Not PayForm Is Nothing AndAlso m.Text = PayForm.Text Then
      PayForm.Focus()
    End If

    If Not TrainForm Is Nothing AndAlso m.Text = TrainForm.Text Then
      TrainForm.Focus()
    Fnd Tf

    If Not SkedForm Is Nothing AndAlso m.Text = SkedForm.Text Then
      SkedForm.Focus()
    End If

    m.Checked = True
  End Sub

  Private Sub CloseAllWindows(ByVal sender As Object, ByVal e As EventArgs)

    If Not EmpForm Is Nothing Then
      EmpForm.Dispose()
    End If
    If Not PayForm Is Nothing Then
      PayForm.Dispose()
    End If
    If Not TrainForm Is Nothing Then
      TrainForm.Dispose()
    End If
    If Not SkedForm Is Nothing Then
      SkedForm.Dispose()
    End If
  End Sub
```

```
Private Sub ByByWindow(ByVal sender As Object, ByVal e As EventArgs)

  If sender Is EmpForm Then
    EmpForm = Nothing
  End If
  If sender Is PayForm Then
    PayForm = Nothing
  End If
  If sender Is TrainForm Then
    TrainForm = Nothing
  End If
  If sender Is SkedForm Then
    SkedForm = Nothing
  End If

  ListWindows(Nothing, Nothing)
End Sub

#End Region
```

Now that you have entered the delegate code, you can enter the code needed in the constructor.

C#

```
public Form1()
{
  InitializeComponent();

  mnuClose.Click    += new EventHandler(this.CloseMe);
  mnuEmp.Click      += new EventHandler(this.OpenWindow);
  mnuSked.Click     += new EventHandler(this.OpenWindow);
  mnuPayroll.Click  += new EventHandler(this.OpenWindow);
  mnuTrain.Click    += new EventHandler(this.OpenWindow);

}
```

VB

```
Public Sub New()
  MyBase.New()

  'This call is required by the Windows Form Designer.
  InitializeComponent()

  AddHandler mnuClose.Click, New EventHandler(AddressOf Me.CloseMe)
  AddHandler mnuEmp.Click, New EventHandler(AddressOf Me.OpenWindow)
  AddHandler mnuSked.Click, New EventHandler(AddressOf Me.OpenWindow)
  AddHandler mnuPayroll.Click, New EventHandler(AddressOf Me.OpenWindow)
  AddHandler mnuTrain.Click, New EventHandler(AddressOf Me.OpenWindow)

End Sub
```

This code is exceeding simple considering what this program can do. As I said before, the bulk of the code is dynamic.

If you can hang on a minute before you run the program, I need to explain what is going on in the code. You will get a much better appreciation of it that way. First, look at the OpenWindow delegate. This method is meant to be called by a menu item only.

NOTE   Because I programmed the OpenWindow delegate, I know this method is meant to be called by a menu item only. You cannot always count on this, however. Someone else may accidentally copy and paste a section of code that uses this delegate for a Button Click event. (The delegate signature is the same.) It is best to test the Sender object before you actually do anything.

The first thing I do is test to make sure that the delegate was called by a MenuItem. Once I know that it is, I assign an internal variable that I can work with by casting the Sender object. Here is the code to do this:

```
MenuItem m;

if(sender is MenuItem)
  m = (MenuItem)sender;
else
  return;
```

TIP   This code should *never* fail. If it does fail, you have a programming error. Instead of quietly exiting like I do here, you should throw an exception for debugging purposes.

Now for the meat of this delegate. The following code is repeated in this method for each child form:

```
if(m == mnuEmp)
{
  if(EmpForm == null)
  {
    EmpForm = new Employee();
    EmpForm.Load      += new EventHandler(this.ListWindows);
    EmpForm.GotFocus  += new EventHandler(this.ListWindows);
    EmpForm.Disposed  += new EventHandler(this.ByByWindow);
    EmpForm.Show();
  }
  else
    EmpForm.Focus();
}
```

I check to see if the user clicked the Employee form menu item. (Reflection in .NET is a wonderful thing.)

NOTE   I show the use here of combining several events into a single delegate. In some cases, this is appropriate, but in others, it is not. I prefer to handle each event with its own delegate. If there is common code, I break it out into a helper function that gets called by each delegate. Among other things, doing this makes the delegate code shorter and easier to read.

Once I know this, I test to see if the form already exists on the desktop. If it does, I bring it into focus. This is the first of two ways this example programmatically brings a form into focus.

If the form does not exist yet, I instantiate it, assign a few delegates, and show the form nonmodally. Notice that I use the same delegate for the Load event and the GotFocus event. The ListWindows delegate tears down and reconstructs the window list according to the open forms.

I chain the disposed event of the form so I can reset the form-variable to null. This is how I keep only one instance of a particular form open at a time.

Now let's look at the ListWindows delegate. For clarity's sake, I don't bother testing for the correct Sender object here. The first thing I do is clear the window list of submenu items. I then add the standard Close All menu item to close all windows and a separator for the actual list of windows.

For each of the forms that is open (as determined by the form references), I add a menu item list to the window list. While I do this, I also dynamically assign the FocusForm delegate to each item in the list.

Once I have the list, I check the Sender object to see which form was instantiated (remember, I chain the Load event for each form to this delegate). The form that was instantiated (or received focus) gets its list item checked. This is how most window lists work. It allows you to see which window is currently active.

This delegate is called anytime a form is instantiated via the form's Load event. It is also called each time the form comes in focus via the GotFocus event. So in theory, if I click a form on the desktop, the window list will reflect this by placing a check mark next to that form.

Notice the delegate that I assign to each menu item in the form window list. It is the FocusForm delegate. Here it is again:

```
private void FocusForm(object sender, EventArgs e)
{
  MenuItem m;

  if(sender is MenuItem)
    m = (MenuItem)sender;
  else
    return;

  foreach(MenuItem mnu in mnuWindow.MenuItems)
    mnu.Checked = false;

  if(EmpForm != null && m.Text == EmpForm.Text)
    EmpForm.Focus();
```

```
    if(PayForm != null && m.Text == PayForm.Text)
      PayForm.Focus();

    if(TrainForm != null && m.Text == TrainForm.Text)
      TrainForm.Focus();

    if(SkedForm != null && m.Text == SkedForm.Text)
      SkedForm.Focus();

   m.Checked = true;
  }
```

Read the code and see if you can guess what it does. It is simple enough.

This delegate is called when a user clicks a form name in the window list. It unchecks all items in the list, tests which name was clicked, and brings that form into focus. This is the second way to bring an existing form into focus via code.

Running the Multiform SDI Example

Let's recap what happens in this example:

1. A user brings up a form via the Edit menu.

2. The form is put into the window list and is defined as being in focus by the check mark next to its name.

3. The user brings up the rest of the forms via the menu list.

4. All the open forms are listed in the window list. The last one up is in focus.

5. The user tries to bring up a form that already exists on the desktop. This is not allowed, but the form the user wanted is brought into focus. This is reflected in the window list.

6. The user chooses another form in the window list that is not checked. This other form is brought into focus, and the window list now reflects this.

7. The user clicks a form on the window, bringing it into focus. The window list reflects this.

8. The user closes a form on the desktop. The window list reflects this, and the user is now able to instantiate this form again via the Edit menu.

9. The user chooses the Close All menu item and all the open windows close. The window list reflects this and the user is able to instantiate all forms again via the Edit menu.

10. The user closes the main menu and the open child forms also close.

Step 10 is accomplished via garbage collection because the form reference variables I have get disposed during the Dispose event for the main form.

OK, now you can run the program and try this out. Test all the items in the previous list and see if you can find the bug. Found it yet?

Open all the forms via the Edit menu. Click each form and check the window list on the main form. The window list should reflect the current child form that is in focus. This works for all forms except the Employee form.

What gives? I assigned the GotFocus event to the correct delegate. Every other form works. The problem is one of the chicken or the egg. The only difference between the Employee form and the others is that the Employee form has controls. Try this: Put a button on the Payroll form and run the program again. You will see that now the Payroll form acts like the Employee form.

The reason is that the form never gets focus. As soon as there is a single control on the form, that control receives the focus. This is, of course, provided that the control *can* receive focus. So how do you get around this?

Replace the code that assigned the GotFocus event of each form to the ListWindows delegate with the form's click event. Your code should look like this:

```
EmpForm.Activated += new EventHandler(this.ListWindows);
```

Do this for each form. This simple change will make the whole system work as it should. Figure 3-4 shows my desktop with all windows open.

So that is the SDI project. In this section I covered one of the two ways you can present data entry forms to a user. I explain the other way in the next section.

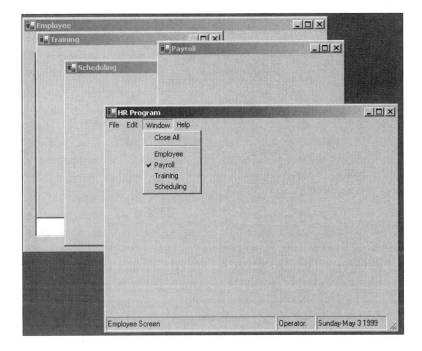

Figure 3-4. All forms in the SDI project shown on the desktop

VB and C# Differences

I would like you to note one thing about the VB code as opposed to the C# code.
Consider these lines of code:

C#

```
if(EmpForm != null && m.Text == EmpForm.Text)
  EmpForm.Focus();
```

VB

```
If Not EmpForm Is Nothing AndAlso m.Text = EmpForm.Text Then
  EmpForm.Focus()
End If
```

In standard VB 6.0 there is no such thing as the keyword AndAlso. In fact, most VB 6.0 programmers would use the keyword And instead. But then again, anyone who has programmed in VB knows that using the keyword And in this case creates a bug.

VB has the unfortunate tendency to evaluate a complete If statement before determining its Boolean value. C++, C, and C# do not do this. These languages allow you to short-circuit a multistatement line. What I mean by this is that if you are testing two statements on one line such as "if A is false and B is false," C# will not test for "B is false" if A turns out to be false. This allows the programmer to write code that, if evaluated, would fail under certain circumstances but not others. This is OK if the first test always fails and if the second test cannot be evaluated.

VB tests both statements before deciding if it should go on. So in this case, if EmpForm equaled nothing, the program would crash on testing the text value of EmpForm, even though technically the If statement already failed on the first test.

This was incredibly annoying[2] in VB 6.0 because it forced you to nest If-Then statements. For years I have been waiting for VB to change to the way C++ worked in this manner. Well, the original beta of VB .NET did change the AND keyword to work properly, but VB programmers complained and Microsoft capitulated. So Microsoft added the keyword AndAlso, which I guess satisfies both camps.

Use the AndAlso keyword often. It makes for more compact and faster-running code.

The Multiple-Document Interface

When you think about it, the SDI as I have shown it here is actually a misnomer. It does, after all, show multiple documents. It just does not show them in a cohesive manner like the MDI interface does.

So what is an MDI program, anyway? An MDI application has a form that acts as a container for any child forms that belong to it. Word 97 is a true MDI application. Excel is also a true MDI application. Figure 3-5 shows you the SDI project you just completed reformulated as an MDI application.

---

2. Soapbox time!

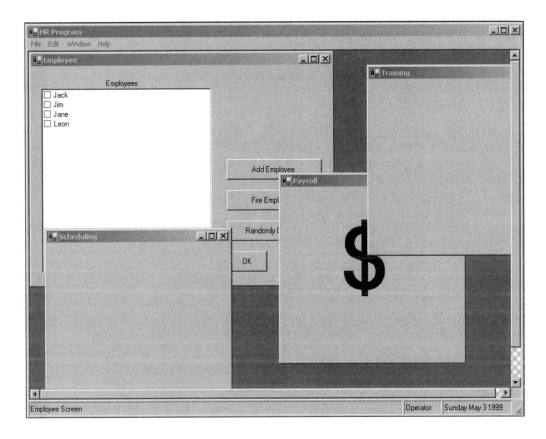

Figure 3-5. The MDI form of the SDI project

It is actually quite easy to convert the SDI application to an MDI application, and I show you how to do so in this section. Once you have finished with the code, you will see that the .NET Framework supports many nice features of MDI applications that you would normally have to program yourself in an SDI environment.

Start a new C# or VB project. Mine is called "MDIapp." While you have this new project open, start up the SDI project you just finished in a different window. You will need to complete the following steps to generate this project:

1. Size the existing form to be 800×600. Name it **UberForm** and change its text to read **HR Program**.

2. Make the form start up in the center of the screen.

3. Change the IsMdiContainer property to true.

4. Copy and paste the MainMenu control from the SDI project to the form on this project. (I love how copy and paste works between .NET projects.)

5. Delete the separator bar from the Window menu choices in the main menu (under the Close All choice).

6. In the Property window for the Window choice, change the MdiList property to true.

7. Add **Tile Horizontally** to the Window menu and name it **mnuHoriz**.

8. Add **Tile Vertically** to the Window menu and name it **mnuVert**.

9. Add **Cascade** to the Window menu and name it **mnuCascade**.

10. Copy and paste the status bar from the SDI project to the main form on this project.

11. Create a new form called **Employee**.

12. Copy and paste the controls from the Employee form in the SDI application to this Employee form.

13. Create a new form called **Payroll**.

14. Create a new form called **Training**.

15. Create a new form called **Scheduling**.

16. Add a label on the Payroll form called **lblCash**. Put a dollar sign ($) in for the Text property. Center the text and set the font at 100 points.

This is it for the visible part of the MDI application. You can now close the SDI project. Listings 3-2a and 3-2b show the code for the MDI application's main form.

Listing 3-2a. C# Code for the MDI Application

```csharp
using System;
using System.Drawing;
using System.Collections;
using System.ComponentModel;
using System.Windows.Forms;
using System.Data;

namespace MDIapp_c
{
  /// <summary>
  /// Summary description for Form1.
  /// </summary>
  public class UberForm : System.Windows.Forms.Form
  {
    private System.Windows.Forms.MainMenu mainMenu1;
    private System.Windows.Forms.MenuItem mnuFile;
    private System.Windows.Forms.MenuItem mnuClose;
    private System.Windows.Forms.MenuItem mnuEdit;
    private System.Windows.Forms.MenuItem mnuEmp;
    private System.Windows.Forms.MenuItem mnuTrain;
    private System.Windows.Forms.MenuItem mnuPayroll;
    private System.Windows.Forms.MenuItem mnuSked;
    private System.Windows.Forms.MenuItem mnuWindow;
    private System.Windows.Forms.MenuItem mnuHelp;
    private System.Windows.Forms.StatusBar statusBar1;
    private System.Windows.Forms.StatusBarPanel statusBarPanel1;
    private System.Windows.Forms.StatusBarPanel statusBarPanel2;
    private System.Windows.Forms.StatusBarPanel statusBarPanel3;
    private System.ComponentModel.Container components = null;
    private System.Windows.Forms.MenuItem mnuHoriz;
    private System.Windows.Forms.MenuItem mnuVert;
    private System.Windows.Forms.MenuItem mnuCascade;
    private System.Windows.Forms.MenuItem mnuCloseAll;

    #region Class Local Variables

    Payroll     PayForm;
    Employee    EmpForm;
    Scheduling  SkedForm;
    Training    TrainForm;

    #endregion
```

```csharp
public UberForm()
{
  InitializeComponent();

  this.Menu = mainMenu1;
  mnuClose.Click     += new EventHandler(this.CloseMe);
  mnuEmp.Click       += new EventHandler(this.OpenWindow);
  mnuSked.Click      += new EventHandler(this.OpenWindow);
  mnuPayroll.Click   += new EventHandler(this.OpenWindow);
  mnuTrain.Click     += new EventHandler(this.OpenWindow);
  mnuCloseAll.Click  += new EventHandler(this.CloseAllWindows);

  mnuHoriz.Click     += new EventHandler(this.ArrangeWindow);
  mnuVert.Click      += new EventHandler(this.ArrangeWindow);
  mnuCascade.Click   += new EventHandler(this.ArrangeWindow);

}

protected override void Dispose( bool disposing )
{
  if( disposing )
  {
    if (components != null)
    {
      components.Dispose();
    }
  }
  base.Dispose( disposing );
}

#region Windows Form Designer generated code
...
...
...

#endregion

[STAThread]
static void Main()
{
  Application.Run(new UberForm());
}
```

```csharp
private void UberForm_Load(object sender, System.EventArgs e)
{
}


#region events

private void CloseMe(object sender, EventArgs e)
{
  this.Close();
}

private void OpenWindow(object sender, EventArgs e)
{
  MenuItem m;

  if(sender is MenuItem)
    m = (MenuItem)sender;
  else
    return;

  if(m == mnuEmp)
  {
    if(EmpForm == null)
    {
      EmpForm = new Employee();
      EmpForm.MdiParent = this;
      EmpForm.Disposed  += new EventHandler(this.ByByWindow);
      EmpForm.Show();
    }
    else
      EmpForm.Focus();
  }

  if(m == mnuTrain)
  {
    if(TrainForm == null)
    {
      TrainForm = new Training();
      TrainForm.MdiParent = this;
      TrainForm.Disposed  += new EventHandler(this.ByByWindow);
      TrainForm.Show();
    }
    else
      TrainForm.Focus();
  }
```

```
      if(m == mnuPayroll)
      {
        if(PayForm == null)
        {
          PayForm = new Payroll();
          PayForm.MdiParent = this;
          PayForm.Disposed  += new EventHandler(this.ByByWindow);
          PayForm.Show();
        }
        else
          PayForm.Focus();
      }

      if(m == mnuSked)
      {
        if(SkedForm == null)
        {
          SkedForm = new Scheduling();
          SkedForm.MdiParent = this;
          SkedForm.Disposed  += new EventHandler(this.ByByWindow);
          SkedForm.Show();
        }
        else
          SkedForm.Focus();
      }

    }

    private void CloseAllWindows(object sender, EventArgs e)
    {
      if(EmpForm != null)
        EmpForm.Dispose();
      if(PayForm != null)
        PayForm.Dispose();
      if(TrainForm != null)
        TrainForm.Dispose();
      if(SkedForm != null)
        SkedForm.Dispose();

    }
```

```
private void ByByWindow(object sender, EventArgs e)
{

  if(sender == EmpForm)
    EmpForm = null;
  if(sender == PayForm)
    PayForm = null;
  if(sender == TrainForm)
    TrainForm = null;
  if(sender == SkedForm)
    SkedForm = null;

}

private void ArrangeWindow(object sender, EventArgs e)
{
  MenuItem m;

  if(sender is MenuItem)
    m = (MenuItem)sender;
  else
    return;

  if(m == mnuHoriz)
    this.LayoutMdi(MdiLayout.TileHorizontal);
  if(m == mnuVert)
    this.LayoutMdi(MdiLayout.TileVertical);
  if(m == mnuCascade)
    this.LayoutMdi(MdiLayout.Cascade);

}

#endregion
}
}
```

Listing 3-2b. VB Code for the MDI Application

```vb
Public Class UberForm
  Inherits System.Windows.Forms.Form

#Region "Class Local Variables"

  Dim PayForm As Payroll
  Dim EmpForm As Employee
  Dim SkedForm As Scheduling
  Dim TrainForm As Training

#End Region

#Region " Windows Form Designer generated code "

  Public Sub New()
    MyBase.New()

    'This call is required by the Windows Form Designer.
    InitializeComponent()

    Me.Menu = mainMenu1
    AddHandler mnuClose.Click, New EventHandler(AddressOf Me.CloseMe)
    AddHandler mnuEmp.Click, New EventHandler(AddressOf Me.OpenWindow)
    AddHandler mnuSked.Click, New EventHandler(AddressOf Me.OpenWindow)
    AddHandler mnuPayroll.Click, New EventHandler(AddressOf Me.OpenWindow)
    AddHandler mnuTrain.Click, New EventHandler(AddressOf Me.OpenWindow)
    AddHandler mnuCloseAll.Click, New EventHandler(AddressOf Me.CloseAllWindows)

    AddHandler mnuHoriz.Click, New EventHandler(AddressOf Me.ArrangeWindow)
    AddHandler mnuVert.Click, New EventHandler(AddressOf Me.ArrangeWindow)
    AddHandler mnuCascade.Click, New EventHandler(AddressOf Me.ArrangeWindow)

  End Sub

  …
  …
  …
#End Region

  Private Sub UberForm_Load(ByVal sender As System.Object, _
                            ByVal e As System.EventArgs) Handles MyBase.Load
  End Sub
```

```vb
#Region "Events"

  Private Sub CloseMe(ByVal sender As Object, ByVal e As EventArgs)
    Me.Close()
  End Sub

  Private Sub OpenWindow(ByVal sender As Object, ByVal e As EventArgs)
    Dim m As MenuItem

    If sender.GetType() Is GetType(MenuItem) Then
      m = CType(sender, MenuItem)
    Else
      Return
    End If

    If m Is mnuEmp Then
      If EmpForm Is Nothing Then
        EmpForm = New Employee()
        AddHandler EmpForm.Disposed, AddressOf Me.ByByWindow
        EmpForm.MdiParent = Me
        EmpForm.Show()
      Else
        EmpForm.Focus()
      End If
    End If

    If m Is mnuTrain Then
      If TrainForm Is Nothing Then
        TrainForm = New Training()
        AddHandler TrainForm.Disposed, AddressOf Me.ByByWindow
        TrainForm.MdiParent = Me
        TrainForm.Show()
      Else
        TrainForm.Focus()
      End If
    End If

    If m Is mnuPayroll Then
      If PayForm Is Nothing Then
        PayForm = New Payroll()
        AddHandler PayForm.Disposed, AddressOf Me.ByByWindow
        PayForm.MdiParent = Me
        PayForm.Show()
```

```
      Else
        PayForm.Focus()
      End If
    End If


    If m Is mnuSked Then
      If SkedForm Is Nothing Then
        SkedForm = New Scheduling()
        AddHandler SkedForm.Disposed, AddressOf Me.ByByWindow
        SkedForm.MdiParent = Me
        SkedForm.Show()
      Else
        SkedForm.Focus()
      End If
    End If


  End Sub

  Private Sub ArrangeWindow(ByVal sender As Object, ByVal e As EventArgs)
    Dim m As MenuItem

    If sender.GetType() Is GetType(MenuItem) Then
      m = CType(sender, MenuItem)
    Else
      Return
    End If


    If m Is mnuHoriz Then
      Me.LayoutMdi(MdiLayout.TileHorizontal)
    End If


    If m Is mnuVert Then
      Me.LayoutMdi(MdiLayout.TileVertical)
    End If


    If m Is mnuCascade Then
      Me.LayoutMdi(MdiLayout.Cascade)
    End If


  End Sub

  Private Sub CloseAllWindows(ByVal sender As Object, ByVal e As EventArgs)
```

```
      If Not EmpForm Is Nothing Then
        EmpForm.Dispose()
      End If
      If Not PayForm Is Nothing Then
        PayForm.Dispose()
      End If
      If Not TrainForm Is Nothing Then
        TrainForm.Dispose()
      End If
      If Not SkedForm Is Nothing Then
        SkedForm.Dispose()
      End If
    End Sub


    Private Sub ByByWindow(ByVal sender As Object, ByVal e As EventArgs)

      If sender Is EmpForm Then
        EmpForm = Nothing
      End If
      If sender Is PayForm Then
        PayForm = Nothing
      End If
      If sender Is TrainForm Then
        TrainForm = Nothing
      End If
      If sender Is SkedForm Then
        SkedForm = Nothing
      End If
    End Sub
#End Region
End Class
```

There is not anywhere near as much to this code. I do not have to keep track of the windows for listing purposes anymore. The .NET Framework does that by using just one property in the menu. I had to capture and dissect all kinds of events in the SDI project to accomplish the same thing.

Notice that when I instantiate each form, I make its MdiParent equal to the main form. This is all I need to do to make a form a child. Leave this line of code out and your child form will be an SDI. This is a great enhancement over VB 6.0, where you had to change the form's property at design time to go from being an MDI child to not. It makes it hard to reuse the same form in two projects both ways.

If you think about it, there is not much you have to do to add a menu option to make this project an SDI or an MDI on the fly. You can do all the rearranging in code. As a matter of fact, you can copy the SDI project's main form code over to this one and do just that if you like. Let me know how you get on, OK?

The Context Menu in MDI Applications

When you write MDI applications, you need to be cognizant of how menus and toolbars are coordinated. If there is a menu for a child window and a menu for the main MDI container form, the two will be merged when the child form opens. The same is true for a toolbar.

But what about pop-up menus? These are normally called *context menus* in .NET. This is another great stride forward from VB 6.0.

VB 6.0 had no menu negotiation, only toolbar negotiation. This means that if you had a child window with its own menu, it would completely replace the main form's menu. This was a pain, but you could get around it. The real pain was in using pop-up menus.

In VB 6.0 a pop-up menu is taken from the main menu. If you had even an invisible menu for pop-up purposes on an MDI child form, it would wipe out the main form's menu. It took me a long time to develop a trick to get around this problem in VB 6.0 by using a surrogate form whose only purpose in life was to provide me with a pop-up menu that did not interfere with the main form's menu.

.NET has no such restriction. As you have seen with the main menu, creating a pop-up menu is just as easy and is not dependent upon any existing control.

The Payroll form has a label with a big dollar sign ($) on it. Type in the following code for the constructor for this form.

C#

```csharp
public Payroll()
{
  InitializeComponent();

  ContextMenu m = new ContextMenu();
  m.MenuItems.Add("Add money to employee");
  m.MenuItems.Add("Remove money from employee");
  m.MenuItems.Add("Give raises to everyone");
  MenuItem mnu = m.MenuItems[m.MenuItems.Count-1];
  mnu.Enabled = false;
  m.MenuItems.Add("Cut in pay");

  lblCash.ContextMenu = m;

}
```

VB

```vb
Public Sub New()
  MyBase.New()

  'This call is required by the Windows Form Designer.
  InitializeComponent()

  Dim m As ContextMenu
  m = New ContextMenu()
  m.MenuItems.Add("Add money to employee")
  m.MenuItems.Add("Remove money from employee")
  m.MenuItems.Add("Give raises to everyone")
  Dim mnu As MenuItem = m.MenuItems(m.MenuItems.Count - 1)
  mnu.Enabled = False
  m.MenuItems.Add("Cut in pay")

  lblCash.ContextMenu = m

End Sub
```

As you can see, it is very easy to create a context menu that pops up when you right-click the dollar sign. This code has nothing to do with the main form.

NOTE   The online help for .NET contains many examples of how to create and use MDI applications. You will also find quite a bit of help on how menus are handled in .NET.

This all I cover in this chapter with regard to creating SDI and MDI applications. As far as which one you should use for your data entry program, this up to you. I prefer an SDI application if the application will have only a few screens that can be filled in one at time. I do not like lots of screens littering my desktop. I use an MDI application if the application will have quite a few screens that can be open at the same time. I like to be able to minimize the whole application if I want.

Making Your Application Available to Everyone

This section deals with two subjects that are more often than not either just glossed over or ignored completely: localization and accessibility.

Localization and *internationalization* are the processes of preparing your program to run in different cultures using multiple languages. This subject is big enough for a whole book, but I just provide you with the basics here.

 TIP   If you think you will run your program in another country, I suggest you read my book *Internationalization and Localization Using Microsoft .NET* (Apress, 2002). In it, I cover localization from soup to nuts.

Most people think of localization as removing the text strings and replacing them with other languages' text strings. As you will see, there is far more to it than that.

Accessibility is another subject that gets short shrift in computer language books. I don't know why. Not to be too mercenary, but there is a big market for accessible programs. An example of an accessible program is a speech recognizer. Research has been going on for years to create one that really works.

Internationalizing Your Program

I guess the first place to start with this topic is design. I have localized many programs after the fact, and quite a few of them needed some major cosmetic surgery. This is mainly due to the differences in the size of a string from one language to another. In general, a control that holds a text string needs to be about twice as long as it normally would. For example, if you have a label on a form whose text reads "Employee Form," it needs to be sized so it can hold 26 letters instead of just 13. This is because in general you need twice as many letters for a string in another language as you do in English. Table 3-1 shows approximately how much a string will grow when translated.

Table 3-1. Buffer Size Growth Based on Original String Length

English	Other Language
1 to 5	100%
6 to 20	70%
20 to 50	30%
> 50	15%

I suppose I could be cynical in analyzing this table by saying that English is terse when using few words, but it is long-winded when speaking volumes. Anyway, I have found that in general this is true.

Internationalizing your program requires that you make the label (or text) longer than normal. Your program may not look as tight graphically when you leave room for internationalization, but it will not have clipped and wrapped text when it is translated, either. If you do not plan correctly, your program could look like a complete mess when you add another language.

Identifying Cultures

Before I get into the specifics of how to localize a program, I first need to go over how to identify your locale. For the purposes of this book, a "locale" is the same as the "culture."

There are two ways to identify a culture. The first is by the language and the country/region. .NET follows International Organization for Standardization (ISO) standards to identify a culture. The language code is a two-letter identifier derived from the ISO 639-1 standard. The region code, which is also a two-letter identifier, is derived from the ISO 3166 standard. The whole ID for a culture is written, for instance, as "es-ES" for Spanish used in Spain or as "en-US" for English used in the United States.

The second way to identify a culture is by the locale identifier (LCID). The LCID is a number that is made up of a primary language identifier, a sublanguage identifier, and a sort order.

You will use both forms of culture identification whenever you deal with localization.

Screen Layout

.NET has the capability to create many versions of the same form. Which version gets displayed depends upon the current thread's CultureInfo setting. I know I have not covered CultureInfo yet, but hang on.

This is a really neat and little-known feature of Windows forms. I like this feature for some reasons and dislike it for others. Here are the pros and cons as I see them.

Pros:

- You can tailor all forms to a particular culture.

- You can insert the correct text in the correct language at design time.

- You can rearrange a form's controls for different cultures at design time.

Cons:

- The process can be unmanageable if many cultures are to be supported.

- The forms may look different between cultures, which makes them harder to support (there is no common interface).

So how does this feature work? Start a new project in either C# or VB. Add some controls to the form so that it looks like the one shown in Figure 3-6.

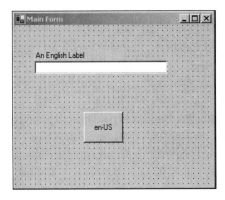

Figure 3-6. A basic form before being localized

As you can see, there is not much here. Now for the fun part. Go into the Properties screen of the form and change the Localizable property to true. While you are at it, change the Language property to English (United States). See Figure 3-7.

Properties	🛛 ×
Form1 System.Windows.Forms.Form	⏷

⊞ AutoScrollMinSize	0, 0
⊞ DockPadding	
⊞ Location	0, 0
⊞ MaximumSize	0, 0
⊞ MinimumSize	0, 0
⊞ Size	**328, 280**
StartPosition	**CenterScreen**
WindowState	Normal
⊟ Misc	
AcceptButton	(none)
CancelButton	(none)
KeyPreview	False
Language	**English (United States** ⏷
Localizable	**True**

Figure 3-7. The Language and Localizable properties of a form

When you changed the Language property, you got a chance to see that .NET supports literally dozens of cultures. Microsoft really did a thorough job with the internationalization features.

You still see what is shown in Figure 3-7. That's fine.

Now change the language to German (Germany). Go to the form, change some of the text, and move the Button over to the left a little. Your form should now look something like the one shown in Figure 3-8.

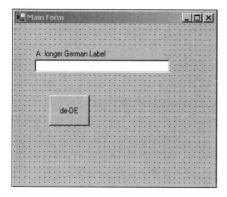

Figure 3-8. The German form

OK, what now? Compile and run the program. You should see the English form (assuming that this is how your computer is set up).

How do you show one form over the other? Go into the code of the form and *before* the InitializeComponent call in the constructor, type in the following lines.

C#

```
Thread.CurrentThread.CurrentUICulture = new CultureInfo("de-DE");
Thread.CurrentThread.CurrentCulture = new CultureInfo("de-DE");
```

VB

```
Thread.CurrentThread.CurrentUICulture = new CultureInfo("de-DE")
Thread.CurrentThread.CurrentCulture = new CultureInfo("de-DE")
```

What this does is change the culture of the current thread from English (assuming it was originally that) to German. You will see on the screen the German version of the form.

Cool! How did that happen?

When you create a form and its Localizable property is set to false, the string that you give to a control's Text property is hard-coded directly into the

InitializeComponent method that is generated by the IDE wizard. I am sure you have seen this when digging through .NET code already.

As soon as you set the Localizable property of the form to true and choose a language, things change. Behind the scenes, .NET creates a resource file and puts the string in there. The InitializeComponent method no longer has hard-coded strings. Instead, it uses the Resources.GetString method to extract the string from the resource file.

When I told you to type in the code to change the culture, I said to put it before the InitializeComponent call. If you put this code after the call, you will not see the German version of the form. This is because the resource file that the Resources.GetString method uses is tied to the current culture of the thread you are working in.

So, you may ask, where are these resource files?

Go to the Solution Explorer window and click the Show All Files icon. You will see the resource files appear under the Form1.cs entry, as shown in Figure 3-9.

Figure 3-9. Solution Explorer showing all files

Notice the name of the files. They are named after the official designation for the languages/regions that you chose: English and German.

Want to change the label text for the German form? Double-click the Form1.de-DE.resx file. You should see the resource editor screen shown in Figure 3-10.

Form1.cs [Design]*	Form1.cs*	**Form1.de-DE.resx***				
Data Tables:		Data:				

data		**Data for data**				
resheader		name	value	comment	type	mimetype
	▶	label1.Size	208, 16	(null)	System.Drawi	(null)
		cmdChange.Location	56, 112	(null)	System.Drawi	(null)
		label1.Text	A longer German Labe	(null)	(null)	(null)
		cmdChange.Text	de-DE	(null)	(null)	(null)
		label1.ImeMode	NoControl	(null)	System.Wind	(null)
	*					

Figure 3-10. The resource editor for the German resource file

Pretty neat, huh? I am sure you are burning to know where these files are stored. If you know that, you can open them with a text editor such as Notepad and try to figure out the format. I will tell you all that and more next.

Externalizing Resources

Resource files come in three flavors: binary, text, and XML. Yes, I know XML is text, but if you have ever read XML, you know it is not anything the casual observer can digest.

Externalizing resources means that all pictures, cursors, fonts, and strings should be stored in a resource file. Most people think of only strings as needing to be externalized. You have to be very careful about pictures, though. Many cultures other than English may find some common icons confusing or even offensive. You need to do some research and find out what is appropriate.

On the confusing front, suppose you are in England writing a shipping and receiving program of some kind. You could have a toolbar with an icon showing a pillar box. Now, in the United States, very few people know what a pillar box is; thus, they would be confused by the picture. A *pillar box* is a British mailbox. Figure 3-11 shows these two different icons for the same device side-by-side.

Figure 3-11. The pillar box is on the left, and the U.S. mailbox is on the right.

The point here is that if you externalize this icon to a resource file, you will be able to put a different icon in each resource file. This allows you to change the look of your program without changing any code at all.

The Basic Text Resource File

The basic resource file is the text resource file. It has the name *<program name>*.txt. You can include only strings in the text resource file. You can create a text resource file with Notepad. The format is like this:

```
EXIT            = Exit
FILE            = File
OPEN            = Open
QUIT            = Quit
TEXT            = Text
SAVE            = Save
CREATE TEXT     = Create Text file for translator
CREATE XML      = Create XML file
```

Each resource is in the form of a key/value pair.

This type of resource file is not very useful, because it can contain only strings. It cannot contain objects such as pictures, cursors, fonts, and so forth. These are the purview of XML and binary resource files.

The XML Resource File

This resource file has the name *<program name>*.resx. Hey! Isn't that the extension of the resource files for the previous German/English form example? Yup. The editor you see is an XML resource file editor provided by .NET. This type of file looks like this:

```
<?xml version="1.0" encoding="utf-8"?>
<root>
  <xsd:schema id="root" targetNamespace="" xmlns=""
 xmlns:xsd=http://www.w3.org/2001/XMLSchema
 xmlns:msdata="urn:schemas-microsoft-com:xml-msdata">
    <xsd:element name="root" msdata:IsDataSet="true">
      <xsd:complexType>
        <xsd:choice maxOccurs="unbounded">
          <xsd:element name="data">
            <xsd:complexType>
```

```
                    <xsd:sequence>
                      <xsd:element name="value" type="xsd:string"
  minOccurs="0" msdata:Ordinal="1" />
                      <xsd:element name="comment" type="xsd:string"
  minOccurs="0" msdata:Ordinal="2" />
                    </xsd:sequence>
                    <xsd:attribute name="name" type="xsd:string" />
                    <xsd:attribute name="type" type="xsd:string" />
                    <xsd:attribute name="mimetype" type="xsd:string" />
                  </xsd:complexType>
                </xsd:element>
                <xsd:element name="resheader">
                  <xsd:complexType>
                    <xsd:sequence>
                      <xsd:element name="value" type="xsd:string"
  minOccurs="0" msdata:Ordinal="1" />
                    </xsd:sequence>
                    <xsd:attribute name="name" type="xsd:string" use="required" />
                  </xsd:complexType>
                </xsd:element>
              </xsd:choice>
            </xsd:complexType>
          </xsd:element>
        </xsd:schema>
        <data name="APPEND">
          <value>Append</value>
        </data>
        <data name="BASICS">
          <value>Basics</value>
        </data>
        <data name="OUTPUT">
          <value>Build Output File(s)</value>
        </data>
        <data name="RESKEY">
          <value>Resource Key</value>
        </data>
        <data name="REMOVE">
          <value>Remove</value>
        </data>
        <data name="BASE NAME">
          <value>Base Name</value>
        </data>
        <data name="RESTEXT">
          <value>Resource Text</value>
```

```xml
    </data>
    <data name="ADD">
      <value>Add</value>
    </data>
    <data name="KEY">
      <value>Key</value>
    </data>
    <data name="FINAL">
      <value>Final</value>
    </data>
    <data name="PICTURES">
      <value>Pictures</value>
    </data>
    <data name="COMMENT">
      <value>Comment</value>
    </data>
    <data name="INPUT FNAME">
      <value>Input Filename</value>
    </data>
    <data name="CULTURE">
      <value>Choose Culture</value>
    </data>
    <data name="PIC COUNT">
      <value>Picture Count</value>
    </data>
    <data name="DATA ERR">
      <value>Data Table was not defined</value>
    </data>
    <data name="STRING COUNT">
      <value>String Count</value>
    </data>
    <data name="EXIT">
      <value>Exit</value>
    </data>
    <data name="FILE">
      <value>File</value>
    </data>
    <data name="OPEN">
      <value>Open</value>
    </data>
    <data name="QUIT">
      <value>Quit</value>
    </data>
    <data name="TEXT">
      <value>Text</value>
```

```
</data>
<data name="SAVE">
  <value>Save</value>
</data>
<data name="CREATE TEXT">
  <value>Create Text file for translator</value>
</data>
<data name="CREATE XML">
  <value>Create XML file</value>
</data>
<data name="CREATE BIN">
  <value>Create Binary File</value>
```

You can read it if you really try. This is only part of the resource file. The rest contains a text representation of a picture. Pretty neat if you ask me.

Describing XML is beyond the scope of this book, but you should become very familiar with it. .NET uses XML extensively for many things. XML is even used to replace COM in client/server applications.

The Binary Resource File

This file has the name format of *<program name>*.resources. It is not a file that you can create directly like the XML file or the text file. It is a compiled version of these two types of files.

NOTE You can create this binary resource file directly using code. My localization book has an extensive example of how to do this. Look at the online help for the ResXResourceWriter class if you are interested.

The .resources file is actually an intermediate step along the way to creating a satellite resource DLL assembly.

How You Use Resource Files

So where are these resource files, how do you make them, and how do you get information out of them? You can make resource files either via the IDE or by hand. I recommend the by-hand method for string resource files for this reason: If you use the IDE to make and edit a resource file, it will be an XML resource file. Most companies do not have the resources to translate a program internally. This means that you will need to send out your resource file to a translation company, which will know nothing about XML.

If you make a text resource file and send it out, it is easy to read and translate. Later on, you can combine the text resource file with the XML resource file to create a single XML or binary resource file.

There is a .NET utility that you should become familiar with called ResGen.exe. It allows you to convert a resource file to and from any of its three forms. It also allows you to perform batch processing and combine several resource files into one. This last part is important when you have an XML file that contains pictures and a text-based resource file that contains the strings.

TIP   The online help explains very well how to use ResGen.exe..

In order for .NET to properly use your resource files, the files must be in the form of a satellite assembly. This is a DLL. Getting the .resources binary file to a DLL is easy. You use the external program AL.exe. Like the ResGen.exe program, the AL.exe program and satellite assemblies are covered pretty well in the online help.[3]

Fallback

.NET uses a fallback mechanism to locate resources. Here is how it works:

1. Look in the *<language>-<country/region>* subdirectory.

2. Look in the *<language>* subdirectory.

3. Look in the assembly itself.

4. Throw an error.

The folks at Microsoft have tried to make the process of finding resources as error-free as possible. If .NET cannot find a resource in one place, it looks in another and on down the line until it has exhausted all possibilities. Normally, your program will include an embedded resource file that contains all the resources for the program's native language. Because all native strings are here, the program should at least find the base untranslated string. This fallback method works very well.

---

3.   I also cover them extensively in my book *Internationalization and Localization Using Microsoft .NET* (Apress, 2002).

Open up Windows Explorer and look in the directory where your last example resides. This is the one that has the German and English screens. If you expand your directory structure, you will see something like the structure shown in Figure 3-12.

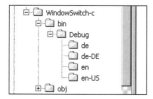

Figure 3-12. The location of resource files

Look in each of these directories and you will find a single file called WindowSwitch-c.resources.dll (this is the name of my file, which is based on the name of my program). This file is the satellite resource file.

Notice the names of the directories. They correspond to the the steps in the fallback scheme.

Obviously, when you release your program it will not have the intervening Bin and Debug directories, so make sure that the resource directories are located directly under the program directory.

If you want to add another language to your program, just make another DLL and create another resource directory to hold it. If the user's computer is changed to the new language, .NET will automatically find the new resource file and you are good to go.

Retrieving Resources

Once you changed the Localizable property of the form to true and added another language, the .NET wizard went ahead and changed the wizard-generated code on you. Open up the code pane for this example and look in the wizard-generated code section. The following is the code that the wizard generated for the label.

C#

```
//
// label1
//
this.label1.AccessibleDescription =
        ((string)(resources.GetObject("label1.AccessibleDescription")));
this.label1.AccessibleName =
        ((string)(resources.GetObject("label1.AccessibleName")));
```

```
this.label1.Anchor = ((System.Windows.Forms.AnchorStyles)
                            (resources.GetObject("label1.Anchor")));
this.label1.AutoSize = ((bool)(resources.GetObject("label1.AutoSize")));
this.label1.Dock = ((System.Windows.Forms.DockStyle)
                            (resources.GetObject("label1.Dock")));
this.label1.Enabled = ((bool)(resources.GetObject("label1.Enabled")));
this.label1.Font =
            ((System.Drawing.Font)(resources.GetObject("label1.Font")));
this.label1.Image =
            ((System.Drawing.Image)(resources.GetObject("label1.Image")));
this.label1.ImageAlign = ((System.Drawing.ContentAlignment)
                            (resources.GetObject("label1.ImageAlign")));
this.label1.ImageIndex = ((int)(resources.GetObject("label1.ImageIndex")));
this.label1.ImeMode = ((System.Windows.Forms.ImeMode)
                            (resources.GetObject("label1.ImeMode")));
this.label1.Location = ((System.Drawing.Point)
                            (resources.GetObject("label1.Location")));
this.label1.Name = "label1";
this.label1.RightToLeft = ((System.Windows.Forms.RightToLeft)
                (resources.GetObject("label1.RightToLeft")));
this.label1.Size =
                ((System.Drawing.Size)(resources.GetObject("label1.Size")));
this.label1.TabIndex = ((int)(resources.GetObject("label1.TabIndex")));
this.label1.Text = resources.GetString("label1.Text");
this.label1.TextAlign = ((System.Drawing.ContentAlignment)
                            (resources.GetObject("label1.TextAlign")));
this.label1.Visible = ((bool)(resources.GetObject("label1.Visible")));
```

What you see here is that all nonstring resources are obtained using the resources.GetObject method. The string is obtained using the resources.GetString method. As a matter of fact, everything about this label is stored in the resource file. That is how the label can move from one form to another. This is very cool and very flexible.

The Globalization Namespace

The Globalization namespace contains all the classes you need for localization. I cover the basics of the Globalization namespace here, but you need to know that this namespace is huge. If you start digging into it, you will find that just about anything in .NET can be localized and quite a bit of the localization work is done for you. If you are going to write an international-aware program, you need to spend some quality time with this namespace.

If you want to localize your program, you will need to include three namespaces: System.Globalization, System.Resources, and System.Threading. Including the other two namespaces precludes you from having to fully qualify every method's name.

Table 3-2 shows you the classes included in the System.Globalization namespace.

Table 3-2. The System.Globalization Namespace

Class	Description
Calendar	Abstract base class that defines time divisions
CompareInfo	Allows you to compare strings in a culture-sensitive manner
CultureInfo	Major class that represents everything about a particular culture
DateTimeFormatInfo	Represents different time/date formats
DaylightTime	Defines daylight saving time around the world
GregorianCalendar	Self-explanatory
HebrewCalendar	Self-explanatory
HijriCalendar	Self-explanatory
JapaneseCalendar	Self-explanatory
JulianCalendar	Self-explanatory
KoreanCalendar	Self-explanatory
TaiwanCalendar	Self-explanatory
ThaiBuddistCalendar	Self-explanatory
NumberFormatInfo	Represents different numerical formats, including currency
RegionInfo	Major class that includes information about a region/country
SortKey	Defines how strings and so forth are sorted
StringInfo	Allows you to parse and iterate strings
TextElementEnumerator	Allows you to enumerate a string
TextInfo	Contains information about specific writing styles

I include the System.Threading namespace so that I can get at the current thread's information.

Before I take you through a simple localized project, I wanted to make you aware that you have a few other things to consider.

Changing the Culture

Earlier I showed you a couple of lines that changed the culture that your program was running in. Normally, your program would detect this from the computer's system settings. Often, you will want to let the user choose the language of his or her choice. It makes your program a little slicker.

You change the current culture through the current thread. You need to create a new culture and assign it to the thread's CurrentUICulture property as follows.

C#

```
CultureInfo DE_culture = new CultureInfo("de-DE");
Thread.CurrentThread.CurrentCulture = DE_culture;
Thread.CurrentThread.CurrentUICulture = DE_culture;
```

VB

```
Dim DE_culture As CultureInfo = New CultureInfo("de-DE")
Thread.CurrentThread.CurrentCulture = DE_culture
Thread.CurrentThread.CurrentUICulture = DE_culture
```

You could have an array of cultures as a variable. You could let the user choose a language from a menu (built up from this array) to change the displayed strings. If you want to get fancy, you can do a directory search and build up the language list from the resource files that you find. This way, you can download a new language to the host computer, and as soon as you are finished, the program will be able to convert into the new language.

There is one thing you need to do besides changing the thread's culture, though: You need to reinitialize the strings of all the controls. It is a good idea to have a control initialization procedure that you can call to do that.

Here is some sample code I took from one of the chapters of my book *Internationalization and Localization Using Microsoft .NET* (Apress, 2002). This sample routine initializes the strings and some icons by getting them from a resource file. This code is in C#.

```csharp
  private void InitStrings()
  {
    ResUtilConsts.rm = new ResourceManager("ResEditor", this.GetType().Assembly);
    sbStatus.Panels[2].Text = DateTime.Now.ToString();
    sbStatus.Panels[1].Width = 100;

    //Tab Pages
    tcResources.TabPages[TEXT_TAB].Text = ResUtilConsts.rm.GetString("TEXT");
    tcResources.TabPages[GRAPHICS_TAB].Text =
ResUtilConsts.rm.GetString("PICTURES");
    tcResources.TabPages[FINAL_TAB].Text = ResUtilConsts.rm.GetString("FINAL");

    //Form Controls
    cmdQuit.Text = ResUtilConsts.rm.GetString("QUIT");
    mnuFile.Text = ResUtilConsts.rm.GetString("FILE");
    mnuOpen.Text = ResUtilConsts.rm.GetString("OPEN");
    mnuAppend.Text = ResUtilConsts.rm.GetString("APPEND");
    mnuExit.Text = ResUtilConsts.rm.GetString("EXIT");

    //do picture tab
    lblPicKey.Text = ResUtilConsts.rm.GetString("KEY");
    lblPictures.Text = ResUtilConsts.rm.GetString("PICTURES");
    cmdAddPic.Text = ResUtilConsts.rm.GetString("ADD");
    cmdDelPic.Text = ResUtilConsts.rm.GetString("REMOVE");

    //Do Final tab
    fraBasics.Text = ResUtilConsts.rm.GetString("BASICS");
    lblInputFname.Text = ResUtilConsts.rm.GetString("INPUT FNAME");
    lblStrCnt.Text = ResUtilConsts.rm.GetString("STRING COUNT");
    lblPicCnt.Text = ResUtilConsts.rm.GetString("PIC COUNT");
    lblCulture.Text = ResUtilConsts.rm.GetString("CULTURE");
    fraOutput.Text = ResUtilConsts.rm.GetString("OUTPUT");
    lblBaseName.Text = ResUtilConsts.rm.GetString("BASE NAME");
    cmdSave.Text = ResUtilConsts.rm.GetString("SAVE");
    chkCreateText.Text = ResUtilConsts.rm.GetString("CREATE TEXT");
    chkCreateXML.Text = ResUtilConsts.rm.GetString("CREATE XML");
    chkCreateBin.Text = ResUtilConsts.rm.GetString("CREATE BIN");

    this.Icon = (Icon)ResUtilConsts.rm.GetObject("Flag");

  }
```

Displaying Dates and Time

People in the United States write the date as month/day/year. The rest of the world does it differently. This has major ramifications for data entry programs. If you only allow a person to input date values in mm/dd/yyyy format, you will get errors when someone in England puts in a birth date of 23/08/68. Make sure your validation code handles this.

Of course, along with the date there is time. Again, the United States is different from the rest of the world. People in the United States use AM/PM to denote the noontime crossover. Most of the rest of the world uses what Americans call *military time*. This is based on a 24-hour clock. So a time of 3:15 PM in the United States is 15:15:00 everywhere else.

Again, your ability to handle time is very important. This is why you should always display dates and time using either the DateTimeFormatInfo specifiers (see the online help) or the methods provided by the DateTime class.

The DateTime class has several methods that format the output of date and time for you:

- ToShortDateString

- ToShortTimeString

- ToLongTimeString

- ToLongDateString

You will find the actual specifier for how these dates and times look by clicking the Start button and selecting Settings ➤ Control Panel ➤ Regional Options.

What about input of dates and times? The answer to that is to use either the provided DateTime picker control, the Calendar control, or some kind of MaskedEdit control. The less freedom that the user has to enter wrong information, the better off you are. The DateTimePicker and Calendar controls are both culture sensitive.

The DateTimePicker normally takes its format information from the system settings. Changing the current thread's culture does not change the way this control displays data. There is a way to do this, though, on a culture-by-culture basis. It takes only a few lines of code on your part, but the manipulations that go on behind the scenes are impressive. Here is some code to make the DateTimePicker display its value depending upon the current thread's culture.

C#

```
DateTimePicker dtp = new DateTimePicker();
DateTimeFormatInfo dt = Thread.CurrentThread.CurrentCulture.DateTimeFormat;
dtp.CustomFormat = dt.ShortDatePattern;
dtp.Format = DateTimePickerFormat.Custom;
```

VB

```
Dim dtp As DateTimePicker = New DateTimePicker()
Dim dt As DateTimeFormatInfo = _
               Thread.CurrentThread.CurrentCulture.DateTimeFormat()
dtp.CustomFormat = dt.ShortDatePattern
dtp.Format = DateTimePickerFormat.Custom
```

I suggest you look at the help for the DateTimeInfo class. It is very instructive.

Displaying Currency and Numbers

So you can display date and time. What about numbers? Here's the scoop:

- The United States uses a period as the decimal separator. Most of the rest of the world uses a comma.

- The United States uses a comma as the thousands separator. Most of the rest of the world uses a period.

When you are allowing input of numbers, you will need to allow for a comma and a period as both the thousands separator and the decimal separator. I have been burned by programs that allow only a period for the decimal separator.

There is a class in the Globalization namespace called NumberFormatInfo. This is similar to the DateTimeFormatInfo class in that it holds all the relevant information for a culture's formatting of numbers and currency.

If you want to print a string representation of a number, you would normally use the ToString method of the object's base class. How many of you know that this method is overloaded? Look at this line of code:

```
MessageBox.Show(123456.ToString("N"));
```

This gives the result 123,456.00.

Now change the culture to German and run the same code:

```
Thread.CurrentThread.CurrentCulture = new CultureInfo("de-DE");
MessageBox.Show(123456.ToString("N"));
```

This gives the result 123.456,00. Notice that the decimal separator and thousands separator are appropriate for the current culture.

You could also do the following to force the output to be different from the current culture:

```
Thread.CurrentThread.CurrentCulture = new CultureInfo("de-DE");
MessageBox.Show(123456.ToString("N", new CultureInfo("en-US")));
```

The output of this is 123,456.00. The ToString method looks at the NumberFormatInfo class contained in the supplied culture for clues as to how to display this number.

When you ask for input of numbers and display this output, you will need to be aware of what methods are culture sensitive.

Different Calendars

You saw from Table 3-2 that there are eight different calendars that .NET knows about. Coverage of converting dates from one calendar to another and back again is beyond the scope of this book, but know that there are ways to do so. The calendars presented in Table 3-2 are the most common ones in use throughout the world today. It is a safe bet that you can find one to fit your target country.

String Sort Order Considerations

Here is something that most programmers are unaware of: Different languages have different sort orders. .NET has different sort orders as well. There is the international sort order, which is case insensitive. In this case, A, b, and C would be sorted as AbC. Normal ASCII sort order would sort this list as ACb.

But what about Finnish sort order? In Finland, V is considered the same level as W. Suppose you have the following list:

Victory

Wake

Woman

Yak

The Finnish sort order would sort the list as follows:

Wake

Victory

Woman

Yak

Look in the SortKey class under the System.Globalization namespace to see the sort order for your language.

The Localized Data-Entry Example

This example makes use of two language resource files for text. It also makes use of culture-aware features of some common controls.

NOTE   This example includes a few pictures. They are included in the code source you can obtain from the Downloads section of the Apress Web site (http://www.apress.com).

The example is an expense report for car mileage. It is a bit simplistic, but you will see some interesting validation code. It is supposed to work in English and in French.

Start a new project in either C# or VB. Follow these steps to put the required controls on the form:

1. Make the form FixedSingle with no minimize or maximize buttons. Name the form **Multilingual** and set the text to **Car Mileage Expense**.

2. Add a PictureBox to the top left of the form and size it to be 32×32. Call it **picUSA**.

3. Add a PictureBox to the top left of the form and size it to be 32×32. Call it **picFRA**.

4. Add a Label called **lblName** whose text reads **Name**. Make the width of the control about 160 pixels.

5. Add a TextBox called **txtName**.

6. Add a Label called **lblBirth** whose text reads **Date of Birth**. Make the width of the control about 160 pixels.

7. Add a DateTimePicker called **dtBirth**.

8. Add a GroupBox called **gb1** whose text reads **Address**.

9. Inside the GroupBox, add a Label called **lblAddr1** whose text reads **Address 1**. Right-justify the text and make the width of the label about 96 pixels.

10. Inside the GroupBox, next to the Label add a TextBox called **txtAddr1**.

11. Inside the GroupBox, add a Label called **lblAddr2** whose text reads **Address 2**. Right-justify the text and make the width of the label about 96 pixels.

12. Inside the GroupBox, next to the Label add a TextBox called **txtAddr2**.

13. Inside the GroupBox, add a Label called **lblAddr3** whose text reads **Address 3**. Right-justify the text and make the width of the label about 96 pixels.

14. Inside the GroupBox, next to the Label add a TextBox called **txtAddr3**.

15. Add a Label called **lblStart** whose text reads **Travel start time**. Make the width of the control about 160 pixels.

16. Add a DateTimePicker called **dtStart**.

17. Add a Label called **lbEnd** whose text reads **Travel end time**. Make the width of the control about 160 pixels.

18. Add a DateTimePicker called **dtEnd**.

19. Add a Label called **lbMiles** whose text reads **Miles Traveled**. Make the width of the control about 160 pixels.

20. Add a TextBox called **txtMiles**.

21. Add a Label whose text reads *** .35 =**. Make the font 12 point and bold.

22. Add a Label called **lbOwed** whose text reads **Amount Owed**. Make the width of the control about 160 pixels.

23. Add a Label called **lbCash**. Make the border FixedSingle and the BackColor Linen.

In case you were wondering where to put all this stuff, see Figure 3-13.

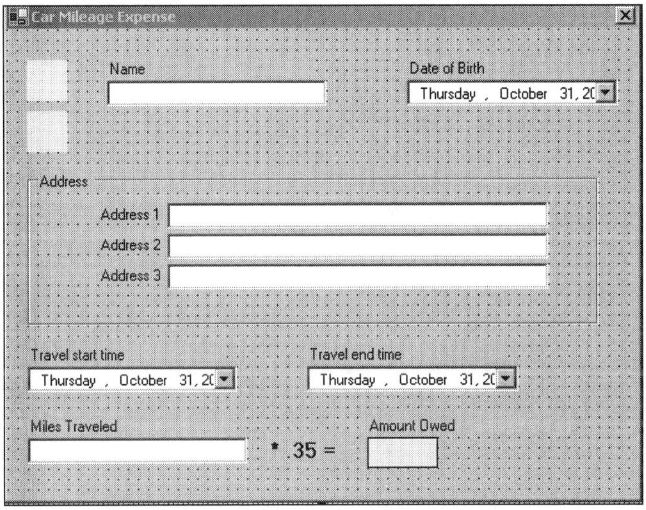

Figure 3-13. The Car Mileage Expense form layout

You sized the text controls so that any translated text will fit in them without being truncated or wrapped. It's a good idea to do this so you won't have to redesign the whole form when you go to another language.

The next thing you are going to do is compile the form. This sets up the necessary directory structure for the resource files. Because you will be working in the debugger, the resource files need to be in the current directory, which is the Debug directory for C# users and the Bin directory for you VB fans.

Your directory structure should look like the one shown in Figure 3-14, which displays both the VB and C# directory structures.

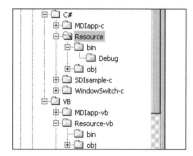

Figure 3-14. The project directory structure for C# and VB

Make two text files in these working directories:

- French.txt

- English.txt

These two files are the text-based resource files for this project. Edit the French.txt file and type in the following lines of text:

```
NAME=(french)Name
DOB=(french)Date of birth
ADDR=(french)Address
ADDR1=(french)Address 1
ADDR2=(french)Address 2
ADDR3=(french)Address 3
STARTTIME=(french)Start Time
ENDTIME=(french)End Time
MILES=(french)Miles
CASHBACK=(french)Cash
CAPTION=(french)Car Milage Expense
```

Save the file. Now open up the English.txt file and type in the following text:

```
NAME=Name
DOB=Date of birth
ADDR=Address
ADDR1=Address 1
ADDR2=Address 2
ADDR3=Address 3
STARTTIME=Start Time
ENDTIME=End Time
```

```
MILES=Miles
CASHBACK=Cash
CAPTION=Car Milage Expense
```

Save this file. As you can see, I don't speak French. However, I'm sure you catch the drift of what I'm doing here.

Whenever you use one of the .NET ancillary console mode programs (there are a whole host of them), you will need to set up the environment properly. Microsoft has provided you with a batch file called CorVars.bat. Find this batch file and put it in the working directory.

Now make your own batch file called ResBuild.bat in this directory. Type the following lines in this new batch file:

```
call corvars.bat
resgen french.txt
resgen english.txt
```

Very simple. Double-click this program and you should see the French.resources and English.resources files appear. Figure 3-15 shows my directory after running this ResBuild.bat program.

Name	Size	Type
BuildRes.bat	1 KB	MS-DOS Batch File
corvars.bat	1 KB	MS-DOS Batch File
english.resources	1 KB	RESOURCES File
English.txt	1 KB	Text Document
FRA.ICO	2 KB	Icon
french.resources	1 KB	RESOURCES File
French.txt	1 KB	Text Document
Resource.exe	14 KB	Application
Resource.pdb	20 KB	Program Debug Dat...
USA.ICO	2 KB	Icon

Figure 3-15. The directory contents after running ResBuild.bat

Notice that along with the resource files, I have a couple of icons.[4]

Now it is time for the code. Listings 3-3a and 3-3b show the code for this form. There is not much actual code here, but some of it is complicated. I cover the code in detail in a bit.

---

4. These icons are on your system somewhere, but if you download the source code from the Downloads section of the Apress Web site (http://www.apress.com), you'll get them supplied to you.

Listing 3-3a. C# Code for the Resource Example

```csharp
using System;
using System.Threading;
using System.Globalization;
using System.Resources;
using System.Drawing;
using System.Collections;
using System.ComponentModel;
using System.Windows.Forms;
using System.Data;

namespace Resource
{
  /// <summary>
  /// Multilingual expense form chapter 3
  /// </summary>
  public class Multilingual : System.Windows.Forms.Form
  {
    #region class local variables

    private enum LANG
    {
      LANG_USA,
      LANG_FRA
    };

    float cash  = 0.0f;
    float miles = 0.0f;

    #endregion

    private System.Windows.Forms.Label lblName;
    private System.Windows.Forms.TextBox txtName;
    private System.Windows.Forms.DateTimePicker dtBirth;
    private System.Windows.Forms.Label lblDOB;
    private System.Windows.Forms.TextBox txtAddr1;
    private System.Windows.Forms.Label lblAddr1;
    private System.Windows.Forms.TextBox txtAddr2;
    private System.Windows.Forms.Label lblAddr2;
    private System.Windows.Forms.TextBox txtAddr3;
    private System.Windows.Forms.Label lblAddr3;
    private System.Windows.Forms.Label lblStart;
    private System.Windows.Forms.DateTimePicker dtStart;
```

```
private System.Windows.Forms.DateTimePicker dtEnd;
private System.Windows.Forms.TextBox txtMiles;
private System.Windows.Forms.Label lblMiles;
private System.Windows.Forms.Label lblOwed;
private System.Windows.Forms.Label lblCash;
private System.Windows.Forms.PictureBox picUSA;
private System.Windows.Forms.PictureBox picFRA;
private System.Windows.Forms.GroupBox gb1;
private System.Windows.Forms.Label lblEnd;
private System.Windows.Forms.Label label1;
private System.ComponentModel.Container components = null;

public Multilingual()
{
  InitializeComponent();

  txtMiles.KeyPress += new KeyPressEventHandler(this.InputValidator);
  txtMiles.KeyUp    += new KeyEventHandler(this.CalculateCash);

  picUSA.BackColor  = Color.Transparent;
  picUSA.SizeMode   = PictureBoxSizeMode.StretchImage;
  picUSA.Image      = Image.FromFile("usa.ico");
  picUSA.Click      += new EventHandler(this.NewLanguage);

  picFRA.BackColor  = Color.Transparent;
  picFRA.SizeMode   = PictureBoxSizeMode.StretchImage;
  picFRA.Image      = Image.FromFile("fra.ico");
  picFRA.Click      += new EventHandler(this.NewLanguage);

}

protected override void Dispose( bool disposing )
{
  if( disposing )
  {
    if (components != null)
    {
      components.Dispose();
    }
  }
  base.Dispose( disposing );
}
```

```
#region Windows Form Designer generated code

...

...

...


#endregion

[STAThread]
static void Main()
{
  Application.Run(new Multilingual());
}

private void Form1_Load(object sender, System.EventArgs e)
{
  InitStrings();
}

private void InitStrings()
{
  ResourceSet rs;

  if(Thread.CurrentThread.CurrentCulture.Name == "fr-FR")
    rs = new ResourceSet("French.resources");
  else
    rs = new ResourceSet("English.resources");

  this.Text        = rs.GetString("CAPTION");
  lblName.Text     = rs.GetString("NAME");
  lblDOB.Text      = rs.GetString("DOB");
  gb1.Text         = rs.GetString("ADDR");
  lblAddr1.Text    = rs.GetString("ADDR1");
  lblAddr2.Text    = rs.GetString("ADDR2");
  lblAddr3.Text    = rs.GetString("ADDR3");
  lblStart.Text    = rs.GetString("STARTTIME");
  lblEnd.Text      = rs.GetString("ENDTIME");
  lblMiles.Text    = rs.GetString("MILES");
  lblOwed.Text     = rs.GetString("CASHBACK");

  rs.Close();
  rs.Dispose();
```

```
  //Adjust the date and time displayed in the pickers
  DateTimeFormatInfo dtf = new DateTimeFormatInfo();
  dtf = Thread.CurrentThread.CurrentCulture.DateTimeFormat;

  dtBirth.CustomFormat = dtf.ShortDatePattern;
  dtBirth.Format = DateTimePickerFormat.Custom;

  dtStart.CustomFormat = dtf.ShortTimePattern;
  dtStart.Format = DateTimePickerFormat.Custom;
  dtStart.ShowUpDown = true;

  dtEnd.CustomFormat = dtf.ShortTimePattern;
  dtEnd.Format = DateTimePickerFormat.Custom;
  dtEnd.ShowUpDown = true;

  lblCash.Text = cash.ToString("N", Thread.CurrentThread.CurrentCulture);
  txtMiles.Text = miles.ToString("N", Thread.CurrentThread.CurrentCulture);

  this.Refresh();
}

#region events


private void NewLanguage(object sender, EventArgs e)
{
  LANG l = LANG.LANG_USA;
  if (sender is PictureBox)
    if (sender == picFRA)
      l = LANG.LANG_FRA;

  if (l == LANG.LANG_FRA)
  {
    Thread.CurrentThread.CurrentCulture = new CultureInfo("fr-FR");
    Thread.CurrentThread.CurrentUICulture = new CultureInfo("fr-FR");
  }
  else
  {
    Thread.CurrentThread.CurrentCulture = new CultureInfo("en-US");
    Thread.CurrentThread.CurrentUICulture = new CultureInfo("en-US");
  }
```

```csharp
      InitStrings();
    }


    private void InputValidator(object sender, KeyPressEventArgs e)
    {
      TextBox t;
      NumberFormatInfo nf = Thread.CurrentThread.CurrentCulture.NumberFormat;

      if(sender is TextBox)
      {
        t = (TextBox)sender;
        if (t == txtMiles)
        {
          //Allow only 0-9 and decimal separator
          if(Char.IsNumber(e.KeyChar))
            e.Handled = false;
          else if(e.KeyChar == Convert.ToChar(nf.NumberDecimalSeparator))
          {
            if(t.Text.IndexOf(Convert.ToChar(nf.NumberDecimalSeparator)) >=0)
              e.Handled = true;
            else
              e.Handled = false;
          }
          else
            e.Handled = true;
        }
      }

    }

    private void CalculateCash(object sender, KeyEventArgs e)
    {
      TextBox t;
      if(sender is TextBox)
      {
        t = (TextBox)sender;
        if (t == txtMiles)
        {
          try
          {
            miles = float.Parse(txtMiles.Text);
            cash = miles * 0.35f;
            lblCash.Text=cash.ToString("N",Thread.CurrentThread.CurrentCulture);
          }
```

```
        catch
        {
          lblCash.Text = "";
        }
      }
    }


  }
  #endregion
}
}
```

Listing 3-3b. VB Code for the Resource Example

```
Option Strict On

Imports System
Imports System.Resources
Imports System.Threading
Imports System.Globalization

Public Class Multilingual
  Inherits System.Windows.Forms.Form

#Region "class local variables"

  Private Enum LANG
    LANG_USA
    LANG_FRA
  End Enum

  Dim cash As Single = 0.0F
  Dim miles As Single = 0.0F

#End Region

#Region " Windows Form Designer generated code "

  Public Sub New()
    MyBase.New()

    InitializeComponent()
```

```vbnet
        AddHandler txtMiles.KeyPress, AddressOf InputValidator
        AddHandler txtMiles.KeyUp, AddressOf CalculateCash

        picUSA.BackColor = Color.Transparent
        picUSA.SizeMode = PictureBoxSizeMode.StretchImage
        picUSA.Image = Image.FromFile("usa.ico")
        AddHandler picUSA.Click, AddressOf NewLanguage

        picFRA.BackColor = Color.Transparent
        picFRA.SizeMode = PictureBoxSizeMode.StretchImage
        picFRA.Image = Image.FromFile("fra.ico")
        AddHandler picFRA.Click, AddressOf NewLanguage

    End Sub

...
...
...
#End Region

    Private Sub Form1_Load(ByVal sender As System.Object, _
                        ByVal e As System.EventArgs) Handles MyBase.Load

    End Sub

    Private Sub InitStrings()
      Dim rs As ResourceSet

      If Thread.CurrentThread.CurrentCulture.Name = "fr-FR" Then
        rs = New ResourceSet("French.resources")
      Else
        rs = New ResourceSet("English.resources")
      End If

      Me.Text = rs.GetString("CAPTION")
      lblName.Text = rs.GetString("NAME")
      lblDOB.Text = rs.GetString("DOB")
      gb1.Text = rs.GetString("ADDR")
      lblAddr1.Text = rs.GetString("ADDR1")
      lblAddr2.Text = rs.GetString("ADDR2")
      lblAddr3.Text = rs.GetString("ADDR3")
```

```
    lblStart.Text = rs.GetString("STARTTIME")
    lblEnd.Text = rs.GetString("ENDTIME")
    lblMiles.Text = rs.GetString("MILES")
    lblOwed.Text = rs.GetString("CASHBACK")

    rs.Close()
    rs.Dispose()

    'Adjust the date and time displayed in the pickers
    Dim dtf As DateTimeFormatInfo = New DateTimeFormatInfo()
    dtf = Thread.CurrentThread.CurrentCulture.DateTimeFormat

    dtBirth.CustomFormat = dtf.ShortDatePattern
    dtBirth.Format = DateTimePickerFormat.Custom

    dtStart.CustomFormat = dtf.ShortTimePattern
    dtStart.Format = DateTimePickerFormat.Custom
    dtStart.ShowUpDown = True

    dtEnd.CustomFormat = dtf.ShortTimePattern
    dtEnd.Format = DateTimePickerFormat.Custom
    dtEnd.ShowUpDown = True

    lblCash.Text = cash.ToString("N", Thread.CurrentThread.CurrentCulture)
    txtMiles.Text = miles.ToString("N", Thread.CurrentThread.CurrentCulture)

    Refresh()
  End Sub

#Region "events"

  Private Sub NewLanguage(ByVal sender As Object, ByVal e As EventArgs)
    Dim l As LANG = LANG.LANG_USA

    If sender.GetType() Is GetType(PictureBox) Then
      If sender Is picFRA Then
        l = LANG.LANG_FRA
      End If
    End If
```

```vb
    If l = LANG.LANG_FRA Then
      Thread.CurrentThread.CurrentCulture = New CultureInfo("fr-FR")
      Thread.CurrentThread.CurrentUICulture = New CultureInfo("fr-FR")
    Else
      Thread.CurrentThread.CurrentCulture = New CultureInfo("en-US")
      Thread.CurrentThread.CurrentUICulture = New CultureInfo("en-US")
    End If


    InitStrings()
  End Sub


  Private Sub InputValidator(ByVal sender As Object, _
                             ByVal e As KeyPressEventArgs)
    Dim t As TextBox
    Dim nf As NumberFormatInfo = _
            Thread.CurrentThread.CurrentCulture.NumberFormat

    If sender.GetType() Is GetType(TextBox) Then
      t = CType(sender, TextBox)
      If t Is txtMiles Then
        'Allow only 0-9 and decimal separator
        If (Char.IsNumber(e.KeyChar)) Then
          e.Handled = False
        ElseIf (e.KeyChar = Convert.ToChar(nf.NumberDecimalSeparator)) Then
          If (t.Text.IndexOf(Convert.ToChar _
                          (nf.NumberDecimalSeparator)) >= 0) Then
            e.Handled = True
          Else
            e.Handled = False
          End If
        Else
          e.Handled = True
        End If
      End If
    End If
  End Sub


  Private Sub CalculateCash(ByVal sender As Object, ByVal e As KeyEventArgs)
    Dim t As TextBox

    If sender.GetType() Is GetType(TextBox) Then
      t = CType(sender, TextBox)
      If t Is txtMiles Then
        Try
          miles = Single.Parse(txtMiles.Text)
```

```
        cash = miles * 0.35F
        lblCash.Text = cash.ToString("N", Thread.CurrentThread.CurrentCulture)
      Catch
        lblCash.Text = ""
      End Try
    End If
  End If


  End Sub
#End Region
End Class
```

Finished? Compile and run the program. The first screen you see should look like Figure 3-16.

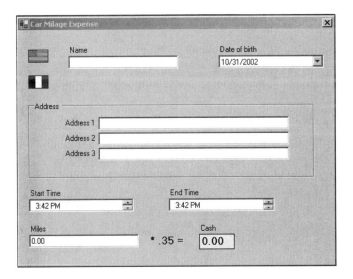

Figure 3-16. The English version of the form

Enter a value (you can use decimals) in the Miles field. You should see that I only allow numbers (and decimal points) and the cash value is calculated automatically. Notice that the calendar and the time controls show the date and time according to U.S. standards.

Click the French flag. Your screen now should look like Figure 3-17.

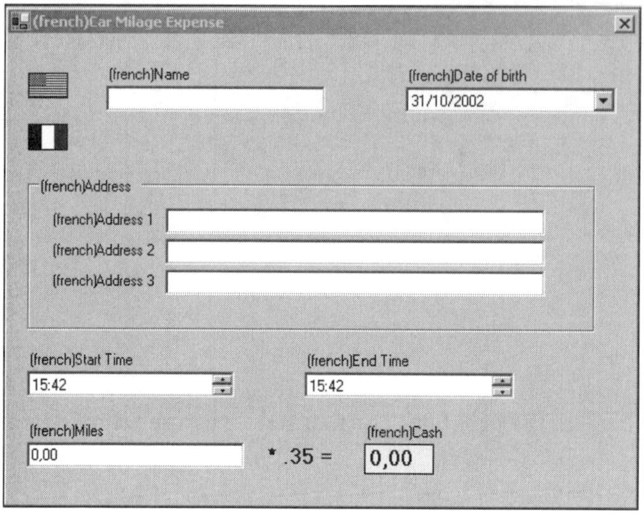

Figure 3-17. The French version of the form

The date format has changed to reflect the norm for France. So has the time. Look at the Miles field and the Cash field. The decimal separator has changed according to the French culture.

Enter in a value in the Miles field. You will not be able to enter in a period anymore for the decimal separator. Only the comma is allowed for this.

Notice that all the text strings have changed to their French equivalents.[5] Click back and forth between the French and English forms. Everything changes as it is supposed to. Well, almost everything. The drop-down calendar is not translated. To get a translated calendar, use the Calendar control instead.

Now to dissect the code. Let's start with the InitStrings method. The first thing I do is to create a resource set that lets me extract resources from a resource file.

> **NOTE**   I am *not* using the approved fallback scheme for this example. Instead, I am using what are called *loose resources*. There is no inherent error protection in this method, and it is nowhere near as robust as the fallback method. However, it has the advantage of being very simple to implement.

Here is the C# code:

---

5. As near as I can do, anyway.

```
ResourceSet rs;

if(Thread.CurrentThread.CurrentCulture.Name == "fr-FR")
  rs = new ResourceSet("French.resources");
else
  rs = new ResourceSet("English.resources");
```

I detect the current culture and open the appropriate resource file. I did *not* rely on knowing which icon was clicked. If you do that, you will get confused when your program gets French resources when the culture is still English. Always rely on the culture setting for stuff like this.

Next, I use the GetString method of the ResoureSet class to fill all the controls' text strings.

Finally, I adjust the DateTimePickers according to the current culture, as follows:

```
//Adjust the date and time displayed in the pickers
DateTimeFormatInfo dtf = new DateTimeFormatInfo();
dtf = Thread.CurrentThread.CurrentCulture.DateTimeFormat;

dtBirth.CustomFormat = dtf.ShortDatePattern;
dtBirth.Format = DateTimePickerFormat.Custom;

dtStart.CustomFormat = dtf.ShortTimePattern;
dtStart.Format = DateTimePickerFormat.Custom;
dtStart.ShowUpDown = true;

dtEnd.CustomFormat = dtf.ShortTimePattern;
dtEnd.Format = DateTimePickerFormat.Custom;
dtEnd.ShowUpDown = true;

lblCash.Text = cash.ToString("N", Thread.CurrentThread.CurrentCulture);
txtMiles.Text = miles.ToString("N", Thread.CurrentThread.CurrentCulture);
```

The CurrentCulture class has classes that describe number formats and date/time formats, among other things. I retrieve the date/time format string and apply the short version of it to the DateTimePickers. Notice that I also convert an internal floating-point variable to a string based on the current culture. This is how you see the comma or period when appropriate.

The last thing I do in this method is refresh the form and its controls. Nowhere in this function am I depending upon any state variables. This is important.

So, what happens when you click the icons? Here is the delegate code:

```
private void NewLanguage(object sender, EventArgs e)
{
  LANG l = LANG.LANG_USA;
  if (sender is PictureBox)
    if (sender == picFRA)
      l = LANG.LANG_FRA;

  if (l == LANG.LANG_FRA)
  {
    Thread.CurrentThread.CurrentCulture = new CultureInfo("fr-FR");
    Thread.CurrentThread.CurrentUICulture = new CultureInfo("fr-FR");
  }
  else
  {
    Thread.CurrentThread.CurrentCulture = new CultureInfo("en-US");
    Thread.CurrentThread.CurrentUICulture = new CultureInfo("en-US");
  }

  InitStrings();
}
```

I detect which PictureBox is clicked and change the culture accordingly. If I got here some other way, I automatically change back to US culture. Because I wrote the code, I should only get here if a PictureBox was clicked. After changing the culture, I call the InitStrings function I just went over. Because I used the DateTimePicker for data and time entries, there is no need for me to write any validation code. It works in all cultures known to .NET.

Now for the data validation part that is *not* known to .NET. I am referring to entering in the mileage for the day's trip. Here is the code:

```
private void InputValidator(object sender, KeyPressEventArgs e)
{
  TextBox t;
  NumberFormatInfo nf = Thread.CurrentThread.CurrentCulture.NumberFormat;

  if(sender is TextBox)
  {
    t = (TextBox)sender;
    if (t == txtMiles)
```

```
  {
    //Allow only 0-9 and decimal separator
    if(Char.IsNumber(e.KeyChar))
      e.Handled = false;
    else if(e.KeyChar == Convert.ToChar(nf.NumberDecimalSeparator))
    {
      if(t.Text.IndexOf(Convert.ToChar(nf.NumberDecimalSeparator)) >=0)
        e.Handled = true;
      else
        e.Handled = false;
    }
    else
      e.Handled = true;
  }
}
}
```

First off, I obtain the number format of the current culture. I need this to determine what the decimal separator is. Once I know this, I can check for it. This is how I allow only what is culturally appropriate to be entered via the keyboard. If the key that is pressed is not a number or the allowed separator, it gets thrown away. This is validation on the fly with an international twist.

This extra piece of code may be confusing you here:

```
if(t.Text.IndexOf(Convert.ToChar(nf.NumberDecimalSeparator)) >=0)
  e.Handled = true;
else
  e.Handled = false;
```

This code is very important and without it I open up a major bug. I leave it up to you to figure out what it does.

In the constructor for this example, I attached a delegate to both the KeyPress and KeyUp events. I did this so I could calculate the money owed on the fly. As the user types in mileage values in the Miles field, the Cash field changes accordingly. Here is the code:

```
private void CalculateCash(object sender, KeyEventArgs e)
{
  TextBox t;
  if(sender is TextBox)
  {
    t = (TextBox)sender;
    if (t == txtMiles)
```

```
    {
      try
      {
        miles = float.Parse(txtMiles.Text);
        cash = miles * 0.35f;
        lblCash.Text=cash.ToString("N",Thread.CurrentThread.CurrentCulture);
      }
      catch
      {
        lblCash.Text = "";
      }
    }
  }
}
```

This is the only place where I use error protection. I have not used error protection so far because these are examples and the code sometimes obscures what I want to show. I use exception handling in subsequent chapters quite a bit, though.

So, here I convert the text representation of a number to an actual number. This Parse method is culturally aware. I then do some simple math and convert the result to a string. If I get here without typing a number, I clear the Cash field. The only way I can get here without typing a number is by typing in a comma or a period as the first digit. If you want, you can make sure you never get to this routine unless you have a valid number by not allowing the decimal separator as the first character in the Miles field. This is what I would do in a real program. Avoid bad programming if you can.

Any questions? No? Good.

Accessibility

The last section dealt with making your program accessible to the international market. But what about making your program accessible to people with disabilities? This section touches on this subject as it relates to data entry screens. This topic deserves a more thorough treatment, though, and I recommend you research it further through the numerous books and Web sites devoted to the subject.

If you are running Windows, you will be able to change how your program works via the Accessibility Options area in the Control Panel. You can enable such features as StickyKeys, which enables you to use the Ctrl, Alt, or Shift key combinations by typing one key at a time. You can also enable a visual cue based on sound alerts.

The Windows accessibility options apply systemwide. What can you do to make your program more accessible? Here are some general guidelines to help you along:

- Allow the user to change to a larger font programwide if desired.

- Keep control clutter to a minimum. Do not overload screens with as many controls as you can fit on them.

- Keep the program flow simple and logical.

- Group data logically and keep related data in one place.

- Use color and shading to emphasize important parts of the screen.

- If you are writing for children, be cognizant of the text you use. Keep things simple.

- Consider programming for low-resolution screens for those with visual impairments.

- Allow the user to assign sounds to certain actions. This is easy to do programmatically.

These general guidelines apply to accessibility, but they also make sense for most regular programming tasks.

Programming Accessibility

The controls in .NET allow you to present accessibility information to any accessible client. What do I mean by this? Suppose you have a text-to-speech processor. As the user moves his or her mouse over the screen, the computer indicates what control the user's mouse is currently hovering over and what the control means. Now, this is easy for something like a TextBox that has a Text property, but what about a picture?

Four properties and one object deal with accessibility in any control. The properties are as follows:

- AccessibleDefaultActionDescription

- AccessibleDescription

- AccessibleName

- AccessibleRole

The descriptions are strings that you can assign to a control that can be read by accessibility clients. These strings could be something like "This button exits the program." The name could be something like "Exit Button."

The AccessibleRole property is an enumeration that describes what the control is. This role is a bit more than just the .NET name of the control. For instance, for a PictureBox, I would choose AccessibleRole.Graphic. For a RichTextBox, I would choose AccessibleRole.Document. Are you starting to get the idea here? These properties allow you to provide meaningful information to an accessible client (such as a text-to-speech processor) so it can help the user to work with your program.

Each control can also be assigned an AccessibleObject. This object has quite a few more properties and methods to help you provide more information to the user.

Accessibility Spy Example

The example I present in this section will give you an idea how an accessibility client can get information about your data entry program. You need to first make sure that you fill in all the pertinent information for the AccessibleRole property and the AccessibleDescription property at a minimum. If you take the time to put this information in each of your controls, you enable an accessibility client to provide an alternate method of relaying information about the control to the user.

This example has two forms. One is a main form that has a few controls on it. You can pretend that this is your complicated data entry form. The second form is an accessibility client. You can pretend that because the user has enabled accessibility for your program, this form has popped up to help the user along.

Start out with a new VB or C# project. Mine is called "Accessibility." You will need to perform the following steps to get going:

1. Place a Button on the form whose text reads **Exit**.

2. Place a Label on the form whose text reads **Name**.

3. Place a TextBox under the Label.

This is it for controls on this form. It is enough to show you what goes on. Figure 3-18 shows this form.

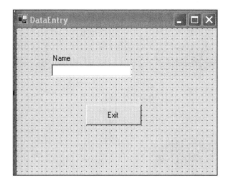

Figure 3-18. A simple form demonstrating accessibility

Click the Exit button and in the Properties window choose PushButton for the AccessibleRole. Type in **Program Exit Button** for the AccessibleDescription. Figure 3-19 shows the Properties window.

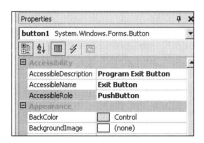

Figure 3-19. Accessible properties

Click the TextBox and choose Text for the AccessibleRole and type in **Name of Employee** for the AccessibleDescription. Leave the AcessibleRole for the Label as is.

Now add a new Windows form to the project called "Spy." Add the following controls:

1. Add a Label whose text reads **Accessible Description**. Make the font Arial, 12 points.

2. Below the Accessible Description label add another Label called **lblDesc**. Change its border style to Fixed3D and its font to Arial, 30 points.

3. Add a Label whose text reads **Text**. Make the font Arial, 12 points.

4. Below the Text label add another Label called **lblText**. Change its border style to Fixed3D and its font to Arial, 30 points.

5. Add a reference to the Microsoft.VisualBasic runtime DLL (C# only).

Your Spy form should look like the one shown in Figure 3-20.

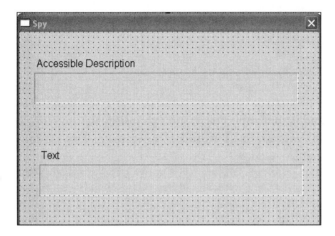

Figure 3-20. The Spy form

Add the following code to your Spy form.

C#

```csharp
private void Spy_Load(object sender, System.EventArgs e)
{
  //This precludes menus because a menu is a component
  foreach(Control c in this.Owner.Controls)
  {
    c.MouseEnter += new EventHandler(this.AccessibleEnter);
    c.MouseLeave += new EventHandler(this.AccessibleLeave);
  }

}

private void AccessibleEnter(object sender, EventArgs e)
{
  Control c;
```

```
    //This precludes menus.  You can include menus if you like
    //by testing for a component.
    if(sender is Control)
      c = (Control)sender;
    else
      return;

    //Don't bother with incidental controls
    if(c.AccessibleRole == AccessibleRole.Default)
      return;

    //Yes, folks, you can use VB commands inside C#
    Microsoft.VisualBasic.Interaction.Beep();

    lblDesc.Text = c.AccessibleDescription;
    lblText.Text = c.Text;
  }

  private void AccessibleLeave(object sender, EventArgs e)
  {

    lblDesc.Text = "";
    lblText.Text = "";
  }
```

VB

```
  Private Sub Spy_Load(ByVal sender As System.Object, _
                    ByVal e As System.EventArgs) Handles MyBase.Load

    'This precludes menus because a menu is a component
    Dim c As Control
    For Each c In Me.Owner.Controls
      AddHandler c.MouseEnter, AddressOf AccessibleEnter
      AddHandler c.MouseLeave, AddressOf AccessibleLeave
    Next

  End Sub

  Private Sub AccessibleEnter(ByVal sender As Object, ByVal e As EventArgs)
    Dim c As Control

    'This precludes menus.  You can include menus if you like
    'by testing for a component.
```

```
    'I cannot test for lineage like in C#
    c = CType(sender, Control)

    'Don't bother with incidental controls
    If c.AccessibleRole = AccessibleRole.Default Then
      Return
    End If

    Beep()

    lblDesc.Text = c.AccessibleDescription
    lblText.Text = c.Text
  End Sub

  Private Sub AccessibleLeave(ByVal sender As Object, ByVal e As EventArgs)

    lblDesc.Text = ""
    lblText.Text = ""
  End Sub
```

Now go back to the main form and add the following code.

C#

```
  #region class local variables

  Spy SpyForm;

  #endregion

  …
  …
  …

  private void Form1_Load(object sender, System.EventArgs e)
  {
    SpyForm = new Spy();
    SpyForm.Owner = this;

    SpyForm.Show();
  }
```

VB

```
Private SpyForm As Spy

Private Sub dataentry_Load(ByVal sender As System.Object, _
                          ByVal e As System.EventArgs) Handles MyBase.Load
   SpyForm = New Spy()
   SpyForm.Owner = Me

   SpyForm.Show()

End Sub
```

Run the project and move your mouse over the controls on the main form. The Spy form should pick this up and give you information about each of the controls on the main form. I used large fonts on the Spy form to help people with visual disabilities.

As you move your mouse over the main form, notice that you are not spying on the Label. Let's look at the code.

The main form instantiates the Spy form and gives it a reference back to itself through the Owner property of the Spy form. Once the Spy form is instantiated I scan the main form for all controls. I then chain a delegate to the MouseEnter and MouseLeave events of each control. The code for this is as follows:

```
//This precludes menus because a menu is a component
foreach(Control c in this.Owner.Controls)
{
  c.MouseEnter += new EventHandler(this.AccessibleEnter);
  c.MouseLeave += new EventHandler(this.AccessibleLeave);
}
```

The code is pretty simple but very effective. The MouseEnter delegate detects the AccessibleRole and shows the Accessible properties on the screen, as shown here:

```
private void AccessibleEnter(object sender, EventArgs e)
{
  Control c;

  //This precludes menus.  You can include menus if you like
  //by testing for a component.
  if(sender is Control)
    c = (Control)sender;
  else
    return;
```

```
    //Don't bother with incidental controls
    if(c.AccessibleRole == AccessibleRole.Default)
      return;

    //Yes, folks, you can use VB commands inside C#
    Microsoft.VisualBasic.Interaction.Beep();

    lblDesc.Text = c.AccessibleDescription;
    lblText.Text = c.Text;
}
```

This is how I ignore the Label on the main form. It has an AccessibleRole of Default.

When I wrote the C# code for this example, I wanted to sound a beep whenever I entered a control. After spending about 30 seconds looking for a C# Beep command, I decided to use the VB one.

TIP   It is not well known that C# programmers can use VB commands if they have a reference to the VB runtime DLL. You will most often use this technique to access the VB string manipulation commands.

Figure 3-21 shows this program in action.

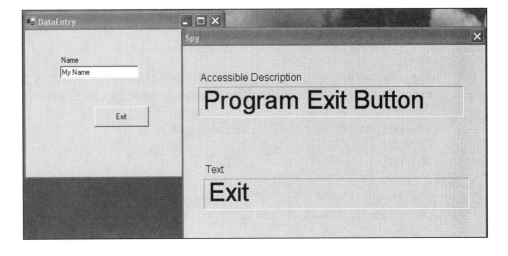

Figure 3-21. The accessibility Spy program in action

As you can see, it does not take much effort to make the main program (your data entry program) accessible for disabled users. I think the Spy program is kind of neat, and I can see all kinds of ways to make it much better.

Summary

In this chapter you learned the ins and outs of various issues associated with data entry screens. The chapter covered the following topics:

- Setting up and using SDI data entry projects

- Setting up and using MDI data entry projects

- Internationalizing your program

- Making your program accessible to people with disabilities

The last two issues often get worked into a program long after it has been released. Spending a little time up front on these issues can save you a lot of time later. You will also have a much better and more maintainable program to show for it.

CHAPTER 4

Keyboard- and Mouse-Based Data Entry

THIS CHAPTER DEALS WITH entering in data using the keyboard and the mouse. Yes I know, you're probably thinking, "Haven't I been typing on the keyboard all along?" Yup, however, you should be aware of the following issues:

- Which key (or keys) is being pressed?

- Which key event should you trap?

- When should you evaluate the key?

- When should you use hot keys?

- When should you use shortcut keys?

I covered some of these topics in Chapters 1, 2, and 3. I further cover trapping key presses in this chapter.

As far as mouse-based data entry goes, so far you have used the mouse to get from one field to another. Using the mouse properly can make screen navigation easier and can also enhance data entry for the user. This mouse-based data entry can be a lot of fun and it can also be rather complicated. I try not to get too complicated in this chapter, but here are some of the things you will see regarding the mouse:

- The mouse events

- Cursor control

- The MouseEventArgs structure

- Drag and drop

- Mouse-based entry validation

- Marquis selection

- GDI+ and the mouse

This last topic, GDI+ and the mouse, is where you will learn some of the more inventive data entry techniques.

The next section covers some more keyboard data-entry functionality.

The Keyboard and You

You have used the keyboard KeyPress event to grant access to or deny certain keys. This is called *on-the-fly validation*. It works quite well in the case of allowing only certain characters to be entered in a TextBox.

The KeyPress event is not the only key event you can use, however. You can use two others: the KeyDown event and the KeyUp event. These events come in the following order:

- KeyDown

- KeyPress

- KeyUp

Why have three events? Because you can get different information about what happened from each event.

The KeyDown event is raised every time a key is pressed. This means that if a user holds a key down, this event is raised for each repeated key.

The KeyUp event is raised when the user lets up on a key. If the user holds down the letter *K* for 20 seconds, you will get a few dozen KeyDown events and only one KeyUp event. In most cases, a KeyDown event is used to initiate some action and a KeyUp event is used to end it.

The KeyPress event is where you trap most of the keystrokes. It gets passed a KeyPressEventArgs object that allows you to compare a key that is pressed against a set of keys that you allow. It also allows you to discard the key if you don't want it.

The KeyDown and KeyUp delegates have the same signature. That is, they both get passed in a KeyEventArgs object. Table 4-1 shows what you get from the KeyEventArgs object.

Table 4-1. KeyEventArgs Properties

Method/Property	Meaning
Alt	True if Alt is pressed; false otherwise
Control	True if Ctrl is pressed; false otherwise
Shift	True if Shift is pressed; false otherwise
Modifiers	Bitwise combination of all modifier keys pressed (see Keys enum)
KeyData	KeyCode combined with modifier keys
KeyValue	Integer representation of KeyData information
KeyCode	The keyboard code for the key pressed
Handled	True if the event was handled; false otherwise

There is quite a bit of information in this object. The following small example should give you a good handle on how you can use these properties.

Open up a new C# or VB Windows project. Mine is called "Keys." Add eight labels, four of which have text in them and the other four of which are empty but have a visible border. Figure 4-1 shows you what your screen should look like.

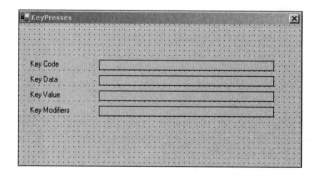

Figure 4-1. The key press display

Can you guess why I did not put any buttons or controls that can receive focus on this form? If I did that, then the form itself could never receive focus and I could not capture key events that happen on the form. (I cover a way around this later in the chapter.)

Now for the code. This is so simple, I show only the C# code here. Make a KeyDown delegate and assign it to the form's KeyDown event.

KeyDown Delegate

```csharp
private void MyKeyDown(object sender, KeyEventArgs e)
{
   keycode.Text = e.KeyCode.ToString();
   keydata.Text = e.KeyData.ToString();
   keyvalue.Text = e.KeyValue.ToString();
   keymod.Text = e.Modifiers.ToString();
}
```

Constructor

```csharp
public frmKeys()
{
   InitializeComponent();

   //This is only valid if the form has focus
   //The form only has focus if there are no visible
   controls that can accept focus on it.
   this.KeyDown += new KeyEventHandler(this.MyKeyDown);
}
```

Compile and run the program. Start pressing keys. When you press Alt-Ctrl-H, you should see something similar to Figure 4-2.

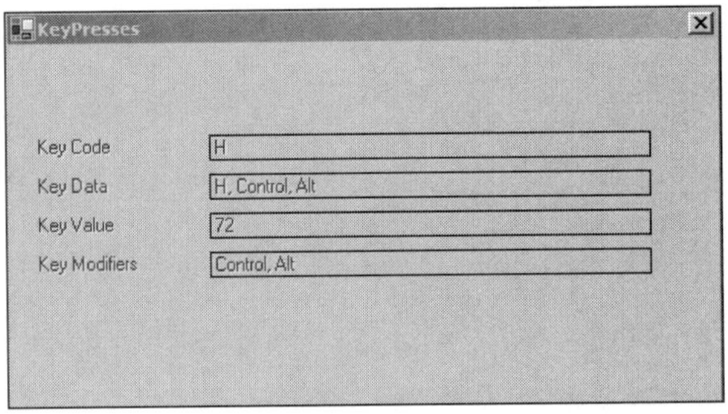

Figure 4-2. The result of pressing keys

What is important to see here, and I am sure you noticed it, is that you get this event for every key that is pressed. So in this case you got three events. You can trap any key or key combination you want.

If you have trapped the KeyDown event and the KeyUp event handler also has the same signature, why trap this KeyUp event? There are two reasons, really. As I already said, the KeyUp event happens only once per key press. It also has one other feature. Suppose you pressed Ctrl-Alt-Enter. How would you know which key was the last up? The KeyUp event will tell you this.

Before I get to the next example I want to mention the KeyPress event. It has a signature that includes the KeyPressEventArgs object. This object does not break down the individual keys that were pressed like the KeyEventArgs object does. It provides only the resulting composite key that was pressed. It gives you an actual Char data type as a result.

What you can do with this event is provide a delegate that checks this value and lets it through or throws it away before the control actually gets it. I have shown you this already in the three previous chapters.

The only good way to see what goes on with these three events is to see the interaction of all three at once. You will do this by extending your "Keys" example:

1. Put all the existing Labels inside a GroupBox on your screen. The GroupBox should read **KeyDown event**.

2. Change the bordered labels to **lblDownCode**, **lblDownData**, **lblDownValue**, and **lblDownMod**, respectively.

3. Add a new Label inside this GroupBox called **lblDownTime**. I set the Label's background color to Linen.

Your screen should look like Figure 4-3.

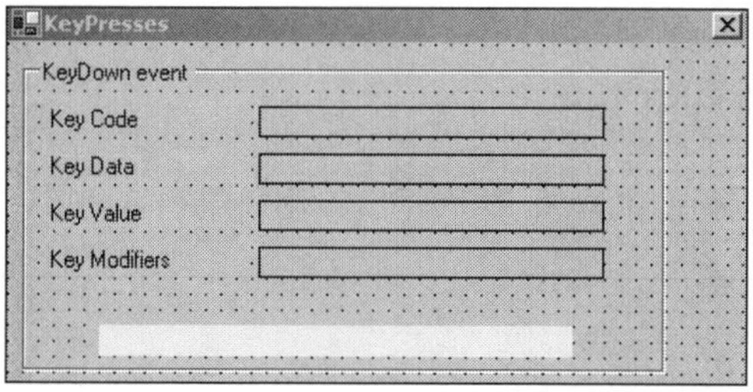

Figure 4-3. The KeyDown GroupBox

Then follow these steps:

1. Add a new Label below the GroupBox whose text reads **Key Press**.

2. Add a new Label called **lblPress** next to the Label you created in step 1.

3. Add a linen-colored Label called **lblPressTime** below the Labels you created in steps 1 and 2.

Your screen should now look like Figure 4-4.

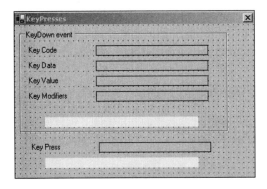

Figure 4-4. Adding a Key Press display

Complete the form by following these steps:

1. Copy the KeyDown GroupBox and add the new GroupBox below the Key Press time label.

2. Change the GroupBox's text to **KeyUp event**.

3. Rename the new time label to **lblUpTime**.

4. Change the bordered labels to **lblUpCode**, **lblUpData**, **lblUpValue**, and **lblUpMod**, respectively.

Figure 4-5 shows the complete form.

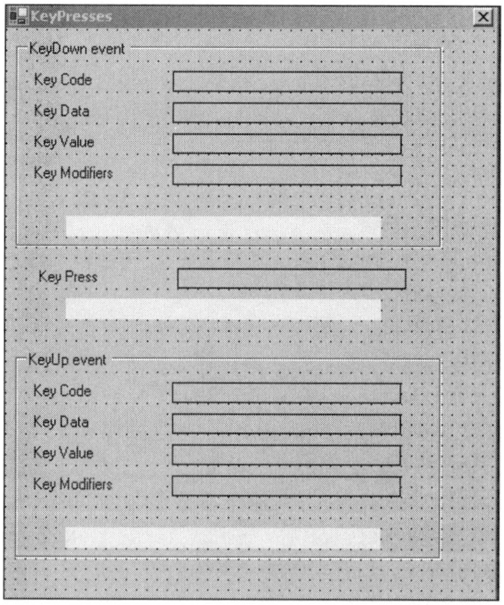

Figure 4-5. The completed key event form

Now for the code. Listings 4-1a and 4-1b show the code for this example.

Listing 4-1a. C# Code for the Complete Keys Example

```csharp
using System;
using System.Threading;
using System.Drawing;
using System.Collections;
using System.ComponentModel;
using System.Windows.Forms;
using System.Data;

namespace Keys_c
{
  /// <summary>
  /// Shows interaction of key events
  /// </summary>
  public class frmKeys : System.Windows.Forms.Form
  {
    private System.Windows.Forms.GroupBox groupBox1;
    private System.Windows.Forms.Label label7;
    private System.Windows.Forms.Label label5;
    private System.Windows.Forms.Label label3;
```

```csharp
                private System.Windows.Forms.Label label2;
                private System.Windows.Forms.Label lblDownTime;
                private System.Windows.Forms.GroupBox groupBox2;
                private System.Windows.Forms.Label lblUpTime;
                private System.Windows.Forms.Label label10;
                private System.Windows.Forms.Label label12;
                private System.Windows.Forms.Label label14;
                private System.Windows.Forms.Label label16;
                private System.Windows.Forms.Label label9;
                private System.Windows.Forms.Label lblPress;
                private System.Windows.Forms.Label lblPressTime;
                private System.Windows.Forms.Label lblUpMod;
                private System.Windows.Forms.Label lblUpValue;
                private System.Windows.Forms.Label lblUpData;
                private System.Windows.Forms.Label lblUpCode;
                private System.Windows.Forms.Label lblDownMod;
                private System.Windows.Forms.Label lblDownValue;
                private System.Windows.Forms.Label lblDownData;
                private System.Windows.Forms.Label lblDownCode;

                private System.ComponentModel.Container components = null;

                public frmKeys()
                {
                  InitializeComponent();

                  //This is only valid if the form has focus
                  //The form only has focus if there are no visible controls on it.
                  this.KeyDown  += new KeyEventHandler(this.MyKeyDown);
                  this.KeyPress += new KeyPressEventHandler(this.MyKeyPress);
                  this.KeyUp    += new KeyEventHandler(this.MyKeyUp);

                }


                protected override void Dispose( bool disposing )
                {
                  if( disposing )
                  {
                    if (components != null)
```

```
    {
      components.Dispose();
    }
  }
  base.Dispose( disposing );
}

#region Windows Form Designer generated code
...
...
...

#endregion


[STAThread]
static void Main()
{
  Application.Run(new frmKeys());
}

private void frmKeys_Load(object sender, System.EventArgs e)
{
}

#region events


private void MyKeyDown(object sender, KeyEventArgs e)
{
  lblDownCode.Text = e.KeyCode.ToString();
  lblDownData.Text = e.KeyData.ToString();
  lblDownValue.Text = e.KeyValue.ToString();
  lblDownMod.Text = e.Modifiers.ToString();

  lblDownTime.Text = DateTime.Now.Ticks.ToString();
  Thread.Sleep(2);

}

private void MyKeyPress(object sender, KeyPressEventArgs e)
{
```

```csharp
        lblPress.Text = e.KeyChar.ToString();
        lblPressTime.Text = DateTime.Now.Ticks.ToString();
        Thread.Sleep(2);

    }

    private void MyKeyUp(object sender, KeyEventArgs e)
    {
        lblUpCode.Text = e.KeyCode.ToString();
        lblUpData.Text = e.KeyData.ToString();
        lblUpValue.Text = e.KeyValue.ToString();
        lblUpMod.Text = e.Modifiers.ToString();

        lblUpTime.Text = DateTime.Now.Ticks.ToString();
        Thread.Sleep(2);

    }

    #endregion

    }
}
```

Listing 4-1b. VB Code for the Complete Keys Example

```vb
Option Strict On

Imports System.Threading

Public Class frmKeys
  Inherits System.Windows.Forms.Form

#Region " Windows Form Designer generated code "
...
...
...
#End Region

    Private Sub frmKeys_Load(ByVal sender As System.Object, _
                        ByVal e As System.EventArgs) Handles MyBase.Load
```

```
        AddHandler Me.KeyDown, AddressOf MyKeyDown
        AddHandler Me.KeyPress, AddressOf MyKeyPress
        AddHandler Me.KeyUp, AddressOf MyKeyUp


    End Sub

#Region "events"


    Private Sub MyKeyDown(ByVal sender As Object, ByVal e As KeyEventArgs)
        lblDownCode.Text = e.KeyCode.ToString()
        lblDownData.Text = e.KeyData.ToString()
        lblDownValue.Text = e.KeyValue.ToString()
        lblDownMod.Text = e.Modifiers.ToString()

        lblDownTime.Text = DateTime.Now.Ticks.ToString()
        Thread.Sleep(2)

    End Sub

    Private Sub MyKeyPress(ByVal sender As Object, ByVal e As KeyPressEventArgs)

        lblPress.Text = e.KeyChar.ToString()
        lblPressTime.Text = DateTime.Now.Ticks.ToString()
        Thread.Sleep(2)

    End Sub

    Private Sub MyKeyUp(ByVal sender As Object, ByVal e As KeyEventArgs)
        lblUpCode.Text = e.KeyCode.ToString()
        lblUpData.Text = e.KeyData.ToString()
        lblUpValue.Text = e.KeyValue.ToString()
        lblUpMod.Text = e.Modifiers.ToString()

        lblUpTime.Text = DateTime.Now.Ticks.ToString()
        Thread.Sleep(2)

    End Sub

#End Region
End Class
```

Notice that I included a reference to the Threading namespace. I make each delegate go to sleep for 2 milliseconds so you can better see the time difference between events.

Run this program and press all kinds of keys while the form is in focus. You will see the order of events, which key in a key combination was pressed first, and which key in a key combination was released last.

Press a key until the key repeat kicks in. You will see the KeyDown delegate get called repeatedly. You can see this by looking at the continuously changing time for this event.

Spend some time with this example and play around with the keyboard. Once you see all the keyboard events in action, you may get some ideas on how to use each event in your data entry program. Although this example is fairly simple in construction, you can use what you learn here in some fairly complicated situations.

There's one thing to remember about the key events (as a matter of fact, this goes for any of the standard class events). You should test to see if the Sender object is valid and if the argument object is valid. With most events, there's a way to manually invoke the event using the On<event> statement. In other words, if you want to invoke the KeyDown delegate you call OnKeyDown with the proper KeyEventArgs argument. The same kind of thing goes for the KeyUp and KeyPress events. For these, you use the OnKeyUp and OnKeyPress methods, respectively. Now, why would you do this for a key event?

What if you allow data to be entered in your program through some other means than the keyboard? For instance, you could be reading information from a file, over the network, via a modem, and so on. You could take one route and bypass your validation code for your specialized TextBox and do something like this:

```
TextBox1.text = SomeValue
```

Doing this bypasses any on-the-fly validation code you may have in the KeyPress delegate. If all you want is numbers in this control, you could force alpha characters in here as well.

A better way is to read each character as it comes in and pass it to the TextBox control via the OnKeyPress method. This way, you can fill the TextBox with information without regard to what that information is. You know that the KeyPress delegate with your validation code will take care if it. (Chapter 6 shows you just this scenario.)

The caveat I was talking about is that the following line of code is perfectly valid.

C#

```
OnKeyPress(null);
```

VB

```
OnKeyPress(Nothing)
```

Your nicely coded KeyPress delegate would crash and burn. If you have decided that your delegate should never get called with a null argument, the best thing you could do is use an assertion as the first line of code in your delegate. An assertion is used only in debug mode. This way, you can put all kinds of boneheaded error-checking code that never gets compiled into the release version of your program. This makes for faster release code. To use assertions, you need to include the System.Diagnostics namespace. Here is the C# code for the KeyDown delegate with an assertion:

```csharp
private void MyKeyDown(object sender, KeyEventArgs e)
{

  Debug.Assert(e != null, "BoneHead call");

  lblDownCode.Text = e.KeyCode.ToString();
  lblDownData.Text = e.KeyData.ToString();
  lblDownValue.Text = e.KeyValue.ToString();
  lblDownMod.Text = e.Modifiers.ToString();

  lblDownTime.Text = DateTime.Now.Ticks.ToString();
  Thread.Sleep(2);
}
```

Check out the System.Diagnostics namespace. It has a gaggle of classes that are very handy for debugging.

A Better Mouse Trap

Now you are an expert on handling incoming messages from the keyboard. The next device I cover in this chapter is the mouse.

You may be thinking that using a mouse is just a side effect of a data entry program. Perhaps you would use the mouse to just move from one field to another. You could also use it to select tabs in a TabControl. Neither of these uses requires any mouse-based code from you. In fact, you can write a perfectly good data entry program without writing any mouse-based code at all. You would, however, be cheating yourself and your customer out of a richer user interface.

The Mouse Events

You can handle six events concerning the mouse. Table 4-2 shows these events.

Table 4-2. Mouse Events and Uses

Event	Argument	Use
MouseDown	MouseEventArgs	Reacts to any mouse button press
MouseUp	MouseEventArgs	Fires when the button is let up
MouseEnter	EventArgs	Fires when the mouse enters a control's boundary
MouseLeave	EventArgs	Fires when the mouse leaves a control's boundary
MouseHover	EventArgs	Fires when the mouse hovers within a control's boundary
MouseMove	MouseEventArgs	Fires every time the mouse moves

Notice that three of these events use the MouseEventArgs class and the others use a plain old EventArgs class. This is because there is no reason for you to know anything about the Enter, Leave, and Hover events, other than the mouse is here. The Move, Down, and Up events let the programmer know what the user was doing with the mouse.

Rather than hash over all the mouse events and what they can do, I think an example is in order. This is a fairly complex example. It is what I consider one of the better types of data entry methods. I say this because the user can accomplish a lot on this screen without ever typing in anything. In fact, the only key I let the user enter is the Delete key.

The first part of this example includes everything you have learned so far about basic controls, keyboard event handling, and mouse event handling. The second part of this example, however, extends the mouse-handling capability by adding some GDI+ capability. As an end result, you will see a familiar interface (these days) and you will also know how to program this type of interface.

Start with a new C# or VB project. Mine is called "MouseTrap."

1. Size the main form to be around 488×424.

2. Change the form's name to **frmMouse**.

3. Make the form start up centered and change the text to **Mouse Event Handlers**.

4. Make the form FixedSingle with no maximize or minimize buttons.

5. Add a StatusBar and call it **sb**.

6. Add a ListBox and call it **lstPics**.

7. Add a Button and call it **cmdAdd**. Change the text to read **Add to Panel**.

8. Add a Panel called **P1**. Make its border style Fixed3D.

Figure 4-6 shows what the form looks like.

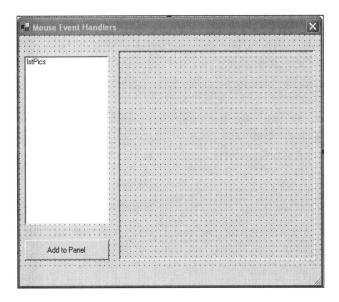

Figure 4-6. All the controls on the MouseTrap form

As you can see, there is not much here. Using these controls, however, you can accomplish more than a fleet of TextBoxes.

TIP This project uses quite a few pictures. You can find them in this book's code, which you can download from the Downloads section of the Apress Web site (http://www.apress.com).

Here is what this example will do:

- Load some pictures of flags into an array and display the text values in the ListBox. The user can multiselect any of the text values in the ListBox.

- When the user clicks the Add button, the pictures will transfer to the Panel. The pictures will be arranged in the Panel similar to a thumbnail view in Windows Explorer.

- When the user passes the mouse over a flag in the Panel, the flag's name will appear on the StatusBar and the cursor will change to a hand.

- The user can select flags for deletion in the Panel by left-clicking them with the mouse. Flags marked for deletion will have a border around them. When the user presses the Delete key, the marked flags are deleted and the remaining flags are rearranged.

This example involves quite a bit of code, so let's get started.

First of all, you will need a class local structure that holds the picture of the flag and its name. You will notice that this structure looks identical to a class. Do you know what the difference is? I suggest you look it up in the online help. The reason I am using a structure is because it is value based and is held on the stack (these are two hints as to the difference between a class and a structure).

C#

```
#region Class Local Variables

//Structs get created on the stack
private struct Symbols
{
  private Image   mflag;
  private string  mDispName;
  public Symbols(string DispName, Image flag)
  {
    mflag = flag;
    mDispName = DispName;
  }
  public Image Flag
  {
    get{return mflag;}
  }
```

```
      public string Name
      {
        get{return mDispName;}
      }
    };
```

```
    #endregion
```

VB

```
#Region "Class Local Variables"

  'Structs get created on the stack
  Private Structure Symbols
    Private mflag As Image
    Private mDispName As String
    Public Sub New(ByVal DispName As String, ByVal flag As Image)
      mflag = flag
      mDispName = DispName
    End Sub
    Public ReadOnly Property Flag() As Image
      Get
        Return mflag
      End Get
    End Property
    Public ReadOnly Property Name() As String
      Get
        Return mDispName
      End Get
    End Property
  End Structure
```

```
#End Region
```

In Chapter 1, I introduced you to a simple way to link one control to another by using the DataSource property. Visual Studio 6.0 allowed you to connect a Data-Source only to a database.

My goal in using the ListBox is to show a list of country names that I have flags for. Now I could have an array of flags and hard-code the names into the ListBox. Then I could extract the flag from the array according to the index of the entry chosen in the ListBox. This works but it is so 1990s.

The more elegant thing to do is use the DataSource property of the ListBox to directly link to an internal array. This internal array, of course, holds a collection of "Symbols" structures I just defined. Look carefully at the constructor code.

C#

```
public frmMouse()
{
  InitializeComponent();

  //Need to use arraylist here.
  ArrayList Pics = new ArrayList();
  Pics.Add(new Symbols("Italy",       Image.FromFile("Italy.ico")));
  Pics.Add(new Symbols("Japan",       Image.FromFile("japan.ico")));
  Pics.Add(new Symbols("Canada",      Image.FromFile("canada.ico")));
  Pics.Add(new Symbols("Germany",     Image.FromFile("germany.ico")));
  Pics.Add(new Symbols("Mexico",      Image.FromFile("mexico.ico")));
  Pics.Add(new Symbols("Norway",      Image.FromFile("norway.ico")));
  Pics.Add(new Symbols("New Zealand", Image.FromFile("nz.ico")));
  Pics.Add(new Symbols("England",     Image.FromFile("england.ico")));
  Pics.Add(new Symbols("USA",         Image.FromFile("usa.ico")));

  lstPics.SelectionMode = SelectionMode.MultiExtended;
  lstPics.DataSource = Pics;
  lstPics.DisplayMember = "Name";
  lstPics.ValueMember = "Flag";

  //Set up the status bar
  sb.Panels.Add("Flag = ");
  sb.Panels[0].AutoSize = StatusBarPanelAutoSize.Spring;
  sb.ShowPanels = true;

  //Transfer the data over.
  cmdAdd.Click += new EventHandler(this.MoveFlags);

  //Make sure the user can see all flags
  P1.AutoScroll = true;

  //Intercept all keyboard strokes before they get to the controls
  this.KeyPreview = true;
  this.KeyDown    += new KeyEventHandler(this.DeleteFlags);

}
```

VB

```
Public Sub New()
  MyBase.New()

  InitializeComponent()

  'Need to use arraylist here.
  Dim Pics As ArrayList = New ArrayList()
  Pics.Add(New Symbols("Italy", Image.FromFile("Italy.ico")))
  Pics.Add(New Symbols("Japan", Image.FromFile("japan.ico")))
  Pics.Add(New Symbols("Canada", Image.FromFile("canada.ico")))
  Pics.Add(New Symbols("Germany", Image.FromFile("germany.ico")))
  Pics.Add(New Symbols("Mexico", Image.FromFile("mexico.ico")))
  Pics.Add(New Symbols("Norway", Image.FromFile("norway.ico")))
  Pics.Add(New Symbols("New Zealand", Image.FromFile("nz.ico")))
  Pics.Add(New Symbols("England", Image.FromFile("england.ico")))
  Pics.Add(New Symbols("USA", Image.FromFile("usa.ico")))

  lstPics.SelectionMode = SelectionMode.MultiExtended
  lstPics.DataSource = Pics
  lstPics.DisplayMember = "Name"
  lstPics.ValueMember = "Flag"

  'Set up the status bar
  sb.Panels.Add("Flag = ")
  sb.Panels(0).AutoSize = StatusBarPanelAutoSize.Spring
  sb.ShowPanels = True

  'Transfer the data over.
  AddHandler cmdAdd.Click, New EventHandler(AddressOf MoveFlags)

  'Make sure the user can see all flags
  P1.AutoScroll = True

  'Intercept all keyboard strokes before they get to the controls
  Me.KeyPreview = True
  AddHandler Me.KeyDown, New KeyEventHandler(AddressOf DeleteFlags)

End Sub
```

As far as the ListBox goes, this code sets it up for MultiSelect and sets the DataSource to the internal ArrayList. Here is what happens when the ListBox is displayed. The string that is displayed in the ListBox is taken from the ListBox's

DisplayMember property. This property is the name of the property of the DataSource that holds the actual string that is displayed. Notice that the Symbols structure has a property called "Name." The value that is associated with that name is pointed to by the ValueMember property of the ListBox. The Symbols structure has a "Flag" property that holds the image associated with the name.

Personally, I think this capability is incredibly cool and saves quite a bit of table lookup code.

The rest of the constructor sets up the status bar and some event handlers. Back in Chapter 3 I said there was no way for a form to get focus once there was a single control on it that allowed the user to do something. This was why I could not use the Focus event on a filled form in the SDI project to signal that the window list should change. Well, the same type of thing applies here. Once I have a control that accepts keystrokes, I cannot normally get a keystroke event from the form. What I need to do is use the KeyPreview property.

This KeyPreview property intercepts all keystrokes destined for controls on that form. I use it here to intercept the Delete key. This way, I can press the Delete key on any part of the form (and its controls) and I can handle it.

Listings 4-2a and 4-2b show the rest of the code. The code contains a helper function that arranges controls in the Panel and the delegates for mouse events and keyboard events.

Listing 4-2a. C# Code for Delegates

```
#region Helper functions

private void ArrangeImages()
{
    int x        = 0;
    int y        = 0;
    int PICSPACE = 10;
    int PICSIZE  = 64;

    //Number of pictures in a row.
    //Do not show a picture if it means we get a horizontal
    //scroll bar
    int NumPicsInWidth = (P1.Size.Width - PICSPACE) /
      (PICSIZE + PICSPACE);
    for (int k = 0; k<= P1.Controls.Count - 1; k++)
    {
        //determine if we are in a new row
        if (k % (NumPicsInWidth) == 0 )
          x = PICSPACE;
```

```
      else
        x = P1.Controls[k - 1].Location.X + PICSIZE + PICSPACE;


      if (k < NumPicsInWidth )
        y = PICSPACE;
      else if (k % (NumPicsInWidth) == 0 )
        y = P1.Controls[k - 1].Location.Y + PICSIZE + PICSPACE;


      P1.Controls[k].Location = new Point(x, y);
    }

  }


#endregion

#region events

private void MoveFlags(object sender, EventArgs e)
{
  foreach(Symbols flg in lstPics.SelectedItems)
  {
    PictureBox p  = new PictureBox();
    p.Size        = new Size(40, 40);
    p.SizeMode    = PictureBoxSizeMode.StretchImage;
    p.MouseDown  += new MouseEventHandler(this.PicMouseDown);
    p.MouseEnter += new EventHandler(this.PicMouseEnter);
    p.MouseLeave += new EventHandler(this.PicMouseLeave);
    p.Cursor      = Cursors.Hand;
    p.Image       = flg.Flag;
    p.Tag         = flg.Name;
    P1.Controls.Add(p);
  }

  ArrangeImages();

}

private void DeleteFlags(object sender, KeyEventArgs e)
{
  if(e.KeyCode == Keys.Delete)
  {
```

```
            //Try this shortcut. It will not work.  Do you know why?
//         foreach(PictureBox p in P1.Controls)
//         {
//            if(p.BorderStyle == BorderStyle.FixedSingle)
//                P1.Controls.Remove(p);
//         }

        PictureBox p;
        bool deleted = true;
        while (deleted)
        {
          deleted = false;
          for(int k=0; k<P1.Controls.Count; k++)
          {
            if(P1.Controls[k] is PictureBox)
            {
              p = (PictureBox)P1.Controls[k];
              if(p.BorderStyle == BorderStyle.FixedSingle)
              {
                P1.Controls.RemoveAt(k);
                deleted = true;
                //Controls.count has changed. Reinitialize the "for" loop
                break;
              }
            }
          }
        }

        ArrangeImages();
      }
    }

    private void PicMouseDown(object sender, MouseEventArgs e)
    {
      PictureBox P;
      if (sender is PictureBox)
        P = (PictureBox)sender;
      else
        return;

      if(e.Button == MouseButtons.Left)
      {
        if(P.BorderStyle == BorderStyle.FixedSingle)
          P.BorderStyle = BorderStyle.None;
```

```
      else
        P.BorderStyle = BorderStyle.FixedSingle;
    }
  }


  private void PicMouseEnter(object sender, EventArgs e)
  {
    if (sender is PictureBox)
    {
      PictureBox P = (PictureBox)sender;
      sb.Panels[0].Text = P.Tag.ToString();
    }
  }


  private void PicMouseLeave(object sender, EventArgs e)
  {
    sb.Panels[0].Text = "";
  }


  #endregion
```

Listing 4-2b. VB Code for Delegates

```
#Region "Helper functions"

  Private Sub ArrangeImages()
    Dim x As Int32 = 0
    Dim y As Int32 = 0
    Dim k As Int32
    Dim PICSPACE As Int32 = 10
    Dim PICSIZE As Int32 = 64


    'Number of pictures in a row.
    'Do not show a picture if it means we get a horizontal
    'scroll bar
    Dim NumPicsInWidth As Int32 = (P1.Size.Width - PICSPACE) \ _
                                  (PICSIZE + PICSPACE)
    'Control collections are zero based.
    'VB type collections are 1 based.
    For k = 0 To P1.Controls.Count - 1
      'determine if we are in a new row
      If k Mod (NumPicsInWidth) = 0 Then
        x = PICSPACE
```

```
        Else
          x = P1.Controls(k - 1).Location.X + PICSIZE + PICSPACE
        End If


        If k < NumPicsInWidth Then
          y = PICSPACE
        ElseIf k Mod (NumPicsInWidth) = 0 Then
          y = P1.Controls(k - 1).Location.Y + PICSIZE + PICSPACE
        End If


        P1.Controls(k).Location = New Point(x, y)
      Next
    End Sub


#End Region

#Region "events"

    Private Sub MoveFlags(ByVal sender As Object, ByVal e As EventArgs)
      Dim flg As Symbols


      For Each flg In lstPics.SelectedItems
        Dim p As PictureBox = New PictureBox()
        p.Size = New Size(40, 40)
        p.SizeMode = PictureBoxSizeMode.StretchImage
        AddHandler p.MouseDown, New MouseEventHandler(AddressOf PicMouseDown)
        AddHandler p.MouseEnter, New EventHandler(AddressOf PicMouseEnter)
        AddHandler p.MouseLeave, New EventHandler(AddressOf PicMouseLeave)
        p.Cursor = Cursors.Hand
        p.Image = flg.Flag
        p.Tag = flg.Name
        P1.Controls.Add(p)
      Next


      ArrangeImages()
    End Sub


    Private Sub DeleteFlags(ByVal sender As Object, ByVal e As KeyEventArgs)

      If e.KeyCode = Keys.Delete Then

        'Try this shortcut. It will not work.  Do you know why?
        'Dim p As PictureBox
        'For Each p In P1.Controls
```

```
    '  If p.BorderStyle = BorderStyle.FixedSingle Then
    '    P1.Controls.Remove(p)
    '  End If
    'Next

    Dim p As PictureBox
    Dim deleted As Boolean = True
    Dim k As Int32
    While (deleted)
      deleted = False
      For k = 0 To P1.Controls.Count - 1
        If P1.Controls(k).GetType() Is GetType(PictureBox) Then
          p = DirectCast(P1.Controls(k), PictureBox)
          If p.BorderStyle = BorderStyle.FixedSingle Then
            P1.Controls.RemoveAt(k)
            deleted = True
            'Controls.count has changed. Reinitialize the "for" loop
            Exit For
          End If
        End If
      Next
    End While

    ArrangeImages()
  End If
End Sub

Private Sub PicMouseDown(ByVal sender As Object, ByVal e As MouseEventArgs)
  Dim P As PictureBox

  If sender.GetType() Is GetType(PictureBox) Then
    P = DirectCast(sender, PictureBox)
  Else
    Return
  End If

  If e.Button = MouseButtons.Left Then
    If P.BorderStyle = BorderStyle.FixedSingle Then
      P.BorderStyle = BorderStyle.None
    Else
      P.BorderStyle = BorderStyle.FixedSingle
    End If
  End If
End Sub
```

```
Private Sub PicMouseEnter(ByVal sender As Object, ByVal e As EventArgs)

  If sender.GetType() Is GetType(PictureBox) Then
    Dim P As PictureBox = CType(sender, PictureBox)
    sb.Panels(0).Text = P.Tag.ToString()
  End If

End Sub

Private Sub PicMouseLeave(ByVal sender As Object, ByVal e As EventArgs)
  sb.Panels(0).Text = ""
End Sub

#End Region
```

Perhaps I should analyze this code a bit. First of all, I like the Panel control a lot. It serves as a great container and has automatic scroll bars. It can hold any type of control and as many controls as you want to put in it.

When you get into some advanced data entry programs, you will find yourself using images quite a bit. Anyway, you will need to arrange whatever controls you put in there in some fashion. The ArrangeImages method has a vertical scroll bar only. Personally, I like this better than two scroll bars on a control—but that is me. Notice that I decide how many controls can fit in the Panel horizontally by first finding out how big the Panel actually is. I do this because I often use a Panel in a form that is sizable. If you anchor the Panel to all sides of its container, you will find that the Panel will grow and shrink in size as its container size changes. This means that you may be able to fit more (or fewer) images horizontally inside the Panel. If this form was sizable (it is not in this example), then I would call the ArrangeImages method during the form's Resize event.

So what happens when the user chooses some flags named in the ListBox and then clicks the Add button? Here is the C# code again:

```
private void MoveFlags(object sender, EventArgs e)
{
  foreach(Symbols flg in lstPics.SelectedItems)
  {
    PictureBox p  = new PictureBox();
    p.Size        = new Size(40, 40);
    p.SizeMode    = PictureBoxSizeMode.StretchImage;
    p.MouseDown  += new MouseEventHandler(this.PicMouseDown);
```

```
    p.MouseEnter  += new EventHandler(this.PicMouseEnter);
    p.MouseLeave  += new EventHandler(this.PicMouseLeave);
    p.Cursor       = Cursors.Hand;
    p.Image        = flg.Flag;
    p.Tag          = flg.Name;
    P1.Controls.Add(p);
  }
  ArrangeImages();
}
```

Remember how the ListBox was set up to use the ArrayList as its DataSource? The DisplayMember was the name property of the Symbols structure and the ValueMember was the image property of the Symbols structure.

As I iterate through the selected items in the ListBox,[1] I create a new PictureBox and assign the ValueMember of the selected item as the image. Very simple but very powerful.

I also assign some standard delegates to each PictureBox I make. When I have done all this, I call the ArrangeImages method, and violá—instant flags! Figure 4-7 shows this example with all the flags in the Panel.

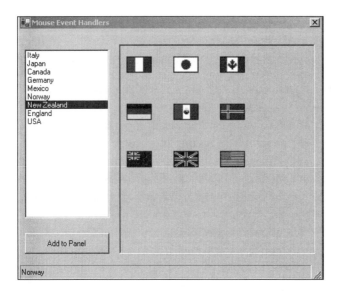

Figure 4-7. All the flags displayed

---

1. Try doing that in VB 6.0!

The Mouse, GDI+, and You

OK, so now you know the basics of the keyboard and the mouse. As you saw from the last example, using graphics can make for a more visually descriptive data entry program. I can see this kind of ListBox/images screen in a hospital-supply program. The list could be the complicated Latin names of surgical instruments and the images could be pictures of the instruments. The images would be a verification of what the user thinks the word means. The Panel could represent the set of instruments a surgeon would need in an operating room. You could also use something like this in an online-store checkout screen.

Anyway, moving on to the GDI+ enhancement: marquis selection. The purpose of this enhancement is to allow the user to drag a rectangle around some of the flags shown in the Panel, thereby selecting them. This is a common enough thing to do in data entry programs that you should learn how to do it.

The method that you will use to draw a rectangle is (funnily enough) Graphics.DrawRectangle. There is one caveat with this method, though: The Rectangle data type argument needs its starting point to be at the top left of the rectangle. It also needs its ending point to be below and to the right of the starting point. Consider the following rectangles as defined in C#:

```csharp
Rectangle r1 = new Rectangle(100, 100, 100, 50);
Rectangle r2 = new Rectangle(100, 100, -100, 50);
Rectangle r3 = new Rectangle(100, 100, 100, -50);
Rectangle r4 = new Rectangle(100, 100, -100, -50);
```

Each of these rectangles is perfectly legal; however, only the first one is valid for the DrawRectangle method. When the user drags the mouse, there is no guarantee that she will start at the top left and end at the bottom right. In fact, all things being equal, there is only a 25% chance of this happening. What you need to do as a programmer is convert the bottom three rectangles to the proper form so that all four values are positive. This is not so easy.

The best way I have found to accomplish this is to create a static class with a method that takes a rectangle and returns a corrected one. Now this class is quite small, as it has no constructor and the single method is short. However, I made it a class because I can see adding a few other static methods to it to handle such things as adding a method to return a rounded version of a sharp-cornered rectangle. Of course, in this case, the return data type would be a region, not a rectangle.

Add a new class to your MouseTrap project and call it "RectangleC." You will need to include the System.Drawing namespace at the top of this class. This class has no constructor and only one static (shared in VB) method. Listings 4-3a and 4-3b show the code for the whole class.

Listing 4-3a. C# Code for the Rectangle Converter Class

```csharp
using System;
using System.Drawing;

namespace MouseTrap_c
{
  /// <summary>
  /// Converts a rectangle that starts at any corner into one that can be drawn by
  /// the Graphics object.
  /// </summary>
  public class RectangleC
  {
    public static Rectangle Convert(Rectangle rect)
    {
      rect.X = rect.X - (Math.Abs(rect.Width) - rect.Width)/2;
      rect.Y = rect.Y - (Math.Abs(rect.Height) - rect.Height)/2;
      rect.Size = new Size(Math.Abs(rect.Width), Math.Abs(rect.Height));

      return rect;
    }
  }
}
```

Listing 4-3b. VB Code for the Rectangle Converter Class

```vb
Option Strict On

Imports System.Drawing

Public Class RectangleC

  Public Shared Function Convert(ByVal rect As Rectangle) As Rectangle

    rect.X = rect.X - CInt((Math.Abs(rect.Width) - rect.Width) / 2)
    rect.Y = rect.Y - CInt((Math.Abs(rect.Height) - rect.Height) / 2)
    rect.Size = New Size(Math.Abs(rect.Width), Math.Abs(rect.Height))

    Return rect
  End Function
End Class
```

Not much here, is there? When I first made this class I had all kinds of math in here. With some patience and advice from friends, I managed to boil it down to what you see here.

Unless you have worked with the GDI+ namespaces before, this may be your first introduction to the Point and Size structures. They are extremely useful and necessary in just about all GDI+ code. It is beyond the scope of this book to fully explain the Point and Size structures and their uses, so I encourage you to look in the online help for more information.

Compile your project and correct any errors you may have. You need this class to compile cleanly before you go any further.

Add the following variable to your class local variables section in the main form.

C#

```
//This is added for marquis selection of flags in the Panel
Rectangle Marquis = Rectangle.Empty;
```

VB

```
'This is added for marquis selection of flags in the Panel
Dim Marquis As Rectangle = Rectangle.Empty
```

I use the static Empty method to create a rectangle of no size. When the Paint delegate sees this, it skips past trying to render this rectangle and choose flags.

Speaking of Paint delegates, you will need to create one for the Panel. Because this is a small example, I use a delegate for the Paint event rather than override it.

Include the following method in your main form's code.

C#

```
private void PanelPaint(object sender, PaintEventArgs e)
{
  Rectangle r = RectangleC.Convert(Marquis);

  if(Marquis != Rectangle.Empty)
  {
    e.Graphics.DrawRectangle(Pens.Red, r);
    foreach(PictureBox P in P1.Controls)
    {
      if(r.Contains(P.Bounds))
        P.BorderStyle = BorderStyle.FixedSingle;
      else
        P.BorderStyle = BorderStyle.None;
    }
  }
}
```

VB

```vb
Private Sub PanelPaint(ByVal sender As Object, ByVal e As PaintEventArgs)
  Dim P As PictureBox
  Dim r As Rectangle = RectangleC.Convert(Marquis)

  If Not Marquis.Equals(Rectangle.Empty) Then
    e.Graphics.DrawRectangle(Pens.Red, r)
    For Each P In P1.Controls
      If r.Contains(P.Bounds) Then
        P.BorderStyle = BorderStyle.FixedSingle
      Else
        P.BorderStyle = BorderStyle.None
      End If
    Next
  End If
End Sub
```

The first thing I do here is to create a rectangle that has the correct starting and ending points. I use the new static RectangleC class to do this.

If the rectangle is not empty, I draw it on the Panel. I then iterate through each of the PictureBoxes in the Panel, looking for those that are completely contained in the bounding rectangle. If I find any, I mark them for deletion. If there are any outside this bounding rectangle, they are unmarked.

You need to know that GDI+ erases the drawing surface before it draws the rectangle. This is one reason that GDI+ is so much easier to use than the direct Windows GDI. You have to do far less to accomplish much more.

Well, you now have a Paint delegate. The trick now is to create the bounding rectangle and make sure this Paint delegate gets called when needed. Add the following three delegates below the Paint delegate.

C#

```csharp
private void PanelMouseDown(object sender, MouseEventArgs e)
{
  if (e.Button != MouseButtons.Left)
    return;

  Marquis = new Rectangle(new Point(e.X, e.Y), Size.Empty);
}
```

```csharp
    private void PanelMouseMove(object sender, MouseEventArgs e)
    {
      if (e.Button != MouseButtons.Left)
        return;

      Marquis.Size = new Size(e.X-Marquis.X, e.Y-Marquis.Y);
      P1.Invalidate();
    }

    private void PanelMouseUp(object sender, MouseEventArgs e)
    {
      Marquis = Rectangle.Empty;
      P1.Invalidate();
    }
```

VB

```vb
  Private Sub PanelMouseDown(ByVal sender As Object, ByVal e As MouseEventArgs)

    If e.Button <> MouseButtons.Left Then Return
    Marquis = New Rectangle(New Point(e.X, e.Y), Size.Empty)
  End Sub

  Private Sub PanelMouseMove(ByVal sender As Object, ByVal e As MouseEventArgs)

    If e.Button <> MouseButtons.Left Then Return

    Marquis.Size = New Size(e.X - Marquis.X, e.Y - Marquis.Y)
    P1.Invalidate()
  End Sub

  Private Sub PanelMouseUp(ByVal sender As Object, ByVal e As MouseEventArgs)

    Marquis = Rectangle.Empty
    P1.Invalidate()
  End Sub
```

Notice that I make use of the MouseEventArgs argument to determine if I am currently painting. I can't tell you how many examples I've seen where the programmer used a global variable to determine if painting was going on.

The MouseDown delegate creates a new rectangle that begins where the user pressed the left mouse button. It has no size to start with.

The MouseMove delegate changes the size of the rectangle according to the current X and Y position of the mouse. There is no need for a variable to tell me if I am drawing; the fact that the left mouse button is down while I am moving it implies this. At the end of this method I invalidate the Panel. This fires the Paint event, which gets handled by the Paint delegate.

The MouseUp delegate simply resets the rectangle and invalidates the screen, which makes the rectangle disappear. All that is left are the flags, some of which may be marked for deletion.

Now to wire the mouse delegates up to the Panel. Add the following code to the constructor.

C#

```
//These delegates are added to facilitate marquis selection
P1.MouseMove += new MouseEventHandler(this.PanelMouseMove);
P1.MouseDown += new MouseEventHandler(this.PanelMouseDown);
P1.MouseUp   += new MouseEventHandler(this.PanelMouseUp);
P1.Paint     += new PaintEventHandler(this.PanelPaint);
```

VB

```
'These delegates are added to facilitate marquis selection
AddHandler P1.MouseMove, New MouseEventHandler(AddressOf PanelMouseMove)
AddHandler P1.MouseDown, New MouseEventHandler(AddressOf PanelMouseDown)
AddHandler P1.MouseUp, New MouseEventHandler(AddressOf PanelMouseUp)
AddHandler P1.MouseMove, New MouseEventHandler(AddressOf PanelMouseMove)
AddHandler P1.Paint, New PaintEventHandler(AddressOf PanelPaint)
```

That's it. Compile and run the program. Figure 4-8 shows marquis selection in action.

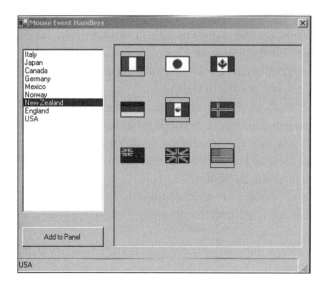

Figure 4-8. Marking flags for deletion via marquis selection

Deleting the Flags

The other mouse-handling delegates for the images are simple enough. As the user left-clicks the picture, I change its border to make it stand out as being selected. When the mouse is run over the picture, I show the name of the flag on the StatusBar. This name comes from the Tag property of the PictureBox. This is also shown in Figure 4-7.

Figure 4-9 shows the screen with four of the flags marked for deletion.

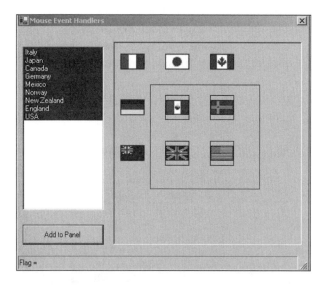

Figure 4-9. Four flags marked for deletion

The user presses the Delete key and the marked flags are deleted. After the deletion, the rest of the flags are rearranged to fill the voids. Here is the C# code for this KeyDown delegate:

```
private void DeleteFlags(object sender, KeyEventArgs e)
{
  if(e.KeyCode == Keys.Delete)
  {

    //Try this shortcut. It will not work.  Do you know why?
//      foreach(PictureBox p in P1.Controls)
//      {
//        if(p.BorderStyle == BorderStyle.FixedSingle)
//          P1.Controls.Remove(p);
//      }

    PictureBox p;
    bool deleted = true;
    while (deleted)
    {
      deleted = false;
      for(int k=0; k<P1.Controls.Count; k++)
      {
        if(P1.Controls[k] is PictureBox)
        {
          p = (PictureBox)P1.Controls[k];
          if(p.BorderStyle == BorderStyle.FixedSingle)
          {
            P1.Controls.RemoveAt(k);
            deleted = true;
            //Controls.count has changed. Reinitialize the "for" loop
            break;
          }
        }
      }
    }
    ArrangeImages();
  }
}
```

I left in some code that I commented out. This code (if it worked) would be more elegant than the code below it. However, it does not work. Your homework is to read up on collections and find out why.

TIP Collections are a big part of the .NET Framework. It would behoove you to learn as much about them as you can.

The ability to remove an object from a collection while iterating over that collection would sure be nice. However, sometimes the brute-force way is best.

Summary

This chapter covered handling keyboard events and mouse events. Proper use of controls along with the data entry tools every computer has (the mouse and keyboard) can provide you with the ability to program a powerful and visually appealing data entry screen.

The addition of some GDI+ code allows you to enhance the user experience. Be aware that the GDI+ code I showed you in this chapter is very minimal. Subsequent chapters deal with other aspects of the GDI+ drawing capability.

Chapter 5 details some of the more complex data entry screens that you often see today. Most of these screens are object oriented in nature and can greatly simplify the user experience.

CHAPTER 5

The Object-Oriented GUI

THIS CHAPTER DEALS WITH entering data into a program using the keyboard (simple) and the mouse (more involved). The last example in Chapter 4 showed how you can use some simple graphics and mouse-based drawing to allow the user to make choices on the screen.

Although Chapter 4 was a bit of a departure from the normal text-based data entry screens, this chapter will take the concept even further. I discuss using the mouse in much more detail for things such as

- Drag-and-drop operations

- Right-click context (pop-up) menu selection

- Control resizing

Of course, advanced use of the mouse involves the use of advanced controls. These controls are what I consider the basis of the object-oriented graphical user interface (GUI). In the next section I explain what I mean by this.

What Is the Object-Oriented GUI?

Suppose you have an auto parts store, and you use a program to handle the front counter sales. Now, I have been to many auto parts stores, and their programs are all pretty much the same. They all look like UNIX dumb terminal leftovers. The screens are text-based and quite often parts are mish-mashed together as if they were all the same. It is obvious that these programs are not programmed in an object-oriented way, and they are not presented in an object-oriented way.

Here's my version of an object-oriented auto parts program:

1. The user chooses which car the customer is referring to in a hierarchical list of some kind.

2. A wire-frame picture of the car appears with major sections outlined in different colors.

3. The user clicks a major section and is able to drill down into subassemblies and finally individual parts.

4. The customer watches this, points to a section, and says, "I don't know the name, but that doohickey over there is what broke."

There can be a few different ways to present this kind of data as you drill down. Probably the final list of parts within a section would be a ListView, as many parts fit multiple cars.

Anyway, you can see that showing information like this is very intuitive. Programming it is actually fairly easy. Each part is an object, which in turn belongs to collections, which represent the sections of the car. Each object would have self-knowledge such as inventory, price, suggested sister parts, and so on. As the inventory of the part is at the reorder stage, it could automatically color itself red or perhaps change its icon to something else. This way, when the user drills down into the parts list, the user can instantly know the status of that part. As each object communicates with the sales portion of the program, it is also communicating with the inventory portion of the program.

You can see that presenting an object-oriented GUI also requires that you program in an object-oriented way. Which controls would you use for this kind of GUI?

Controls That Play Major Roles in an Object-Oriented GUI

The .NET IDE contains quite a few controls, most of which I am sure you have used. But have you used them to present data in an object-oriented fashion? Here are some of the controls I use for modern data entry programs:

- ContextMenu

- Floating ToolBar

- ListView

- TreeView

- PictureBox

- Panel

- Splitter

- Graphical Calendar

I use the ContextMenu because it is a common way for an object to allow the user to tell it to do something. A ContextMenu can be part of an object; it does not need to belong to a form.

 NOTE   Yes, a form is an object. It is a special kind of object, though, and most programmers (especially VB 6.0 programmers) do not think of it this way. Everyone knows that a form can contain a MainMenu and a ToolBar, but not many people extend this idea to a simple class as well.

A floating, dockable ToolBar can look to the user to be a separate object that can be acted on. A ToolBar does not necessarily need to be attached to any particular form.

You'll often use the TreeView, ListView, Panel, and PictureBox together to show more graphical views of the data. Oftentimes, you'll add a Splitter to enable the user to resize controls on a particular form.

Using Controls in an Object-Oriented Way

Let's take some of these controls and play around with them. I think that once you see some examples, you'll better understand what I'm talking about.

The first control you will use is the ContextMenu. Now, as you probably know, you can make a pop-up menu and attach it to any visible control. For instance, you can have a TreeView or ListView control that has a pop-up menu attached to it. The problem with this, though, is that you may want different menu choices and actions based on the node that is currently selected (I cover nodes shortly). If you have a control that contains nodes that represent different objects, you are forced to either have the same choices for all objects (perhaps some would be grayed-out) or reprogram the pop-up menu based on the node that is active. Either way, you are not using the full capability of .NET to both program and present data in an object-oriented manner.

Suppose you want to present different views of an object. These views could take the form of a node in a TreeView in one screen and a CheckBox in another, and perhaps an Image in yet another screen. If you create a pop-up menu that allows actions on that object in one view, the user will expect the same functionality in all views. In the auto parts store scenario, such an action could be to display the price of the part the object represents. Attaching the pop-up menu to a control is not the best choice in this scenario. The best choice is to have the object know what it needs to do when the user wants a pop-up menu.

Start a new VB or C# project. Mine is called "ContainedControls." This project includes the default form and one additional class. This project shows you how to have an object use its own pop-up menu instead of your having to program one for each control that will contain this object.

For discussion purposes, this object is a part in an auto parts store. The idea is to have this part get all its own information from a database (a pretend database, in this case) and present itself to the user in different forms. You will see from the example that the main form contains very little code. Most of the code is in the object's class. Start out by putting the following controls on the form:

1. Add a TreeView and call it **Tree**.

2. Add a GroupBox whose text reads **Parts**.

3. Add three check boxes inside the GroupBox. Name them **chkP1**, **chkP2**, and **chkP3**, respectively.

4. Add three PictureBoxes below the GroupBox. Name them **picA**, **picB**, and **picC**, respectively.

5. Add a button called **cmdQuit** whose text reads **Quit**.

Your form should look like the one shown in Figure 5-1.

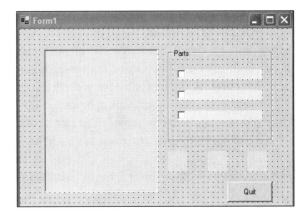

Figure 5-1. The main form showing controls

Before you start entering the code for this form, you will need a class that represents the parts that this form will show. Add a new class called "SomePart." Even for a class that does virtually nothing real, it needs to use classes from quite a few different namespaces. Make sure you have the following namespaces in this class.

C#

```
using System;
using System.Collections;
using System.Drawing;
using System.Drawing.Drawing2D;
using System.Windows.Forms;
```

VB

```
Option Strict On

Imports System
Imports System.Drawing
Imports System.Drawing.Drawing2D
Imports System.Collections
Imports System.Windows.Forms
```

I love collections, and Microsoft has heeded my wishes and made a lot more specific collection classes.[1] I use the ArrayList in this class, which needs the Collections namespace. I also use some imaging classes, which need the Drawing namespaces.

You may be wondering why I use the Forms namespace. The answer is that I need it to reference the ContextMenu class.

 NOTE Including the namespaces at the top of the file does *not* add any extra code to the program. A namespace is not a library. You can think of a namespace as local calling area. It lets you reference classes within the namespace without using the fully qualified name of the class. It is similar to dialing a number without the area code.

This class has the ability to provide its name, its price, and a picture of itself. To accomplish this, you need some internal variables.

---

1. I'm sure they didn't know anything of my wishes, but I'm pleased by the result anyway.

C#

```csharp
private ContextMenu mnu = new ContextMenu();
private Decimal     mPrice;
private string      mIdentifier;
private string      mToolsNeeded;
private ArrayList   mAr;
private Image       mImg;
static  int         mPartsCount=0;

private struct menu_item
{
  public MenuItem m;
  public string   s;
  public void DoSomething(string Title)
  {
    if(s != null)
      MessageBox.Show(s, Title);
    else
      MessageBox.Show("No Action", Title);
  }
}
```

VB

```vb
Private mnu As ContextMenu = New ContextMenu()
Private mPrice As Decimal
Private mIdentifier As String
Private mToolsNeeded As String
Private mAr As ArrayList
Private mImg As Image
Shared mPartsCount As Int32 = 0

Private Structure menu_item
  Public m As MenuItem
  Public s As String
  Public Sub DoSomething(ByVal Title As String)
    If Not s Is Nothing Then
      MessageBox.Show(s, Title)
    Else
      MessageBox.Show("No Action", Title)
    End If
  End Sub
End Structure
```

The structure holds both the MenuItem and a string. The string is used in the DoSomething method. If this were a real application, the DoSomething method would perhaps do something real such as talk back to the inventory software and decrease the count of this item when the customer bought it. Right now, this method just displays some string in a message box.

The constructor for this class initializes data and initializes individual MenuItem objects. Each MenuItem and its associated string are kept in a menu_item structure that is added to a collection of menu_items. The constructor and setup code follows.

C#

```csharp
public SomePart()
{
  mPartsCount += 1;
  GetData();
  InitMenu();
}

// This private function is supposed to get the record for
// this part from the database and set up whatever fields are necessary
private void GetData()
{
  //Fake getting this from the database
  mPrice = 54.952M + mPartsCount;
  mToolsNeeded = "Linemans pliers\n Phillips screwdriver\n Half a brain";
  mIdentifier = "Some Part #" + mPartsCount.ToString();

  mImg = Image.FromFile(mPartsCount.ToString() + ".ico");

}

private void InitMenu()
{
  mAr = new ArrayList();
  menu_item m;

  m = new menu_item();
  m.m = new MenuItem("Customer Price", new EventHandler(this.MenuHandler));
  m.s = "Customer Price = " + mPrice.ToString("C");
  mAr.Add(m);
```

```
        m = new menu_item();
        m.m = new MenuItem("Tools Needed", new EventHandler(this.MenuHandler));
        m.s = "Suggested Tools = " + mToolsNeeded;
        mAr.Add(m);

        for(int k=0; k<mPartsCount; k++)
        {
          m = new menu_item();
          m.m = new MenuItem("Item #" + k.ToString(),
                                    new EventHandler(this.MenuHandler));
          mAr.Add(m);
        }

        mAr.TrimToSize();

    }

    private void MenuHandler(object sender, EventArgs e)
    {
      MenuItem m = (MenuItem)sender;

      foreach(menu_item menu in mAr)
      {
        if (menu.m == m)
          menu.DoSomething(mIdentifier);
      }
    }
```

VB

```
  Public Sub New()
    mPartsCount += 1
    GetData()
    InitMenu()
  End Sub

  ' This private function is supposed to get the record for
  ' this part from the database and set up whatever fields are necessary
  Private Sub GetData()
    'Fake getting this from the database
    mPrice = CType(54.952, Decimal) + mPartsCount
    mToolsNeeded = "Linemans pliers\n Phillips screwdriver\n Half a brain"
    mIdentifier = "Some Part #" + mPartsCount.ToString()
```

```
      mImg = Image.FromFile(mPartsCount.ToString() + ".ico")

  End Sub


  Private Sub InitMenu()
    mAr = New ArrayList()
    Dim m As menu_item
    Dim k As Int32

    m = New menu_item()
    m.m = New MenuItem("Customer Price", New EventHandler(AddressOf MenuHandler))
    m.s = "Customer Price = " + mPrice.ToString("C")
    mAr.Add(m)

    m = New menu_item()
    m.m = New MenuItem("Tools Needed", New EventHandler(AddressOf MenuHandler))
    m.s = "Suggested Tools = " + mToolsNeeded
    mAr.Add(m)

    For k = 0 To mPartsCount - 1
      m = New menu_item()
      m.m = New MenuItem("Item #" + k.ToString(), _
                         New EventHandler(AddressOf MenuHandler))
      mAr.Add(m)
    Next

    mAr.TrimToSize()

  End Sub

  Private Sub MenuHandler(ByVal sender As Object, ByVal e As EventArgs)
    Dim m As MenuItem = DirectCast(sender, MenuItem)
    Dim menu As menu_item

    For Each menu In mAr
      If Object.Equals(menu.m, m) Then
        menu.DoSomething(mIdentifier)
      End If
    Next
  End Sub
```

Note that in the MenuHandler code, the C# version is able to use the double equals sign (= =) to detect if the MenuItem chosen is the same as one in the array of menu_items. The VB code has no such construct. You need to use the Object.Equals method.

The last pieces of code in this class are the properties and a method that actually displays the menu.

C#

```csharp
public void ShowMenu(Control c, Point p)
{
  foreach(menu_item m in mAr)
  {
    mnu.MenuItems.Add(m.m);
  }

  mnu.Show(c, p);
  mnu.MenuItems.Clear();
}

public Decimal Price { get{ return mPrice; } }
public string  ID    { get{ return mIdentifier; } }
public Image   img   { get{ return mImg; } }
```

VB

```vb
Public Sub ShowMenu(ByVal c As Control, ByVal p As Point)
  Dim m As menu_item

  For Each m In mAr
    mnu.MenuItems.Add(m.m)
  Next

  mnu.Show(c, p)
  mnu.MenuItems.Clear()
End Sub

Public ReadOnly Property Price() As Decimal
  Get
    Return mPrice
  End Get
End Property

Public ReadOnly Property ID() As String
  Get
    Return mIdentifier
  End Get
End Property
```

```
Public ReadOnly Property img() As Image
  Get
    Return mImg
  End Get
End Property
```

Note here also how the C# code is much more compact than the VB code for the same functionality.

When I show the menu, I enumerate through all the menu_item structures held in the ArrayList. Each MenuItem found is added to the ContextMenu, which is then displayed at the position passed in.

Building the menu in this manner allows me to use code that is independent of how many menu items this object wants to show. As you can see from the InitMenu method, each object has a different menu with different choices. This is to simulate object initialization from a database.

Note the static (shared in VB) variable that is used as a cross-object counter. This is a handy way to count instances of a class. I suggest you read up on it in the online help.

Using the Object

Now it is time to program the form that uses this class. The first thing to do is to double-click the Quit button and add some code in the generated delegate to close out the application. Use the form's Close method for this.

Because this example is intended to show how an object can pop up a menu that is tailored to itself, you will need some way to notify the object that it must do this. Normally the user would right-click a control to invoke the pop-up menu.

When you create each object you will place it in a TreeView, a CheckBox, and an image control. When the user right-clicks any of these controls, he or she should see the same pop-up menu for an object no matter where the object is.

First, add a class local variable to the form that represents the class.

C#

```
SomePart Engine;
```

VB

```
Dim Engine As SomePart
```

Add the following code to the form that handles the right-click event for any control that holds an instance of the SomePart class.

C#

```
#region Mouse Events

private void RightClick(object sender, MouseEventArgs e)
{
  if(e.Button != MouseButtons.Right)
    return;

  if(sender is TreeView)
    Engine = (SomePart)Tree.SelectedNode.Tag;
  else if(sender is PictureBox)
  {
    PictureBox p = (PictureBox)sender;
    Engine = (SomePart)p.Tag;
  }
  else if(sender is CheckBox)
  {
    CheckBox c = (CheckBox)sender;
    Engine = (SomePart)c.Tag;
  }

  Engine.ShowMenu((Control)sender, new Point(e.X, e.Y) );

}

#endregion
```

VB

```
#Region "Mouse Events"

  Private Sub RightClick(ByVal sender As Object, ByVal e As MouseEventArgs)

    If e.Button <> MouseButtons.Right Then Return

    If sender.GetType() Is GetType(TreeView) Then
      Engine = CType(Tree.SelectedNode.Tag, SomePart)
    ElseIf sender.GetType() Is GetType(PictureBox) Then
      Dim p As PictureBox = CType(sender, PictureBox)
      Engine = CType(p.Tag, SomePart)
    ElseIf sender.GetType() Is GetType(CheckBox) Then
      Dim c As CheckBox = CType(sender, CheckBox)
      Engine = CType(c.Tag, SomePart)
    End If
```

```
Engine.ShowMenu(CType(sender, Control), New Point(e.X, e.Y))

End Sub

#End Region
```

You can see from this delegate that I check for the type of control that invoked this method. Once I know that information, I create a reference to the object that is associated with that control. In this case, the Tag property of each control holds the object.

The last thing I do here is tell the object to show its pop-up menu at the current mouse position. If the object had no pop-up menu, this method would still run just fine. This code works for all instances of the SomeParts object.

Now that you have the delegate coded, it is time to add the constructor code.

C#

```
public Form1()
{
  InitializeComponent();

  Tree.MouseDown  += new MouseEventHandler(this.RightClick);
  chkP1.MouseDown += new MouseEventHandler(this.RightClick);
  chkP2.MouseDown += new MouseEventHandler(this.RightClick);
  chkP3.MouseDown += new MouseEventHandler(this.RightClick);
  picA.MouseDown  += new MouseEventHandler(this.RightClick);
  picB.MouseDown  += new MouseEventHandler(this.RightClick);
  picC.MouseDown  += new MouseEventHandler(this.RightClick);

  SomePart part;

  //Put the first part in the tree and the checkbox and the image
  part = new SomePart();
  TreeNode Node = new TreeNode();
  Node.Text = part.ID;
  Node.Tag = part;
  Tree.Nodes.Add(Node);
  chkP1.Text=part.ID;
  chkP1.Tag = part;
  picA.Image = part.img;
  picA.Tag = part;
```

```
        part = new SomePart();
        Node = new TreeNode();
        Node.Text = part.ID;
        Node.Tag = part;
        Tree.Nodes.Add(Node);
        chkP2.Text=part.ID;
        chkP2.Tag = part;
        picB.Image = part.img;
        picB.Tag = part;

        part = new SomePart();
        Node = new TreeNode();
        Node.Text = part.ID;
        Node.Tag = part;
        Tree.Nodes.Add(Node);
        chkP3.Text=part.ID;
        chkP3.Tag = part;
        picC.Image = part.img;
        picC.Tag = part;

    }
```

VB

```
Public Sub New()
  MyBase.New()

    'This call is required by the Windows Form Designer.
    InitializeComponent()

    AddHandler Tree.MouseDown, AddressOf RightClick
    AddHandler chkP1.MouseDown, AddressOf RightClick
    AddHandler chkP2.MouseDown, AddressOf RightClick
    AddHandler chkP3.MouseDown, AddressOf RightClick
    AddHandler picA.MouseDown, AddressOf RightClick
    AddHandler picB.MouseDown, AddressOf RightClick
    AddHandler picC.MouseDown, AddressOf RightClick
    Dim part As SomePart

    'Put the first part in the tree and the checkbox and the image
    part = New SomePart()
    Dim Node As TreeNode = New TreeNode()
```

```
Node.Text = part.ID
Node.Tag = part
Tree.Nodes.Add(Node)
chkP1.Text = part.ID
chkP1.Tag = part
picA.Image = part.img
picA.Tag = part

part = New SomePart()
Node = New TreeNode()
Node.Text = part.ID
Node.Tag = part
Tree.Nodes.Add(Node)
chkP2.Text = part.ID
chkP2.Tag = part
picB.Image = part.img
picB.Tag = part

part = New SomePart()
Node = New TreeNode()
Node.Text = part.ID
Node.Tag = part
Tree.Nodes.Add(Node)
chkP3.Text = part.ID
chkP3.Tag = part
picC.Image = part.img
picC.Tag = part
```

```
End Sub
```

Each control gets assigned the same delegate for the MouseDown event. I create three different engine parts and add each one to the TreeView, CheckBox, and Image controls. Note that I use the Tag property of each control to hold the object's instance. I also get all information, such as the name of the object and its picture, directly from each object.

The code in this form has no idea what object is called or what its image is. This is the way it should be to provide the most programming flexibility.

This is all the code you need for the form. Compile and run the project. Your initial screen should look like Figure 5-2.

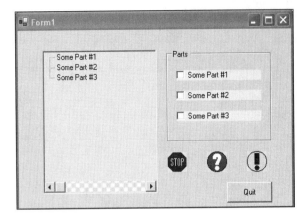

Figure 5-2. A running form

The images you see here are included with the code for this book, which you can get from the Downloads section of the Apress Web site (http://www.apress.com). Right-click the representation of each object and you will see the appropriate pop-up menu. Figure 5-3 shows the pop-up menu for Some Part #1 in the TreeView.

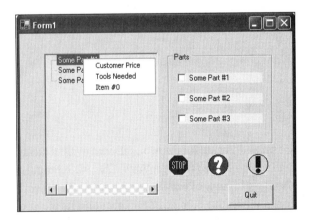

Figure 5-3. The pop-up menu for Some Part #1 in the TreeView

Figure 5-4 shows the pop-up menu for Some Part #2 in the Image view. You can see that the objects behave differently by the number of menu items in the menu.

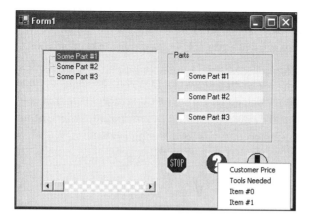

Figure 5-4. The pop-up menu for Some Part #2 in the Image view

Figure 5-5 shows what happens when you click the second CheckBox and choose the customer price.

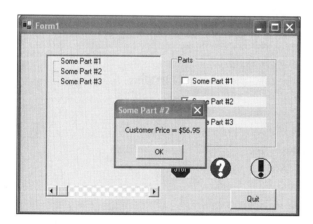

Figure 5-5. An actual menu choice

The code that activates this message box is not in the form but in the object itself. As you start activating the pop-up menu for each object, you will find that each behaves as it should, no matter where the object resides. This is the object-oriented way of displaying information. The user expects this kind of behavior. Until .NET came along, it was difficult to program this kind of behavior without all kinds of code.

Nowhere in the form's code do I change the behavior of the object based on which object was chosen or on where the object was shown. This is the object-oriented way of programming this kind of code. If the object has no pop-up menu, so be it. It just does not show.

By the way, the SomePart class was constructed so that you can easily change out the MessageBox displayed here with some more meaningful action. This is important down the line as you add database or other functionality. Adding other functionality does not require you to change the form's code at all.

Manipulating Data with the ListView Control

So far in this book you have seen the use of a TreeView control and a ListView control in separate examples. What I have shown you is the tip of the iceberg as far as these controls go. Making full use of all the capabilities of the TreeView and ListView controls is the secret to a really good object-oriented GUI.

Here are some things you have not seen with these controls that, when used, really spice up a user interface:

- Multiple levels in the TreeView

- Pictures in TreeView nodes and ListView cells

- Drag-and-drop capability in the TreeView and ListView

- Node manipulation in the TreeView

- Cell manipulation in the ListView

- Different ListView views

- Virtual nodes and views

- Background and foreground color manipulation

Getting to know the TreeView control and how to use it effectively is really worthwhile. Now, you can consult the online help for TreeView and ListView examples, but you will find them lacking in cohesiveness. What you need to know is how all these items work together to provide a complete data entry and manipulation screen. This is what I show you in the next section.

Different Views of Data with the ListView Control

The ListView control allows you to present data in one of four ways:

- Large icons

- Small icons

- Small icons in a vertical list

- Report view

You see the ListView control all the time when you use a computer. The right pane in Windows Explorer is a ListView.

If you are a VB 6.0 veteran, you will have undoubtedly used the ListView. The .NET version is somewhat different in its setup, however, and requires familiarity with collections and how they work.[2]

The ListView consists of the visible control, which includes many methods and properties. To add any data to this control, you need to add records to an ItemList collection. There is a method in the ListView class that you can use to add items directly to the list. There is also a method to add an array of ListViewItems to the control. Here is how to do it.

C#

```
ListView lvw = new ListView();
lvw.Items.Add("First Item");
lvw.Items.Add( new ListViewItem("Second Item"));
ListViewItem[] items = new ListViewItem[3] {
                        new ListViewItem("fourth Item"),
                        new ListViewItem("fifth Item"),
                        new ListViewItem("sixth Item")};
lvw.Items.AddRange(items);
```

VB

```
Dim lvw As ListView = New ListView()
lvw.Items.Add("First Item")
lvw.Items.Add(New ListViewItem("Second Item"))
```

---

2. There are those collections again!

```
Dim items() As ListViewItem = New ListViewItem(2) { _
                      New ListViewItem("fourth Item"), _
                      New ListViewItem("fifth Item"), _
                      New ListViewItem("sixth Item")}
lvw.Items.AddRange(items)
```

This code shows the various ways to add items to a ListView. I have found, however, that I often want to keep several sets of data that I can swap in and out of the ListView. For instance, I may want to show a list of all 1,000 people in the San Francisco office. I may also want to instantly switch the view with a list of all 870 people in the Boston office. Constantly going back and forth to the database, creating ListItems, and adding them to the ListView can be tedious and slow.

In the next example, you will create a class that allows you to swap a ListView list with another one. The output may not be very jazzy, but this is the first step toward a more involved and more graphical data entry program than you have seen thus far in the book.

Start a new project in either C# or VB. Mine is called "ListViewSwap."

1. Add a ListView control named **lv** to the form.

2. Add a Button named **cmdSwap** to the form. Change its text to **Swap**.

3. Make sure the form starts in the center of the screen.

Figure 5-6 shows what this form should look like.

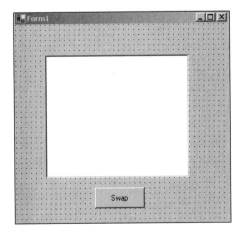

Figure 5-6. A simple ListView form

Now for the ListView collection class. Add a new class called "LvItems" to the project. Listings 5-1a and 5-1b show the code for this class.

Listing 5-1a. C# Code for the LvItems Class

```csharp
using System;
using System.Windows.Forms;
using System.Collections;

namespace ListViewSwap_c
{
  /// <summary>
  /// Summary description for LvItems.
  /// </summary>
  public class LvItems
  {
    private ArrayList mCol;

    public LvItems()
    {
      mCol = new ArrayList();
    }

    /// <summary>
    /// Add a string to an array of ListViewItems
    /// </summary>
    /// <param name="val"></param>
    public void Add(string val)
    {
      mCol.Add(new ListViewItem(val));
    }

    /// <summary>
    /// Add a ListViewItem to an array of ListViewItems
    /// </summary>
    /// <param name="val"></param>
    public void Add(ListViewItem val)
    {
      mCol.Add(val);
    }
```

```
    /// <summary>
    /// Gets a ListViewItem array
    /// </summary>
    public ListViewItem[] Items
    {
      get
      {
        mCol.TrimToSize();
        ListViewItem[] lvw = new ListViewItem[mCol.Count];
        mCol.CopyTo(lvw, 0);
        return lvw;
      }
    }
  }
}
```

Listing 5-1b. VB Code for the LvItems Class

```
Option Strict On

Imports System
Imports System.Windows.Forms
Imports System.Collections

Public Class LvItems

  Private mCol As ArrayList

  Public Sub New()
    mCol = New ArrayList()
  End Sub

  ' <summary>
  ' Add a string to an array of ListViewItems
  ' </summary>
  ' <param name="val"></param>
  Public Sub Add(ByVal val As String)
    mCol.Add(New ListViewItem(val))
  End Sub
```

```vb
' <summary>
' Add a ListViewItem to an array of ListViewItems
' </summary>
' <param name="val"></param>
Public Sub Add(ByVal val As ListViewItem)
    mCol.Add(val)
End Sub


' <summary>
' Gets a ListViewItem array
' </summary>
Public ReadOnly Property Items() As ListViewItem()
    Get
        mCol.TrimToSize()
        Dim lvw(mCol.Count - 1) As ListViewItem
        mCol.CopyTo(lvw, 0)
        Return lvw
    End Get
End Property
End Class
```

I called this a collection class. It is missing a few methods, however. Strictly speaking, a collection class needs a way to enumerate over its internal list. It also should have a remove method and way to get a single item as well. I have not put these methods in here because they are not needed for my purposes.

The reason for using this class as opposed to just a generic array or collection is type safety. Using this class, it is impossible to hold anything other than a ListViewItem. A normal ArrayList or generic collection can hold any number of any data type. It is best to enforce type safety whenever you can.

Now it is time to add the code for the main form. First, add some local variables.

C#

```csharp
#region class local variables

LvItems lvw1;
LvItems lvw2;
LvItems SwapList;

#endregion
```

VB

```
#Region "class local variables"

  Private lvw1 As LvItems
  Private lvw2 As LvItems
  Private SwapList As LvItems

#End Region
```

You can probably guess what the code will do from looking at the variables. I instantiate two LvItems objects to hold different sets of data. The swap list is what I will display in the ListView. The constructor for this form follows.

C#

```
public Form1()
{
  InitializeComponent();

  //Show details with two columns
  lv.View = View.Details;
  lv.Columns.Add("First Item", -2, HorizontalAlignment.Center);
  lv.Columns.Add("Sub Item",   -2, HorizontalAlignment.Center);

  //Add individual items to the first stored list
  lvw1 = new LvItems();
  lvw1.Add("1     I belong to LC1");
  lvw1.Add("2     I belong to LC1");
  lvw1.Add("3     I belong to LC1");

  //Add an item to the first list that has a subitem
  ListViewItem k = new ListViewItem();
  k.Text = "4     Parent Item";
  k.SubItems.Add("Sub Item 1");
  lvw1.Add(k);

  //Add items to the second stored list
  lvw2 = new LvItems();
  lvw2.Add("1   I belong to LC2");
  lvw2.Add("2   I belong to LC2");
  lvw2.Add("3   I belong to LC2");

  lv.Items.AddRange(lvw1.Items);
}
```

VB

```vb
Public Sub New()
  MyBase.New()

  InitializeComponent()

  'Show details with two columns
  lv.View = View.Details
  lv.Columns.Add("First Item", -2, HorizontalAlignment.Center)
  lv.Columns.Add("Sub Item", -2, HorizontalAlignment.Center)

  'Add individual items to the first stored list
  lvw1 = New LvItems()
  lvw1.Add("1       I belong to LC1")
  lvw1.Add("2       I belong to LC1")
  lvw1.Add("3       I belong to LC1")

  'Add an item to the first list that has a subitem
  Dim k As ListViewItem = New ListViewItem()
  k.Text = "4      Parent Item"
  k.SubItems.Add("Sub Item 1")
  lvw1.Add(k)

  'Add items to the second stored list
  lvw2 = New LvItems()
  lvw2.Add("1   I belong to LC2")
  lvw2.Add("2   I belong to LC2")
  lvw2.Add("3   I belong to LC2")

  lv.Items.AddRange(lvw1.Items)

End Sub
```

I set up the list to have two columns. I then add some records to each of the LvItems objects. I even add a ListViewItem that has a subitem just to show that this is possible as well.

The last line in this constructor goes out to the ListViewItem collection object and retrieves an array of ListViewItems that are then added to the list. If I want to swap this list out for another, I need a little more code. This code is included in the following delegate. I got this delegate definition generated automatically for me by double-clicking on the cmdSwap button on the form.

C#

```csharp
private void cmdSwap_Click(object sender, System.EventArgs e)
{
    SwapList = (SwapList == lvw2) ? lvw1 : lvw2;
    lv.Items.Clear();
    lv.Items.AddRange(SwapList.Items);
}
```

VB

```vb
Private Sub cmdSwap_Click(ByVal sender As System.Object, _
                          ByVal e As System.EventArgs) Handles cmdSwap.Click

    If SwapList Is lvw2 Then
        SwapList = lvw1
    Else
        SwapList = lvw2
    End If
    lv.Items.Clear()
    lv.Items.AddRange(SwapList.Items)

End Sub
```

What I do here is reference a different list than the one contained in the SwapList. I then clear the ListView control and retrieve the new array of ListViewItems. Try this code out.

There is not much here and it has little "wow" factor. However, this method of storing ListViewItems and swapping them out with existing ones in a control will be very important. Think about it a little and you will find that you can adapt this kind of class to store any kind of type-safe list.

In the next section you'll move on to more involved uses for the ListView.

Changing How the ListView Works

In this section I present an example that uses the ListView control in several different ways. I am not going to fall into the usual trap of supplying just a few short lines of setup code, however.

Creating different views of the ListView control also necessitates creating different uses. Perhaps a detail view would be used one way, and a large icon view would be used another way. It is how you use the different views that makes this control so flexible, not just how you display the data.

This section's example is a demonstration of how you could use a ListView control in a movie rental program. Quite a bit of the example's functionality is behind the scenes. You will notice that as you run the program, you are not required to use the keyboard for any data entry. You do it all with the mouse. Here is what you will see in this example:

- A ListView in Detail mode

- A ListView in LargeIcon mode

- Getting data from a file on disk

- Storing data as objects and collections of objects

- Manipulating objects via mouse actions

- The drag-and-drop capability of the TreeView and PictureBox

- Using the ComboBox effectively in an object-oriented way

Along the way, I point out some important details that you can use in your future code.

The ListView Project

Start a new C# or VB project. Mine is called "MovieList."

NOTE   This example uses a few text and image files. If you download the code for this example from the Downloads section of the Apress Web site (http://www.apress.com), you will get these files. If you decide not to enter the code by hand (entering by hand is recommended), at least follow the code description. There are some concepts introduced here that are crucial to understanding how this program works. These concepts will be very useful in any future .NET programming you do.

You will need to make the following changes to the main form. Figure 5-7 shows what the form should look like.

1. Size the form to be 700×450. Start-up should be Center Screen.

2. Add a Label that reads **Movie genre**.

3. Add a ComboBox below the Label called **cmbGenre**.

4. Add a Label that reads **Rentals**. Center the text within the Label.

5. Add a ListView control below the Rentals Label called **lstRentals**.

6. Add a Label that reads **For Sale**. Center the text within the Label.

7. Add a ListView control below the For Sale Label called **lstSold**.

8. Add a PictureBox called **picRental**.

9. Add a Label below the PictureBox that reads **Rental Check Out**.

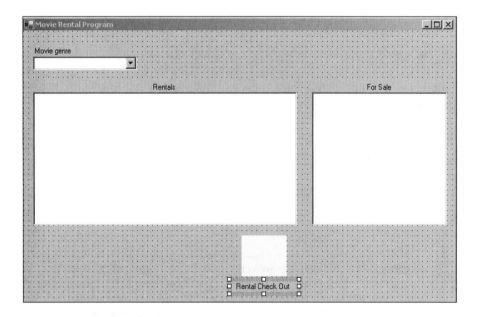

Figure 5-7. A video rental form

This form is not anything that I would sell as a rental package. It is intended to show how the ListView controls work and how all of these controls can interact with each other.

What would an object-oriented program be without objects? You will need to add three additional classes to make this program work. Add the following classes to your project:

- Movie

- MovieList

- ListViewSorter

To rent movies, this program will need a Movie object. This object holds only a few items of information, such as the movie title and the rental price. A real program would need a whole host of properties. The code for this class follows.

C#

```csharp
using System;

namespace MovieList_c
{
  /// <summary>
  /// Summary description for Movie.
  /// </summary>
  public class Movie
  {
    private string  mName;
    private Decimal mSalePrice;
    private Decimal mRentalPrice;

    public Movie(string name)
    {
      mName  = name;
      mSalePrice = 12.95m;
      mRentalPrice = 3.40m;
    }

    public string  Name       { get { return mName; } }
    public Decimal SalePrice   { get { return mSalePrice; } }
    public Decimal RentalPrice { get { return mRentalPrice; } }
  }
}
```

VB

```vb
Option Strict On

Public Class Movie
```

```
    Private mName As String
    Private mSalePrice As Decimal
    Private mRentalPrice As Decimal

    Public Sub New(ByVal name As String)
      mName = name
      mSalePrice = 12.95D
      mRentalPrice = 3.4D
    End Sub

    Public ReadOnly Property Name() As String
      Get
        Return mName
      End Get
    End Property

    Public ReadOnly Property SalePrice() As Decimal
      Get
        Return mSalePrice
      End Get
    End Property

    Public ReadOnly Property RentalPrice() As Decimal
      Get
        Return mRentalPrice
      End Get
    End Property
  End Class
```

Now that you have a Movie object, what do you do with it? You could put it in a collection of movies, but that would mean that at some point you would need to enumerate over that movie collection to find the one you want. This works but it requires code.

In thinking about the design of this example, I knew that I would be working with ListViewItems as my major object. After all, I have two ListView controls that work *only* with ListViewItems as objects. A ListViewItems has a Tag property. This Tag property was designed to hold an object whose data relates to the ListViewItem. In the case of this example, I store the Movie object in the ListViewItem.Tag property of each record shown in the ListView control. This gives me direct access to the movie in question without having to search through some unrelated collection.

The next class to fill in is the MovieList class. This class does several things. The basis of the class is the same as the class I showed you in the previous example; it is designed to hold a collection of ListViewItem objects. I have added the following functionality to this class:

- Gets its data from a text file in the current directory

- Parses each line of the text file into a ListViewItem with associated subitems

- Instantiates a Movie object for each ListViewItem and saves it in the ListViewItem.Tag property

- Removes a ListViewItem from the collection

- Changes a property of a single ListViewItem in the collection

The code in Listings 5-2a and 5-2b show this MovieList class. Read the code carefully to see what I am doing.

Listing 5-2a. C# Code for the MovieList Class

```csharp
using System;
using System.IO;
using System.Collections;
using System.Windows.Forms;

namespace MovieList_c
{
  /// <summary>
  /// Summary description for MovieList.
  /// </summary>
  public class MovieList
  {
    private const string OUT = "Out";
    private const string INHOUSE = "In";

    private ArrayList mCol;
    private char      mDelimiter = '^';
    private string    mGenre;

    public MovieList()
    {
      mCol = new ArrayList();
    }

    public MovieList(string fname)
    {
      string buffer;
```

```
      mCol = new ArrayList();
      FileInfo fIn = new FileInfo(fname);
      try
      {
        StreamReader sr = new StreamReader( fIn.OpenRead() );
        while (sr.Peek() != -1)
        {
          buffer = sr.ReadLine();
          string[] List = buffer.Split(mDelimiter);
          if(List.GetLength(0) == 1)
          {
            if(buffer != string.Empty)
              mGenre = buffer;
          }
          else if(List.GetLength(0) > 1)
          {
            ListViewItem l = new ListViewItem(List);
            l.Tag = new Movie(l.Text);
            mCol.Add(l);
          }
        }
        sr.Close();
      }
      catch(Exception e)
      {
        MessageBox.Show("Unable to read file " + fname);
        throw e;
      }
    }


    public override string ToString() { return mGenre; }
    public string Genre { get{return mGenre;} }


    /// <summary>
    /// Add a string to an array of ListViewItems
    /// </summary>
    /// <param name="val"></param>
    public void Add(string val)
    {
      mCol.Add(new ListViewItem(val));
    }


    /// <summary>
    /// Add a ListViewItem to an array of ListViewItems
```

```csharp
/// </summary>
/// <param name="val"></param>
public void Add(ListViewItem val)
{
  mCol.Add(val);
}


/// <summary>
/// Remove a ListViewItem from the array of ListViewItems
/// </summary>
/// <param name="val"></param>
public void Remove(ListViewItem val)
{
  mCol.Remove(val);
}


/// <summary>
/// Checkout a movie
/// </summary>
/// <param name="val"></param>
public bool CheckOut(ListViewItem val)
{
  string stock = val.SubItems[val.SubItems.Count-1].Text;

  if(stock == OUT)
    return false;

  mCol.Remove(val);
  val.SubItems[val.SubItems.Count-1].Text = OUT;
  mCol.Add(val);
  return true;
}


/// <summary>
/// Gets a ListViewItem array
/// </summary>
public ListViewItem[] Items
{
  get
  {
    mCol.TrimToSize();
    ListViewItem[] lvw = new ListViewItem[mCol.Count];
    mCol.CopyTo(lvw, 0);
    return lvw;
```

```
        }
      }
    }
  }
}
```

Listing 5-2b. VB Code for the MovieList Class

```vb
Option Strict On

Imports System
Imports System.IO
Imports System.Collections
Imports System.Windows.Forms


Public Class MovieList

  Private Const OUT As String = "Out"
  Private Const INHOUSE As String = "In"

  Private mCol As ArrayList
  Private mDelimiter As Char = "^"c
  Private mGenre As String

  Public Sub New()
    mCol = New ArrayList()
  End Sub

  Public Sub New(ByVal fname As String)
    Dim buffer As String

    mCol = New ArrayList()
    Dim fIn As FileInfo = New FileInfo(fname)
    Try
      Dim sr As StreamReader = New StreamReader(fIn.OpenRead())
      While (sr.Peek() <> -1)
        buffer = sr.ReadLine()
        Dim List() As String = buffer.Split(mDelimiter)
        If List.GetLength(0) = 1 Then
          If (buffer <> String.Empty) Then
            mGenre = buffer
          End If
        ElseIf List.GetLength(0) > 1 Then
          Dim l As ListViewItem = New ListViewItem(List)
          l.Tag = New Movie(l.Text)
```

```
        mCol.Add(l)
      End If
    End While
    sr.Close()
  Catch e As Exception
    MessageBox.Show("Unable to read file " + fname)
    Throw e
  End Try
End Sub


Public Overrides Function ToString() As String
  Return mGenre
End Function


Public ReadOnly Property Genre() As String
  Get
    Return mGenre
  End Get
End Property


Public Sub Add(ByVal val As String)
  mCol.Add(New ListViewItem(val))
End Sub


Public Sub Add(ByVal val As ListViewItem)
  mCol.Add(val)
End Sub


Public Sub Remove(ByVal val As ListViewItem)
  mCol.Remove(val)
End Sub


Public Function CheckOut(ByVal val As ListViewItem) As Boolean
  Dim stock As String = val.SubItems(val.SubItems.Count - 1).Text

  If stock = OUT Then
    Return False
  End If

  mCol.Remove(val)
  val.SubItems(val.SubItems.Count - 1).Text = OUT
  mCol.Add(val)
  Return True
End Function
```

```
    Public ReadOnly Property Items() As ListViewItem()
      Get
        mCol.TrimToSize()
        Dim lvw(mCol.Count) As ListViewItem
        mCol.CopyTo(lvw, 0)
        Return lvw
      End Get
    End Property

  End Class
```

Let's dissect this class a little. Look at the constructor. Inside of a Try-Catch block I open a text file, read it in line by line, and create ListItems from the contents of each line. Here is the relevant C# code:

```csharp
    StreamReader sr = new StreamReader( fIn.OpenRead() );
    while (sr.Peek() != -1)
    {
      buffer = sr.ReadLine();
      string[] List = buffer.Split(mDelimiter);
      if(List.GetLength(0) == 1)
      {
        if(buffer != string.Empty)
          mGenre = buffer;
      }
      else if(List.GetLength(0) > 1)
      {
        ListViewItem l = new ListViewItem(List);
        l.Tag = new Movie(l.Text);
        mCol.Add(l);
      }
    }
```

At the top of this file I declared a delimiter constant to be the caret symbol. If you look through the file, you will see that each line uses this symbol for a delimiter. Here is the ActionMovie.txt file:

```
Action Movies

StageCoach^1932^94^VHS^In
Speed^1994^120^8mm^Out
Alien^1986^98^DVD^In
Train Robber^1923^36^VHS^In
```

The first line of this file is the genre of movies. The code detects this because there are no delimiters in this line. The other four lines are delimited records. As each one is read in, I create an array of strings to represent each field in the record. I then add each array en masse to the constructor of the ListViewItem class, which automatically creates a ListViewItem and as many ListViewSubItem objects as needed. This ListViewItem is then added to the total collection. The first line I read in gets assigned to the Genre variable.

There is one other line of code in this class that I would like to draw your attention to. Here is the C# code:

```
public override string ToString() { return mGenre; }
```

Would you believe me if I told you that without this line of code, the whole program would not work as it does? You will learn the reason for this in a bit. For now, see the sidebar "Overriding the ToString() Method" for an explanation.

I will leave the third class, ListViewSorter, for a bit later.

Overriding the ToString() Method

I use a ComboBox in the main form to choose the genre of movie that should be displayed in the movie list. Bring up the help file for the ComboBox and you will see that it allows you to add only an object to its item list. The only kind of code I have ever seen with a ComboBox loads a string as an item is something like this:

```
ComboBox cmb = new ComboBox();
cmb.Items.Add("First Choice");
cmb.Items.Add("Second Choice");
cmb.Items.Add("Third Choice");
```

If the programmer needs to know what item was chosen, he or she looks at the selected index property and does something based on that. Perhaps the programmer even compares the text property to some lookup table and performs an action based on the index of the lookup. Although this kind of code works, it is not what the authors of this control intended.

Read the help carefully for the Add function of this control. It says that the string displayed is the object's ToString() method. Suppose you add a bunch of PictureBoxes to this list like so:

```
ComboBox cmb = new ComboBox();
cmb.Items.Add(new PictureBox());
cmb.Items.Add(new PictureBox());
cmb.Items.Add(new PictureBox());
```

This is perfectly valid code. If you look at the result, you see a ComboBox that has the following entries:

```
System.Windows.Forms.PictureBox
System.Windows.Forms.PictureBox
System.Windows.Forms.PictureBox
```

What you see is the text you get from the PictureBox.ToString() method. Now in the case of this example, I created a class that overrides the ToString() method that returns the genre of the movie list. Normally, it would have returned the name of the class. When I add instances of this class (objects) to the ComboBox list, the ComboBox will get the displayed text from the ToString() method and will look to the user as if I entered in strings only.

Adding the object directly to the Item list of the ComboBox allows me to get the SelectedItem, cast it to the proper data type, and then call a method directly. There is no lookup involved. In fact, my program does not even know, or keep track of, what or how many objects are in the ComboBox. This is way cool!

The Main Movie Form Code

You have the supporting guts of this project done. Now it is time to add the code for the main form. Start out with some class local variables.

C#

```
#region class local variables

MovieList ActionMovies;
MovieList DramaMovies;
MovieList ComedyMovies;
ImageList BigIcons;

#endregion
```

VB

```
#Region "class local variables"

  Private ActionMovies As MovieList
  Private DramaMovies As MovieList
  Private ComedyMovies As MovieList
  Private BigIcons As ImageList

#End Region
```

As you can see, I have three types of movies. I also have an ImageList that I use for the icon display ListView control. Before I add any constructor code I will need some delegates to call. The mouse does a lot of work in this program, so I have quite a few mouse event handlers. Most of them are used for drag-and-drop operations.

C#

```csharp
#region Delegates

private void GenreClick(object sender, EventArgs e)
{
  ComboBox cmb = (ComboBox)sender;
  GetList((MovieList)cmb.SelectedItem);
}

private void MovieRentalStartDrag(object sender, ItemDragEventArgs e)
{
  lstRentals.DoDragDrop(e.Item, DragDropEffects.Move);
}

private void MovieRentalDragAcross(object sender, DragEventArgs e)
{
  e.Effect = DragDropEffects.Move;
}

private void MovieDragInto(object sender, DragEventArgs e)
{
  //The data must come from the lstRentals ListView
  object o = e.Data.GetData(DataFormats.Serializable);
  if(o is ListViewItem)
  {
    ListViewItem l = (ListViewItem)o;
    if (l.ListView == lstRentals)
      e.Effect = DragDropEffects.All;
    else
      e.Effect = DragDropEffects.None;
  }
}
```

```
private void RentalCartDrop(object sender, DragEventArgs e)
{
  object o = e.Data.GetData(DataFormats.Serializable);
  ListViewItem l = (ListViewItem)o;

  DialogResult dr = MessageBox.Show("Confirm Rental of " + l.Text,
                                    "Rent Video",
                                    MessageBoxButtons.YesNo);
  if(dr == DialogResult.No)
    return;

  //Look at the genre combo box to see which movie list to delete this
  //ListViewItem from.
  MovieList m = (MovieList)cmbGenre.SelectedItem;
  if(!m.CheckOut(l))
    MessageBox.Show("This Movie is already out.");

}

private void MovieSoldDrop(object sender, DragEventArgs e)
{
  object o = e.Data.GetData(DataFormats.Serializable);
  ListViewItem l = (ListViewItem)o;

  DialogResult dr = MessageBox.Show("Are you sure you want to sell " +
                                    l.Text + "?" ,
                                    "Sell This Video",
                                    MessageBoxButtons.YesNo);
  if(dr == DialogResult.No)
    return;

  //Very important!!  If I did not remove this ListViewItem from the source
  //list I would need to clone this ListViewItem before I add it to the
  //lstSold control.
  lstRentals.Items.Remove(l);
  lstSold.Items.Add((ListViewItem)l);
  lstSold.Items[lstSold.Items.Count-1].ImageIndex = 0;
```

```
      //Look at the genre combo box to see which movie list to delete this
      //ListViewItem from.
      MovieList m = (MovieList)cmbGenre.SelectedItem;
      m.Remove(l);


    }


    #endregion
```

VB

```
#Region "Delegates"

  Private Sub GenreClick(ByVal sender As Object, ByVal e As EventArgs)
    Dim cmb As ComboBox = CType(sender, ComboBox)
    GetList(CType(cmb.SelectedItem, MovieList))
  End Sub


  Private Sub MovieRentalStartDrag(ByVal sender As Object, _
                                   ByVal e As ItemDragEventArgs)
    lstRentals.DoDragDrop(e.Item, DragDropEffects.Move)
  End Sub


  Private Sub MovieRentalDragAcross(ByVal sender As Object, _
                                    ByVal e As DragEventArgs)
    e.Effect = DragDropEffects.Move
  End Sub


  Private Sub MovieDragInto(ByVal sender As Object, ByVal e As DragEventArgs)
    'The data must come from the lstRentals ListView
    Dim o As Object = e.Data.GetData(DataFormats.Serializable)
    If o.GetType() Is GetType(ListViewItem) Then
      Dim l As ListViewItem = DirectCast(o, ListViewItem)
      If (l.ListView Is lstRentals) Then
        e.Effect = DragDropEffects.All
      Else
        e.Effect = DragDropEffects.None
      End If
    End If
  End Sub
```

```
Private Sub RentalCartDrop(ByVal sender As Object, ByVal e As DragEventArgs)
  Dim o As Object = e.Data.GetData(DataFormats.Serializable)
  Dim l As ListViewItem = DirectCast(o, ListViewItem)

  Dim dr As DialogResult = MessageBox.Show("Confirm Rental of " + l.Text, _
                                "Rent Video", _
                                MessageBoxButtons.YesNo)
  If dr = DialogResult.No Then
    Return
  End If


  'Look at the genre combo box to see which movie list to delete this
  'ListViewItem from.
  Dim m As MovieList = CType(cmbGenre.SelectedItem, MovieList)
  If Not m.CheckOut(l) Then
    MessageBox.Show("This Movie is already out.")
  End If
End Sub

Private Sub MovieSoldDrop(ByVal sender As Object, ByVal e As DragEventArgs)
  Dim o As Object = e.Data.GetData(DataFormats.Serializable)
  Dim l As ListViewItem = DirectCast(o, ListViewItem)

  Dim dr As DialogResult = MessageBox.Show("Are you sure you want to sell " + _
                                l.Text + "?", _
                                "Sell This Video", _
                                MessageBoxButtons.YesNo)
  If dr = DialogResult.No Then
    Return
  End If

  'Very important!!  If I did not remove this ListViewItem from the source
  'list I would need to clone this ListViewItem before I add it to the
  'lstSold control.
  lstRentals.Items.Remove(l)
  lstSold.Items.Add(DirectCast(l, ListViewItem))
  lstSold.Items(lstSold.Items.Count - 1).ImageIndex = 0
```

```
        'Look at the genre combo box to see which movie list to delete this
        'ListViewItem from.
        Dim m As MovieList = CType(cmbGenre.SelectedItem, MovieList)
        m.Remove(1)

    End Sub

#End Region
```

Most of these delegates take care of the housekeeping during drag-and-drop operations.

The GenreClick method calls GetList. This helper function follows.

C#

```
    private void GetList(MovieList list)
    {
      lstRentals.BeginUpdate();
      lstRentals.Items.Clear();
      lstRentals.Items.AddRange(list.Items);
      lstRentals.EndUpdate();
    }
```

VB

```
    Private Sub GetList(ByVal list As MovieList)
      lstRentals.BeginUpdate()
      lstRentals.Items.Clear()
      lstRentals.Items.AddRange(list.Items)
      lstRentals.EndUpdate()
    End Sub
```

Several things need to happen for a drag-and-drop operation to work:

• The source object must be serializable. Most .NET objects are, but if you want to drag and drop your own object, it must inherit from the ISerializable interface.

• You must hook to an event (usually MouseDown) where you use the DoDrag method. This method needs the object being dragged and the DragEffects enumeration you want. Note that the ListView has a special ItemDrag event that I use here to start the process.

- You must set up the receiving control to allow drop operations. You do this with the AllowDrop property.

- Hook up to the DragEnter event for the destination control. Here you will detect the object being dragged and either allow the operation to continue or deny it.

- Hook up to the DragDrop event in the destination control and perform whatever operation is needed with the data from the source object.

You can hook into some other events with drag and drop, but the preceding list covers the basics.

Along the way, you need to know a couple of things. First, you need to know that the DragEffects enumeration allows you to specify if you want the operation to be a copy, move, or cancelled. If you use DragEffects.None, you will effectively cancel the drag operation.

Second, you need to know how to get the data that you are transferring over. There are a few standard data types that the drag-and-drop operation knows about. These types are the most common types of data to be moved. Some of the data types are as follows:

- Bitmap

- CSV format text

- HTML

- Text

You should be aware of a whole host of other data types. See the online help for the DataFormats class. If your object does not fall into one of these nice categories, then you will need to use DataFormats.Serializable like I did. This returns an object that you will need to cast to the proper data type before you can use it.

Note that in the MovieSoldDrop event, I remove the ListViewItem object from its source ListView control before I add it to the destination ListView control. I need to do this because common sense dictates that it should only be in one bin at a time. Also, I need to do this because the object can be in only one ListView control at a time. If I want it in both, I need to clone the ListViewItem before I add it to the second control.

The last thing I do in the drag-and-drop operation here is to remove the ListViewItem object from its MovieList collection. Now, as I change genres using the ComboBox, I will not see this movie again when I reload its genre collection.

TIP This section has presented a number of tasks you will need to do and items you will need to watch out for when you design a data entry screen that has interaction between controls. Whatever you do needs to make sense to the user and it also needs to make sense programmatically.

If you ran the program now, nothing would happen. Although this seems to happen all too often with released code, at least you can say you know something was left out here. You will need to fill in the constructor with initialization code.

Listings 5-3a and 5-3b show the code for the constructor. Note that I am doing a little exception handling in here as far as reading in the movie files go.

Listing 5-3a. C# Constructor Initialization Code

```csharp
public Form1()
{
  InitializeComponent();

  //Get the movie ListViewItems
  try   { ActionMovies = new MovieList("ActionMovies.txt"); }
  catch { ActionMovies = null; }

  try   { DramaMovies = new MovieList("DramaMovies.txt"); }
  catch { DramaMovies = null; }

  try   { ComedyMovies = new MovieList("ComedyMovies.txt"); }
  catch { ComedyMovies = null; }

  //Set up the rental ListView
  lstRentals.View = View.Details;
  lstRentals.AllowColumnReorder = true;
  lstRentals.GridLines = true;
  lstRentals.FullRowSelect = true;
  lstRentals.AllowDrop = true;
  lstRentals.ItemDrag     += new
      ItemDragEventHandler
     (this.MovieRentalStartDrag);
  lstRentals.DragEnter    += new
     DragEventHandler
     (this.MovieRentalDragAcross);
  lstRentals.Columns.Add("Title",        -2, HorizontalAlignment.Center);
  lstRentals.Columns.Add("Release Date", -2, HorizontalAlignment.Center);
```

```
lstRentals.Columns.Add("Running Time", -2, HorizontalAlignment.Center);
lstRentals.Columns.Add("Format",       -2, HorizontalAlignment.Center);
lstRentals.Columns.Add("In Stock",     -2, HorizontalAlignment.Center);

//Now set up the For-Sale ListView
BigIcons = new ImageList();
BigIcons.Images.Add(Image.FromFile("movie.bmp"));
lstSold.LargeImageList = BigIcons;
lstSold.View = View.LargeIcon;
lstSold.AllowDrop = true;
lstSold.DragEnter += new DragEventHandler(MovieDragInto);
lstSold.DragDrop  += new DragEventHandler(MovieSoldDrop);

//Fill the rental box
picRental.SizeMode = PictureBoxSizeMode.StretchImage;
picRental.Image = Image.FromFile("cart.bmp");
picRental.AllowDrop = true;
picRental.DragEnter += new DragEventHandler(MovieDragInto);
picRental.DragDrop  += new DragEventHandler(this.RentalCartDrop);

//Fill the ComboBox.  This MUST be done after setting up the
//rental listView control
if(ActionMovies != null) cmbGenre.Items.Add(ActionMovies);
if(DramaMovies != null) cmbGenre.Items.Add(DramaMovies);
if(ComedyMovies != null) cmbGenre.Items.Add(ComedyMovies);
cmbGenre.SelectedIndexChanged += new EventHandler(this.GenreClick);
//Setting the index automatically fires the event
cmbGenre.SelectedIndex = 0;


}
```

Listing 5-3b. VB Constructor Initialization Code

```
Public Sub New()
  MyBase.New()

  'This call is required by the Windows Form Designer.
  InitializeComponent()

  'Get the movie ListViewItems
  Try
    ActionMovies = New MovieList("ActionMovies.txt")
  Catch
    ActionMovies = Nothing
  End Try
```

```
Try
  DramaMovies = New MovieList("DramaMovies.txt")
Catch
  DramaMovies = Nothing
End Try


Try
  ComedyMovies = New MovieList("ComedyMovies.txt")
Catch
  ComedyMovies = Nothing
End Try



'Set up the rental ListView
lstRentals.View = View.Details
lstRentals.AllowColumnReorder = True
lstRentals.GridLines = True
lstRentals.FullRowSelect = True
lstRentals.AllowDrop = True
AddHandler lstRentals.ItemDrag, New ItemDragEventHandler _
                              (AddressOf MovieRentalStartDrag)
AddHandler lstRentals.DragEnter, New DragEventHandler _
                              (AddressOf MovieRentalDragAcross)

lstRentals.Columns.Add("Title", -2, HorizontalAlignment.Center)
lstRentals.Columns.Add("Release Date", -2, HorizontalAlignment.Center)
lstRentals.Columns.Add("Running Time", -2, HorizontalAlignment.Center)
lstRentals.Columns.Add("Format", -2, HorizontalAlignment.Center)
lstRentals.Columns.Add("In Stock", -2, HorizontalAlignment.Center)

'Now set up the For-Sale ListView
BigIcons = New ImageList()
BigIcons.Images.Add(Image.FromFile("movie.bmp"))
lstSold.LargeImageList = BigIcons
lstSold.View = View.LargeIcon
lstSold.AllowDrop = True
AddHandler lstSold.DragEnter, New DragEventHandler(AddressOf MovieDragInto)
AddHandler lstSold.DragDrop, New DragEventHandler(AddressOf MovieSoldDrop)

'Fill the rental box
picRental.SizeMode = PictureBoxSizeMode.StretchImage
picRental.Image = Image.FromFile("cart.bmp")
picRental.AllowDrop = True
AddHandler picRental.DragEnter, New DragEventHandler(AddressOf MovieDragInto)
AddHandler picRental.DragDrop, New DragEventHandler(AddressOf RentalCartDrop)
```

```
'Fill the ComboBox.  This MUST be done after setting up the
'rental listView control
If Not ActionMovies Is Nothing Then cmbGenre.Items.Add(ActionMovies)
If Not DramaMovies Is Nothing Then cmbGenre.Items.Add(DramaMovies)
If Not ComedyMovies Is Nothing Then cmbGenre.Items.Add(ComedyMovies)
AddHandler cmbGenre.SelectedIndexChanged, New EventHandler _
                                        (AddressOf GenreClick)
'Setting the index automatically fires the event
cmbGenre.SelectedIndex = 0

End Sub
```

Let's look at what's going on here. First, I initialize three MovieList objects. If the objects fail to initialize properly, I set these objects to null. By doing this, I allow the program to run correctly with only one or two valid MovieLists. The most likely reason for a MovieList object failing to initialize properly is an inability to read the text file.

After this, I initialize the two ListView controls and I put a picture of a shopping cart in the PictureBox control. Notice that I set up this PictureBox for drag-and-drop operations as well. The last thing I do in this constructor is fill the ComboBox. Here is the code again:

```
//Fill the ComboBox.  This MUST be done after setting up the
//rental listView control
if(ActionMovies != null) cmbGenre.Items.Add(ActionMovies);
if(DramaMovies != null) cmbGenre.Items.Add(DramaMovies);
if(ComedyMovies != null) cmbGenre.Items.Add(ComedyMovies);
cmbGenre.SelectedIndexChanged += new EventHandler(this.GenreClick);
//Setting the index automatically fires the event
cmbGenre.SelectedIndex = 0;
```

If the MovieList object is not null (nothing in VB) I add the object to the ComboBox. Remember how I overrode the ToString() method in the MovieList class? The ComboBox gets the text to display from the ToString method of the object that I add.

Once I set the event handler, I set the SelectedIndex property to the first item. Doing this programmatically automatically calls the delegate for the event handler. This is why this operation is left until last. If I did it before finishing the setup, I would have bugs galore.

Run the program and play with it. Figure 5-8 shows this form as it is running.

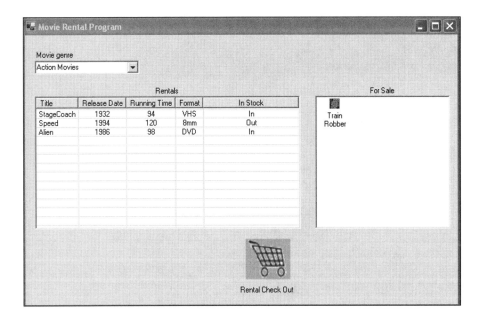

Figure 5-8. Running the video rental form

This form does everything you would expect it to, with perhaps a few exceptions. You are not able to reverse a checkout and you are not able to put a movie from the For Sale bin back into the Rentals bin. You have enough knowledge to do this yourself if you are so inclined.

Play around with the Rentals ListView. You are able to swap columns. You are not able to sort them, though. Sorting columns is a common thing in this kind of control and your users will expect it.

You can set up sorting by hooking into the ColumnClick event and reversing the current sort order. This allows you to click a column and go from a descending sort to an ascending sort. The problem with this is that it sorts only on the first column. I know that when I come across ListViews like this, I expect to click any column and have the list sorted according to that column. This last piece of code accomplishes this.

Remember the ListViewSorter class I had you make? I bet you forgot all about that. Currently it has no code in it. What follows is the code for this class.

C#

```csharp
using System;
using System.Windows.Forms;
using System.Collections;

namespace MovieList_c
{
  /// <summary>
  /// This class sorts a ListView control by column
  /// </summary>
  public class ListViewSorter: IComparer
  {
    private int      mCol;
    private SortOrder mOrder;

    public ListViewSorter(int column, SortOrder order)
    {
      mCol=column;
      mOrder = order;
    }
    public int Compare(object x, object y)
    {
      int returnVal = String.Compare(((ListViewItem)x).SubItems[mCol].Text,
        ((ListViewItem)y).SubItems[mCol].Text);
      if(mOrder == SortOrder.Descending)
        return (returnVal *= -1);
      else
        return returnVal;
    }
  }
}
```

VB

```vb
Option Strict On
Imports System.Windows.Forms
Imports System.Collections

Public Class ListViewSorter
  Implements IComparer
```

```
Dim mCol As Integer
Dim mOrder As SortOrder

Public Sub New(ByVal column As Integer, ByVal order As SortOrder)
  mCol = column
  mOrder = order
End Sub


Public Function Compare(ByVal x As Object, ByVal y As Object) As Integer _
                      Implements System.Collections.IComparer.Compare
  Dim returnVal As Integer = String.Compare( _
                      (CType(x, ListViewItem)).SubItems(mCol).Text, _
                      (CType(y, ListViewItem).SubItems(mCol).Text))
  If mOrder = SortOrder.Descending Then
    returnVal *= -1
    Return returnVal
  Else
    Return returnVal
  End If
End Function


End Class
```

This class allows you to override the normal compare routine of the ListView. Add the following delegate to the main form.

C#

```csharp
private void ColumnSort(object sender, ColumnClickEventArgs e)
{
  ListView lvw = (ListView)sender;
  ArrayList SortList = (ArrayList)lvw.Tag;
  SortList[e.Column] = (SortOrder)SortList[e.Column] ==
                    SortOrder.Ascending ?
                    SortOrder.Descending :
                    SortOrder.Ascending;
  lvw.Sorting = (SortOrder)SortList[e.Column];

  lvw.BeginUpdate();
  lvw.ListViewItemSorter = new ListViewSorter(e.Column, lvw.Sorting);
  lvw.Sort();
  lvw.EndUpdate();
}
```

VB

```
Private Sub ColumnSort(ByVal sender As Object, ByVal e As ColumnClickEventArgs)
  Dim lvw As ListView = CType(sender, ListView)
  Dim SortList As ArrayList = CType(lvw.Tag, ArrayList)
  SortList(e.Column) = IIf(DirectCast(SortList(e.Column), SortOrder) = _
                                          SortOrder.Ascending, _
                                          SortOrder.Descending, _
                                          SortOrder.Ascending)
  lvw.Sorting = DirectCast(SortList(e.Column), SortOrder)

  lvw.BeginUpdate()
  lvw.ListViewItemSorter = New ListViewSorter(e.Column, lvw.Sorting)
  lvw.Sort()
  lvw.EndUpdate()
End Sub
```

What I have here is an array of sort orders for each column in the ListView. Depending on which column you select, this method gets the last sort order for that column and changes it to the opposite order. It then redirects the ListViewItemSorter property to use the ListViewSorter class, which sorts the ListView based on the column and sort order passed in. Notice that the sort order array was retrieved from the Tag property of the ListView control.

To make this all work, add the following code to the constructor just below where you initialized the lstRentals ListView control.

C#

```
ArrayList order = new ArrayList();
for(int k=0; k<lstRentals.Columns.Count; k++)
  order.Insert(k, SortOrder.Ascending);
order.TrimToSize();
lstRentals.Tag = order;
lstRentals.ColumnClick += new ColumnClickEventHandler(ColumnSort);
```

VB

```
'Make something that will hold the current sort order for the current column
Dim order As ArrayList = New ArrayList()
Dim k As Integer
For k = 0 To lstRentals.Columns.Count - 1
  order.Insert(k, SortOrder.Ascending)
Next
order.TrimToSize()
```

```
lstRentals.Tag = order
AddHandler lstRentals.ColumnClick, New ColumnClickEventHandler _
                              (AddressOf ColumnSort)
```

Notice that I keep the sort order array as a part of the ListView control. Doing this obviates the need for me to keep any global variables, and it also eliminates the need to keep track of which array belongs to which ListView control. The ColumnSort delegate does not care which ListView control needs sorting, nor does it care how many columns that control has.

TIP   It is always best to keep all data and functionality concerning an object within that object itself. This basically makes your object self-aware and able to handle its own needs.

Now you can run the program and click different columns in the lstRentals ListView control. You will be able to sort in ascending or descending order based on the column that you clicked. This functionality is not just a nicety in data entry programs; it is required.

One note here. Click the column header for the running time. See that the sort order is 98, 94, 36, 120 for descending and the reverse for ascending. How can this be? Take a piece of paper and the ASCII chart and compare the text representations of these numbers. You will see that the order is correct (120 begins with a 1 so its sort order is first).

What to do? In order to fix things like this, you will need to make a compare routine for each column. If you have a column of numbers, you will need to sort according to numerical order.

Manipulating Data with the TreeView Control

The TreeView control is my favorite one to use in data entry programs. It allows you to present data in a hierarchical format. It also allows the user to see quite a bit of data in a small space or, if needed, the user can filter what he or she sees by collapsing parent nodes. It has the capability to move data within itself hierarchically, and it also supports drag and drop.

The TreeView control used in conjunction with the ListView control can make for a very powerful and intuitive data entry screen. You can think of the TreeView control as a detail view of the ListView control, only turned 90 degrees vertically. Here is what I mean.

Suppose you set up a ListView control with four columns. The first column is the ListViewItems and the other three columns are SubItems of the first one. You can do the same thing with a TreeView control. The first column would equate to a root node. The SubItems of the ListView would equate to child nodes of the parent root node.

Sometimes it is worthwhile to present different views of data to the user. After all, data entry programs are not only about entering data into some screen. They also encompass ways to present data to the user.

This next example uses a TreeView, a PictureBox, and a ListView control to present a mock photo album screen. It allows transfer of data from the ListView control to the TreeView control while the PictureBox is used to view the actual photo.

You may be wondering where the data entry part comes in. After all, the only thing I allow is transfer of a ListView control item over to a TreeView. If you think about it, this is a form of data entry. The TreeView is used to categorize the photographs. The ListView shows you all the photos in no particular order. You could easily make a form that pops up based on a right-click on the ListView item. This form would then require input from the user as to which category or categories the picture should belong. This kind of form is classic data entry. I think it is more intuitive, however, for the user to drag his or her picture over to a TreeView that contains a hierarchical list of categories.

 NOTE   Keep in mind that although this form of drag and drop is intuitive and requires little training, it can be slow. When you design your program, the TreeView drag-and-drop data entry could be your main form of data entry. You could also include a "speed screen" form that allows the more advanced user to do the same thing only with more traditional (and sometimes faster) data entry forms. You will need to balance usability with ease of use.

This example uses quite a few external bitmaps and icons that you can download from the Downloads section of the Apress Web site (http://www.apress.com).

Start a new C# or VB project. Mine is called "Photo." You will need to perform the following steps to set up your project:

1. Size the main form to be 700×500. Make the form start at Center Screen, and set the FormBorderStyle to FixedSingle.

2. Add a Label that reads **Photo Classifications**. Center this text in the Label.

3. Below the Photo Classifications Label, add a TreeView control called **tvPics**.

4. Add a Label that reads **All photos**. Center this text in the Label.

5. Below the All photos Label, add a ListView control called **lvPics**.

6. Below the lvPics ListView control, add a PictureBox called **pic**.

Your form should look like Figure 5-9.

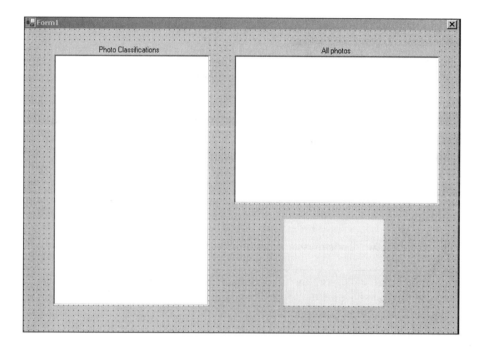

Figure 5-9. The main form for the Photo project

As you can see, there is not much here. Even though this screen may look sparse, an awful lot of information will be presented here. Quite a bit of data validation goes on in the background too.

You will need to add the following classes to your project:

- ListViewSorter

- Photo

- PhotoList

Your Solution Explorer should look like Figure 5-10.

Figure 5-10. Solution Explorer for the Photo project

The C# screen shot would have the .cs extension instead of the .vb extension. But you know that already, don't you?

Anyway, did you notice some similarities in the classes I include here? They are essentially the same as in the previous MovieView project. In fact, the ListViewSorter class is identical.

CAUTION   Code reuse at work here!

Here is the ListViewSorter code.

C#

```csharp
using System;
using System.Windows.Forms;
using System.Collections;

namespace Photo_c
{
  /// <summary>
  /// This class sorts a ListView control by column
  /// </summary>
  public class ListViewSorter: IComparer
  {
    private int       mCol;
    private SortOrder mOrder;
```

```csharp
    public ListViewSorter(int column, SortOrder order)
    {
      mCol=column;
      mOrder = order;
    }
    public int Compare(object x, object y)
    {
      int returnVal = String.Compare(((ListViewItem)x).SubItems[mCol].Text,
        ((ListViewItem)y).SubItems[mCol].Text);
      if(mOrder == SortOrder.Descending)
        return (returnVal *= -1);
      else
        return returnVal;
    }
  }
}
```

VB

```vb
Option Strict On
Imports System.Windows.Forms
Imports System.Collections

Public Class ListViewSorter
  Implements IComparer

  Dim mCol As Integer
  Dim mOrder As SortOrder

  Public Sub New(ByVal column As Integer, ByVal order As SortOrder)
    mCol = column
    mOrder = order
  End Sub

  Public Function Compare(ByVal x As Object, ByVal y As Object) As Integer _
                       Implements System.Collections.IComparer.Compare
    Dim returnVal As Integer = String.Compare( _
                          (CType(x, ListViewItem)).SubItems(mCol).Text, _
                          (CType(y, ListViewItem).SubItems(mCol).Text))
    If mOrder = SortOrder.Descending Then
      returnVal *= -1
      Return returnVal
```

```
      Else
        Return returnVal
      End If
   End Function
End Class
```

I went through this code in the last example, so I won't repeat myself here.
I will say this, however: This class is handy to have around whenever you work with
ListView controls. You can easily change it to accommodate different cultures'
sorting styles.

The Photo class code follows.

C#

```csharp
using System;
using System.IO;
using System.Drawing;

namespace Photo_c
{
  /// <summary>
  /// class that has a photographic memory :)
  /// </summary>
  public class Photo
  {
    Image mPic;
    string mName;
    string mLocation;
    string mDateShot;

    public Photo(string picname)
    {
      mPic = Image.FromFile(picname);
      mName = Path.GetFileNameWithoutExtension(picname);
      mDateShot = DateTime.Today.ToShortDateString();
      mLocation = mName;
    }
```

```
    public override string ToString(){ return "Photo"; }

    public string Location  { get {return mLocation;} }
    public string Name      { get {return mName;} }
    public string Date      { get {return mDateShot;} }
    public Image Picture    { get {return mPic;} }
  }
}
```

VB

```
Option Strict On
Imports System.IO
Imports System.Drawing

Public Class Photo

  Dim mPic As Image
  Dim mName As String
  Dim mLocation As String
  Dim mDateShot As String

  Public Sub New(ByVal picname As String)
    mPic = Image.FromFile(picname)
    mName = Path.GetFileNameWithoutExtension(picname)
    mDateShot = DateTime.Today.ToShortDateString()
    mLocation = mName
  End Sub

  Public Overrides Function ToString() As String
    Return "Photo"
  End Function

  Public ReadOnly Property Location() As String
    Get
      Return mLocation
    End Get
  End Property
```

```
    Public ReadOnly Property Name() As String
       Get
          Return mName
       End Get
    End Property

    Public ReadOnly Property DateShot() As String
       Get
          Return mDateShot
       End Get
    End Property

    Public ReadOnly Property Picture() As Image
       Get
          Return mPic
       End Get
    End Property
End Class
```

This class, when instantiated, creates an object that holds an image. It has a few properties and overrides the ToString method. Obviously, a real application would need quite a few more properties. In fact, some of the properties you may want to expose are properties of the image itself.

TIP   Refer to my book *GDI+ Programming in C# and VB .NET* (Apress, 2002) for a detailed discussion on what properties you can get from a .jpg, .gif, or other type of image file. You'll be surprised at the wealth of information these image standards afford.[3]

Remember that I overrode the ToString method in the last example. Here I do it for a different reason.

The last class to be filled in is the PhotoList class.

---

3.   Shameless plug here!

C#

```csharp
using System;
using System.Drawing;
using System.Collections;
using System.Windows.Forms;

namespace Photo_c
{
  /// <summary>
  /// Class that holds all photographs regardless of classification
  /// </summary>
  public class PhotoList
  {
    ArrayList mPics;

    public PhotoList()
    {
      mPics = new ArrayList();

      //Normally you would detect these pictures and load them.
      mPics.Add(new Photo("desert1.jpg"));
      mPics.Add(new Photo("desert2.jpg"));
      mPics.Add(new Photo("desert3.jpg"));
      mPics.Add(new Photo("fields1.jpg"));
      mPics.Add(new Photo("fields2.jpg"));
      mPics.Add(new Photo("flowers1.jpg"));
      mPics.Add(new Photo("flowers2.jpg"));
      mPics.Add(new Photo("flowers3.jpg"));
      mPics.Add(new Photo("flowers4.jpg"));
      mPics.Add(new Photo("sea1.jpg"));
      mPics.Add(new Photo("sea2.jpg"));
      mPics.Add(new Photo("sea3.jpg"));
      mPics.Add(new Photo("sea4.jpg"));
      mPics.Add(new Photo("spring1.jpg"));
      mPics.Add(new Photo("spring2.jpg"));
      mPics.Add(new Photo("spring3.jpg"));
      mPics.TrimToSize();
    }
```

```
/// <summary>
/// Gets an Image array
/// </summary>
public ListViewItem[] Items
{
  get
  {
    mPics.TrimToSize();
    ListViewItem[] lst = new ListViewItem[mPics.Count];


    ArrayList aList = new ArrayList();
    foreach(Photo p in mPics)
    {
      ListViewItem l = new ListViewItem(p.Name);
      l.Tag = p;
      l.SubItems.Add(p.Date);
      l.SubItems.Add(p.Location);
      l.SubItems.Add("JPG");

      aList.Add(l);
    }
    aList.TrimToSize();
    aList.CopyTo(lst, 0);
    return lst;
  }
}
}
}
```

VB

```
Option Strict On

Imports System.Drawing
Imports System.Collections
Imports System.Windows.Forms

Public Class PhotoList

  Dim mPics As ArrayList
```

```vbnet
Public Sub New()
  mPics = New ArrayList()

  'Normally you would detect these pictures and load them.
  mPics.Add(New Photo("desert1.jpg"))
  mPics.Add(New Photo("desert2.jpg"))
  mPics.Add(New Photo("desert3.jpg"))
  mPics.Add(New Photo("fields1.jpg"))
  mPics.Add(New Photo("fields2.jpg"))
  mPics.Add(New Photo("flowers1.jpg"))
  mPics.Add(New Photo("flowers2.jpg"))
  mPics.Add(New Photo("flowers3.jpg"))
  mPics.Add(New Photo("flowers4.jpg"))
  mPics.Add(New Photo("sea1.jpg"))
  mPics.Add(New Photo("sea2.jpg"))
  mPics.Add(New Photo("sea3.jpg"))
  mPics.Add(New Photo("sea4.jpg"))
  mPics.Add(New Photo("spring1.jpg"))
  mPics.Add(New Photo("spring2.jpg"))
  mPics.Add(New Photo("spring3.jpg"))
  mPics.TrimToSize()
End Sub

'/// <summary>
'/// Gets an Image array
'/// </summary>
Public ReadOnly Property Items() As ListViewItem()
  Get
    mPics.TrimToSize()
    Dim lst(mPics.Count - 1) As ListViewItem
    Dim aList As ArrayList = New ArrayList()
    Dim p As Photo
    For Each p In mPics
      Dim l As ListViewItem = New ListViewItem(p.Name)
      l.Tag = p
      l.SubItems.Add(p.DateShot)
      l.SubItems.Add(p.Location)
      l.SubItems.Add("JPG")
```

```
      aList.Add(l)
    Next
    aList.TrimToSize()
    aList.CopyTo(lst, 0)
    Return lst
  End Get
End Property


End Class
```

The constructor for this class instantiates some Photo objects, which contain photographs.

Because I use this class only in conjunction with a ListView control, I have a single Items property that returns an array of ListViewItem objects. If I decide to use this class to fill the TreeView as well, I turn this property into a function and overload it with another version that returns an array of nodes. I could even return an array of images if I like. You are not limited by what I do here.[4]

Compile your program and fix any errors you may have. (You should not have any errors.)

The code for the main form is pretty extensive. You will work your way through it from the bottom of the code on up to the constructor. First, though, add the following class local variable.

C#

```
    PhotoList Piclist;
```

VB

```
  Dim Piclist As PhotoList
```

This is the only class local variable you will need. The next thing to add is the delegate code for the ListView control. They consist of drag and drop, column sort, and row select methods.

---

4. You are welcome to use and abuse this code. If what you do turns out good, give me credit somewhere. If it turns out bad, I had nothing to do with it.

C#

```
#region ListView Delegates

private void RowSelect(object sender, EventArgs e)
{
  Debug.Assert(sender == lvPics,
             "Only the lvPics ListView control can activate this delegate");
  Debug.Assert(lvPics.SelectedIndices.Count <= 1,
             "only one item can be selected");

  if(lvPics.SelectedIndices.Count == 1)
  {
    Photo p = (Photo)lvPics.SelectedItems[0].Tag;
    pic.Image = p.Picture;
  }
}

private void ColumnSort(object sender, ColumnClickEventArgs e)
{
  ListView lvw = (ListView)sender;
  ArrayList SortList = (ArrayList)lvw.Tag;
  SortList[e.Column] = (SortOrder)SortList[e.Column] ==
                        SortOrder.Ascending ?
                        SortOrder.Descending :
                        SortOrder.Ascending;
  lvw.Sorting = (SortOrder)SortList[e.Column];

  lvw.BeginUpdate();
  lvw.ListViewItemSorter = new ListViewSorter(e.Column, lvw.Sorting);
  lvw.Sort();
  lvw.EndUpdate();
}

private void PhotoStartDrag(object sender, ItemDragEventArgs e)
{
  if(sender == lvPics)
    lvPics.DoDragDrop(e.Item, DragDropEffects.Move );
}
```

```csharp
    private void PhotoDragAcross(object sender, DragEventArgs e)
    {
      if(sender == lvPics)
        e.Effect = DragDropEffects.Move;
    }


    #endregion
```

VB

```vb
#Region "ListView Delegates"

  Private Sub RowSelect(ByVal sender As Object, ByVal e As EventArgs)
    Debug.Assert(sender Is lvPics, _
                 "Only the lvPics ListView control can activate this delegate")
    Debug.Assert(lvPics.SelectedIndices.Count <= 1, _
                 "only one item can be selected")

    If lvPics.SelectedIndices.Count = 1 Then
      Dim p As Photo = DirectCast(lvPics.SelectedItems(0).Tag, Photo)
      pic.Image = p.Picture
    End If
  End Sub

  Private Sub ColumnSort(ByVal sender As Object, _
                         ByVal e As ColumnClickEventArgs)
    Dim lvw As ListView = CType(sender, ListView)
    Dim SortList As ArrayList = CType(lvw.Tag, ArrayList)
    SortList(e.Column) = IIf(DirectCast(SortList(e.Column), SortOrder) = _
                                             SortOrder.Ascending, _
                                             SortOrder.Descending, _
                                             SortOrder.Ascending)
    lvw.Sorting = DirectCast(SortList(e.Column), SortOrder)

    lvw.BeginUpdate()
    lvw.ListViewItemSorter = New ListViewSorter(e.Column, lvw.Sorting)
    lvw.Sort()
    lvw.EndUpdate()
  End Sub
```

```
Private Sub PhotoStartDrag(ByVal sender As Object, _
                           ByVal e As ItemDragEventArgs)
   If sender Is lvPics Then
     lvPics.DoDragDrop(e.Item, DragDropEffects.Move)
   End If
End Sub


Private Sub PhotoDragAcross(ByVal sender As Object, ByVal e As DragEventArgs)
   If sender Is lvPics Then
     e.Effect = DragDropEffects.Move
   End If
End Sub
```

#End Region

The RowSelect delegate has the following code in it:

```
Debug.Assert(sender == lvPics,
          "Only the lvPics ListView control can activate this delegate");
Debug.Assert(lvPics.SelectedIndices.Count <= 1,
          "only one item can be selected");
```

I have mentioned this before, but I will reiterate it here: If you have code that is supposed to run only under certain conditions, you should use assertion code to detect any wrongdoing. The assertion code is compiled out of the released version to increase speed. Now, I could have added code to make sure that the sender is the correct type, but that would only really be needed if this were a multicast delegate. That is, it would only be needed if this delegate were designed to be used by more than one control. In this case, I designed this delegate to be used only by the lvPics ListView control. My test-engineering department would find an error in usage by seeing the assertion.

Also note that I allow only one item to be selected. I take care of this in the initialization routine by setting the MultiSelect property to false. If I forgot to do this, the test engineer would undoubtedly try to select multiple items and he or she would get an assertion error. Getting this error would alert me (the programmer) to the fact that I made a boneheaded omission.

Even though the ListView control does not accept drop operations, I still attach a delegate to the DragEnter event. I do this so I can set the drag effects to something that represent copying an object. This is strictly a cosmetic thing and adds no real functionality to the code.

The following code is the delegate code for the TreeView control.

C#

```csharp
#region TreeView Delegates

private void NodeSelect(object sender, TreeViewEventArgs e)
{
  Debug.Assert(sender == tvPics,
            "Only the tvPics TreeView control can activate this delegate");

  if(e.Node.Tag != null)
  {
    Photo p = (Photo)e.Node.Tag;
    pic.Image = p.Picture;
  }
  else
    pic.Image = null;
}

private void TreeDragInto(object sender, DragEventArgs e)
{
  e.Effect = DragDropEffects.All;

}

private void TreeDragDrop(object sender, DragEventArgs e)
{
  //The x and y values are in form coordinates
  tvPics.SelectedNode = tvPics.GetNodeAt(tvPics.PointToClient
                                      (new Point(e.X, e.Y)));
  if(tvPics.SelectedNode == null)
  {
    MessageBox.Show("You need to drop this item on a node.");
    return;
  }

  //Normally you would detect the source data against the drop node
  //If the source data did not belong there then flag an error
  if(tvPics.SelectedNode.Parent == null)
  {
    MessageBox.Show("You cannot drop this item on the root node.");
    return;
  }
```

```
    if(tvPics.SelectedNode.Tag != null)
    {
      MessageBox.Show("You cannot drop a photo on a photo.");
      return;
    }

    //Get the object being passed.
    //I use a ListView object as the carrier since Photo is not serializable
    //A serializable object must be able to serialize all data within
    object o = e.Data.GetData(DataFormats.Serializable);
    ListViewItem l = (ListViewItem)o;
    Photo snap = (Photo)l.Tag;

    tvPics.BeginUpdate();
    TreeNode n = new TreeNode(snap.Name);
    n.Tag = snap;
    n.SelectedImageIndex = 2;
    n.ImageIndex = 2;
    tvPics.SelectedNode.Nodes.Add(n);
    tvPics.SelectedNode.Expand();
    tvPics.EndUpdate();

  }

  private void TreeExpandCollapse(object sender, TreeViewEventArgs e)
  {
    if(e.Action == TreeViewAction.Expand)
      e.Node.SelectedImageIndex = 1;

    if(e.Action == TreeViewAction.Collapse)
      e.Node.SelectedImageIndex = 0;

  }
  #endregion
```

VB

```
#Region "TreeView Delegates"

  Private Sub NodeSelect(ByVal sender As Object, ByVal e As TreeViewEventArgs)
    Debug.Assert(sender Is tvPics, _
                "Only the tvPics TreeView control can activate this delegate")
```

```
   If Not e.Node.Tag Is Nothing Then
     Dim p As Photo = DirectCast(e.Node.Tag, Photo)
     pic.Image = p.Picture
   Else
     pic.Image = Nothing
   End If
End Sub


Private Sub TreeDragInto(ByVal sender As Object, ByVal e As DragEventArgs)
  e.Effect = DragDropEffects.All
End Sub


Private Sub TreeDragDrop(ByVal sender As Object, ByVal e As DragEventArgs)
  'The x and y values are in form coordinates
  tvPics.SelectedNode = tvPics.GetNodeAt(tvPics.PointToClient _
                                     (New Point(e.X, e.Y)))
  If tvPics.SelectedNode Is Nothing Then
    MessageBox.Show("You need to drop this item on a node.")
    Return
  End If


  'Normally you would detect the source data against the drop node
  'If the source data did not belong there then flag an error
  If tvPics.SelectedNode.Parent Is Nothing Then
    MessageBox.Show("You cannot drop this item on the root node.")
    Return
  End If


  If Not tvPics.SelectedNode.Tag Is Nothing Then
    MessageBox.Show("You cannot drop a photo on a photo.")
    Return
  End If


  'Get the object being passed.
  'I use a ListView object as the carrier since Photo is not serializable
  'A serializable object must be able to serialize all data within
  Dim o As Object = e.Data.GetData(DataFormats.Serializable)
  Dim l As ListViewItem = DirectCast(o, ListViewItem)
  Dim snap As Photo = DirectCast(l.Tag, Photo)
```

```
    tvPics.BeginUpdate()
    Dim n As TreeNode = New TreeNode(snap.Name)
    n.Tag = snap
    n.SelectedImageIndex = 2
    n.ImageIndex = 2
    tvPics.SelectedNode.Nodes.Add(n)
    tvPics.SelectedNode.Expand()
    tvPics.EndUpdate()

  End Sub


  Private Sub TreeExpandCollapse(ByVal sender As Object, _
                                 ByVal e As TreeViewEventArgs)
    If e.Action = TreeViewAction.Expand Then
      e.Node.SelectedImageIndex = 1
    End If

    If e.Action = TreeViewAction.Collapse Then
      e.Node.SelectedImageIndex = 0
    End If
  End Sub
#End Region
```

There is quite a bit of complicated code here.

The TreeDragDrop routine checks to see if it is permissible to drop a photo on a particular node. If not, I flag an error with a message box and abort the operation. If the operation is allowed to proceed, I create a new node, add it to the drop node, and set the new node's Tag property to hold the Photo object.

The NodeSelect routine checks the current node for a tag. If the current node's tag is null, I clear the PictureBox. If the current node is not null, I cast the Tag object into the Photo object and display the photo in the PictureBox. This is simple enough, but it has its problems, as I will show soon.

The TreeExpandCollapse routine changes the icon shown at the node being expanded or collapsed. I use an open folder icon for expanded nodes and a closed folder icon for collapsed nodes. This gives the user some visual feedback in the TreeView.

Now on to the initialization code for the form. Add the following code region to your main form.

C#

```
#region Setup routines

private void SetupListView()
{
  //Set up the photo ListView
  lvPics.View = View.Details;
  lvPics.AllowColumnReorder = true;
  lvPics.GridLines = true;
  lvPics.FullRowSelect = true;
  lvPics.AllowDrop = true;
  lvPics.MultiSelect = false;
  lvPics.SelectedIndexChanged += new EventHandler(this.RowSelect);
  lvPics.ItemDrag      += new ItemDragEventHandler(this.PhotoStartDrag);
  lvPics.DragEnter     += new DragEventHandler(this.PhotoDragAcross);
  lvPics.Columns.Add("Name",      -2, HorizontalAlignment.Center);
  lvPics.Columns.Add("Date",      -2, HorizontalAlignment.Center);
  lvPics.Columns.Add("Location",  -2, HorizontalAlignment.Center);
  lvPics.Columns.Add("Format",    -2, HorizontalAlignment.Center);
  //Account for extra pixel created by column separator
  int width = (lvPics.Width - lvPics.Columns.Count) / lvPics.Columns.Count;
  foreach(ColumnHeader c in lvPics.Columns)
    c.Width = width;

  //Make something that will hold the current
  //sort order for the current column
  ArrayList order = new ArrayList();
  for(int k=0; k<lvPics.Columns.Count; k++)
    order.Insert(k, SortOrder.Ascending);
  order.TrimToSize();
  lvPics.Tag = order;
  lvPics.ColumnClick += new ColumnClickEventHandler(ColumnSort);

  //Fill the ListView
  lvPics.BeginUpdate();
  lvPics.Items.Clear();
  lvPics.Items.AddRange(Piclist.Items);
  lvPics.EndUpdate();

}
```

```csharp
  private void SetupTree()
  {
    ImageList iList = new ImageList();
    iList.Images.Add(Image.FromFile("closed.ico"));
    iList.Images.Add(Image.FromFile("open.ico"));
    iList.Images.Add(Image.FromFile("camera.ico"));

    tvPics.AllowDrop = true;
    tvPics.ImageList = iList;
    tvPics.HideSelection = false;
    tvPics.HotTracking = true;   //This is limiting
    tvPics.AfterSelect   += new TreeViewEventHandler(NodeSelect);
    tvPics.AfterExpand   += new TreeViewEventHandler(TreeExpandCollapse);
    tvPics.AfterCollapse += new TreeViewEventHandler(TreeExpandCollapse);
    tvPics.DragEnter     += new DragEventHandler(TreeDragInto);
    tvPics.DragDrop      += new DragEventHandler(TreeDragDrop);

    //Add some root nodes
    TreeNode root = new TreeNode("All Photos");
    root.Nodes.Add("Seascapes");
    root.Nodes.Add("Desert Scenes");
    root.Nodes.Add("Flowers");
    root.Nodes.Add("Spring");
    root.Expand();
    tvPics.Nodes.Add(root);
  }
```

VB

```vb
#Region "Setup routines"

  Private Sub SetupListView()
    'Set up the photo ListView
    lvPics.View = View.Details
    lvPics.AllowColumnReorder = True
    lvPics.GridLines = True
    lvPics.FullRowSelect = True
    lvPics.AllowDrop = True
    lvPics.MultiSelect = False
    AddHandler lvPics.SelectedIndexChanged, _
                   New EventHandler(AddressOf RowSelect)
```

```
                AddHandler lvPics.ItemDrag, _
                        New ItemDragEventHandler(AddressOf PhotoStartDrag)
                AddHandler lvPics.DragEnter, _
                        New DragEventHandler(AddressOf PhotoDragAcross)
                lvPics.Columns.Add("Name", -2, HorizontalAlignment.Center)
                lvPics.Columns.Add("Date", -2, HorizontalAlignment.Center)
                lvPics.Columns.Add("Location", -2, HorizontalAlignment.Center)
                lvPics.Columns.Add("Format", -2, HorizontalAlignment.Center)
                'Account for extra pixel created by column separator
                Dim c As ColumnHeader
                Dim width As Integer
                width = (lvPics.Width - lvPics.Columns.Count) \ lvPics.Columns.Count
                For Each c In lvPics.Columns
                  c.Width = width
                Next

                'Make something that will hold the current sort order for the current column
                Dim order As ArrayList = New ArrayList()
                Dim k As Integer
                For k = 0 To lvPics.Columns.Count - 1
                  order.Insert(k, SortOrder.Ascending)
                Next
                order.TrimToSize()
                lvPics.Tag = order
                AddHandler lvPics.ColumnClick, _
                        New ColumnClickEventHandler(AddressOf ColumnSort)

                'Fill the ListView
                lvPics.BeginUpdate()
                lvPics.Items.Clear()
                lvPics.Items.AddRange(Piclist.Items)
                lvPics.EndUpdate()

            End Sub

            Private Sub SetupTree()
              Dim iList As ImageList = New ImageList()
              iList.Images.Add(Image.FromFile("closed.ico"))
              iList.Images.Add(Image.FromFile("open.ico"))
              iList.Images.Add(Image.FromFile("camera.ico"))
```

```
tvPics.AllowDrop = True
tvPics.ImageList = iList
tvPics.HideSelection = False
tvPics.HotTracking = True  'This is limiting
AddHandler tvPics.AfterSelect, _
                New TreeViewEventHandler(AddressOf NodeSelect)
AddHandler tvPics.AfterExpand, _
                New TreeViewEventHandler(AddressOf TreeExpandCollapse)
AddHandler tvPics.AfterCollapse, _
                New TreeViewEventHandler(AddressOf TreeExpandCollapse)
AddHandler tvPics.DragEnter, _
                New DragEventHandler(AddressOf TreeDragInto)
AddHandler tvPics.DragDrop, _
                New DragEventHandler(AddressOf TreeDragDrop)

'Add some root nodes
Dim root As TreeNode = New TreeNode("All Photos")
root.Nodes.Add("Seascapes")
root.Nodes.Add("Desert Scenes")
root.Nodes.Add("Flowers")
root.Nodes.Add("Spring")
root.Expand()
tvPics.Nodes.Add(root)


  End Sub
#End Region
```

First, I'll pick apart the ListView setup. This is pretty much the same as the setup for the previous MovieList example. I set up the number of columns, change the width to match each column to be evenly divided across the width of the control, and fill it with ListViewItems from the PhotoList object. Notice that I also add the necessary code to sort based on the column chosen.

I set up the TreeView with static nodes that represent photograph categories. Normally, you would make this tree with perhaps only the root node. The user would set up the categories in a different screen. It is best if the user can have as much control over a program like this as possible.

The TreeView uses three icons. One represents an expanded node, one represents a collapsed node, and one represents a picture. I hook into the AfterExpand and AfterCollapse events to change these icons accordingly. This is a nicety that makes your program just a little better. Because I want to do drag-and-drop operations, I hook into the appropriate events for this functionality.

The constructor should look like the following.

C#

```
public Form1()
{
  InitializeComponent();

  Piclist = new PhotoList();

  pic.SizeMode = PictureBoxSizeMode.StretchImage;
  SetupListView();
  SetupTree();
}
```

VB

```
Public Sub New()
  MyBase.New()

  'This call is required by the Windows Form Designer.
  InitializeComponent()

  Piclist = New PhotoList()

  pic.SizeMode = PictureBoxSizeMode.StretchImage
  SetupListView()
  SetupTree()

End Sub
```

Now your program is complete. Compile and run the program. Your initial screen should look like the one shown in Figure 5-11.

Here you see each photograph and some associated properties. If you have been reading the code, you should know that I am hard-coding the format field. As I mentioned, though, you can obtain this information and much more from the file itself.

Try dragging a photograph over to the TreeView without dropping it on a node. Figure 5-12 is what you should see.

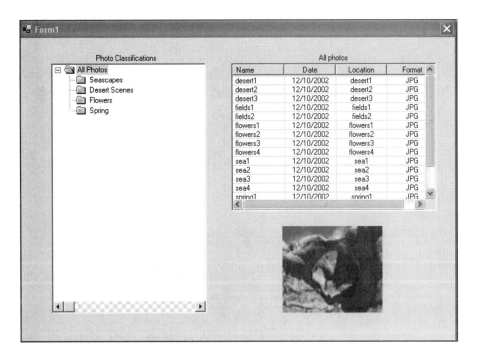

Figure 5-11. Running the Photo example

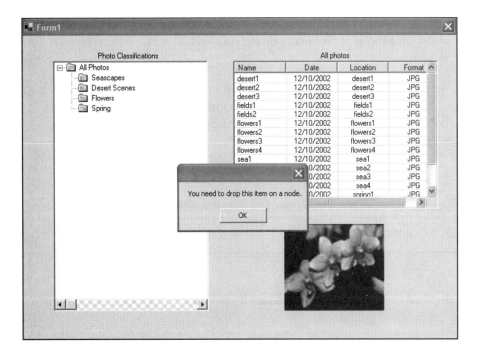

Figure 5-12. Bad drop zone

Now try dropping a photograph on the root node All Photos. You should see the message in Figure 5-13.

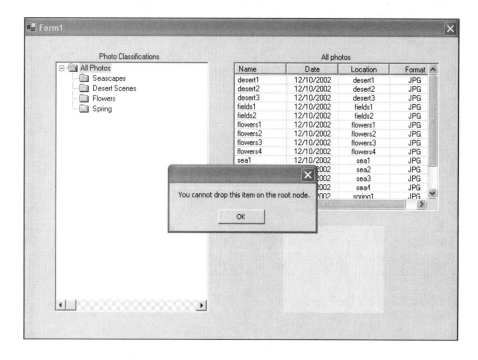

Figure 5-13. Try dropping the photo on the root node.

What do you notice about the drag-and-drop operation? As you drag and drop onto a tree node, there is no feedback to tell you that you are on a node. There is also no feedback to tell you that you cannot drop onto a node before you release the mouse button.

CROSS-REFERENCE   I cover the TreeView control in great detail in Chapter 9 and also in Chapter 10. Chapter 10 covers using the TreeView in a multithreaded way.

As I said (and demonstrated) before, if you can steer the user along a data entry path, you should do so.

There's actually no need at all for these two error messages. Wouldn't it be nice if while you were dragging the photograph over the tree, the node under the mouse would highlight? Wouldn't it also be nice to highlight only the nodes that can accept the photographs? If you were able to do these two things, you could get rid of some postdrop validation code and an annoying error message for the user. Try adding the following delegate to the TreeView delegate region.

C#

```csharp
private void TreeDragOver(object sender, DragEventArgs e)
{
  //Stop this from happening when over a node that
  //is not allowed to be dropped on
  TreeNode node = tvPics.GetNodeAt(tvPics.PointToClient
                                   (new Point(e.X, e.Y)));
  if(node.Tag == null)
  {
    tvPics.Focus();  //Problem with this is that it fires an event
    tvPics.SelectedNode = node;
    e.Effect = DragDropEffects.All;
  }
  else e.Effect = DragDropEffects.None;
}
```

VB

```vb
Private Sub TreeDragOver(ByVal sender As Object, ByVal e As DragEventArgs)
  'Stop this from happening when over a node that
  'is not allowed to be dropped on
  Dim node As TreeNode = tvPics.GetNodeAt(tvPics.PointToClient _
                                 (New Point(e.X, e.Y)))
  If node.Tag Is Nothing Then
    tvPics.Focus()  'Problem with this is that it fires an event
    tvPics.SelectedNode = node
    e.Effect = DragDropEffects.All
  Else
    e.Effect = DragDropEffects.None
  End If
End Sub
```

In this code, I first instantiate a new TreeNode based on the position of the mouse. If the node has a valid tag, I set the focus to the TreeView control and set the selected node to the new node under the mouse. This means that I allow you to only drop a photograph on a node that is not a photograph. If the drop node is not valid, I set the drop effects to none so it is impossible to drop the photo. Thus, the drop zone error message never gets run.

Add the following delegate hook in the SetupTree code.

C#

```
tvPics.DragOver      += new DragEventHandler(TreeDragOver);
```

VB

```
AddHandler tvPics.DragOver, New DragEventHandler(AddressOf TreeDragOver)
```

Also, add this line of code in the same method.

C#

```
root.Tag = "Root Node";
```

VB

```
root.Tag = "Root Node"
```

You need to change one last thing. Change the code in the NodeSelect delegate to accommodate the new tag for the root node when showing pictures. This will blank out the PictureBox when a nonpicture node is selected. Here is the new delegate.

C#

```
private void NodeSelect(object sender, TreeViewEventArgs e)
{
  Debug.Assert(sender == tvPics,
            "Only the tvPics TreeView control can activate this delegate");

  if(e.Node.Tag != null && e.Node.Tag.ToString() == "Photo")
  {
    Photo p = (Photo)e.Node.Tag;
    pic.Image = p.Picture;
  }
  else
    pic.Image = null;
}
```

VB

```
Private Sub NodeSelect(ByVal sender As Object, ByVal e As TreeViewEventArgs)
  Debug.Assert(sender Is tvPics, _
              "Only the tvPics TreeView control can activate this delegate")

  If (Not e.Node.Tag Is Nothing) AndAlso e.Node.Tag.ToString() = "Photo" Then
     '     If Not e.Node.Tag Is Nothing Then
    Dim p As Photo = DirectCast(e.Node.Tag, Photo)
    pic.Image = p.Picture
  Else
    pic.Image = Nothing
  End If
End Sub
```

There is a very important point in this VB code. All you VB 6.0 programmers, *pay attention!*

You *must* use the AndAlso operator when comparing the tag here. In VB 6.0 the "and" operator does not mean the same thing as in C or C++, or C# or any other "C" family language. In VB 6.0 the whole line gets evaluated, even if the first logical test is not satisfied. In other languages, you are allowed to have an illegal test for the second half of the IF statement if the first half does not pass. This is because in other languages the evaluation of the IF statement is stopped when one of the tests is invalid. This technique is called "short-circuiting the expression" and programmers use it all the time.

Unfortunately, Microsoft decided to carry this quirk/bug/aggravation of VB 6.0 with them into VB .NET. In a nod to good programming, though, Microsoft did include the AndAlso operator, which acts like the "and" operator in C# and other languages.

Anyway, if you did not use the AndAlso operator here, your program would crash inexplicably and I would get all the blame.[5]

Highlighting Nodes

Before I move on to the next subject, I want to say one last thing about the TreeDragOver delegate. This is the one that highlights the node under the cursor while you are dragging a photo. There is a line in here that sets the focus to the TreeView control. If you comment this line out and run the program, you will still get highlighting, but it will be gray.

---

5. Actually, I welcome bug reports. If I did something wrong, please let me know.

In the SetupTree function I include a line of code to set the HideSelection property to false. It is this property that allows the gray selection of the node even without setting the focus to the node.

Try commenting this HideSelection code out, and also comment out the set focus line in the TreeDragOver function. Now when you drag an item over a node, you will not see any highlighting at all.

My point here is this: Leave the HideSelection code in there and cut out the set focus code. Adding the set focus code will definitely cause problems later when 6 months down the line you or someone else will write a delegate that hooks to the GotFocus event of your TreeView. All of a sudden, tons of code will run at the wrong time when you drag an object over your nodes. Forcing the tree to get focus in this code will fire the GotFocus event.

Although it is nice to see the node properly selected, it is not worth the headache of possible future bugs. Use the "HideSelection = false" method of highlighting instead.

Anchoring and Docking

Sounds the name of a store at the mall, doesn't it? "Anchoring and Docking Scandinavian Furniture." (Just kidding.)

In order to present the best form to your user, you will need to take into consideration the size and resolution of the host computer screen. The best way to do this is to make your form presentable at a resolution of 800×600 and then allow the user to size the form to the dimensions he or she wants. You do this via the anchoring capability of the .NET controls. I choose 800×600 because this is the minimum reasonable resolution you should expect the user to have.

Normally in VB 6.0, you resized controls on your form through the Resize event with lots of code, or you bought a resizer control. In my VB 6.0 days I went the latter route. I tried the resize code route, but it was very problematic and the code changed whenever I added or deleted a control. I just could not get the fine-tuning I wanted. Well, I am glad to see that Microsoft has included anchoring capability as well as docking capability with .NET.

Although these two properties of any .NET control are really nice, they really come into play when used with the Splitter control. You should be familiar with the Splitter, as you use it whenever you split a screen in Word, Excel, or even Outlook. The Splitter allows you to manually resize controls within a form. You can even use the Splitter to resize controls within other controls.

Open up a new project in .NET. Mine is called "AnchorDock." In this example I want to show you how to make a multipanel form whose contents are resized according to the size of the form and also according to a couple of Splitters inside the form. Because the form is intended to be resized, you should set a minimum size to the form. I set mine to 200×200. This keeps the user from making the form so small that the controls look funny.

Quite often you want to create a form that has multiple sections. This example has three sections. The first is at the bottom of the form. The second is the top-left part of the form, and the third is the top-right part of the form. Add the following controls in the following order:

1. Add a RichTextBox called **rcT** to the form. Set its docking style to Bottom.

2. Add a Splitter control above the RichTextBox. Set the Cursor property to Hsplit and set the docking style to Bottom. Change the color of the Splitter to something like Fuchsia.

3. Add a TreeView control above the Splitter and call it **T1**. Set the docking style to Left and the border style to FixedSingle.

4. Add a Splitter control to the right of the TreeView. Set the Cursor property to Vsplit and set the docking style to Left. Change the color of the Splitter to something like Fuchsia.

5. Add a Panel on the remaining part of the form. Set its docking style to Fill. Set the AutoScroll property to true.

6. Add a PictureBox called **Pic** to the top-left part of the panel. Its anchor properties should be Top and Left. Color the background something like Teal.

You should see something that looks like Figure 5-14.

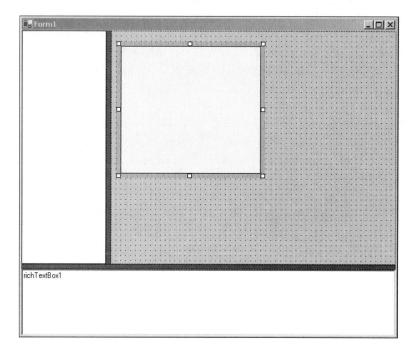

Figure 5-14. A tripanel display

Add the following delegate to the code.

C#

```csharp
private void DisplaySize(object sender, EventArgs e)
{
  rcT.AppendText("Picture Size = " + Pic.Size.ToString() + "\n");
  rcT.AppendText("Panel size = " + panel1.Size.ToString() + "\n\n");
}
```

VB

```vb
Private Sub DisplaySize(ByVal sender As Object, ByVal e As EventArgs)
  rcT.AppendText("Picture Size = " + Pic.Size.ToString() + "\n")
  rcT.AppendText("Panel size = " + panel1.Size.ToString() + "\n\n")
End Sub
```

This displays the size of the PictureBox and the Panel whenever a Resize event occurs. Which Resize event? Add the following code to the constructor.

C#

```csharp
public Form1()
{
  InitializeComponent();

  //Fill the tree view
  TreeNode node = new TreeNode("Base Inventory");
  node.Nodes.Add("Laptop 234");
  node.Nodes.Add("Desktop 831");
  node.Nodes.Add("68030 Emulator");
  node.Expand();
  T1.Nodes.Add(node);


  // uncomment this next line to make the aspect ratio of bitmap real
  //Pic.SizeMode = PictureBoxSizeMode.AutoSize;
  Pic.Size = panel1.Size;
  //Comment this next line of code out for correct aspect ratio
  Pic.SizeMode = PictureBoxSizeMode.StretchImage;
  Pic.Image = Image.FromFile("floorplan.bmp");

  this.Resize += new EventHandler(this.DisplaySize);
  foreach(Control c in this.Controls)
    c.Resize += new EventHandler(this.DisplaySize);
}
```

VB

```vb
Public Sub New()
  MyBase.New()

  InitializeComponent()

  'Fill the tree view
  Dim node As TreeNode = New TreeNode("Base Inventory")
  node.Nodes.Add("Laptop 234")
  node.Nodes.Add("Desktop 831")
  node.Nodes.Add("68030 Emulator")
  node.Expand()
  T1.Nodes.Add(node)
```

```
' uncomment this next line to make the aspect ratio of bitmap real
'Pic.SizeMode = PictureBoxSizeMode.AutoSize;
Pic.Size = panel1.Size
'Comment this next line of code out for correct aspect ratio
Pic.SizeMode = PictureBoxSizeMode.StretchImage
Pic.Image = Image.FromFile("floorplan.bmp")

'       me.Resize += new EventHandler(this.DisplaySize);
Dim c As Control
For Each c In Me.Controls
  AddHandler c.Resize, New EventHandler(AddressOf DisplaySize)
Next
End Sub
```

This code adds some nodes to the tree, sets up the PictureBox with a bitmap, and hooks the delegate you just added into the Resize event of all controls on the form.

Figure 5-15 shows the form running.

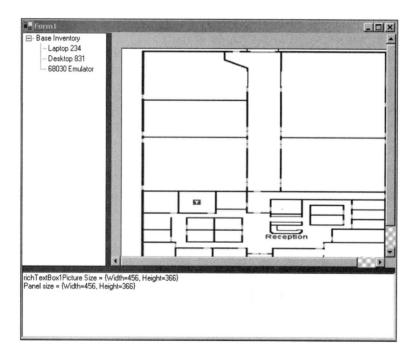

Figure 5-15. Running the tripanel form

This form represents a snapshot of an inventory control system. The inventory is shown in the TreeView, and the map showing the placement of each piece of the inventory is shown in the bitmap. The bottom text box serves as a running location of inventory as it is being moved about.

Normally, you would place other PictureBoxes with icons on the bitmap to show the placement. I leave that to you. Also, right now the bottom text box shows only the size of a few controls as you resize the form and move the Splitters.

This example demonstrates that it is not too hard to create a form that is flexible enough to comply with most screen resolutions and user preferences. This is very important in data entry programs and in most other Windows programs.

Summary

This has been quite a chapter. I covered two basic controls: the TreeView and the ListView. Used together in the right way, these controls can provide you with a powerful and graphical way to display and manipulate data.

Remember that the easier you make data entry, the more accepted your program will be by users. Data entry need not be just about text boxes and date fields. Drag-and-drop capability is also a form of data entry, and a powerful one at that.

This chapter introduced you to the object-oriented way to program a user interface. The examples presented use collections and objects that contain other objects. The code in this chapter is as independent of the objects it acted on as I could make it. Yours should be too.

The next chapter covers data and data sources in depth.

CHAPTER 6

Advanced Data Entry

IN CHAPTER 5 you looked at data entry programs from a GUI point of view. You already knew the basics of text and simple form-based data entry screens. Chapter 5 expanded on this knowledge by introducing some more advanced data entry screens.

This chapter aims to do the same sort of thing with the data itself. So far you have seen raw data in the form of user-entered text or a file on the hard drive. You should not be complacent in thinking that that all data is either from a database or a keyboard, however. There are other kinds of data you should be aware of. Identifying and handling different forms of data is what this chapter is all about.

The Database

So, where does data come from? Like most people, I know where babies come from, and I even know some of the biology involved. I am not an obstetrician, however. Well, as with babies, I know some things about databases such as how to connect to them, extract data from them, and save data to them. I even know a few things about how databases work. I am not an ODBC expert, however.

When most people think of data entry programs, they think of databases. The usual question then becomes, "Is it Oracle or SQL?" Most of the tragically uninformed also have very strong opinions on which database is best or fastest. You know the kind of people I'm talking about.

To me, a database is somewhere to store data to and retrieve data from. I can set up a pretty good structure and I can write some SQL code, but I leave performance to the experts. As far as experts go, there are many books on the subject, the better of which come from Apress, the publisher of this book.

Because the database is tied so closely to the data entry program, I thought it wise to take you through how to use the database in your data entry program. In-depth coverage of all the nuances of ADO.NET is beyond the scope of this book, but I think you will get a good feeling of how it is done from this chapter.

ADO.NET Background

ADO.NET consists of basically four layers:

- *Connection object:* This object connects to a data source.

- *Command object:* This object executes commands (usually SQL) on the data source.

- *DataReader object:* This object provides a high-speed, forward read-only access to your data.

- *DataAdapter object:* This object populates a DataSet and also allows you to update a data source.

The Connection object connects with the data source in two ways. The first is a highly optimized provider called the SQL Server .NET Data Provider. The second is a more general provider called the OLE DB .NET Data Provider.

The general OLE DB provider will work with just about any modern database out there. If you were to use Oracle or some other powerful database, you would get a specialized provider just for that.

 NOTE There are more than a few wizards and such to help you set up database access in .NET. In this chapter, however, I stick to doing it from code only. If you want to see these wizards and data controls at work, I suggest you look through the online help files.

Here is how you set up the Connection object.

C#

```
string Provider = "Provider=Microsoft.Jet.OLEDB.4.0;Data Source=MyDB.MDB";
OleDbConnection myConn = new OleDbConnection(Provider);
```

VB

```
Dim Provider As String
Provider = "Provider=Microsoft.Jet.OLEDB.4.0;Data Source=MyDB.MDB"
Dim myConn As OleDbConnection = New OleDbConnection(Provider)
```

This code sets up a connection to a Microsoft Access database using the Jet database engine. Until recently, Access was the database provided by Microsoft in its Office package. Access is commonly used and actually does very well for most applications.

So, after the connection comes the command. You need to add the following to your code to set up the Command object and have it execute.

C#

```csharp
string strSQL = "SELECT * FROM autoparts" ;
OleDbCommand myCmd = new OleDbCommand( strSQL, myConn );
OleDbDataReader datareader = null;
myConn.Open();
datareader = myCmd.ExecuteReader();
```

VB

```vb
Dim myConn As OleDbConnection = New OleDbConnection(Provider)
Dim myCmd As OleDbCommand = New OleDbCommand(strSQL, myConn)
Dim datareader As OleDbDataReader = Nothing
myConn.Open()
datareader = myCmd.ExecuteReader()
```

You can see from this code snippet that I am associating a SQL statement with the Connection object. I then create a DataReader object, open the connection, and invoke the Command object. There is one object left in this list: the DataSet object. I cover that object in detail shortly. For now, you will generate a small example to populate a ListBox that uses the code I just showed you.

This example is compact and very speedy. It uses the forward read-only DataReader to get data from the database and then put it in the table. It is enough to get you going if you are new to ADO.NET.

Start a new project in VB or C#. Mine is called "DB_data." You will need to download this book's code from the Downloads section of the Apress Web site (http://www.apress.com) to get the database.

Add a ListBox to your form and make the form start in the center of the screen. Listings 6-1a and 6-2b show the code for the form's load event for this project. Before that, however, you need to add some namespaces.

C#

```csharp
using System;
using System.Diagnostics;
using System.Drawing;
using System.Collections;
using System.ComponentModel;
using System.Windows.Forms;
using System.Data;
using System.Data.OleDb;
```

VB

```
Imports System
Imports System.Diagnostics
Imports System.Drawing
Imports System.Collections
Imports System.ComponentModel
Imports System.Windows.Forms
Imports System.Data
Imports System.Data.OleDb
```

There is no initialization of variables or controls, so let's jump straight to the form's load event in Listings 6-1a and 6-1b.

Listing 6-1a. C# Code for the Form's Load Event

```csharp
private void Form1_Load(object sender, System.EventArgs e)
{
    string Provider = "Provider=Microsoft.Jet.OLEDB.4.0;Data Source=MyDB.MDB";
    // create Objects of ADOConnection and ADOCommand
    OleDbConnection myConn = new OleDbConnection(Provider);
    string strSQL = "SELECT * FROM autoparts" ;
    OleDbCommand myCmd = new OleDbCommand( strSQL, myConn );
    OleDbDataReader datareader = null;
    try
    {
      myConn.Open();
      datareader = myCmd.ExecuteReader();
      while (datareader.Read() )
      {
        lstParts.Items.Add(datareader["au_PartName"]);
      }
    }
    catch (Exception ex)
    {
      MessageBox.Show("Database Error: {0}", ex.Message);
    }
    finally
    {
      myConn.Close();
    }
}
```

Listing 6-1b. VB Code for the Form's Load Event

```
Private Sub Form1_Load(ByVal sender As System.Object, _
                       ByVal e As System.EventArgs) Handles MyBase.Load
   Dim Provider As String

   Provider = "Provider=Microsoft.Jet.OLEDB.4.0;Data Source=MyDB.MDB"
   Dim strSQL As String = "SELECT * FROM autoparts"
   ' create Objects of ADOConnection and ADOCommand
   Dim myConn As OleDbConnection = New OleDbConnection(Provider)
   Dim myCmd As OleDbCommand = New OleDbCommand(strSQL, myConn)
   Dim datareader As OleDbDataReader = Nothing

   Try
     myConn.Open()
     datareader = myCmd.ExecuteReader()
     While datareader.Read()
       lstParts.Items.Add(datareader("au_PartName"))
     End While
   Catch ex As Exception
     MessageBox.Show("Database Error: {0}", ex.Message)
   Finally
     myConn.Close()
   End Try
End Sub
```

You open and read the database inside a Try-Catch block. You should always do any data access from within an error-handling block.

Notice that the read loop does not test for end-of-file and it also does not increment the database cursor. This is a big change from ADO, where you had to increment the cursor within the loop. I can't tell you how many times over the years I forgot to increment the cursor and got stuck in an endless loop. Figure 6-1 shows the result of this example.

Figure 6-1. The result of the database example

Using the DataGrid Control

So, is this the best way to get data from a database? For some cases, maybe it is. However, there is a DataGrid control that allows you to connect it as a direct view into the database table. You would use this control for smaller monolithic programs for direct manipulation of your database.

The DataGrid control is very powerful indeed. In fact, it is not too hard to write a program that uses the DataGrid control as a complete front-end for any number of databases. You could write your own Microsoft SQL Server database GUI. In this chapter, I do not go this far, though. What I will do is show you the basics, and if you want to take it further you can consult the online help.

The DataGrid control is a control that lets you look into a database via a DataSet. You can think of a DataSet as a collection of DataTables. These DataTables represent the tables in your database.

When most people think of the DataGrid, they think only of databases. This control is much more powerful than that, though. It can also view data from XML files. In addition, you can fill it with data from any other source you can think of. All you need to do is create a table, get your data from someplace, and create new rows from this data. Once you put the table in a DataSet, you set the DataSource property of the grid to this DataSet and you are done—instant GUI.

So what else can a basic DataGrid control do? How about this:

- It can read data from just about any database.

- It can update, insert, and delete data in the database.

- It can provide drill-down capabilities to view hierarchical tables.

- It can provide validation capabilities for data and for referential integrity.

It would not be hard to write a small book just on the DataGrid control and its capabilities.

I would like to extend the previous example a little by replacing the ListBox with the DataGrid control. I will also add another table to the MyDB.mdb Access database. If you download the code for this example from the Downloads section of the Apress Web site (http://www.apress.com), you will also get the new database file.

Start a new project in VB or C#. Mine is called "DB_Grid."

1. Add a DataGrid control called **dg1**.

2. Add a Button called **cmdParts** to the form. Change its text to read **Parts**.

3. Add a Button called **cmdInventory** to the form. Change its text to read **Inventory**.

4. Add a Button called **cmdBoth** to the form. Change its text to read **Both**.

5. Add a Button called **cmdCommit** to the form. Change its text to read **Commit**.

Your form should look like the one shown in Figure 6-2.

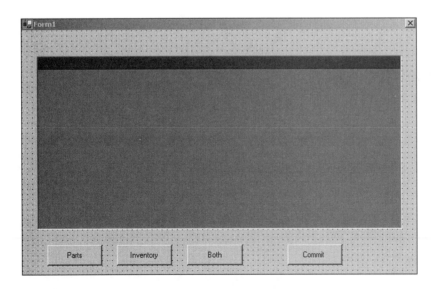

Figure 6-2. The DataGrid form setup

One of the neat things about ADO.NET is the *disconnected recordset*. What this means is that you can get data from a source, put it into the DataSet, and then disconnect the DataSet from the source. This allows you to have a nonpersistent connection to a database. Where is this handy? How about in client/server applications? You can do hit-and-run data gathering from different sources without keeping the TCP/IP connection open. How about ASP.NET? You can get data from a Web site, and if the connection goes down, you can still work with the data at hand. I think this is really cool.

I show you in the code for this example how to use a disconnected recordset. I then change the program slightly so you can change data in the database. This requires a persistent DataSet connection.

First, add some namespaces so you can get all the correct classes and methods without having to use fully qualified names.

C#

```
using System;
using System.Drawing;
using System.Collections;
using System.ComponentModel;
using System.Windows.Forms;
using System.Data;
using System.Data.SqlClient;
using System.Data.OleDb;
```

VB

```
Imports System
Imports System.Drawing
Imports System.Collections
Imports System.ComponentModel
Imports System.Windows.Forms
Imports System.Data
Imports System.Data.SqlClient
Imports System.Data.OleDb
```

Now add the class variables.

C#

```
#region class local variables

string Provider = "Provider=Microsoft.Jet.OLEDB.4.0;Data Source=MyDB.MDB";
OleDbConnection MyDB_Conn;
OleDbDataAdapter SQL_parts;
OleDbDataAdapter SQL_inv;
OleDbCommandBuilder OLE_Parts;
OleDbCommandBuilder OLE_Inv;

#endregion
```

VB

```
#Region "class local variables"

  Dim Provider As String = _
                "Provider=Microsoft.Jet.OLEDB.4.0;Data Source=MyDB.MDB"
  Dim MyDB_Conn As OleDbConnection
  Dim SQL_parts As OleDbDataAdapter
  Dim SQL_inv As OleDbDataAdapter
  Dim OLE_Parts As OleDbCommandBuilder
  Dim OLE_Inv As OleDbCommandBuilder

#End Region
```

What I have here is a connection to the database, a couple of adapters that connect directly to tables in the database, a couple of SQL command builders, and a connection string. You can see from the connection string that the database is an Access database and that I use the Jet database engine to connect.

I could easily change this to a SQL server database by using a SQLDataAdapter object and changing the provider string to

```
string Provider =
  " Data Source=localhost;Integrated
    Security=SSPI;Initial Catalog=MyDB";
```

I would also need to change the OleDbConnection to SQLDbConnection and the OleDbCommandBuilder to SQLDbCommandBuilder.

If you are starting to think about this, you will see that you could build a database connection class that takes data from any database based upon an enumeration. This enumeration would include values such as DB_ORACLE, DB_MSACCESS, and DB_SQL.[1]

Next, add the following delegates that correspond to the buttons.

C#

```
#region events

private void ViewParts(object sender, EventArgs e)
{
  dg1.SetDataBinding(dg1.DataSource, "AutoParts");
}

private void ViewInventory(object sender, EventArgs e)
{
  dg1.SetDataBinding(dg1.DataSource, "Inventory");
}

private void ViewBoth(object sender, EventArgs e)
{
  //Setting this to a null string forces the top
  //level view.
  dg1.SetDataBinding(dg1.DataSource, "");
  dg1.Expand(-1);
}

private void CommitChanges(object sender, EventArgs e)
{

}

#endregion
```

VB

```
#Region "events"

  Private Sub ViewParts(ByVal sender As Object, ByVal e As EventArgs)
    dg1.SetDataBinding(dg1.DataSource, "AutoParts")
  End Sub
```

---

1. In fact, this is routine and should be done to abstract the data from the source.

```
Private Sub ViewInventory(ByVal sender As Object, ByVal e As EventArgs)
  dg1.SetDataBinding(dg1.DataSource, "Inventory")
End Sub

Private Sub ViewBoth(ByVal sender As Object, ByVal e As EventArgs)
  'Setting this to a null string forces the top
  'level view.
  dg1.SetDataBinding(dg1.DataSource, "")
  dg1.Expand(-1)
End Sub

Private Sub CommitChanges(ByVal sender As Object, ByVal e As EventArgs)

End Sub

#End Region
```

These methods may seem a bit confusing right now, but basically they swap out the table that is currently being displayed. I left the CommitChanges method blank for now. You will fill it in later.

The last piece of code to add is the initialization code in the constructor. Here it is.

 NOTE I intentionally left out any Try-Catch blocks to make the code easier to read. In a real program, you would need to add exception handling to any database manipulation code.

C#

```
public Form1()
{
  InitializeComponent();

  cmdParts.Click      += new EventHandler(this.ViewParts);
  cmdInventory.Click  += new EventHandler(this.ViewInventory);
  cmdBoth.Click       += new EventHandler(this.ViewBoth);
  cmdCommit.Click     += new EventHandler(this.CommitChanges);
  cmdCommit.Enabled = false;
```

```
//First thing to do is establish the connection
MyDB_Conn = new OleDbConnection(Provider);

//Now create some SQL statements that get data from different tables
SQL_parts = new OleDbDataAdapter( "SELECT * FROM AutoParts", MyDB_Conn );
SQL_parts.SelectCommand =
            new OleDbCommand("SELECT * FROM AutoParts", MyDB_Conn );
OLE_Parts = new OleDbCommandBuilder(SQL_parts);

SQL_inv   = new OleDbDataAdapter( "SELECT * FROM Inventory", MyDB_Conn );
SQL_inv.SelectCommand =
            new OleDbCommand("SELECT * FROM Inventory", MyDB_Conn );
OLE_Inv   = new OleDbCommandBuilder(SQL_inv);

//You now have your SQL statements that get all data from both
//tables in the database.  Create a data set and add 2 tables
DataSet DS = new DataSet();
DataTable Parts   = new DataTable("AutoParts");
DataTable Inv     = new DataTable("Inventory");
DS.Tables.Add(Parts);
DS.Tables.Add(Inv);

MyDB_Conn.Open();

//Use the SQL data adapters to fill the tables via the SQL statements
SQL_parts.Fill(DS, "AutoParts");
SQL_inv.Fill(DS, "Inventory");

//Normally I would put this at the end.  I put it here
//to prove a point... The data set is disconnected and you
//can still work with it after the connection is gone.
//If you need to update the database you will need to keep
//this connection.
MyDB_Conn.Close();
MyDB_Conn.Dispose();

//Once I have the data tables filled in the data set I can manipulate the
//existing columns.
Parts.Columns[0].Caption    = "ID";
Parts.Columns[0].ColumnName = "ID";
Parts.Columns[1].Caption    = "Name";
Parts.Columns[1].ColumnName = "Name";
Parts.Columns[2].Caption    = "Vehicle ID";
Parts.Columns[2].ColumnName = "Vehicle ID";
```

```
      Parts.Columns[3].Caption     = "Notes";
      Parts.Columns[3].ColumnName = "Notes";
      //Make the last 2 columns invisible
      Parts.Columns[4].ColumnMapping = MappingType.Hidden;
      Parts.Columns[5].ColumnMapping = MappingType.Hidden;

      Inv.Columns[0].Caption     = "Part Num";
      Inv.Columns[0].ColumnName  = "Part Num";
      Inv.Columns[1].Caption     = "Current Count";
      Inv.Columns[1].ColumnName  = "Current Count";
      Inv.Columns[2].Caption     = "Reorder Count";
      Inv.Columns[2].ColumnName  = "Reorder Count";

      //Bind the table in the data source to the grid display
      dg1.SetDataBinding(DS, "AutoParts");

      //This object takes up space.  Get rid of it.
      DS.Dispose();
   }
```

VB

```
  Public Sub New()
    MyBase.New()

    InitializeComponent()

    AddHandler cmdParts.Click, New EventHandler(AddressOf ViewParts)
    AddHandler cmdInventory.Click, New EventHandler(AddressOf ViewInventory)
    AddHandler cmdBoth.Click, New EventHandler(AddressOf ViewBoth)
    AddHandler cmdCommit.Click, New EventHandler(AddressOf CommitChanges)
    cmdCommit.Enabled = False

    'First thing to do is establish the connection
    MyDB_Conn = New OleDbConnection(Provider)

    'Now create some SQL statements that get data from different tables
    SQL_parts = New OleDbDataAdapter("SELECT * FROM AutoParts", MyDB_Conn)
    SQL_parts.SelectCommand = _
            New OleDbCommand("SELECT * FROM AutoParts", MyDB_Conn)
    OLE_Parts = New OleDbCommandBuilder(SQL_parts)
```

```
SQL_inv = New OleDbDataAdapter("SELECT * FROM Inventory", MyDB_Conn)
SQL_inv.SelectCommand = _
        New OleDbCommand("SELECT * FROM Inventory", MyDB_Conn)
OLE_Inv = New OleDbCommandBuilder(SQL_inv)

'You now have your SQL statements that get all data from both
'tables in the database.  Create a data set and add 2 tables
Dim DS As DataSet = New DataSet()
Dim Parts As DataTable = New DataTable("AutoParts")
Dim Inv As DataTable = New DataTable("Inventory")
DS.Tables.Add(Parts)
DS.Tables.Add(Inv)

MyDB_Conn.Open()

'Use the SQL data adapters to fill the tables via the SQL statements
SQL_parts.Fill(DS, "AutoParts")
SQL_inv.Fill(DS, "Inventory")

'Normally I would put this at the end.  I put it here
'to prove a point... The data set is disconnected and you
'can still work with it after the connection is gone.
'If you need to update the database you will need to keep
'this connection.
MyDB_Conn.Close()
MyDB_Conn.Dispose()

'Once I have the data tables filled in the data set I can manipulate the
'existing columns.
Parts.Columns(0).Caption = "ID"
Parts.Columns(0).ColumnName = "ID"
Parts.Columns(1).Caption = "Name"
Parts.Columns(1).ColumnName = "Name"
Parts.Columns(2).Caption = "Vehicle ID"
Parts.Columns(2).ColumnName = "Vehicle ID"
Parts.Columns(3).Caption = "Notes"
Parts.Columns(3).ColumnName = "Notes"
'Make the last 2 columns invisible
Parts.Columns(4).ColumnMapping = MappingType.Hidden
Parts.Columns(5).ColumnMapping = MappingType.Hidden
```

```
    Inv.Columns(0).Caption = "Part Num"
    Inv.Columns(0).ColumnName = "Part Num"
    Inv.Columns(1).Caption = "Current Count"
    Inv.Columns(1).ColumnName = "Current Count"
    Inv.Columns(2).Caption = "Reorder Count"
    Inv.Columns(2).ColumnName = "Reorder Count"


    'Bind the table in the data source to the grid display
    dg1.SetDataBinding(DS, "AutoParts")

    'This object takes up space.  Get rid of it.
    DS.Dispose()
End Sub
```

This code does a lot of things. Let's dissect it. Get out the scalpel and hemostat.

After some initialization of the buttons, I connect to the database, prepare the data adapters, and set some SQL commands. Here's the C# code:

```
//First thing to do is establish the connection
MyDB_Conn = new OleDbConnection(Provider);

//Now create some SQL statements that get data from different tables
SQL_parts = new OleDbDataAdapter( "SELECT * FROM AutoParts", MyDB_Conn );
SQL_parts.SelectCommand =
            new OleDbCommand("SELECT * FROM AutoParts", MyDB_Conn );
OLE_Parts = new OleDbCommandBuilder(SQL_parts);

SQL_inv   = new OleDbDataAdapter( "SELECT * FROM Inventory", MyDB_Conn );
SQL_inv.SelectCommand =
            new OleDbCommand("SELECT * FROM Inventory", MyDB_Conn );
OLE_Inv   = new OleDbCommandBuilder(SQL_inv);
```

You can see from this code that I have the simplest of SQL commands: Get everything from a particular table. There are two tacks you can take here. One is to get all information and selectively show it. The other is to get only the information you want to show by using more selective SQL statements. I take the first approach here in order to show how to hide data in the DataGrid.

Be aware that when you get all data from a table, the process will be slower and take more memory than a selective data retrieval. If you need to show pieces of data based on changing criteria (such as login rights or data filtering), however, you would be better off getting all the data and hiding what is not necessary. Like everything, though, you may have to adjust your data-gathering scheme if you are working with really huge databases.

I go into detail regarding the CommandBuilder object in a bit. So, here I have a connection to the database and data adapters for individual tables in the database. Next, I create the tables, add them to the database, get the data, and end the connection. Here is the C# code:

```
//You now have your SQL statements that get all data from both
//tables in the database.  Create a data set and add 2 tables
DataSet DS = new DataSet();
DataTable Parts    = new DataTable("AutoParts");
DataTable Inv      = new DataTable("Inventory");
DS.Tables.Add(Parts);
DS.Tables.Add(Inv);

MyDB_Conn.Open();

//Use the SQL data adapters to fill the tables via the SQL statements
SQL_parts.Fill(DS, "AutoParts");
SQL_inv.Fill(DS, "Inventory");

//Normally I would put this at the end.  I put it here
//to prove a point... The data set is disconnected and you
//can still work with it after the connection is gone.
//If you need to update the database you will need to keep
//this connection.
MyDB_Conn.Close();
MyDB_Conn.Dispose();
```

I have a parts table and an inventory table whose contents I bring into DataTables. I then add the DataTables to the DataSet collection.

After I open the connection to the database, I fill the tables using the SQL statements in the respective data adapters. I then kill the connection. The rest of the code in the constructor simply changes some column names and sets the table that is displayed first. The fact that I can manipulate and show the DataSet proves after killing the connection to the database that this is indeed a disconnected DataSet.

You are starting to work with objects now that take up appreciable amounts of memory. Although it is good practice to dispose of unused objects, it is especially important to get rid of memory hogs if they are not needed. Change the Dispose method of your form to reflect what I have here.

C#

```csharp
protected override void Dispose( bool disposing )
{
  if( disposing )
  {
    if (components != null)
    {
      components.Dispose();
    }
    if(MyDB_Conn != null)
    {
      MyDB_Conn.Close();
      MyDB_Conn.Dispose();
    }
    if(SQL_inv != null)
      SQL_inv.Dispose();
    if(SQL_parts != null)
      SQL_parts.Dispose();
  }
  base.Dispose( disposing );
}
```

VB

```vb
Protected Overloads Overrides Sub Dispose(ByVal disposing As Boolean)
  If disposing Then
    If Not (components Is Nothing) Then
      components.Dispose()
    End If
    If Not MyDB_Conn Is Nothing Then
      MyDB_Conn.Close()
      MyDB_Conn.Dispose()
    End If
    If Not SQL_inv Is Nothing Then
      SQL_inv.Dispose()
    End If
    If Not SQL_parts Is Nothing Then
      SQL_parts.Dispose()
    End If
  End If
  MyBase.Dispose(disposing)
End Sub
```

Compile and run your program. Figure 6-3 shows the form after the Parts button is clicked.

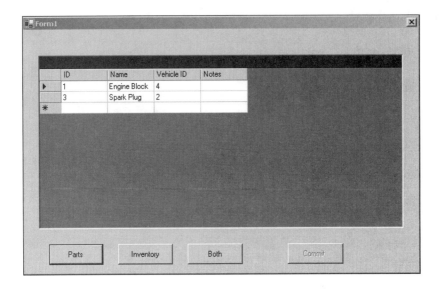

Figure 6-3. The Parts table

The column headers are not the actual field names in the table because I changed them in the code.

Figure 6-4 shows the form after the Inventory button is clicked.

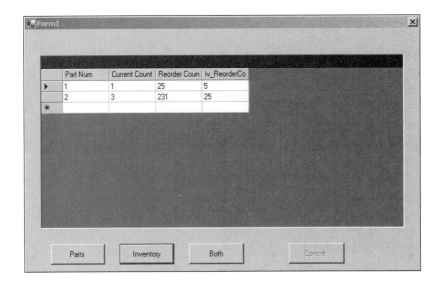

Figure 6-4. The Inventory table

You can see that I did not change the last field column here. The column header shows the actual field name in the table.

Figure 6-5 shows the form when the Both button is clicked.

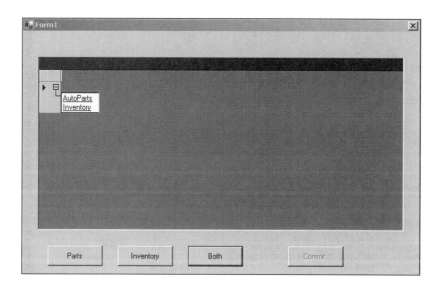

Figure 6-5. Both tables shown

If you click the hyperlink you will drill down into the individual tables. When you do this you will also be able to come back to this screen by using the navigation icon on the DataGrid.

OK. That was pretty cool and not too complicated. Of course, this is the DataGrid at its simplest. In a real auto parts application, I may have several more tables that provide links into other tables. I could then use these links to make parent/child references in the DataGrid control for drill-down capability.

So what about the grayed-out Commit button? In the constructor I killed the connection after getting the data to prove that the DataSet was really disconnected. I am now going to ask you to reverse that code and add some more code to the Commit button delegate to enable updating of the data. Here is the corrected constructor.

C#

```csharp
public Form1()
{
  InitializeComponent();

  cmdParts.Click      += new EventHandler(this.ViewParts);
  cmdInventory.Click  += new EventHandler(this.ViewInventory);
  cmdBoth.Click       += new EventHandler(this.ViewBoth);
  cmdCommit.Click     += new EventHandler(this.CommitChanges);
//    cmdCommit.Enabled = false;

  //First thing to do is establish the connection
  MyDB_Conn = new OleDbConnection(Provider);

  //Now create some SQL statements that get data from different tables
  SQL_parts = new OleDbDataAdapter( "SELECT * FROM AutoParts", MyDB_Conn );
  SQL_parts.SelectCommand =
            new OleDbCommand("SELECT * FROM AutoParts", MyDB_Conn );
  OLE_Parts = new OleDbCommandBuilder(SQL_parts);

  SQL_inv   = new OleDbDataAdapter( "SELECT * FROM Inventory", MyDB_Conn );
  SQL_inv.SelectCommand =
            new OleDbCommand("SELECT * FROM Inventory", MyDB_Conn );
  OLE_Inv   = new OleDbCommandBuilder(SQL_inv);

  //You now have your SQL statements that get all data from both
  //tables in the database.  Create a data set and add 2 tables
  DataSet DS = new DataSet();
  DataTable Parts   = new DataTable("AutoParts");
  DataTable Inv     = new DataTable("Inventory");
  DS.Tables.Add(Parts);
  DS.Tables.Add(Inv);

  MyDB_Conn.Open();

  //Use the SQL data adapters to fill the tables via the SQL statements
  SQL_parts.Fill(DS, "AutoParts");
  SQL_inv.Fill(DS, "Inventory");
```

```
//        //Normally I would put this at the end.  I put it here
//        //to prove a point... The data set is disconnected and you
//        //can still work with it after the connection is gone.
//        //If you need to update the database you will need to keep
//        //this connection.
//      MyDB_Conn.Close();
//      MyDB_Conn.Dispose();


        //Once I have the data tables filled in the data set I can manipulate the
        //existing columns.
        Parts.Columns[0].Caption    = "ID";
        Parts.Columns[0].ColumnName = "ID";
        Parts.Columns[1].Caption    = "Name";
        Parts.Columns[1].ColumnName = "Name";
        Parts.Columns[2].Caption    = "Vehicle ID";
        Parts.Columns[2].ColumnName = "Vehicle ID";
        Parts.Columns[3].Caption    = "Notes";
        Parts.Columns[3].ColumnName = "Notes";
        //Make the last 2 columns invisible
        Parts.Columns[4].ColumnMapping = MappingType.Hidden;
        Parts.Columns[5].ColumnMapping = MappingType.Hidden;


//      Inv.Columns[0].Caption      = "Part Num";
//      Inv.Columns[0].ColumnName   = "Part Num";
//      Inv.Columns[1].Caption      = "Current Count";
//      Inv.Columns[1].ColumnName   = "Current Count";
//      Inv.Columns[2].Caption      = "Reorder Count";
//      Inv.Columns[2].ColumnName   = "Reorder Count";


        //Bind the table in the data source to the grid display
        dg1.SetDataBinding(DS, "AutoParts");

        //This object takes up space.  Get rid of them.
        DS.Dispose();
    }
```

VB

```vb
Public Sub New()
  MyBase.New()

  InitializeComponent()

  AddHandler cmdParts.Click, New EventHandler(AddressOf ViewParts)
  AddHandler cmdInventory.Click, New EventHandler(AddressOf ViewInventory)
  AddHandler cmdBoth.Click, New EventHandler(AddressOf ViewBoth)
  AddHandler cmdCommit.Click, New EventHandler(AddressOf CommitChanges)
  'cmdCommit.Enabled = False

  'First thing to do is establish the connection
  MyDB_Conn = New OleDbConnection(Provider)

  'Now create some SQL statements that get data from different tables
  SQL_parts = New OleDbDataAdapter("SELECT * FROM AutoParts", MyDB_Conn)
  SQL_parts.SelectCommand = _
            New OleDbCommand("SELECT * FROM AutoParts", MyDB_Conn)
  OLE_Parts = New OleDbCommandBuilder(SQL_parts)

  SQL_inv = New OleDbDataAdapter("SELECT * FROM Inventory", MyDB_Conn)
  SQL_inv.SelectCommand = _
            New OleDbCommand("SELECT * FROM Inventory", MyDB_Conn)
  OLE_Inv = New OleDbCommandBuilder(SQL_inv)

  'You now have your SQL statements that get all data from both
  'tables in the database.  Create a data set and add 2 tables
  Dim DS As DataSet = New DataSet()
  Dim Parts As DataTable = New DataTable("AutoParts")
  Dim Inv As DataTable = New DataTable("Inventory")
  DS.Tables.Add(Parts)
  DS.Tables.Add(Inv)

  MyDB_Conn.Open()

  'Use the SQL data adapters to fill the tables via the SQL statements
  SQL_parts.Fill(DS, "AutoParts")
  SQL_inv.Fill(DS, "Inventory")
```

```
''Normally I would put this at the end.  I put it here
''to prove a point... The data set is disconnected and you
''can still work with it after the connection is gone.
''If you need to update the database you will need to keep
''this connection.
'MyDB_Conn.Close()
'MyDB_Conn.Dispose()

'Once I have the data tables filled in the data set I can manipulate the
'existing columns.
Parts.Columns(0).Caption = "ID"
Parts.Columns(0).ColumnName = "ID"
Parts.Columns(1).Caption = "Name"
Parts.Columns(1).ColumnName = "Name"
Parts.Columns(2).Caption = "Vehicle ID"
Parts.Columns(2).ColumnName = "Vehicle ID"
Parts.Columns(3).Caption = "Notes"
Parts.Columns(3).ColumnName = "Notes"
'Make the last 2 columns invisible
Parts.Columns(4).ColumnMapping = MappingType.Hidden
Parts.Columns(5).ColumnMapping = MappingType.Hidden

'Inv.Columns(0).Caption = "Part Num"
'Inv.Columns(0).ColumnName = "Part Num"
'Inv.Columns(1).Caption = "Current Count"
'Inv.Columns(1).ColumnName = "Current Count"
'Inv.Columns(2).Caption = "Reorder Count"
'Inv.Columns(2).ColumnName = "Reorder Count"

'Bind the table in the data source to the grid display
dg1.SetDataBinding(DS, "AutoParts")

'This object takes up space.  Get rid of them.
DS.Dispose()
End Sub
```

Add the following code to your Commit delegate.

C#

```csharp
private void CommitChanges(object sender, EventArgs e)
{
  DataSet DS = (DataSet)dg1.DataSource;
  DataSet DS_Change = DS.GetChanges(DataRowState.Modified);
  //If no changes then obviously no new data set is formed
  if(DS_Change != null)
  {
    if(!DS_Change.HasErrors)
    {
      //get the data adapter and call update
      try
      {
        SQL_inv.Update(DS_Change, "Inventory");
        MessageBox.Show("Saving Inventory data successful!");
      }
      catch (Exception ex)
      {
        MessageBox.Show("Error Saving Inventory data\n{0}", ex.Message);
      }
    }
  }
}
```

VB

```vb
Private Sub CommitChanges(ByVal sender As Object, ByVal e As EventArgs)
  Dim DS As DataSet = CType(dg1.DataSource, DataSet)
  Dim DS_Change As DataSet = DS.GetChanges(DataRowState.Modified)
  If Not DS_Change Is Nothing Then
    If Not DS_Change.HasErrors Then
      'get the data adapter and call update
      Try
        SQL_inv.Update(DS_Change, "Inventory")
        MessageBox.Show("Saving Inventory data successful!")
      Catch ex As Exception
        MessageBox.Show("Error Saving Inventory data\n{0}", ex.Message)
      End Try
    End If
  End If
End Sub
```

In the constructor I commented out the code that changes the column headers for the Inventory table. If you look at the new delegate code, you will see that I tell the data adapter to update the table with the new modified DataSet. There are no explicit SQL statements in here that do this.

The data adapter has the ability to generate common SQL statements for you, such as Update and Insert, based upon the table you are accessing. This is really cool and convenient. Some requirements need to be met first, though:

- The table you are updating must have a unique primary key. An autoincrement key is best.

- The column names must match the field names in the table you are updating.

Now these restrictions are not too bad, as quite a few DataGrid applications would have tables with primary keys and it may be OK to display the raw field name. However, what do you do in the case where you want to update a free-form table and your grid is nicely formatted with user-friendly names and such? What then?

Providing Your Own SQL Commands

You see in this example that the OleDbDataAdapter (and any data adapter) can automatically generate its own SQL commands for deleting, updating, and inserting data. If you are not willing to live with the restrictions, then you must provide your own SQL commands to perform these tasks. Table 6-1 shows the properties you must set in order for the Update method to work when you do not use the OleDbCommandBuilder.

Table 6-1. OleDbDataAdapter SQL Commands

OleDbAdapter Property	How to Use
DeleteCommand	Provide a SQL command to delete records from a table.
UpdateCommand	Provide a SQL command to update records in a table.
InsertCommand	Provide a SQL command to insert records in a table.
SelectCommand	Provide a SQL command to get records form a table.

When you get a changed DataSet from the DataSet.GetChanges method and then call the OleDbDataAdapter.Update command, the appropriate Delete, Update, and Insert commands will be used to reconcile these changes with the actual table.

To me this seems a logical, step-by-step approach to working with databases. It is much more fun than the old ADO I used in VB 6.0.

Please note that in this example I allowed for updates only to the inventory table. I provided an OleDbCommandBuilder object for the parts table but never called the Update method. It seemed, though, to the user, that this table could be updated and changes saved. This is because I did not include any data or field restriction code. As I said before, this DataGrid can be a complicated beast when used to its fullest extent. The next section covers some of the data validation and data restriction capabilities of the DataGrid.

DataGrid Validation

All the examples I see for grids and so forth appear to be single purpose. That is, they lead you through some specific example, and if your needs are a little different, you seem to be left hanging.

The next example makes use of the grid in a slightly different way. Not all your data comes directly from a database. In fact, ADO.NET allows you to fill in tables of data manually. This means that your data can come from any source or from multiple sources.

The best way to get data in anything other than a simple application is to abstract the data from the application. This means that your application does not know where the data comes from and does not care. This allows you to change the data source with no changes in the code that manages the data. This is a good thing, and it is what you should work toward.

As far as the DataGrid goes, it offers you the ability to edit fields, accept changes, roll back changes, restrict data types, and provide validation events. I have not shown you much of the validation end, but this example will take care of that. Here is what you will see in this example:

- A public class that contains information about a particular town

- A static class that returns town objects on demand

- Abstraction of data gathering and updating from data management

- DataTable restriction code

- A DataGrid event handler to detect a cell click

- A DataTable event handler to validate new data

- An error object in a DataGrid control

Start a new project in C# or VB. Mine is called "GridRestrict." Add a single DataGrid control to the form and call it **dg1**. Figure 6-6 shows you the layout.

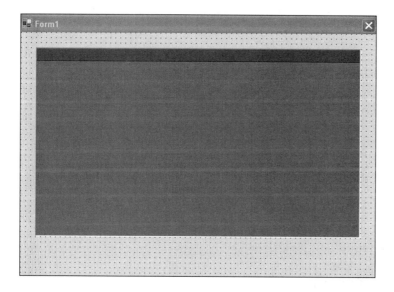

Figure 6-6. The grid restriction example layout

That was not too complicated, was it? Here is where the tricky bit comes in:

1. Add a class called **Towns** to the project.

2. Add a class called **Town** to the project.

3. In the C# project, add a reference to the Microsoft Visual Basic .NET runtime.

The Town class holds information about a particular town. For this project, I picked just a few properties that a town has. You can add more if you like. Here is the code.

C#

```csharp
using System;

namespace GridRestrict_c
{
  /// <summary>
  /// This class contains information about a town.
  /// </summary>
  public class Town
  {
    private string mName;
    private string mCounty;
    private string mState;
    private string mMayor;
    private string mZip;
    private float  mMillRate;

    public string Name
    {
      get { return mName; }
      set { mName = value; }
    }

    public string County
    {
      get { return mCounty; }
      set { mCounty = value; }
    }

    public string State
    {
      get { return mState; }
      set { mState = value; }
    }

    public string Mayor
    {
      get { return mMayor; }
      set { mMayor = value; }
    }
```

```csharp
    public string Zip
    {
      get { return mZip; }
      set { mZip = value; }
    }

    public float MillRate
    {
      get { return mMillRate; }
      set { mMillRate = value; }
    }

  }
}
```

VB

```vb
Option Strict On

Public Class Town

  Private mName As String
  Private mCounty As String
  Private mState As String
  Private mMayor As String
  Private mZip As String
  Private mMillRate As Single

  Public Property Name() As String
    Get
      Return mName
    End Get
    Set(ByVal Value As String)
      mName = Value
    End Set
  End Property

  Public Property County() As String
    Get
      Return mCounty
    End Get
    Set(ByVal Value As String)
      mCounty = Value
    End Set
  End Property
```

```
        Public Property State() As String
          Get
            Return mState
          End Get
          Set(ByVal Value As String)
            mState = Value
          End Set
        End Property

        Public Property Mayor() As String
          Get
            Return mMayor
          End Get
          Set(ByVal Value As String)
            mMayor = Value
          End Set
        End Property

        Public Property Zip() As String
          Get
            Return mZip
          End Get
          Set(ByVal Value As String)
            mZip = Value
          End Set
        End Property

        Public Property MillRate() As Single
          Get
            Return mMillRate
          End Get
          Set(ByVal Value As Single)
            mMillRate = Value
          End Set
        End Property
    End Class
```

Objects instantiated from this class serve as the basic data container that is known to all parts of the program. You will see what I mean shortly.

As you can see, this class is nothing more than a way to store data, add to it, and retrieve it. The next class is a factory class that creates these Town objects upon demand. As soon as a property is called in this class, the constructor is run and an internal table is filled with data.

The data that I get does not come from a database table. It is instead filled in manually by me in the code. Why do that? I am trying to show you that data can come from anywhere. The code that fills in the data table is easily interchanged with code that gets data from a database, an XML Web service, or something else.

Listings 6-2a and 6-2b show the complete code for the Towns class.

Listing 6-2a. C# Code for the Towns Class

```csharp
using System;
using System.Data;

namespace GridRestrict_c
{
  /// <summary>
  /// static class that gets information about towns in a state from
  /// an Access Database.
  ///
  /// This is an abstraction of the data from the main program.  I can change the
  /// way data is obtained and its source at any time without having to change
  /// the interface to the data from the outside.  This is a good thing!
  /// </summary>
  public class Towns
  {
    private static DataSet DS;

    static Towns()
    {
      DS = new DataSet();
      DS.Tables.Add(GetData());
    }


    public bool Update(Town t)
    {
      //Code in here updates the database and
      //merges the new and old dataset
      return true;
    }
```

```csharp
#region public static properties

public static float MinAllowedMillRate { get { return 12f; } }
public static float MaxAllowedMillRate { get { return 99f; } }


  public static Town Hartford
{
  get
  {
    Town t = null;
    DataTable dt = DS.Tables["TownInfo"];
    foreach(DataRow r in dt.Rows)
    {
      if(r["Name"].ToString() == "Hartford")
      {
        t = FillFromRow(r);
        break;
      }
    }
    return t;
  }
}

public static Town LosAngeles
{
  get
  {
    Town t = null;
    DataTable dt = DS.Tables["TownInfo"];
    foreach(DataRow r in dt.Rows)
    {
      if(r["Name"].ToString() == "Los Angeles")
      {
        t = FillFromRow(r);
        break;
      }
    }
    return t;
  }
}
```

```csharp
public static Town Orlando
{
  get
  {
    Town t = null;
    DataTable dt = DS.Tables["TownInfo"];
    foreach(DataRow r in dt.Rows)
    {
      if(r["Name"].ToString() == "Orlando")
      {
        t = FillFromRow(r);
        break;
      }
    }
    return t;
  }
}


#endregion


#region local methods

private static Town FillFromRow(DataRow r)
{
  Town t = new Town();
  t.Name     = (string)r["Name"];
  t.State    = (string)r["State"];
  t.County   = (string)r["County"];
  t.Mayor    = (string)r["Mayor"];
  t.Zip      = (string)r["Zip"];
  t.MillRate = (float)r["MillRate"];
  return t;
}

private static DataTable GetData()
{
  //Let's pretend that we are getting this data from a database table.
  //For now this shows that you can make the table by hand if you want to.
  //You can also get the data from an INI file, CFG file, or XML WEB service.
  //Any way you get the data it can be arranged in a table that has specific
  //demands.
```

```
// Create a new DataTable.
DataTable  dt = new DataTable("TownInfo");
DataColumn dc;
DataRow    dr;

// Create town name
dc           = new DataColumn();
dc.DataType  = System.Type.GetType("System.String");
dc.ColumnName = "Name";
dc.ReadOnly  = true;
dc.Unique    = true;
// Add the column to the DataColumnCollection.
dt.Columns.Add(dc);

// Create state town is in
dc           = new DataColumn();
dc.DataType  = System.Type.GetType("System.String");
dc.ColumnName = "State";
dc.ReadOnly  = false;
dc.Unique    = false;
dt.Columns.Add(dc);

// Create county town is in
dc           = new DataColumn();
dc.DataType  = System.Type.GetType("System.String");
dc.ColumnName = "County";
dc.ReadOnly  = false;
dc.Unique    = false;
dt.Columns.Add(dc);

// Create mayor of town
dc           = new DataColumn();
dc.DataType  = System.Type.GetType("System.String");
dc.ColumnName = "Mayor";
dc.ReadOnly  = false;
dc.Unique    = false;
dt.Columns.Add(dc);

// Create town zip code
dc           = new DataColumn();
dc.DataType  = System.Type.GetType("System.String");
dc.ColumnName = "Zip";
dc.ReadOnly  = false;
dc.Unique    = true;
dt.Columns.Add(dc);
```

```
    // Create town mill rate
    dc             = new DataColumn();
    dc.DataType    = System.Type.GetType("System.Single");
    dc.ColumnName  = "MillRate";
    dc.ReadOnly    = false;
    dc.Unique      = false;
    dt.Columns.Add(dc);

    // Create 4 DataRow objects that represent towns.  Add them to the table
    dt.Rows.Add(new object[] {"Hartford", "CT", "Hartford",
                              "Mike", "06011", 45.23f } );
    dt.Rows.Add(new object[] {"Los Angeles", "CA", "LA",
                              "Fred", "23456", 64.85f } );
    dt.Rows.Add(new object[] {"Orlando", "FL", "Kissimmee",
                              "Mikey", "45376", 25.00f } );

    return dt;
  }

  #endregion

}
}
```

Listing 6-2b. VB Code for the Towns Class

```
Option Strict On

Public Class Towns

  ' static class that get information about towns in a state from
  ' an Access Database.
  '
  ' This is an abstraction of the data from the main program.  I can change the
  ' way data is obtained and its source at any time without having to change the
  ' interface to the data from the outside.  This is a good thing!
  Private Shared DS As DataSet

  Shared Sub New()
    DS = New DataSet()
    DS.Tables.Add(GetData())
  End Sub
```

```vbnet
Public Function Update(ByVal t As Town) As Boolean
  'Code in here updates the database and
  'merges the new and old dataset
  Return True
End Function

#Region "public static properties"

Public Shared ReadOnly Property MinAllowedMillRate() As Single
  Get
    Return 12.0F
  End Get
End Property

Public Shared ReadOnly Property MaxAllowedMillRate() As Single
  Get
    Return 99.0F
  End Get
End Property

Public Shared ReadOnly Property Hartford() As Town
  Get
    Dim t As Town = Nothing
    Dim dt As DataTable = DS.Tables("TownInfo")
    Dim r As DataRow
    For Each r In dt.Rows
      If r("Name").ToString() = "Hartford" Then
        t = FillFromRow(r)
        Exit For
      End If
    Next
    Return t
  End Get
End Property

Public Shared ReadOnly Property LosAngeles() As Town
  Get
    Dim t As Town = Nothing
    Dim dt As DataTable = DS.Tables("TownInfo")
    Dim r As DataRow
    For Each r In dt.Rows
```

```vbnet
         If r("Name").ToString() = "Los Angeles" Then
           t = FillFromRow(r)
           Exit For
         End If
       Next
       Return t
    End Get
  End Property


  Public Shared ReadOnly Property Orlando() As Town
    Get
       Dim t As Town = Nothing
       Dim dt As DataTable = DS.Tables("TownInfo")
       Dim r As DataRow
       For Each r In dt.Rows
         If r("Name").ToString() = "Orlando" Then
           t = FillFromRow(r)
           Exit For
         End If
       Next
       Return t
    End Get
  End Property


#End Region


#Region "local methods"

  Private Shared Function FillFromRow(ByVal r As DataRow) As Town
    Dim t As Town = New Town()
    t.Name = CType(r("Name"), String)
    t.State = CType(r("State"), String)
    t.County = CType(r("County"), String)
    t.Mayor = CType(r("Mayor"), String)
    t.Zip = CType(r("Zip"), String)
    t.MillRate = CType(r("MillRate"), Single)
    Return t
  End Function

  Private Shared Function GetData() As DataTable
    'Let's pretend that we are getting this data from a database table.
    'For now this shows that you can make the table by hand if you want to.
    'You can also get the data from an INI file, CFG file, or XML WEB service.
    'Any way you get the data it can be arranged in a table that has specific
    'demands.

    ' Create a new DataTable.
```

```
Dim dt As DataTable = New DataTable("TownInfo")
Dim dc As DataColumn
Dim dr As DataRow

' Create town name
dc = New DataColumn()
dc.DataType = System.Type.GetType("System.String")
dc.ColumnName = "Name"
dc.ReadOnly = True
dc.Unique = True
dt.Columns.Add(dc)

' Create state town is in
dc = New DataColumn()
dc.DataType = System.Type.GetType("System.String")
dc.ColumnName = "State"
dc.ReadOnly = False
dc.Unique = False
dt.Columns.Add(dc)

' Create county town is in
dc = New DataColumn()
dc.DataType = System.Type.GetType("System.String")
dc.ColumnName = "County"
dc.ReadOnly = False
dc.Unique = False
dt.Columns.Add(dc)

' Create mayor of town
dc = New DataColumn()
dc.DataType = System.Type.GetType("System.String")
dc.ColumnName = "Mayor"
dc.ReadOnly = False
dc.Unique = False
dt.Columns.Add(dc)

' Create town zip code
dc = New DataColumn()
dc.DataType = System.Type.GetType("System.String")
dc.ColumnName = "Zip"
dc.ReadOnly = False
dc.Unique = True
dt.Columns.Add(dc)
```

```
    ' Create town mill rate
    dc = New DataColumn()
    dc.DataType = System.Type.GetType("System.Single")
    dc.ColumnName = "MillRate"
    dc.ReadOnly = False
    dc.Unique = False
    dt.Columns.Add(dc)

    ' Create 4 DataRow objects that represent towns.  Add them to the table
    dt.Rows.Add(New Object() {"Hartford", "CT", "Hartford", _
                              "Mike", "06011", 45.23F})
    dt.Rows.Add(New Object() {"Los Angeles", "CA", "LA", _
                              "Fred", "23456", 64.85F})
    dt.Rows.Add(New Object() {"Orlando", "FL", "Kissimmee", _
                              "Mikey", "45376", 25.0F})

    Return dt
  End Function
#End Region
End Class
```

Let's look at this class a little more closely. This class is called a *static* class in C# and a *shared* class in VB.

 TIP Static methods, variables, and constructors are very handy indeed. I suggest you look up further examples on how to use them.

A class that has static methods or properties allows you to call these methods without instantiating the class. Have you ever played around with the Colors class, the Pens class, or the Brushes class in GDI+? These three classes are prime examples of static classes. For instance, you can get a color from the Colors class without instantiating the class first:

```
This.BackColor = Colors.Red;
```

This makes it seem as if you are just getting a color. A lot is going on behind the scenes, though.

For my Towns class, I can make this call directly:

```
Dim MyTown as Town = Towns.Orlando
```

I never instantiated an object of Towns. How was I able to return a Town object without explicitly loading the data? The answer is the static (shared) constructor.

If you have a normal constructor, you will need to instantiate the object before this constructor gets called. What I have done here is added the static (shared) keyword to the constructor definition. This means that this constructor will run once, and only once, when a static method is called. Suppose I did this:

```
Dim MyTown as Town = Towns.Orlando
Dim MyTown2 as Town = Towns.Hartford
```

The static constructor will get called only once. Therefore, I get the data only once.

Note that this class contains a method to update a Town object. This method is not static, so you need to instantiate an object of this class before you use it.

If I were to fill out this Update method, I would include a normal constructor that set up some other parameters I may need. This Update method would also include code to accept or reject changes to the Town object and merge those changes with the static DataSet. This way, the next time I call the property that returns a particular Town object, I get the changed data.

This kind of programming allows you to get and save data blindly. The presentation code has no idea how the data is saved, and it does not care. It only cares that the new data it saved for Orlando, for example, would also appear the next time it got an Orlando Town object.

The code for the form consists of three sections: a section that initializes data in the constructor, a section that handles events, and a section that makes the table for the DataGrid. The third section is as follows. Add this code to your form.

C#

```
#region internal methods

private DataTable MakeTable()
{
  // Create a new DataTable.
  DataTable dt = new DataTable("SomeTowns");
  DataColumn dc;
  DataRow dr;

  dc = new DataColumn();
  dc.DataType= System.Type.GetType("System.String");
  dc.ColumnName = "Town Name";
  dc.Caption = "Town Name";
  dc.ReadOnly = true;
  dc.Unique = true;
  dt.Columns.Add(dc);
```

```
    dc = new DataColumn();
    dc.DataType= System.Type.GetType("System.String");
    dc.ColumnName = "State";
    dc.Caption = "State";
    dc.ReadOnly = true;
    dc.Unique = false;
    dt.Columns.Add(dc);

    dc = new DataColumn();
    dc.DataType= System.Type.GetType("System.String");
    dc.ColumnName = "County Name";
    dc.Caption = "County Name";
    dc.ReadOnly = true;
    dc.Unique = false;
    dt.Columns.Add(dc);

    dc = new DataColumn();
    dc.DataType= System.Type.GetType("System.Single");
    dc.ColumnName = "MillRate";
    dc.Caption = "MillRate";
    dc.ReadOnly = false;
    dc.Unique = false;
    dt.Columns.Add(dc);

    return dt;
  }
  #endregion
```

VB

```
#Region "internal methods"

  Private Function MakeTable() As DataTable
    ' Create a new DataTable.
    Dim dt As DataTable = New DataTable("SomeTowns")
    Dim dc As DataColumn
    Dim dr As DataRow

    dc = New DataColumn()
    dc.DataType = System.Type.GetType("System.String")
    dc.ColumnName = "Town Name"
    dc.Caption = "Town Name"
    dc.ReadOnly = True
    dc.Unique = True
    dt.Columns.Add(dc)
```

```
    dc = New DataColumn()
    dc.DataType = System.Type.GetType("System.String")
    dc.ColumnName = "State"
    dc.Caption = "State"
    dc.ReadOnly = True
    dc.Unique = False
    dt.Columns.Add(dc)

    dc = New DataColumn()
    dc.DataType = System.Type.GetType("System.String")
    dc.ColumnName = "County Name"
    dc.Caption = "County Name"
    dc.ReadOnly = True
    dc.Unique = False
    dt.Columns.Add(dc)

    dc = New DataColumn()
    dc.DataType = System.Type.GetType("System.Single")
    dc.ColumnName = "MillRate"
    dc.Caption = "MillRate"
    dc.ReadOnly = False
    dc.Unique = False
    dt.Columns.Add(dc)

    Return dt
  End Function

#End Region
```

Look at this code closely. The grid has columns that are set up for particular data types. All of the columns are read-only except for the MillRate column. Also note that the town name must be unique. These are constraints that I put on the DataGrid to help me with data entry and validation. The grid will not allow me to enter in any data that is not the correct data type. It will also not allow any cells to be edited that are read-only. With just these few properties, I have effectively shut down the user from doing anything he or she should not be allowed to do. There are some exceptions, of course, that I cover shortly.

This next section of code contains the delegates to handle some grid and table events.

C#

```
    #region event code
```

```csharp
private void DataChanged(object sender, DataColumnChangeEventArgs e)
{
  DataTable dt = (DataTable)sender;
  if (e.Column.ColumnName.Equals("MillRate"))
  {
    if ((float)e.ProposedValue < Towns.MinAllowedMillRate ||
        (float)e.ProposedValue > Towns.MaxAllowedMillRate)
    {
      e.Row.RowError =
            "You tried to enter a value outside accepted parameters!";
      string s = "Mill Rate cannot be < " +
                  Towns.MinAllowedMillRate.ToString() +
                  "\n Mill Rate cannot be > " +
                  Towns.MaxAllowedMillRate.ToString();
      e.Row.SetColumnError(e.Column, s);

      //An error object is put up next to the row and cell
      dt.RejectChanges();
      //Yes folks, you can use VB commands in C#.
      Microsoft.VisualBasic.Interaction.Beep();
    }
    else
      dt.AcceptChanges();
  }
}


private void Grid_MouseDown(object sender, MouseEventArgs e)
{
  // Use the DataGrid control's HitTest method with the x and y properties.
  //I use this event to clear errors in the current row.
  DataGrid.HitTestInfo GridHit = dg1.HitTest(e.X,e.Y);

  if(GridHit.Type == DataGrid.HitTestType.Cell)
  {
    DataSet DS = (DataSet)dg1.DataSource;
    if(DS.HasErrors)
    {
      DataTable DT = DS.Tables[dg1.DataMember];
      DT.Rows[GridHit.Row].ClearErrors();
    }
  }
}

#endregion
```

VB

```vb
#Region "event code"

    Private Sub DataChanged(ByVal sender As Object, _
                            ByVal e As DataColumnChangeEventArgs)
        Dim dt As DataTable = CType(sender, DataTable)

        If e.Column.ColumnName.Equals("MillRate") Then
            If CType(e.ProposedValue, Single) < Towns.MinAllowedMillRate Or _
                CType(e.ProposedValue, Single) > Towns.MaxAllowedMillRate Then
                e.Row.RowError = _
                    "You tried to enter a value outside accepted parameters!"
                Dim s As String = "Mill Rate cannot be < " + _
                        Towns.MinAllowedMillRate.ToString() + _
                        "\n Mill Rate cannot be > " + _
                        Towns.MaxAllowedMillRate.ToString()
                e.Row.SetColumnError(e.Column, s)

                'An error object is put up next to the row and cell
                dt.RejectChanges()
                Beep()
            Else
                dt.AcceptChanges()
            End If
        End If
    End Sub

    Private Sub Grid_MouseDown(ByVal sender As Object, _
                            ByVal e As MouseEventArgs)
        ' Use the DataGrid control's HitTest method with the x and y properties.
        'I use this event to clear errors in the current row.
        Dim GridHit As DataGrid.HitTestInfo = dg1.HitTest(e.X, e.Y)

        If GridHit.Type = DataGrid.HitTestType.Cell Then
            Dim DS As DataSet = CType(dg1.DataSource, DataSet)
            If DS.HasErrors Then
                Dim DT As DataTable = DS.Tables(dg1.DataMember)
                DT.Rows(GridHit.Row).ClearErrors()
            End If
        End If
    End Sub
#End Region
```

These two routines are my data validation routines. The first one, DataChanged(), detects the cell that was changed. If it is a MillRate cell, then I see if the new value is within range. If the new value is not within range, I set the error object for the row and for the cell. I then reject the change, which brings back the previous value and makes the computer beep.

> **NOTE** It is possible to use VB commands in a C# program. I had you add a reference to the Visual Basic DLL at the start of the project. The C# code here calls a VB Beep command. C# has no beep command. You are able to use things like the VB string functions if you like. Some built-in methods are easier to use in VB, and .NET allows you to access them.

The second delegate, Grid_MouseDown(), has code that detects the cell the user clicked in. Once I know that a cell was clicked, I determine if the DataSet had errorsOnce. Fill in the following constructor code to see how this works.

C#

```csharp
public Form1()
{
  InitializeComponent();

  //Create a new data set with a table
  DataSet   DS  = new DataSet();
  DataTable DT  = MakeTable();

  Town t = Towns.Hartford;
  DT.Rows.Add(new object[] {t.Name, t.State, t.County, t.MillRate});
  t = Towns.LosAngeles;
  DT.Rows.Add(new object[] {t.Name, t.State, t.County, t.MillRate});
  t = Towns.Orlando;
  DT.Rows.Add(new object[] {t.Name, t.State, t.County, t.MillRate});
  DT.AcceptChanges();  //A base comparison to reject changes if necessary

  //Add table to data set
  //Only one table so assign source directly to it.
  DS.Tables.Add(DT);
  dg1.DataSource = DS;
  dg1.DataMember = "SomeTowns";
```

```
        DT.ColumnChanged += new DataColumnChangeEventHandler(this.DataChanged);
        dg1.MouseDown    += new MouseEventHandler(this.Grid_MouseDown);

    }
```

VB

```
Public Sub New()
    MyBase.New()

    InitializeComponent()

    'Create a new data set with a table
    Dim DS As DataSet = New DataSet()
    Dim DT As DataTable = MakeTable()

    Dim t As Town = Towns.Hartford
    DT.Rows.Add(New Object() {t.Name, t.State, t.County, t.MillRate})
    t = Towns.LosAngeles
    DT.Rows.Add(New Object() {t.Name, t.State, t.County, t.MillRate})
    t = Towns.Orlando
    DT.Rows.Add(New Object() {t.Name, t.State, t.County, t.MillRate})
    DT.AcceptChanges() 'A base comparison to reject changes if necessary

    'Add table to data set
    'Only one table so assign source directly to it.
    DS.Tables.Add(DT)
    dg1.DataSource = DS
    dg1.DataMember = "SomeTowns"

    AddHandler DT.ColumnChanged, _
            New DataColumnChangeEventHandler(AddressOf DataChanged)
    AddHandler dg1.MouseDown, _
            New MouseEventHandler(AddressOf Grid_MouseDown)

End Sub
```

Once I get the data from the static methods and add them to the table as rows, I accept the changes. This sets up a baseline for any changes that come along later. If the validation code finds that the changes are illegal, it calls the RejectChanges method. Otherwise it calls the AcceptChanges method again to create a new baseline.

Compile and run the code. Your screen should look like the one shown in Figure 6-7.

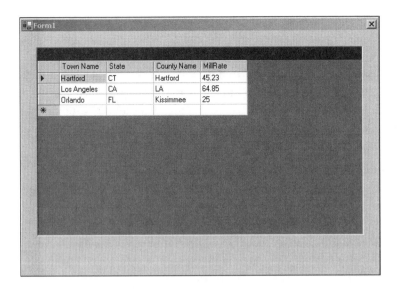

Figure 6-7. The initial screen

Try to change some values. You will see that you are locked out of all columns except for the MillRate column. Try changing the mill rate for a town to some string value. The grid will not allow it.

Try to change the mill rate for a town to 5. Your screen should look like Figure 6-8.

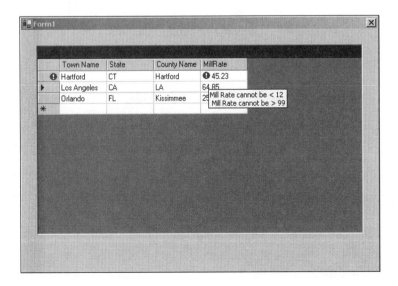

Figure 6-8. An error in the cell

You see the error icon appear at both the row level and at the cell itself. Figure 6-8 shows the cell error. Also note that the new illegal value you entered was rolled back.

Click the mouse in any cell and the error icons disappear. This is what you want to happen. These error icons do not indicate a current error in this case (the code reversed that); they just show that an error occurred. If the user got rid of these icons before viewing them, no harm would be done.

Using the DataGrid and Disconnected Data

The example in the previous section showed you how to use disconnected data as a data source for the DataGrid control. Normally, when programmers think of ADO.NET and the DataGrid control, they think of disconnected data as using a DataSet. Though I used a DataSet here to hold the DataGrid data, it had nothing to do with the classic idea of a disconnected recordset.

My data for this example came from a class that served up the Town object via static methods. If you have a program that has fairly constant data, such as towns in a state, a static class is a great way to access this data.

The static class in the example used a DataSet with a DataTable to hold data. I did this for convenience, as the DataSet is transactional. I can accept any changes to it or reject them. If I use my own data structures, I need quite a bit of code to replicate this functionality that I get for free.

Other Data Sources

Data can take many forms. You have seen data entered from the keyboard. You have seen data entered via the mouse. You have now seen data that comes from a database. What about other data sources? Here are a few different sources of data:

- Serial connections

- USB devices

- Internet

- Remoting

- Barcode readers

- Data acquisition cards

Let's first take a peek at serial connections.

RS-232 Data

I have done quite a bit of serial communication work in just about all programming languages. When .NET came out, I went searching through the namespaces and lists of controls and did not find any reference at all to any RS-232 device. Bummer!

After thinking about it for a while, I realized that serial connections are becoming a thing of the past, at least in the mainstream programming world. More and more devices are leaning toward TCP/IP or USB communication. If you need to talk to a device via an RS-232 device or a modem, though, what can you do?

If you have been using VB 6.0 you already have the answer: Use the MSComm control. This RS-232 and modem OCX has been around for ages. It is a bit outdated these days, but it still works . . . somewhat OK.

Working with the MSComm control (or for that matter, any OCX control) requires a little diversion from normal .NET operating parameters. You will need to use the Component Object Model Interoperability (COM Interop) capability of .NET.

The COM Interop capability of .NET allows you to generate a .NET program that acts as a client or a server to any IDispatch-based COM object. Essentially, you can take an OCX, or perhaps an ActiveX EXE server made in VB 6.0, and use it in a .NET program. This is great news for those of you who want to migrate to .NET slowly—you are still able to use some of your legacy code as is.

The Platform Invocation Services (PInvoke) and COM Interop capabilities of .NET are quite involved, and it would take a whole book to describe them to you. In the case of COM Interop, it is easier to show you how to use it than to tell you what is going on behind the scenes. The next small example shows you how to include and set up the MSComm serial control in a C# program.

NOTE   To follow along with this example, you need to have Visual Studio 6.0 installed on your machine. Even if you do not have Visual Studio 6.0 installed, this example is still good to look at, as it is applicable to any OCX control you may want to use.

Start a new project. Mine is called "MSComm." Once you have the form on your screen, you will need to get a reference to the MSComm RS-232 control.

1. Go to the form and bring the Toolbox into view.

2. Right-click the Toolbox and choose Customize Toolbox.

3. Choose the COM Components tab in the Customize Toolbox window and check the Microsoft Communications Control option, as shown in Figure 6-9.

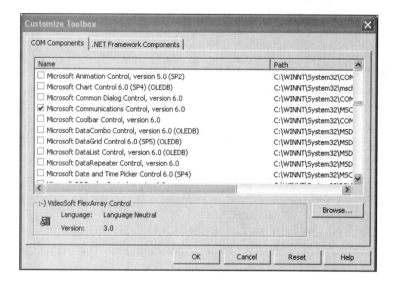

Figure 6-9. Choosing the Microsoft Communications Control in the COM Components tab

Notice that I have the Microsoft Communications Control, version 6.0 highlighted in this window. Double-click it and click OK to select it. Your Toolbox should now have this control in it. Drag the control over to your form and you will see the phone icon on your form.

Notice that adding this control automatically added a couple of references for you, as shown in Figure 6-10.

Figure 6-10. New Communications Control references

Change the name of the control from AxMSComm1 to COM1.

Now that you have an MSComm control on your form, you can write some code to use it. Listing 6-3 presents code for the constructor and code to handle the input event of the control.

Listing 6-3. C# Code for the MSComm Constructor and Delegate

```
public Form1()
{
  InitializeComponent();

  COM1.CommPort    = 1;
  COM1.Handshaking = MSCommLib.HandshakeConstants.comRTSXOnXOff;
  COM1.Settings    = "9600, 0, 7, 1";
  COM1.InputMode   = MSCommLib.InputModeConstants.comInputModeText;
  COM1.InputLen    = 0;
  COM1.NullDiscard = false;
  COM1.OnComm      += new EventHandler(this.CommEvent);
}

private void CommEvent(object sender, EventArgs e)
{
  if (COM1.InBufferCount <= 0)
    return;

  //Do some processing and validation here.
}
```

I don't bother presenting the VB code here, because it is virtually identical to the C# code. I would like to note one thing in this code snippet. I set the NullDiscard property to false. In case you have not run across it yet, null can be a very important character. It is especially important in the RS-232 world. For instance, if you were to program a Class 1 fax program, you would use a string of a few thousand nulls as training characters. If this property were set to true (by default), you would never be able to train to the sending fax machine.

Null has also become very important in the last several years with the rise in importance of Unicode character storage. For the uninitiated, Unicode is used in VB 6.0 and in .NET to hold internal representations of characters. In simple terms, Unicode is a 2-byte representation of a character.

You may have heard of the American Standard Code for Information Interchange (ASCII) coding scheme. Since the dawn of time,[2] ASCII has defined the characters you can type in a computer and the binary representation of their storage. ASCII

---

2. Many years, anyway.

relies on a 256-byte set of characters whose lower 127 bytes are fixed as the normal Latin/English character set. In order to handle multiple languages, a code page scheme was developed to represent characters of another language. For instance, if you switched your code page to CP1251, you would get a set of Russian characters.

Using ASCII to save strings of characters is all but dead. Since Windows NT, most programs store characters as Unicode. As you can guess, though, there has to be some compatibility between ASCII and Unicode. There is. The normal IBM code page 437 for Latin/US English is at the beginning of the Unicode character set. To be compliant with the 4-byte rule of Unicode, the first 2 bytes are null (i.e., 0x00 in hex). So the Unicode representation of the letter *N* is 0x004E. The ASCII representation of this letter is 0x4E.

 TIP As a programmer, you should be thoroughly familiar with Unicode. The standard is published on the Web at `http://www.unicode.org` and there are numerous tomes available regarding Unicode.

So the upshot of all this Unicode stuff is that you may get a Unicode data stream from an RS-232 device (such as another computer), and if you discard null characters you will get only half the information.[3]

Incidental Data

You can treat the other sources of data I mentioned earlier, such as USB devices and barcode readers, in the same way as RS-232 data. Basically, you are getting a data stream from an outside source. Most likely, you will have an interface DLL that comes with a third-party barcode reader or USB device. These DLLs will often have all the necessary methods to allow you to get the data from the device.

Once you have the data, your program should not care where the data came from. It only needs to know how to handle and validate the data. Too often I have seen programs that have the data gathering code hopelessly intertwined with the data management code. This is so wrong.

If you are going to get data from an external source, you should encapsulate the method of getting the data in a class. This class should have an interface that the rest of the program could use to access that data.

Here's a real live "for-instance" situation. I work for a company that interfaces with high-end biometric identification devices (e.g., fingerprint scan, iris scan,

---

3. My wife often claims that she talks in Unicode and I only listen in ASCII!

hand geometry, and so forth). One of these devices has several ways to communicate with the outside world: serial connection, modem, and network IP. My programmatic interface to this device is not dependent upon the method of communication. I have a self-contained class that detects how the device is connected to my PC. This class saves data to the same internal structure whether it is talking via RS-232, network, or modem. This class has an interface to the outside world that serves up data the same way no matter how it was obtained. I use this program with up to several hundred devices, all of which are a mix of RS-232 and network devices. I make no changes in my code based on the communication method. If the RS-232 protocol was enhanced for speed, I would need to change only this one class to take advantage of that.

What I am saying here is that you should not choke if someone asks you to create a program whose data is not in a database. Encapsulate and debug the data gathering class, and then move on to the rest of the code. Once you get the data, you are in familiar territory.

File-Based Data

File-based data includes normal text files, .ini files, binary files, XML files, and so forth. Basically, file-based data is anything that resides on a disk and is not highly specialized like a database file.

Since Windows 95 came out with its registry-based storage system, .ini files have been officially declared obsolete by Microsoft. As you well know, though, .ini files have not been abandoned by programmers, and even Microsoft uses them extensively. .NET and XML may actually put .ini files to bed for good, however.

XML and .ini configuration files are a subject unto themselves, and I discuss them in detail in Chapter 9. The files I discuss in this chapter are normal text and binary files.

You saw the use of text-based files in Chapter 5. That was just the tip of the iceberg.

File I/O and Streams

What is a stream? If you are thinking about fishing, you need to concentrate harder on this book. The water analogy is not that far off, however. If you were to put a piece of wood in an unknown stream, where would it end up? Would it end up in a lake, a pond, or perhaps the ocean? You would not know, and the action of throwing the piece of wood in the stream has nothing to do with where it ends up.

The same is true for a stream in .NET. A *stream* is a baseless form of storage. You can write to a stream, and the information could end up in a database, a file, memory, or perhaps the Internet. So far, you have seen file-based I/O; I show you stream-based I/O next.

Start a new Windows project in either C# or VB. Mine is called "Union." You hard-core C programmers should get a premonition about this example by the name I used for it. Anyway, this is basically a GUI-less example. I show you how to write data to a stream and read data from a stream. The stream will be attached to a few different methods of storage. For this example I use binary I/O. Text I/O is much the same, if not easier.

First make sure you have the following namespaces.

C#

```
using System;
using System.Drawing;
using System.Collections;
using System.ComponentModel;
using System.Windows.Forms;
using System.Data;
using System.Runtime.InteropServices;
using System.IO;
```

VB

```
Imports System
Imports System.Drawing
Imports System.Collections
Imports System.ComponentModel
Imports System.Windows.Forms
Imports System.Data
Imports System.Runtime.InteropServices
Imports System.IO
```

Start out with some class variables, as follows.

C#

```
#region class local variables

public struct SalaryBenefits
{
  private int    mVacationDays;
  private int    mSickDays;
  public int VacationDays
```

```
    {
      get{return mVacationDays;}
      set{mVacationDays = value;}
    }
    public int SickDays
    {
      get{return mSickDays;}
      set{mSickDays = value;}
    }
    public int DaysOff {get{return mSickDays + mVacationDays;}}
  }

  FileStream    FS;
  BinaryReader  BR;
  BinaryWriter  BW;

  private byte[] Buffer = new byte[1000];

  #endregion
```

VB

```
#Region "class local variables"

  Public Structure SalaryBenefits
    Private mVacationDays As Integer
    Private mSickDays As Integer
    Public Property VacationDays() As Integer
      Get
        Return mVacationDays
      End Get
      Set(ByVal Value As Integer)
        mVacationDays = Value
      End Set
    End Property
    Public Property SickDays() As Integer
      Get
        Return mSickDays
      End Get
      Set(ByVal Value As Integer)
        mSickDays = Value
      End Set
    End Property
```

```
   Public ReadOnly Property DaysOff() As Integer
      Get
         Return mSickDays + mVacationDays
      End Get
   End Property
End Structure


Dim FS As FileStream
Dim BR As BinaryReader
Dim BW As BinaryWriter
Dim SR As StreamReader
Dim SW As StreamWriter


Private Buffer(1000) As Byte

#End Region
```

I include a structure here as a way to store internal data. I will be reading and writing vacation and sick days for an employee. The last variable in this list is an array of bytes. You experienced programmers can probably guess what this variable is for. The rest of you will have to wait and see.

Add the following region of code to your form. This code reads and writes binary data to a file.

C#

```
#region Read/Write File via normal way

private void WriteNormalBinary()
{
    FS = new FileStream("SalaryFile", FileMode.OpenOrCreate);
    BW = new BinaryWriter(FS);

    SalaryBenefits x = new SalaryBenefits();
    x.VacationDays = 82;
    x.SickDays = 31;
    BW.Write(x.VacationDays);
    BW.Write(x.SickDays);
    BW.Flush();
    BW.Close();

}
```

```
private void ReadNormalBinary()
{
  FS = new FileStream("SalaryFile", FileMode.Open);
  BR = new BinaryReader(FS);

  SalaryBenefits y = new SalaryBenefits();
  y.VacationDays = BR.ReadInt32();
  y.SickDays = BR.ReadInt32();
}

#endregion
```

VB

```
#Region "Read/Write File via normal way"

  Private Sub WriteNormalBinary()
    FS = New FileStream("SalaryFile", FileMode.OpenOrCreate)
    BW = New BinaryWriter(FS)

    Dim x As SalaryBenefits = New SalaryBenefits()
    x.VacationDays = 82
    x.SickDays = 31
    BW.Write(x.VacationDays)
    BW.Write(x.SickDays)
    BW.Flush()
    BW.Close()
  End Sub

  Private Sub ReadNormalBinary()
    FS = New FileStream("SalaryFile", FileMode.Open)
    BR = New BinaryReader(FS)

    Dim y As SalaryBenefits = New SalaryBenefits()
    y.VacationDays = BR.ReadInt32()
    y.SickDays = BR.ReadInt32()
  End Sub

#End Region
```

Add this code to your Form_Load routine.

C#

```
private void Form1_Load(object sender, System.EventArgs e)
{
  WriteNormalBinary();
  ReadNormalBinary();

}
```

VB

```
Private Sub Form1_Load(ByVal sender As System.Object, _
                       ByVal e As System.EventArgs) Handles MyBase.Load

  WriteNormalBinary()
  ReadNormalBinary()

End Sub
```

Step through the code with your debugger. Here is what happens during the write:

1. A file stream is created and a binary writer is wrapped around it.

2. An instance of the Benefits structure is created and filled with data.

3. Each property of the structure is written to the file.

The read operation is just the reverse. I wrap a file stream in a binary reader and read each value into the structure. What would happen if I read the values in reverse order? Well, because both values are the same data type (integers), the numbers would just be switched around. However, if one of the values was an integer and the other was a double and you read them in reverse, you would not get anything predictable. In fact, you may get an error.

Remember, you need to know what you are doing with binary flat files like this. The advantage of a binary flat file over a database for small amounts of data is speed. Reading and writing flat binary files is incredibly fast.

Want to go faster? How about reading and writing to memory? Nothing is faster than that.[4] Add the following region of code to your form.

---

4. Except maybe The Flash!

C#

```csharp
#region read/write to memory stream normal way

private void WriteMemNormalBinary()
{
  MemoryStream MS = new MemoryStream(Buffer);
  BW = new BinaryWriter(MS);

  SalaryBenefits x = new SalaryBenefits();
  x.VacationDays = 36;
  x.SickDays = 17;
  BW.Write(x.VacationDays);
  BW.Write(x.SickDays);
  BW.Flush();
  BW.Close();

}

private void ReadMemNormalBinary()
{
  MemoryStream MS = new MemoryStream(Buffer);
  BR = new BinaryReader(MS);

  SalaryBenefits y = new SalaryBenefits();
  y.VacationDays = BR.ReadInt32();
  y.SickDays = BR.ReadInt32();
}
#endregion
```

VB

```vb
#Region "read/write to memory stream normal way"

  Private Sub WriteMemNormalBinary()
    Dim MS As MemoryStream = New MemoryStream(Buffer)
    BW = New BinaryWriter(MS)

    Dim x As SalaryBenefits = New SalaryBenefits()
    x.VacationDays = 36
    x.SickDays = 17
    BW.Write(x.VacationDays)
    BW.Write(x.SickDays)
    BW.Flush()
    BW.Close()
```

```
    End Sub

  Private Sub ReadMemNormalBinary()
    Dim MS As MemoryStream = New MemoryStream(Buffer)
    BR = New BinaryReader(MS)

    Dim y As SalaryBenefits = New SalaryBenefits()
    y.VacationDays = BR.ReadInt32()
    y.SickDays = BR.ReadInt32()
  End Sub
#End Region
```

Call these two functions in the Form_Load event. Here is what it should look like now.

C#

```
    private void Form1_Load(object sender, System.EventArgs e)
    {
      WriteNormalBinary();
      ReadNormalBinary();

      WriteMemNormalBinary();
      ReadMemNormalBinary();
    }
```

VB

```
  Private Sub Form1_Load(ByVal sender As System.Object, _
                      ByVal e As System.EventArgs) Handles MyBase.Load

    WriteNormalBinary()
    ReadNormalBinary()

    WriteMemNormalBinary()
    ReadMemNormalBinary()
  End Sub
```

The buffer that I created in the variables section is what I use to store my data. This is very interesting because it acts as virtual storage. Remember the RAM disk days of DOS?

NOTE What is DOS, you say? For those of us old enough to remember, a RAM disk was used extensively to hold data for quick retrieval. I used to know a guy who would transfer a goodly chunk of his 20MB hard drive to RAM disk upon start-up just to get the extra speed out of his IBM 20MHz 286.

Note that the code to read and write is exactly the same once I have instantiated the stream. In fact, if I called the memory stream the same name as the file stream, the code would differ in only one line. This is the power of streams. Once you have instantiated it, your code does not need to care where the data is going.

I encourage you to use streams over basic file I/O, as streams provide a more flexible way of handling data. It is no big deal to encapsulate the reading and writing of data in a class and just instantiate the class with the stream you want the data to go to.

A Better Database

Let me tell you a story. A long time ago, a young programmer (yours truly) wanted a faster database than was available at the time (the time being the days of the 386 computer). This programmer decided to write his own binary database using routines written in C. After much trial and error, this programmer used Unions to perform high-speed data transfer to and from the database. When I was playing around with file I/O in .NET, I wanted to see if I could do the same sort of thing. The answer is . . . kind of.

For those of you who do not know what a Union is, here is the long answer. Remember the Benefits structure? It had two variables. Whenever I wanted to write the data in the structure to the stream, I needed to call the write function twice, once for each variable. What if I had 20 variables? The code to write this stream would get very large.

Suppose I could arrange the structure so that I only needed to write one variable to the stream, and this variable would automatically contain the information in all the other variables. A *Union* is a data structure in which each variable resides in the same address space. Figure 6-11 shows a normal memory map of sequential data stored in a structure.

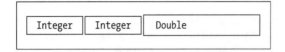

Figure 6-11. Sequential data stored in a structure

A Union allows the kind of data mapping shown in Figure 6-12.

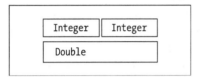

Figure 6-12. An overlapping data structure

If I was able to achieve the structure shown in Figure 6-12, I would need to save only one piece of data to the stream. This would be the double value. If I read back the double value, I would then get the two integer values.

To achieve this type of data structure, I need to know quite a bit about the sizes of internal data. I also need to be sure that the size of an integer does not change from language to language as I use this structure. For instance, I know that an integer in .NET is 4 bytes and a double is 8 bytes. This is very convenient, as I can fit two integers in the space of a double. What if I used this .NET structure in a VB 6.0 program? An integer in VB 6.0 is 2 bytes. I would need to pass in a VB 6.0 long data type, which is 4 bytes.

So now that I have explained a Union, how do you go about making one? Add this structure to your class variables section.

C#

```
//Must use only value types.  Cannot mix in reference types
[ StructLayout( LayoutKind.Explicit )]
  public struct UnionBenefits
{
  [ FieldOffset(0)]
  public int     VacationDays;
  [ FieldOffset(4)]
  public int     SickDays;
  [ FieldOffset(0)]
  public double  DaysOff;
}
```

VB

```
<StructLayout(LayoutKind.Explicit)> _
Public Structure UnionBenefits
  <FieldOffset(0)> Public VacationDays As Integer
  <FieldOffset(4)> Public SickDays As Integer
  <FieldOffset(0)> Public DaysOff As Double
End Structure
```

Interesting, eh? The Interop services namespace defines the StructLayout attributes. As you can see here, I lay out the VacationDays variable at offset 0. Because this is an integer, I lay out the next variable, SickDays, at offset 4. An integer takes 4 bytes. This makes them sequential. The next variable is a double, which is 8 bytes. I lay this out at offset 0. This variable overlays the two integers exactly, just like what is shown in Figure 6-12.

Add the following code regions to your form.

C#

```
#region Read/Write File via fake union

private void WriteViaUnion()
{
  UnionBenefits x = new UnionBenefits();
  x.SickDays = 5;
  x.VacationDays = 15;

  FS = new FileStream("UnionFile", FileMode.OpenOrCreate);
  BW = new BinaryWriter(FS);
  BW.Write(x.DaysOff);
  BW.Flush();
  BW.Close();

}

private void ReadViaUnion()
{
  FS = new FileStream("UnionFile", FileMode.Open);

  UnionBenefits y = new UnionBenefits();
  BR = new BinaryReader(FS);
  y.DaysOff = BR.ReadDouble();

}
```

```
    #endregion

    #region read/write to memory stream via fake union

    private void WriteMemViaUnion()
    {
      UnionBenefits x = new UnionBenefits();
      x.SickDays = 33;
      x.VacationDays = 66;

      MemoryStream MS = new MemoryStream(Buffer);
      BW = new BinaryWriter(MS);
      BW.Write(x.DaysOff);
      BW.Flush();
      BW.Close();

    }

    private void ReadMemViaUnion()
    {
      MemoryStream MS = new MemoryStream(Buffer);

      UnionBenefits y = new UnionBenefits();
      BR = new BinaryReader(MS);
      y.DaysOff = BR.ReadDouble();

    }

    #endregion
```

VB

```
#Region "Read/Write File via fake union"

  Private Sub WriteViaUnion()
    Dim x As UnionBenefits = New UnionBenefits()
    x.SickDays = 5
    x.VacationDays = 15

    FS = New FileStream("UnionFile", FileMode.OpenOrCreate)
    BW = New BinaryWriter(FS)
    BW.Write(x.DaysOff)
    BW.Flush()
    BW.Close()
```

```
    End Sub

    Private Sub ReadViaUnion()
      FS = New FileStream("UnionFile", FileMode.Open)

      Dim y As UnionBenefits = New UnionBenefits()
      BR = New BinaryReader(FS)
      y.DaysOff = BR.ReadDouble()

    End Sub

#End Region

#Region "read/write to memory stream via fake union"

    Private Sub WriteMemViaUnion()
      Dim x As UnionBenefits = New UnionBenefits()
      x.SickDays = 33
      x.VacationDays = 66

      Dim MS As MemoryStream = New MemoryStream(Buffer)
      BW = New BinaryWriter(MS)
      BW.Write(x.DaysOff)
      BW.Flush()
      BW.Close()

    End Sub

    Private Sub ReadMemViaUnion()
      Dim MS As MemoryStream = New MemoryStream(Buffer)

      Dim y As UnionBenefits = New UnionBenefits()
      BR = New BinaryReader(MS)
      y.DaysOff = BR.ReadDouble()

    End Sub

#End Region
```

Of course, you will need to call the following methods.

C#

```csharp
private void Form1_Load(object sender, System.EventArgs e)
{
  WriteNormalBinary();
  ReadNormalBinary();

  WriteViaUnion();
  ReadViaUnion();

  WriteMemNormalBinary();
  ReadMemNormalBinary();

  WriteMemViaUnion();
  ReadMemViaUnion();

}
```

VB

```vb
Private Sub Form1_Load(ByVal sender As System.Object, _
                    ByVal e As System.EventArgs) Handles MyBase.Load

  WriteNormalBinary()
  ReadNormalBinary()

  WriteViaUnion()
  ReadViaUnion()

  WriteMemNormalBinary()
  ReadMemNormalBinary()

  WriteMemViaUnion()
  ReadMemViaUnion()

End Sub
```

Here is what happens:

- SickDays and VacationDays are initialized.

- The DaysOff variable is saved to the stream.

That's it. I needed to save and retrieve only one variable. Figure 6-13 shows the variable list as I am about to save the structure.

Name	Value	Type
⊞ BW	{System.IO.BinaryWriter}	System.IC
⊞ this	{Unions_c.Form1}	Unions_c.
⊟ x	{Unions_c.Form1.UnionBenefits}	Unions_c.
⊟ System.ValueType	{Unions_c.Form1.UnionBenefits}	System.V
VacationDays	66	int
SickDays	33	int
DaysOff	7.00258611344623E-313	double

Figure 6-13. The overlapped benefits structure

You can see from Figure 6-13 that the DaysOff variable means nothing at all if you interpret it as a double.

There are some caveats to this method of data storage. The main one is that you cannot overlay value data types with reference data types. That is, you cannot overlay a string over several integers. This is the only major drawback that I see. There is actually a way around this that involves using two structures and overloaded methods. If you are interested in this using this type of data storage, I leave it up to you to figure out the workaround.

Summary

This chapter explained some of the more advanced data entry and storage techniques available to you. I covered the use of database access and its interaction with the DataGrid. I also showed you how to use the DataGrid with just about any data source you can come up with. While I was on the subject of DataGrids, I introduced you to the static or shared class. This important class type is used extensively in .NET.

In this chapter I also covered other types of data sources, such as USB devices, RS-232, and so forth. You saw that once you get the data into your program, you can treat it like any other data you get such as that from a database.

The last part of this chapter dealt with data streams and how you can apply them to file storage, memory storage, or whatever. I showed you how to fake a simple C-like Union using the Interop services namespace of .NET. Unions can be a very fast alternative to parsing data.

So far, you have worked within the confines of what .NET provides you. The next chapter deals with ways to extend the data validation capabilities of .NET.

Error Handling

SO FAR IN THIS BOOK I have stayed away from any involved error handling. This was mainly to get rid of any extraneous code that was not directly related to the task at hand. However, I cannot hold off any longer. I do not want you to think that you can just go out programming and hope for the best.

No matter how good a programmer you are, you will need to provide some means of handling errors that occur. Here are some main sources of errors:

- Coding bugs

- Inability to open files

- Coding bugs

- Wrong user input

- Coding bugs

- Unexpected data

- Coding bugs

As far as this book is concerned, error handling goes hand in hand with data validation. After all, if your data is always good, there is no need to validate and no need to throw errors.

Showing Basic Errors

The basic method of handling errors when entering data is the ErrorProvider object. You saw this object a few times in Chapter 6, but I never really explained it.

Basically, the ErrorProvider is a small icon that you can associate with any visible control on your form. All you need to do is instantiate a new version of it and tell it which control to sit next to. The user sees a small blinking icon next to the offending field. When the mouse hovers over the icon, a ToolTip text message appears with some relevant information.

My thoughts on this ErrorProvider control have gone from "This is pretty cool" to "This is cute but not terribly useful." I concede that the control does have some uses, though.

Have you ever filled in a Web page with information needed to complete a transaction? Oftentimes when you leave something out, the same Web page comes back with a little error icon next to the fields you forgot (or failed) to fill in. This is useful to let the user know what he or she needs to do to remedy the situation. The ErrorProvider control for Windows Forms programs serves basically the same function.

In the ASP world, a user fills in fields in a Web page. When the user clicks OK, that Web page gets posted back to the server, and then it gets validated as a whole. If the Web page has any errors, it gets transferred back to the user's PC with error icons attached.

Windows Forms programs work a little differently. Most times you are able to validate a field during data entry or immediately after. There is no need for any ErrorProvider control in this case, as you will sound the klaxons and prevent the user from continuing on until the error is fixed.

There are times, though, when this control is useful. If you want, or need, to stave off validation until a whole form's worth of fields are entered, then you could use this control to flag several fields that may be in error. This is validation at the end of data entry.

When you have a form whose fields are validated at the end of the data entry phase, this is usually because many fields on the form are interrelated or maybe some fields are required to be filled in. Each field cannot be validated on its own, but the form must be validated as a whole. Try this simple example.

Make a new project. Mine is called "ErrProvider." Add the following controls:

1. Add a Label whose text reads **Name**.

2. Add a TextBox called **txtName** below this Label.

3. Add a Label whose text reads **Address**.

4. Add a TextBox called **txtAddr** below this Label.

5. Add a Label whose text reads **Favorite movie**.

6. Add a CheckedListBox called **lstMovies** below this Label.

7. Add a Button called **cmdSave** whose text reads **Save**.

Your form should look like the one shown in Figure 7-1.

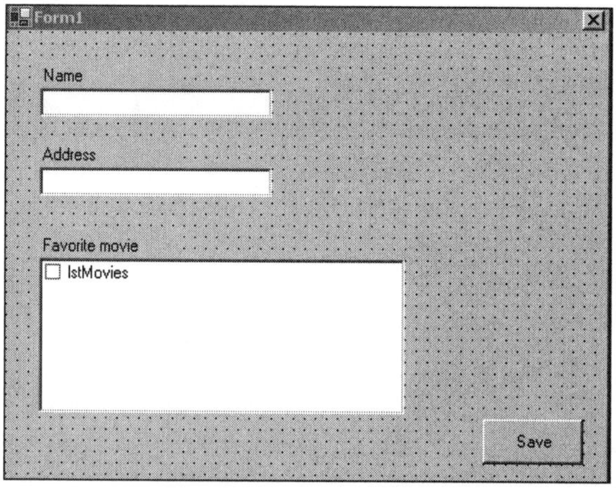

Figure 7-1. An error provider form

Before I have you add the ErrorProvider code, I want you to click each control on this form and look at the Properties page. For instance, if you click the CheckedListBox control, your Properties page should look like the one shown in Figure 7-2.

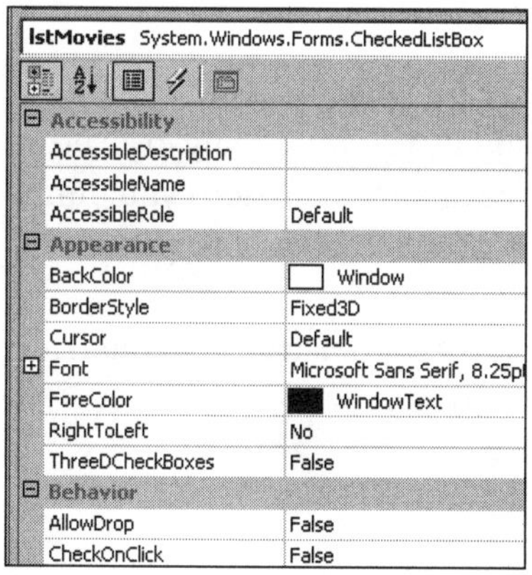

Figure 7-2. The CheckedListBox properties before adding an ErrorProvider control

Now add an ErrorProvider object to your form and call it **Err**. Click your CheckedListBox again and notice that there are some new properties, as shown in Figure 7-3.

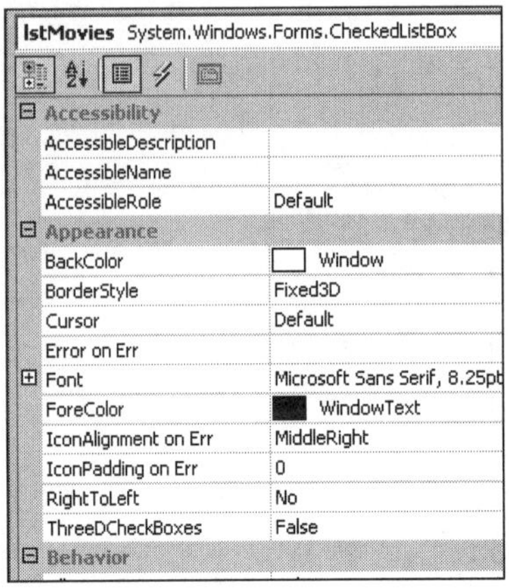

Figure 7-3. The CheckedListBox properties after adding an ErrorProvider control

These new properties have been added to all the controls on your form:

- Error on Err

- IconAlignment on Err

- IconPadding on Err

These are design-time properties only and you can't change them in code or at runtime. They're here to provide you with the capability of hard-coding in an error display while you're laying out the form. This is nice of Microsoft, don't you think? The only properties I would use are the icon placement and icon padding properties. The text should be flexible and code based.

Anyway, double-click the cmdSave button and get the delegate generated for you. Your filled-in delegate should look like the following.

C#

```csharp
private void cmdSave_Click(object sender, System.EventArgs e)
{
    if(txtName.Text == string.Empty)
        Err.SetError(txtName, "Cannot save form without a name");
    else
        Err.SetError(txtName, "");
```

```csharp
    if(txtAddr.Text == string.Empty)
      Err.SetError(txtAddr, "Cannot save form without an address");
    else
      Err.SetError(txtAddr, "");

    if(lstMovies.SelectedIndices.Count == 0)
      Err.SetError(lstMovies, "Cannot save form without a favorite movie");
    else
      Err.SetError(lstMovies, "");
  }
```

VB

```vb
  Private Sub cmdSave_Click(ByVal sender As System.Object, _
                            ByVal e As System.EventArgs) Handles cmdSave.Click

    If (txtName.Text = String.Empty) Then
      Err.SetError(txtName, "Cannot save form without a name")
    Else
      Err.SetError(txtName, "")
    End If

    If (txtAddr.Text = String.Empty) Then
      Err.SetError(txtAddr, "Cannot save form without an address")
    Else
      Err.SetError(txtAddr, "")
    End If

    If (lstMovies.SelectedIndices.Count = 0) Then
      Err.SetError(lstMovies, "Cannot save form without a favorite movie")
    Else
      Err.SetError(lstMovies, "")
    End If
  End Sub
```

Now add some code to fill in the CheckedListBox.

C#

```csharp
private void Form1_Load(object sender, System.EventArgs e)
{
  lstMovies.Items.Add("Dumbo");
  lstMovies.Items.Add("WindTalkers");
  lstMovies.Items.Add("Paper Chase");
  lstMovies.Items.Add("War Of The Worlds");
  lstMovies.Items.Add("LOTR");

}
```

VB

```vb
Private Sub Form1_Load(ByVal sender As System.Object, _
                       ByVal e As System.EventArgs) Handles MyBase.Load

  lstMovies.Items.Add("Dumbo")
  lstMovies.Items.Add("WindTalkers")
  lstMovies.Items.Add("Paper Chase")
  lstMovies.Items.Add("War Of The Worlds")
  lstMovies.Items.Add("LOTR")

End Sub
```

Run the program and click the Save button. Your screen should look like the one shown in Figure 7-4.

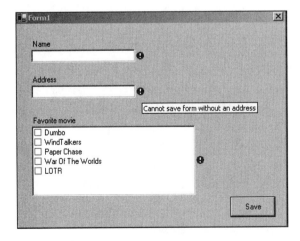

Figure 7-4. A form with errors

If you add some text to one of the TextBoxes or check a movie, the corresponding error will go away when you click the Save button again.

ErrorProvider Uses

Although the ErrorProvider is good for this kind of scenario, I prefer to use a more in-your-face error-handling method when possible.

If you have a form with many fields that just need to be filled in, the ErrorProvider is OK to use. For this form, however, I prefer to pop up a dialog box as well that shows the user the error of his or her ways in as explicit terms as possible. There is not much information you can provide in an ErrorProvider's ToolTip text box.

The Error Dialog Box

Have you ever come across an error like the one shown in Figure 7-5?

Figure 7-5. An obtuse error

I have seen errors like this many times. Click OK and your program just disappears. This is not too friendly. It is, however, all too common.

When you create error messages, be mindful of the following:

- The error message should provide a good description of the error.

- The error message should suggest a way for the user to fix the problem.

- The error message should provide a way for your program to get around the error or gracefully exit if the error is a showstopper.

The next example (in C# only) shows a better way to display an error with gentle prodding. Open up a new project and call it "ErrDialog." Figure 7-6 shows the form after you have added the following controls:

1. Add a Label that reads **Start Time**.

2. Add a TextBox called **txtStart**.

3. Add a Label that reads **End Time**.

4. Add a TextBox called **txtEnd**.

5. Add a Label called **lblTicks**. Make its BorderStyle FixedSingle and center the text.

6. Add a Timer to the form.

7. Add a Button called **cmdOK**. It should read **OK**.

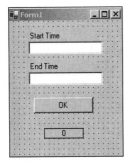

Figure 7-6. The ErrDialog form

Double-click the Timer to get the timer1_Tick delegate.

Listing 7-1 shows the code for the whole form (except for the wizard code). There is not much here, but there is enough to show what I need.

Listing 7-1. C# Code for the ErrDialog Example

```
using System;
using System.Drawing;
using System.Collections;
using System.ComponentModel;
using System.Windows.Forms;
using System.Data;
```

```
namespace ErrDialog_c
{
  public class Form1 : System.Windows.Forms.Form
  {
    private System.Windows.Forms.Timer timer1;
    private System.Windows.Forms.Label lblTicks;
    private System.Windows.Forms.Button cmdOK;
    private System.Windows.Forms.Label label1;
    private System.Windows.Forms.TextBox txtStart;
    private System.Windows.Forms.Label label2;
    private System.Windows.Forms.TextBox txtEnd;
    private System.ComponentModel.IContainer components;

    public Form1()
    {
      InitializeComponent();

      timer1.Interval = 1000;
      timer1.Start();
      cmdOK.Click += new EventHandler(this.OK_Click);

      txtStart.Text = DateTime.Now.ToShortTimeString();
      txtEnd.Text   = DateTime.Now.AddMinutes(-1).ToShortTimeString();
    }

    protected override void Dispose( bool disposing )
    {
      if( disposing )
      {
        if (components != null)
        {
          components.Dispose();
        }
      }
      base.Dispose( disposing );
    }

    #region Windows Form Designer generated code
    ...
    ...
    ...
    #endregion
```

```
[STAThread]
static void Main()
{
  Application.Run(new Form1());
}

private void timer1_Tick(object sender, System.EventArgs e)
{
  lblTicks.Text = (int.Parse(lblTicks.Text)+1).ToString();
}

private void Form1_Load(object sender, System.EventArgs e)
{
}

private void OK_Click(object sender, EventArgs e)
{
  DialogResult Retval;
  string msg;

  msg =  "The end time field has an incorrect value.\n";
  msg += "The end time must be later than the start time\n\n";
  msg += "Press 'Yes' to automatically adjust the end time";

  Retval = MessageBox.Show( msg,
                            "Incorrect End Time",
                            MessageBoxButtons.YesNo,
                            MessageBoxIcon.Error);
  if(Retval == DialogResult.Yes)
    txtEnd.Text =
          DateTime.Parse(txtStart.Text).AddMinutes(1).ToShortTimeString();
  txtEnd.SelectAll();
  txtEnd.Focus();
  }
 }
}
```

Run the program and click the OK button. Figure 7-7 shows a much better dialog box than the one in Figure 7-5.

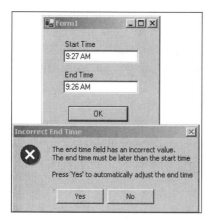

Figure 7-7. A better dialog box

This error dialog box tells the user explicitly what is wrong and what needs to be done to correct the problem. In this case, the program is able to automatically correct the problem for the user and offers to do so.

If the user clicks Yes, the end time will change to the start time plus 1 minute, the End Time TextBox will be highlighted, and the text inside will be selected. If the user clicks No, the same thing will happen, except the time will not be adjusted.

The user has been led back to the offending field and the field is ready to be edited. I have come across many instances where this kind of nice error handling has been possible but not used. You should show users errors like this whenever possible.

The Modality of the Error Dialog Box

I had you add a timer to the form that displays the seconds as they tick by. I did this to prove a point. When the MessageBox is invoked, it is *modal*. That is to say, you cannot do anything else in your program until you get rid of the dialog box. Does this mean that your program stops running? It appears to, as the next line of code after the MessageBox appears does not get run until the MessageBox goes away. However, look at the Label that holds the result of the time tick event.

The timer keeps ticking away, and the Label is updated with the new time while the MessageBox is still on the screen. This tells you that your program still responds to events, as it normally should. This is good news if you happen to be communicating with some RS-232 device at the time you pop up this message. Of course, any other thread that happens to be running on the side still continues on as normal.

There is one thing missing from the MessageBox dialog box: It has no provision for a Help button. Even the IDE debugger has a Help button on its MessageBox. Why leave it off here?[1] There is also no provision to add your own buttons to the dialog box. The VB 6.0 MessageBox dialog box was much more comprehensive in this respect.

TIP Although it is not recommended by Microsoft, you can still use the VB 6.0 MsgBox command. If you need the extra functionality, it may be useful to you. See the online help for information on how to use the MsgBox command.

You may find the built-in MessageBox to be limiting in its use. For instance, you may want to add a Help button or maybe some user-defined buttons. Perhaps you would like the dialog box to be nonmodal but still reside on top of the form. You can do all of this if you roll your own MessageBox form. You already have the knowledge to do this, and it could definitely enhance your programs that use it.

Advanced Error Reporting

So, you can now flash errors to the user. You know how to detect any user-entered data that is wrong, and you can politely show the user the error of his or her ways.

What about errors that have nothing to do with user input? These are errors such as unexpected coding bugs (yes, you can catch these at runtime), bad data coming in from some RS-232 port, or perhaps a security breach in your program. How do you handle errors such as these? Let's look to the System.Diagnostics namespace for the answers.

Using the Diagnostic Capabilities of .NET

The first thing I want to cover is the EventLogger. You may or may not be aware that since Windows 2000, there are system event log files and extensions to the Windows application programming interface (API) that allow you to read, write, create, and delete these log files.

The three basic log files are called Application, Security, and System. These three files are often written to by the operating system and also by various third-party

---

1. Sometimes I do not understand decisions like this.

programs. If you look at these log files, you can find some interesting information. You can also find some useless and outdated information.

I am not going to tell you where these files are until after this next small example. Well, OK, on my Windows XP machine they are located in the WINNT\System32\Config folder of my C: drive. If you want to find where your files are located, perform a search for "SysEvent.evt" on your root drive. You should see quite a few files in this directory.

The main method of the EventLog class is, of course, the WriteEntry command. This is an overloaded method that allows you to enter the following information:

- A string detailing what happened

- An EventLogEntryType enumeration that indicates what kind of event this is

- An EventID, which is a user-defined integer that you can use identify an event

- A category, which is a user-defined integer that you can use to categorize an event

The only thing you really need is the string detailing what happened. This next example, though, will use everything but the category.

 NOTE   The EventLogger is not really the place to put all messages you wish to save to disk. For instance, if you want to record information in a file to be sent back to you, the event log is not the place. The event log is used mainly for recording installation details and program start-up, shutdown, and security details.

Start a new C# or VB Windows program. Mine is called "Logging." Put a Button on the main form called **cmdLogin** and make the text read **Login**. Double-click this Button to get the click delegate.

Add another form called **Login** to the project. Add the following controls:

1. Add a Label that reads **Login Name.**

2. Add a TextBox called **txtName** below the Label.

3. Add a Label that reads **Password.**

4. Add a TextBox called **txtPass** below the Password Label. Make the MaxLength equal 5 and change the PasswordChar to *.

5. Add a Button called **cmdOK** to the form. Change its text to **OK**.

6. Add a Button called **cmdCancel** to the form. Change its text to **Cancel**.

7. Double-click the two Buttons to get the click delegates.

Your login form should look like the one shown in Figure 7-8.

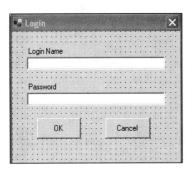

Figure 7-8. The login form

So, now you have two forms with essentially no code. Before you add code to these forms, you will need to add a class to your project called "EventLogger."

This class has static (shared in VB) methods that write certain things to a predetermined event file. Listings 7-2a and 7-2b show the code for this class.

Listing 7-2a. C# Code for the EventLogger Class

```
using System;
using System.Diagnostics;

namespace Logging_c
{
  /// <summary>
  /// Summary description for EventLogger.
  /// </summary>
```

```csharp
public class EventLogger
{
  private const int LE_Error      = 1;
  private const int LE_BadEntry   = 2;
  private const int LE_Started    = 3;
  private const int LE_Ended      = 4;
  private const int LE_Login      = 5;
  private const int LE_Logout     = 6;
  private const string ProdName   = "Logger";
  private const string SourceName = "Test Logger";

  static EventLog DataLog;

  static EventLogger()
  {
    if(!EventLog.SourceExists(ProdName))
      EventLog.CreateEventSource(ProdName, SourceName);

    //It is possible to enable an event to notify you of
    //a log entry being written
    DataLog = new EventLog();
    DataLog.Source = SourceName;
    DataLog.EnableRaisingEvents = true;
    DataLog.EntryWritten += new EntryWrittenEventHandler(EventLogWritten);

  }

  private static void EventLogWritten(object sender, EntryWrittenEventArgs e)
  {
    string s = string.Empty;
    switch(e.Entry.EventID)
    {
      case LE_Error:
        s="Error Event Written";
        break;
      case LE_BadEntry:
        s="Bad Entry Event Written";
        break;
      case LE_Started:
        s="Program Started Event Written";
        break;
```

```
    case LE_Ended:
      s="Program Ended Event Written";
      break;
    case LE_Login:
      s="Login Event Written";
      break;
    case LE_Logout:
      s="Logout Event Written";
      break;
    default:
      s="Event Written";
      break;
  }
  System.Windows.Forms.MessageBox.Show(s);
}

public static void ProgramStart()
{
  //Write to the log file that the program was started
  DataLog.WriteEntry("Program Started",
                     EventLogEntryType.Information, LE_Started);
}

public static void ProgramEnd()
{
  //Write to the log file that the program was started
  DataLog.WriteEntry("Program Ended",
                     EventLogEntryType.Information, LE_Started);
}

public static void LoginOK(string LoginName)
{
  DataLog.WriteEntry("Successful Login:" + LoginName,
                     EventLogEntryType.SuccessAudit, LE_Login);
}

public static void LoginFailed(string LoginName)
{
  DataLog.WriteEntry("Failed Login:" + LoginName,
                     EventLogEntryType.FailureAudit, LE_Login);
}
```

```csharp
    public static void LoginCanceled(string LoginName)
    {
      if (LoginName == String.Empty)
        LoginName = "Unknown Login Name";

      DataLog.WriteEntry("Failed Login:" + LoginName,
                         EventLogEntryType.FailureAudit, LE_Login);
    }

    public static void LogoutOK(string LoginName)
    {
      DataLog.WriteEntry("Successful Logout:" + LoginName,
                         EventLogEntryType.SuccessAudit, LE_Logout);
    }
  }
}
```

Listing 7-2b. VB Code for the EventLogger Class

```vb
Option Strict On

Imports System
Imports System.Diagnostics

Public Class EventLogger

  Private Const LE_Error As Int32 = 1
  Private Const LE_BadEntry As Int32 = 2
  Private Const LE_Started As Int32 = 3
  Private Const LE_Ended As Int32 = 4
  Private Const LE_Login As Int32 = 5
  Private Const LE_Logout As Int32 = 6
  Private Const ProdName As String = "Logger"
  Private Const SourceName As String = "Test Logger"

  Shared DataLog As EventLog

  Shared Sub New()
    If Not EventLog.SourceExists(ProdName) Then
      EventLog.CreateEventSource(ProdName, SourceName)
    End If
```

```vbnet
    'It is possible to enable an event to notify you of
    'a log entry being written
    DataLog = New EventLog()
    DataLog.Source = SourceName
    DataLog.EnableRaisingEvents = True
    AddHandler DataLog.EntryWritten, New _
                        EntryWrittenEventHandler(AddressOf EventLogWritten)
End Sub

Private Shared Sub EventLogWritten(ByVal sender As Object, _
                                   ByVal e As EntryWrittenEventArgs)
   Dim s As String = String.Empty
   Select Case (e.Entry.EventID)
     Case LE_Error
       s = "Error Event Written"
     Case LE_BadEntry
       s = "Bad Entry Event Written"
     Case LE_Started
       s = "Program Started Event Written"
     Case LE_Ended
       s = "Program Ended Event Written"
     Case LE_Login
       s = "Login Event Written"
     Case LE_Logout
       s = "Logout Event Written"
     Case Else
       s = "Event Written"
   End Select
   System.Windows.Forms.MessageBox.Show(s)
End Sub

Public Shared Sub ProgramStart()
   'Write to the log file that the program was started
   DataLog.WriteEntry("Program Started", _
                   EventLogEntryType.Information, LE_Started)
End Sub

Public Shared Sub ProgramEnd()
   'Write to the log file that the program was started
   DataLog.WriteEntry("Program Ended", _
                   EventLogEntryType.Information, LE_Started)
End Sub
```

```
Public Shared Sub LoginOK(ByVal LoginName As String)
   DataLog.WriteEntry("Successful Login:" + LoginName, _
                      EventLogEntryType.SuccessAudit, LE_Login)
End Sub

Public Shared Sub LoginFailed(ByVal LoginName As String)
   DataLog.WriteEntry("Failed Login:" + LoginName, _
                      EventLogEntryType.FailureAudit, LE_Login)
End Sub

Public Shared Sub LoginCanceled(ByVal LoginName As String)
   If LoginName = String.Empty Then
     LoginName = "Unknown Login Name"
   End If

   DataLog.WriteEntry("Failed Login:" + LoginName, _
                      EventLogEntryType.FailureAudit, LE_Login)
End Sub

Public Shared Sub LogoutOK(ByVal LoginName As String)
   DataLog.WriteEntry("Successful Logout:" + LoginName, _
                      EventLogEntryType.SuccessAudit, LE_Logout)
End Sub

End Class
```

Let's see what's going on in this class. The static constructor is guaranteed to run the first time I use any of the methods in this class. The constructor looks for an existing log source name. If this source name does not exist, then it creates a log file with the corresponding source name. It is possible to have a single log file accessed through many sources. This way, if you have a client/server program running on your machine, you could make one source the client source and one source the server source. They would both write to the same log file and you could distinguish them when reading the log file based on source name.

How does .NET know if a source exists? The API call that is wrapped by the EventLog.SourceExists static method looks in the registry for the source name. An event log file does not have any source name associated with the file itself. You will find event log entries in the registry under HKEY_LOCAL_MACHINE/SYSTEM/ControlSet001/Services/EventLog. Figure 7-9 shows my registry after running this finished example.

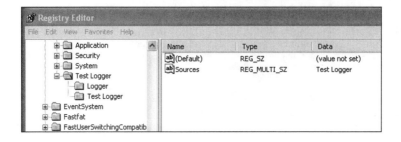

Figure 7-9. My registry entry for the event logger source

If the source does not exist, I make a new log file with the corresponding source. I enable log events and assign a delegate to capture those events.

Each static method in this class writes a value to the log file with a special event code. The log event handler looks at this code to determine what was written to disk.

Normally, you would not enable events for writing log file entries. There is no point in doing so, and it takes time. I do it here to show you what is going on.

The next code to fill in is the login form. Because you got the wizard to make the click delegates for the buttons, you only need to fill in the click event code. Here it is.

C#

```csharp
private void cmdOK_Click(object sender, System.EventArgs e)
{
  const bool LoginOK = true; //Causes unreachable code

  //First put in some code to evaluate if login succeeded
  if(LoginOK)
    EventLogger.LoginOK(txtName.Text);
  else
    EventLogger.LoginFailed(txtName.Text);

  this.Close();
}

private void cmdCancel_Click(object sender, System.EventArgs e)
{
  EventLogger.LoginCanceled(txtName.Text);
  this.Close();
}
```

VB

```
Private Sub cmdOK_Click(ByVal sender As System.Object, _
                        ByVal e As System.EventArgs) Handles cmdOK.Click
    Const LoginOK As Boolean = True    'Causes unreachable code

    'First put in some code to evaluate if login succeeded
    If LoginOK Then
      EventLogger.LoginOK(txtName.Text)
    Else
      EventLogger.LoginFailed(txtName.Text)
    End If

    Me.Close()

End Sub

Private Sub cmdCancel_Click(ByVal sender As System.Object, _
                        ByVal e As System.EventArgs) Handles cmdCancel.Click
    EventLogger.LoginCanceled(txtName.Text)
    Me.Close()
End Sub
```

As you can see, there is not much here. All I do is call a static method on the event logger based on the click event. No validation code here.

The next piece of code to add is the code for the main form. Again, there is not much here. Just make sure your Form_Load and button click event handlers look like this.

C#

```
private void Form1_Load(object sender, System.EventArgs e)
{
    EventLogger.ProgramStart();
}

private void cmdLogin_Click(object sender, System.EventArgs e)
{
    Login frm = new Login();
    frm.ShowDialog();
}
```

VB

```
Private Sub cmdLogin_Click(ByVal sender As System.Object, _
                          ByVal e As System.EventArgs) Handles cmdLogin.Click
   Dim frm As Login = New Login()
   frm.ShowDialog()

End Sub


Private Sub Form1_Load(ByVal sender As System.Object, _
                      ByVal e As System.EventArgs) Handles MyBase.Load
   EventLogger.ProgramStart()
End Sub
```

I also have a method to write to the log file upon program close. You will do this in the Dispose method of the main form. Add this line of code to the main form's Dispose method just before the end of the procedure:

```
   EventLogger.ProgramEnd();
```

Lose the semicolon for VB.

There you have it. Run the program and try to log in, or click Cancel on the login form. You should see some message boxes appear when log events are being written to the file.

You have two ways to view the file. You can use the EventLog methods to extract events and create your own event viewer. You can also use the supplied Event Viewer that comes with the Windows operating system. To access the Event Viewer, click the Start button and select Control Panel ➤ Administrative Tools ➤ Event Viewer. Figure 7-10 shows the Event Viewer looking at the Test Logger event file.

If you double-click any of the events, you can see the text that was written to this event. You can also set some parameters for the log file in here. For instance, you can set the maximum size of this file. It is a first-in first-out rotation.

The log file is good for keeping permanent records (within limits) of events on a certain machine. I often use it for just the purpose this example shows: program start-up and shutdown, and security. The real logger is the Trace function of .NET.

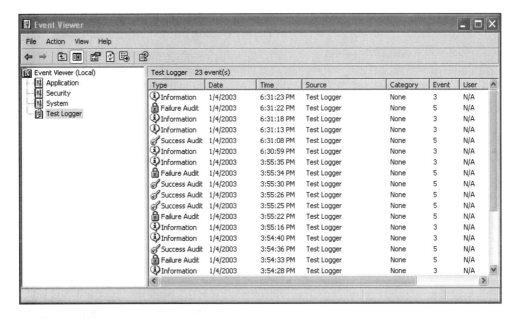

Figure 7-10. The Event Viewer

Instrumenting Your Code

My version of Microsoft Word flags "instrumenting" as not being a word. You would think that the .NET folks would incorporate their own lexicon into the Word dictionary . . . but I digress.

Instrumenting is the process of enabling your code to report status about things that happen in your code during runtime. Although you use the Debug class mainly for the development stage, you use the Trace class for collecting data out in the field. Here is what happens during a trace in Windows Forms:

1. You define a trace listener or use the default listener.

2. You add the listener to the Listeners collection.

3. You define the level of tracing according to the TraceLevel enumeration.

4. You add trace statements at strategic points in your code.

5. You turn on tracing via a configuration file or via a code switch.

This is the general idea. The actual implementation is somewhat more involved. So, what would you trace? Here are some things I have found to be essential tracing material:

- Success or failure of launching other programs from within code

- Modem initialization strings and return messages

- Database reading and writing

- RS-232 input and output

- Hardware initialization status

Once you get the hang of tracing your code, you will find it indispensable for troubleshooting problems in the field. It is no big deal to have tracing off by default and then turned on by a configuration file. This is the preferred method—let me tell you why. You could have several listeners in the Listeners collection. Some of these listeners could (read: should) be writing some information to a file. File I/O takes time, and if you have a trace switch set to verbose, you would be writing every trace message you have to every listener you have. This could severely impact performance.

Here is the trick to using tracing. Make sure you use a switch to turn tracing on and off. Use conditional trace writes based on the four levels of tracing. Use a configuration file to turn the trace levels on.

Your Own TraceListener

Although several types of trace listeners are available to you natively, there are some instances when you will want to make your own. In these cases, you would inherit from the TraceListener class and override the necessary methods, and perhaps add a few of your own.

When I started playing around with tracing, I wanted to send trace output to a console window. I like console windows. Unfortunately, you cannot do this in a Windows application; you can do it only in a console application. When you have a Windows application, all writes to the console go to the Debug window in the IDE and they vanish when running the executable. What to do? I could take the easy route and make the next example a console application. But I really wanted to do the console thing in a Windows application, so I came up with this example.

Start a new Windows project in C# or in VB. Mine is called "Tracing." You will need a second form to simulate the console window. Setup consists of the following steps:

1. Add a TextBox called **txtInput** to the main form.

2. Make this TextBox Multiline.

3. Add a Button called **cmdEnable** to the main form. The text should read **Enable Trace**.

4. Add a Button called **cmdDisable** to the main form. The text should read **Disable Trace**.

5. Add a Button called **cmdQuit** to the main form. The text should read **Quit**.

6. Make the form start in the center of the screen.

Your form should look like Figure 7-11.

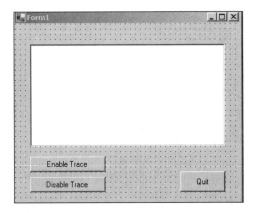

Figure 7-11. The main form for the Tracing project

The next thing to add is another form called **console**. This form should have a single TextBox on it called **txtOut**. Make this TextBox Multiline and set its Docking property to Fill.

You will also need to set the form's FormBorderStyle to FixedToolWindow. You should see a form whose contents are taken up with the TextBox. Because this is a tool window, the border is very small and contains a small *X* to kill the form.

There is not much code in this form. Listings 7-3a and 7-3b show the code for this form minus much of the wizard-generated code.

Listing 7-3a. C# Code for the Console Form

```csharp
using System;
using System.IO;
using System.Drawing;
using System.Collections;
using System.ComponentModel;
using System.Windows.Forms;
namespace Tracing_c
{

  public class console : System.Windows.Forms.Form
  {

    private bool mAlive;

    private System.Windows.Forms.TextBox txtOut;
    private System.ComponentModel.Container components = null;

    public console()
    {
      InitializeComponent();
      this.Text          = "Console Output";
      txtOut.BackColor       = Color.Black;
      txtOut.ForeColor = Color.White;
      mAlive             = true;
      this.Hide();
    }

    protected override void Dispose( bool disposing )
    {
      if( disposing )
      {
        if(components != null)
        {
          components.Dispose();
        }
      }
      base.Dispose( disposing );
      mAlive = false;
    }
```

```
    #region Windows Form Designer generated code
    …
    …
    …
    #endregion

    private void console_Load(object sender, System.EventArgs e)
    {
    }

    public bool IsAlive { get{return mAlive;} }
    public void Out(string buffer)
    {
      this.Show();
      txtOut.AppendText(buffer);
    }

    public void OutL(string buffer)
    {
      this.Show();
      txtOut.AppendText(buffer + "\r\n");
    }

    public void Clear()
    {
      txtOut.Text = string.Empty;
    }

  }
}
```

Listing 7-3b. VB Code for the Console Form

```
Option Strict On
Imports System.IO

Public Class console
  Inherits System.Windows.Forms.Form

  Private mAlive As Boolean

#Region " Windows Form Designer generated code "
```

```
    Public Sub New()
      MyBase.New()

      InitializeComponent()
      mAlive = True
      Me.Hide()

    End Sub


    'Form overrides dispose to clean up the component list.
    Protected Overloads Overrides Sub Dispose(ByVal disposing As Boolean)
      If disposing Then
        If Not (components Is Nothing) Then
          components.Dispose()
        End If
      End If
      MyBase.Dispose(disposing)
      mAlive = False
    End Sub


  ...
  ...
  ...


#End Region

    Public ReadOnly Property IsAlive() As Boolean
      Get
        Return mAlive
      End Get
    End Property

    Public Sub Out(ByVal buffer As String)
      Me.Show()
      txtOut.AppendText(buffer)
    End Sub

    Public Sub OutL(ByVal buffer As String)
      Me.Show()
      txtOut.AppendText(buffer + vbCrLf)
    End Sub
```

```
    Public Sub Clear()
        txtOut.Text = String.Empty
    End Sub
End Class
```

This class has a method to output a line of text to the TextBox and one to output a line of text followed by a carriage return/linefeed. If you look at the Trace class, you will see that this follows the methods in there that allow you to just pump out information or to output information a line at a time.

Note the IsAlive property. You may be wondering why I need this. I will tell you shortly.

Back to the main form. First, you need to add some namespace references.

C#

```
using System.ComponentModel;
using System.Windows.Forms;
using System.Data;
using System.Diagnostics;
using System.IO;
```

VB

```
Imports System.Data
Imports System.Diagnostics
Imports System.IO
```

Next, you need some class local variables.

C#

```
    #region class local variables
    TraceSwitch Tsw;
    #endregion
```

VB

```
#Region "class local variables"
    Dim Tsw As TraceSwitch
#End Region
```

Then you need some delegates to handle various events. Add the following code block to your main form.

C#

```csharp
#region events

private void EnableTrace(object sender, EventArgs e)
{
  Tsw.Level = TraceLevel.Verbose;
  Trace.WriteLineIf(Tsw.TraceVerbose, DateTime.Now.ToString() +
                                  " Tracing enabled");
}

private void DisableTrace(object sender, EventArgs e)
{
  Trace.WriteLineIf(Tsw.TraceVerbose, DateTime.Now.ToString() +
    " Tracing Disabled");
  Tsw.Level = TraceLevel.Off;
}

private void Quit(object sender, EventArgs e)
{
  Trace.WriteLineIf(Tsw.TraceVerbose, DateTime.Now.ToString() +
    " Program Closed");
  Trace.Close();
  this.Close();
}

private void KeyPress(object sender, KeyPressEventArgs e)
{
  if(e.KeyChar == (char)13)
    Trace.WriteLineIf(Tsw.TraceVerbose, string.Empty);
  else
    Trace.WriteIf(Tsw.TraceVerbose, e.KeyChar.ToString());
}
#endregion
```

VB

```vbnet
#Region "events"

  Private Sub EnableTrace(ByVal sender As Object, ByVal e As EventArgs)
    Tsw.Level = TraceLevel.Verbose
    Trace.WriteLineIf(Tsw.TraceVerbose, DateTime.Now.ToString() + _
                                  " Tracing enabled")
  End Sub
```

```vbnet
    Private Sub DisableTrace(ByVal sender As Object, ByVal e As EventArgs)
        Trace.WriteLineIf(Tsw.TraceVerbose, DateTime.Now.ToString() + _
            " Tracing Disabled")
        Tsw.Level = TraceLevel.Off
    End Sub

    Private Sub Quit(ByVal sender As Object, ByVal e As EventArgs)
        Trace.WriteLineIf(Tsw.TraceVerbose, DateTime.Now.ToString() + _
            " Program Closed")
        Trace.Close()
        Me.Close()
    End Sub

    Private Shadows Sub KeyPress(ByVal sender As Object, _
                                 ByVal e As KeyPressEventArgs)
        If e.KeyChar = ChrW(13) Then
            Trace.WriteLineIf(Tsw.TraceVerbose, String.Empty)
        Else
            Trace.WriteIf(Tsw.TraceVerbose, e.KeyChar.ToString())
        End If
    End Sub
#End Region
```

When the Enable button is clicked, I turn on tracing to the maximum level. You should be aware that each level also turns on the levels below it.

When the Disable button is clicked, I write a trace message and turn off tracing. You can see from the code that I use a version of the WriteLine method that checks for the trace level before writing. This is handy but it comes with a warning. The runtime engine will check to see if the trace message can be displayed even if the trace level is not active. This means that the whole line had better work all the time or you could throw an exception. So if you want to display the division of two numbers, you should make sure the divisor is not zero.

Next, add a trace line to the Form_Load delegate.

C#

```csharp
    private void Form1_Load(object sender, System.EventArgs e)
    {
        //You should not see this anywhere in any trace logs
        Trace.WriteLineIf(Tsw.TraceVerbose, "Program Started");
    }
```

VB

```
Private Sub Form1_Load(ByVal sender As System.Object, _
                       ByVal e As System.EventArgs) Handles MyBase.Load
  'You should not see this anywhere in any trace logs
  Trace.WriteLineIf(Tsw.TraceVerbose, "Program Started")
End Sub
```

Normally, you will not see this trace line anywhere, because the initialization routine has the trace switch turned off at start-up.

To send trace output to the console form, you need to make a new kind of trace listener. To do so, you need to add a new class to the main form. Add it below the class local variables section of the main form.

C#

```
public class NewListener : TraceListener
{
  console con = new console();
  public NewListener()
  {
    con = null;
  }
  public override void Write(string s)
  {
    if(con == null || !con.IsAlive)
      con = new console();

    con.Out(s);
  }
  public override void WriteLine(string s)
  {
    if(con == null || !con.IsAlive)
      con = new console();

    con.OutL(s);
  }
  public override void Close()
  {
    if(con != null)
    {
      con.Close();
      con = null;
    }
  }
}
```

```
    public void clear()
    {
      if(con != null)
        con.Clear();
    }
  }
```

VB

```
  Public Class NewListener
    Inherits TraceListener

    Dim con As console = New console()

    Public Sub New()
      con = Nothing
    End Sub

    Public Overloads Overrides Sub Write(ByVal s As String)
      If con Is Nothing OrElse Not con.IsAlive Then
        con = New console()
      End If
      con.Out(s)
    End Sub

    Public Overloads Overrides Sub WriteLine(ByVal s As String)
      If con Is Nothing OrElse Not con.IsAlive Then
        con = New console()
      End If
      con.OutL(s)
    End Sub

    Public Overloads Overrides Sub Close()
      If Not con Is Nothing Then
        con.Close()
        con = Nothing
      End If
    End Sub

    Public Sub clear()
      If Not con Is Nothing Then
        con.Clear()
      End If
    End Sub
  End Class
```

This class inherits from the TraceListener abstract base class. It overrides two of the Write methods and adds its own Clear method. Look in the online help to see which methods are required to be overridden and which are optional.

Now you can see from this code why I needed the IsAlive method in the console form. Every time a message is written to the console form, I need to know if the form exists or not. If it does not exist, then I create it and write to it. This way, the user can kill the console form any time, and if tracing is enabled my program will not crash but will instead pop the form back up.

Now add the following constructor code.

C#

```csharp
public Form1()
{
  InitializeComponent();

  Tsw = new TraceSwitch("VerboseTrace", "Trace data read/write");

  Stream myFile = File.Create("TestFile.txt");
  Trace.Listeners.Add(new TextWriterTraceListener(myFile));
  Trace.Listeners.Add(new NewListener());
  Trace.AutoFlush = true;

  txtInput.KeyPress += new KeyPressEventHandler(this.KeyPress);
  cmdEnable.Click   += new EventHandler(this.EnableTrace);
  cmdDisable.Click  += new EventHandler(this.DisableTrace);
  cmdQuit.Click     += new EventHandler(this.Quit);
}
```

VB

```vb
Public Sub New()
  MyBase.New()

  InitializeComponent()

  Tsw = New TraceSwitch("VerboseTrace", "Trace data read/write")

  Dim myFile As Stream = File.Create("TestFile.txt")
  Trace.Listeners.Add(New TextWriterTraceListener(myFile))
  Trace.Listeners.Add(New NewListener())
  Trace.AutoFlush = True
```

```
AddHandler txtInput.KeyPress, New KeyPressEventHandler(AddressOf KeyPress)
AddHandler cmdEnable.Click, New EventHandler(AddressOf EnableTrace)
AddHandler cmdDisable.Click, New EventHandler(AddressOf DisableTrace)
AddHandler cmdQuit.Click, New EventHandler(AddressOf Quit)


End Sub
```

This constructor sets up the trace listeners and adds them to the collection. Note that I have three listeners. The default listener writes to the Debug window in the IDE. I have a listener that writes to a file. I have a listener that writes to the console form. Whenever I use the Trace.WriteLineIf method, the output goes to all three. This is pretty cool, don't you think?

Now run the program and start typing in the text box. Click the Enable button and continue typing. You should see the result of your typing in the console window as well, as shown in Figure 7-12.

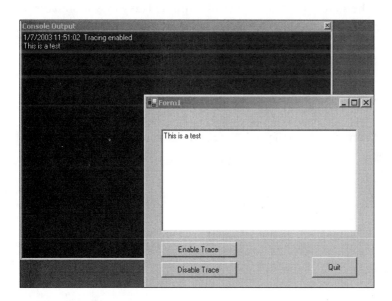

Figure 7-12. Tracing is enabled.

Kill the console window and continue typing. The console window will pop back up again. Disable tracing and the window stays up but nothing is written to it.

This is a pretty neat way to do debugging in the field. Quite often it is handy to have a console window on the screen where you can see what is going on in real time. I have used this many times to capture communication between some device and my program. I can tell pretty quickly if something is wrong and where the problem is.

Note the contents of the trace text file. It has the same information as the screen shown in Figure 7-12 does.

NOTE   C# users will find the text file in the Debug directory under the BIN directory for this project. VB users will find it in the BIN directory.

The Runtime Switch

When you create a program, you do not want any special buttons on the form to turn tracing on and off. The better way is to have your program read a configuration file and determine the state of the trace switch at runtime. This way, you shut down the program, edit the configuration file switch, and turn on the program, and you have instant tracing.

Add an XML file to your project called *<application name>*.exe.config.

NOTE   Because I denote my examples with -c or -vb, my .config files are called Tracing-c.exe.config and Tracing-vb.exe.config.

The contents of this file are as follows:

```xml
<?xml version="1.0" encoding="utf-8" ?>
<configuration>
  <system.diagnostics>
    <switches>
      <!-- "0"=off, "1"=errors, "2"=errors+warnings,
           "3"=detailed error info, "4"=verbose -->
      <add name="VerboseTrace" value="4"/>
    </switches>
  </system.diagnostics>
</configuration>
```

Spelling and case matter here. Although this file is created in your project directory, it needs to reside in the same directory as your executable.

VB users should copy this file to the BIN directory under their Tracing project directory. C# users should copy this file to the BIN\Debug directory under their Tracing project directory.

Now run your program and the trace message in the Form_Load delegate gets written to the console screen. In fact, the console screen appears at start-up.

You can change the value in this configuration file to reflect any of the four allowable values. This way, you can control tracing at the customer site when needed.

Throwing Errors

I know that up to now my examples have been seriously lacking in error checking. That's because I don't write buggy code.

Seriously, I have avoided major error checking because it sometimes gets in the way of what I really want to show you. However, error checking is very important to any professional-level program.

There is something called *exception handling* in .NET, where you can wrap some code inside a Try-Catch-Finally block. Any errors that happen because of this code—no matter how serious—will cause the code to end up in the Catch portion of the Try-Catch-Finally block. This is good because it is here that you can detect what happened and do something nice about it.

The Generic Error

Most of the examples I have seen concerning throwing and catching errors have been really simplistic. They go something like this.

C#

```csharp
try
{
  StreamReader file = new StreamReader("MyFile.txt");
  string s = file.ReadLine();
  int x = int.Parse(s);
  s = file.ReadLine();
  int y = int.Parse(s);

  int z = x/y;
  MessageBox.Show("The value of X/Y is " + x.ToString());

}
```

```
    catch
    {
      MessageBox.Show("Some error happened");
      this.Close();
    }
```

VB

```
Try
    Dim file As StreamReader = New StreamReader("MyFile.txt")
    Dim s As String = file.ReadLine()
    Dim x As Int32 = Int32.Parse(s)
    s = file.ReadLine()
    Dim y As Int32 = Int32.Parse(s)

    Dim z As Int32 = CInt(x / y)
    MessageBox.Show("The value of X/Y is " + x.ToString())

Catch
    MessageBox.Show("Some error happened")
    Me.Close()
End Try
```

This is catching errors at its simplest. No error trapping at all would have given you a better understanding of what happened.

Essentially, three things could have gone wrong here:

- The file might not exist. This would make the StreamReader instantiation fail.

- The file might exist but be empty. This would make the read return a null string, which causes an error in the parse line.

- The value of "y" might be zero, which throws an error during the division.

How would you know what happened and how would you present the error to the user? Well, you could catch an error. Change the Catch block to read as follows.

C#

```
    catch(Exception ex)
    {
      MessageBox.Show(ex.Message);
      this.Close();
    }
```

VB

```
Catch ex As Exception
  MessageBox.Show(ex.Message)
  Me.Close()
End Try
```

You are now catching the general exception. This is better, but it can still cause some confusion. For instance, if the error caught was in the parsing of the string to an integer, you would get the error shown in Figure 7-13.

Figure 7-13. A confusing error

Do you know which error this is? I don't. It could have come from either of the two parsing operations.

This next code shows a much more detailed Catch block. It includes specific error catching and detailed error messages.

C#

```
catch(IOException ex)
{
  MessageBox.Show("File I/O Exception: " + ex.Message);
}
catch(ArgumentNullException ex)
{
  MessageBox.Show("Parse Error: Null string\n" + ex.Message);
}
catch(FormatException ex)
{
  MessageBox.Show("Parse Error: string was not numeric\n" + ex.Message);
}
catch(DivideByZeroException ex)
{
  MessageBox.Show("Math error: 'y' was zero\n" + ex.Message);
}
```

```
catch(Exception ex)
{
  MessageBox.Show(ex.Message);
}
```

VB

```
Catch ex As IOException
  MessageBox.Show("File I/O Exception: " + ex.Message)
Catch ex As ArgumentNullException
  MessageBox.Show("Parse Error: Null string\n" + ex.Message)
Catch ex As FormatException
  MessageBox.Show("Parse Error: string was not numeric\n" + ex.Message)
Catch ex As DivideByZeroException
  MessageBox.Show("Math error: 'y' was zero\n" + ex.Message)
Catch ex As Exception
  MessageBox.Show(ex.Message)
End Try
```

As you can see, I catch almost every error that can happen within the Try block. The only thing I can't tell you is which parse line threw the ArgumentNullException or FormatException. This is the preferred method of catching errors. First try to catch the most specific errors and then catch the most general one. This is kind of like a switch-case block in C# (Select-Case in VB), where the last case statement is the default. You have something to fall back on if none of the others is run.

So, is this better than the simple Exception catch? Maybe a little, as it gives more detailed messages, but this code is awfully long and busy. Can you see doing this for every method? Also, what happens in the case of an error (besides showing a message) if there is a failure?

Catching Errors Before They Happen

The better way to catch errors like this is before they happen. I can easily adjust this example, where I am opening up a file, reading the contents, parsing some values, and doing a division, so it is more readable and also more robust. Here is what this example should look like.

C#

```csharp
try
{
  int x, y, z;
  StreamReader file = new StreamReader("MyFile.txt");
  string s = file.ReadLine();
  if(s == string.Empty || s == null)
    throw new ApplicationException("First line was empty");

  x = int.Parse(s);
  s = file.ReadLine();
  if(s == string.Empty || s == null)
    throw new ApplicationException("Second line was empty");

  y = int.Parse(s);
  if(y != 0)
  {
    z = x/y;
    MessageBox.Show("The value of X/Y is " + z.ToString());
  }
  else
    MessageBox.Show("Unable to divide numbers");
}
catch(ApplicationException ex)
{
  MessageBox.Show(ex.Message);
  //Put a trace message here
}
catch(IOException ex)
{
  MessageBox.Show("File I/O Exception: " + ex.Message);
  //Put a trace message here
}
catch(Exception ex)
{
  MessageBox.Show(ex.Message);
  //Put a trace message here
}
```

VB

```vb
Try
  Dim file As StreamReader = New StreamReader("MyFile.txt")
  Dim s As String = file.ReadLine()
  If s = String.Empty Or s Is Nothing Then
    Throw New ApplicationException("First line was empty")
  End If
  Dim x As Int32 = Int32.Parse(s)
  s = file.ReadLine()
  If s = String.Empty Or s Is Nothing Then
    Throw New ApplicationException("second line was empty")
  End If
  Dim y As Int32 = Int32.Parse(s)
  If y <> 0 Then
    Dim z As Int32 = CInt(x / y)
    MessageBox.Show("The value of X/Y is " + x.ToString())
  Else
    MessageBox.Show("Unable to divide numbers")
  End If
Catch ex As IOException
  MessageBox.Show("File I/O Exception: " + ex.Message)
  'Put a trace message here
Catch ex As ApplicationException
  MessageBox.Show(ex.Message)
  'Put a trace message here
Catch ex As Exception
  MessageBox.Show(ex.Message)
  'Put a trace message here
End Try
```

This code has fewer catches, and it can also catch which line of parse code was invalid. I put some simple error checking in the Try block before I did any major operations. The only thing I can't check for is some unknown I/O error when opening the file. I may not have permission, the file may not exist, and so on. For this I still need to catch the IOException.

By the way, there should be no excuse for a divide by zero exception to appear. Anytime you think that you may have a divisor of zero, check before you do the math. Many programs have blown up due to a divide by zero error that was not caught.

The Finally Block

There is more to the Try-Catch block. There is a Finally block that you can also add. The Finally block is interesting in that is it guaranteed to run no matter what. You can take advantage of this in several ways, as I demonstrate in this section.

The Finally block comes last after the Try-Catch block. Its main use is to take care of some housekeeping that may have been skipped over during the Try block. As you have probably figured out, the Try-Catch block jumps over any subsequent code in the Try block if there is an error. There is no way to go back to this code.

Before I go on, I must tell you about one gotcha related to Try blocks. Any object that you want to access outside of the Try block must be defined outside of the Try block. Here is what I mean.

C#

```csharp
private void foo()
{
  try
  {
    StreamReader file = new StreamReader("MyFile.txt");
    file.Close();
  }
  catch(Exception ex)
  {
    MessageBox.Show(ex.Message);
  }

  file.Close();
}
```

VB

```
Private Sub foo()
  Try
    Dim file As StreamReader = New StreamReader("MyFile.txt")
    file.Close()
  Catch ex As Exception
    MessageBox.Show(ex.Message)
  End Try

  File.Close()
End Sub
```

If the StreamReader initialization fails, the first attempt at closing the file will not get run. If you try to compile this code, however, you will get an error stating that the compiler does not recognize the variable "file". This variable was defined inside the Try block and that is the extent of its scope. To have the compiler recognize this "file" variable, I need to define it before the Try block as follows.

C#

```
private void foo()
{
  StreamReader file;
  try
  {
    file = new StreamReader("MyFile.txt");
    file.Close();
  }
  catch(Exception ex)
  {
    MessageBox.Show(ex.Message);
  }

  if(file != null)
    file.Close();
}
```

VB

```
Private Sub foo()
  Dim file As StreamReader
```

```
    Try
      File = New StreamReader("MyFile.txt")
      file.Close()
    Catch ex As Exception
      MessageBox.Show(ex.Message)
    End Try

    If Not file Is Nothing Then
      file.Close()
    End If
  End Sub
```

Now the compiler will be happy. By the way, I made sure that the "file" object was null before I closed it outside of the Try block. I did not do this while inside the Try block. Anyone know why?[2]

Now when you wrap the last few lines in a Finally block, your program should also work. Here is the code.

C#

```
    private void foo()
    {
      StreamReader file;
      try
      {
        file = new StreamReader("MyFile.txt");
        file.Close();
      }
      catch(Exception ex)
      {
        MessageBox.Show(ex.Message);
      }
      finally
      {
        if(file != null)
          file.Close();
      }
    }
```

---

2. Because inside the Try block I know that this object is not null. There's no need to check.

VB

```vb
Private Sub foo()
  Dim file As StreamReader

  Try
    File = New StreamReader("MyFile.txt")
    file.Close()
  Catch ex As Exception
    MessageBox.Show(ex.Message)
  Finally
    If Not file Is Nothing Then
      file.Close()
    End If
  End Try
End Sub
```

You may be wondering what the point of the Finally block is. In this case, the point is to get rid of the first instance of closing the file. You see the Finally block is guaranteed to run no matter what. So whether the Try block was successful or not, the file object would still get released before the method ended. This next bit of code shows the true power of this concept.

C#

```csharp
private void FooBar()
{
  StreamReader file = null;
  SolidBrush B     = new SolidBrush(Color.Azure);
  Pen P            = new Pen(B, 3);
  Font F           = new Font("Arial", 12);
  Graphics G       = null;

  try
  {
    G = Graphics.FromHwnd(this.Handle);
    file = new StreamReader("MyFile.txt");
    string s = file.ReadLine();
    G.DrawString(s, F, B, 10, 20);
    // Do some funky stuff with the pen here
    // Also do some extensive code
    //...
    //...
    if(s == "The End")
      return;
```

```
    s = file.ReadLine();
    // Do some more stuff with the pen here
    // Also do some more extensive code
    //...
    //...
    G.DrawString(s, F, B, 30, 20);

  }
  catch(Exception ex)
  {
    MessageBox.Show(ex.Message);
  }
  finally
  {
    if(G != null)
      G.Dispose();
    if(F != null)
      F.Dispose();
    if(P != null)
      P.Dispose();
    if(B != null)
      B.Dispose();
    if(file != null)
      file.Close();
  }
}
```

VB

```
Private Sub FooBar()
  Dim file As StreamReader = Nothing
  Dim B As SolidBrush = New SolidBrush(Color.Azure)
  Dim P As Pen = New Pen(B, 3)
  Dim F As Font = New Font("Arial", 12)
  Dim G As Graphics = Nothing

  Try
    G = Graphics.FromHwnd(Me.Handle)
    file = New StreamReader("MyFile.txt")
    Dim s As String = file.ReadLine()
    G.DrawString(s, F, B, 10, 20)
    ' Do some funky stuff with the pen here
    ' Also do some extensive code
    '...
    '...
```

```vbnet
        If s = "The End" Then
            Return
        End If


        s = file.ReadLine()
        ' Do some more stuff with the pen here
        ' Also do some more extensive code
        '...
        '...
        G.DrawString(s, F, B, 30, 20)

    Catch ex As Exception
        MessageBox.Show(ex.Message)
    Finally
        If Not G Is Nothing Then
            G.Dispose()
        End If
        If Not F Is Nothing Then
            F.Dispose()
        End If
        If Not P Is Nothing Then
            P.Dispose()
        End If
        If Not B Is Nothing Then
            B.Dispose()
        End If
        If Not file Is Nothing Then
            file.Close()
        End If
        end try
End Sub
```

In this method I instantiate quite a few objects that take up memory. Because it is always nice to clean up after myself, I dispose of these objects in the Finally block.

NOTE The common language runtime's (CLR's) garbage collector (GC) takes care of cleaning up managed resources, but it does this in its own sweet time. If you forget to dispose of managed resources, the GC will eventually get around to it. However, if you open a serial port or some raw GDI object such as a brush, you will need to get rid of it once you are done. The GC does not know about this stuff and will happily let you leak memory until your machine screams for mercy and your customers demand their money back.

Now, what is interesting is that there are some return statements in the Try block that bail out of the code depending on some value. This kind of thing happens all the time in software.

I use the Finally block here to make sure that these objects are disposed of before I leave this method. Even though I told the compiler I wanted to return halfway through the code, the Finally block still gets run.

Quite often I will use a Try-Finally block just for this purpose in some complicated or long methods. It is easy to instantiate objects, work with them for a week, and then forget to dispose of them at the end of your code. If you create the Finally block and dispose of every object you create at the same time you type in the code to create them, you will not make that mistake.

 NOTE The code for all this Try-Catch stuff is included in the code for this book, which you can obtain from the Downloads section of the Apress Web site (http://www.apress.com). The project is called "PlayCatch."

Summary

In this chapter I covered error handling and the controls and methods that .NET offers to help you. Handling and showing errors in an elegant way is very important to any program you write. I would venture to say that handling errors is even more important in a data entry program. People are, after all, prone to making mistakes. The more information you can give users about their mistakes in the form of an error and a possible correction, the better. You learned how to accomplish this by using message boxes and even by creating your own dialog boxes.

In this chapter you also learned about the ErrorProvider object and its limited usefulness. You explored how to use the EventLog capability of .NET.

Troubleshooting capability in the field is very important to any professional program. I showed you how to use the trace capability of .NET to instrument your code in a helpful manner.

Finally, I demonstrated the Try-Catch-Finally block form of error catching/handling. You saw some very useful tips for catching specific errors and disposing of objects that you may have forgotten about.

The next chapter covers advanced data validation. This is where you depart from the basic .NET controls and use some specific validation controls similar to what ASP.NET has.

CHAPTER 8

Advanced Validation and Custom Data Validation Controls

I TOOK A BREAK in Chapter 7 to discuss error handling. Although it may not be thought of traditionally as part of the world of data entry, error handling is even more important than normal in this arena.

This chapter covers some of the more advanced topics of data validation. You will see the Masked Edit control that was popular in VB 6.0. You will also see how to use the regular expression capability of .NET to generate short and sweet expressions for complicated data validation. Finally, you will learn how to make your own data validation control similar to the one that comes with ASP.NET.

In the next section you'll explore the most advanced, and the most flexible, of the data validation techniques: regular expressions.

Regular Expressions in .NET

To my mind there is nothing regular about regular expressions. Consider this regular expression: `href\s*=\s*(?:""(?<1>[^""]*)""|(?<1>\S+).`[1] Now what is so regular about this? I think that the expression "Find all the href="..." values and their locations in a string" is a lot more regular.

Although my English language expression may seem more regular and is certainly more humanly readable, the .NET Framework interprets the actual regular expression very nicely. As you know, being a programmer forces you to talk to the computer in its own language.[2] Make no mistake, "Regular Expression" may not be a language, but it has a syntax just like any another computer language such as C# or VB.

So, what are regular expressions used for and how do you use them in .NET? Regular expressions are used to parse strings. However, this is a bit simplistic. Parsing

---

1. I extracted this example from the online help
2. This is not *Star Trek* . . . yet.

strings brings to mind reading a line of text and extracting a substring from that text. Parsing also brings to mind extracting information from a comma-delimited file.

Regular expressions are much more than just parsing, though. Regular expressions in .NET can extract, insert, change, and delete any pattern in any string either forward or backward. This is powerful stuff.

Were regular expressions invented for .NET? No, they have been around longer than I have been programming, which is a very long time. For those real oldies who used the code editor Brief, regular expressions were a part of daily programming life. Those of you from the UNIX world dreamed in regular expression syntax.

The RegularExpressions Namespace

A whole namespace is devoted to regular expressions and their use: System.Text.RegularExpressions. In here you will find eight classes and one enumeration devoted to regular expressions. You will even find an event that you can hook to for custom validation during a matching operation. I go over these classes lightly in this section just to give you an idea of what they are used for. After this I charge headlong into the geeky world of regular expression usage.

The Capture class provides a result from a regular expression's subexpression capture. This means that if you use regular expressions to extract a substring, this is where you would find the answer. This class is *immutable,* meaning its properties cannot be changed. You will not be able to instantiate this class, and it does not appear by magic. Instead, you get an instance of this class from the CaptureCollection class.

The CaptureCollection class is a collection of Capture classes.[3] So, as you probably guessed, this is a collection of the entire set of substrings returned by a particular regular expression search.

If you have a complicated regular expression that includes more than one substring search, how do you get the instances of the Capture class? You can't get them all from a CaptureCollection, because this gives you only the Capture instances for a single subexpression. What you need is a group.

The Group class is used to hold a collection of CaptureCollections. At the very least it will hold a collection of one Capture object. At most it will hold as many CaptureCollections as are needed by the expression.

NOTE   You definitely should know that collections could contain collections ad infinitum. If you don't, then study the collection classes for some more examples.

---

3.   Did you guess that?

Of course, you cannot have a Group object without a collection of Group objects to hold it. This is the GroupCollection class. It contains a set of groups resulting from a regular expression match.

If you were to supply a regular expression to the framework to evaluate, you would naturally need an object as a result. This object is the Match class. The Match class is derived from the Group class, which is in turn derived from the Capture class. Therefore, the Match class holds all the results from a single regular expression call. It is in the returned Match object that you start digging for your results.

The last biggie in this list of classes is the Regex class. This class holds the regular expression that you need evaluated. If you call Regex.Match with a regular expression, you will get back a Match object. Check the Success property of this object for any hits.

The Regular Expression Syntax

Before I go on, you need to know a little about the regular expression syntax. First in the list are the escape characters. An *escape character* is a backslash followed by a special character or set of characters. For instance, in C-derived languages the escape character \n means newline, which most of the time gets converted to a carriage return/linefeed pair. Table 8-1 contains a list of regular expression escape characters.

Table 8-1. Regular Expression Escape Characters

Character Sequence	Meaning
\a	Bell character.
\b	Backspace or word boundary.
\t	Tab.
\r	Carriage return.
\v	Vertical tab.
\f	Form feed.
\n	Newline.
\e	Escape.
\0nnn	*nn* represents an octal number. The whole expression represents an octal number.
\0xnn	*nn* represents a hex number. The hex number is an ASCII character.
\cA	ASCII control character. This is Ctrl-A.

There are a few other characters, including back references, that are beyond the scope of this book. This next table is your first foray into the simple use of regular expressions. Table 8-2 contains a list of character matching commands.

Table 8-2. Character Matching Commands

Command	Meaning
[abcd]	Matches anything in the brackets.
[^abcd]	Matches anything *not* in the brackets.
[0-9]	The dash is used as an extender; same as [0123456789].
.	The period matches any character.
\p{name}	Matches any character in the named character class.
\P{name}	Matches any character *not* in the named character class.
\w	Matches any word or character that follows.
\W	Matches any word or character that *does not* follow.
\s	Matches any white space character.
\S	Matches any non-white-space character.
\d	Matches any decimal digit; same as [0-9].
\D	Matches any nondecimal character; same as [^0-9].

Is this all you need to know about the grammar? No. There is a set of commands called *quantifiers* that you can use to add additional information to the search pattern. The quantifiers apply only to that group or character class that precedes them. So, for example, I could have the expression [abcd]?. This means that the question mark quantifier acts on the bracket pattern. In this case, instead of finding all matches of abcd, it only finds only zero or one match. Table 8-3 shows the list of quantifiers.

Table 8-3. Regular Expression Quantifiers

Character(s)	Meaning
*	Zero or more matches
+	One or more matches
?	Zero or one match
{n}	Exactly *n* matches
{n,}	At least *n* matches
{n,m}	At least *n* but no more than *m* matches
*?	Gets first match that consumes the fewest repeats
+?	Specifies as few repeats as possible but at least one repeat
??	Gets match using zero repeats if possible
{n}?	Same as {n}
{n,}?	Gets at least *n* matches with as few repeats as possible
{n,m}?	Gets at least *n* to *m* matches with as few repeats as possible

Notice the overuse of the question mark? This is called the *lazy quantifier*. Usually the regular expression engine is greedy; it tries to find as many matches as possible with the constraints you gave it. The lazy quantifier tells the engine to match only what is necessary to achieve a match and nothing more. In essence, a quantifier token tells the parser how many times the previous expression should be matched. Once you start working with regular expressions, you will see that without quantifiers you can get major performance hits when running the regular expression engine. The trick is to be as specific as possible in your expression.

Here are some examples of regular expressions and their results. The text I am searching for in these examples is the same. The text being searched is the same between examples also. The only thing that changes is the quantifiers. If you are unfamiliar with regular expressions, hopefully this will clarify things for you.

Make a small console application in either VB or C#. The code for this application is shown here.

C#

```
using System;
using System.Text.RegularExpressions;

namespace RegX_c
{
  class Class1
  {
    [STAThread]
    static void Main(string[] args)
    {
      Regex r  = new Regex("Sp[ace] [1-9]*");

      for (Match m = r.Match("Space 1999 Spac 1999 Spa 1999 Sp 1999");
m.Success; m = m.NextMatch())
        Console.WriteLine(m.Value);

      Console.ReadLine();
    }
  }
}
```

VB

```
Option Strict On

Imports System
Imports System.Text.RegularExpressions

Module Module1

  Sub Main()
    Dim m As Match
    Dim text As String = "Space 1999 Spac 1999 Spa 1999 Sp 1999"

    Dim r As Regex = New Regex("Sp[ace] [1-9]*")

    m = r.Match(text)
    While m.Success
      Console.WriteLine(m.Value)
      m = m.NextMatch()
    End While
```

```
    Console.ReadLine()
  End Sub

End Module
```

I have here a text string that consists of several variations of the title to an old TV show called *Space 1999*. I have also instantiated a Regex object with the regular expression that determines the strings I am looking for. Here is the result of running this example:

```
Spa 1999
```

Exciting, isn't it? The regular expression told the parser to look for any strings that matched the *s*, followed by the *p*, followed by the *a*, followed by a space, followed by zero or more matches of the digits 1–9. Now, you're probably wondering, why didn't the parse spit back the actual text "Space 1999"?

When you are looking for something in brackets, it means match anything in there starting with the first character in the brackets. Because I had no quantifiers for the brackets, the default is to find only one match. The first character in the brackets is *a*, and this is what it started with. Note that the brackets represent one character position in the string. So, what happened is that the parser looked for "Spa 1999" as a first try, got a hit, and bailed out.

Change the regular expression to this:

```
"Sp[ace]? [1-9]*"
```

Now run the program and you should get the following results:

```
Spa 1999
Sp 1999
```

Why the two results? I had you add a ? quantifier to the bracketed text. Table 8-3 states that ? means find zero or one matches. So the parser first found zero matches in the form of "Sp 1999" and then it found one match in the form of "Spa 1999". Again, it spit these matches out and bailed. The parser did no more than what you told it to do.

Change the regular expression to this:

```
"Sp[ace]+ [1-9]*"
```

All you are doing is swapping out the ? quantifier with a + quantifier. Here are the results:

```
Space 1999
Spac 1999
Spa 1999
```

The + quantifier tells the parser to find one or more matches. It found all three. Remember that this quantifier has to find at least one match to succeed. Now change the quantifier from + to * like this:

```
"Sp[ace]* [1-9]*"
```

This means find zero or more matches. Here are the results:

```
Space 1999
Spac 1999
Spa 1999
Sp 1999
```

The parser found everything. The "Sp 1999" answer is the result of finding zero matches. The other answers are the result of finding the "or more" matches.

The three quantifiers ?, *, and + are like wild cards. You need to be careful with them because they could take up more time than you think and force your computer to come to a grinding halt. The only one that is really safe here is ?, the lazy quantifier. However, even this quantifier can return results you may not be looking for.

Exact Matching

If you have a situation where you are looking for an exact number of hits, use exact matching. Change the regular expression again to this:

```
Sp[ace]{2} [1-9]*"
```

What you are doing here is telling the parser to find an exact match of two characters in the brackets in any order. Here is what it found:

```
Spac 1999
```

This does not tell you much. How about changing your search string to this:

```
"Space 1999 Spca 1999 Spac 1999 Spa 1999 Sp 1999"
```

You added an alternate spelling of "Spac" with "Spca". It uses the same two characters but swapped. Here is the result:

```
Spca 1999
Spac 1999
```

As you can see, the numerical quantifier does not care about the order of the characters in the brackets. It will ruthlessly hunt down any variation and tell you about it.

So, is this all there is to regular expressions? Not by a long shot. In fact, many articles and books are dedicated to the subject. I know a few people who pride themselves on inventing the most complicated-looking regular expressions you could imagine. I have a plan in mind for you regarding regular expressions, however, so I will show you only a little more.

Text Replacement

There are two more features of regular expressions you need to know about: search-and-replace and search-and-delete. They are actually the same thing, but you can treat them as different here. Search and delete is actually search and replace with an empty string.

The Regex class has several static functions. These static functions allow you to input a regular expression and get an answer without having to compile the regular expression first. In this case, you will be using the overloaded function called Regex.Replace.

Essentially, this static function creates a one-time use of a Regex class, uses it for the intended purpose, and then throws it away. Here is a simple replacement function using one of the overloaded versions of the Regex.Replace method.

C#

```csharp
private static void Replace()
{
  //Replace all instances of the word could with the word should
  string OrgString = "This could be done. It could be accomplished now. " +
                     "I couldn't get it done in time";
  string SearchPattern = "could ";
  string ReplacePattern = "should ";

  Console.WriteLine(OrgString + "\n\n");
  Console.WriteLine(Regex.Replace(OrgString, SearchPattern, ReplacePattern));

  Console.ReadLine();
}
```

VB

```vb
Sub Replace()
  'Replace all instances of the word could with the word should
  Dim OrgString As String = "This could be done. " + _
                            "It could be accomplished now. " + _
                            "I couldn't get it done in time"
  Dim SearchPattern As String = "could "
  Dim ReplacePattern As String = "should "

  Console.WriteLine(OrgString + vbCrLf + vbCrLf)
  Console.WriteLine(Regex.Replace(OrgString, SearchPattern, ReplacePattern))

  Console.ReadLine()
End Sub
```

This is about as simple as a replacement can get. I search for any instance of the string "could" and replace it with the string "should". I include the space in the search string to avoid the hit on the word "couldn't".

Suppose the first word of a sentence was capitalized? This replace expression would miss it. An easy way to fix this problem is to use the replace function twice.

C#

```csharp
private static void Replace2()
{
  //Replace all instances of the word could with the word should
  string OrgString     = "Could it be done? It could be done now.";

  Console.WriteLine(OrgString + "\n");
  OrgString = Regex.Replace(OrgString, "Could", "Should");
  Console.WriteLine(Regex.Replace(OrgString, "could", "should"));

  Console.ReadLine();
}
```

VB

```vb
Sub Replace2()
  'Replace all instances of the word could with the word should
  Dim OrgString As String = "Could it be done? It could be done now."
```

Advanced Validation and Custom Data Validation Controls

```
      Console.WriteLine(OrgString + "\n")
      OrgString = Regex.Replace(OrgString, "Could", "Should")
      Console.WriteLine(Regex.Replace(OrgString, "could", "should"))

      Console.ReadLine()
   End Sub
```

The output of this function is as follows:

```
Could it be done? It could be done now.
Should it be done? It should be done now.
```

This is simple text replacement. You can get quite a bit more complicated. If you want to know more about text replacement, I suggest the reams of information available on the Internet or in the online help.

So, why am I covering regular expressions? Validation.

Regular Expression Validation

Now you know a little about regular expressions. Take my word for it, this introduction only scratches the surface. Now what?

Remember the validation routines for TextBox input? A few of them that you have seen look for patterns of characters using conditional statements in code. What about replacing those statements with regular expressions? Here are some common things to validate for in text box input:

- Accept only nonnumeric characters.

- Accept only numeric characters.

- Accept characters in a certain order.

- Accept dates based on the culture setting.

- Match a registration key that is entered in a specific format.

- Allow US-style ZIP codes.

- Allow only US-style phone numbers.

- Allow international phone numbers.

- Validate a URI.

- Validate an IP address.

- Accept passwords that must have at least six characters of which two are numbers.

Some of this stuff can be quite lengthy to validate using code. Much of it can be boiled down to a single line of code using a regular expression. Table 8-4 shows some common regular expressions and what they do.

Table 8-4. Common Data Validation Expressions

Expression	Meaning
[0-9]	Matches any single number within a string
\d	Matches any single number within a string
[^0-9]	Matches any single nonnumeric character within a string
\D	Matches any single nonnumeric character within a string
[A-Za-z]	Matches any uppercase or lowercase letter in a string
\d{5}(-\d{4})?	Matches U.S. 5-digit ZIP code or 5+4-digit ZIP code
1-[2-9]{1}\d{2}-\d{3}-\d{4}	Matches U.S.-style phone number (i.e., n-nnn-nnn-nnnn)
\d{1,3}\.\d{1,3}\.\d{1,3}\.\d{1,3}	Matches IP address format (not actual addresses)
([\w-]+)@([\w-]+\.)+[A-Za-z]{2,3}	Matches common e-mail addresses

These are only a few of the things you can do with regular expressions. If you want to find a period, then you need to escape it like this: \.. Unless it is inside a set of brackets, just use the period by itself. The \w construct is the same as using [A-Za-z0-9_]. Notice that I used [\w-]—this allows me to trap on any word character, including the dash.

In case you were wondering about the phone number expression, area codes cannot start with a 0 or 1. Therefore, I allow only 2 through 9 at the start of an area code. Note also that the phone number expression allows only one format. You can lengthen this regular expression considerably by allowing more formats such as a dash or a slash between numbers, or perhaps by making the area code optional.

There is one other thing to note here. If you are testing a whole string, it is best to anchor the regular expression at the beginning and at the end. Use a caret (^) as the first character in the expression and use a dollar sign ($) as the last. This allows you to test the string inclusive.

So, how do you use these regular expressions to validate something? Try these methods.

C#

```
//Matches string of consecutive numbers
private static bool IsInteger(string number)
{
  return(Regex.IsMatch(number, "^[+-]?[0-9]+$"));
}


//Matches string of consecutive letters
private static bool IsAlpha(string str)
{
  return(Regex.IsMatch(str, "^[A-Za-z]+$"));
}


//Checks for format of 5 or 5+4 zip code
private static bool IsValidZip(string code)
{
  return(Regex.IsMatch(code, "^\\d{5}(-\\d{4})?$"));
}


//Checks for format of most all email addresses
private static bool IsValidEmail(string email)
{
  return(Regex.IsMatch(email, "^([\\w-]+)@([\\w-]+\\.)+[A-Za-z]{2,3}$"));
}


//Checks for format of USA phone number
private static bool IsValidPhone(string phone)
{
  return(Regex.IsMatch(phone, "^([\\w-]+)@([\\w-]+\\.)+[A-Za-z]{2,3}$"));
}
```

```
//Checks for format of USA date
//separators = /-.
//format = xx/xx/xxxx or xx/xx/xx
//Month and day must be within correct calendar range
//Year can be anything either 2 or 4 digits
private static bool IsValidUSAdate(string dt)
{
    return(Regex.IsMatch(dt, "^(0[1-9]|1[0-2])[./-]" +
                             "(0[1-9]|1[0-9]|2[0-9]|3[0-1])" +
                             "[./-](\\d{2}|\\d{4})$"));
}


//Checks for format of military time
private static bool IsValidMilitaryTime(string tm)
{
    return(Regex.IsMatch(tm, "^([0-1][0-9]|2[0-3]):[0-5][0-9]$"));
    // ([0-1][0-9]|2[0-3]) Check for 00-19 OR 20-23 as hours
    // [0-5][0-9]          Check for 00-59 as minutes
}


//Checks for format of password
//format = 6-15 characters
//          Must include 2 consecutive digits
//          Must include at least one lowercase letter
//          Must include at least one uppercase letter
private static bool IsPasswordFormatValid(string Pword)
{
    return(Regex.IsMatch(Pword,"^(?=.*\\d{2})(?=.*[a-z])(?=.*[A-Z]).{6,15}$"));
    // ?= means look ahead in the string for what follows
    // (?=.*\\d{2}) Starting at the beginning find zero or more of any
    //              character and at 2 consecutive digits in the string.
    // (?=.*[a-z])  Starting at the beginning find zero or more of any
    //              character and a lowercase letter somewhere in the string.
    // (?=.*[A-Z])  Starting at the beginning find zero or more of any
    //              character and an uppercase letter somewhere in the string.
    // .{6,15}      With all else being equal, There must be between 6 and 15
    //              characters in the string
}
```

VB

```vb
'Matches string of consecutive numbers
Function IsInteger(ByVal number As String) As Boolean
  Return (Regex.IsMatch(number, "^[+-]?[0-9]+$"))
End Function


'Matches string of consecutive letters
Function IsAlpha(ByVal str As String) As Boolean
  Return (Regex.IsMatch(str, "^[A-Za-z]+$"))
End Function


'Checks for format of 5 or 5+4 zip code
Function IsValidZip(ByVal code As String) As Boolean
  Return (Regex.IsMatch(code, "^\\d{5}(-\\d{4})?$"))
End Function


'Checks for format of most all email addresses
Function IsValidEmail(ByVal email As String) As Boolean
  Return (Regex.IsMatch(email, "^([\\w-]+)@([\\w-]+\\.)+[A-Za-z]{2,3}$"))
End Function


'Checks for format of USA phone number
Function IsValidPhone(ByVal phone As String) As Boolean
  Return (Regex.IsMatch(phone, "^([\\w-]+)@([\\w-]+\\.)+[A-Za-z]{2,3}$"))
End Function


'Checks for format of USA date
'separators = /-.
'format = xx/xx/xxxx or xx/xx/xx
'Month and day must be within correct calendar range
'Year can be anything either 2 or 4 digits
Function IsValidUSAdate(ByVal dt As String) As Boolean
  Return (Regex.IsMatch(dt, "^(0[1-9]|1[0-2])[./-]" + _
                            "(0[1-9]|1[0-9]|2[0-9]|3[0-1])" _
                            "[./-](\\d{2}|\\d{4})$"))
End Function


'Checks for format of military time
Function IsValidMilitaryTime(ByVal tm As String) As Boolean
  Return (Regex.IsMatch(tm, "^([0-1][0-9]|2[0-3]):[0-5][0-9]$"))
  ' ([0-1][0-9]|2[0-3]) Check for 00-19 OR 20-23 as hours
  ' [0-5][0-9]          Check for 00-59 as minutes
End Function
```

```
'Checks for format of password
'format = 6-15 characters
'          Must, include 2 consecutive digits
'          Must include at least one lowercase letter
'          Must include at least one uppercase letter
Function IsPasswordFormatValid(ByVal Pword As String) As Boolean
  Return (Regex.IsMatch(Pword, "^(?=.*\\d{2})(?=.*[a-z])(?=.*[A-Z]).{6,15}$"))
   ' ?= means look ahead in the string for what follows
   ' (?=.*\\d{2}) Starting at the beginning find zero or more of any
   '                character and at 2 consecutive digits in the string.
   ' (?=.*[a-z])  Starting at the beginning find zero or more of any
   '                character and a lowercase letter somewhere in the string.
   ' (?=.*[A-Z])  Starting at the beginning find zero or more of any
   '                character and an uppercase letter somewhere in the string.
   ' .{6,15}      With all else being equal, There must be between 6 and 15
   '                characters in the string
End Function
```

Every single one of these methods works. Check them out. Try coding some of these regular expressions and see how much space they take up.

Probably the most obscure one here is the password checker. It uses a construct I have not explicitly covered. The regular expression parser has the capability to look forward in a string from its cursor point or look behind it. I am using the positive look-ahead search character set (?=pattern). The comments explain what the construct is doing. For further details on other subexpression patterns like this, I suggest you consult the online help.

Some of these expressions can be tricky, but they have so much power to get you what you want. As a contrast, look at the following code. This is an alternate way of validating the password as opposed to the regular expression.

C#

```
private static bool LongWayPassword(string Pword)
{
  //Check length first
  if(Pword.Length < 6 || Pword.Length > 15)
    return false;

  string upper = "ABCDEFGHIJKLMNOPQRSTUVWXYZ";
  string lower = upper.ToLower();
  bool FoundUpper = false;
  bool FoundLower = false;
  int  NumsFound  = 0;
```

```csharp
      char[] chars = Pword.ToCharArray();
      foreach(char c in chars)
      {
        //look for at least one uppercase letter
        if(Char.IsUpper(c))
          FoundUpper = true;
        //look for at least one lowercase letter
        if(Char.IsLower(c))
          FoundLower = true;
        if(Char.IsNumber(c))
          NumsFound++;
      }
      if(FoundUpper && FoundLower && NumsFound > 1)
        return true;
      else
        return false;
    }
```

VB

```vb
  Function LongWayPassword(ByVal Pword As String) As Boolean
    'Check length first
    If Pword.Length < 6 Or Pword.Length > 15 Then
      Return False
    End If

    Dim upper As String = "ABCDEFGHIJKLMNOPQRSTUVWXYZ"
    Dim lower As String = upper.ToLower()
    Dim FoundUpper As Boolean = False
    Dim FoundLower As Boolean = False
    Dim NumsFound As Int32 = 0

    Dim chars() As Char = Pword.ToCharArray()
    Dim c As Char
    For Each c In chars
      'look for at least one uppercase letter
      If Char.IsUpper(c) Then
        FoundUpper = True
      End If
      'look for at least one lowercase letter
      If Char.IsLower(c) Then
        FoundLower = True
      End If
```

```
      If Char.IsNumber(c) Then
        NumsFound += 1
      End If
    Next
    If FoundUpper And FoundLower And NumsFound > 1 Then
      Return True
    Else
      Return False
    End If
  End Function
```

So, for the C# code I saved some 20 lines of code by using the regular expression. For the VB code I saved about 25 lines of code. I saved not only code but also bugs. As you know, every line of code entered is a potential bug.

Regular expressions are not only a powerful but also an efficient way to perform search missions, as you saw with the password example. Wouldn't it be nice to have a TextBox that you could enter a regular expression as a property to be run against during validation? That's coming up toward the end of the chapter. For now, let's look at a very powerful control called the Masked Edit control.

The Masked Edit Control

The Masked Edit control is not native to .NET. Normally, I am reluctant to discuss third-party controls because most programmers will not have access to them. This one is different, however.

The Masked Edit control comes with Visual Studio 6.0. I would imagine that nearly everyone who is using .NET and is reading this book has Visual Studio 6.0 or 5.0 on his or her machine.

The fact that this control comes from Visual Studio 6.0, specifically from VB 6.0, should tell you something. It is an OCX; therefore, it is a COM control. Because it is not native to .NET, you will not see it on your Toolbox. You can get it easily enough, though, by following these steps:

1. Open up a Windows Forms project.

2. Bring the Toolbox into view.

3. Right-click the Toolbox and choose Customize Toolbox.

4. Choose the COM Components tab.

5. Select Microsoft Masked Edit Control, version 6.0.

Figure 8-1 shows the Customize Toolbox window.

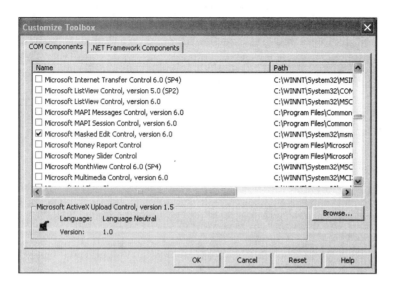

Figure 8-1. Choosing the Masked Edit control

Click OK and you should now have the Masked Edit control in your Toolbox. Figure 8-2 shows what it looks like.

Figure 8-2. The Masked Edit control in the Toolbox

You should also notice that two references were also added: AxInterop.MSMask and Interop.MSMask. Now, you already know that .NET talks to VB programs and OCXs via the Interop services, right? If not, you should. You can easily go along and code a perfectly good program without knowing how .NET is talking to this control, but to truly excel at this game you should know what is going on. Coverage of Interop is beyond the scope of this book, but I do urge you to spend some time learning at least the basics of how the COM Interop services work. OK, enough of that.

This control looks like a normal TextBox when dropped on a form. It has some enhancements, though. You can set a masked property to validate input and also to format output. You can even add some visual cues in the form of literal characters. For instance, you can make the box display the dashes for a normal phone number. I could add a mask in this form: ##/##/##. This is a typical date mask. The front slashes appear on the control as visual cues. Figure 8-3 shows this.

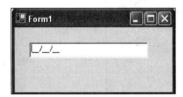

Figure 8-3. The Masked Edit control with a date mask

As you type in numbers, the cursor will skip over the slashes and put the numbers where they belong. Isn't this so much easier than hooking into the Paint and KeyPress events? The mask is easy to change as well.

You can mask just about any set of characters you like. Be aware, though, that the masking you can do here is not even close to the validation you can do using regular expressions. Table 8-5 shows the masking characters available for this control.

Table 8-5. Masking Characters for the Masked Edit Control

Character	Meaning
#	Digit placeholder
.	Decimal placeholder based on culture settings
,	Thousand separator based on culture settings
:	Time separator based on culture settings
/	Date separator based on culture settings
\	Escapes the next character as a literal
&	Character placeholder

Table 8-5. Masking Characters for the Masked Edit Control (Continued)

Character	Meaning
<	Converts all characters to lowercase
>	Converts all characters to uppercase
A	Required alphanumeric character
a	Optional alphanumeric character
9	Optional digit placeholder
C	Works like the & character
?	Letter placeholder (upper- or lowercase)

If you enter any character that is not valid according to the mask, it rejects that character. This is just like setting the Handled property of a TextBox to true during the KeyPress event. If you want to trap this rejection, you can hook into the ValidationError event.

All this is really nice, don't you think? Well, guess what?

It does not work properly in .NET!

Now, I know that quite a few of you VB programmers are probably sitting there in disbelief, so I will prove it to you. First, I will show you the sequence of events (literally) and the resulting Text property when you use this control in a VB 6.0 program. You can try this out if you want to see how it works, but suffice it to say that this is exceedingly easy VB 6.0 code.

VB 6.0

```
Private Sub me1_GotFocus()
  L.AddItem "m1 got focus event"
End Sub


Private Sub me1_LostFocus()
  L.AddItem "m1 lost focus event"
End Sub


Private Sub me1_ValidationError(InvalidText As String, StartPosition As Integer)
  L.AddItem "m1 validation error even " & me1.Text
End Sub
```

```
'===========================================================
Private Sub me2_GotFocus()
  L.AddItem "m2 got focus event"
End Sub

Private Sub me2_LostFocus()
  L.AddItem "m2 lost focus event"
End Sub

Private Sub me2_ValidationError(InvalidText As String, StartPosition As Integer)
  L.AddItem "m2 validation error event " & me2.Text
End Sub
```

Figure 8-4 shows the result of running this code.

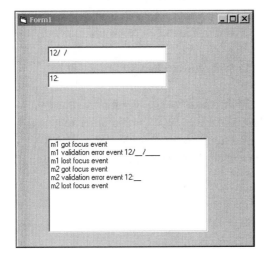

Figure 8-4. VB 6.0 using Masked Edit control

You can see that the events are in the following correct order:

1. The control got focus.

2. A validation error event fired because I left the control too early.

3. The second control got focus.

4. A validation error event fired because I left the control too early.

5. The first control got focus.

This is what you would expect, and it is what you get. Notice that when I display the Text property of the control, I get the text entered as well as the visual cues. I went from control to control by using the Tab key.

Now let's do the same thing in C# and in VB. Believe it or not, this control behaves slightly differently in the two languages.

Start a new project in either C# or in VB. Mine is called "MaskedEdit." Add the following controls and properties:

1. Add a Label whose text reads **Enter Date**.

2. Below this Label add a Masked Edit control called **meDate**. Change its TabIndex to 0. Change its mask to 9#/9#/####.

3. Add a Label whose text reads **Enter Military Time**.

4. Below this Label add a Masked Edit control called **meTime**. Change its TabIndex to 1. Change its mask to ##:##.

5. Add a ListBox called **L**. Change its TabStop property to false.

Figure 8-5 shows what this looks like.

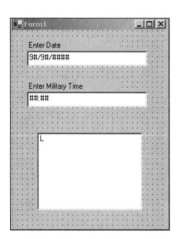

Figure 8-5. .NET Masked Edit control test

The code for this project is similar to the code for the VB 6.0 project. Listings 8-1a and 8-1b show the code for the Form_Load event handler and also for the delegates that handle the enter, leave, and validation error events.

Listing 8-1a. C# Code for the Masked Edit Control Test Program

```csharp
private void Form1_Load(object sender, System.EventArgs e)
{
  meDate.ValidationError +=
              new MaskEdBoxEvents_ValidationErrorEventHandler(DateErr);
  meDate.Enter += new EventHandler(DateEnter);
  meDate.Leave += new EventHandler(DateLeave);

  meTime.ValidationError +=
              new MaskEdBoxEvents_ValidationErrorEventHandler(TimeErr);
  meTime.Enter += new EventHandler(TimeEnter);
  meTime.Leave += new EventHandler(TimeLeave);

}

#region Masked Edit events

private void DateEnter(object sender, EventArgs e)
{
  L.Items.Add("Date got focus");
}

private void DateLeave(object sender, EventArgs e)
{
  L.Items.Add("Date left");
  L.Items.Add("Date Text = " + meDate.Text);
}

private void DateErr(object sender, MaskEdBoxEvents_ValidationErrorEvent e)
{
  L.Items.Add("Date validation error");
}

private void TimeEnter(object sender, EventArgs e)
{
  L.Items.Add("Time got focus");
}

private void TimeLeave(object sender, EventArgs e)
{
  L.Items.Add("Time left");
  L.Items.Add("Time Text = " + meTime.Text);
}
```

```csharp
private void TimeErr(object sender, MaskEdBoxEvents_ValidationErrorEvent e)
{
  L.Items.Add("Time validation error");
}


#endregion
```

Listing 8-1b. VB Code for the Masked Edit Control Test Program

```vb
Private Sub Form1_Load(ByVal sender As System.Object, _
                       ByVal e As System.EventArgs) Handles MyBase.Load

  AddHandler meDate.ValidationError, _
          New MaskEdBoxEvents_ValidationErrorEventHandler(AddressOf DateErr)
  AddHandler meDate.Enter, New EventHandler(AddressOf DateEnter)
  AddHandler meDate.Leave, New EventHandler(AddressOf DateLeave)

  AddHandler meTime.ValidationError, _
          New MaskEdBoxEvents_ValidationErrorEventHandler(AddressOf TimeErr)
  AddHandler meTime.Enter, New EventHandler(AddressOf TimeEnter)
  AddHandler meTime.Leave, New EventHandler(AddressOf TimeLeave)

End Sub

#Region "Masked Edit events"

  Private Sub DateEnter(ByVal sender As Object, ByVal e As EventArgs)
    L.Items.Add("Date got focus")
  End Sub

  Private Sub DateLeave(ByVal sender As Object, ByVal e As EventArgs)
    L.Items.Add("Date left")
    L.Items.Add("Date Text = " + meDate.Text)
  End Sub

  Private Sub DateErr(ByVal sender As Object, _
                      ByVal e As MaskEdBoxEvents_ValidationErrorEvent)
    L.Items.Add("Date validation error")
  End Sub

  Private Sub TimeEnter(ByVal sender As Object, ByVal e As EventArgs)
    L.Items.Add("Time got focus")
  End Sub
```

```
    Private Sub TimeLeave(ByVal sender As Object, ByVal e As EventArgs)
      L.Items.Add("Time left")
      L.Items.Add("Time Text = " + meTime.Text)
    End Sub

    Private Sub TimeErr(ByVal sender As Object, _
                        ByVal e As MaskEdBoxEvents_ValidationErrorEvent)
      L.Items.Add("Time validation error")
    End Sub

#End Region
```

Compile and run the program. Type in a few valid characters in the date field and tab over to the time field. Type a few valid characters in the time field and tab back over to the date field. Figure 8-6 shows the result of this.

Figure 8-6. .NET rendition of the Masked Edit control test

As you can see, the events are in the following order:

1. The date field got focus.

2. The date field lost focus.

3. The time field got focus.

4. The date field fired a validation error.

5. The time field lost focus.

6. The date field got focus.

7. The time field fired a validation error.

Talk about a time lag! The validation error event is not fired until the next control already has focus. The reason I would use this event is to bring focus back to the offending control if not enough characters were entered. The control itself takes care of any error while you are still in the control, but this event is the way for you to know if the control has enough characters.

Imagine this. What do you think would happen if I had the following code for these two controls?

C#

```csharp
private void DateErr(object sender, MaskEdBoxEvents_ValidationErrorEvent e)
{
  L.Items.Add("Date validation error");
  meDate.Focus();
}
private void TimeErr(object sender, MaskEdBoxEvents_ValidationErrorEvent e)
{
  L.Items.Add("Time validation error");
  meTime.Focus();
}
```

VB

```vb
Private Sub DateEnter(ByVal sender As Object, ByVal e As EventArgs)
  L.Items.Add("Date got focus")
  meDate.Focus()
End Sub
Private Sub TimeErr(ByVal sender As Object, _
                    ByVal e As MaskEdBoxEvents_ValidationErrorEvent)
  L.Items.Add("Time validation error")
  meTime.Focus()
End Sub
```

All I did was set the focus back to the offending control. Let me tell you what happens here: complete lockup. Because the events come out of order, the validation code for the date control sets focus back to the date control when focus is already in the time control. This makes the time control validation error code return focus back to the time control. You have set up a game of high-speed ping-pong. You can spend days trying to overcome this, but it can't be done without lots of code. Eliminating lots of code is the whole point of using this control.

Notice in Figure 8-6 that when I printed out the Text property of each control, all I got was an empty string. There is no way to get at the Text property of this control in .NET.

Now for the difference in using this control between C# and VB. The Text property does not even show up in the C# IntelliSense. It does in VB .NET.

So, why didn't I just tell you that this control does not work? Because you needed to feel the pain I went through trying to get it to work. Really, I show you this because I don't want you to think that this control can save you hours of programming and that it's the answer to most of your data entry and validation problems. It isn't.

Does it end here? Is there any hope? No and yes. How about making your own Masked Edit control?

Rolling Your Own Masked Edit Control

Because you can't use the VB 6.0–supplied Masked Edit control, how about making your own? This is such a useful control that it is well worth taking the time to cover it here.

I liked the idea of the Masked Edit control and its features. Here is what you will be programming as features in this control:

- Ability to have predefined mask formats

- Ability to have user-defined mask formats (limited)

- Ability to have no mask and accept anything

- Ability to have a validation error event that fires before the control loses focus

- Ability to suppress the validation error event (which fires only during validation) by setting the TextBox.CausesValidation property to false

- Ability to have visual cues so the user knows how many characters to input

- Ability to allow literals that cannot be deleted

All this can be yours for only $19.95! And if you call now, I will throw in another control for free!

I must warn you about writing this control and its associated test program. It is not easy, and you have to take care to do everything perfectly or your control will crash. Here we go.

Start a new C# or VB Windows control library. This is not a normal Windows project—it is a user control that you will modify heavily. Mine is called "CustomMask."

> **NOTE** In the code for this chapter (you can download the code for this book from the Downloads section of the Apress Web site at http://www.apress.com), you will see that the VB project is called CustomMask-vb and the C# project is called CustomMask-c. I tell you this because you may see two of the same controls in the .NET control library after you write the test program.

There is no user interface to this control. What you see on the screen is a small borderless window. I show you how to get rid of it shortly. For now, look at the code generated for you.

> **CAUTION** Whatever you do, don't double-click the form to get to the code. You will get the Form_Load event delegate definition and the delegate code as well. You will be making some changes to the code, which will cause some errors in the wizard-generated code, and you will then need to get rid of this code by hand.

This class derives from System.Windows.Forms.UserControl. This is fine for most user controls, but what I want to do here is derive from the TextBox. This allows me to extend the TextBox properties. Here are the before and after class definitions. (Be sure to add System.Text and System.Text.RegularExpressions namespace references.)

C# Class Definition Before the Change

```
public class UserControl1 : System.Windows.Forms.UserControl
{
...
}
```

C# Class Definition After the Change

```
public class MaskedTextBox_C : System.Windows.Forms.TextBox
{
...
}
```

VB Class Definition Before the Change

```
Public Class UserControl1
    Inherits System.Windows.Forms.UserControl
...
End Class
```

VB Class Definition After the Change

```
Public Class MaskedTextBox_VB
  Inherits System.Windows.Forms.TextBox
...
End Class
```

As you can see, the code now inherits from the TextBox class. If you try to view the form, you will not be able to because it does not exist anymore.

Now it is time to add some class local variables. Some of these will be public so you will be able to see them in your test form. Here they are.

C#

```
#region local variables

public event ValidationErrorEventHandler ValidationError;

public enum FormatType
{
  None,
  Date,
  Numbers,
  Alpha
};
string       mUserMask;
FormatType   mFmt            = FormatType.None;
char         mNumberPlace    = '#';
char         mCue            = '_';
string       mRegNum         = "[0-9]";
```

```
char        mAlphaPlace    = '?';
string      mRegAlpha      = "[A-Za-z]";
string      mAnything      = ".*";
string      mRegExpression = string.Empty;
StringBuilder mText        = new StringBuilder();
int         mValidationErrors;

#endregion
```

VB

```
#Region "local variables"

  Public Event ValidationError As ValidationErrorEventHandler

  Public Enum FormatType
    None
    DateFormat
    Numbers
    Alpha
  End Enum

  Dim mUserMask As String
  Dim mFmt As FormatType = FormatType.None
  Dim mNumberPlace As Char = "#"c
  Dim mCue As Char = "_"c
  Dim mRegNum As String = "[0-9]"
  Dim mAlphaPlace As Char = "?"c
  Dim mRegAlpha As String = "[A-Za-z]"
  Dim mAnything As String = ".*"
  Dim mRegExpression As String = String.Empty
  Dim mText As StringBuilder = New StringBuilder()
  Dim mValidationErrors As Int32

#End Region
```

The Format enumeration is used for the Format property you will code next. This enumeration allows anyone using this control to choose an easy-to-see format rather than entering in a number. You will see this more clearly when you get to the client portion of this project.

Remember the regular expressions? As you can see from this variable list, you will use them extensively in this control.

Now it is time to add two new properties, Format and Mask. Here is the code.

C#

```csharp
#region New properties

/// <summary>
/// Sets one of three formats
/// Date must be ##/##/####
/// Numbers must be 0-9 exactly 8 digits.
/// Alpha must be A-Z or a-z, exactly 8 digits
/// </summary>
public FormatType Format
{
  get{return mFmt;}
  set
  {
    mFmt = value;
    mText = new StringBuilder();

    if(mFmt == FormatType.None)
    {
      mUserMask = "";
      mRegExpression = mAnything;
    }
    else if(mFmt == FormatType.Date)
    {
      mUserMask = "##/##/####";
      mText.Append("__/__/____");
      mRegExpression = "\\d{2}/\\d{2}/\\d{4}";
    }
    else if(mFmt == FormatType.Alpha)
    {
      mUserMask = "????????";
      mRegExpression = mRegAlpha + "{8}";
      mText.Append("_____");
    }
    else if(mFmt == FormatType.Numbers)
    {
      mUserMask = "########";
      mRegExpression = mRegNum + "{8}";
      mText.Append("_____");
    }
    Mask = mUserMask;
  }
}
```

```csharp
/// <summary>
/// If the Format property is set then
/// this property is invalid
/// Mask properties recognized are:
///    # for number
///    ? for alpha (upper or lowercase)
/// all other characters are literals
/// </summary>
public string Mask
{
  get{return mUserMask;}
  set
  {
    if(mFmt == FormatType.None)
    {
      mRegExpression = string.Empty;
      mText = new StringBuilder();
      mUserMask = value;
      char[] chars = mUserMask.ToCharArray();
      foreach(char c in chars)
      {
        if(c == mNumberPlace)
        {
          mRegExpression += mRegNum;
          mText.Append(mCue);
        }
        else if(c == mAlphaPlace)
        {
          mRegExpression += mRegAlpha;
          mText.Append(mCue);
        }
        else
        {
          mRegExpression += c.ToString();
          mText.Append(c);
        }
      }
    }
    this.Text = mText.ToString();
  }
}

#endregion
```

VB

```vb
#Region "New properties"

  Public Property Format() As FormatType
    Get
      Return mFmt
    End Get
    Set(ByVal Value As FormatType)
      mFmt = Value
      mText = New StringBuilder()

      If mFmt = FormatType.None Then
        mUserMask = ""
        mRegExpression = mAnything
      ElseIf mFmt = FormatType.DateFormat Then
        mUserMask = "##/##/####"
        mText.Append("__/__/____")
        mRegExpression = "\\d{2}/\\d{2}/\\d{4}"
      ElseIf mFmt = FormatType.Alpha Then
        mUserMask = "????????"
        mRegExpression = mRegAlpha + "{8}"
        mText.Append("_____")
      ElseIf mFmt = FormatType.Numbers Then
        mUserMask = "########"
        mRegExpression = mRegNum + "{8}"
        mText.Append("_____")
      End If
      Mask = mUserMask
    End Set
  End Property

  Public Property Mask() As String
    Get
      Return mUserMask
    End Get
    Set(ByVal Value As String)
      If mFmt = FormatType.None Then
        mRegExpression = String.Empty
        mText = New StringBuilder()
        mUserMask = Value
        Dim chars() As Char = mUserMask.ToCharArray()
        Dim c As Char
        For Each c In chars
```

```
        If c = mNumberPlace Then
          mRegExpression += mRegNum
          mText.Append(mCue)
        ElseIf c = mAlphaPlace Then
          mRegExpression += mRegAlpha
          mText.Append(mCue)
        Else
          mRegExpression += c.ToString()
          mText.Append(c)
        End If
      Next
      Me.Text = mText.ToString()
    End If
  End Set
End Property

#End Region
```

Let's look at these properties in some detail. The Format property builds a regular expression based on the type of data allowed in. At the same time, it builds the string to be shown in the TextBox. I am using the underscore (_) character as a visual cue for the user. If you want, you can add another property to allow the user to choose his or her cue.

In the interest of limiting the code I need, I limited the alpha and numeric formats to only eight characters. Also note that I am not allowing any optional numbers or optional alpha characters.

The Mask property is dependent upon what the user chooses for the Format property. If the user chooses a format of None, then this property accepts the user format. I allow only # and ? as replacement characters. All other characters entered are treated as literal and cannot be changed by the user during runtime. A literal is defined as a character that appears at its correct position in the control, and it cannot be deleted or overwritten.

Notice that this Mask property builds the correct regular expression string, as it looks at each character in the input mask. At the same time, I am also building the text that is to be displayed in the control during runtime.

The next bit of code you will need takes care of the user entering in characters during runtime. I also have a delete routine in here.

C#

```
#region Helper stuff

public string EnterLetter(ref int position, char c)
{
  //User pressed delete key
  if((int)c == 8)
  {
    position--;
    return DeleteLetter(ref position);
  }

  //User trying to go beyond bounds
  if(position >= mText.Length)
    return mText.ToString();

  //If we have hit a literal then advance one
  //Do this in a loop in case there are more literals.
  if(mText[position] != mCue)
    position++;

  //check to see if the character is ok
  if(mUserMask[position] == mNumberPlace)
  {
    if(Regex.IsMatch(c.ToString(), mRegNum))
    {
      mText[position] = c;
      position ++;
    }
  }
  else if(mUserMask[position] == mAlphaPlace)
  {
    if(Regex.IsMatch(c.ToString(), mRegAlpha))
    {
      mText[position] = c;
      position ++;
    }
  }

  return mText.ToString();
}
```

```
public string DeleteLetter(ref int pos)
{
  //If the character to be deleted is a cue then bail out
  if(mText[pos] != mCue)
  {
    //If the character to be deleted is valid then change it back to a cue
    if(mUserMask[pos] == mNumberPlace || mUserMask[pos] == mAlphaPlace)
      mText[pos] = mCue;
  }
  return mText.ToString();
}


#endregion
```

VB

```
#Region "Helper stuff"

  Public Function EnterLetter(ByRef position As Int32, _
                              ByVal c As Char) As String
    'User pressed delete key
    If Val(c) = 8 Then
      position -= 1
      Return DeleteLetter(position)
    End If

    'User trying to go beyond bounds
    If position >= mText.Length Then
      Return mText.ToString()
    End If

    'If we have hit a literal then advance one
    'Do this in a loop in case there are more literals.
    If mText.Chars(position) <> mCue Then
      position += 1
    End If

    'check to see if the character is ok
    If mUserMask.Chars(position) = mNumberPlace Then
      If Regex.IsMatch(c.ToString(), mRegNum) Then
        mText.Chars(position) = c
        position += 1
      End If
```

```
      ElseIf mUserMask.Chars(position) = mAlphaPlace Then
        If Regex.IsMatch(c.ToString(), mRegAlpha) Then
          mText.Chars(position) = c
          position += 1
        End If
      End If


      Return mText.ToString()
    End Function

    Public Function DeleteLetter(ByRef pos As Int32) As String
      'If the character to be deleted is a cue then bail out
      If mText.Chars(pos) <> mCue Then
        'If the character to be deleted is valid then change it back to a cue
        If mUserMask.Chars(pos) = mNumberPlace Or _
          mUserMask.Chars(pos) = mAlphaPlace Then
          mText.Chars(pos) = mCue
        End If
      End If
      Return mText.ToString()
    End Function

#End Region
```

Let's look at the EnterLetter routine first. The first thing I do here is check for a backspace. If I find it, I decrement the position pointer and call the Delete function, which returns the corrected string.

If the character puts me over the allowed length, I disallow the character and return the original string. If the character is about to overwrite a cue character, I advance the pointer and then add the character to the string. If the character is in a spot where I have a regular expression character, I use the Regex object to decide if it is a match. If so, I replace the character in the internal string and return that string. If this character does not match, I ignore it and return the original string.

This EnterLetter routine is called from the KeyPress event handler. The only way for me to ignore any character is to set the KeyPressEventArgs.Handled property to true. As you will see, I do this for every character that comes in.

The DeleteLetter routine replaces the deleted character with a cue character. It will not replace a literal with a cue character. This prevents the control from deleting literals.

NOTE   This control can handle only one literal character in a row. There is no checking for multiple literals in a row, and there is no looping to allow this. If you enter two literals in a row while testing this control, it will explode. The point of this example is to show you how it is done, not to do it all for you. You have the knowledge to enhance this control and make it robust if you so desire.

The next region of code to be added contains the various event handlers for the TextBox. You will be adding handlers for the following events:

- TextBox.Enter

- TextBox.Leave

- TextBox.KeyDown

- TextBox.KeyPress

Here is the code for these delegates.

C#

```csharp
#region hooked events

private void MaskBoxEnter(object sender, EventArgs e)
{
  this.Text = mText.ToString();
  this.SelectionLength=0;
}

private void MaskBoxLeave(object sender, EventArgs e)
{
  if(mUserMask == string.Empty)
  {
    mText = new StringBuilder(this.Text);
  }
}
```

```csharp
    private void MaskBoxKeyDown(object sender, KeyEventArgs e)
    {
      //No mask so let in any character
      if(mUserMask == string.Empty)
        return;

      int pos = this.SelectionStart;
      if(e.KeyData == Keys.Delete)
      {
        this.Text = DeleteLetter(ref pos);
        this.SelectionStart = pos;
      }
      e.Handled = true;
    }

    private void MaskBoxKeyPress(object sender, KeyPressEventArgs e)
    {
      //No mask so let in any character
      if(mUserMask == string.Empty)
        return;

      int pos = this.SelectionStart;
      this.Text = EnterLetter(ref pos, e.KeyChar);
      e.Handled = true;
      this.SelectionStart = pos;
    }

    #endregion
```

VB

```vb
#Region "hooked events"

  Private Sub MaskBoxEnter(ByVal sender As Object, ByVal e As EventArgs)
    Me.Text = mText.ToString()
    Me.SelectionLength = 0
  End Sub

  Private Sub MaskBoxLeave(ByVal sender As Object, ByVal e As EventArgs)
    If mUserMask = String.Empty Then
      mText = New StringBuilder(Me.Text)
    End If
  End Sub
```

```vbnet
Private Sub MaskBoxKeyDown(ByVal sender As Object, ByVal e As KeyEventArgs)
  'No mask so let in any character
  If mUserMask = String.Empty Then
    Return
  End If

  Dim pos As Int32 = Me.SelectionStart
  If e.KeyData = Keys.Delete Then
    Me.Text = DeleteLetter(pos)
    Me.SelectionStart = pos
  End If
  e.Handled = True
End Sub

Private Sub MaskBoxKeyPress(ByVal sender As Object, _
                            ByVal e As KeyPressEventArgs)
  'No mask so let in any character
  If mUserMask = String.Empty Then
    Return
  End If

  Dim pos As Int32 = Me.SelectionStart
  Me.Text = EnterLetter(pos, e.KeyChar)
  e.Handled = True
  Me.SelectionStart = pos
End Sub
```

#End Region

I hook into the KeyDown event for the sole purpose of trapping the Delete key. I use the SelectionStart property to determine where the cursor is in the control. I set the text of the control to the string that gets returned from the Delete function. I then set the Handled property to true to disallow the multiple keystrokes bug.

The Enter function sets the selection length to zero to prevent the whole string from being selected. It also sets the text of the box to the current version of text held in memory.

The KeyPress handler lets in any character if no mask or format is provided. This lets the control act as a normal TextBox. The rest of this function gets the new string from the EnterLetter function and resets the position of the cursor in the control.

TIP There is no explicit property to retrieve the cursor position in a TextBox control. Instead, use the SelectionStart property, which gives you the point at which the next character gets entered.

So, now you have all the new properties and event handlers necessary for a Masked Edit control. Just wire up the delegates in the class constructor.

C#

```csharp
public MaskedTextBox_C()
{
  InitializeComponent();

  mValidationErrors      = 0;
  this.Enter            += new EventHandler(MaskBoxEnter);
  this.Leave            += new EventHandler(MaskBoxLeave);
  this.KeyDown          += new KeyEventHandler(MaskBoxKeyDown);
  this.KeyPress         += new KeyPressEventHandler(MaskBoxKeyPress);
}
```

VB

```vb
Public Sub New()
  MyBase.New()

  InitializeComponent()

  mValidationErrors = 0
  AddHandler Me.Enter, New EventHandler(AddressOf MaskBoxEnter)
  AddHandler Me.Leave, New EventHandler(AddressOf MaskBoxLeave)
  AddHandler Me.KeyDown, New KeyEventHandler(AddressOf MaskBoxKeyDown)
  AddHandler Me.KeyPress, New KeyPressEventHandler(AddressOf MaskBoxKeyPress)

End Sub
```

There it is. You now have a control that extends the properties of the TextBox with two extra ones allowing for masking. If you enter a mask, this control will validate each character entered against that mask. In a little while, you will be testing this control. There is one thing missing, however.

What happens when the user tabs out of this control before everything is entered? You get no warning that a problem has occurred. After all, there are missing characters and you need to know this. The solution is to add an event.

The event that you will add is called ValidationErrorEvent. This event will get fired if two conditions are met: if the user leaves a control and if that controls text does not match the supplied mask. I will be firing this event from within the Validated event that comes with the TextBox control. I do this for two reasons:

- The Validated event can be suppressed by setting the CausesValidation property of the TextBox to false. This also suppresses my new event.

- The Validated event is called before the Leave event to allow the user to stop focus from transferring to another control if he or she so wishes.

Before I have you enter the new event code, I suggest that you look over the numerous examples in the online help. Like I keep saying, you can program away happily without knowing what really goes on, but to understand things like events and delegates you need to dig in. The effort is well worth it.

I could have written this event using the .NET-supplied EventHandler and the accompanying EventArgs. This is boring, though, not to mention uninformative. So in order to make some new type of event arguments, you will need to generate a new class that is derived from the class EventArgs. Put this class code above the class code for your control. Along with this class, you will need to define a delegate for a client to hook into.

C#

```csharp
public class ValidationErrorEventArgs : EventArgs
{

  private string mMask;
  private string mText;

  public ValidationErrorEventArgs(string mask, string OffendingText)
  {
    mMask = mask;
    mText = OffendingText;
  }

  public string Mask{get{return mMask;}}
  public string Text{get{return mText;}}
}
public delegate void ValidationErrorEventHandler(object sender,
                                        ValidationErrorEventArgs e);
```

VB

```
Public Class ValidationErrorEventArgs
  Inherits EventArgs

  Private mMask As String
  Private mText As String

  Public Sub New(ByVal mask As String, ByVal OffendingText As String)
    mMask = mask
    mText = OffendingText
  End Sub

  Public ReadOnly Property Mask() As String
    Get
      Return mMask
    End Get
  End Property

  Public ReadOnly Property Text() As String
    Get
      Return mText
    End Get
  End Property

End Class
Public Delegate Sub ValidationErrorEventHandler(ByVal sender As Object, _
                                       ByVal e As _
                                       ValidationErrorEventArgs)
```

Now that you have this class, you will need to provide an On*xxx* method that goes with the event. Enter the following region of code.

C#

```
#region OnXXX event stuff

public void RaiseError()
{
  ValidationErrorEventArgs e = new ValidationErrorEventArgs(mUserMask,
    mText.ToString());
  OnValidationError(e);
}
```

```csharp
  protected virtual void OnValidationError(ValidationErrorEventArgs e)
  {
    ValidationError(this, e);
  }

  #endregion
```

VB

```vb
#Region "OnXXX event stuff"

  Public Sub RaiseError()
    Dim e As ValidationErrorEventArgs = _
        New ValidationErrorEventArgs(mUserMask, mText.ToString())
    OnValidationError(e)
  End Sub

  Protected Sub OnValidationError(ByVal e As ValidationErrorEventArgs)
    RaiseEvent ValidationError(Me, e)
  End Sub

#End Region
```

You must call the OnValidationError method to raise the event. This is required and you will be flogged if you do not do it this way (see the online help).

I include the RaiseEvent method for ease of use. Notice that I pass in the current mask and text so the client can determine the problem from ValidationErrorEventArgs.

Because I need to call this from inside the Validation event, I need to wire this event up. At the same time, I also wire up a delegate to my new event so I can keep track of how many times matching failed in this control.

Add these two delegates to your "hooked events" region.

C#

```csharp
  private void MaskBoxValidated(object sender, EventArgs e)
  {
    if(!Regex.IsMatch(mText.ToString(), mRegExpression))
      RaiseError();
  }
```

```
//Special event to handle case of no one connecting to my delegate
//avoids a null reference
private void DefaultHandler(object sender, ValidationErrorEventArgs e)
{
  mValidationErrors++;
}
```

VB

```
Private Sub MaskBoxValidated(ByVal sender As Object, ByVal e As EventArgs)
  If Not Regex.IsMatch(mText.ToString(), mRegExpression) Then
    RaiseError()
  End If
End Sub

'Special event to handle case of no one connecting to my delegate
'avoids a null reference
Private Sub DefaultHandler(ByVal sender As Object, _
                           ByVal e As ValidationErrorEventArgs)
  mValidationErrors += 1
End Sub
```

By the way, connecting to my own event avoids a nasty null reference bug in case the client decides not to use this event.

The MaskBoxValidated event handler uses the regular expression engine to evaluate the whole text to the mask. If this match fails, then I start the ball rolling and fire the event.

Of course, in order to catch the Validated event you need to connect to it. Add the following lines to your constructor.

C#

```
this.Validated      += new EventHandler(MaskBoxValidated);
this.ValidationError += new ValidationErrorEventHandler(DefaultHandler);
```

VB

```
AddHandler Me.Validated, New EventHandler(AddressOf MaskBoxValidated)
AddHandler Me.ValidationError, _
          New ValidationErrorEventHandler(AddressOf DefaultHandler)
```

There you are. A shiny new Masked Edit control. Compile it and make sure you have no syntax bugs. Because this is part of a control library, you will end up with a DLL after compilation. You will bring this DLL into your Toolbox when you make the client.

Testing the Masked Edit Control

Testing the new control is simple. Start a new Windows Forms project in C# or VB. Mine is called "MaskClient." Note here that I can use the VB control in the C# project or vice versa. This is the CLR at work.

You will need to add the control to your Toolbox. You can make a new Toolbox tab or use one of the existing ones. I use the General tab. Bring up the General tab on the Toolbox. Right-click the tab and choose Customize Toolbox. Choose the .NET Framework Components tab in the Customize Toolbox dialog box.

If you are writing in VB, click Browse and look for your DLL in the BIN subdirectory of your project. Select it and click OK on the dialog box. If you are writing in C# you will find the DLL in the BIN\Debug subdirectory of your project. Figure 8-7 shows the dialog box after you have chosen the control.

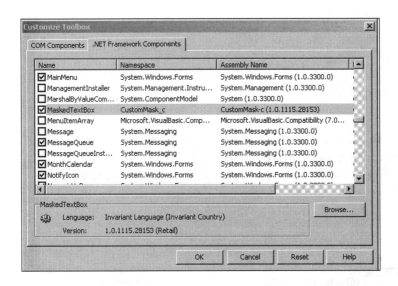

Figure 8-7. Choosing the new control

Figure 8-8 shows what your Toolbox should now look like.

Figure 8-8. The new control in the Toolbox

You have a single gear to work with. You can change this icon if you want. See the online help for assistance.

Drag this control over to the form and call it **me1**. Drag another control such as a TextBox over to the form as well. This other control allows you to leave the Masked Edit control and catch the Validate event. Your form should look like the one shown in Figure 8-9.

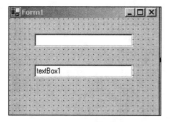

Figure 8-9. The test form

You can see that this new control looks the same as the TextBox. Click the Masked Edit control and look at the properties. You should see the two new properties at the bottom of the list. Click the Format property and the enumeration will appear (see Figure 8-10).

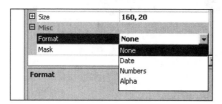

Figure 8-10. The new properties

If you choose one of the formats and click in the mask, you will see the correct mask appear for that format. You will also see the correct text appear in the box. This is pretty cool!

Choose None for a format and enter the following mask property: ##?/#?/##. This means allow two numbers, one alpha, a literal, a number, an alpha, a literal, and two numbers. Run the program and your form should look like Figure 8-11.

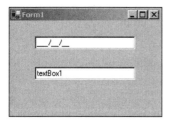

Figure 8-11. The running form

Enter in some characters in the edit box and you will see that only those corresponding to the mask are allowed. You will also see the control skip over the literals. Try deleting and backspacing over characters. Pretty neat, huh? Now tab out to the next control. You will not know that this control failed.

Double-click the form and add the following code.

C#

```
private void Form1_Load(object sender, System.EventArgs e)
{
  me1.ValidationError += new ValidationErrorEventHandler(MaskValid);
}

private void MaskValid(object sender, ValidationErrorEventArgs e)
{
  MessageBox.Show(e.Mask + "   " + e.Text);
}
```

VB

```
Private Sub Form1_Load(ByVal sender As System.Object, _
                    ByVal e As System.EventArgs) Handles MyBase.Load
  AddHandler me1.ValidationError, _
          New ValidationErrorEventHandler(AddressOf Valid)
End Sub
```

```
Private Sub Valid(ByVal sender As Object, ByVal e As ValidationErrorEventArgs)
    MessageBox.Show(e.Mask + "  " + e.Text)
End Sub
```

Now run the form again, enter some values in the mask control, and tab over to the next control. You will need to make sure that you reference the namespace of the control you created. Figure 8-12 shows the results.

Figure 8-12. Mask results

When you tab out of the control without the correct values in it, ValidateErrorEvent gets fired. If the control was valid, you would not get this event. Now this event gives you the opportunity to restore focus to this control. It allows you to be strict and lock up the whole form unless the control has the correct values.

That's it for this Masked Edit control and test program. What do you think? Pretty neat, isn't it? I can see doing this for quite a few different controls. I can see making controls that are target specific, such as a control that handles only e-mail addresses. Perhaps you want a control that's used only for login purposes. You could make the mask accept some obtuse set of characters in a certain order. You could make this login control write to a special file whenever someone tries to hack into your program. You could make this login control shut down and reformat the hard drive if three unsuccessful attempts at logging in were detected. You could . . .

There is also another way to do this kind of thing. You could go the same route as the ErrorProvider control. You could make a control that extends properties of any control you want.

Extending Control Properties

You can do two things about making your own validation controls in .NET. One of them is to make a completely new control by building on an existing control. This is what you did in the last example. The other thing you can do is add a few new properties to a control without making a new one altogether. This is called extending the control.

The neat thing about this extension is that it can work with any control you like. Want a for-instance? How about the ToolTip control? I have not discussed this control in any detail, so how about the ErrorProvider control?

As you know from previous chapters, the ErrorProvider control is something that you plop down on your form and it appears in the tray below the form. It does not appear on the form itself. In case you have not been paying attention, as soon as you put the ErrorProvider control on the form, every visible control on the form has several new properties that are related to the ErrorProvider control. Try a new project with several controls on it and look at the Properties page. Now add an ErrorProvider to your form. Your several controls now have a few extra properties related to the ErrorProvider.

The ErrorProvider is a class that inherits from Component and also implements the IExtenderProvider interface. It is set up to extend the properties of any control on the current form. The ToolTip control does the same thing.

Extending the properties of a control offers you a big advantage over making your own control. The code works the same (within limits) for any control. It also allows you to turn any control on your form into . . . SuperControl!

This next example contains two classes that extend a TextBox control. The first class provides properties that make the control accept only numbers or only numbers within a certain range. The second class provides a regular expression property for validation before focus leaves the control.

By the way, both of these classes allow the TextBox to work as normal by using a Required property. This allows you to have 50 TextBoxes on the screen and use the extensions on only a few of them.

I start the next section by introducing you to my buddy Vlad the validator.

The Number Validation Extender

Start a new project in either C# or VB. Make sure it is a class library that you are starting. You want to end up with a DLL that you can put in your Toolbox as a new control. The name of my project is "Vlad."

This class has no user interface (obviously), so I will get right down to the code. The first thing to do is add a reference to the System.Windows.Forms DLL. You do this in the project window. Figure 8-13 shows the project after the reference has been added.

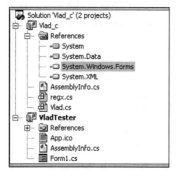

Figure 8-13. A reference to the form's DLL

You will notice that my solution has two projects. You will add the test project later.

The next thing to add is some namespace references to your code.

C#

```
using System;
using System.Collections;
using System.Windows.Forms;
using System.ComponentModel;
using System.Text.RegularExpressions;
```

VB

```
Option Strict On

Imports System
Imports System.Collections
Imports System.Windows.Forms
Imports System.ComponentModel
Imports System.Text.RegularExpressions
```

As you can see, you will be using regular expressions again.

TIP The first part of this chapter covers regular expressions. Reading the first part of this chapter makes this part so much more understandable.

Next is the class definition. I use some specialized attributes for these classes. I also use some for the properties within. I suggest you read up on attributes before you go any further. (At least read up a little so you know what attributes are.) Here is the class definition.

C#

```
[ProvideProperty("Required",          typeof(Control))]
[ProvideProperty("RangeValueRequired", typeof(Control))]
[ProvideProperty("MinValue",          typeof(Control))]
[ProvideProperty("MaxValue",          typeof(Control))]
public class NumberValidate : Component, IExtenderProvider
{
…
}
```

VB

```
<ProvideProperty("Required", GetType(Control)), _
 ProvideProperty("RangeValueRequired", GetType(Control)), _
 ProvideProperty("MinValue", GetType(Control)), _
 ProvideProperty("MaxValue", GetType(Control))> _
Public Class NumberValidate
  Inherits Component
  Implements IExtenderProvider
…
End Class
```

I am telling any control that looks in here (using reflection) that I am providing four properties:

- *Required:* This tells that control to accept only numbers.

- *RangeValueRequired:* This tells the control to accept numbers in the supplied range.

- *MinValue:* This is the minimum value for the range.

- *MaxValue:* This is the maximum value for the range.

Whenever you implement the IExtenderProvider interface, you need to override the CanExtend property. Add the following code inside the class block.

C#

```csharp
bool IExtenderProvider.CanExtend(object target)
{
  if (target is TextBox)
  {
    TextBox t = (TextBox)target;
    tp.Active = true;
    return true;
  }
  else
    return false;
}
```

VB

```vb
Function CanExtend(ByVal target As Object) As Boolean _
                  Implements IExtenderProvider.CanExtend
  If TypeOf target Is TextBox Then
    Dim t As TextBox = CType(target, TextBox)
    tp.Active = True
    Return True
  Else
    Return False
  End If
End Function
```

I have set the control type I will be extending to a TextBox. If you like, you can extend any control you want. How about extending the RichTextBox with a class that does spell checking on the fly? You can do a lot with extenders.

OK, you have the properties defined that appear in the Properties page of the extended control. You also have narrowed the set of extended control to all TextBoxes. It is time to add the guts to this class. Be sure to add the following locals region.

C#

```csharp
#region locals

// holds Key - value pair for efficient retrieval
//Holds all properties of all controls that use this extender.
private System.Collections.Hashtable CustomProps =
                  new System.Collections.Hashtable();
```

```
ErrorProvider er = new ErrorProvider();
ToolTip      tp = new ToolTip();

//Holds all the custom properties of a control
private class Props
{
  public bool Required     = false;
  public bool RangeRequired = false;
  public Decimal  MinVal    = 0;
  public Decimal  MaxVal    = 999;
}

#endregion
```

VB

```
#Region "locals"

  ' holds Key - value pair for efficient retrieval
  'Holds all properties of all controls that use this extender.
  Private CustomProps As System.Collections.Hashtable = _
                      New System.Collections.Hashtable()

  Private er As ErrorProvider = New ErrorProvider()
  Private tp As ToolTip = New ToolTip()

  'Holds all the custom properties of a control
  Private Class Props
    Public Required As Boolean = False
    Public RangeRequired As Boolean = False
    Public MinVal As Decimal = 0
    Public MaxVal As Decimal = 999
  End Class

#End Region
```

Next, I add the delegates for the events I will use. Vlad will hook into the KeyPress event and the Validating event. Here is the delegate region of code.

C#

```csharp
#region events

private void KeyPress(object sender, KeyPressEventArgs e)
{
  //Allow backspace
  if(e.KeyChar == (char)8)
    return;

  //Allow 0-9
  if(!Regex.IsMatch(e.KeyChar.ToString(), "[0-9]"))
    e.Handled = true;
}

private void ValidateProp(object sender, CancelEventArgs e)
{
  Control ctl = (Control)sender;

  //Reset the error
  er.SetError(ctl, "");

  if(GetRequired(ctl))
  {
    if(ctl.Text == string.Empty)
    {
      er.SetError(ctl, "No value was entered when one was required");
      return;
    }

    if(GetRangeValueRequired(ctl))
    {
      Props p = (Props)CustomProps[ctl];
      try
      {
        if(Decimal.Parse(ctl.Text) < p.MinVal)
          er.SetError(ctl, "Value entered is less than minimum value");
      }
      catch
      {
        er.SetError(ctl, "Value is non-numeric");
      }
```

```
        try
        {
          if(Decimal.Parse(ctl.Text) > p.MaxVal)
            er.SetError(ctl, "Value entered is greater than minimum value");
        }
        catch
        {
          er.SetError(ctl, "Value is non-numeric");
        }
      }
    }
  }

  #endregion
```

VB

```
#Region "events"

  Private Sub KeyPress(ByVal sender As Object, ByVal e As KeyPressEventArgs)
    'Allow backspace
    If e.KeyChar = Chr(8) Then
      Return
    End If

    'Allow 0-9
    If Not Regex.IsMatch(e.KeyChar.ToString(), "[0-9]") Then
      e.Handled = True
    End If
  End Sub

  Private Sub ValidateProp(ByVal sender As Object, ByVal e As CancelEventArgs)
    Dim ctl As Control = CType(sender, Control)

    'Reset the error
    er.SetError(ctl, "")

    If GetRequired(ctl) Then
      If ctl.Text = String.Empty Then
        er.SetError(ctl, "No value was entered when one was required")
        Return
      End If
```

```
      If GetRangeValueRequired(ctl) Then
        Dim p As Props = CType(CustomProps(ctl), Props)
      If GetRangeValueRequired(ctl) Then
        Dim p As Props = CType(CustomProps(ctl), Props)
        If IsNumeric(ctl.Text) Then
          If Decimal.Parse(ctl.Text) < p.MinVal Then
            er.SetError(ctl, "Value entered is less than minimum value")
          End If
          If Decimal.Parse(ctl.Text) > p.MaxVal Then
            er.SetError(ctl, "Value entered is greater than minimum value")
          End If
        Else
          er.SetError(ctl, "Value is non-numeric")
        End If
      End If
      End If
    End If
  End Sub

#End Region
```

The KeyPress delegate uses the regular expression engine to validate only numbers. I allow a backspace in here as well. The Validating delegate checks to see if validating is required and if the validation should be range sensitive.

Notice here that I choose to instantiate a new ErrorProvider within my extender. If something is wrong, I set the ErrorProvider text and flash the icon next to the offending control.

If you want, you can prevent the control from losing focus in the case of an error. This is problematic, though, because if you try to exit the program while the control is invalid, you will not be able to. One solution I have seen to this "exit" problem is to walk the stack and find the WM_CLOSE message as the reason you are leaving the control. I think that setting an error is just fine.

The error text says nothing about how the control should be used. In fact, how is the user supposed to know that this control needs only numbers within a certain range? The answer is to use the ToolTip control. You saw in the locals region that I included a ToolTip control. Enter the following code, which fills the text.

C#

```csharp
private void SetToolTip(Control ctl)
{
  string tip = string.Empty;
  Props p = (Props)CustomProps[ctl];
  if(p.Required)
    tip = "Validation of numbers required";
  if(p.RangeRequired)
  {
    tip += " / Number range required";
    tip += " / Min value = " + p.MinVal.ToString();
    tip += " / Max value = " + p.MaxVal.ToString();
  }
  tp.SetToolTip(ctl, tip);
}
```

VB

```vb
Private Sub SetToolTip(ByVal ctl As Control)
  Dim tip As String = String.Empty
  Dim p As Props = CType(CustomProps(ctl), Props)
  If p.Required Then
    tip = "Validation of numbers required"
  End If
  If p.RangeRequired Then
    tip += " / Number range required"
    tip += " / Min value = " + p.MinVal.ToString()
    tip += " / Max value = " + p.MaxVal.ToString()
  End If
  tp.SetToolTip(ctl, tip)
End Sub
```

As you can see, I change the text to reflect the properties set for this control. Anytime one of the properties is changed, I call this method.

When you define a property using attributes, you need a property get and set function to go with it. The name of the function must be the name of the property preceded by the word "Get" or "Set." Here is the code region for the Required property.

C#

```
#region Required property

public bool GetRequired(Control ctl)
{
  if(CustomProps.Contains(ctl))
  {
    Props p = (Props)CustomProps[ctl];
    SetToolTip(ctl);
    return p.Required;
  }
  else
    return false;
}

public void SetRequired(Control ctl, bool val)
{
  if(CustomProps.Contains(ctl))
  {
    Props p = (Props)CustomProps[ctl];
    if(val == p.Required)
      return;

    p.Required = val;
    CustomProps[ctl] = p;
    SetToolTip(ctl);
    if(val)
    {
      ctl.KeyPress    += new KeyPressEventHandler(KeyPress);
      ctl.Validating += new CancelEventHandler(ValidateProp);
    }
    else
    {
      ctl.KeyPress    -= new KeyPressEventHandler(KeyPress);
      ctl.Validating -= new CancelEventHandler(ValidateProp);
    }
  }
  else
  {
    Props p = new Props();
    p.Required = val;
```

```
      CustomProps.Add(ctl, p);
      SetToolTip(ctl);
      ctl.Validating += new CancelEventHandler(ValidateProp);
    }
  }

  #endregion
```

VB

```
#Region "Required property"

  Public Function GetRequired(ByVal ctl As Control) As Boolean
    If CustomProps.Contains(ctl) Then
      Dim p As Props = CType(CustomProps(ctl), Props)
      SetToolTip(ctl)
      Return p.Required
    End If
    Return False
  End Function

  Public Sub SetRequired(ByVal ctl As Control, ByVal val As Boolean)
    If CustomProps.Contains(ctl) Then
      Dim p As Props = CType(CustomProps(ctl), Props)
      If val = p.Required Then
        Return
      End If

      p.Required = val
      CustomProps(ctl) = p
      SetToolTip(ctl)
      If val Then
        AddHandler ctl.KeyPress, _
                New KeyPressEventHandler(AddressOf KeyPress)
        AddHandler ctl.Validating, _
                New CancelEventHandler(AddressOf ValidateProp)
      Else
        RemoveHandler ctl.KeyPress, _
                New KeyPressEventHandler(AddressOf KeyPress)
        RemoveHandler ctl.Validating, _
                New CancelEventHandler(AddressOf ValidateProp)
      End If
```

```
      Else
        Dim p As Props = New Props()
        p.Required = val

        CustomProps.Add(ctl, p)
        SetToolTip(ctl)
        AddHandler ctl.Validating, New CancelEventHandler(AddressOf ValidateProp)
      End If
    End Sub

#End Region
```

Interesting code, this is. Note that I instantiated a hash table in the locals region. I also made a small class that holds the properties. I use the hash table because it accepts a key/value pair. The key in this case is the Control object and the value is the property object instated from the Props class. Hash tables are also extremely fast data structures.

The Get function looks to see if the hash table contains a set of properties for this control. If not, I return a default value of false.[4] The Set function again looks to see if this control already contains a set of properties. If so, I get these properties, make the change, and then store this property back in the hash table. If this Set function does not find the Set properties in the hash table, I instantiate a new set of properties, change the individual property I need, and store it in the hash table. Note that I set the ToolTip property in each of these functions.

If the user sets the Required property to true, I wire up the delegates to the correct events. If not, I unwire them. Doing this obviates the need for my delegates to test whether or not they should be validating. This is the preferred method.

Next on the list are the RangeValueRequired properties.

C#

```
#region RangeValue required

//Get method for range required
public bool GetRangeValueRequired(Control ctl)
{
    //This makes best use of a hashtable for quick retrieval
    if(CustomProps.Contains(ctl))
```

---

4. I would not hard-code values like this in a real program.

```
    {
      Props p = (Props)CustomProps[ctl];
      SetToolTip(ctl);
      return p.RangeRequired;
    }
    else
      return false;
}

//Set method for Range required
public void SetRangeValueRequired(Control ctl, bool val)
{
  if(CustomProps.Contains(ctl))
  {
    //See if this property is already correctly set
    Props p = (Props)CustomProps[ctl];
    if(val == p.RangeRequired)
      return;

    //Set this property and add it back to the list
    p.RangeRequired = val;
    CustomProps[ctl] = p;
    if(val)
    {
      ctl.KeyPress   += new KeyPressEventHandler(KeyPress);
      ctl.Validating += new CancelEventHandler(ValidateProp);
    }
    else
    {
      ctl.KeyPress   -= new KeyPressEventHandler(KeyPress);
      ctl.Validating -= new CancelEventHandler(ValidateProp);
    }
    SetToolTip(ctl);
  }
  else
  {
    //Set this property and add it to the list
    Props p = new Props();
    p.RangeRequired = val;
    CustomProps.Add(ctl, p);
    if(val)
      ctl.KeyPress += new KeyPressEventHandler(KeyPress);
```

```
        SetToolTip(ctl);
      }
    }


    #endregion
```

VB

```
#Region "RangeValue required"

  'Get method for range required
  Public Function GetRangeValueRequired(ByVal ctl As Control) As Boolean
    'This makes best use of a hashtable for quick retrieval
    If CustomProps.Contains(ctl) Then
      Dim p As Props = CType(CustomProps(ctl), Props)
      SetToolTip(ctl)
      Return p.RangeRequired
    End If
    Return False
  End Function

  'Set method for Range required
  Public Sub SetRangeValueRequired(ByVal ctl As Control, ByVal val As Boolean)
    If CustomProps.Contains(ctl) Then
      'See if this property is already correctly set
      Dim p As Props = CType(CustomProps(ctl), Props)
      If val = p.RangeRequired Then
        Return
      End If

      'Set this property and add it back to the list
      p.RangeRequired = val
      CustomProps(ctl) = p
      If val Then
        AddHandler ctl.KeyPress, _
                New KeyPressEventHandler(AddressOf KeyPress)
        AddHandler ctl.Validating, _
                New CancelEventHandler(AddressOf ValidateProp)
      Else
        RemoveHandler ctl.KeyPress, _
                New KeyPressEventHandler(AddressOf KeyPress)
        RemoveHandler ctl.Validating, _
                New CancelEventHandler(AddressOf ValidateProp)
      End If
```

```
      SetToolTip(ctl)
    Else
      'Set this property and add it to the list
      Dim p As Props = New Props()
      p.RangeRequired = val
      CustomProps.Add(ctl, p)
      If val Then
        AddHandler ctl.KeyPress, New KeyPressEventHandler(AddressOf KeyPress)
      End If
      SetToolTip(ctl)
    End If
  End Sub

#End Region
```

This code is much the same as the code for the Required property. One last piece of code is needed here. The following is the code for the minimum and maximum value properties.

C#

```
#region Min and Max Values

public Decimal GetMinValue(Control ctl)
{
  if(CustomProps.Contains(ctl))
  {
    Props p = (Props)CustomProps[ctl];
    SetToolTip(ctl);
    return p.MinVal;
  }
  else
    return 0;
}

[DefaultValue(0)]
public void SetMinValue(Control ctl, Decimal val)
{
  if(val < 0)
    val = 0;
```

```
    if(CustomProps.Contains(ctl))
    {
      Props p = (Props)CustomProps[ctl];
      p.MinVal = val;
      CustomProps[ctl] = p;
      SetToolTip(ctl);
    }
    else
    {
      Props p = new Props();
      p.MinVal = val;
      CustomProps.Add(ctl, p);
      SetToolTip(ctl);
    }
}

public Decimal GetMaxValue(Control ctl)
{
    if(CustomProps.Contains(ctl))
    {
      Props p = (Props)CustomProps[ctl];
      SetToolTip(ctl);
      return p.MaxVal;
    }
    else
      return 999;
}

[DefaultValue(999)]
public void SetMaxValue(Control ctl, Decimal val)
{
    if(val > 999)
      val = 999;

    if(CustomProps.Contains(ctl))
    {
      Props p = (Props)CustomProps[ctl];
      p.MaxVal = val;
      CustomProps[ctl] = p;
      SetToolTip(ctl);
    }
```

```
    else
    {
      Props p = new Props();
      p.MaxVal = val;
      CustomProps.Add(ctl, p);
      SetToolTip(ctl);
    }
  }

  #endregion
```

VB

```
#Region "Min and Max Values"

  Public Function GetMinValue(ByVal ctl As Control) As Decimal
    If CustomProps.Contains(ctl) Then
      Dim p As Props = CType(CustomProps(ctl), Props)
      SetToolTip(ctl)
      Return p.MinVal
    End If
    Return 0
  End Function


  '   <DefaultValue(0)>_
  Public Sub SetMinValue(ByVal ctl As Control, ByVal val As Decimal)
    If val < 0 Then val = 0

    If CustomProps.Contains(ctl) Then
      Dim p As Props = CType(CustomProps(ctl), Props)
      p.MinVal = val
      CustomProps(ctl) = p
      SetToolTip(ctl)
    Else
      Dim p As Props = New Props()
      p.MinVal = val
      CustomProps.Add(ctl, p)
      SetToolTip(ctl)
    End If
  End Sub
```

```
Public Function GetMaxValue(ByVal ctl As Control) As Decimal
  If (CustomProps.Contains(ctl)) Then
    Dim p As Props = CType(CustomProps(ctl), Props)
    SetToolTip(ctl)
    Return p.MaxVal
  End If
  Return 999
End Function

' [DefaultValue(999)]
Public Sub SetMaxValue(ByVal ctl As Control, ByVal val As Decimal)
  If val > 999 Then val = 999

  If CustomProps.Contains(ctl) Then
    Dim p As Props = CType(CustomProps(ctl), Props)
    p.MaxVal = val
    CustomProps(ctl) = p
    SetToolTip(ctl)
  Else
    Dim p As Props = New Props()
    p.MaxVal = val
    CustomProps.Add(ctl, p)
    SetToolTip(ctl)
  End If
End Sub

#End Region
```

Note that in this region I use attributes on the Set properties to define a default value.

OK, that's it for this extender. What you have is a control that you can load into your Toolbox and drag onto a form. If this control sees a TextBox on the form, the TextBox will get these four new properties.

If the new properties are set correctly, you will not be able to enter any letters into the TextBox. You can also set the range of numbers allowed. This control provides a custom ToolTip for the TextBox and also provides a custom ErrorProvider control. You have everything you need to get going.

Now for the testing part. Actually, do you want to test this before adding the next extender class? Yes? OK.

Testing the NumberExtender Control

Add another project to your Vlad solution space. Make this project a Windows Forms project. Also make this the start-up project. Then add two controls to this form. Make sure that one of the controls is a TextBox. If you look at the properties of the TextBox, you will see this is your normal, everyday TextBox.

Now for the magic. While you are in the form, open up the Toolbox. Right-click the Toolbox and choose the .NET Framework Components tab, as shown in Figure 8-14. This is just like choosing the custom TextBox you made in the last example.

Browse to the BIN directory under the VB project (BIN\Debug under the C# project) and double-click Vlad.dll, as shown in Figure 8-14.[5]

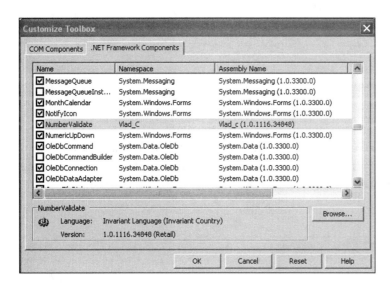

Figure 8-14. Choosing the new validation control

Click OK and you should have this control in your Toolbox. Now drag this control over to your form. Make sure that you clear the default text from this control. Figure 8-15 shows the Properties screen for the TextBox after adding the control to the form.

---

5. Because I have both VB and C# controls, I differentiated them with -C and -VB.

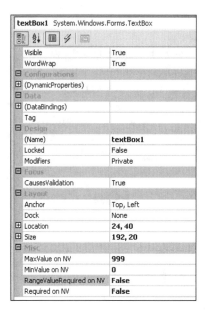

Figure 8-15. New properties added to control

See that the default properties came up correctly?

Enable the two required properties and change the MinValue to 50 and the MaxValue to 55. Now run the program. Figure 8-16 shows my form after I exited the TextBox with an invalid entry.

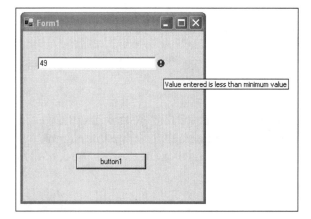

Figure 8-16. An invalid entry

Notice that the ErrorProvider has appeared next to the offending TextBox. I moused over the ErrorProvider icon and I got the message you see here.

How is the user supposed to know what is required in the TextBox? This is where the ToolTip text comes in. Hover your mouse over the TextBox and your screen should look like Figure 8-17.

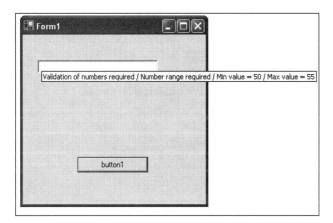

Figure 8-17. ToolTip help

This text changes based on what the values were for validating this control. Pretty cool, isn't it? Well, I think so anyway.

Now back to the second validation control.

The Regular Expression Validator

Here is a cool control that I decided to make separate from the NumberValidator. Add a new class to the Vlad project called **RegxValidate**. This class also extends the TextBox control, but with two properties this time. The first property is a Required property and the second is a Mask property. The code for this is much the same as for the NumberValidator. There are a few enhancements, though, that I explain shortly. First, enter the code in Listings 8-2a and 8-2b.

Listing 8-2a. C# Code for the Regx Class

```csharp
using System;
using System.Collections;
using System.Windows.Forms;
using System.ComponentModel;
using System.Text.RegularExpressions;
using System.Diagnostics;

namespace Vlad_c
{
  /// <summary>
  /// Allow user to enter a regular expression for validation purposes
  /// </summary>

  [ProvideProperty("Required",          typeof(Control))]
  [ProvideProperty("RegularExpression", typeof(Control))]
  public class RegxValidate: Component, IExtenderProvider
  {

    #region locals

    // holds Key - value pair for efficient retrieval
    //Holds all properties of all controls that use this extender.
    private System.Collections.Hashtable CustomProps  =
                         new System.Collections.Hashtable();

    ErrorProvider er = new ErrorProvider();
    ToolTip       tp = new ToolTip();

    //Holds all the custom properties of a control
    private class Props
    {
      public bool Required  = false;
      public string Regx    = ".*";
    }

    #endregion

    public RegxValidate()
    {
    }
```

```csharp
bool IExtenderProvider.CanExtend(object target)
{
  //Target can be anything; like a ComboBox if needed
  //Target can be multiple things also
  if (target is TextBox)
  {
    return true;
  }
  else
    return false;
}


#region Required property

public bool GetRequired(Control ctl)
{
  if(CustomProps.Contains(ctl))
  {
    Props p = (Props)CustomProps[ctl];
    SetToolTip(ctl);
    return p.Required;
  }
  else
    return false;
}


public void SetRequired(Control ctl, bool val)
{
  if(CustomProps.Contains(ctl))
  {
    Props p = (Props)CustomProps[ctl];
    if(val == p.Required)
      return;

    p.Required = val;
    CustomProps[ctl] = p;
    SetToolTip(ctl);
    if(val)
      ctl.Validating += new CancelEventHandler(ValidateProp);
    else
      ctl.Validating -= new CancelEventHandler(ValidateProp);
  }
```

```csharp
    else
    {
      Props p = new Props();
      p.Required = val;

      CustomProps.Add(ctl, p);
      SetToolTip(ctl);
      ctl.Validating += new CancelEventHandler(ValidateProp);
    }
}


#endregion

#region Regular Expression property

public string GetRegularExpression(Control ctl)
{
  if(CustomProps.Contains(ctl))
  {
    Props p = (Props)CustomProps[ctl];
    SetToolTip(ctl);
    return p.Regx;
  }
  else
    return ".*";
}


[DefaultValue("")]
public void SetRegularExpression(Control ctl, string val)
{
  //Put something here to verify that regular expression is valid
  try
  {
    Regex.IsMatch("abcdefg", val);
  }
  catch(Exception e)
  {
    string err = "Invalid Regular Expression on:\n";
    err += ctl.Name + "\n\n" + e.Message;
    MessageBox.Show(err);
    er.SetError(ctl, "Invalid Regular Expression!!");
    return;
  }
```

```csharp
    if(CustomProps.Contains(ctl))
    {
      Props p = (Props)CustomProps[ctl];
      p.Regx = val;
      CustomProps[ctl] = p;
    }
    else
    {
      Props p = new Props();
      p.Regx = val;
      CustomProps.Add(ctl, p);
    }
    SetToolTip(ctl);
  }

#endregion

#region events

private void ValidateProp(object sender, CancelEventArgs e)
{
  Control ctl = (Control)sender;

  //Reset the error
  er.SetError(ctl, "");

  if(GetRequired(ctl))
  {
    Props p = (Props)CustomProps[ctl];
    if(!Regex.IsMatch(ctl.Text, p.Regx))
      er.SetError(ctl, "Value did not match input restrictions");
    return;
  }
}

#endregion

#region other stuff
```

```csharp
      private void SetToolTip(Control ctl)
      {
        string tip = string.Empty;
        tp.Active = false;
        SetTooltipActive();
        Props p = (Props)CustomProps[ctl];
        if(p.Required)
          tip = "Regular Expression validation: " + p.Regx ;
        tp.SetToolTip(ctl, tip);
      }

      [Conditional("DEBUG")]
      private void SetTooltipActive()
      {
        tp.Active = true;
      }

      #endregion
   }
}
```

Listing 8-2b. VB Code for the Regx Class

```vb
Option Strict On

Imports System
Imports System.Collections
Imports System.Windows.Forms
Imports System.ComponentModel
Imports System.Text.RegularExpressions

<ProvideProperty("Required", GetType(Control)), _
 ProvideProperty("RegularExpression", GetType(Control))> _
Public Class RegxValidate
  Inherits Component
  Implements IExtenderProvider

#Region "locals"

  ' holds Key - value pair for efficient retrieval
  'Holds all properties of all controls that use this extender.
  Private CustomProps As System.Collections.Hashtable = _
                             New System.Collections.Hashtable()
```

```vbnet
    Private er As ErrorProvider = New ErrorProvider()
    Private tp As ToolTip = New ToolTip()

    'Holds all the custom properties of a control
    Private Class Props
      Public Required As Boolean = False
      Public Regx As String = ".*"
    End Class

#End Region

    Public Sub New()

    End Sub

    Function CanExtend(ByVal target As Object) As _
                     Boolean Implements IExtenderProvider.CanExtend
      'Target can be anything; like a ComboBox if needed
      'Target can be multiple things also
      If TypeOf target Is TextBox Then
        Return True
      Else
        Return False
      End If
    End Function

#Region "Required property"

    Public Function GetRequired(ByVal ctl As Control) As Boolean
      If CustomProps.Contains(ctl) Then
        Dim p As Props = CType(CustomProps(ctl), Props)
        SetToolTip(ctl)
        Return p.Required
      End If
      Return False
    End Function

    Public Sub SetRequired(ByVal ctl As Control, ByVal val As Boolean)
      If CustomProps.Contains(ctl) Then
        Dim p As Props = CType(CustomProps(ctl), Props)
        If val = p.Required Then
          Return
        End If
```

```vb
      p.Required = val
     CustomProps(ctl) = p
     SetToolTip(ctl)
     If val Then
       AddHandler ctl.Validating, _
                 New CancelEventHandler(AddressOf ValidateProp)
     Else
       RemoveHandler ctl.Validating, _
                 New CancelEventHandler(AddressOf ValidateProp)
     End If
   Else
     Dim p As Props = New Props()
     p.Required = val

     CustomProps.Add(ctl, p)
     SetToolTip(ctl)
     AddHandler ctl.Validating, New CancelEventHandler(AddressOf ValidateProp)
   End If
 End Sub

#End Region

#Region "Regular Expression property"

 Public Function GetRegularExpression(ByVal ctl As Control) As String
   If CustomProps.Contains(ctl) Then
     Dim p As Props = CType(CustomProps(ctl), Props)
     SetToolTip(ctl)
     Return p.Regx
   Else
     Return ".*"
   End If
 End Function

 <DefaultValue("")> _
 Public Sub SetRegularExpression(ByVal ctl As Control, ByVal val As String)
   'Put something here to verify that regular expression is valid
   Try
     Regex.IsMatch("abcdefg", val)
   Catch e As Exception
     Dim err As String = "Invalid Regular Expression on:" + vbCrLf
     err += ctl.Name + vbCrLf + vbCrLf + e.Message
     MessageBox.Show(err)
     er.SetError(ctl, "Invalid Regular Expression!!")
```

```vbnet
      Return
    End Try


    If CustomProps.Contains(ctl) Then
      Dim p As Props = CType(CustomProps(ctl), Props)
      p.Regx = val
      CustomProps(ctl) = p
    Else
      Dim p As Props = New Props()
      p.Regx = val
      CustomProps.Add(ctl, p)
    End If
    SetToolTip(ctl)
  End Sub

#End Region

#Region "events"

  Private Sub ValidateProp(ByVal sender As Object, ByVal e As CancelEventArgs)
    Dim ctl As Control = CType(sender, Control)

    'Reset the error
    er.SetError(ctl, "")

    If GetRequired(ctl) Then
      Dim p As Props = CType(CustomProps(ctl), Props)
      If Not Regex.IsMatch(ctl.Text, p.Regx) Then
        er.SetError(ctl, "Value did not match input restrictions")
      End If
      Return
    End If
  End Sub

#End Region

#Region "other stuff"

  Private Sub SetToolTip(ByVal ctl As Control)
    Dim tip As String = String.Empty
    tp.Active = False
    SetTooltipActive()
    Dim p As Props = CType(CustomProps(ctl), Props)
```

```
   If p.Required Then
     tip = "Regular Expression validation: " + p.Regx
   End If
   tp.SetToolTip(ctl, tip)
End Sub

<Conditional("DEBUG")> _
Private Sub SetTooltipActive()
   tp.Active = True
End Sub

#End Region
End Class
```

Let's look at some interesting code. I decided that I do not want the designer of the form that this component goes on to have a problem with regular expressions. After all, not everyone has read the first part of this chapter and is now an expert.

It is all too easy to enter in a regular expression that cannot be parsed. What do you do then? I have code in the SetRegularExpression method to trap this error. Here is the C# code.

C#

```
...

   //Put something here to verify that regular expression is valid
   try
   {
     Regex.IsMatch("abcdefg", val);
   }
   catch(Exception e)
   {
     string err = "Invalid Regular Expression on:\n";
     err += ctl.Name + "\n\n" + e.Message;
     MessageBox.Show(err);
     er.SetError(ctl, "Invalid Regular Expression!!");
     return;
   }

...
```

Because I have no way of parsing a regular expression, I figured I would let the regular expression engine take a look at it. As you can see, I wrap a simple call to the parser in a Try-Catch block. If this call fails, the regular expression passed in was in error. I then pop up a message box with a descriptive error and at the same time I add an error icon next to the control.

Now test this new control. Compile this code and make sure you get no errors. Go into the tester project you have in this solution and remove the number validation control from the form. Also go into the Toolbox and delete this control from the Toolbox. Exit out of the IDE as a whole.

NOTE   I tested this on a few different machines. On some I needed to reload the IDE and on some I did not. Just to be safe, reload the IDE before you reload the control.

Customize the Toolbox with the same Vlad class you did before. You should now have two new controls. Figure 8-18 shows this.

Figure 8-18. Two new controls

Drag the RegxValidate control over to your form and you are ready to go.

The neat thing about all this new error code is that it happens at design time. Figure 8-19 shows my form at design time when I enter in the following regular expression: **[0-9+**. Enter this in and click another property or on the form itself.

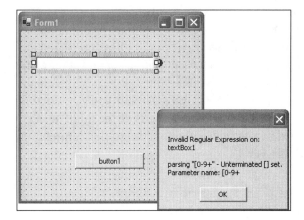

Figure 8-19. Design-time errors

See the nice error box? If the expression was good, I would not get this problem. Now just in case you click OK and then get an important phone call and forget what you were doing, I added the error icon to this control. See it in the back there? Figure 8-20 shows the text for this error during design time.

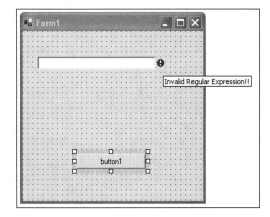

Figure 8-20. The error icon at design time

Now there is no way you cannot tell me that this is really cool. It is quite helpful as well. When you come back from your Mountain Dew break, you have a visual cue that you may have forgotten to correct a regular expression problem.

Special Debug Code

Look at the code for this class carefully and you will see that I have added some special debug code in the form of a ToolTip.

When most users use this control, they will have no clue about regular expressions. The designer of the form will (hopefully) have included some training and a help file. This help file will tell the user what data is valid for this control. As you know, you can enter some pretty hairy regular expressions that may require some weird data pattern to be entered. Showing the user the regular expression that his or her data will be checked against is at best useless. It is also rather unfriendly.

Wouldn't it be nice to offer some ToolTip text for the test engineers? They should, after all, know something about regular expressions. They can at least call you over to see what could be wrong.

Here is the C# code that allows this to happen. The VB code is much the same.

C#

```
#region other stuff

private void SetToolTip(Control ctl)
{
  string tip = string.Empty;
  tp.Active = false;
  SetTooltipActive();
  Props p = (Props)CustomProps[ctl];
  if(p.Required)
    tip = "Regular Expression validation: " + p.Regx ;
  tp.SetToolTip(ctl, tip);
}

[Conditional("DEBUG")]
private void SetTooltipActive()
{
  tp.Active = true;
}

#endregion
```

I used the Conditional attribute, which tests for the DEBUG compiler directive. If the debug version of this code is run, the SetToolTipActive method will get called. Otherwise, the line of code that calls this function never gets compiled. Now I think this is a neat feature.

Notice that in the SetToolTip method I set the ToolTip to be inactive. The next line of code is the call to the method that sets it to be active. If you made a release version of this code, you would never see this ToolTip. Figure 8-21 shows this ToolTip in action.

Figure 8-21. Debug code showing the regular expression

Both you and your test engineers will love this feature.

Before you leave this section, you will need to test the functionality of this control. I leave it up to you to enter in any regular expression you like and prove to yourself that it works. Try the regular expression shown in Figure 8-21. Remember that this control does not do on-the-fly validation. It validates only when you leave the control.

Summary

This was a fun chapter. It provided you with an introduction to regular expressions. The regular expression syntax allows you to match or replace anything in a string. This is a powerful tool and I presented only the basics to you here.

I also showed you how you could use the Masked Edit control that comes with VB 6.0. You could use it if it worked, that is. For some reason, it does not work properly in .NET and it can give you some nasty ping-pong bugs.

The Masked Edit control is a nice idea, so I showed you how to make your own. At the same time, I showed you how to put the regular expressions to good use as a validation technique.

I finished the chapter with an explanation of how to write control extenders. These extenders allow you to add properties to any existing control you choose.

The next chapter deals with the subject of XML data and how to validate it.

CHAPTER 9

XML Data Entry and Validation

THE LAST CHAPTER was a lot of fun, what with playing around with new and extended controls and all.

This chapter is the last of the "how to validate data" chapters. You pretty much know all there is to know by now concerning data entry and validation with user-entered data. I even covered some of the ways you can get machine input such as RS-232 input and file I/O.

What I have not covered yet is Extensible Markup Language (XML). That is what this chapter is all about . . . kind of. I am not going to go into great depth about XML, so I expect you to know the basics of XML and how a well-formed XML document should look.

What Is XML to .NET?

Normally, XML is covered along with Web services and Internet programming technologies such as ASP.NET. You will find many large and imposing books that discuss XML to death, along with how to use it in the Internet space. What I am concerned with here is how XML is used in the Windows Forms "space," if you will.

Traditionally, a Windows application uses the following types of files for storage:

- CSV text files

- Binary files

- Databases

- INI files

You normally don't think of using XML files for a desktop application. However, this is gaining more favor among developers and it's a big part of .NET. The .NET Framework uses XML files extensively for configuration files. You saw this in Chapter 7 when you turned tracing on and off using an XML configuration file.

XML files are used as a transport medium in .NET to allow interprocess communication through simple firewalls. XML is text-based and, as such, is let through port 80 on a server. This is changing, though, as XML firewalls are becoming more the norm these days.

XML is also used by .NET as a transport medium for client/server programs even if they reside on the same machine. Coverage of Remoting is beyond the scope of this book, but I will give you this tidbit: Remoting can change from a fast binary protocol to a slower XML-based SOAP protocol with a single line change in a configuration file. There is no need to write two transport stacks—.NET does it all for you.

In this chapter I cover how to read, write, and use XML files, and how to validate them. I do not go into any great depth with XML. Entire books are devoted to that subject.

The System.Xml Namespace

The System.Xml namespace contains almost 40 classes and a few interfaces to help with your XML needs. It is comprehensive, to say the least. In this section I concentrate on a few of those classes and interfaces.

The first thing I cover is writing to an XML file. One of the things XML files are good for is configuration data. They are fast replacing .ini files for this purpose. Of course, configuration data does not necessarily contain only string data. This may seem like a contradiction because an XML file is a text file. However, an XML file can have a great deal of data that is not string data but is represented by strings. Take the resource file, for instance. In .NET a resource file is often an XML file. I have built resource files with only .jpg files in them. If you were to look at the file, you would see an incredibly huge string for each .jpg file.

One of the nice things about the .NET XML classes is the XmlConvert class, which can convert strongly typed data into strings and back again. You will see this in the next example.

Wide-Open Data

Before I start on this simple example, I want to mention one thing. I hope you are wondering how secure XML files are. After all, they are text files that anyone can open and read using any text editor. In fact, quite a few XML files have descriptive tags that let you glean some pretty useful information.

There are ways you can secure XML files, and I use a method to secure some of the data in an XML file in the next example. I do not go too deep into encryption here, so I suggest that you read up on the cryptography capabilities of .NET. They are quite extensive.

Writing XML Data

Start a new Windows project in either C# or VB. Mine is called "WriteXML." Follow these steps to add a few controls on the default form:

1. Add a Label that reads **Configuration Date**.

2. Add a Label called **lblDate** below the Configuration Data Label. Make the BorderStyle FixedSingle.

3. Add a Label whose text reads **IP Address**.

4. Add a TextBox called **txtIP** below the IP Address Label.

5. Add a Label whose text reads **Mode**.

6. Add a ComboBox called **cmbMode** below the Mode Label.

7. Add a Label whose text reads **Password**.

8. Add a TextBox called **txtPass** below the Password Label.

9. Add a Label whose text reads **Time zone offset**.

10. Add a TextBox called **txtOffset** below the Time zone offset Label.

11. Add a Label whose text reads **Relay Delay**.

12. Add a TextBox called **txtRelay** below the Relay Delay Label.

13. Add a Button called **cmdWrite**. Change its text to **Write XML**.

Your form should look like the one shown in Figure 9-1.

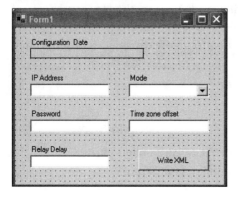

Figure 9-1. The XMLWriter form

This form represents a typical subset of configuration data for an embedded controller of some type.

Now as I inferred earlier, XML files are wide open to hacking by anyone with a text editor. With that in mind, I would be crazy to save a password to an XML file as is. The first thing I need to do code-wise is create a static encryption class that will encrypt and decrypt any string passed to it.

Add a new class to your project called "Classify." Listings 9-1a and 9-1b show the complete code for this class.

Listing 9-1a. C# Code for the Classify Static Class

```
using System;
using System.IO;
using System.Text;
using System.Security.Cryptography;

namespace WriteXML_c
{
  /// <summary>
  /// Summary description for Classify.
  /// </summary>
  public class Classify
  {

    #region class local variables

    private static string EncryptKey = "CryptoManiac";
```

```
  private static MD5CryptoServiceProvider hashmd5;
  private static TripleDESCryptoServiceProvider des;
  private static byte[] pwdhash;

  #endregion

  static Classify()
  {
    hashmd5 = new MD5CryptoServiceProvider();
    pwdhash = hashmd5.ComputeHash(ASCIIEncoding.ASCII.GetBytes(EncryptKey));

    //implement DES3 encryption
    des = new TripleDESCryptoServiceProvider();
    des.Key = pwdhash;
    des.Mode = CipherMode.ECB; //CBC, CFB
  }

  public static string Encrypt(string OriginalString)
  {
    byte[] buff = ASCIIEncoding.ASCII.GetBytes(OriginalString);
    return Convert.ToBase64String(des.CreateEncryptor().
                                  TransformFinalBlock(buff, 0,
                                  buff.Length));
  }

  public static string Decrypt(string EncryptedString)
  {
    byte[] buff = Convert.FromBase64String(EncryptedString);
    return ASCIIEncoding.ASCII.GetString(des.CreateDecryptor().
                                  TransformFinalBlock(buff, 0,
                                  buff.Length));
  }
 }
}
```

Listing 9-1b. VB Code for the Classify Static Class

```
Option Strict On

Imports System.IO
Imports System.Text
Imports System.Security.Cryptography
```

```vb
Public Class Classify

#Region "class local variables"

  Private Shared EncryptKey As String = "CryptoManiac"
  Private Shared hashmd5 As MD5CryptoServiceProvider
  Private Shared des As TripleDESCryptoServiceProvider
  Private Shared pwdhash() As Byte

#End Region

  Shared Sub New()
    hashmd5 = New MD5CryptoServiceProvider()
    pwdhash = hashmd5.ComputeHash(ASCIIEncoding.ASCII.GetBytes(EncryptKey))

    'implement DES3 encryption
    des = New TripleDESCryptoServiceProvider()
    des.Key = pwdhash
    des.Mode = CipherMode.ECB
  End Sub

  Public Shared Function Encrypt(ByVal OriginalString As String) As String
    Dim buff() As Byte = ASCIIEncoding.ASCII.GetBytes(OriginalString)
    Return Convert.ToBase64String(des.CreateEncryptor(). _
                                    TransformFinalBlock(buff, 0, _
                                    buff.Length))
  End Function

  Public Shared Function Decrypt(ByVal EncryptedString As String) As String
    Dim buff() As Byte = Convert.FromBase64String(EncryptedString)
    Return ASCIIEncoding.ASCII.GetString(des.CreateDecryptor(). _
                                    TransformFinalBlock(buff, 0, _
                                    buff.Length))
  End Function
End Class
```

Although this is not a book about encryption, I cannot really talk about data without at least mentioning the topic. This class is just about the simplest way to encrypt and decrypt a string in .NET.

As you can see, I use triple Data Encryption Standard (DES) encryption. I have a character-based key that I start out with, which in this case is the word "CryptoManiac." This gets encoded into a hash, which is then given as the key to the DES service provider object.

Using static (shared in VB) methods and a static constructor allow me to set up the DES encryption class just once and use it many times. You know by now my fondness for static classes, and this is a perfect use for one.

All I need to do to encrypt a string is call the Encrypt method. I can also decrypt the string using the same class. Of course, I need the correct key to decrypt the string.

NOTE If you were to release this code, a programmer could easily get the encrypting key by reading the intermediate language (IL) code. If you want to seriously use encryption, you should also use an obfuscator for the IL code. A few obfuscators are available. In addition to using an obfuscator, you should hide the encrypting key by building the string out of a series of bytes that are added via a series of method calls. This way, a programmer cannot use a hex editor and see the word "CryptoManiac" glaring at him or her on the screen.

Now for the main form's code. This is pretty short, so I present all of the code in Listings 9-2a and 9-2b. The Windows-generated code is deleted here for clarity.

Listing 9-2a. C# Code for the Main Form

```csharp
using System;
using System.Drawing;
using System.Collections;
using System.ComponentModel;
using System.Windows.Forms;
using System.Text;
using System.Xml;
using System.Data;

namespace WriteXML_c
{
  public class Form1 : System.Windows.Forms.Form
  {
    #region vars
```

```
string fname = "Output.xml";
enum MODE
{
  None,
  OnLine,
  OffLine,
  Dumb
}

#endregion

private System.Windows.Forms.Button cmdWrite;
private System.Windows.Forms.Label label1;
private System.Windows.Forms.Label lblFirst;
private System.Windows.Forms.Label lblDate;
private System.Windows.Forms.Label label3;
private System.Windows.Forms.Label label4;
private System.Windows.Forms.ComboBox cmbMode;
private System.Windows.Forms.TextBox txtIP;
private System.Windows.Forms.TextBox txtOffset;
private System.Windows.Forms.TextBox txtPass;
private System.Windows.Forms.Label label5;
private System.Windows.Forms.TextBox txtRelay;
private System.Windows.Forms.Label label2;

private System.ComponentModel.Container components = null;

public Form1()
{
  InitializeComponent();

  lblDate.Text = DateTime.Now.ToLongDateString();
  cmbMode.Items.Add(MODE.Dumb);
  cmbMode.Items.Add(MODE.OffLine);
  cmbMode.Items.Add(MODE.OnLine);
  cmbMode.Items.Add(MODE.None);
  cmbMode.SelectedIndex = 0;

  txtIP.Text = "123.456.789.13";
  txtPass.Text = "Abc56def";
  txtOffset.Text = "-34";
  txtRelay.Text = "21.8";
```

```csharp
      cmdWrite.Click += new EventHandler(this.WriteXMLFile);


}

protected override void Dispose( bool disposing )
{
  if( disposing )
  {
    if (components != null)
    {
      components.Dispose();
    }
  }
  base.Dispose( disposing );
}

#region Windows Form Designer generated code
...
...
...

#endregion

[STAThread]
static void Main()
{
  Application.Run(new Form1());
}

private void Form1_Load(object sender, System.EventArgs e)
{
}

private void WriteXMLFile(object sender, EventArgs e)
{
  double    RelayDelay;
  DateTime  date;
  string    IP;
  MODE      mode;
  int       TZ_Offset;
  string    Pword;
```

```
//I am going to be really bad here and assume that all user-filled-in
//fields are going to convert properly
date        = Convert.ToDateTime(lblDate.Text);
IP          = txtIP.Text;
mode        = (MODE)cmbMode.SelectedItem;
TZ_Offset   = int.Parse(txtOffset.Text);
Pword       = Classify.Encrypt(txtPass.Text);
RelayDelay  = Convert.ToDouble(txtRelay.Text);

//This is your basic well-formed XML file.
XmlTextWriter w = new XmlTextWriter(fname, Encoding.UTF8);
w.Formatting = Formatting.Indented;

w.WriteStartDocument();
w.WriteStartElement("Device_Configuration");

w.WriteElementString("ConfigDate", XmlConvert.ToString(date));
w.WriteElementString("IP", txtIP.Text);
w.WriteElementString("Mode", cmbMode.SelectedItem.ToString());
w.WriteElementString("PassWord", Pword);
w.WriteElementString("TimeZoneOffset", XmlConvert.ToString(TZ_Offset));
w.WriteElementString("RelayDelay", XmlConvert.ToString(RelayDelay));

w.WriteEndElement();
w.WriteEndDocument();

w.Flush();
w.Close();
      }
   }
}
```

Listing 9-2b. VB Code for the Main Form

```
Option Strict On
Imports System
Imports System.Drawing
Imports System.Collections
Imports System.ComponentModel
Imports System.Windows.Forms
Imports System.Text
Imports System.Xml
Imports System.Data
```

```
Public Class Form1
    Inherits System.Windows.Forms.Form

#Region "vars"

    Private fname As String = "Output.xml"
    Enum MODE
        None
        OnLine
        OffLine
        Dumb
    End Enum

#End Region

#Region " Windows Form Designer generated code "

    Public Sub New()
        MyBase.New()

        InitializeComponent()

        lblDate.Text = DateTime.Now.ToLongDateString()
        cmbMode.Items.Add(MODE.Dumb)
        cmbMode.Items.Add(MODE.OffLine)
        cmbMode.Items.Add(MODE.OnLine)
        cmbMode.Items.Add(MODE.None)
        cmbMode.SelectedIndex = 0

        txtIP.Text = "123.456.789.13"
        txtPass.Text = "Abc56def"
        txtOffset.Text = "-34"
        txtRelay.Text = "21.8"

        AddHandler cmdWrite.Click, New EventHandler(AddressOf Me.WriteXMLFile)

    End Sub

    ...
    ...
    ...


#End Region
```

```vb
        Private Sub Form1_Load(ByVal sender As System.Object, _
                                ByVal e As System.EventArgs) Handles MyBase.Load

        End Sub

        Private Sub WriteXMLFile(ByVal sender As Object, ByVal e As EventArgs)
            Dim RelayDelay As Double
            Dim dte As DateTime
            Dim IP As String
            Dim mode As MODE
            Dim TZ_Offset As Int32
            Dim Pword As String

            'I am going to be really bad here and assume that all user-filled-in
            'fields are going to convert properly
            dte = Convert.ToDateTime(lblDate.Text)
            IP = txtIP.Text
            mode = CType(cmbMode.SelectedItem, MODE)
            TZ_Offset = Int32.Parse(txtOffset.Text)
            Pword = Classify.Encrypt(txtPass.Text)
            RelayDelay = Convert.ToDouble(txtRelay.Text)

            'This is your basic well-formed XML file.
            Dim w As XmlTextWriter = New XmlTextWriter(fname, Encoding.UTF8)
            w.Formatting = Formatting.Indented

            w.WriteStartDocument()
            w.WriteStartElement("Device_Configuration")

            w.WriteElementString("ConfigDate", XmlConvert.ToString(dte))
            w.WriteElementString("IP", txtIP.Text)
            w.WriteElementString("Mode", cmbMode.SelectedItem.ToString())
            w.WriteElementString("PassWord", Pword)
            w.WriteElementString("TimeZoneOffset", XmlConvert.ToString(TZ_Offset))
            w.WriteElementString("RelayDelay", XmlConvert.ToString(RelayDelay))

            w.WriteEndElement()
            w.WriteEndDocument()

            w.Flush()
            w.Close()
        End Sub
    End Class
```

Compile and run the program. Your form should look like the one shown in Figure 9-2.

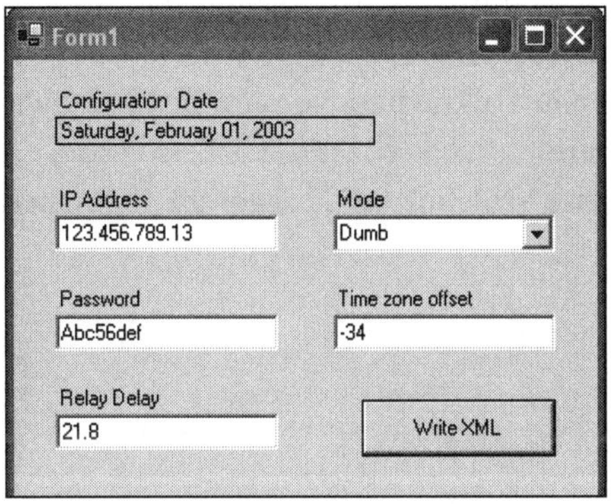

Figure 9-2. The running form

Let's look at the code. First of all, I fill in the text boxes with some values for you. You are free to change these values if you like. I have tried to include a smattering of all the standard data types in .NET. The IP Address is a string. The Mode is an enumeration. The Password is a string, and the Time zone offset is an integer. The Relay Delay is a double.

I did not include any validation on these fields. Changing the values to something other than what is expected will crash the program.

The following piece of C# code is responsible for writing the file:

```
XmlTextWriter w = new XmlTextWriter(fname, Encoding.UTF8);
w.Formatting = Formatting.Indented;

w.WriteStartDocument();
w.WriteStartElement("Device_Configuration");

w.WriteElementString("ConfigDate", XmlConvert.ToString(date));
w.WriteElementString("IP", txtIP.Text);
w.WriteElementString("Mode", cmbMode.SelectedItem.ToString());
w.WriteElementString("PassWord", Pword);
w.WriteElementString("TimeZoneOffset", XmlConvert.ToString(TZ_Offset));
w.WriteElementString("RelayDelay", XmlConvert.ToString(RelayDelay));

w.WriteEndElement();
w.WriteEndDocument();
```

Notice that I use the XmlConvert routines to convert the strongly typed data to a string that is suitable for saving in an XML file. Now the string that you get out of this conversion is not always the same as what you would get out of using the plain Convert functions. This is important to remember if you are wondering why I use this specialized class. Most notably, the date is converted to a format that is not what you would expect from a date-to-string conversion.

Notice also that I save the encrypted version of the password to the XML file. It would not do to have the raw password here.

So what happens when you click the Write XML button? You get the following result:

```xml
<?xml version="1.0" encoding="utf-8"?>
<Device_Configuration>
  <ConfigDate>2003-02-01T00:00:00.0000000-05:00</ConfigDate>
  <IP>123.456.789.13</IP>
  <Mode>Dumb</Mode>
  <PassWord>aXIHM6wwE6HXiEmkPOz42g==</PassWord>
  <TimeZoneOffset>-34</TimeZoneOffset>
  <RelayDelay>21.8</RelayDelay>
</Device_Configuration>
```

Each piece of data is tagged correctly and the password is encrypted. The date is also in a format that XML parsers can understand.

By the way, you will find this file in the Debug directory of your C# project and in the BIN directory of your VB project.

Using the XmlTextWrite like I have here to write an XML file is much like writing a bunch of If-EndIf statements in VB. Let me show you the pertinent code again, only this time with some indentation so you can see what I mean:

```
XmlTextWriter w = new XmlTextWriter(fname, Encoding.UTF8);
  w.Formatting = Formatting.Indented;
  w.WriteStartDocument();
    w.WriteStartElement("Device_Configuration");

      w.WriteElementString("ConfigDate", XmlConvert.ToString(date));
      w.WriteElementString("IP", txtIP.Text);
      w.WriteElementString("Mode", cmbMode.SelectedItem.ToString());
      w.WriteElementString("PassWord", Pword);
      w.WriteElementString("TimeZoneOffset", XmlConvert.ToString(TZ_Offset));
      w.WriteElementString("RelayDelay", XmlConvert.ToString(RelayDelay));
```

```
        w.WriteEndElement();
      w.WriteEndDocument();
    w.Flush();
    w.Close();
```

I bracket the whole file with a start document command and an end document command. This document command has a nested element command, which in turn has some nested strings. If you keep this kind of format, you will be fairly safe.

So, what is a quick way to tell if your resulting document is well-formed? Try opening it with an Internet browser. If the document is missing necessary elements, then the browser will choke.

Those of you who write in HTML or XML quite often are used to writing documents that are well-formed. You can, however, write an XML document that contains all the information you are looking for and it is not well-formed at all. If you do this, you can still read it using an XmlTextReader. So what's the point of the well-formed document? The point is that you also want other programs to read your XML file. If you can make it standard, then no one has to call you up to get the format. This is a big plus.

Reading and Validating What You Wrote

OK, now you know how to write a simple XML configuration file. How do you read it back? By using the XmlTextReader, of course.

The XmlTextReader class has about eight hundred million members that let you do all kinds of stuff. I use only a few here to show you a simple reader and validation procedure. The XmlTextReader is a forward-only, nonvalidating reader. It is intended to be used for high-speed access to XML documents whose contents are known by you to be well-formed. This class is also handy because it does not require a schema or a document type definition (DTD).

On to the next part of this example. Add a new Button to your form called **cmdRead**. Its text should be **Read XML**. Figure 9-3 shows this addition.

You need to go back into this form and add some new code. Because you will use some regular expressions for validation, you need to include the System.Text.RegularExpressions namespace at the top of your form.

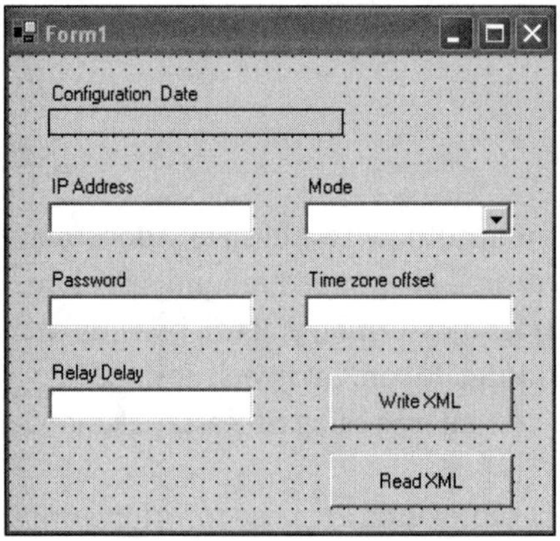

Figure 9-3. The new Read XML button

Add the following enumeration to your form's local variables region.

C#

```csharp
//Added for read
enum CONFIG_STATE
{
  C_UNKNOWN,
  C_DATE,
  C_IP,
  C_MODE,
  C_PASS,
  C_OFFSET,
  C_RELAY
}
```

VB

```vb
'Added for read
Enum CONFIG_STATE
  C_UNKNOWN
  C_DATE
  C_IP
  C_MODE
  C_PASS
  C_OFFSET
    C_RELAY
End Enum
```

You use this enumeration to determine what state the code is in while reading the XML file.

You need to add some code to your constructor. Here it is with the new code in bold.

C#

```csharp
public Form1()
{
    InitializeComponent();

    lblDate.Text = DateTime.Now.ToLongDateString();
    cmbMode.Items.Add(MODE.Dumb);
    cmbMode.Items.Add(MODE.OffLine);
    cmbMode.Items.Add(MODE.OnLine);
    cmbMode.Items.Add(MODE.None);
    cmbMode.SelectedIndex = 0;

    txtIP.Text = "123.456.789.13";
    txtPass.Text = "Abc56def";
    txtOffset.Text = "-34";
    txtRelay.Text = "21.8";

    cmdWrite.Click += new EventHandler(this.WriteXMLFile);

    //=========== New read code =============
    cmdRead.Enabled = false;
    cmdRead.Click += new EventHandler(this.ReadXMLFile);
}
```

VB

```vb
Public Sub New()
    MyBase.New()

    InitializeComponent()

    lblDate.Text = DateTime.Now.ToLongDateString()
    cmbMode.Items.Add(MODE.Dumb)
    cmbMode.Items.Add(MODE.OffLine)
    cmbMode.Items.Add(MODE.OnLine)
    cmbMode.Items.Add(MODE.None)
    cmbMode.SelectedIndex = 0
```

```
        txtIP.Text = "123.456.789.13"
        txtPass.Text = "Abc56def"
        txtOffset.Text = "-34"
        txtRelay.Text = "21.8"

        AddHandler cmdWrite.Click, New EventHandler(AddressOf Me.WriteXMLFile)

        '=========== New read code =============
        cmdRead.Enabled = False
        AddHandler cmdRead.Click, New EventHandler(AddressOf Me.ReadXMLFile)
    End Sub
```

This disables the Read XML button until you have written the file to disk. It also wires up the ReadXMLFile delegate to the click event handler of this button.

Now add the following piece of code to the bottom of your existing WriteXMLFile method.

C#

```
        //enable read code
        cmbMode.SelectedIndex = 3;
        cmdRead.Enabled    = true;
        cmdWrite.Enabled   = false;
        txtIP.Text         = "";
        txtPass.Text       = "";
        txtOffset.Text     = "";
        txtRelay.Text      = "";
        lblDate.Text       = "";
```

VB

```
        'enable read code
        cmbMode.SelectedIndex = 3
        cmdRead.Enabled = True
        cmdWrite.Enabled = False
        txtIP.Text = ""
        txtPass.Text = ""
        txtOffset.Text = ""
        txtRelay.Text = ""
        lblDate.Text = ""
```

This code clears the screen, disables the Write XML button, and enables the Read XML button. The last bit of code to add, of course, is the ReadXMLFile method.

C#

```csharp
private void ReadXMLFile(object sender, EventArgs e)
{
  double       RelayDelay  = 0.0;;
  DateTime     date        = DateTime.Today.AddYears(-28);
  string       IP          = "INVALID IP";
  MODE         mode        = MODE.None;
  int          TZ_Offset   = 0;
  string       Pword       = string.Empty;
  bool         Config      = false;
  CONFIG_STATE cs          = CONFIG_STATE.C_UNKNOWN;

  //I use a state machine based upon the CONFIG_STATE value.
  //This is but one way to do this.
  XmlTextReader r = new XmlTextReader(fname);
  //Ignore all white space
  r.WhitespaceHandling = WhitespaceHandling.None;
  while (r.Read())
  {
    switch (r.NodeType)
    {
      case XmlNodeType.Element:
        if(r.Name == "Device_Configuration")
          Config = true;
        else
        {
          if(Config)
          {
            switch(r.Name)
            {
              case "ConfigDate":
                cs = CONFIG_STATE.C_DATE;
                break;
              case "IP":
                cs = CONFIG_STATE.C_IP;
                break;
              case "Mode":
                cs = CONFIG_STATE.C_MODE;
                break;
              case "PassWord":
                cs = CONFIG_STATE.C_PASS;
                break;
```

```
              case "TimeZoneOffset":
                cs = CONFIG_STATE.C_OFFSET;
                break;
              case "RelayDelay":
                cs = CONFIG_STATE.C_RELAY;
                break;
          }
        }
      }
    break;
  case XmlNodeType.Text:
    if(Config)
    {
      switch(cs)
      {
        case CONFIG_STATE.C_DATE:
          date = XmlConvert.ToDateTime(r.Value);
          break;
        case CONFIG_STATE.C_IP:
          if(Regex.IsMatch(r.Value,
                        "^\\d{1,3}.\\d{1,3}.\\d{1,3}.\\d{1,3}$"))
            IP = r.Value;
          break;
        case CONFIG_STATE.C_MODE:
          switch(r.Value)
          {
            case "Dumb":
              mode = MODE.Dumb;
              break;
            case "OnLine":
              mode = MODE.OnLine;
              break;
            case "OffLine":
              mode = MODE.OffLine;
              break;
            case "None":
            default:
              mode = MODE.None;
              break;
          }
          break;
        case CONFIG_STATE.C_PASS:
          Pword = Classify.Decrypt(r.Value);
          break;
```

```
                    case CONFIG_STATE.C_OFFSET:
                      //Do some validation
                      if(Regex.IsMatch(r.Value, "^[0-9+-]+$"))
                        TZ_Offset = XmlConvert.ToInt32(r.Value);
                      break;
                    case CONFIG_STATE.C_RELAY:
                      //Do some validation
                      if(Regex.IsMatch(r.Value, "^[0-9+-.]+$"))
                        RelayDelay = XmlConvert.ToDouble(r.Value);
                      break;
                  }
                }
                break;
            }
          }
          r.Close();
          txtIP.Text        = IP;
          txtPass.Text      = Pword;
          txtOffset.Text    = TZ_Offset.ToString();
          txtRelay.Text     = RelayDelay.ToString();
          lblDate.Text      = date.ToLongDateString();
          for(int k=0; k<cmbMode.Items.Count; k++)
          {
            if((MODE)cmbMode.Items[k] == mode)
            {
              cmbMode.SelectedIndex = k;
              break;
            }
          }
          cmdWrite.Enabled = true;
          cmdRead.Enabled  = false;
      }
```

VB

```
  Private Sub ReadXMLFile(ByVal sender As Object, ByVal e As EventArgs)
    Dim RelayDelay As Double = 0.0
    Dim dte As DateTime = DateTime.Today.AddYears(-28)
    Dim IP As String = "INVALID IP"
    Dim mode As MODE = mode.None
    Dim TZ_Offset As Int32 = 0
    Dim Pword As String = String.Empty
    Dim Config As Boolean = False
    Dim cs As CONFIG_STATE = CONFIG_STATE.C_UNKNOWN
```

```
'I use a state machine based upon the CONFIG_STATE value.
'This is but one way to do this.
Dim r As XmlTextReader = New XmlTextReader(fname)
'Ignore all white space
r.WhitespaceHandling = WhitespaceHandling.None
While r.Read()
  Select Case r.NodeType
    Case XmlNodeType.Element
      If r.Name = "Device_Configuration" Then
        Config = True
      Else
        If Config Then
          Select Case r.Name
            Case "ConfigDate"
              cs = CONFIG_STATE.C_DATE
            Case "IP"
              cs = CONFIG_STATE.C_IP
            Case "Mode"
              cs = CONFIG_STATE.C_MODE
            Case "PassWord"
              cs = CONFIG_STATE.C_PASS
            Case "TimeZoneOffset"
              cs = CONFIG_STATE.C_OFFSET
            Case "RelayDelay"
              cs = CONFIG_STATE.C_RELAY
          End Select
        End If
      End If
    case XmlNodeType.Text:
    If Config Then
      Select Case cs
        Case CONFIG_STATE.C_DATE
          dte = XmlConvert.ToDateTime(r.Value)
        Case CONFIG_STATE.C_IP
          If Regex.IsMatch(r.Value, _
                        "^\d{1,3}.\d{1,3}.\d{1,3}.\d{1,3}$") Then
            IP = r.Value
          End If
        Case CONFIG_STATE.C_MODE
          Select Case r.Value
            Case "Dumb"
              mode = mode.Dumb
            Case "OnLine"
              mode = mode.OnLine
```

```
                Case "OffLine"
                    mode = mode.OffLine
                Case "None"
                    mode = mode.None
              End Select
          Case CONFIG_STATE.C_PASS
            Pword = Classify.Decrypt(r.Value)
          Case CONFIG_STATE.C_OFFSET
            'Do some validation
            If Regex.IsMatch(r.Value, "^[0-9+-]+$") Then
              TZ_Offset = XmlConvert.ToInt32(r.Value)
            End If
            case CONFIG_STATE.C_RELAY:
              'Do some validation
              If Regex.IsMatch(r.Value, "^[0-9+-.]+$") Then
                RelayDelay = XmlConvert.ToDouble(r.Value)
            End If
        End Select
      End If
  End Select
End While
r.Close()
txtIP.Text = IP
txtPass.Text = Pword
txtOffset.Text = TZ_Offset.ToString()
txtRelay.Text = RelayDelay.ToString()
lblDate.Text = dte.ToLongDateString()
Dim k As Int32
For k = 0 To cmbMode.Items.Count - 1
  If CType(cmbMode.Items(k), MODE) = mode Then
    cmbMode.SelectedIndex = k
    Exit For
  End If
Next
cmdWrite.Enabled = True
cmdRead.Enabled = False
End Sub
```

This is a lot of code just to read a few lines of XML data. Let's examine it.

For those of you familiar with the Simple API for XML (SAX) reader method, the XmlTextReader is much the same. The big difference, though, is that while the SAX reader "pushed" nodes in the form of events, this reader pulls nodes from the XML file.

Quite a few types of nodes are available that I can trap, but because this is a very simple XML file, I trap only the elements and their values.

The first thing I want to know is if this is a device configuration file. If not, I fall through all the code as the reader traverses the file. Once I know that this is a device configuration file, I set a flag and crank up the state machine.

I look at each element name to see if it jibes with what I expect out of this file. If so, I set the machine state and wait for the next iteration of the read cycle. If this next iteration is a value (it should always be some kind of value in my XML file), I convert the value to the proper data type according to the state machine value.

Notice that before I convert the numerical values, I use the regular expression parser to validate that the data is in the correct form. I do this for the IP address as well.

TIP   Regular expressions are a *big* part of data validation. See Chapter 8 for more involved uses of regular expressions.

I do this conversion process until the XML file has been read completely. The only thing that I cannot convert explicitly is the enumerated value that I save to the file.

Enumerated Values in XML Files

You have two ways to save the enumerated value in the XML file. The first way is to convert the enumeration to an integer and save the integer to the file. This method makes for much less code in converting the value back. There is one big problem with doing this, though.

Suppose I had saved the enumeration value in the file, and then 6 months later I inserted another enumerated value in the middle of the Enum definition in my program. The next time I read in the integer from the XML file and convert to an enumeration, I could be one off. This can be an elusive and possibly destructive bug to have.

The second way—the way I chose to implement—is to save the text form of the enumeration to the XML file. Although this takes a little bit of code to restore from the file, it actually saves two bugs. The first bug it eliminates is the addition/subtraction of an enumerated value in the definition. The second bug it eliminates is the deletion of the enumerated value itself. If the code does not find the enumeration match, it defaults to whatever I initialized the value at.

Validating Using the XmlTextReader

It may seem like overkill, but you can see from this reader code that I converted the string value from the XML file into a strong data type then converted it back so I could display it in the TextBox. I did this to prove a point.

Most of the time when you save data to an XML file, it will be nonstring data. You will need to do the conversion process back and forth as you write and read the data.

As I noted earlier, the XmlTextReader is not a validating reader. Everything it pulls in is text. You must do the validation yourself. You can see from the example that this validation is not hard, but it can be time consuming. Suppose I had quite a bit of data in all different kinds of formats that I wanted to read from an XML file. The better way to go would be to have some kind of easy validation while the file was being read. Well, it just so happens that .NET provides you with one: the XmlValidatingReader.

The XmlValidatingReader

The XmlValidatingReader sits on top of the XmlTextReader and validates each node according to a schema. Now you can validate against a DTD as well, or even make a validating reader that validates against nothing.

I am going to show you one way to validate XML data as it is being read in. I will validate against an external XML schema file. If at the end of this section you find validation of XML interesting, I suggest you spend some quality time with the online help. Although it is important, what I am about to show you is just the tip of the XML and Extensible Schema Definition (XSD) iceberg.

So, what is XML validation? Here is what you *can* do with validation:

- Validate the data type.

- Validate that the right tags are in the correct owning blocks.

- Validate the minimum number of times an element appears.

- Validate the maximum amount of times an element appears.

What you *cannot* do is validate your data against regular expressions. You will still need to do that manually. XML validation automates a big part of reading an XML file, however.

The best way to explain how an XmlValidatingReader works is to show you by example. In this section I expand on the previous example by adding schema support for the method that reads the XML file.

Start with a brand-new C# or VB project. Mine is called "ValidateXML." The form is almost the same as that in the previous example, with the addition of one more major control. I copied the form layout of the previous project to the Clipboard and pasted it on the new form for this project. Here are the manual instructions if you did not complete the last example:

1. Add a Label that reads **Configuration Date.**

2. Add a Label called **lblDate** below the Configuration Date Label. Make the BorderStyle FixedSingle.

3. Add a Label whose text reads **IP Address.**

4. Add a TextBox called **txtIP** below the IP Address Label.

5. Add a Label whose text reads **Mode.**

6. Add a ComboBox called **cmbMode** below the Mode Label.

7. Add a Label whose text reads **Password.**

8. Add a TextBox called **txtPass** below the Password Label.

9. Add a Label whose text reads **Time zone offset.**

10. Add a TextBox called **txtOffset** below the Time zone offset Label.

11. Add a Label whose text reads **Relay Delay.**

12. Add a TextBox called **txtRelay** below the Relay Delay Label.

13. Add a Button called **cmbWrite.** Change the text to **Write XML.**

14. Add a Label whose text reads **Read Results.** Center the text in the control.

15. Add a RichTextBox to the form and call it **rcResults.**

Your new form should look like the one shown in Figure 9-4.

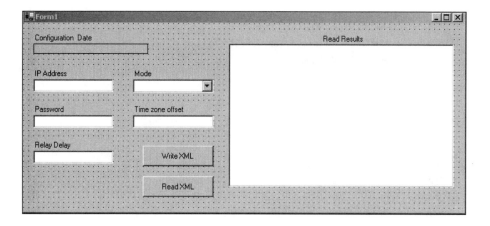

Figure 9-4. The new form for the validating reader

I use the RichTextBox to display the (good and bad) results of reading the file. Double-click the two buttons to get the delegates created for you.

Now, a validating reader needs a schema to work with. You could make one via code, but the easier way is to use the XML designer provided by .NET. Although your XML data file may change, the schema should remain static once you have your validation rules in place.

Make sure that you have the following code in your constructor.

C#

```
lblDate.Text = DateTime.Now.ToLongDateString();
cmbMode.Items.Add(MODE.Dumb);
cmbMode.Items.Add(MODE.OffLine);
cmbMode.Items.Add(MODE.OnLine);
cmbMode.Items.Add(MODE.None);
cmbMode.SelectedIndex = 0;

txtIP.Text = "123.456.789.13";
txtPass.Text = "Abc56def";
txtOffset.Text = "-34";
txtRelay.Text = "21.8";
```

VB

```
lblDate.Text = DateTime.Now.ToLongDateString()
cmbMode.Items.Add(MODE.Dumb)
cmbMode.Items.Add(MODE.OffLine)
cmbMode.Items.Add(MODE.OnLine)
cmbMode.Items.Add(MODE.None)
cmbMode.SelectedIndex = 0

txtIP.Text = "123.456.789.13"
txtPass.Text = "Abc56def"
txtOffset.Text = "-34"
txtRelay.Text = "21.8"
```

Making the Schema

Go to the Solution Explorer window and add a new XML Schema to your project. You will see a blank page with two tabs at the bottom left of the page. One tab is for viewing the controls for the page and the other is for viewing the actual XML code generated by said controls. Name this new XML Schema **ConfigDevice.xsd**. Figure 9-5 shows my Solution Explorer window after I added the new item.

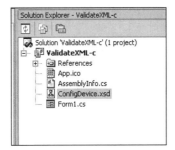

Figure 9-5. The new XML Schema file

Now for the fun part. Drop a complex type control onto your schema form. Name it **ConfigDevice**. Click the first box under the letters *CT* and you will see a drop-down control. Click this control and choose an element. Call it **ConfigDate** and choose a type of DateTime in the cell next to it.

Table 9-1 shows the elements that you need to add to this control.

Table 9-1. Elements for the ConfigDevice Complex Type Control

Element	Type
ConfigDate	DateTime
IP	string
Mode	string
PassWord	string
TimeZoneOffset	integer
RelayDelay	double

Once you have finished adding the elements, drag over an element from the Toolbox and drop it on your XML form. The element name should be "Device_Configuration". The type of this element should be ConfigDevice. You choose the type from the drop-down box in the cell to the right of the name. Once you do this, the rest of this element box should fill itself in for you automatically.

Figure 9-6 shows these two controls as they are filled in on the XML form.

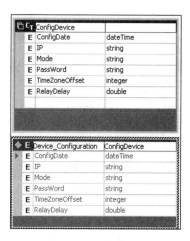

Figure 9-6. XML controls

You made a user-defined type called "ConfigDevice." The members of this new type are the elements and associated types that you typed in. Once this was complete, you dropped a new element on the form. You gave it a name and assigned its type to the new user-defined type.

You can think of this as defining a structure with certain public variables. You then define a new variable whose type is this new structure. You have done it hundreds of times in code; now you are doing it using XML blocks.

There is one more thing you need to do to this schema. You will want to make sure that the XML file you are checking actually has the values you are looking for. You will also want to see those values only once in the XML file.

Click the element ConfigDate in the complex type control. Go over to the Properties screen and enter **1** as the minOccurs value. Enter **1** also for the maxOccurs value. Do this for all the elements in the complex type.

Click the XML tab at the bottom of your XML form. Your code should look like Figure 9-7.

```xml
<?xml version="1.0" encoding="utf-8" ?>
<xs:schema id="ConfigDevice" targetNamespace="http://tempuri.org/ConfigDevice.xsd"
           elementFormDefault="qualified" xmlns="http://tempuri.org/ConfigDevice.xsd"
           xmlns:mstns="http://tempuri.org/ConfigDevice.xsd"
           xmlns:xs="http://www.w3.org/2001/XMLSchema">
  <xs:complexType name="ConfigDevice">
    <xs:sequence>
      <xs:element name="ConfigDate" type="xs:dateTime" minOccurs="1" maxOccurs="1" />
      <xs:element name="IP" type="xs:string" maxOccurs="1" minOccurs="1" />
      <xs:element name="Mode" type="xs:string" minOccurs="1" maxOccurs="1" />
      <xs:element name="PassWord" type="xs:string" maxOccurs="1" minOccurs="1" />
      <xs:element name="TimeZoneOffset" type="xs:integer" minOccurs="1" maxOccurs="1" />
      <xs:element name="RelayDelay" type="xs:double" maxOccurs="1" minOccurs="1" />
    </xs:sequence>
  </xs:complexType>
  <xs:element name="Device_Configuration" type="ConfigDevice"></xs:element>
</xs:schema>
```

Figure 9-7. XML output for the XSD file

I like working with schema files because the syntax is the same as an XML file. A DTD uses a different syntax.

If you want to, you can embed this XML Schema at the top of an XML data file. This will give you a single XML file for transport that includes data and validation requirements. This is called an *inline schema*.

You need to go to Windows Explorer and copy this XSD file to the BIN directory if you are working in VB or to the BIN\Debug directory if you are working in C#.

The Validation Form's Code

You need to add the following namespace references to your code.

C#

```csharp
using System.Xml;
using System.IO;
using System.Xml.Schema;
```

VB

```vb
Imports System.Xml
Imports System.IO
Imports System.Xml.Schema
```

I include the IO namespace because I will use a stream to read the file. Add the following variables block.

C#

```csharp
#region vars

string XMLfname    = "ConfigDevice.xml";
string XSDfname    = "ConfigDevice.xsd";
string NameSpace   = "http://tempuri.org/ConfigDevice.xsd";
enum MODE
{
  None,
  OnLine,
  OffLine,
  Dumb
}

#endregion
```

VB

```vb
#Region "vars"

  Private XMLfname As String = "ConfigDevice.xml"
  Private XSDfname As String = "ConfigDevice.xsd"
  Private nmSpace As String = "http://tempuri.org/ConfigDevice.xsd"
  Private Enum MODE
    None
    OnLine
    OffLine
    Dumb
  End Enum

#End Region
```

I include a namespace in both the XSD and XML files so they can reference the correct schema file.

The next thing to add is the code to write the XML file.

C#

```csharp
private void WriteXMLFile()
{
  double     RelayDelay;
  DateTime   date;
  string     IP;
  MODE       mode;
  Decimal     TZ_Offset;
  string     Pword;

  //I am going to be really bad here and assume that all user-filled-in
  //fields are going to convert properly
  date       = Convert.ToDateTime(lblDate.Text);
  IP         = txtIP.Text;
  mode       = (MODE)cmbMode.SelectedItem;
  TZ_Offset  = int.Parse(txtOffset.Text);
  Pword      = txtPass.Text;
  RelayDelay = Convert.ToDouble(txtRelay.Text);

  //This is your basic well-formed XML file.
  XmlTextWriter w = new XmlTextWriter(XMLfname, null);
  w.Formatting = Formatting.Indented;
  w.WriteStartDocument();
```

```
            w.WriteStartElement("Device_Configuration", NameSpace);

            //Uncomment the short date line and comment the one above to cause
            //an XML validation error in the read routine
            w.WriteStartElement("ConfigDate");
            w.WriteString(XmlConvert.ToString(date));
//          w.WriteString(date.ToShortDateString());
            w.WriteEndElement();

            w.WriteStartElement("IP");
            w.WriteString(txtIP.Text);
            w.WriteEndElement();

            w.WriteStartElement("Mode");
            w.WriteString(cmbMode.SelectedItem.ToString());
            w.WriteEndElement();

            w.WriteStartElement("PassWord");
            w.WriteString(Pword);
            w.WriteEndElement();

            w.WriteStartElement("TimeZoneOffset");
            w.WriteString(XmlConvert.ToString(TZ_Offset));
            w.WriteEndElement();

            w.WriteStartElement("RelayDelay");
            w.WriteString(XmlConvert.ToString(RelayDelay));
            w.WriteEndElement();

            w.WriteEndElement();
            w.WriteEndDocument();
            w.Flush();
            w.Close();

            //enable read code
            cmbMode.SelectedIndex = 3;
            cmdRead.Enabled   = true;
            cmdWrite.Enabled  = false;
        }
```

VB

```vb
Private Sub WriteXMLFile()
    Dim RelayDelay As Double
    Dim dte As DateTime
    Dim IP As String
    Dim mode As MODE
    Dim TZ_Offset As Decimal
    Dim Pword As String

    'I am going to be really bad here and assume that all user-filled-in
    'fields are going to convert properly
    dte = Convert.ToDateTime(lblDate.Text)
    IP = txtIP.Text
    mode - CType(cmbMode.SelectedItem, MODE)
    TZ_Offset = Int32.Parse(txtOffset.Text)
    Pword = txtPass.Text
    RelayDelay = Convert.ToDouble(txtRelay.Text)

    'This is your basic well-formed XML file.
    Dim w As XmlTextWriter = New XmlTextWriter(XMLfname, Nothing)
    w.Formatting = Formatting.Indented
    w.WriteStartDocument()

    w.WriteStartElement("Device_Configuration", nmSpace)

    'Uncomment the short date line and comment the one above to cause
    'an XML validation error in the read routine
    w.WriteStartElement("ConfigDate")
    w.WriteString(XmlConvert.ToString(dte))
    'w.WriteString(dte.ToShortDateString())
    w.WriteEndElement()

    w.WriteStartElement("IP")
    w.WriteString(txtIP.Text)
    w.WriteEndElement()

    w.WriteStartElement("Mode")
    w.WriteString(cmbMode.SelectedItem.ToString())
    w.WriteEndElement()
```

```
    w.WriteStartElement("PassWord")
    w.WriteString(Pword)
    w.WriteEndElement()

    w.WriteStartElement("TimeZoneOffset")
    w.WriteString(XmlConvert.ToString(TZ_Offset))
    w.WriteEndElement()

    w.WriteStartElement("RelayDelay")
    w.WriteString(XmlConvert.ToString(RelayDelay))
    w.WriteEndElement()

    w.WriteEndElement()
    w.WriteEndDocument()
    w.Flush()
    w.Close()

    'enable read code
    cmbMode.SelectedIndex = 3
    cmdRead.Enabled = True
    cmdWrite.Enabled = False
End Sub
```

I am writing to the XML file a little differently from the previous example. In that example I used the WriteElementString method. Here I explicitly write the start element tag, write its value, and then write the end element tag.

The only real difference here from the last example is that I am not encrypting the password. You have that class and you can use it if you like.

Next is the XML reader. I first show you the code then explain what is going on. This code region includes two methods.

C#

```
#region Read XML file

private void ReadXMLFile ()
{
    double    RelayDelay;
    DateTime  date;
    string    IP;
    MODE      mode;
    decimal   TZ_Offset;
    string    Pword;
```

```
try
{
  //open up a stream and feed it to the XmlTextReader
  StreamReader sRdr          = new StreamReader(XMLfname);
  XmlTextReader tRdr         = new XmlTextReader(sRdr);

  //Instantiate a new schemas collection
  //Add this one schema to the collection
  //A collection means that you can validate this XML file against any
  //number of schemas.  You would do this if you were reading the file
  //piecemeal
  XmlSchemaCollection Schemas = new XmlSchemaCollection();
  Schemas.Add(null, XSDfname);

  //Instantiate a new validating reader.  This validates for data type
  //and presence.
  //Add the schemas collection to the validating reader and funnel the
  //XmlTextReader through it.
  //wire up an ad-hoc validation delegate to catch any validation errors
  XmlValidatingReader vRdr   = new XmlValidatingReader(tRdr);
  vRdr.ValidationType        = ValidationType.Schema;
  vRdr.ValidationEventHandler += new ValidationEventHandler(ValXML);
  vRdr.Schemas.Add(Schemas);

  //Read the XML file through the validator
  object node;
  while (vRdr.Read())
  {
    node = null;
    if (vRdr.LocalName.Equals("ConfigDate"))
    {
      node = vRdr.ReadTypedValue();
      if(node != null)
        date = (DateTime)node;
    }
    if (vRdr.LocalName.Equals("RelayDelay"))
    {
      node = vRdr.ReadTypedValue();
      if(node != null)
        RelayDelay = (double)node;
    }
```

```
            if (vRdr.LocalName.Equals("TimeZoneOffset"))
            {
              node = vRdr.ReadTypedValue();
              if(node != null)
                TZ_Offset = (decimal)node;
            }
            if (vRdr.LocalName.Equals("PassWord"))
            {
              node = vRdr.ReadTypedValue();
              if(node != null)
                Pword = (string)node;
            }
            if (vRdr.LocalName.Equals("Mode"))
            {
              node = vRdr.ReadTypedValue();
//            mode = (string)node;
            }
            if (vRdr.LocalName.Equals("IP"))
            {
              node = vRdr.ReadTypedValue();
              if(node != null)
                IP = (string)node;
            }
            if(node != null)
            {
              rcResults.AppendText(vRdr.LocalName + "\n");
              rcResults.AppendText(node.GetType().ToString() + "\n");
              rcResults.AppendText(node.ToString() + "\n\n");
            }


        }
        vRdr.Close();
        tRdr.Close();
        sRdr.Close();
    }
    catch (Exception e)
    {
        //The handler will catch malformed XML docs.
        //It is not intended to catch bad data.  That is the delegate's job
        MessageBox.Show("Exception analyzing Config file: " + e.Message);
    }
}
```

```csharp
    private void ValXML(Object sender, ValidationEventArgs e)
    {
      //This delegate will ONLY catch bad data.  It will not catch
      //a malformed XML document!!
      rcResults.AppendText(e.Message + "\n\n");
    }

    #endregion
```

VB

```vbnet
#Region "Read XML file"

  Private Sub ReadXMLFile()
    Dim RelayDelay As Double
    Dim dte As DateTime
    Dim IP As String
    Dim mode As MODE
    Dim TZ_Offset As Decimal
    Dim Pword As String

    Try
      'open up a stream and feed it to the XmlTextReader
      Dim sRdr As StreamReader = New StreamReader(XMLfname)
      Dim tRdr As XmlTextReader = New XmlTextReader(sRdr)

      'Instantiate a new schemas collection
      'Add this one schema to the collection
      'A collection means that you can validate this XML file against any
      'number of schemas.  You would do this if you were reading the file
      'piecemeal
      Dim Schemas As XmlSchemaCollection = New XmlSchemaCollection()
      Schemas.Add(Nothing, XSDfname)

      'Instantiate a new validating reader.  This validates for data type
      'and presence.
      'Add the schemas collection to the validating reader and funnel the
      'XmlTextReader through it.
      'wire up an ad-hoc validation delegate to catch any validation errors
      Dim vRdr As XmlValidatingReader = New XmlValidatingReader(tRdr)
      vRdr.ValidationType = ValidationType.Schema
      AddHandler vRdr.ValidationEventHandler, _
                                  New ValidationEventHandler(AddressOf ValXML)
      vRdr.Schemas.Add(Schemas)
```

```
'Read the XML file through the validator
Dim node As Object
While vRdr.Read()
  node = Nothing
  If vRdr.LocalName.Equals("ConfigDate") Then
    node = vRdr.ReadTypedValue()
    If Not node Is Nothing Then
      dte = CType(node, DateTime)
    End If
  End If
  If vRdr.LocalName.Equals("RelayDelay") Then
    node = vRdr.ReadTypedValue()
    If Not node Is Nothing Then
      RelayDelay = CType(node, Double)
    End If
  End If
  If vRdr.LocalName.Equals("TimeZoneOffset") Then
    node = vRdr.ReadTypedValue()
    If Not node Is Nothing Then
      TZ_Offset = CType(node, Decimal)
    End If
  End If

  If vRdr.LocalName.Equals("PassWord") Then
    node = vRdr.ReadTypedValue()
    If Not node Is Nothing Then
      Pword = CType(node, String)
    End If
  End If
  If (vRdr.LocalName.Equals("Mode")) Then
    node = vRdr.ReadTypedValue()
    '              mode = (string)node;
  End If
  If vRdr.LocalName.Equals("IP") Then
    node = vRdr.ReadTypedValue()
    If Not node Is Nothing Then
      IP = CType(node, String)
    End If
  End If
  If Not node Is Nothing Then
    rcResults.AppendText(vRdr.LocalName + vbCrLf)
    rcResults.AppendText(node.GetType().ToString() + vbCrLf)
    rcResults.AppendText(node.ToString() + vbCrLf + vbCrLf)
  End If
```

```
      End While
      vRdr.Close()
      tRdr.Close()
      sRdr.Close()
    Catch e As Exception
      'The handler will catch malformed XML docs.
      'It is not intended to catch bad data.  That is the delegate's job
      MessageBox.Show("Exception analyzing Config file: " + e.Message)
    End Try
  End Sub

  Private Sub ValXML(ByVal sender As Object, ByVal e As ValidationEventArgs)
    'This delegate will ONLY catch bad data.  It will not catch
    'a malformed XML document!!
    rcResults.AppendText(e.Message + vbCrLf + vbCrLf)
  End Sub

#End Region
```

This code creates a new XmlTextReader that is fed by the StreamReader. I then create a schema collection and add the schema I just created to it.

The next thing I do is create an XmlValidatingReader, tell it how to validate the XML file, and wire up a validation error handler. I pass the schemas collection to this validating reader.

Because I am passing a collection of schemas to the reader, it is safe to infer that this reader can validate the XML file against any number of schemas. In fact, that is true. If you have a huge XML data file, you may want to validate chunks of it against different schemas.

As I read the XML file, I look for a particular tag and then cast the string directly to the variable I need. Here is the RelayDelay repeated.

C#

```
            if (vRdr.LocalName.Equals("RelayDelay"))
            {
              node = vRdr.ReadTypedValue();
              if(node != null)
                RelayDelay = (double)node;
            }
```

In the previous example I needed to check this value with the regular expression parser to make sure it was the correct data type. Here I can safely assume it is because the ValidationEventHandler delegate would have caught any data type errors.

Once I know the nodes are valid, I write some statistics to the TextBox screen. Here is the code for that.

VB

```
If Not node Is Nothing Then
  rcResults.AppendText(vRdr.LocalName + vbCrLf)
  rcResults.AppendText(node.GetType().ToString() + vbCrLf)
  rcResults.AppendText(node.ToString() + vbCrLf + vbCrLf)
End If
```

The LocalName is the element name. Besides this, I show the data type that the schema expects and the actual value of the node. If there are any problems with data type or missing data, I handle the problem in the delegate.

Enter the following code, which wires up the buttons.

C#

```
#region events

private void cmdWrite_Click(object sender, System.EventArgs e)
{
  WriteXMLFile();
}

private void cmdRead_Click(object sender, System.EventArgs e)
{
  ReadXMLFile();
}

#endregion
```

VB

```
#Region "events"

  Private Sub cmdWrite_Click_1(ByVal sender As System.Object, _
                               ByVal e As System.EventArgs) _
                               Handles cmdWrite.Click
    WriteXMLFile()
  End Sub
```

```
Private Sub cmdRead_Click_1(ByVal sender As System.Object, _
                            ByVal e As System.EventArgs) _
                            Handles cmdRead.Click
    ReadXMLFile()
End Sub

#End Region
```

Compile and run the program. Click the Write XML button then the Read XML button. Figure 9-8 shows the form after reading the XML file.

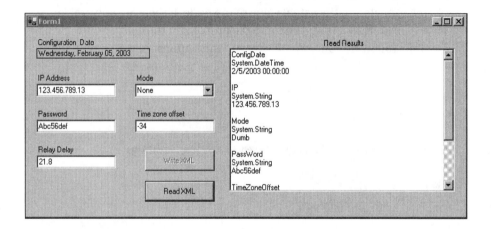

Figure 9-8. The validated XML form

All's well here. Now make a slight change to the code to write to the XML file. This is where you write the ConfigDate string to the file.

C#

```
    w.WriteStartElement("ConfigDate");
//    w.WriteString(XmlConvert.ToString(date));
    w.WriteString(date.ToShortDateString());
    w.WriteEndElement();
```

The VB code is the same minus the semicolon.

What I am doing here is saving a raw date string to the XML file. Run the program and you should see the screen shown in Figure 9-9.

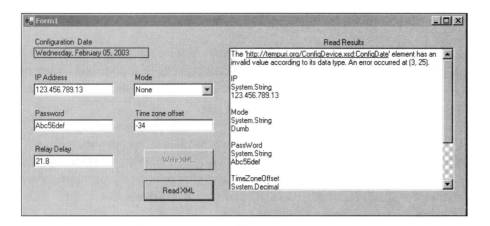

Figure 9-9. An error in XML validation

You can see that the validation handler caught the problem and the error displays on the screen.

 NOTE The XmlValidatingReader catches *only* validation errors. If you have a malformed XML file, the XmlValidatingReader will not catch that. It will instead throw an exception. You may want to read in the XML file first and check for well-formedness before letting the XmlValidatingReader take a look at it.

I suggest playing around a little with the code to see what errors you can catch.

Other Types of XML Data

As I mentioned earlier, this chapter only scratches the surface of XML data files. There are other kinds of XML data files.

If you think about it, these last two examples used XML as a minidatabase. If you have worked with ADO, you know that ADO can save data to an XML file as a database. Some programs do this. In .NET you can save a data set to an XML file.

Another common use of XML files is object persistence. When an object in .NET is saved to disk, it can be saved as an XML file. This is *serialization*. Though coverage of serialization is beyond the scope of this book, this technique has quite a few uses. It also has some drawbacks, such as not saving private fields and type information. I suggest you view the copious online help entries for more information on this subject.

Summary

This chapter showed you some simple uses for XML files. You saw how to write and read XML files. You learned how to convert data types back and forth from XML text to strict data types. You also learned in the first example how to validate XML data as it is being read in.

The second example showed you how to use a schema with an XmlValidatingReader to automatically validate the data type of the node you are reading. This makes reading XML files much more automatic and less error-prone.

The next chapter is all about keeping the user happy. Your programs may need to do quite a bit of processing, and giving your users the illusion of speed will be important in your programs.

CHAPTER 10

Keeping Users Happy

CHAPTER 9 COVERED how to use XML files in your data entry and validation programs. It was the last of the "how to validate" chapters.

This chapter deals with scalability issues in relation to the user interface. What do I mean by this? If you have a huge database and several concurrent clients running your program, your program may encounter some slowdown in the user interface.

The following major rule applies to building a user interface: Never keep the user waiting. This means do not freeze the user interface while something is going on behind the scenes. Even if your program is not really all that fast, you can give the perception of speed to the user. That is what this chapter is all about.

In this chapter I provide you with some tips regarding Windows Forms controls. I also spend some time covering threading. For most of you VB 6.0 users, threading is a new concept. It is also something you have been waiting years for.

Speeding Up the Controls

Before I delved into .NET, the most recent language I worked in was VB 6.0. I created some large GUI-based projects in VB 6.0, and along the way I came up against some frustrating speed barriers.

When I first started using .NET, I wanted to experiment with some of the controls common to both languages. I wanted to know if Microsoft removed some of those barriers I came across in VB 6.0. The answer is both yes and no.

I mainly wanted to experiment with the TreeView control. As I have mentioned before in this book, I like this control. I think it shows the most information in the smallest space. I also think it shows hierarchical relationships the best of all the controls. If you think about it, quite a bit of data is hierarchical in nature.

The VB 6.0 TreeView

To start off, I will show you some code for a VB 6.0 project that tests the performance of the VB 6.0 TreeView. I want to give you a baseline to compare .NET to. After you have examined this project and its results, you will build the same project in .NET.

I don't expect you to have VB 6.0, so I just show you the code and the results in this section. Listing 10-1 shows the code for the VB 6.0 Tree Tester project.

Listing 10-1. VB 6.0 Code for the Tree Tester Project

```
Option Explicit

Dim tmr As Single

Private Sub cmdClear_Click()
  Dim Count As Long

  Count = Tree.Nodes.Count
  MousePointer = vbHourglass
  DoEvents
  tmr = Timer
  Tree.Nodes.Clear

  lblClear.Caption = (Timer - tmr) & " seconds to clear " & Count & " Nodes)"
  MousePointer = vbNormal

End Sub

Private Sub cmdFill_Click()
  Dim k      As Integer
  Dim Count As Long
  Dim max    As Long

  MousePointer = vbHourglass
  DoEvents
  max = Val(txtMax.Text)
  Count = Tree.Nodes.Count
  tmr = Timer
  For k = Count To Count + max
    Tree.Nodes.Add , , "Key" & k, "Node " & k
  Next

  lblFill.Caption = (Timer - tmr) & " seconds to fill " & max & " Nodes)"
  MousePointer = vbNormal

End Sub

Private Sub Form_Load()
  txtMax = 1000
End Sub
```

```
Private Sub txtMax_KeyPress(KeyAscii As Integer)

  If KeyAscii < 48 Or KeyAscii > 57 Then
    KeyAscii = 0
  End If

End Sub
```

This code is fairly simple. It creates several thousand nodes in a tree and then clears the tree. The time to do both is displayed in some labels on the form. Figure 10-1 shows this form after adding 1,000 nodes.

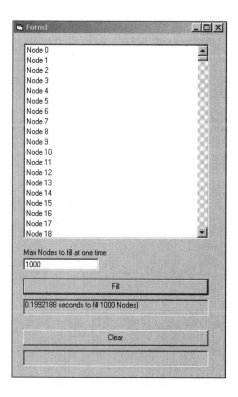

Figure 10-1. Adding 1,000 nodes to a VB 6.0 tree

You can see that it took just two-tenths of a second to fill the tree with 1,000 root nodes. Why root nodes? Suppose a corporation has 1,000 employees. Each employee would be a root node and each employee would have child nodes representing a range of items, such as subordinate personnel.

Anyway, you can see that this did not take long at all. I must tell you that 1,000 nodes is not much, though. I have programs that work with trees containing more than 40,000 nodes.[1] If you extrapolate, you will find that 40,000 nodes take 8 seconds to load. This is unacceptable in an enterprise program.

How long does it take to clear this tree? See Figure 10-2 for the answer.

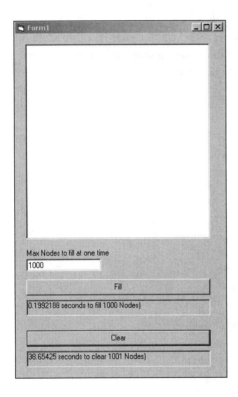

Figure 10-2. Clearing 1,000 nodes in VB 6.0 tree

Yup, that's right. It takes almost 40 seconds to clear 1,000 root nodes from a TreeView control in VB 6.0. For 40,000 nodes, it would take almost a half-hour to clear this screen. For 100,000 nodes, it would take 2.7 days to clear this control. Are you willing to wait that long? I would have rebooted the machine after a few seconds.

Now I know you may not believe me, so I included this VB 6.0 project in this book's code so you can try it yourself. You can download the code for this book from the Downloads section of the Apress Web site (http://www.apress.com).

---

1. Think large colleges.

You may be wondering how I solved the slowdown problem. I didn't. I was only able to ameliorate it by using some Windows API calls to freeze the tree window and manually clear the tree. This helped a lot, but the control is still unworkable for large amounts of data. I finally fixed this problem in VB 6.0 by buying a third-party TreeView control. It's lightning fast in both loading and clearing.

While I was playing around with the TreeView control in VB 6.0 trying to get it to run faster, I noticed something about the TreeView that I put to good use. I will tell you what it is when I cover the TreeView control for .NET.

The .NET TreeView Tester

In this section you will compare the performance of the VB 6.0 TreeView control and the .NET TreeView control.

Start a new VB or C# project. Mine is called "TreeTest." You will need to add a number of controls:

1. Add a TreeView control and call it **Tree**.

2. Add a Label whose text reads **Max nodes to fill in at one time** below the TreeView.

3. Add a TextBox called **txtMax**. Its text should read **1000**.

4. Add a Button called **cmdFill**. Its text should read **Fill**.

5. Add a Label called **lblFill**. Set its BorderStyle to FixedSingle.

6. Add a Button called **cmdClear**. Its text should read **Clear**.

7. Add a Label called **lblClear**. Set its BorderStyle to FixedSingle.

Figure 10-3 shows what the form should look like.

Figure 10-3. Tree tester form

You need to double-click the buttons to get the delegates generated for you. The code is exceedingly simple and follows the code for the VB 6.0 tester. The only thing you need to enter is the code for the button click delegates.

C#

```
private void cmdFill_Click(object sender, System.EventArgs e)
{
  DateTime  tmr;
  TimeSpan  ts;
  int       NumNodes = int.Parse(txtMax.Text);

  lblFill.Text  = "";
  lblClear.Text = "";
  Application.DoEvents();
  this.Cursor = Cursors.WaitCursor;
  tmr = DateTime.Now;
  for(int k=0; k< NumNodes; k++)
    Tree.Nodes.Add("Node " + k.ToString());
  ts = DateTime.Now - tmr;
  lblFill.Text = ts.TotalSeconds.ToString() + " seconds to add " +
                   NumNodes.ToString() + " Nodes ";
```

```
    this.Cursor = Cursors.Arrow;
  }

  private void cmdClear_Click(object sender, System.EventArgs e)
  {
    DateTime tmr = DateTime.Now;
    TimeSpan ts;
    string   NodeCount = Tree.Nodes.Count.ToString();

    this.Cursor = Cursors.WaitCursor;
    Tree.Nodes.Clear();
    this.Cursor = Cursors.Arrow;

    ts = DateTime.Now - tmr;
    lblClear.Text = ts.TotalSeconds.ToString() +
    " seconds to clear " + NodeCount + " Nodes ";
  }
```

VB

```
  Private Sub cmdFill_Click(ByVal sender As System.Object, _
                        ByVal e As System.EventArgs) Handles cmdFill.Click
    Dim tmr As DateTime = DateTime.Now
    Dim ts As TimeSpan
    Dim NumNodes As Int32 = Int32.Parse(txtMax.Text)
    Dim k As Int32

    lblFill.Text = ""
    lblClear.Text = ""
    Application.DoEvents()
    Me.Cursor = Cursors.WaitCursor
    tmr = DateTime.Now
    '    Tree.BeginUpdate()
    For k = 0 To NumNodes
      Tree.Nodes.Add("Node " + k.ToString())
    Next
    '    Tree.EndUpdate()
    ts = DateTime.Now.Subtract(tmr)
    lblFill.Text = ts.TotalSeconds.ToString() + " seconds to add " + _
    NumNodes.ToString() + " Nodes "
    Me.Cursor = Cursors.Arrow

  End Sub
```

```
Private Sub cmdClear_Click(ByVal sender As System.Object, _
                           ByVal e As System.EventArgs) Handles cmdClear.Click
    Dim tmr As DateTime = DateTime.Now
    Dim ts As TimeSpan
    Dim NodeCount As String = Tree.Nodes.Count.ToString()

    Me.Cursor = Cursors.WaitCursor
    '      Tree.BeginUpdate()
    Tree.Nodes.Clear()
    '      Tree.EndUpdate()
    Me.Cursor = Cursors.Arrow

    ts = DateTime.Now.Subtract(tmr)
    lblClear.Text = ts.TotalSeconds.ToString() + " seconds to clear " + _
                    NodeCount + " Nodes "

End Sub
```

Notice that I change the cursor to an hourglass before I do any work. You should do this to indicate that your program has not locked up. Don't forget to change it back.

Run the program and click the Fill and Clear buttons. Figure 10-4 shows the results from my laptop.

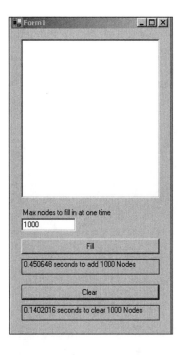

Figure 10-4. Filling and clearing 1,000 nodes

The .NET version is significantly better than the VB 6.0 version in clearing nodes. In fact, the .NET control clears nodes some 99% faster than the VB 6.0 control.

I hope you noticed that filling the .NET control took more than twice as long as filling the VB 6.0 control. Now does this extrapolate linearly if you add, say, 10,000 nodes? Run your program and add an extra 0 to the text box. Click the Fill button. Figure 10-5 shows what happened on my machine.

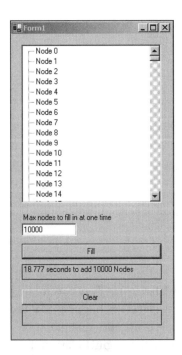

Figure 10-5. Adding 10,000 nodes

You can see that it didn't take 4 seconds to add ten times the number of nodes—it took 18 seconds! Are your customers going to wait around for that? I think not.

I hesitate to click the Clear button, but what the hey. Figure 10-6 shows the results of this action.

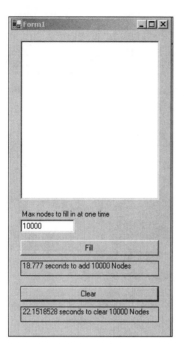

Figure 10-6. Clearing 10,000 nodes

Again, this task is not a linear extrapolation.

Remember that I said I was able to speed up the VB 6.0 TreeView control by using some API commands to freeze the window? Well, it just so happens that the .NET TreeView control has these commands built in as properties that greatly increase the speed of this control. These commands are the BeginUpdate and EndUpdate properties. Here is the code with the new properties entered.

C#

```
private void cmdFill_Click(object sender, System.EventArgs e)
{
    DateTime  tmr;
    TimeSpan  ts;
    int       NumNodes = int.Parse(txtMax.Text);

    lblFill.Text  = "";
    lblClear.Text = "";
    Application.DoEvents();
    this.Cursor = Cursors.WaitCursor;
    tmr = DateTime.Now;
    Tree.BeginUpdate();
```

```
      for(int k=0; k< NumNodes; k++)
        Tree.Nodes.Add("Node " + k.ToString());
      Tree.EndUpdate();
      ts = DateTime.Now - tmr;
      lblFill.Text = ts.TotalSeconds.ToString() + " seconds to add " +
                     NumNodes.ToString() + " Nodes ";
      this.Cursor = Cursors.Arrow;
   }


   private void cmdClear_Click(object sender, System.EventArgs e)
   {
      DateTime tmr = DateTime.Now;
      TimeSpan ts;
      string   NodeCount = Tree.Nodes.Count.ToString();

      this.Cursor = Cursors.WaitCursor;
      Tree.BeginUpdate();
      Tree.Nodes.Clear();
      Tree.EndUpdate();
      this.Cursor = Cursors.Arrow;

      ts = DateTime.Now - tmr;
      lblClear.Text = ts.TotalSeconds.ToString() +
      " seconds to clear " + NodeCount + " Nodes ";
   }
```

VB

```
  Private Sub cmdFill_Click(ByVal sender As System.Object, _
                            ByVal e As System.EventArgs) Handles cmdFill.Click
    Dim tmr As DateTime = DateTime.Now
    Dim ts As TimeSpan
    Dim NumNodes As Int32 = Int32.Parse(txtMax.Text)
    Dim k As Int32

    lblFill.Text = ""
    lblClear.Text = ""
    Application.DoEvents()
    Me.Cursor = Cursors.WaitCursor
    tmr = DateTime.Now
    Tree.BeginUpdate()
    For k = 0 To NumNodes
      Tree.Nodes.Add("Node " + k.ToString())
    Next
```

```
Tree.EndUpdate()
ts = DateTime.Now.Subtract(tmr)
lblFill.Text = ts.TotalSeconds.ToString() + " seconds to add " + _
NumNodes.ToString() + " Nodes "
Me.Cursor = Cursors.Arrow

End Sub

Private Sub cmdClear_Click(ByVal sender As System.Object, _
                        ByVal e As System.EventArgs) Handles cmdClear.Click
    Dim tmr As DateTime = DateTime.Now
    Dim ts As TimeSpan
    Dim NodeCount As String = Tree.Nodes.Count.ToString()

    Me.Cursor = Cursors.WaitCursor
    Tree.BeginUpdate()
    Tree.Nodes.Clear()
    Tree.EndUpdate()
    Me.Cursor = Cursors.Arrow

    ts = DateTime.Now.Subtract(tmr)
    lblClear.Text = ts.TotalSeconds.ToString() + " seconds to clear " + _
                NodeCount + " Nodes "

End Sub
```

Once you have entered these four lines of code, try running the program at 10,000 nodes again. Table 10-1 shows the results of my adding and clearing root nodes in the TreeView control after adding this code.

Table 10-1. Adding and Clearing Nodes in a TreeView Control

Number of Nodes	Fill Time (Seconds)	Clear Time (Seconds)
1,000	.08	.07
10,000	6.39	5.86
20,000	31.89	30.13
30,000	73.38	70.04
40,000	129.53	125.52
50,000	201.18	196.03

I was going to do 100,000 nodes, but I do not have the time. This book needs to get out.

Clearing the TreeView in a Flash

Unfortunately, there is not much you can do to physically increase the speed of adding nodes to a tree. There is, however, one thing you can do to allow the tree to clear in an instant.

I have been stressing all along that I am adding root nodes to this tree. What would happen if you have a single root node that acts as a header for all the pretend users you are adding to this tree? Let's see.

You will comment out the code loop that generates the root nodes for the tree. You will then add some code to make a single root node and add the 10,000 or so nodes as child nodes to this one root node. Here is the code. The changed code is in bold.

C#

```
private void cmdFill_Click(object sender, System.EventArgs e)
{
  DateTime  tmr;
  TimeSpan  ts;
  int       NumNodes = int.Parse(txtMax.Text);

  lblFill.Text  = "";
  lblClear.Text = "";
  Application.DoEvents();
  this.Cursor = Cursors.WaitCursor;
  tmr = DateTime.Now;
  Tree.BeginUpdate();
  //Add only root nodes
  //      for(int k=0; k< NumNodes; k++)
  //        Tree.Nodes.Add("Node " + k.ToString());

  //Add a single root node and many child nodes.
  TreeNode HeaderNode = Tree.Nodes.Add("User Header Node");
  for(int k=0; k< NumNodes; k++)
    HeaderNode.Nodes.Add("Node " + k.ToString());
  HeaderNode.Expand();
```

```
    Tree.EndUpdate();
    ts = DateTime.Now - tmr;
    lblFill.Text = ts.TotalSeconds.ToString() + " seconds to add " +
      NumNodes.ToString() + " Nodes ";
    this.Cursor = Cursors.Arrow;
  }
```

VB

```
  Private Sub cmdFill_Click(ByVal sender As System.Object, _
                         ByVal e As System.EventArgs) Handles cmdFill.Click
    Dim tmr As DateTime = DateTime.Now
    Dim ts As TimeSpan
    Dim NumNodes As Int32 = Int32.Parse(txtMax.Text)
    Dim k As Int32

    lblFill.Text = ""
    lblClear.Text = ""
    Application.DoEvents()
    Me.Cursor = Cursors.WaitCursor
    tmr = DateTime.Now
    Tree.BeginUpdate()
    'Add only root nodes
    'For k = 0 To NumNodes
    '  Tree.Nodes.Add("Node " + k.ToString())
    'Next
    Dim HeaderNode As TreeNode = Tree.Nodes.Add("User Header Node")
    For k = 0 To NumNodes
      HeaderNode.Nodes.Add("Node " + k.ToString())
    Next
    HeaderNode.Expand()

    Tree.EndUpdate()
    ts = DateTime.Now.Subtract(tmr)
    lblFill.Text = ts.TotalSeconds.ToString() + " seconds to add " + _
    NumNodes.ToString() + " Nodes "
    Me.Cursor = Cursors.Arrow

  End Sub
```

This is a simple change that has major ramifications for the speed of your
program. Compile and run the code now. Figure 10-7 shows what happens when
I add and clear 25,000 nodes in my TreeView.

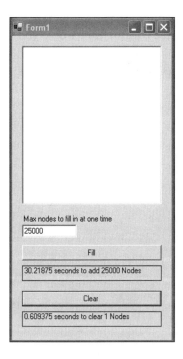

Figure 10-7. Clearing 25,000 nodes with one root node

Your eyes do not deceive you. This small code change cleared 25,000 nodes in the tree in under a second. Now we are getting somewhere.

The 30 seconds to fill 25,000 records, though, is really distracting and makes the TreeView control unusable for major databases.

Increasing Apparent TreeView Fill Speed

Because I can't really increase the fill speed of the TreeView, how about fooling the user into thinking that the tree is already filled? If reality doesn't work, smoke and mirrors just might.

The first thing you can do is show the user that something is actually going on. Take the 10,000-node example. It takes almost 6 seconds to fill the TreeView with nodes. During this time you show an hourglass cursor. This is a start, but you can do more.

If the user is able to see some of the data, he or she could start viewing this data while the rest of the screen is filling up. You did this at the start of this example, before you added the BeginUpdate and EndUpdate commands. Each node was shown as it was created. The problem with this is that it greatly slowed down the system as the tree had to repaint while each node was being added.

The VisibleCount property in the TreeView control allows you to tell how many nodes it takes to fill the *visible* portion of the tree control. How would you use this property to your advantage?

I have made one last change to this example's tree fill code. The new code is in bold.

C#

```csharp
private void cmdFill_Click(object sender, System.EventArgs e)
{
    DateTime   tmr;
    TimeSpan   ts;
    int        NumNodes = int.Parse(txtMax.Text);

    lblFill.Text  = "";
    lblClear.Text = "";
    Application.DoEvents();
    this.Cursor = Cursors.WaitCursor;
    tmr = DateTime.Now;
//    Tree.BeginUpdate();
    //-------------------------------------------------------------------
    //Add only root nodes
    //      for(int k=0; k< NumNodes; k++)
    //        Tree.Nodes.Add("Node " + k.ToString());
    //-------------------------------------------------------------------


    //-------------------------------------------------------------------
    //Add a single root node and many child nodes.
//    TreeNode HeaderNode = Tree.Nodes.Add("User Header Node");
//    for(int k=0; k< NumNodes; k++)
//      HeaderNode.Nodes.Add("Node " + k.ToString());
//    HeaderNode.Expand();
    //-------------------------------------------------------------------

    //Add nodes and show them before shutting down the tree pane update
    bool AllowUpdate = true;
    TreeNode HeaderNode = Tree.Nodes.Add("User Header Node");
    for(int k=0; k< NumNodes; k++)
    {
```

```
      if(AllowUpdate && HeaderNode.Nodes.Count > Tree.VisibleCount)
      {
        HeaderNode.Expand();
        Application.DoEvents();
        Tree.BeginUpdate();
        AllowUpdate = false;
      }
      HeaderNode.Nodes.Add("Node " + k.ToString());
    }
    Tree.EndUpdate();
    ts = DateTime.Now - tmr;
    lblFill.Text = ts.TotalSeconds.ToString() + " seconds to add " +
      NumNodes.ToString() + " Nodes ";
    this.Cursor = Cursors.Arrow;
  }
```

VB

```
Private Sub cmdFill_Click(ByVal sender As System.Object, _
                    ByVal e As System.EventArgs) Handles cmdFill.Click
  Dim tmr As DateTime = DateTime.Now
  Dim ts As TimeSpan
  Dim NumNodes As Int32 = Int32.Parse(txtMax.Text)
  Dim k As Int32

  lblFill.Text = ""
  lblClear.Text = ""
  Application.DoEvents()
  Me.Cursor = Cursors.WaitCursor
  tmr = DateTime.Now
  '    Tree.BeginUpdate()
  '----------------------------------------------------------------------
  'Add only root nodes
  'For k = 0 To NumNodes
  ' Tree.Nodes.Add("Node " + k.ToString())
  'Next
  'For k = 0 To NumNodes
  ' Tree.Nodes.Add("Node " + k.ToString())
  'Next
```

```
'------------------------------------------------------------------------
'Add a single root node and many child nodes
'Dim HeaderNode As TreeNode = Tree.Nodes.Add("User Header Node")
'For k = 0 To NumNodes
'   HeaderNode.Nodes.Add("Node " + k.ToString())
'Next
'HeaderNode.Expand()
'------------------------------------------------------------------------


'Add nodes and show them before shutting down the tree pane update
Dim AllowUpdate As Boolean = True
Dim HeaderNode As TreeNode = Tree.Nodes.Add("User Header Node")
For k = 0 To NumNodes
  If AllowUpdate AndAlso HeaderNode.Nodes.Count > Tree.VisibleCount Then
    HeaderNode.Expand()
    Application.DoEvents()
    Tree.BeginUpdate()
    AllowUpdate = False
  End If
  HeaderNode.Nodes.Add("Node " + k.ToString())
Next


Tree.EndUpdate()
ts = DateTime.Now.Subtract(tmr)
lblFill.Text = ts.TotalSeconds.ToString() + " seconds to add " + _
NumNodes.ToString() + " Nodes "
Me.Cursor = Cursors.Arrow


End Sub
```

Previous code has been commented out and new code has been added.

What I am doing here is allowing the tree to refresh itself for every node added until I see that the visible portion of the tree has all the nodes it can display. At this point, I shut down the tree repainting and add nodes as before.

Compile and run this program now. Figure 10-8 shows my results.

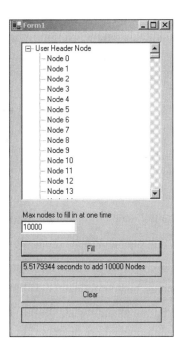

Figure 10-8. Showing some nodes

When you run this example, you will see the nodes appear immediately, and the total fill time does not suffer. After all, you are showing the fill for only about 15 or so nodes.

Although you have not decreased the time to fill the tree, you have decreased the time the user waits before seeing something. Believe me, this makes a huge difference to the apparent speed of the program.

Filling a True Tree Hierarchy

So far I have talked about a tree in terms of root nodes only. I showed you the problems with having thousands of root nodes added that were somewhat ameliorated by using a master root node and many subnodes. This is a trick to get around a deficiency in the TreeView control that comes with .NET. In reality we are still talking about many single root nodes.

This is not real life, however. Real programs use many root nodes and many subnodes within subnodes. Data can be a complicated thing when you are trying to display interrelated information.

Here is a contrived but common scenario. A superstore has an inventory database that contains every item in the store. This store sells clothing and toys. This is what your data could look like:

A Toys Header Node
    Electronic Toys
        Many Brands
    Video Games
        Many Brands
    Battery-Powered Toys
        Many Brands
    Plush Toys
        Many Brands
    Action Figures
        Many Brands
  Board Games
        Many Brands
    Models
        Many Brands
A Clothing Header Node
    Footwear
        Many Brands
    Jackets
        Many Brands
    Tops
        Many Brands
    Pants
        Many Brands
    Underwear
        Many Brands
    Gloves/Hats
        Many Brands
    Sweaters
        Many Brands

Each of these first-level subnodes could have hundreds of thousands of subnodes. It would not be unusual to end up with many thousands of total nodes in your tree.

When you have a situation like this, you need to sit and think a bit before you go about writing code to fill your tree. No matter what you do, there may be an unacceptable delay in getting and displaying the information. There is one approach, though, that can greatly reduce the time need to display information in a TreeView control: Don't get or show the information until needed.

If someone goes into your inventory program and wants to know only about board games, there is no need to waste time getting information about all the other inventory items. You can let the user know these items exist and then get the other items only when the user calls for them.

Making a Virtual Tree

The trick to making the user think there is data when there is none yet to be shown is to use virtual nodes. This is not something included with the TreeView; you need to program it yourself.

This next example shows the store inventory problem. It has a TreeView that includes over 25,000 nodes. I will show you the "fill it all at once" method and the "smoke and mirrors" method of presenting the data.

Start a new C# or VB Windows program. Mine is called "QuickTreeFill." Next, add these items:

1. Add a TreeView control called **Tree**.

2. Add a Button called **cmdFill**. Its text should read **Fill Normal**.

3. Add a Button called **cmdFillFast**. Its text should read **Fill Fast**.

4. Add a Button called **cmdClear**. Its text should read **Clear**.

Figure 10-9 shows what the form looks like.

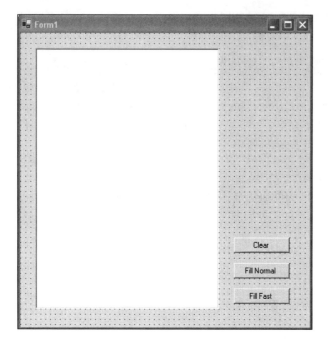

Figure 10-9. The new tree fill form

Before you add any code to the form, you will need to add a new class called "Inventory." This class holds some classes and structures that represent the data you will be working with. Listings 10-2a and 10-2b show the complete code for this class.

Listing 10-2a. C# Code for the Inventory Class

```csharp
using System;
using System.Collections;

namespace QuickTreeFill_c
{
  /// <summary>
  /// Summary description for Inventory.
  /// </summary>
  ///
```

```
public struct Brand
{
  public Brand(string name)
  {
    BrandName = name;
  }
  public string BrandName;
}


public class Toys
{
  public Items BatteryPowered  = new Items(1000, "BatteryPowered");
  public Items Electronic      = new Items(500,  "Electronic");
  public Items BoardGames      = new Items(1000,  "BoardGames");
  public Items Video           = new Items(2000, "Video");
  public Items Models          = new Items(1000,  "Models");
  public Items Plush           = new Items(3000, "Plush");
  public Items ActionFigures   = new Items(250,  "ActionFigures");

  public struct Items
  {
    public ArrayList Brands;
    public Items(int amount, string kind)
    {
      Brands = new ArrayList();
      for(int k=0; k<amount; k++)
        Brands.Add(new Brand(kind + " Brand " + k.ToString()));
    }
  }
}


public class Clothing
{
  public Items Footwear   = new Items(500,   "Footwear");
  public Items Jackets    = new Items(600,    "Jackets");
  public Items Tops       = new Items(4800,  "Tops");
  public Items Pants      = new Items(1000, "Pants");
  public Items Underwear  = new Items(100,    "Underwear");
  public Items GlovesHats = new Items(5000,   "GlovesHats");
  public Items Sweaters   = new Items(2000,   "Sweaters");
```

```
      public struct Items
      {
        public ArrayList Brands;
        public Items(int amount, string kind)
        {
          Brands = new ArrayList();
          for(int k=0; k<amount; k++)
            Brands.Add(new Brand(kind + " Brand " + k.ToString()));
        }
      }
    }
  }
}
```

Listing 10-2b. VB Code for the Inventory Class

```
Option Strict On

Imports System.Collections


Public Structure Brand
  Public Sub New(ByVal name As String)
    BrandName = name
  End Sub
  Public BrandName As String
End Structure

Public Class Toys
  Public BatteryPowered As Items = New Items(1000, "BatteryPowered")
  Public Electronic As Items = New Items(500, "Electronic")
  Public BoardGames As Items = New Items(1000, "BoardGames")
  Public Video As Items = New Items(2000, "Video")
  Public Models As Items = New Items(1000, "Models")
  Public Plush As Items = New Items(3000, "Plush")
  Public ActionFigures As Items = New Items(250, "ActionFigures")

  Public Structure Items
    Public Brands As ArrayList
    Public Sub New(ByVal amount As Int32, ByVal kind As String)
      Brands = New ArrayList()
      Dim k As Int32
      For k = 0 To amount
        Brands.Add(New Brand(kind + " Brand " + k.ToString()))
      Next
```

```
    End Sub
  End Structure
End Class


Public Class Clothing
  Public Footwear As Items = New Items(500, "Footwear")
  Public Jackets As Items = New Items(600, "Jackets")
  Public Tops As Items = New Items(4800, "Tops")
  Public Pants As Items = New Items(1000, "Pants")
  Public Underwear As Items = New Items(100, "Underwear")
  Public GlovesHats As Items = New Items(5000, "GlovesHats")
  Public Sweaters As Items = New Items(2000, "Sweaters")

  Public Structure Items
    Public Brands As ArrayList
    Public Sub New(ByVal amount As Int32, ByVal kind As String)
      Brands = New ArrayList()
      Dim k As Int32
      For k = 0 To amount
        Brands.Add(New Brand(kind + " Brand " + k.ToString()))
      Next
    End Sub
  End Structure
End Class
```

I use a class to hold an ArrayList containing thousands of items. Although this is not reality, it does serve the purpose.

Now it is time to add some code to the main form. Make sure that you have a reference to the System.Collections namespace at the top of your code. First off, you will need some class local variables.

C#

```
    #region class local variables

    private Toys toys;
    private Clothing Clothes;
    private enum NodeLevel
    {
      AllToys,
      AllClothes,
      ToyBrand,
      ClothingBrand,
      BatteryToys,
```

```
            ElectronicToys,
            BoardGameToys,
            VideoToys,
            PlushToys,
            ModelToys,
            FigureToys,
            ClothingFootwear,
            ClothingTops,
            ClothingJackets,
            ClothingSweaters,
            ClothingPants,
            ClothingGloves
        }

    #cndregion
```

VB

```
#Region "class local variables"

  Private toys As Toys
  Private Clothes As Clothing
  Private Enum NodeLevel
    AllToys
    AllClothes
    ToyBrand
    ClothingBrand
    BatteryToys
    ElectronicToys
    BoardGameToys
    VideoToys
    PlushToys
    ModelToys
    FigureToys
    ClothingFootwear
    ClothingTops
    ClothingJackets
    ClothingSweaters
    ClothingPants
    ClothingGloves
  End Enum

#End Region
```

There is a property in the TreeNode class that lets you get the full path of where it is in the tree. I prefer not to use this, though. I want to know exactly what kind of node I am on at any moment. I use the NodeLevel enum for that. You will see just how I use it soon.

Next, you need to add some helper functions.

C#

```
#region Helper functions

private void ClearTree(object sender, EventArgs e)
{
  Tree.Nodes.Clear();
  cmdFill.Enabled     = true;
  cmdFillFast.Enabled = true;
}

private void UpdateTree(ArrayList Brands, TreeNode ClickedNode)
{
  bool AllowUpdate = true;

  this.Cursor = Cursors.WaitCursor;
  foreach(Brand x in Brands)
  {
    ClickedNode.Nodes.Add(x.BrandName);
    if(AllowUpdate && ClickedNode.Nodes.Count > Tree.VisibleCount)
    {
      AllowUpdate = false;
      ExpandThisNode(ClickedNode);
      Tree.BeginUpdate();
    }
  }
  Tree.EndUpdate();
  this.Cursor = Cursors.Arrow;
}

private void ExpandThisNode(TreeNode node)
{
  Tree.BeforeExpand -= new TreeViewCancelEventHandler(FillSubNodes);
  node.Expand();
  Tree.BeforeExpand += new TreeViewCancelEventHandler(FillSubNodes);
  Application.DoEvents();
}

#endregion
```

VB

```vb
#Region "Helper functions"

  Private Sub ClearTree(ByVal sender As Object, ByVal e As EventArgs)
    Tree.Nodes.Clear()
    cmdFill.Enabled = True
    cmdFillFast.Enabled = True
  End Sub

  Private Sub UpdateTree(ByVal Brands As ArrayList, ByVal ClickedNode As TreeNode)
    Dim AllowUpdate As Boolean = True

    Me.Cursor = Cursors.WaitCursor
    Dim x As Brand
    For Each x In Brands
      ClickedNode.Nodes.Add(x.BrandName)
      If AllowUpdate AndAlso ClickedNode.Nodes.Count > Tree.VisibleCount Then
        AllowUpdate = False
        ExpandThisNode(ClickedNode)
        Tree.BeginUpdate()
      End If
    Next
    Tree.EndUpdate()
    Me.Cursor = Cursors.Arrow
  End Sub

  Private Sub ExpandThisNode(ByVal node As TreeNode)
    RemoveHandler Tree.BeforeExpand, New
    TreeViewCancelEventHandler(AddressOf FillSubNodes)
    node.Expand()
    AddHandler Tree.BeforeExpand, New
    TreeViewCancelEventHandler(AddressOf FillSubNodes)
    Application.DoEvents()
  End Sub

#End Region
```

The ClearTree function is a delegate that handles the Clear button click event. The UpdateTree function adds subnodes to a node that is passed in by argument. You can see that I take each brand and add it to the ClickedNode. While I do this, I keep track of the number of nodes, and when I get past the VisibleCount, I turn off the TreeView repainting. This allows me to show something to the user while he or she waits for data to appear.

Note the ExpandThisNode routine. Why do I need this? I have a delegate assigned to the Expand event (you will see this code in a bit). When I call the node.Expand() function, it will fire this event and I will be back in my delegate. I end up in a circular loop. Before I call the node.Expand method, I need to turn off the Expand delegate and then turn it back on afterward.

The form contains two buttons. The first is the Clear button. You just coded the delegate for that button. The second is the Fill Normal button. Clicking this button gets all the data and fills in all the nodes. The code for these buttons follows.

C#

```csharp
#region fill the tree slow

private void FillWholeTree(object sender, EventArgs e)
{
  Tree.BeforeExpand   -= new TreeViewCancelEventHandler(FillSubNodes);

  cmdFill.Enabled = false;
  cmdFillFast.Enabled = false;
  this.Cursor = Cursors.WaitCursor;
  Tree.Nodes.Clear();
  Tree.BeginUpdate();

  //------ Do Toys -------
  TreeNode ThisNode;
  TreeNode AllToys = Tree.Nodes.Add("All Toys");
  AllToys.Tag = NodeLevel.AllToys;
  TreeNode node = AllToys.Nodes.Add("Action Figures");
  node.Tag = NodeLevel.FigureToys;
  foreach(Brand x in toys.ActionFigures.Brands)
    ThisNode = node.Nodes.Add(x.BrandName);

  node = AllToys.Nodes.Add("Battery Powered Toys");
  foreach(Brand x in toys.BatteryPowered.Brands)
    node.Nodes.Add(x.BrandName);

  node = AllToys.Nodes.Add("Board Games");
  foreach(Brand x in toys.BoardGames.Brands)
    node.Nodes.Add(x.BrandName);

  node = AllToys.Nodes.Add("Electronic Games");
  foreach(Brand x in toys.Electronic.Brands)
    node.Nodes.Add(x.BrandName);
```

```
            node = AllToys.Nodes.Add("Models");
            foreach(Brand x in toys.Models.Brands)
              node.Nodes.Add(x.BrandName);

            node = AllToys.Nodes.Add("Plush Toys");
            foreach(Brand x in toys.Plush.Brands)
              node.Nodes.Add(x.BrandName);

            node = AllToys.Nodes.Add("Video Games");
            foreach(Brand x in toys.Video.Brands)
              node.Nodes.Add(x.BrandName);

            // --------- Do Clothing ---------
            TreeNode AllClothes = Tree.Nodes.Add("All Clothes");
            node = AllClothes.Nodes.Add("Footwear");
            foreach(Brand x in Clothes.Footwear.Brands)
              node.Nodes.Add(x.BrandName);

            node = AllClothes.Nodes.Add("Gloves and Hats");
            foreach(Brand x in Clothes.GlovesHats.Brands)
              node.Nodes.Add(x.BrandName);

            node = AllClothes.Nodes.Add("Jackets");
            foreach(Brand x in Clothes.Jackets.Brands)
              node.Nodes.Add(x.BrandName);

            node = AllClothes.Nodes.Add("Pants");
            foreach(Brand x in Clothes.Pants.Brands)
              node.Nodes.Add(x.BrandName);

            node = AllClothes.Nodes.Add("Sweaters");
            foreach(Brand x in Clothes.Sweaters.Brands)
              node.Nodes.Add(x.BrandName);

            node = AllClothes.Nodes.Add("Tops");
            foreach(Brand x in Clothes.Tops.Brands)
              node.Nodes.Add(x.BrandName);

            Tree.EndUpdate();
            this.Cursor = Cursors.Arrow;
        }
        #endregion
```

VB

```vb
#Region "fill the tree slow"

  Private Sub FillWholeTree(ByVal sender As Object, ByVal e As EventArgs)
    Dim x As Brand

    RemoveHandler Tree.BeforeExpand, New
    TreeViewCancelEventHandler(AddressOf FillSubNodes)

    Me.Cursor = Cursors.WaitCursor
    Tree.Nodes.Clear()
    Tree.BeginUpdate()

    '------ Do Toys -------
    Dim ThisNode As TreeNode
    Dim AllToys As TreeNode = Tree.Nodes.Add("All Toys")
    AllToys.Tag = NodeLevel.AllToys
    Dim node As TreeNode = AllToys.Nodes.Add("Action Figures")
    node.Tag = NodeLevel.FigureToys
    For Each x In toys.ActionFigures.Brands
      ThisNode = node.Nodes.Add(x.BrandName)
    Next

    node = AllToys.Nodes.Add("Battery Powered Toys")
    For Each x In toys.BatteryPowered.Brands
      node.Nodes.Add(x.BrandName)
    Next

    node = AllToys.Nodes.Add("Board Games")
    For Each x In toys.BoardGames.Brands
      node.Nodes.Add(x.BrandName)
    Next

    node = AllToys.Nodes.Add("Electronic Games")
    For Each x In toys.Electronic.Brands
      node.Nodes.Add(x.BrandName)
    Next

    node = AllToys.Nodes.Add("Models")
    For Each x In toys.Models.Brands
      node.Nodes.Add(x.BrandName)
    Next
```

```
node = AllToys.Nodes.Add("Plush Toys")
For Each x In toys.Plush.Brands
  node.Nodes.Add(x.BrandName)
Next


node = AllToys.Nodes.Add("Video Games")
For Each x In toys.Video.Brands
  node.Nodes.Add(x.BrandName)
Next


' --------- Do Clothing ---------
Dim AllClothes As TreeNode = Tree.Nodes.Add("All Clothes")
node = AllClothes.Nodes.Add("Footwear")
For Each x In Clothes.Footwear.Brands
  node.Nodes.Add(x.BrandName)
Next


node = AllClothes.Nodes.Add("Gloves and Hats")
For Each x In Clothes.GlovesHats.Brands
  node.Nodes.Add(x.BrandName)
Next


node = AllClothes.Nodes.Add("Jackets")
For Each x In Clothes.Jackets.Brands
  node.Nodes.Add(x.BrandName)
Next


node = AllClothes.Nodes.Add("Pants")
For Each x In Clothes.Pants.Brands
  node.Nodes.Add(x.BrandName)
Next


node = AllClothes.Nodes.Add("Sweaters")
For Each x In Clothes.Sweaters.Brands
  node.Nodes.Add(x.BrandName)
Next


node = AllClothes.Nodes.Add("Tops")
For Each x In Clothes.Tops.Brands
  node.Nodes.Add(x.BrandName)
Next
```

```
    Tree.EndUpdate()
    Me.Cursor = Cursors.Arrow

  End Sub

#End Region
```

This code should not be new to you. It simply runs through each collection of inventory items and adds nodes to the tree. I shut down the update of the tree at the start and give the user a wait cursor to look at while I am adding nodes. The next region of code is the interesting one.

Enter the following code, which handles the smoke and mirrors action to make the user believe the data is all there and ready to view.

C#

```
#region Smoke and Mirrors

private void FillTreeFast(object sender, EventArgs e)
{
  cmdFill.Enabled     = false;
  cmdFillFast.Enabled = false;
  Tree.BeforeExpand    += new TreeViewCancelEventHandler(FillSubNodes);

  Tree.Nodes.Clear();
  Tree.BeginUpdate();
  TreeNode node = Tree.Nodes.Add("All Toys");
  node.Tag = NodeLevel.AllToys;
  node.Nodes.Add("VirtualNode");
  node = Tree.Nodes.Add("All Clothes");
  node.Tag = NodeLevel.AllClothes;
  node.Nodes.Add("VirtualNode");
  Tree.EndUpdate();

}

private void FillSubNodes(object sender, TreeViewCancelEventArgs e)
{
  TreeNode  ClickedNode = e.Node;
  TreeNode  node;
  NodeLevel l = (NodeLevel)ClickedNode.Tag;
```

```
      ClickedNode.Nodes.Clear();
      switch(l)
      {
        case NodeLevel.AllToys:
          node = ClickedNode.Nodes.Add("Battery Powered Toys");
          node.Tag = NodeLevel.BatteryToys;
          node.Nodes.Add("VirtualNode");
          node = ClickedNode.Nodes.Add("Board Games");
          node.Tag = NodeLevel.BoardGameToys;
          node.Nodes.Add("VirtualNode");
          node = ClickedNode.Nodes.Add("Electronic Games");
          node.Tag = NodeLevel.ElectronicToys;
          node.Nodes.Add("VirtualNode");
          node = ClickedNode.Nodes.Add("Models");
          node.Tag = NodeLevel.ModelToys;
          node.Nodes.Add("VirtualNode");
          node = ClickedNode.Nodes.Add("Plush Toys");
          node.Tag = NodeLevel.PlushToys;
          node.Nodes.Add("VirtualNode");
          node = ClickedNode.Nodes.Add("Video Games");
          node.Tag = NodeLevel.VideoToys;
          node.Nodes.Add("VirtualNode");
          break;
        case NodeLevel.AllClothes:
          node = ClickedNode.Nodes.Add("Gloves and Hats");
          node.Tag = NodeLevel.ClothingGloves;
          node.Nodes.Add("VirtualNode");
          node = ClickedNode.Nodes.Add("Jackets");
          node.Tag = NodeLevel.ClothingJackets;
          node.Nodes.Add("VirtualNode");
          node = ClickedNode.Nodes.Add("Pants");
          node.Tag = NodeLevel.ClothingPants;
          node.Nodes.Add("VirtualNode");
          node = ClickedNode.Nodes.Add("Sweaters");
          node.Tag = NodeLevel.ClothingSweaters;
          node.Nodes.Add("VirtualNode");
          node = ClickedNode.Nodes.Add("Tops");
          node.Tag = NodeLevel.ClothingTops;
          node.Nodes.Add("VirtualNode");
          break;
        case NodeLevel.ModelToys:
          UpdateTree(toys.Models.Brands, ClickedNode);
          break;
```

```
      case NodeLevel.BatteryToys:
        UpdateTree(toys.BatteryPowered.Brands, ClickedNode);
        break;
      case NodeLevel.BoardGameToys:
        UpdateTree(toys.BoardGames.Brands, ClickedNode);
        break;
      case NodeLevel.ElectronicToys:
        UpdateTree(toys.Electronic.Brands, ClickedNode);
        break;
      case NodeLevel.FigureToys:
        UpdateTree(toys.ActionFigures.Brands, ClickedNode);
        break;
      case NodeLevel.PlushToys:
        UpdateTree(toys.Plush.Brands, ClickedNode);
        break;
      case NodeLevel.VideoToys:
        UpdateTree(toys.Video.Brands, ClickedNode);
        break;
      case NodeLevel.ClothingFootwear:
        UpdateTree(Clothes.Footwear.Brands, ClickedNode);
        break;
      case NodeLevel.ClothingGloves:
        UpdateTree(Clothes.GlovesHats.Brands, ClickedNode);
        break;
      case NodeLevel.ClothingJackets:
        UpdateTree(Clothes.Jackets.Brands, ClickedNode);
        break;
      case NodeLevel.ClothingPants:
        UpdateTree(Clothes.Pants.Brands, ClickedNode);
        break;
      case NodeLevel.ClothingSweaters:
        UpdateTree(Clothes.Sweaters.Brands, ClickedNode);
        break;
      case NodeLevel.ClothingTops:
        UpdateTree(Clothes.Tops.Brands, ClickedNode);
        break;
    }
  }
#endregion
```

VB

```
#Region "Smoke and Mirrors"

  Private Sub FillTreeFast(ByVal sender As Object, ByVal e As EventArgs)
    cmdFill.Enabled = False
    cmdFillFast.Enabled = False
    AddHandler Tree.BeforeExpand, _
             New TreeViewCancelEventHandler(AddressOf FillSubNodes)
    Tree.Nodes.Clear()
    Tree.BeginUpdate()
    Dim node As TreeNode = Tree.Nodes.Add("All Toys")
    node.Tag = NodeLevel.AllToys
    node.Nodes.Add("VirtualNode")
    node = Tree.Nodes.Add("All Clothes")
    node.Tag = NodeLevel.AllClothes
    node.Nodes.Add("VirtualNode")
    Tree.EndUpdate()

  End Sub

  Private Sub FillSubNodes(ByVal sender As Object, _
                           ByVal e As TreeViewCancelEventArgs)
    Dim ClickedNode As TreeNode = e.Node
    Dim node As TreeNode
    Dim l As NodeLevel = CType(ClickedNode.Tag, NodeLevel)

    ClickedNode.Nodes.Clear()
    Select Case l
      Case NodeLevel.AllToys
        node = ClickedNode.Nodes.Add("Battery Powered Toys")
        node.Tag = NodeLevel.BatteryToys
        node.Nodes.Add("VirtualNode")
        node = ClickedNode.Nodes.Add("Board Games")
        node.Tag = NodeLevel.BoardGameToys
        node.Nodes.Add("VirtualNode")
        node = ClickedNode.Nodes.Add("Electronic Games")
        node.Tag = NodeLevel.ElectronicToys
        node.Nodes.Add("VirtualNode")
        node = ClickedNode.Nodes.Add("Models")
        node.Tag = NodeLevel.ModelToys
        node.Nodes.Add("VirtualNode")
        node = ClickedNode.Nodes.Add("Plush Toys")
        node.Tag = NodeLevel.PlushToys
```

```
    node.Nodes.Add("VirtualNode")
    node = ClickedNode.Nodes.Add("Video Games")
    node.Tag = NodeLevel.VideoToys
    node.Nodes.Add("VirtualNode")
  Case NodeLevel.AllClothes
    node = ClickedNode.Nodes.Add("Gloves and Hats")
    node.Tag = NodeLevel.ClothingGloves
    node.Nodes.Add("VirtualNode")
    node = ClickedNode.Nodes.Add("Jackets")
    node.Tag = NodeLevel.ClothingJackets
    node.Nodes.Add("VirtualNode")
    node = ClickedNode.Nodes.Add("Pants")
    node.Tag = NodeLevel.ClothingPants
    node.Nodes.Add("VirtualNode")
    node = ClickedNode.Nodes.Add("Sweaters")
    node.Tag = NodeLevel.ClothingSweaters
    node.Nodes.Add("VirtualNode")
    node = ClickedNode.Nodes.Add("Tops")
    node.Tag = NodeLevel.ClothingTops
    node.Nodes.Add("VirtualNode")
  Case NodeLevel.ModelToys
    UpdateTree(toys.Models.Brands, ClickedNode)
  Case NodeLevel.BatteryToys
    UpdateTree(toys.BatteryPowered.Brands, ClickedNode)
  Case NodeLevel.BoardGameToys
    UpdateTree(toys.BoardGames.Brands, ClickedNode)
  Case NodeLevel.ElectronicToys
    UpdateTree(toys.Electronic.Brands, ClickedNode)
  Case NodeLevel.FigureToys
    UpdateTree(toys.ActionFigures.Brands, ClickedNode)
  Case NodeLevel.PlushToys
    UpdateTree(toys.Plush.Brands, ClickedNode)
  Case NodeLevel.VideoToys
    UpdateTree(toys.Video.Brands, ClickedNode)
  Case NodeLevel.ClothingFootwear
    UpdateTree(Clothes.Footwear.Brands, ClickedNode)
  Case NodeLevel.ClothingGloves
    UpdateTree(Clothes.GlovesHats.Brands, ClickedNode)
  Case NodeLevel.ClothingJackets
    UpdateTree(Clothes.Jackets.Brands, ClickedNode)
  Case NodeLevel.ClothingPants
    UpdateTree(Clothes.Pants.Brands, ClickedNode)
  Case NodeLevel.ClothingSweaters
    UpdateTree(Clothes.Sweaters.Brands, ClickedNode)
```

```
      Case NodeLevel.ClothingTops
         UpdateTree(Clothes.Tops.Brands, ClickedNode)
      End Select
   End Sub
#End Region
```

Here is an explanation of what happens when the user clicks the Fill Fast button. First, I fill only the top two nodes of the tree, the Toys and Clothing header nodes. While I do this, I add a virtual node under each of these two header nodes. This forces the TreeView control to add a plus sign (+) next to the two header nodes. As all computer users from Windows 95 on know, clicking the plus sign shows more data below the node. I have effectively given the user the impression of speed (showing only two nodes is fast) and access to further data.

The next method, FillSubNodes, is where all the real action happens. This is the delegate for the TreeView control's BeforeExpand event (you will wire this up shortly). The first thing I do here is prevent updating of the tree. I then clear out all the subnodes from this node. This does two things. On start-up, it gets rid of the virtual node. If this was expanded and collapsed previously, it gets rid of all the sub-nodes under this node. I then get the data again from the database (my collections in this case). The data is always "live."

Depending on which node was clicked, I add a single subnode with a virtual node or I add all the nodes contained in the appropriate collection. Notice that I use the NodeLevel enumeration to determine which node was clicked. Whenever I create a node, I save the node's type in the node's Tag property.

Now it is time to wire up the delegates in the form's constructor.

C#

```
public Form1()
{
  InitializeComponent();

  toys             = new Toys();
  Clothes          = new Clothing();
  cmdClear.Click   += new EventHandler(ClearTree);
  cmdFill.Click    += new EventHandler(FillWholeTree);
  cmdFillFast.Click += new EventHandler(FillTreeFast);
}
```

VB

```
Public Sub New()
  MyBase.New()

  InitializeComponent()

  toys = New Toys()
  Clothes = New Clothing()
  AddHandler cmdClear.Click, New EventHandler(AddressOf ClearTree)
  AddHandler cmdFill.Click, New EventHandler(AddressOf FillWholeTree)
  AddHandler cmdFillFast.Click, New EventHandler(AddressOf FillTreeFast)

End Sub
```

I instantiate the data classes first. This takes almost no time at all. I then wire up the delegates for the button click events.

Running the Fast TreeView

Compile and run the program. Click the Fill Normal button and note the wait necessary for the tree to fill.

Now click the Clear button and then the Fill Fast button. You will see the top two nodes appear instantly. Each time you go deeper into the tree by expanding nodes, you are getting data as you need it. The data is obtained and put in the tree very fast. Any slowdown is negligible because you are getting at most 5,000 nodes instead of 25,000 nodes, as is the case with the fill slow method.

Using virtual nodes is a good way to break up the data presentation task into small chunks. Chances are that a user will want to see only a small subset of data anyway, and you may never need to display most of the data you have. The point is, the user does not know this and is generally happy with the speed.

TIP I have used this technique many times in my code. I recently did a project, however, that had the potential of over 100,000 nodes, and this method started to get slow. I bought a third-party TreeView control that is the best thing since sliced bread. It is very fast in adding nodes and instantaneous in deleting them.

So, is this it for speeding up the interface? No. I used a TreeView control as an example. You can use some of the same techniques with other data presentation controls. The most powerful tool you can use to speed up the GUI is threading.

Multithreading

Be careful what you wish for, you just might get it. VB programmers have been grousing about the lack of free threading for years through many versions of VB. Well, now you have it.

The threading model in .NET allows you to get into a world of trouble with bugs that are hard to track down and performance penalties that you may not be aware of. It takes quite a bit of careful programming to use threading effectively.

There are a number of ways to use multithreading to your advantage. In this section I show you just one of them.

 NOTE   This section is not by any means a complete treatise on multi-threading. I expect you to know something about multithreading before you start. The most lucid explanation on multithreading I have found is in Dan Appleman's book *Moving to VB .NET: Strategies, Concepts, and Code, Second Edition* (Apress, 2003).

This method uses multithreading to enhance a Windows Forms control so it frees up more time for the user to do something else if needed. Multithreading with Windows Forms controls is not the easiest of tasks. You need to do quite a bit of marshaling of data back and forth between threads to get things to work correctly.

Enhancing the TreeView Control with Multithreading

Before I start on multithreading, I want to mention three methods that all controls have. These methods are specific to multithreading:

- BeginInvoke

- Invoke

- EndInvoke

The BeginInvoke method allows a thread to call a delegate asynchronously on a control that was created on another thread. In other words, if you had a TreeView control created on thread 1, thread 2 could call a delegate on thread 1 that is attached to the TreeView control on thread 1. Because BeginInvoke is asynchronous, thread 2 is not blocked while the delegate on thread 1 is running.

The Invoke method does the same thing as the BeginInvoke method, except the calling thread is blocked until the delegate returns. This is a synchronous call.

The EndInvoke method uses an IAsyncResult object that results from the BeginInvoke method call. Because the BeginInvoke method call is asynchronous, you may not get this result back right away. If you make a call to EndInvoke and the delegate you called from the BeginInvoke method is not ready, the EndInvoke method will block until the delegate finishes. You need be somewhat careful with the EndInvoke method because your thread could be blocked for quite some time. The IAsyncResult object contains state information about the thread operation. It allows calling threads to be signaled when an operation is completed.

With that information under your belt, it is time to start the multithreading project. Here is what it does:

- It creates a user control that is based on the TreeView control.

- It allows the user to pass in an array of strings that will be turned into nodes in this control.

- The user control will have two threads running to manage the addition of nodes to the TreeView control.

- The threads will work in such a way as to allow the user to continue with the GUI while nodes are being added to the tree.

- A test program will be added to the solution that proves it is working.

Start with a new C# or VB project. Mine is called "QuickTree." This project is a Windows Control Library project—it is *not* a Windows Forms project. Perform the following steps:

1. Change the name of the user control class to **QuickTree.cs**.

2. Change the name of the class itself to **QuickTree**.

3. Add a TreeView control to the user control form.

4. Call the TreeView control **tree**. Change the Dock property to Fill.

Figure 10-10 shows the Solution Explorer window.

Figure 10-10. The QuickTree solution space

Don't worry that two projects are indicated. The second one is the tester you will code later.

When you change the name of the class in the code pane, it should read as follows.

C#

```
public class QuickTree : System.Windows.Forms.UserControl
```

VB

```
Public Class QuickTree
    Inherits System.Windows.Forms.UserControl
```

You first need to add some statements to this class that reference the proper namespaces.

C#

```
using System;
using System.Collections;
using System.ComponentModel;
using System.Drawing;
using System.Data;
using System.Windows.Forms;
using System.Threading;
```

VB

```vbnet
Option Strict On

Imports System
Imports System.Collections
Imports System.ComponentModel
Imports System.Drawing
Imports System.Data
Imports System.Windows.Forms
Imports System.Threading
```

Here is something for you C# developers to do. The TreeView control that you added to this user control is private to this user control. You need to make it public. You do this so that any client that uses this new UserControl will still be able to manipulate the tree normally, as well as through the extra methods you will provide.

Now add some variables to this class.

C#

```csharp
#region vars

private delegate void NodeAddDelegate(TreeNode[] tnodes);
private           NodeAddDelegate NodeDelegate;

private           EventHandler    onFillComplete;
public event      EventHandler    FillComplete;

private           ArrayList       tnodes;
private           TreeNode        BaseNode;
private           Thread          FillThread;
private           bool            filling;
private           bool            WaitForFill;

#endregion
```

VB

```
#Region "vars"

    Private Delegate Sub NodeAddDelegate(ByVal tnodes() As TreeNode)
    Private NodeDelegate As NodeAddDelegate

    Private on_FillComplete As EventHandler
    Public Event FillComplete As EventHandler

    Private tnodes As ArrayList
    Private BaseNode As TreeNode
    Private FillThread As Thread
    Private filling As Boolean
    Private WaitForFill As Boolean

#End Region
```

I declare a delegate that takes as an argument an array of TreeNodes. This delegate adds the tree nodes to the TreeView control. For speed, it adds them using the TreeView.AddRange method.

I also declare an event handler called onFillComplete. (The VB name is slightly different because of VB's annoying habit of being case insensitive.) I then declare an event called FillComplete. I use this event to notify the client that the tree has been filled using the multithreaded method. This is not necessary, but it is nice to let the client know when you are done.

Finally, I declare a thread and some control variables.

Let's start off the real code with some extra properties and methods that an external client can use in addition to the normal TreeView methods.

C#

```
    #region properties/methods

    public bool OK2Fill
    {
      get{return !filling;}
    }

    public ArrayList Strings
    {
      set{tnodes = (ArrayList)value.Clone();}
    }
```

```csharp
public void StartFill(TreeNode node)
{
  BaseNode = node;

  //Do not interrupt a fill
  if(filling)
    return;

  //Make sure that someone actually put this control on the form
  //This could have been called without initializing the tree.
  if(tree.IsHandleCreated)
  {
    filling = true;
    FillThread = new Thread(new ThreadStart(tnodeThread));
    FillThread.Start();
  }
  else
    WaitForFill = true;
}

public void StopFill()
{
  //Obviously if I am not filling then no need to join threads
  if (!filling)
  {
    return;
  }

  if (FillThread.IsAlive)
  {
    FillThread.Abort();
    FillThread.Join();
  }

  FillThread = null;
  filling = false;
}

#endregion
```

VB

```vb
#Region "properties/methods"

  Public ReadOnly Property OK2Fill() As Boolean
    Get
      Return Not filling
    End Get
  End Property

  Public WriteOnly Property Strings() As ArrayList
    Set(ByVal Value As ArrayList)
      tnodes = CType(Value.Clone(), ArrayList)
    End Set
  End Property

  Public Sub StartFill(ByVal node As TreeNode)
    BaseNode = node

    'Do not interrupt a fill
    If filling Then Return

    'Make sure that someone actually put this control on the form
    'This could have been called without initializing the tree.
    If (tree.IsHandleCreated) Then
      filling = True
      FillThread = New Thread(New ThreadStart(AddressOf tnodeThread))
      FillThread.Start()
    Else
      WaitForFill = True
    End If
  End Sub

  Public Sub StopFill()
    'Obviously if I am not filling then no need to join threads
    If Not filling Then Return

    If FillThread.IsAlive Then
      FillThread.Abort()
      FillThread.Join()
    End If
```

```
        FillThread = Nothing
        filling = False
    End Sub
```

```
#End Region
```

There is some interesting code in here. I have a property that lets the client know if it is OK to monkey around with the TreeView control directly. Because I send nodes over to this control for a multithreaded add, I can easily do this several times in a row before the first add is finished. Also, because the TreeView control is public, the client could easily do something like clear the control before it is finished. Although I am not going to stop direct manipulation of the tree, I will let the client know if it is OK.

The second property in this region is one that copies an array of strings into memory. I use this list of strings to convert to TreeNodes, which are added to the tree asynchronously.

The next method is the StartFill method, which checks to see if the tree is actually created yet by checking for its handle. If everything is OK, I spin up a new thread and let it rip. If the handle is not yet created, I set the control variable that allows the thread to start after the handle has been created. You will see this bit of code shortly.

The StopFill method checks to see if the thread is alive and running. If so, it stops the thread and blocks the calling thread until this one is finished. You can add a timeout to the join method in case the calling thread is hung. This allows you to kill the thread based on a timeout.

The next region of code to add contains the event handlers and delegates.

C#

```csharp
#region events/Delegates

//If the user kills the program before the tree has filled then you will
//need to stop the fill first.  This is why the Base.OnHandleDestroyed
//is called after the stop fill.
protected override void OnHandleDestroyed(EventArgs e)
{
  if (!tree.RecreatingHandle)
    StopFill();
  base.OnHandleDestroyed(e);
}
```

```csharp
//This overridden method sort of delays things a little if the calling program
//was too aggressive and started a fill before the tree was ready to accept it
protected override void OnHandleCreated(EventArgs e)
{
  base.OnHandleCreated(e);
  if(WaitForFill)
  {
    WaitForFill = false;
    StartFill(BaseNode);
  }
}

//This method is called via a BeginInvoke by the background
//thread
private void AddNodes(TreeNode[] tnodes)
{
  tree.BeginUpdate();

  if(BaseNode != null)
  {
    BaseNode.Nodes.AddRange(tnodes);
    BaseNode.Expand();
  }
  else
    tree.Nodes.AddRange(tnodes);

  tree.EndUpdate();
}

//This method is called by the background thread when it is
//finished handing over all the nodes it needs to add.
private void OnFillComplete(object sender, EventArgs e)
{
  //Only call this delegate if someone has hooked up to it
  //otherwise it is null and you will get a major crash.  C# ONLY!!
  if(FillComplete != null)
    FillComplete(sender, e);
}

#endregion
```

VB

```vb
#Region "events/Delegates"

  'If the user kills the program before the tree has filled then you will
  'need to stop the fill first.  This is why the Base.OnHandleDestroyed
  'is called after the stop fill.
  Protected Overrides Sub OnHandleDestroyed(ByVal e As EventArgs)
    If Not tree.RecreatingHandle Then
      StopFill()
    End If
    MyBase.OnHandleDestroyed(e)
  End Sub


  'This overridden method sort of delays things a little if the calling program
  'was too aggressive and started a fill before the tree was ready to accept it
  Protected Overrides Sub OnHandleCreated(ByVal e As EventArgs)
    MyBase.OnHandleCreated(e)
    If WaitForFill Then
      WaitForFill = False
      StartFill(BaseNode)
    End If
  End Sub


  'This method is called via a BeginInvoke by the background
  'thread
  Private Sub AddNodes(ByVal tnodes() As TreeNode)
    tree.BeginUpdate()

    If Not BaseNode Is Nothing Then
      BaseNode.Nodes.AddRange(tnodes)
      BaseNode.Expand()
    Else
      tree.Nodes.AddRange(tnodes)
    End If

    tree.EndUpdate()
  End Sub
```

```
'This method is called by the background thread when it is
'finished handing over all the nodes it needs to add.
Private Sub OnFillComplete(ByVal sender As Object, ByVal e As EventArgs)
  'Only call this delegate if someone has hooked up to it
  'otherwise it is null and you will get a major crash.
  RaiseEvent FillComplete(sender, e)
End Sub
```

```
#End Region
```

Here is where some tricky work goes on.

The first two methods override the OnHandleCreated and OnHandleDestroyed methods. I override the OnHandleCreated method to allow a deferred fill. Remember, the StartFill method checked to see if the tree handle was created, and if not it set the WaitForFill variable. Well, this event handler catches the creation of the handle, and if this variable was set it starts the fill process. This is a way to make sure that the client does not have to wait around for the control to be created before starting the fill.

The OnHandleDestroyed event is used to kill the worker thread before the tree is destroyed. If you did not use this event and you killed the window containing this control while the thread was running, your program would crash. Notice that I defer the call to the base method until after stopping the thread. Remember that the Thread.Join method blocks the calling thread (this one) before returning. By deferring the call to the base method until after the join has returned, I make sure that the window is not destroyed before it is time.

The AddNodes method is nothing you haven't seen before. It takes an array of nodes and adds it to a base node. If the base node does not exist, it adds all the nodes as root nodes. We all know by now that adding a few thousand root nodes makes for an oppressively long time to clear the tree. This is why the StartFill method takes a node as an argument. It allows this control to add nodes to an already existing node. This makes the clear method very fast.

The OnFillComplete delegate is used to raise an event while in the current thread. This delegate is called by the worker thread when it is done. As I stated earlier, this method is not necessary, but it does make things consistent because the event is raised by the calling thread rather than the worker thread.

Notice that this C# version of this method checks to see if a client has connected to this event before calling it. If you did not check for null here, your program would crash if no client wired up a delegate to this event.

TIP Nowhere in the .NET help examples is this null checking mentioned or done. All the help examples work because all the clients they provide connect to the events that were fired. Remember this tip—it will get you when you try to raise an event and no one is listening.

The VB code does not check for null here, as the internal VB code takes care of this if no one is listening.[2]

The next region of code to add contains the worker thread.

C#

```csharp
#region Worker Thread

private void tnodeThread()
{
  ArrayList NodeList = new ArrayList();
  Array NodeArray;

  try
  {
    tnodes.TrimToSize();
    for(int k=0; k<tnodes.Count; k++)
    {
      NodeList.Add(new TreeNode((string)tnodes[k]));
      if(decimal.Remainder((decimal)NodeList.Count, 20) == 0)
      {
        NodeArray = Array.CreateInstance(typeof(TreeNode), NodeList.Count);
        NodeList.CopyTo(NodeArray);
        IAsyncResult r = this.BeginInvoke(NodeDelegate,
                                          new object[] {NodeArray});
        NodeList.Clear();
        //Sleep for 300 milliseconds to pretend we are doing something
        //really complicated
        Thread.Sleep(300);
      }
    }
```

---

2. This is one of the annoying differences between VB and C#. Sometimes C# is better and sometimes VB comes out ahead. VB wins this one in my mind.

```csharp
    if(NodeList.Count > 0)
    {
      NodeArray = Array.CreateInstance(typeof(TreeNode), NodeList.Count);
      NodeList.CopyTo(NodeArray);
      IAsyncResult r = this.BeginInvoke(NodeDelegate,
                                        new object[] {NodeArray});
    }
  }
  finally
  {
    filling = false;
    //I could raise the event from here but it would be coming from
    //a different thread.  If a client did not know this was a multithreaded
    //control then it could expect the event to be raised from the same
    //thread that the client is in.
    BeginInvoke(onFillComplete, new object[] {this, EventArgs.Empty});
  }

}

#endregion
```

VB

```vbnet
#Region "Worker Thread"

  Private Sub tnodeThread()
    Dim NodeList As ArrayList = New ArrayList()
    Dim NodeArray As Array
    Dim k As Int32

    Try
      tnodes.TrimToSize()
      For k = 0 To tnodes.Count - 1
        NodeList.Add(New TreeNode(CType(tnodes(k), String)))
        If Decimal.Remainder(CType(NodeList.Count, Decimal), 20) = 0 Then
          NodeArray = Array.CreateInstance(GetType(TreeNode), NodeList.Count)
          NodeList.CopyTo(NodeArray)
          Dim r As IAsyncResult = Me.BeginInvoke(NodeDelegate, _
                                          New Object() {NodeArray})
          NodeList.Clear()
          'Sleep for 300 milliseconds to pretend we are doing something
          'really(complicated)
          Thread.Sleep(300)
        End If
```

```
      Next
      If NodeList.Count > 0 Then
        NodeArray = Array.CreateInstance(GetType(TreeNode), NodeList.Count)
        NodeList.CopyTo(NodeArray)
        Dim r As IAsyncResult = Me.BeginInvoke(NodeDelegate, _
                                        New Object() {NodeArray})
      End If
    Finally
      filling = False

      'I could raise the event from here but it would be coming from
      'a different thread.  If a client did not know this was a multithreaded
      'control then it could expect the event to be raised from the same
      'thread that the client is in.
      BeginInvoke(on_FillComplete, New Object() {Me, EventArgs.Empty})
    End Try

  End Sub

#End Region
```

This thread consists of only a single method. First, I wrap the code in a Try-Finally block. This ensures that the "filling" variable gets reset and the FillComplete delegate gets called before I leave this method. No matter what, the Finally clause guarantees this.

I make an array of nodes and add the strings as nodes one by one into the array. Once the array has 20 items, I create a simple array of nodes that gets passed to the NodeDelegate via the BeginInvoke call.

You can see that I clear the node list array after I make the call. Using the Decimal.Remainder function allows me to comment out the NodeList.Clear() call and keep adding to the list if I want while sending 20 nodes at a time to the delegate. I chose 20 as an arbitrary number.

Most worker threads are in existence because they do a lot of work and you don't want the user to have to wait around for it to be done. This thread does not do so much work. To simulate a lot of work, I added a call to a sleep method. This call slows down the filling of the tree and lets you better see the effect of the background thread.

Because this thread sleeps for a while, I know as a programmer that the worker thread that adds nodes to the tree is done at the end of this sleep time. I am assuming that it is safe to continue on with my work. In reality, I should be calling EndInvoke with IAsyncResult from the BeginInvoke method. The EndInvoke call in this case should come after the sleep call. This ensures that the worker thread is actually done before I continue on. If the worker thread is not done, the EndInvoke method blocks the main thread from continuing until the worker thread finishes. Just to be safe, you should always call EndInvoke after calling BeginInvoke. You avoid so many problems that way.

Notice that I do not add nodes to the TreeView control on this thread. Instead, I marshal the nodes over to the calling thread via the BeginInvoke method. This allows the thread that made the tree to add the nodes. You really need to do this with a Windows Forms control. You do not have complete control over the control, and you may create a conflict or a deadlock if the control is trying to do something (such as clear 10,000 root nodes) while another thread is busy adding nodes. It is always preferable to do any manipulation of a Windows Forms control on the thread it was created on.

TIP Always manipulate a control on the thread it was created on to avoid any potential conflict.

The last thing to do is wire up all the delegates in the constructor. Here is the code.

C#

```csharp
public QuickTree()
{
    InitializeComponent();

    tnodes         = new ArrayList();
    NodeDelegate   = new NodeAddDelegate(AddNodes);
    onFillComplete = new EventHandler(OnFillComplete);
    filling        = false;
}
```

VB

```vb
Public Sub New()
    MyBase.New()

    'This call is required by the Windows Form Designer.
    InitializeComponent()
```

```
    tnodes = New ArrayList()
    NodeDelegate = New NodeAddDelegate(AddressOf AddNodes)
    on_FillComplete = New EventHandler(AddressOf OnFillComplete)
    filling = False

End Sub
```

There you have it. You now have a TreeView control that has been enhanced with a method that adds nodes via a worker thread. It allows you to add many thousands of nodes while still working in the GUI. How about trying it out?

Testing the Enhanced TreeView Control

The first thing you need to do is compile the new control. This will end up as a DLL in the BIN directory for you VB fans and in the BIN\Debug directory for you C# folks.

Add a new project to your QuickTree solution. Call this project **QuickTreeTester**. Right-click this new project and make it the start-up project for the solution. Your solution space should look similar to Figure 10-11.

Figure 10-11. A complete solution space

Size the default form to be about 570×470. Also make this form start in the center of the screen.

Before you add any controls to your form, you need to add your new user control to the Toolbox. You did this several times in Chapter 8, so I go over it lightly here.

Right-click the Toolbox while in the General tab. There is nothing in this tab, so it is easy to see when you have added a control.

Choose the Customize Toolbox choice and click the .NET Framework Components tab. In this tab, click the Browse button and choose the QuickTree DLL that is in either your BIN subdirectory or the BIN\Debug subdirectory for your project.

Once you have double-clicked the control, it will appear in your Toolbox browser, as shown in Figure 10-12.

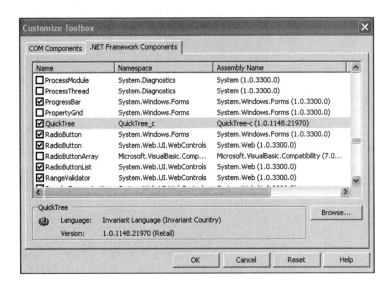

Figure 10-12. The Customize Toolbox screen

Click OK and your new control will appear in your Toolbox.
Now it's time to add some controls to this test form:

1. Add a GroupBox to the left side of the form. Size it to fit almost the entire left side of the form. Change its text to **Node Tester**.

2. Inside the GroupBox, add a Label whose text reads **Multithreaded Nodes**. Center the text in the Label.

3. Inside the GroupBox, add your new QuickTree user control. It should look like a TreeView control when you drop it on the form. Name this control **qt**.

4. Inside the GroupBox, add a Label whose text reads **Nodes** under the QuickTree control.

5. Inside the GroupBox, add a TextBox called **txtNodes** next to the Label. Enter **1000** in the Text property.

6. Inside the GroupBox, add a Button called **cmdFill**. Its text should read **Fill**.

7. Next to the GroupBox, add a RichTextBox.

8. Below the RichTextBox, add a Panel called **P1**.

Figure 10-13 shows what the form looks like.

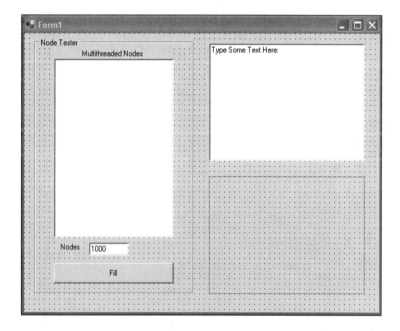

Figure 10-13. The new multithreaded tree tester

You are able to fill in the TextBox with some number of nodes that you want in the tree. The RichTextBox gives you something to do while the nodes are being added. You will use the Panel as a place to scribble some picture with your mouse while nodes are being added. If the multithreading works as planned, you should be able to type or scribble while seeing nodes being added to the tree in chunks of 20.

NOTE   I will show you code that sets up the Panel for drawing with the mouse. Some of the code to accomplish this with the mouse will be fairly advanced. Some of this code is similar to an example I wrote for my book *GDI+ Programming with C# and VB .NET* (Apress, 2002). If you are interested in all the capabilities of GDI+ in .NET, I encourage you to pick up this book.[3]

Now for the tester code. You need the following namespace references.

C#

```csharp
using System;
using System.Drawing;
using System.Collections;
using System.ComponentModel;
using System.Windows.Forms;
using System.Data;
using System.Threading;
using System.Drawing.Drawing2D;
```

VB

```vb
Option Strict On

Imports System
Imports System.Collections
Imports System.ComponentModel
Imports System.Drawing
Imports System.Data
Imports System.Windows.Forms
Imports System.Threading
Imports System.Drawing.Drawing2D
```

Next, of course, is the local variable section.

---

3.   Another shameless plug. But really, GDI+ is very interesting.

C#

```
#region Class local storage

private Point        mStartPoint;
private Point        mLastPoint;
private GraphicsPath mPath;
private Rectangle    mInvalidRect;

#endregion
```

VB

```
#Region "vars"

  Private Delegate Sub NodeAddDelegate(ByVal tnodes() As TreeNode)
  Private NodeDelegate As NodeAddDelegate

  Private on_FillComplete As EventHandler
  Public Event FillComplete As EventHandler

  Private tnodes As ArrayList
  Private BaseNode As TreeNode
  Private FillThread As Thread
  Private filling As Boolean
  Private WaitForFill As Boolean

#End Region
```

You need to add the following methods. Add them below the Form_Load event handler.

C#

```
private void AllowNumbers(object sender, KeyPressEventArgs e)
{
  if(!Char.IsNumber(e.KeyChar) && e.KeyChar != (char)8 )
    e.Handled = true;
}
```

```csharp
    private void TreeComplete(object sender, EventArgs e)
    {
      MessageBox.Show("Tree is done filling");
    }


    private void FillTree(object sender, EventArgs e)
    {
      ArrayList s = new ArrayList();
      int x = int.Parse(txtNodes.Text);

      for(int k=0; k<x; k++)
        s.Add(k.ToString());
      s.TrimToSize();

      //Do not try to bypass the fill without knowing that it is ok
      if(qt.OK2Fill)
      {
        qt.tree.Nodes.Clear();
        TreeNode n = qt.tree.Nodes.Add("BaseNode");
        qt.Strings = s;
        qt.StartFill(n);
      }
    }
```

VB

```vb
  Private Sub AllowNumbers(ByVal sender As Object, ByVal e As KeyPressEventArgs)
    If Not Char.IsNumber(e.KeyChar) AndAlso e.KeyChar <> 8.ToString() Then
      e.Handled = True
    End If
  End Sub

  Private Sub TreeComplete(ByVal sender As Object, ByVal e As EventArgs)
    MessageBox.Show("Tree is done filling")
  End Sub

  Private Sub FillTree(ByVal sender As Object, ByVal e As EventArgs)
    Dim s As ArrayList = New ArrayList()
    Dim x As Int32 = Int32.Parse(txtNodes.Text)
    Dim k As Int32
```

```
   For k = 0 To x - 1
     s.Add(k.ToString())
   Next
   s.TrimToSize()

   'Do not try to bypass the fill without knowing that it is ok
   If qt.OK2Fill Then
     qt.tree.Nodes.Clear()
     Dim n As TreeNode = qt.tree.Nodes.Add("BaseNode")
     qt.Strings = s
     qt.StartFill(n)
   End If
 End Sub
```

The AllowNumbers method allows only digits to be entered in the TextBox. You have seen me do this several different ways, including using regular expressions. As my mother says, "There is more than one way to skin a cat."

The TreeComplete delegate connects to the event that is fired by the user control QuickTree. All I do here is pop up a message box to tell you it is done.

The FillTree method starts the ball rolling. It creates an array of strings that are passed into the QuickTree control. Note that I add a base node directly to the tree before I start filling it in. Also notice that I ask the control if it is OK to start playing around with it.

This next region of code handles the painting of the Panel control.

C#

```
#region Panel Painting code

private void PanelPaint(object sender, PaintEventArgs e)
{
  Graphics G = e.Graphics;

  G.SmoothingMode = SmoothingMode.HighSpeed;

  if (mPath.PointCount > 0)
    G.DrawPath(Pens.Black, mPath);

  G.DrawRectangle(Pens.Red, 0, 0, P1.Width-1, P1.Height-1);
}
```

```
private void M_Down(object sender, MouseEventArgs m)
{
  if (m.Button == MouseButtons.Left)
  {
    mStartPoint  = new Point(m.X, m.Y);
    mLastPoint   = mStartPoint;
    mPath  = new GraphicsPath();
    P1.Invalidate();
  }
}


private void M_Up(object sender, MouseEventArgs m)
{
  mPath.CloseFigure();
  P1.Cursor       = Cursors.Default;

  P1.Invalidate();
}


private void M_Move(object sender, MouseEventArgs m)
{
  if(m.Button == MouseButtons.Left)
  {
    mPath.AddLine(mLastPoint.X, mLastPoint.Y, m.X, m.Y);
    mLastPoint.X = m.X;
    mLastPoint.Y = m.Y;

    mInvalidRect = Rectangle.Truncate(mPath.GetBounds());
    mInvalidRect.Inflate( new Size(2, 2) );
    P1.Invalidate(mInvalidRect);
  }
}


#endregion
```

VB

```
#Region "Panel Painting code"

  Private Sub PanelPaint(ByVal sender As Object, ByVal e As PaintEventArgs)
    Dim G As Graphics = e.Graphics

    G.SmoothingMode = SmoothingMode.HighSpeed
```

```
      If mPath.PointCount > 0 Then
        G.DrawPath(Pens.Black, mPath)
      End If

      G.DrawRectangle(Pens.Red, 0, 0, P1.Width - 1, P1.Height - 1)
    End Sub

    Private Sub M_Down(ByVal sender As Object, ByVal m As MouseEventArgs)
      If m.Button = MouseButtons.Left Then
        mStartPoint = New Point(m.X, m.Y)
        mLastPoint = mStartPoint
        mPath = New GraphicsPath()
        P1.Invalidate()
      End If
    End Sub

    Private Sub M_Up(ByVal sender As Object, ByVal m As MouseEventArgs)
      mPath.CloseFigure()
      P1.Cursor = Cursors.Default

      P1.Invalidate()
    End Sub

    Private Sub M_Move(ByVal sender As Object, ByVal m As MouseEventArgs)
      If m.Button = MouseButtons.Left Then
        mPath.AddLine(mLastPoint.X, mLastPoint.Y, m.X, m.Y)
        mLastPoint.X = m.X
        mLastPoint.Y = m.Y

        mInvalidRect = Rectangle.Truncate(mPath.GetBounds())
        mInvalidRect.Inflate(New Size(2, 2))
        P1.Invalidate(mInvalidRect)
      End If
    End Sub

#End Region
```

Here is what is happening. The M_Down, M_Move, and M_Up methods connect to the appropriate events for the Panel. The M_Down delegate creates a Point structure and initializes a GraphicsPath. The M_Move delegate takes note of the mouse position and creates a line that extends from the last known mouse position to the current position. This line then gets added to the GraphicsPath and the Panel is invalidated. Before I invalidate the Panel, I calculate the size of a rectangle that will hold the GraphicsPath. This rectangle gets sent to the Invalidate command. I do this to minimize the amount of drawing that is done on the screen. It creates less flicker and faster drawing. The M_Up method closes the GraphicsPath by connecting the end point directly to the start point. It then does one last Invalidate of the Panel.

When the Panel is invalidated, the OnPaint event for the control gets fired. I handle this event with the PanelPaint delegate. This delegate makes sure that the painting is done as fast as possible. It then draws the path using a black pen. (The Pens class is static. Remember static classes?) I check first to see if there are any points in the GraphicsPath. You could have clicked the mouse here and created nothing. I also draw a red border around the Panel to give it some definition.

The last thing to do is wire up all the delegates and perform some initialization. This is done in the constructor.

C#

```csharp
public Form1()
{
  InitializeComponent();

  //Set Drawing Panel Properties
  P1.BackColor       = Color.Bisque;
  P1.Paint          += new PaintEventHandler(this.PanelPaint);
  P1.MouseDown      += new MouseEventHandler(this.M_Down);
  P1.MouseUp        += new MouseEventHandler(this.M_Up);
  P1.MouseMove      += new MouseEventHandler(this.M_Move);
  mPath = new GraphicsPath();

  //Set double buffer to ameliorate screen flicker
  this.SetStyle(ControlStyles.AllPaintingInWmPaint,true);
  this.SetStyle(ControlStyles.DoubleBuffer,true);

  cmdFill.Click     += new EventHandler(FillTree);
  txtNodes.KeyPress += new KeyPressEventHandler(AllowNumbers);
  qt.FillComplete   += new EventHandler(TreeComplete);
}
```

VB

```vb
Public Sub New()
  MyBase.New()

  'This call is required by the Windows Form Designer.
  InitializeComponent()
```

```
'Set Drawing Panel Properties
P1.BackColor = Color.Bisque
AddHandler P1.Paint, New PaintEventHandler(AddressOf PanelPaint)
AddHandler P1.MouseDown, New MouseEventHandler(AddressOf M_Down)
AddHandler P1.MouseUp, New MouseEventHandler(AddressOf M_Up)
AddHandler P1.MouseMove, New MouseEventHandler(AddressOf M_Move)
mPath = New GraphicsPath()

'Set double buffer to ameliorate screen flicker
Me.SetStyle(ControlStyles.AllPaintingInWmPaint, True)
Me.SetStyle(ControlStyles.DoubleBuffer, True)

AddHandler cmdFill.Click, New EventHandler(AddressOf FillTree)
AddHandler txtNodes.KeyPress, New KeyPressEventHandler(AddressOf _
                                        AllowNumbers)
AddHandler qt.FillComplete, New EventHandler(AddressOf TreeComplete)

End Sub
```

I color the Panel and set the ControlStyles of the form itself. The ControlStyles I chose here allow for double buffering of the drawing. Double buffering virtually eliminates flicker when repainting the screen. I also wire up the new event from the QuickTree control as well as the button in the tester screen.

Testing the Multithreaded Control

It is now time to put this multithreaded TreeView to a test. Compile the program and fix any errors. If you cannot fix any errors, then download the code for this program from the Downloads section of the Apress Web site (http://www.apress.com). I guarantee it works.

Figure 10-14 shows the form as I am drawing on the Panel and typing in the RichTextBox.

If this was an e-book, I could perhaps animate this picture and show you that the nodes are being added and I am drawing at the same time. Maybe next year.

At some point while you are typing or scribbling, you will see a message pop up stating that all the nodes are there. Figure 10-15 shows this.

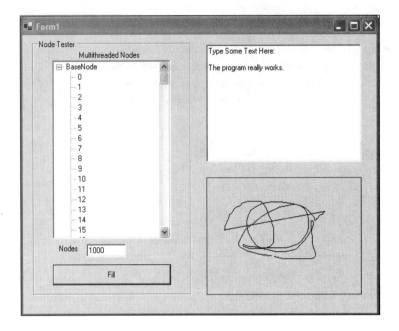

Figure 10-14. Doing three things at once

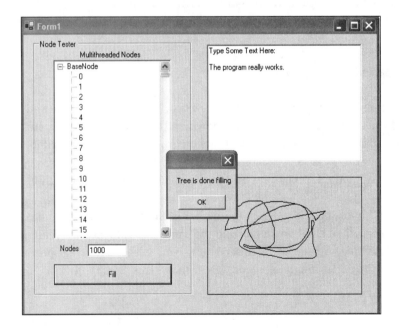

Figure 10-15. The multithreaded node addition finishes.

You can prove to yourself that you are constantly adding nodes by dragging down the scroll thumb while nodes are being added. You will see the thumb scrolling back up until it is done.

I chose the drawing panel as a test because it requires quite a bit of system time in the form of events. None of the mouse events seems to hinder or slow down the filling of the tree.

Multithreading is cool. Have I forgotten anything, though? What about race conditions between threads?

A Conflict of Interest

I use two variables in the worker thread, the Filling variable and the tnodes array, that can cause problems between it and the main thread. It is entirely possible for these variables to be changed by one thread while the other is trying to use them.

The Filling variable is not so bad. The main thread does not fiddle with this while the worker thread is running. Also, the main thread looks at this variable only after starting the worker thread. If the worker thread changes it from true to false while the main thread is trying to use it, no big deal. The main thread will just bail out of the StartFill method if false or continue if true. Because the worker thread changes this variable only when it is finished, no damage will be done.

The tnodes array is another matter. This is one reason I added the OK2Fill property to this control. I am giving the client a chance to be nice and not change anything with the tree while stuff is going on. This is not enough, however.

Suppose the client altered the strings that are the basis for the tnodes array while the worker thread was filling the tree. Some undesirable effects would happen. Your first line of defense here is to alter the Strings property of the control.

C#

```csharp
public ArrayList Strings
{
  set
  {
    if(!filling)
      tnodes = (ArrayList)value.Clone();
  }
}
```

VB

```
Public WriteOnly Property Strings() As ArrayList
  Set(ByVal Value As ArrayList)
    If Not filling Then
      tnodes = CType(Value.Clone(), ArrayList)
    End If
  End Set
End Property
```

Here I made sure that I was not in the process of filling the tree before changing the tnodes list. Again, the Filling variable could be changing while this property is using it, but by then the worker thread is done with the tnodes array and it does not matter.

Now you are probably thinking about using a SyncLock to block a thread from using any shared variables while another thread is using them. This works, of course, but it is not necessary here. There is no need to block threads here if you think about what is going on in the program.

If this program was more complicated (such as appending nodes while the first set was being added), then the code would differ a lot and perhaps then you would need some more variables that would require locking between threads.

This program is simple and, as such, it does not need a lot of thread synchronizing. You can soon get yourself into hot water, however. Try your thread legs out with small programs like this, and then graduate to full-bore multiprocessor/multithreaded programs only after you have learned what to do and what not to do.

Summary

This chapter dealt with speeding up the user experience when it concerns the GUI. Many controls (mainly the TreeView) have some limitations when it comes to large amounts of data. You learned how to overcome several limitations of the TreeView control by using virtual nodes and getting data only when you are ready to show it. You also learned how to use multithreading with Windows Forms controls in the last part of the chapter.

Multithreading allows you to fill in a control with copious amounts of data while still allowing the user to navigate the screen. You saw that it was possible to fill in a TreeView control and draw on the screen using a mouse at the same time. Although the program's user may not appreciate the finer points of multithreading, the user will appreciate the fact that he or she does not need to go have lunch while trying to display data.

I demonstrated how to improve performance with just the TreeView control. I hope you don't think that this is the only control that you can improve. You can apply the techniques I covered in this chapter, especially multithreading, to most of the controls that come with .NET.

This is the last of the "how-to" chapters. The next chapter takes you through a complete program using many of the lessons from the preceding chapters. It pulls all the information together for you.

CHAPTER 11

Pulling It All Together

THIS IS THE LAST CHAPTER in this book. All the previous chapters dealt with individual aspects of data entry and validation. Although I have tried to provide some good examples, sometimes it really hits home when you see a complete data entry project. That is what this chapter is all about.

Before you start the chapter, I need to tell you that the code for this project is extensive. In fact, it is too extensive to include all the code in the chapter. I strongly suggest that you download the code for this project from the Downloads section of the Apress Web site (http://www.apress.com) before you continue.

The Golf Project

I have been looking around for some time for a good golf score tracker program.[1] There are a few good ones out there, but being cheap I wanted the best one to be free. Failing to find a free one, I decided I would program one myself.

I really like this program. In fact, I like it so much I am not going to complete it for you. You will get about 70% of it, though, which is certainly enough for you to complete your own version if you so desire.

This project is an MDI application. As it stands, it includes two child windows and several modal dialog boxes. I really like MDI applications because the interface is self-contained and easy to work with.

The data structure of this program is collection based. Now, I have talked about and used collections throughout this book. All the collections I have used to this point have come with .NET. Some have little or no type safety, such as the generic SortedList collection. Some of them are *strongly typed,* such as the Controls collection contained in every control. The Controls collection can only have objects that derive from System.Windows.Forms.Control. If you try to add an integer to the Controls collection, you will get an error. Strongly typed collections make for robust code.

This project uses several collections that you create yourself. These collections are strongly typed. Rolling your own collections has several advantages, which I explain later. These data collections are gathered from a database layer. This database layer abstracts the data persistence from the rest of the program, which allows you the most flexibility when it comes to working with databases.

---

1. I recently got hooked . . . and sliced, and so on.

Although I have included a database abstraction class in this example, I have not filled it in. You can use any data storage medium you like. Whether you use SQL Server or a plain CSV text file for storage makes no difference to the rest of the program.

I use exception handling where appropriate, and I also use assertions to make sure that I am not making any bonehead mistakes.

I use a menu, which has standard appropriate choices. I also use the ErrorProvider object to call attention to any validation problems.

I use a DataGrid to provide a view into the data structures. The DataGrid I use is set up differently than ones you may have seen before. This is further proof of the flexibility of the DataGrid control. I, of course, use the TreeView as another way of looking at data.

So, where to start? As I already mentioned, this project is far too large for me to provide complete creation instructions. For those of you reading this in a bookstore or on an airplane, I describe the screens here.

If you are looking at the project now, you see the Solution Explorer window shown in Figure 11-1.

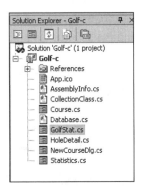

Figure 11-1. The Golf project in Solution Explorer

You can see that I have five forms and two classes. The Database class contains the data abstraction code. The Collections class contains all the data structures for this project.

Figure 11-2 shows the initial MDI main screen. There is nothing special about making an MDI form. In fact, all you need to do is set the IsMdiContainer property to true.

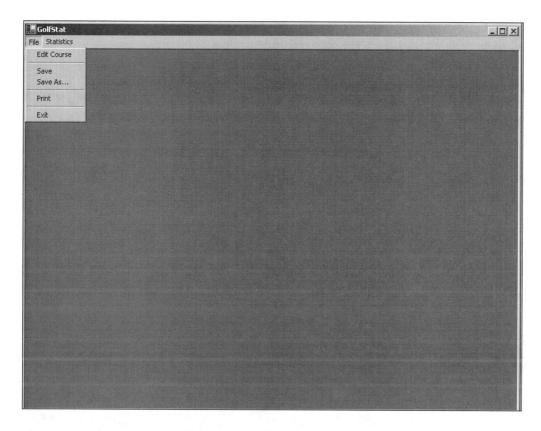

Figure 11-2. The MDI container for the Golf project

The menu is fairly intuitive. I did not fill out the Save or Print choices. Printing is beyond the scope of this book.[2]

Now, if you thought that making a form an MDI container was difficult, then you will think that making a form an MDI child is twice as hard. All you need to do to make a form an MDI child is set the MdiParent property to the parent MDI container form. This is not a design-time property; it is a runtime property.

Now that you know you make a form an MDI child at runtime, what does this tell you? You could easily add a menu option to your main form to change all MDI child forms into normal forms. Voila! You now have an instant SDI application. There is no way to do that in VB 6.0.[3] I started the size of the main form to fit an 800×600 screen.

---

2. Printing is, however, within the scope of my previous book, *GDI+ Programming in C# and VB .NET* (Apress, 2002).

3. Not without some serious side trips to the API.

The next form is the course editor form. It is a child MDI form that pops up when you choose Edit Course. Figure 11-3 shows this form.

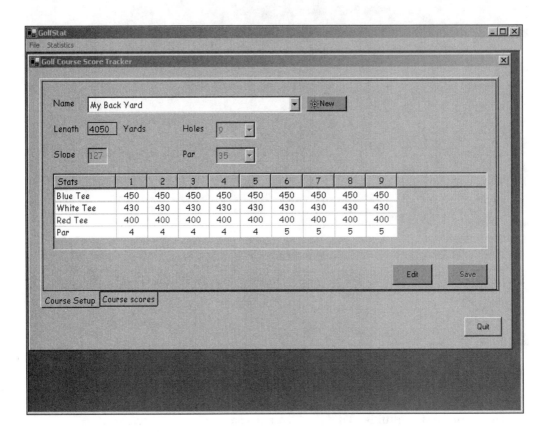

Figure 11-3. *The course editor form*

I use a ListView control to show the tee distances. The course ComboBox allows you to choose which course to edit. If the user clicks the Edit button, the controls become enabled for changing. As you see it now, the course cannot be edited. This avoids any error handling when the user is trying to edit course values when he or she is not in edit mode. Instead of telling the user he or she cannot change any values, just don't allow it. If the user wants to edit the values of the tee distances, the user just clicks the first column of the row he or she wants to edit.

If you navigate to the second tab, Course scores, you see the tab shown in Figure 11-4.

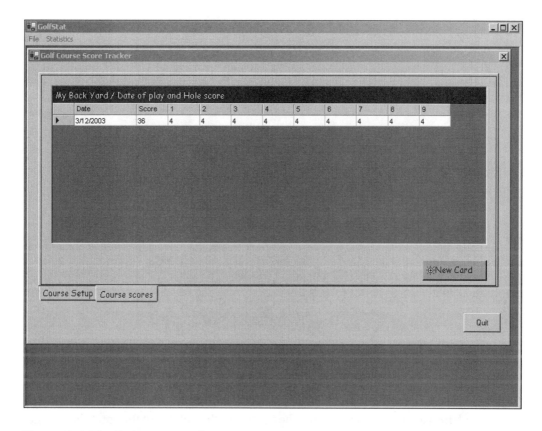

Figure 11-4. The Course scores tab

What you see here is a DataGrid. What you do *not* see here is the new row for the DataGrid. When I first started playing with the DataGrid, it took me a long time to figure out how to prevent the new row from automatically being added. Once I got that, it was child's play.

Clicking the New Card button will automatically add a new row to the DataGrid. It is not just a new row, though. Behind the scenes I create a new ScoreCard object, populate it with the requisite number of Hole objects, and then display it as a new row. You will see the code for this soon.

The next screen in this set is the HoleDetail screen. This program would not be much good if I was not able to use it to track more than just the individual hole scores. I am able to type a number into an individual cell or double-click the cell to bring up the screen shown in Figure 11-5.

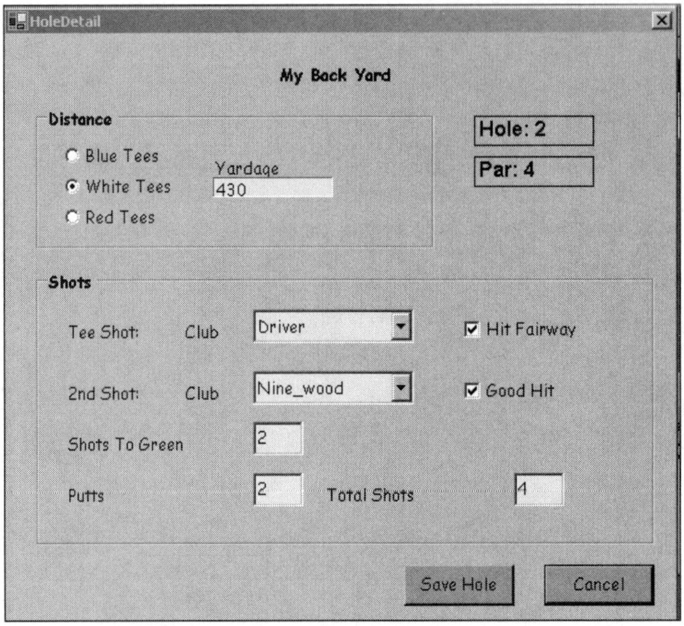

Figure 11-5. The HoleDetail screen

Some of the statistics I keep are standard and some are ones I feel will help me with my game. In any case, when the user saves the hole, I put the Total Shots score in the cell that he or she clicked to get here. Allowing the user to keep his or her scores both ways gives the most flexibility.

The last screen I have is a Statistics screen, as shown in Figure 11-6.

As you can see, I use a TreeView control to look at courses as top-level nodes and individual scorecards as subnodes. This is a slightly different view from using a ListView or DataGrid.

As the user clicks individual scorecards, the appropriate statistics are calculated and displayed. If the user clicks a course, the aggregate statistics for all rounds played on that course are calculated and displayed.

This kind of display allows me to look at things from a holistic point of view or drill down and get the gritty details.

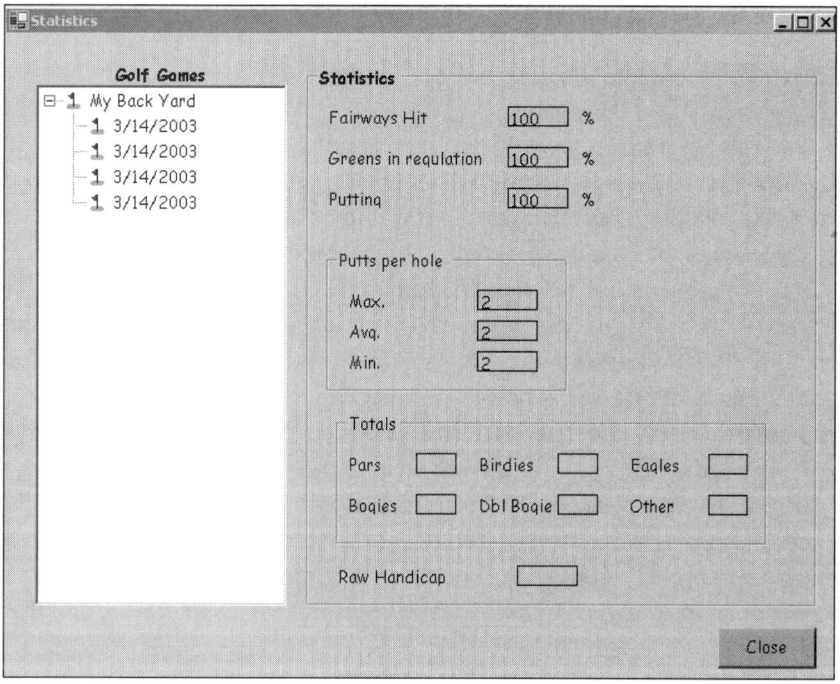

Figure 11-6. The Statistics screen

The Data Structures

You should start programming this project by looking at the data structures. As I mentioned, they are a set of collections based on some abstracted database. The collections are homegrown for two reasons:

- The collections are strongly typed.

- The collections can have certain functionality exposed or not when used as assemblies.

The last reason is why I use homegrown collections the most. Consider that a collection has these five methods in common:

- A way to add an object

- A way to delete an object

- A way to iterate over the collection using a foreach construct

- A way to get a single object from the collection

- A way to get a count of objects in the collection

The methods are Add, Remove, Item, and Count.

If I made a DLL that exposed some collection of GolfCourses, I would not want to expose a raw collection because the client would be able to call the Add and Remove functions of the collection directly. There would be no way for the DLL to track what is going in and out of the collection.

A better way would be to make your own collection and expose only the Count and Item properties. Adding and removing an object from the collection should be done by methods in the class that holds the collection. This allows you to control what gets added to the collection, and it also allows you to do some other processing that may be needed when something is added to or deleted from the collection. You can limit the exposure of some object's method with the Friend keyword in VB and the Internal keyword in C#.

Listings 11-1a and 11-1b show the code for the IHoleDetails collection. Note that a collection of an item has the suffix *s*. The object is called IHoleDetail and the collection is called IHoleDetails.

Listing 11-1a. C# Code for the IHoleDetails Collection Classes

```
#region Hole Detail collection Classes

public class IHoleDetailInfos : IEnumerable
{
  //Slower than Hash table but more flexible
  //Can get item three ways
  //Most like VB type collection
  private SortedList mCol;

  public IHoleDetailInfos()
  {
    mCol = new  SortedList();
  }

  #region collection methods

  // enables foreach processing
  private mEnum GetEnumerator()
  {
    return new mEnum(this);
  }
```

```csharp
//Property count
public int Count
{
  get { return mCol.Count; }
}

// ----- add method ------
public void Add(IHoleDetailInfo hole)
{
  mCol.Add(hole.ToString(), hole);
  mCol.TrimToSize();
}

// ----- overloaded remove method ------
public void Remove(int Index)
{
  mCol.RemoveAt(Index);
}
public void Remove(string key)
{
  mCol.Remove(key);
}

// ----- overloaded item method ------
public IHoleDetailInfo Item(int index)
{
  return (IHoleDetailInfo) mCol.GetByIndex(index);
}
public IHoleDetailInfo Item(string key)
{
  return (IHoleDetailInfo) mCol[key];
}

#endregion

#region enumeration methods

// Implement the GetEnumerator() method:
IEnumerator IEnumerable.GetEnumerator()
{
  return GetEnumerator();
}
```

```csharp
    // Declare the enumerator and implement the IEnumerator interface:
    private class mEnum: IEnumerator
    {
      private int nIndex;
      private IHoleDetailInfos collection;

      // constructor. make the collection
      public mEnum(IHoleDetailInfos coll)
      {
        collection = coll;
        nIndex = -1;
      }

      // start over
      public void Reset()
      {
        nIndex = -1;
      }

      // bump up the index
      public bool MoveNext()
      {
        nIndex++;
        return(nIndex <  collection.mCol.Count);
      }

      // get the current object
      // The current property on the IEnumerator interface:
      object IEnumerator.Current
      {
        get { return(collection.mCol.GetByIndex(nIndex)); }
      }
    }

  #endregion
}


public class IHoleDetailInfo
{
  #region Locals
```

```csharp
private YardMarker  mTeeBox;
private int         mHole;
private int         mPar;
private GolfClubs   mTeeClub;
private GolfClubs   mSecondClub;
private bool        mHitfairway;
private bool        mGood2Shot;
private int         mShots2Green;
private int         mPutts;
private int         mTotalShots;

#endregion

public IHoleDetailInfo()
{
  mTotalShots = 0;
}

public override string ToString()
{
  return mHole.ToString();
}

#region Properties

public YardMarker TeeBox
{
  get{return mTeeBox;}
  set{mTeeBox = value;}
}

public GolfClubs ScondClub
{
  get{return mSecondClub;}
  set{mSecondClub = value;}
}

public GolfClubs TeeClub
{
  get{return mTeeClub;}
  set{mTeeClub = value;}
}
```

```
public bool GoodSecondShot
{
  get{return mGood2Shot;}
  set{mGood2Shot = value;}
}

public bool HitFairway
{
  get{return mHitfairway;}
  set{mHitfairway = value;}
}

public int TotalShots
{
  get{return mTotalShots;}
  set{mTotalShots = value;}
}

public int Putts
{
  get{return mPutts;}
  set{mPutts = value;}
}

public int ShotsToGreen
{
  get{return mShots2Green;}
  set{mShots2Green = value;}
}

public bool GreenInReg
{
  get{return((mPar - mShots2Green >= 2) ? true : false);}
}

public int Par
{
  get{return mPar;}
  set{mPar = value;}
}
```

```
  public int Hole
  {
    get{return mHole;}
    set{mHole = value;}
  }

  #endregion
}

#endregion
```

Listing 11-1b. VB Code for the IHoleDetails Collection Classes

```vb
#Region "Hole Detail collection Classes"

Public Class IHoleDetailInfos
  Implements IEnumerable

  'Slower than Hash table but more flexible
  'Can get item three ways
  'Most like VB type collection
  Private mCol As SortedList

  Public Sub New()
    mCol = New SortedList()
  End Sub

  ' enables foreach processing
  Private Function GetMyEnumerator() As mEnum
    Return New mEnum(Me)
  End Function

  ' Implement the GetEnumerator() method:
  Public Function GetEnumerator() As IEnumerator Implements
   IEnumerable.GetEnumerator
    Return GetMyEnumerator()
  End Function

  'Property count
  Public ReadOnly Property Count() As Int32
    Get
      Return mCol.Count
    End Get
  End Property
```

```
' ----- add method ------
Public Sub Add(ByVal hole As IHoleDetailInfo)
  mCol.Add(hole.ToString(), hole)
  mCol.TrimToSize()
End Sub


' ----- overloaded remove method ------
Public Sub Remove(ByVal Index As Int32)
  mCol.RemoveAt(Index)
End Sub


Public Sub Remove(ByVal key As String)
  mCol.Remove(key)
End Sub


' ----- overloaded item method ------
Public Function Item(ByVal index As Int32) As IHoleDetailInfo
  Return CType(mCol.GetByIndex(index), IHoleDetailInfo)
End Function


Public Function Item(ByVal key As String) As IHoleDetailInfo
  Return CType(mCol(key), IHoleDetailInfo)
End Function


' Declare the enumerator and implement the IEnumerator interface:
Private Class mEnum
  Implements IEnumerator


  Private nIndex As Int32
  Private collection As IHoleDetailInfos


  ' constructor. make the collection
  Public Sub New(ByVal coll As IHoleDetailInfos)
    collection = coll
    nIndex = -1
  End Sub


  ' start over
  Public Sub Reset() Implements IEnumerator.Reset
    nIndex = -1
  End Sub
```

```vbnet
    ' bump up the index
    Public Function MoveNext() As Boolean Implements IEnumerator.MoveNext
      nIndex += 1
      Return (nIndex < collection.mCol.Count)
    End Function


    ' The current property on the IEnumerator interface:
    Public ReadOnly Property Current() As Object Implements IEnumerator.Current
      Get
        Return collection.mCol.GetByIndex(nIndex)
      End Get
    End Property
  End Class

End Class


Public Class IHoleDetailInfo

#Region "Locals"

  Private mTeeBox As YardMarker
  Private mHole As Int32
  Private mPar As Int32
  Private mTeeClub As GolfClubs
  Private mSecondClub As GolfClubs
  Private mHitfairway As Boolean
  Private mGood2Shot As Boolean
  Private mShots2Green As Int32
  Private mPutts As Int32
  Private mTotalShots As Int32

#End Region

  Public Sub New()
    mTotalShots = 0
  End Sub

  Public Overrides Function ToString() As String
    Return mHole.ToString()
  End Function

#Region "Properties"
```

```
Public ReadOnly Property GreenInReg() As Boolean
  Get
    Return (IIf(mPar - mShots2Green >= 2, True, False))
  End Get
End Property

Public Property TeeBox() As YardMarker
  Get
    Return mTeeBox
  End Get
  Set(ByVal Value As YardMarker)
    mTeeBox = Value
  End Set
End Property

Public Property ScondClub() As GolfClubs
  Get
    Return mSecondClub
  End Get
  Set(ByVal Value As GolfClubs)
    mSecondClub = Value
  End Set
End Property

Public Property TeeClub() As GolfClubs
  Get
    Return mTeeClub
  End Get
  Set(ByVal Value As GolfClubs)
    mTeeClub = Value
  End Set
End Property

Public Property GoodSecondShot() As Boolean
  Get
    Return mGood2Shot
  End Get
  Set(ByVal Value As Boolean)
    mGood2Shot = Value
  End Set
End Property
```

```
Public Property HitFairway() As Boolean
  Get
    Return mHitfairway
  End Get
  Set(ByVal Value As Boolean)
    mHitfairway = Value
  End Set
End Property


Public Property TotalShots() As Int32
  Get
    Return mTotalShots
  End Get
  Set(ByVal Value As Int32)
    mTotalShots = Value
  End Set
End Property


Public Property Putts() As Int32
  Get
    Return mPutts
  End Get
  Set(ByVal Value As Int32)
    mPutts = Value
  End Set
End Property


Public Property ShotsToGreen() As Int32
  Get
    Return mShots2Green
  End Get
  Set(ByVal Value As Int32)
    mShots2Green = Value
  End Set
End Property


Public Property Par() As Int32
  Get
    Return mPar
  End Get
  Set(ByVal Value As Int32)
    mPar = Value
  End Set
End Property
```

```
Public Property Hole() As Int32
  Get
    Return mHole
  End Get
  Set(ByVal Value As Int32)
    mHole = Value
  End Set
End Property

#End Region
End Class
```

I have three such sets of classes: one for the individual holes, one for the scorecard, and one for the golf course itself. Figure 11-7 shows the graphical view of the data structure.

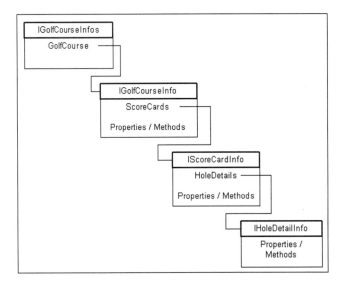

Figure 11-7. The data structure for the Golf project

What you have here is a collection of GolfCourse objects. Each of these GolfCourse objects has a collection of ScoreCard objects. Each of these ScoreCard objects has a collection of HoleDetail objects. Collections of collections of collections.

There is nothing too exciting about the IHoleDetail object except for one thing: I override the ToString() method. You have seen me do this before. I do it so that I can add an IHoleDetail object to a ComboBox list. The ComboBox always uses the ToString() method as the text to show in the control.

Examining the Collection

The collection is a bit more exciting. Notice that the IHoleDetails collection implements the IEnumerable interface.[4] I use a SortedList as the base collection for all the homegrown collections in this project. I do this because you can get and remove objects via an index or a key. It has the added benefit of keeping the list sorted, which can come in handy. The methods I have in here are as follows:

- Count

- Add

- Remove

- Item

These are the classic collection methods.

The IEnumerable interface gives me the ability to enumerate over the collection using the foreach construct. This code implements the following functions:

- *Reset:* Enumeration is done in a forward-only fashion. This function starts at the beginning.

- *MoveNext:* This function bumps up the index into the collection. It also makes sure you cannot go past the end of the collection.

- *Current:* This function returns the current object in the collection as defined by the index.

Here is the code for the IScoreCardInfo object.

C#

```
public class IScoreCardInfo
{
  public IHoleDetailInfos holes;
  private DateTime mDate;
```

---

4. Refresh your memory about the difference between a class and an interface.

```
public IScoreCardInfo()
{
  holes = new IHoleDetailInfos();
  mDate = DateTime.Now;
}

public IScoreCardInfo(int numHoles)
{
  holes = new IHoleDetailInfos();
  IHoleDetailInfo h;
  for(int k=0; k<numHoles; k++)
  {
    h = new IHoleDetailInfo();
    h.TotalShots = 0;
    h.Hole   = k+1;
    h.Putts = 0;
    holes.Add(h);
  }

  mDate = DateTime.Now;
}

public DateTime PlayDate
{
  get{return mDate;}
  set{mDate = value;}
}

public int RoundScore
{
  get
  {
    int score = 0;
    foreach(IHoleDetailInfo h in holes)
      score += h.TotalShots;
    return score;
  }
}
}
```

VB

```vb
Public Class IScoreCardInfo

  Public holes As IHoleDetailInfos
  Private mDate As DateTime

  Public Sub New()
    holes = New IHoleDetailInfos()
    mDate = DateTime.Now
  End Sub

  Public Sub New(ByVal numHoles As Int32)

    holes = New IHoleDetailInfos()
    Dim h As IHoleDetailInfo
    Dim k As Int32
    For k = 0 To numHoles - 1
      h = New IHoleDetailInfo()
      h.TotalShots = 0
      h.Hole = k + 1
      h.Putts = 0
      holes.Add(h)
    Next

    mDate = DateTime.Now
  End Sub

  Public Property PlayDate() As DateTime
    Get
      Return mDate
    End Get
    Set(ByVal Value As DateTime)
      mDate = Value
    End Set
  End Property
```

```
    Public ReadOnly Property RoundScore() As Int32
      Get
        Dim score As Int32 = 0
        Dim h As IHoleDetailInfo
        For Each h In holes
          score += h.TotalShots
        Next
        Return score
      End Get
    End Property
End Class
```

You can see that there is a public collection of IHoleDetailInfo objects. Each scorecard has its own collection. The constructor is responsible for making this collection and initializing some variables.

Notice also that the RoundScore property of this object gets the score in real time. It enumerates over its collection of holes and totals the individual scores. If I did not implement the IEnumerable interface on the IHoleDetails object, I would not be able to do this.

The final collection here is the GolfCourse collection. This contains a list of tee distances and a collection of scorecards. I refer you to the book's code (which you can download from the Downloads section of the Apress Web site at http://www.apress.com) to see this.

The rest of this CollectionClass code contains a static Globals class and some enums. The Globals class is an interesting way to have global variables within a program. It is even thread-safe because I only read variables from it.

The Database Class

I have a class that acts as a buffer between the program and the database. As I mentioned, I do not keep a database for this project, but the code in this class demonstrates how to work with whatever database you do use. This database class shows how to construct the golf course from the holes to the scorecards on up.

Listings 11-2a and 11-2b show the complete database class.

Listing 11-2a. C# Code for the Database Class

```csharp
using System;

namespace Golf_c
{
  /// <summary>
  /// This is the database abstraction code.
  /// Note that the rest of the program knows nothing
  /// about the database or even that there is one.
  /// The only thing it knows about is the GolfCourse collection
  /// </summary>
  public class Database
  {

    #region locals

    public ICourseInfos GolfCourses;

    #endregion

    public Database()
    {
      GolfCourses = new ICourseInfos();

      //You could either put some code here to get the complete database at the
      //start or make a method that needs to be called explicitly to
      //do it. This database, even after years of playing, would be very small.
      //Caching the whole thing in memory is not a big deal.

      //This simulates getting the data from a database.
      GetGolfCourses();
    }

    public void SaveCourse(ICourseInfo GolfCourse)
    {

      if(GolfCourses.Item(GolfCourse.Name) == null)
        GolfCourses.Add(GolfCourse);
```

```
      //Put some code in here to save to a database.
    }

    private void GetGolfCourses()
    {
      //Go out to the database and get the golf course info here
      ICourseInfo course = new ICourseInfo();
      course.NumberOfHoles  = 9;
      course.Name           = "My Back Yard";
      course.Par            = CoursePar._35;
      course.Slope          = 127;

      Tees tee;
      for(int k=0; k<course.Hole.Count; k++)
      {
        tee = (Tees)course.Hole[k];
        tee.BlueDistance    = 450;
        tee.WhiteDistance   = 430;
        tee.RedDistance     = 400;
        tee.Par             = k<5 ? 4 : 5;
        tee.HoleNumber      = k+1;
      }

      IScoreCardInfo card = new IScoreCardInfo();
      card.PlayDate = DateTime.Now;

      IHoleDetailInfo detail;
      for(int k=0; k<course.NumberOfHoles; k++)
      {
        detail = new IHoleDetailInfo();
        detail.Hole = k+1;
        detail.TeeClub = GolfClubs.Driver;
        detail.HitFairway = true;
        detail.ScondClub = GolfClubs.Nine_wood;
        detail.GoodSecondShot = true;
        detail.ShotsToGreen = 2;
        detail.Putts = 2;
        detail.TotalShots = 4;
        detail.Par = ((Tees)course.Hole[k]).Par;
        detail.TeeBox = YardMarker.White;
        card.holes.Add(detail);
      }
```

```
     course.ScoreCards.Add(card);

     GolfCourses.Add(course);

   }
 }
}
```

Listing 11-2b. VB Code for the Database Class

```vb
Option Strict On

' This is the database abstraction code.
' Note that the rest of the program knows nothing
' about the database or even that there is one.
' The only thing it knows about is the GolfCourse collection
' This database abstraction includes some multithreaded code.
Public Class Database

#Region "locals"

  Public GolfCourses As ICourseInfos

#End Region

  Public Sub New()
    GolfCourses = New ICourseInfos()

    'You could either put some code here to get the complete database at the
    'start or make a method that needs to be called explicitly to
    'do it. This database, even after years of playing, would be very small.
    'Caching the whole thing in memory is not a big deal.

    'This simulates getting the data from a database.

    GetGolfCourses()
  End Sub

  Public Sub SaveCourse(ByVal GolfCourse As ICourseInfo)

    If GolfCourses.Item(GolfCourse.Name) Is Nothing Then
      GolfCourses.Add(GolfCourse)
    End If
```

```vbnet
        'Put some code in here to save to a database.
    End Sub

    Private Sub GetGolfCourses()
        'Go out to the database and get the golf course info here
        Dim course As ICourseInfo = New ICourseInfo()
        course.NumberOfHoles = 9
        course.Name = "My Back Yard"
        course.Par = CoursePar._35
        course.Slope = 127

        Dim tee As Tees
        Dim k As Int32
        For k = 0 To course.Hole.Count - 1
            tee = CType(course.Hole(k), Tees)
            tee.BlueDistance = 450
            tee.WhiteDistance = 430
            tee.RedDistance = 400
            If k < 5 Then
                tee.Par = 4
            Else
                tee.Par = 5
            End If
            tee.HoleNumber = k + 1
        Next

        Dim card As IScoreCardInfo = New IScoreCardInfo()
        card.PlayDate = DateTime.Now

        Dim detail As IHoleDetailInfo

        For k = 0 To course.NumberOfHoles - 1
            detail = New IHoleDetailInfo()
            detail.Hole = k + 1
            detail.TeeClub = GolfClubs.Driver
            detail.HitFairway = True
            detail.ScondClub = GolfClubs.Nine_wood
            detail.GoodSecondShot = True
            detail.ShotsToGreen = 2
            detail.Putts = 2
            detail.TotalShots = 4
            detail.Par = (CType(course.Hole(k), Tees)).Par
            detail.TeeBox = YardMarker.White
            card.holes.Add(detail)
```

```
      Next
      course.ScoreCards.Add(card)

      GolfCourses.Add(course)

    End Sub

End Class
```

What I have here is a class local variable that holds the collection of golf courses associated with this database. When the constructor is called, I go and create a single IGolfCourseInfo object on the fly that has just one IScoreCardInfo object.

You can see from this code how easy it is to work with homegrown collections. Try adding an object to the GolfCourses collection that is not an IGolfCourseInfo object. You will get a compiler error. You never even get to run the code.

If you had a simple collection such as an ArrayList, you would be able to put any object in it. This would cause problems down the line. Catching errors at compile time is the way to go if you can.

Starting Up the Program

The initial screen for this program is the MDI parent screen, of course. Let's look at the code for that.

Basically, what I have in this class is a class local variable called "db" that is an instantiated database object. Now when I bring up some of these other child forms, such as the course form or the statistics form, I need access to this database object. After all, it is not only the interface to the actual database, but also it is the keeper of the GolfCourses collection.

Although I have quite a few items in the menu, only a few are wired up to anything. They are the menu choices to open up a course for editing and to view statistics. Here is the code to instantiate these two child forms.

C#

```csharp
private void EditCourse(object sender, EventArgs e)
{
  Course frm = new Course();
  frm.MdiParent = this;
  frm.Show();
}
```

```csharp
private void Stats(object sender, EventArgs e)
{
  Statistics frm = new Statistics();
  frm.MdiParent  = this;
  frm.Show();
}
```

VB

```vb
Private Sub EditCourse(ByVal sender As Object, ByVal e As EventArgs)
  Dim frm As Course = New Course()
  frm.MdiParent = Me
  frm.Show()
End Sub

Private Sub Stats(ByVal sender As Object, ByVal e As EventArgs)
  Dim frm As Statistics = New Statistics()
  frm.MdiParent = Me
  frm.Show()
End Sub
```

All I do is make a new object of the child form I want and set its MdiParent property to the current form. Setting the MdiParent property does two things. First, it tells .NET that this is a child form and that it should reside in the parent's container. Second, it gives the child form a mechanism to call back into the parent form whenever it needs to.

Calling back into the parent form is how the child forms access the database object. It is also a standard way for child forms to communicate with each other. In this case, the parent form acts as an intermediary for child-to-child communication.

The first child form you will look at is the courses form. This form has a tab control that separates editing of the course itself and the course scores. Let's look at the first tab again, as shown in Figure 11-8.

The first thing you may notice is that I swapped the location of the tabs via code. The design-time version of this form has the tabs on the top. For a program like this, I prefer the Excel tab locations.

This form is currently in edit mode. As soon as I click the Edit button, I disable it and I also disable the ability to create a new course. This prevents the user from doing anything he or she should not do. It also prevents me from having to write tons of code that checks if a certain operation is allowed if I am in edit mode. I just do not allow it.

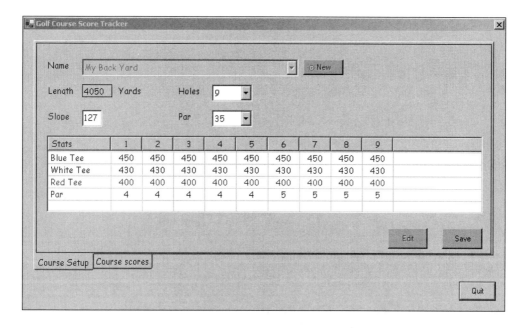

Figure 11-8. The Course Setup tab

While in edit mode, I enable the Holes, Par, and Slope fields, as well as the Save button. Now, I could have made the Holes and the Par fields TextBoxes and left it at that. If I did that, though, I would need to write a fair bit of validation code to make sure that the choices matched a certain range. I would have the added problem that the range of Par values differs if you have 9 or 18 holes.

The best thing to do is what I do here. I use the CoursePar enumeration from the Collections class to fill in the Par ComboBox. This enum contains all the common possibilities for either 9 or 18 holes of golf. If the user chooses 9 holes, then I clear the Par ComboBox and refill it with the appropriate values.

Listings 11-3a and 11-3b show the initialization code for the Course Setup tab and the delegate that handles the Holes ComboBox click event.

Listing 11-3a. C# Code for the Course Setup Tab and cmbHoles Click Event

```csharp
private void GolfCourseTabSetup()
{

    lblLength.BackColor = Color.LightGray;

    //Slope must be between 55 and 155
    txtSlope.MaxLength  = Globals.SlopeLen;
    txtSlope.KeyPress  += new KeyPressEventHandler(this.SlopeKeyPress);
    txtSlope.Validating += new CancelEventHandler(this.SlopeValidate);
```

```csharp
      cmdNew.BackColor  = Color.SandyBrown;
      cmdNew.Font       = cmdQuit.Font;
      cmdNew.Image      = Image.FromFile("new.ico");
      cmdNew.Click      += new EventHandler(this.NewCourse);

      cmdSave.BackColor = Color.SandyBrown;
      cmdSave.Font      = cmdQuit.Font;
      cmdSave.Click     += new EventHandler(this.SaveCourse);
      cmdSave.Enabled   = false;

      cmdEdit.BackColor = Color.SandyBrown;
      cmdEdit.Font      = cmdQuit.Font;
      cmdEdit.Click     += new EventHandler(this.EditCourse);

      cmbPar.DropDownStyle = ComboBoxStyle.DropDownList;

      cmbHoles.DropDownStyle = ComboBoxStyle.DropDownList;
      cmbHoles.Items.Add(Globals.NineHoles);
      cmbHoles.Items.Add(Globals.EighteenHoles);
      cmbHoles.SelectedIndexChanged += new EventHandler(this.SelectPar);
      cmbHoles.SelectedIndex = 1;

      cmbCourseName.MaxLength = 60;
      cmbCourseName.DropDownStyle = ComboBoxStyle.DropDownList;
      cmbCourseName.SelectedIndexChanged += new EventHandler(ChangeCourse);
      foreach(ICourseInfo c in mParent.db.GolfCourses)
      {
        cmbCourseName.Items.Add(c);
      }
      if(cmbCourseName.Items.Count>0)
        cmbCourseName.SelectedIndex = 0;

      lstTees.MouseUp += new MouseEventHandler(EditTeeBox);
    }

    private void SelectPar(object sender, EventArgs e)
    {
      Debug.Assert(sender == cmbHoles,
                  "SelectPar method called by wrong control");

      cmbPar.BeginUpdate();
      cmbPar.Items.Clear();
      if((int)cmbHoles.SelectedItem == Globals.NineHoles)
```

```
    {
      cmbPar.Items.Add((int)CoursePar._36);
      cmbPar.Items.Add((int)CoursePar._35);
      cmbPar.Items.Add((int)CoursePar._27);
    }
    else
    {
      cmbPar.Items.Add((int)CoursePar._72);
      cmbPar.Items.Add((int)CoursePar._71);
      cmbPar.Items.Add((int)CoursePar._70);
      cmbPar.Items.Add((int)CoursePar._54);
    }
    cmbPar.SelectedIndex = 0;
    cmbPar.EndUpdate();

    //While I am in here I need to create the listview on the fly
    //The listview depends upon the number of holes
    if(ThisCourse != null)
      Debug.WriteLine(ThisCourse.Name);

    if(ThisCourse != null && !cmdEdit.Enabled)
      ThisCourse.NumberOfHoles = (int)cmbHoles.SelectedItem;

    SetupTeeList();
  }
```

Listing 11-3b. VB Code for the Course Setup Tab and cmbHoles Click Event

```
Private Sub GolfCourseTabSetup()

  lblLength.BackColor = Color.LightGray

  'Slope must be between 55 and 155
  txtSlope.MaxLength = Globals.SlopeLen
  AddHandler txtSlope.KeyPress, New KeyPressEventHandler(AddressOf SlopeKeyPress)
  AddHandler txtSlope.Validating, New CancelEventHandler(AddressOf SlopeValidate)

  cmdNew.BackColor = Color.SandyBrown
  cmdNew.Font = cmdQuit.Font
  cmdNew.Image = Image.FromFile("new.ico")
  AddHandler cmdNew.Click, New EventHandler(AddressOf NewCourse)
```

```
        cmdSave.BackColor = Color.SandyBrown
        cmdSave.Font = cmdQuit.Font
        AddHandler cmdSave.Click, New EventHandler(AddressOf SaveCourse)
        cmdSave.Enabled = False

        cmdEdit.BackColor = Color.SandyBrown
        cmdEdit.Font = cmdQuit.Font
        AddHandler cmdEdit.Click, New EventHandler(AddressOf EditCourse)

        cmbPar.DropDownStyle = ComboBoxStyle.DropDownList

        cmbHoles.DropDownStyle = ComboBoxStyle.DropDownList
        cmbHoles.Items.Add(Globals.NineHoles)
        cmbHoles.Items.Add(Globals.EighteenHoles)
        AddHandler cmbHoles.SelectedIndexChanged, _
                          New EventHandler(AddressOf SelectPar)
        cmbHoles.SelectedIndex = 1

        cmbCourseName.MaxLength = 60
        cmbCourseName.DropDownStyle = ComboBoxStyle.DropDownList
        AddHandler cmbCourseName.SelectedIndexChanged, _
                          New EventHandler(AddressOf ChangeCourse)
      Dim c As ICourseInfo
      For Each c In mParent.db.GolfCourses

         cmbCourseName.Items.Add(c)
      Next
      If cmbCourseName.Items.Count > 0 Then
         cmbCourseName.SelectedIndex = 0
      End If

      AddHandler lstTees.MouseUp, New MouseEventHandler(AddressOf EditTeeBox)


    Private Sub SelectPar(ByVal sender As Object, ByVal e As EventArgs)
      Debug.Assert(sender Is cmbHoles, _
                "SelectPar method called by wrong control")

      cmbPar.BeginUpdate()
      cmbPar.Items.Clear()
      If CType(cmbHoles.SelectedItem, Int32) = Globals.NineHoles Then
```

```
    cmbPar.Items.Add(CType(CoursePar._36, Int32))
    cmbPar.Items.Add(CType(CoursePar._35, Int32))
    cmbPar.Items.Add(CType(CoursePar._27, Int32))

  Else
    cmbPar.Items.Add((CType(CoursePar._72, Int32)))
    cmbPar.Items.Add(CType(CoursePar._71, Int32))
    cmbPar.Items.Add(CType(CoursePar._70, Int32))
    cmbPar.Items.Add(CType(CoursePar._54, Int32))
  End If
  cmbPar.SelectedIndex = 0
  cmbPar.EndUpdate()

  'While I am in here I need to create the listview on the fly
  'The listview depends upon the number of holes

  If Not ThisCourse Is Nothing And Not cmdEdit.Enabled Then
    ThisCourse.NumberOfHoles = CType(cmbHoles.SelectedItem, Int32)
  End If

  SetupTeeList()
End Sub
```

The setup routine makes sure that I have a validation and KeyPress handler for the Slope field. It also goes out to the static Globals class and gets the maximum length that the field can be. Doing this allows me to change the Slope parameters in the Globals class, and all other code that uses these parameters will change automatically.

You may be wondering why I did not do any setup of the cmbPar ComboBox in the setup routine, yet when the program runs this field is set up correctly. Note the code that sets up the cmbHoles ComboBox:

```
    cmbHoles.DropDownStyle = ComboBoxStyle.DropDownList;
    cmbHoles.Items.Add(Globals.NineHoles);
    cmbHoles.Items.Add(Globals.EighteenHoles);
    cmbHoles.SelectedIndexChanged += new EventHandler(this.SelectPar);
    cmbHoles.SelectedIndex = 1;
```

I wire up the delegate and then set the selected item to a value. Setting the SelectedIndex value automatically fires the SelectedIndexChanged event. I rely on the delegate to set up the cmbPar ComboBox correctly. If I had reversed these last two lines of code, the program would not work correctly.

I override the ToString method in several classes. The ICourseInfo class is one of them. Note this code:

```
foreach(ICourseInfo c in mParent.db.GolfCourses)
{
  cmbCourseName.Items.Add(c);
}
```

I am adding the ICourseInfo object directly to the cmbCourseName ComboBox. The ComboBox uses the ToString method of the object to display information about the object. You saw me demonstrate this in previous chapters.

The delegate shown here is no big surprise. Note, though, that I use the Debug.Assert function to make sure that this delegate is not being called by something that should not call it. This assertion code will get compiled out of the release code.

Here is the code that handles the Slope field.

C#

```
private void SlopeKeyPress(object sender, KeyPressEventArgs e)
{
  Debug.Assert(sender == txtSlope,
            "SlopeKeyPress method called by wrong control");

  if(e.KeyChar < '0' || e.KeyChar > '9')
    e.Handled = true;

  //0 cannot be leading digit
  if(txtSlope.Text == "" && e.KeyChar == '0')
    e.Handled = true;
}

private void SlopeValidate(object sender, CancelEventArgs e)
{
  Debug.Assert(sender == txtSlope,
            "SlopeValidate method called by wrong control");

  try
  {
    int slope = int.Parse(txtSlope.Text);
    if(slope < Globals.MinSlope || slope > Globals.MaxSlope)
    {
      err.SetError(txtSlope, "Slope must be between 55 and 155");
      e.Cancel = true;
    }
```

```
      }
      catch
      {
        err.SetError(txtSlope, "BUG: Slope must be an integer");
        e.Cancel = true;
      }

      if(e.Cancel)
        txtSlope.SelectAll();
      else
        err.SetError(txtSlope, "");
    }
```

VB

```
  Private Sub SlopeKeyPress(ByVal sender As Object, ByVal e As KeyPressEventArgs)
    Debug.Assert(sender Is txtSlope, _
                 "SlopeKeyPress method called by wrong control")

    If e.KeyChar < "0" Or e.KeyChar > "9" Then
      e.Handled = True
    End If

    '0 cannot be leading digit
    If txtSlope.Text = "" AndAlso e.KeyChar = "0" Then
      e.Handled = True
    End If
  End Sub

  Private Sub SlopeValidate(ByVal sender As Object, ByVal e As CancelEventArgs)
    Debug.Assert(sender Is txtSlope, _
                 "SlopeValidate method called by wrong control")

    Try
      Dim slope As Int32 = Int32.Parse(txtSlope.Text)
      If slope < Globals.MinSlope Or slope > Globals.MaxSlope Then
        err.SetError(txtSlope, "Slope must be between 55 and 155")
        e.Cancel = True
      End If
    Catch
      err.SetError(txtSlope, "BUG: Slope must be an integer")
      e.Cancel = True
    End Try
```

```
If (e.Cancel) Then
   txtSlope.SelectAll()
Else
   err.SetError(txtSlope, "")
End If
End Sub
```

You can see here that I use the ErrorProvider control to note any problems with the validation of this field. I use this error control within the confines of a Try-Catch block. In previous chapters I used Catch blocks to show message boxes. As you see here, the Catch block is also a good place to put an ErrorProvider control.

By the way, do you know what error I am catching here? Yup, the integer parse. I could have tested for the TextBox value to be an integer before trying to parse. This is an alternate way.

Examining the Course Scores Tab

The next tab contains quite a bit of setup and event handling. Figure 11-9 shows the Course scores tab.

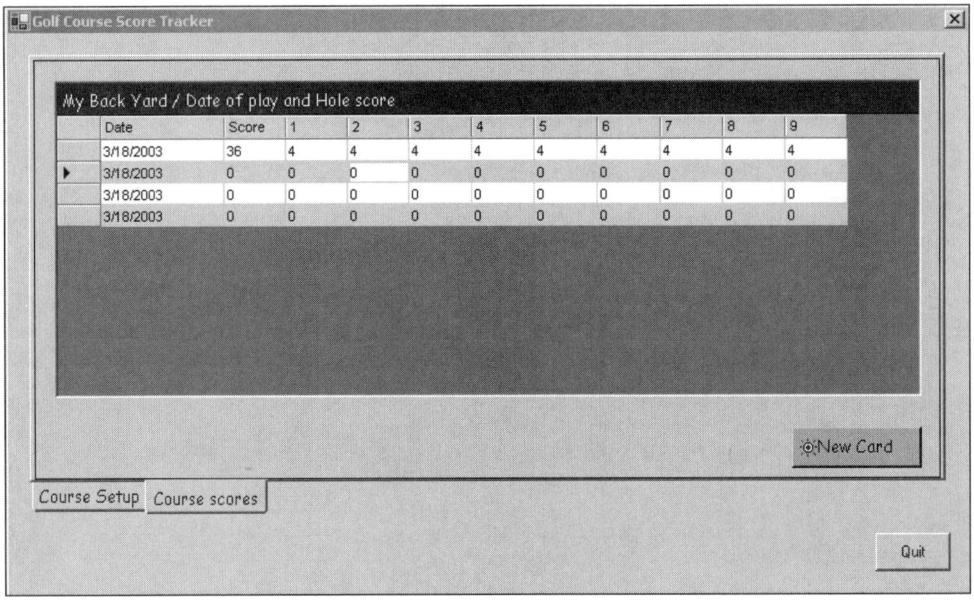

Figure 11-9. The Course scores tab in action

As you can see, I started with an original scorecard and then clicked the New Card button several times. Each time I clicked this button I added a new IScoreCardInfo object to the ScoreCard collection within the current course.

Notice that there is no new record indicator on the DataGrid. I prevent the user from generating a new record by using the DataGrid. I want complete control over what is happening.

Listings 11-4a and 11-4b show the code that gets run when the user switches from the Course Setup tab to the Course scores tab.

Listing 11-4a. C# Code for the Course Scores Tab Setup

```csharp
private void AddScoreCardStyle()
{
  //First clear the existing one out
  dg1.TableStyles.Clear();

  DataGridTableStyle ts1 = new DataGridTableStyle();
  ts1.MappingName = "Course Score";
  // Set other properties.
  ts1.AlternatingBackColor = Color.LightGray;
  //
  // Add textbox column style so we can catch textbox mouse clicks
  DataGridTextBoxColumn TextCol = new DataGridTextBoxColumn();
  TextCol.MappingName        = "Date";
  TextCol.HeaderText         = "Date";
  TextCol.Width              = 100;
  TextCol.TextBox.Validating += new CancelEventHandler(DateCellValidating);
  TextCol.TextBox.DoubleClick += new EventHandler(CellDateClick);
  TextCol.TextBox.KeyPress    += new KeyPressEventHandler(CellDateKeyPress);
  ts1.GridColumnStyles.Add(TextCol);

  TextCol = new DataGridTextBoxColumn();
  TextCol.MappingName        = "Score";
  TextCol.HeaderText         = "Score";
  TextCol.Width              = 50;
  TextCol.TextBox.Enabled    = false;
  ts1.GridColumnStyles.Add(TextCol);

  for(int k=1; k<ThisCourse.NumberOfHoles+1; k++)
  {
    TextCol = new DataGridTextBoxColumn();
    TextCol.MappingName        = k.ToString();
    TextCol.HeaderText         = k.ToString();
    TextCol.Width              = 50;
```

```
      TextCol.TextBox.MaxLength   = 2;
      TextCol.TextBox.DoubleClick += new EventHandler(HoleScoreDblClick);
      TextCol.TextBox.KeyPress    += new KeyPressEventHandler(HoleScoreEntry);
      TextCol.TextBox.Validating  += new CancelEventHandler(HoleScoreValidate);
      ts1.GridColumnStyles.Add(TextCol);
    }
    dg1.TableStyles.Add(ts1);
  }

  private void SetupScoreCardDatagrid()
  {
    //This must be set up based upon the scorecard collection within
    //the thiscourse object. As each cell is clicked it brings up a hole
    //detail. If the user chooses not to click a cell he can in-place edit
    //just the total score. Either way anytime a cell is edited I will need
    //to change something in the iholedetail object that belongs to this hole.

    Debug.Assert(ThisCourse != null, "Must have a valid course");

    //Generate a column style collection that makes each cell a text box.
    AddScoreCardStyle();

    DataColumn dc;
    //Set the datasource to null at start.
    dg1.DataSource = null;
    DataSet DS = new DataSet();

    //Top-level table
    DataTable DT  = new DataTable("Course Score");
    dc = new DataColumn("Date", System.Type.GetType("System.DateTime"));
    DT.Columns.Add(dc);
    dc = new DataColumn("Score", System.Type.GetType("System.Int32"));
    DT.Columns.Add(dc);
    for(int k=1; k<ThisCourse.NumberOfHoles+1; k++)
    {
      dc = new DataColumn(k.ToString(), System.Type.GetType("System.Int32"));
      DT.Columns.Add(dc);
    }

    //<<<<<<<<<<<<<<<<<<<<<<<<<<<<<<<<<<>>>>>>>>>>>>>>>>>>>>>>>>>>>>>>>>>>
    //Add something here to catch if the number of holedetail objects exceeds
    //the number of holes in the course. If so then write to an error file.
    //<<<<<<<<<<<<<<<<<<<<<<<<<<<<<<<<<<>>>>>>>>>>>>>>>>>>>>>>>>>>>>>>>>>>
```

```csharp
ArrayList scores = new ArrayList();
foreach(IScoreCardInfo s in ThisCourse.ScoreCards)
{
  scores.Clear();
  scores.Add(s.PlayDate.ToShortDateString());
  scores.Add(s.RoundScore);
  foreach(IHoleDetailInfo h in s.holes)
  {
    //Remember that the basis for this collection is a SortedList so it
    //should come out in order.
    scores.Add(h.TotalShots);
  }
  DT.Rows.Add(scores.ToArray());
}


DS.Tables.Add(DT);

dg1.CaptionText = cmbCourseName.Text + " / Date of play and Hole score ";
dg1.CaptionFont = new Font("Comic Sans MS", 10);
dg1.Font = new Font("Arial", 8);
dg1.DataSource = DS;
dg1.DataMember = "Course Score";
dg1.CurrentCellChanged += new EventHandler(this.CellChanged);

//Remember binding the property of one control to the property of another.
//This was managed by a PropertyManager object.  When you have an
//object that derives from the IList interface such as a collection,
//then each of these objects has a CurrencyManager. I am changing the
//data view object that belongs to this data source's datamember
//(The table name in this case).  I am making sure that the user cannot
//add a new row using this dataview.  See the online help
//"Consumers of Data on Windows Forms" for more explanation.
CurrencyManager cm = (CurrencyManager)this.BindingContext[dg1.DataSource,
                                                 dg1.DataMember];
((DataView)cm.List).AllowNew = false;

cmdNewCard.BackColor = Color.SandyBrown;
cmdNewCard.Click += new EventHandler(NewCard);

}
```

Listing 11-4b. VB Code for the Course Scores Tab Setup

```vb
Private Sub AddScoreCardStyle()

    'First clear the existing one out
    dg1.TableStyles.Clear()

    Dim ts1 As DataGridTableStyle = New DataGridTableStyle()
    ts1.MappingName = "Course Score"
    ' Set other properties.
    ts1.AlternatingBackColor = Color.LightGray
    '
    ' Add textbox column style so we can catch textbox mouse clicks
    Dim TextCol As DataGridTextBoxColumn = New DataGridTextBoxColumn()
    TextCol.MappingName = "Date"
    TextCol.HeaderText = "Date"
    TextCol.Width = 100
    AddHandler TextCol.TextBox.Validating, _
                New CancelEventHandler(AddressOf DateCellValidating)
    AddHandler TextCol.TextBox.DoubleClick, _
                New EventHandler(AddressOf CellDateClick)
    AddHandler TextCol.TextBox.KeyPress, _
                New KeyPressEventHandler(AddressOf CellDateKeyPress)
    ts1.GridColumnStyles.Add(TextCol)

    TextCol = New DataGridTextBoxColumn()
    TextCol.MappingName = "Score"
    TextCol.HeaderText = "Score"
    TextCol.Width = 50
    TextCol.TextBox.Enabled = False
    ts1.GridColumnStyles.Add(TextCol)

    Dim k As Int32
    For k = 1 To ThisCourse.NumberOfHoles + 1
        TextCol = New DataGridTextBoxColumn()
        TextCol.MappingName = k.ToString()
        TextCol.HeaderText = k.ToString()
        TextCol.Width = 50
        TextCol.TextBox.MaxLength = 2
        AddHandler TextCol.TextBox.DoubleClick, _
                New EventHandler(AddressOf HoleScoreDblClick)
        AddHandler TextCol.TextBox.KeyPress, _
                New KeyPressEventHandler(AddressOf HoleScoreEntry)
```

```
      AddHandler TextCol.TextBox.Validating, _
                  New CancelEventHandler(AddressOf HoleScoreValidate)
    ts1.GridColumnStyles.Add(TextCol)
  Next
  dg1.TableStyles.Add(ts1)
End Sub


Private Sub SetupScoreCardDatagrid()
  'This must be set up based upon the scorecard collection within
  'the thiscourse object. as each cell is clicked it brings up a hole
  'detail. If the user chooses not to click a cell he can in-place edit
  'just the total score. Either way anytime a cell is edited I will need
  'to change something in the iholedetail object that belongs to this hole.

  Debug.Assert(Not ThisCourse Is Nothing, "Must have a valid course")


  'Generate a column style collection that makes each cell a text box.
  AddScoreCardStyle()


  Dim dc As DataColumn
  'Set the datasource to null at start.
  dg1.DataSource = Nothing
  Dim DS As DataSet = New DataSet()


  'Top-level table
  Dim DT As DataTable = New DataTable("Course Score")
  dc = New DataColumn("Date", System.Type.GetType("System.DateTime"))
  DT.Columns.Add(dc)
  dc = New DataColumn("Score", System.Type.GetType("System.Int32"))
  DT.Columns.Add(dc)
  Dim k As Int32
  For k = 1 To ThisCourse.NumberOfHoles
    dc = New DataColumn(k.ToString(), System.Type.GetType("System.Int32"))
    DT.Columns.Add(dc)
  Next


  '<<<<<<<<<<<<<<<<<<<<<<<<<<<<<<<<<<<>>>>>>>>>>>>>>>>>>>>>>>>>>>>>>>>>>>
  'Add something here to catch if the number of holedetail objects exceeds
  'the number of holes in the course. If so then write to an error file.
  '<<<<<<<<<<<<<<<<<<<<<<<<<<<<<<<<<<<>>>>>>>>>>>>>>>>>>>>>>>>>>>>>>>>>>>


  Dim scores As ArrayList = New ArrayList()
  Dim s As IScoreCardInfo
  For Each s In ThisCourse.ScoreCards
```

```
      scores.Clear()
      scores.Add(s.PlayDate.ToShortDateString())
      scores.Add(s.RoundScore)
      Dim h As IHoleDetailInfo
      For Each h In s.holes
        'Remember that the basis for this collection is a SortedList so it
        'should come out in order.
        scores.Add(h.TotalShots)
      Next
      DT.Rows.Add(scores.ToArray())
    Next

    DS.Tables.Add(DT)

    dg1.CaptionText = cmbCourseName.Text + " / Date of play and Hole score "
    dg1.CaptionFont = New Font("Comic Sans MS", 10)
    dg1.Font = New Font("Arial", 8)
    dg1.DataSource = DS
    dg1.DataMember = "Course Score"
    AddHandler dg1.CurrentCellChanged, New EventHandler(AddressOf CellChanged)

    'Remember binding the property of one control to the property of another.
    'This was managed by a PropertyManager object.  When you have an
    'object that derives from the IList interface such as a collection,
    'then each of these objects has a CurrencyManager. I am changing the
    'data view object that belongs to this data source's datamember
    '(The table name in this case).  I am making sure that the user cannot
    'add a new row using this dataview.  See the online help
    '"Consumers of Data on Windows Forms" for more explanation.
    Dim cm As CurrencyManager = CType(Me.BindingContext(dg1.DataSource, _
                                            dg1.DataMember), _
                                            CurrencyManager)
    Dim dv As DataView = CType(cm.List, DataView)
    dv.AllowNew = False

    cmdNewCard.BackColor = Color.SandyBrown
    AddHandler cmdNewCard.Click, New EventHandler(AddressOf NewCard)

  End Sub
```

The first function here is designed to set up a certain view of the DataGrid. I set it up so that each cell is a TextBox. Once I have done that, I can attach delegates to the TextBox events. This is how I am able to get the HoleDetail screen to pop up when the user double-clicks a cell.

NOTE It actually takes three clicks to bring up the HoleDetail screen. This is because the first click turns the cell into a TextBox. At this point, a double-click is caught by the TextBox delegate. You can think of this as one click to chose the cell and a double-click to edit it.

Consider these two lines of code from the SetupScoreCardDatagrid method:

```
CurrencyManager cm = (CurrencyManager)this.BindingContext[dg1.DataSource,
                                                          dg1.DataMember];
((DataView)cm.List).AllowNew = false;
```

The CurrencyManager is the object that handles a data view of a DataGrid. In this case, I am telling the data view for this DataGrid to disallow automatic addition of new rows. Pretty cool, isn't it?

The AddCardStyle method is responsible for setting up the DataGrid so that it shows the correct number of cells according to how many holes the course has. This makes the grids dynamic and presents a nicer interface than if I just clamped everything to 18 holes. It also sets up the cell style and wires up some delegates to catch TextBox events. Notice that I do more than just catch the double-click event. I also catch the Validating and KeyPress events. I do this so that the user can just enter the hole's score by typing directly into the cell. I give the user the option of detailing the hole statistics or just recording the score.

I find that giving users some choice in what data is entered and how it is entered gives the impression that you put some thought into the program. Many times I have seen programs that are aimed at computer novices only. This may be OK for first-time users, but as people get familiar with your program, they will start searching for ways to speed up data entry. Adding alternate ways to input data can make a big difference.

Note that in this setup I disable the TextBox for the Total Score. Once the user clicks in this cell, the TextBox associated with this cell is activated and the cell goes gray, which indicates that the user cannot enter data in it.

Validating Cell Entry

Let's take a quick look at some of the data validation routines for the DataGrid cells.

C#

```csharp
private void CellDateClick(object sender, EventArgs e)
{
  //Handle double-clicking on the date field
  //If you want you can bring up a calendar dialog here to make it
  //easy for the user to pick a date
}

private void CellDateKeyPress(object sender, KeyPressEventArgs e)
{
  //Handle entering data in the date field
  if(!Regex.IsMatch(e.KeyChar.ToString(), "[0-9/-]"))
    e.Handled = true;
}

private void DateCellValidating(object sender, CancelEventArgs e)
{
  Debug.Assert(sender is TextBox,
    "Sender must be a datagrid cell that is a textbox");

  string DateMatch = "[0-1]?[0-9]/[0-3]?[0-9]/[0-9]{4}$";
  if(Regex.IsMatch(((TextBox)sender).Text, DateMatch))
    if(ThisCard != null)
      ThisCard.PlayDate = DateTime.Parse(((TextBox)sender).Text);
  else
    e.Cancel = true;
}

private void HoleScoreEntry(object sender, KeyPressEventArgs e)
{
  if(!Char.IsDigit(e.KeyChar))
    e.Handled = true;
}

private void HoleScoreValidate(object sender, CancelEventArgs e)
{
  Debug.Assert(sender is TextBox,
               "Sender must be a datagrid cell that is a textbox");
```

```
    if(ThisCard != null && ThisHole != null)
    {
      ThisHole.TotalShots = int.Parse(((TextBox)sender).Text);
      dg1[dg1.CurrentCell.RowNumber, 1] = ThisCard.RoundScore;
    }
  }

  private void CellChanged(object sender, EventArgs e)
  {
    try
    {
      ThisCard = ThisCourse.ScoreCards.Item(dg1.CurrentCell.RowNumber);
      ThisHole = ThisCard.holes.Item(dg1.CurrentCell.ColumnNumber-2);
    }
    catch
    {
      ThisCard = null;
      ThisHole = null;
    }
  }
```

VB

```
Private Sub CellDateClick(ByVal sender As Object, ByVal e As EventArgs)
  'Handle double-clicking on the date field
  'If you want you can bring up a calendar dialog here to make it
  'easy for the user to pick a date
End Sub

Private Sub CellDateKeyPress(ByVal sender As Object, _
                          ByVal e As KeyPressEventArgs)
  'Handle entering data in the date field
  If Not Regex.IsMatch(e.KeyChar.ToString(), "[0-9/-]") Then
    e.Handled = True
  End If
End Sub

Private Sub DateCellValidating(ByVal sender As Object, _
                          ByVal e As CancelEventArgs)
  Debug.Assert(TypeOf (sender) Is TextBox, _
      "Sender must be a datagrid cell that is a textbox")
```

```vbnet
      Dim DateMatch As String = "[0-1]?[0-9]/[0-3]?[0-9]/[0-9]{4}$"
      If Regex.IsMatch((CType(sender, TextBox)).Text, DateMatch) Then
        If Not ThisCard Is Nothing Then
          ThisCard.PlayDate = DateTime.Parse((CType(sender, TextBox)).Text)
        Else
          e.Cancel = True
        End If
      End If
    End Sub


    Private Sub HoleScoreEntry(ByVal sender As Object, _
                               ByVal e As KeyPressEventArgs)
      If Not Char.IsDigit(e.KeyChar) Then
        e.Handled = True
      End If
    End Sub


    Private Sub HoleScoreValidate(ByVal sender As Object, _
                                  ByVal e As CancelEventArgs)
      Debug.Assert(TypeOf (sender) Is TextBox, _
                "Sender must be a datagrid cell that is a textbox")

      If Not ThisCard Is Nothing AndAlso Not ThisHole Is Nothing Then
        ThisHole.TotalShots = Int32.Parse((CType(sender, TextBox).Text))
        dg1(dg1.CurrentCell.RowNumber, 1) = ThisCard.RoundScore
      End If
    End Sub


    Private Sub CellChanged(ByVal sender As Object, ByVal e As EventArgs)
      Try
        ThisCard = ThisCourse.ScoreCards.Item(dg1.CurrentCell.RowNumber)
        ThisHole = ThisCard.holes.Item(dg1.CurrentCell.ColumnNumber - 2)
      Catch
        ThisCard = Nothing
        ThisHole = Nothing
      End Try
    End Sub
```

I make use of the regular expression engine to validate dates and some key presses. I spent much of Chapter 9 on regular expressions. I must tell you that it really does pay to learn this syntax. It can save so much code.

The Hole Detail Screen

If the user decides he or she wants to enter statistics for each hole played, he or she needs only double-click in one of the cells that holds the hole score. The user will then see the screen shown in Figure 11-10.

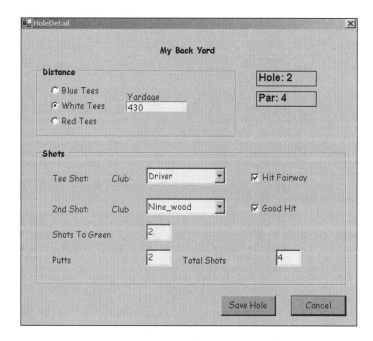

Figure 11-10. The HoleDetail screen shows statistics for each hole played.

This detail screen is the user interface to the IHoleDetail object. The user is not able to enter any value for the yardage. The program does that when the user chooses a radio button. This is restrictive data entry, and there is no reason to add any validation handlers for this data. Whatever the user chooses as his or her tee color is correct.

The Shots GroupBox contains several fields. I decided to use ComboBoxes for the clubs as these are always known quantities. The Shots To Green and Putts fields could be any numeric value. The Total Shots field is the same.

I make good use of controls that steer the user to a predetermined valid entry. The RadioBoxes are not gratuitous and scattered. CheckBoxes are used as Boolean fields to note the quality of the shot. No elaboration is needed here.

Three fields need validation. I first set the field length to 3 for each of these fields. If someone makes more than 99 shots on any one hole, that person needs a new hobby. Next, I trap the KeyPress event to make sure that only numbers are allowed. Listings 11-5a and 11-5b show the constructor and delegates for this form.

Listing 11-5a. C# Code for the HoleDetail Screen

```
public HoleDetail(ref ICourseInfo ThisCourse, ref IHoleDetailInfo hole)
{
  InitializeComponent();

  //Don't forget to initialize tab order and speedkeys, etc.
  this.BackColor = Color.LightGreen;
  cmdSave.BackColor = Color.SandyBrown;
  cmdCancel.BackColor = Color.SandyBrown;

  mHole - hole;
  lblCourse.Text = ThisCourse.Name;
  foreach(Tees tee in ThisCourse.Hole)
  {
    if(tee.HoleNumber == mHole.Hole)
    {
      distance = tee;
      break;
    }
  }

  lblHole.Text = "Hole: " + mHole.Hole.ToString();
  lblPar.Text  = "Par: "  + mHole.Par.ToString();

  optBlue.CheckedChanged += new EventHandler(this.YardClick);
  optWhite.CheckedChanged += new EventHandler(this.YardClick);
  optRed.CheckedChanged += new EventHandler(this.YardClick);
  switch(hole.TeeBox)
  {
    case YardMarker.Blue:
      optBlue.Checked = true;
      TeeBox = YardMarker.Blue;
      break;
    case YardMarker.Red:
      optRed.Checked = true;
      TeeBox = YardMarker.Red;
      break;
```

```
        case YardMarker.White:
        default:
          optWhite.Checked = true;
          TeeBox = YardMarker.White;
          break;
      }

      //This is how you enumerate an enumeration
      //Bet you didn't know you could do this.
      GolfClubs G = GolfClubs.One_iron;
      while(G <= GolfClubs.Putter)
      {
        cmbFirstClub.Items.Add(G);
        if(mHole.TeeClub == G)
          cmbFirstClub.SelectedIndex = cmbFirstClub.Items.Count-1;

        cmbSecondClub.Items.Add(G);
        if(mHole.ScondClub == G)
          cmbSecondClub.SelectedIndex = cmbSecondClub.Items.Count-1;

        G++;
      }

      cmdSave.DialogResult    = DialogResult.OK;
      cmdCancel.DialogResult  = DialogResult.Cancel;
      cmdSave.Click           += new EventHandler(SaveHole);

      chkFairway.Checked  = hole.HitFairway;
      chkGoodHit.Checked  = hole.GoodSecondShot;
      txtShots2Green.MaxLength = 3;
      txtShots2Green.Text = hole.ShotsToGreen.ToString();
      txtShots2Green.KeyPress += new KeyPressEventHandler(OnlyNumbers);
      txtPutts.MaxLength = 3;
      txtPutts.Text       = hole.Putts.ToString();
      txtPutts.KeyPress   += new KeyPressEventHandler(OnlyNumbers);
      txtTotal.MaxLength = 3;
      txtTotal.Text       = hole.TotalShots.ToString();
      txtTotal.KeyPress   += new KeyPressEventHandler(OnlyNumbers);

      //Consider adding a databinding or validation to the totals
      //text box so it automatically totals the shots2green and putts TextBoxes.
    }

    #region events
```

```csharp
private void OnlyNumbers(object sender, KeyPressEventArgs e)
{
  //Allow only positive numbers
  if(!char.IsDigit(e.KeyChar))
    e.Handled = true;
}

 private void YardClick(object sender, EventArgs e)
{
  if(optBlue.Checked)
  {
    txtYards.Text = distance.BlueDistance.ToString();
    TeeBox = YardMarker.Blue;
  }
  else if(optWhite.Checked)
  {
    txtYards.Text = distance.WhiteDistance.ToString();
    TeeBox = YardMarker.White;
  }
  else if(optRed.Checked)
  {
    txtYards.Text = distance.RedDistance.ToString();
    TeeBox = YardMarker.Blue;
  }

}

private void SaveHole(object sender, EventArgs e)
{
  if(txtPutts.Text != string.Empty)
    mHole.Putts = int.Parse(txtPutts.Text);
  else
    mHole.Putts = 0;
  if(txtShots2Green.Text != string.Empty)
    mHole.ShotsToGreen = int.Parse(txtShots2Green.Text);
  else
    mHole.ShotsToGreen = 0;
  if(txtTotal.Text != string.Empty)
    mHole.TotalShots = int.Parse(txtTotal.Text);
  else
    mHole.TotalShots = 0;
  mHole.GoodSecondShot = chkFairway.Checked;
  mHole.GoodSecondShot = chkGoodHit.Checked;
  mHole.TeeBox = TeeBox;
```

```
        mHole.TeeClub = (GolfClubs)cmbFirstClub.SelectedItem;
        mHole.ScondClub = (GolfClubs)cmbSecondClub.SelectedItem;
    }

    #endregion
```

Listing 11-5b. VB Code for the HoleDetail Screen

```
Public Sub New(ByRef ThisCourse As ICourseInfo, ByRef hole As IHoleDetailInfo)
    MyBase.New()

    'This call is required by the Windows Form Designer.
    InitializeComponent()

    'Don't forget to initialize tab order and speedkeys, etc.
    BackColor = Color.LightGreen
    cmdSave.BackColor = Color.SandyBrown
    cmdCancel.BackColor = Color.SandyBrown

    mHole = hole
    lblCourse.Text = ThisCourse.Name
    Dim Tee As Tees
    For Each Tee In ThisCourse.Hole
        If Tee.HoleNumber = mHole.Hole Then
            distance = Tee
            Exit For
        End If
    Next

    lblHole.Text = "Hole: " + mHole.Hole.ToString()
    lblPar.Text = "Par: " + mHole.Par.ToString()

    AddHandler optBlue.CheckedChanged, New EventHandler(AddressOf YardClick)
    AddHandler optWhite.CheckedChanged, New EventHandler(AddressOf YardClick)
    AddHandler optRed.CheckedChanged, New EventHandler(AddressOf YardClick)
    Select Case hole.TeeBox
        Case YardMarker.Blue
            optBlue.Checked = True
            TeeBox = YardMarker.Blue
        Case YardMarker.Red
            optRed.Checked = True
            TeeBox = YardMarker.Red
```

```
      Case YardMarker.White
        optWhite.Checked = True
        TeeBox = YardMarker.White
    End Select

    'This is how you enumerate an enumeration
    'Bet you didn't know you could do this.
    Dim G As GolfClubs = GolfClubs.One_iron
    While G <= GolfClubs.Putter
      cmbFirstClub.Items.Add(G)
      If mHole.TeeClub = G Then
        cmbFirstClub.SelectedIndex = cmbFirstClub.Items.Count - 1
      End If

      cmbSecondClub.Items.Add(G)
      If mHole.ScondClub = G Then
        cmbSecondClub.SelectedIndex = cmbSecondClub.Items.Count - 1
      End If

      G += 1
    End While

    cmdSave.DialogResult = DialogResult.OK
    cmdCancel.DialogResult = DialogResult.Cancel
    AddHandler cmdSave.Click, New EventHandler(AddressOf SaveHole)

    chkFairway.Checked = hole.HitFairway
    chkGoodHit.Checked = hole.GoodSecondShot
    txtShots2Green.MaxLength = 3
    txtShots2Green.Text = hole.ShotsToGreen.ToString()
    AddHandler txtShots2Green.KeyPress, _
                        New KeyPressEventHandler(AddressOf OnlyNumbers)
    txtPutts.MaxLength = 3
    txtPutts.Text = hole.Putts.ToString()
    AddHandler txtPutts.KeyPress, _
                        New KeyPressEventHandler(AddressOf OnlyNumbers)
    txtTotal.MaxLength = 3
    txtTotal.Text = hole.TotalShots.ToString()
    AddHandler txtTotal.KeyPress, _
                        New KeyPressEventHandler(AddressOf OnlyNumbers)
```

```
    'Consider adding a databinding or validation to the totals text box
    'so it automatically totals the shots2green and putts TextBoxes.

  End Sub

#Region "events"

  Private Sub OnlyNumbers(ByVal sender As Object, ByVal e As KeyPressEventArgs)
    'Allow only positive numbers
    If Not Char.IsDigit(e.KeyChar) Then
      e.Handled = True
    End If
  End Sub

  Private Sub YardClick(ByVal sender As Object, ByVal e As EventArgs)
    If optBlue.Checked Then
      txtYards.Text = distance.BlueDistance.ToString()
      TeeBox = YardMarker.Blue
    ElseIf optWhite.Checked Then
      txtYards.Text = distance.WhiteDistance.ToString()
      TeeBox = YardMarker.White
    ElseIf optRed.Checked Then
      txtYards.Text = distance.RedDistance.ToString()
      TeeBox = YardMarker.Blue
    End If
  End Sub

  Private Sub SaveHole(ByVal sender As Object, ByVal e As EventArgs)
    mHole.GoodSecondShot = chkFairway.Checked
    mHole.GoodSecondShot = chkGoodHit.Checked
    mHole.TeeBox = TeeBox
    mHole.TeeClub = CType(cmbFirstClub.SelectedItem, GolfClubs)
    If txtPutts.Text = String.Empty Then
      mHole.Putts = 0
    Else
      mHole.Putts = Int32.Parse(txtPutts.Text)
    End If
    mHole.ScondClub = CType(cmbSecondClub.SelectedItem, GolfClubs)
    If txtShots2Green.Text = String.Empty Then
      mHole.ShotsToGreen = 0
    Else
      mHole.ShotsToGreen = Int32.Parse(txtShots2Green.Text)
    End If
```

```
    If txtTotal.Text = String.Empty Then
      mHole.TotalShots = 0
    Else
      mHole.TotalShots = Int32.Parse(txtTotal.Text)
    End If
  End Sub


#End Region
```

You can see that the code for this form is not difficult at all. In fact, proper use of controls has actually eliminated quite a bit of validation code.

NOTE   I did not include any tab index or speed key setup. I trust that you know to do this as a first step in aiding the user to navigate your screens.

The last screen I present in this project is the Statistics screen. In this screen I show the avid golfer where his or her game falls short (or left, or right, or in the pond, or . . .). Figure 11-11 shows this screen with some scorecards added to the original one.

I will tell you now that I did not add the code for the Totals GroupBox statistics. I also did not calculate the raw handicap. My intention with this form is to show you how to present a different view to the user.

You have seen this view in the form of the DataGrid page. There I displayed the scorecard in a row-by-row format. Each cell contained only some of the information you see in Figure 11-11. For instance, the date was a cell in the DataGrid page, and here it is a node in a tree. Also, the only detailed information I gave in the DataGrid form was the individual hole total. You could gather some of this information from the DataGrid using a calculator and a piece of paper, but that is not what that view is for.

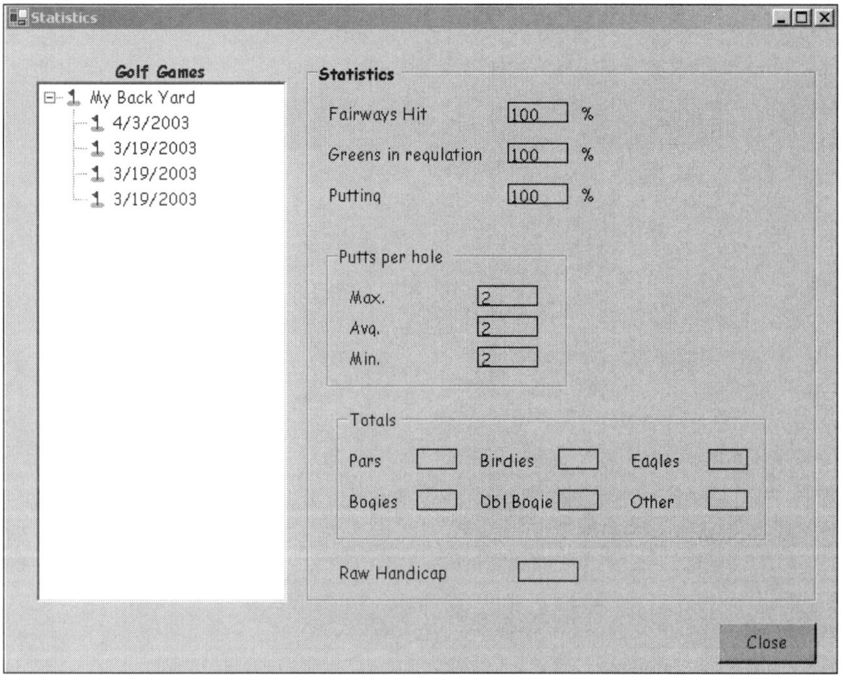

Figure 11-11. The Statistics screen for an avid golfer

Let's look at how I set up this form. Listings 11-6a and 11-6b show all the relevant code for this form.

Listing 11-6a. C# Code for the Statistics Form

```csharp
#region locals

private GolfStat        mParent;
private ICourseInfo     ThisCourse;
private IScoreCardInfo  ThisCard;
private IHoleDetailInfo ThisHole;

#endregion

public Statistics()
{
  InitializeComponent();
  Init();
}
```

```
private void Statistics_Load(object sender, System.EventArgs e)
{
  mParent = (GolfStat)this.MdiParent;
  SetupTree();
}


#region Setup

private void Init()
{
  this.BackColor = Color.LightGreen;
  cmdClose.BackColor = Color.SandyBrown;
  cmdClose.Text = "&Close";
  cmdClose.TabIndex = 0;
  cmdClose.Click += new EventHandler(CloseMe);
  imgIcons.Images.Add(Image.FromFile("flag.ico"));
}


private void SetupTree()
{
  TreeNode CourseNode;
  TreeNode CardNode;

  tvwCourse.Nodes.Clear();
  tvwCourse.BeginUpdate();

  tvwCourse.ImageList = imgIcons;
  tvwCourse.ImageIndex = 0;
  tvwCourse.SelectedImageIndex = 0;
  foreach(ICourseInfo c in mParent.db.GolfCourses)
  {
    CourseNode = tvwCourse.Nodes.Add(c.Name);
    CourseNode.Tag = c;
    foreach(IScoreCardInfo card in c.ScoreCards)
    {
      CardNode = CourseNode.Nodes.Add(card.PlayDate.ToShortDateString());
      CardNode.Tag = card;
    }
  }

  tvwCourse.AfterSelect += new TreeViewEventHandler(CourseStats);
  tvwCourse.EndUpdate();
}
```

```
#endregion

#region events

public void CloseMe(object sender, EventArgs e)
{
  this.Close();
}

private void CourseStats(object s, TreeViewEventArgs e)
{
  float FairwaysHit = 0;
  float GreensInReg = 0;
  float Putting    = 0;
  float MaxPutts    = 0;
  float MinPutts    = 99;
  float AvgPutts    = 0;

  if(e.Node.Tag is IScoreCardInfo)
  {
    ThisCard = (IScoreCardInfo)e.Node.Tag;
    foreach(IHoleDetailInfo h in ThisCard.holes)
    {
      FairwaysHit += h.HitFairway ? 1 : 0;
      GreensInReg += h.GreenInReg ? 1 : 0;
      Putting     += h.Putts;
      if(h.Putts > MaxPutts) MaxPutts = h.Putts;
      if(h.Putts < MinPutts) MinPutts = h.Putts;
      AvgPutts     += h.Putts;
    }
    FairwaysHit /= ThisCard.holes.Count;
    Putting /= (ThisCard.holes.Count * 2);
    GreensInReg /= ThisCard.holes.Count;
    AvgPutts     /= ThisCard.holes.Count;

    lblFairwaysHit.Text = (FairwaysHit*100).ToString();
    lblGreens.Text = (GreensInReg*100).ToString();
    lblPutting.Text = (Putting*100).ToString();
    lblMaxPutts.Text = MaxPutts.ToString();
    lblAvgPutts.Text = AvgPutts.ToString();
    lblMinPutts.Text = MinPutts.ToString();
```

```
        //I will let you figure out the rest of the stats. :)


    }
  }
  #endregion
```

Listing 11-6b. VB Code for the Statistics Form

```vb
#Region "locals"

  Private mParent As GolfStat
  Private ThisCourse As ICourseInfo
  Private ThisCard As IScoreCardInfo
  Private ThisHole As IHoleDetailInfo

#End Region

  Public Sub New()
    MyBase.New()

    'This call is required by the Windows Form Designer.
    InitializeComponent()
    Init()

  End Sub

  Private Sub Statistics_Load(ByVal sender As System.Object, _
                              ByVal e As System.EventArgs) Handles MyBase.Load
    mParent = CType(Me.MdiParent, GolfStat)
    SetupTree()

  End Sub

#Region "Setup"

  Private Sub Init()
    BackColor = Color.LightGreen
    cmdClose.BackColor = Color.SandyBrown
    cmdClose.Text = "&Close"
    cmdClose.TabIndex = 0
    AddHandler cmdClose.Click, New EventHandler(AddressOf CloseMe)
    imgIcons.Images.Add(Image.FromFile("flag.ico"))
  End Sub
```

```vbnet
    Private Sub SetupTree()
      Dim CourseNode As TreeNode
      Dim CardNode As TreeNode

      tvwCourse.Nodes.Clear()
      tvwCourse.BeginUpdate()

      tvwCourse.ImageList = imgIcons
      tvwCourse.ImageIndex = 0
      tvwCourse.SelectedImageIndex = 0
      Dim c As ICourseInfo
      For Each c In mParent.db.GolfCourses
        CourseNode = tvwCourse.Nodes.Add(c.Name)
        CourseNode.Tag = c
        Dim card As IScoreCardInfo
        For Each card In c.ScoreCards
          CardNode = CourseNode.Nodes.Add(card.PlayDate.ToShortDateString())
          CardNode.Tag = card
        Next
      Next

      AddHandler tvwCourse.AfterSelect, _
                          New TreeViewEventHandler(AddressOf CourseStats)
      tvwCourse.EndUpdate()
    End Sub


#End Region

#Region "events"

    Public Sub CloseMe(ByVal s As Object, ByVal e As EventArgs)
      Close()
    End Sub

    Private Sub CourseStats(ByVal s As Object, ByVal e As TreeViewEventArgs)
      Dim FairwaysHit As Single = 0
      Dim GreensInReg As Single = 0
      Dim Putting As Single = 0
      Dim MaxPutts As Single = 0
      Dim MinPutts As Single = 99
      Dim AvgPutts As Single = 0
```

```
If TypeOf (e.Node.Tag) Is IScoreCardInfo Then

  ThisCard = CType(e.Node.Tag, IScoreCardInfo)
  Dim h As IHoleDetailInfo
  For Each h In ThisCard.holes
    If h.HitFairway Then FairwaysHit += 1
    If h.GreenInReg Then GreensInReg += 1
    Putting += h.Putts
    If h.Putts > MaxPutts Then MaxPutts = h.Putts
    If h.Putts < MinPutts Then MinPutts = h.Putts
    AvgPutts += h.Putts
  Next
  FairwaysHit /= ThisCard.holes.Count
  Putting /= (ThisCard.holes.Count * 2)
  GreensInReg /= ThisCard.holes.Count
  AvgPutts /= ThisCard.holes.Count

  lblFairwaysHit.Text = (FairwaysHit * 100).ToString()
  lblGreens.Text = (GreensInReg * 100).ToString()
  lblPutting.Text = (Putting * 100).ToString()
  lblMaxPutts.Text = MaxPutts.ToString()
  lblAvgPutts.Text = AvgPutts.ToString()
  lblMinPutts.Text = MinPutts.ToString()

  'I will let you figure out the rest of the stats. :)

  End If
End Sub
#End Region
```

This code enumerates through each scorecard in each golf course and displays them as nodes in the tree. As the user clicks a scorecard node, I calculate some statistics and show them on the screen.

Here is the code snippet to fill the tree:

```
foreach(ICourseInfo c in mParent.db.GolfCourses)
{
  CourseNode = tvwCourse.Nodes.Add(c.Name);
  CourseNode.Tag = c;
  foreach(IScoreCardInfo card in c.ScoreCards)
  {
    CardNode = CourseNode.Nodes.Add(card.PlayDate.ToShortDateString());
    CardNode.Tag = card;
  }
}
```

You can see from this code that I use the node's Tag property to contain the actual object in question. As the user selects a node in the tree, I test the Tag object to see if it is an IScoreCardInfo object. If so, I gather some aggregate statistics for each hole played for that scorecard.

Summary

The intention of this chapter was to demonstrate one way a data entry project is put together. You saw how to make your own collections and fill them from any kind of data storage. I showed you how to present data in several different forms, depending on what you want the user to do.

Included in this project are aspects from most of the chapters in this book. Data entry is apparent in the forms and their flow. Data validation is shown in the KeyPress and Validation event delegates.

Although the Golf project is by no means a complete project, it is complete enough to show you how everything in this book ties together.

Application Blocks

I HAVE A QUESTION for you: What are the two most common things you program into every project you make? My guess is data access and error handling. It also seems as if you need to rewrite or tweak your past data access modules every time you start a new project. The same thing seems to happen with error handling code. Whatever you had before never seems to fit quite right.

You and I are not the only ones with this problem. Some bright engineers at Microsoft (along with extensive outside help) have invented some additions to your code library. They are called the *Application Blocks for .NET*. As of the publication date of this book there are two of them:

- Data Access Application Block

- Exception Management Application Block

I have included both of these in projects, and believe me, they save quite a bit of work.

Although I covered database access in a minor way in this book, I do not intend to go over the Data Access Application Block in any detail. I do, however, cover the Exception Management Application Block enough so you can download it and use it right away. In this chapter, I show you a teaser. Both Application Blocks are fully documented and include sample code.

Finding the Application Blocks

You will find the setup files on the MSDN Web site. Follow this link to get to the download section of the site: `http://msdn.microsoft.com/library/default.asp?url=/library/en-us/dnbda/html/emab-rm.asp`.

These .msi files are each under 1MB. It takes a short time to download them. Follow these steps to install the Exception Management Application Block:

1. Double-click the .msi install file to start the installation process.

2. Choose the directory for the new folder where all the new code will reside.

3. Once the code finishes installing, click the Start button and check the Programs menu for the "Microsoft Application Blocks for .NET\Exception Management" choice.

One nice thing to note is that not only do you get sample source code for using these classes, but you also get the source code for the classes. If you want to see really well-thought-out code from a team of excellent programmers, I suggest you study the source code for both the Exception Management and Data Access classes.

Once you have downloaded and installed the classes, you need to bring up the C# or VB projects to make the necessary DLLs.

Making the Necessary DLLs for Exception Management

You need to make two DLLs to use in all your future projects. First off, follow the links in your Start menu to the Exception Management Application Block project. Figure A-1 shows the C# project as loaded in my IDE.

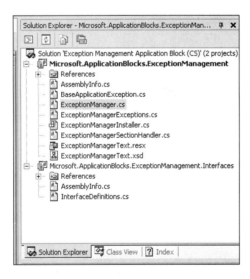

Figure A-1. The Exception Management Application Block project

As you can see here, this solution consists of two projects. One takes care of all the code behind the scenes and the other exposes the interfaces that you write to. You need to build both of these projects. They will end up as DLLs that you reference in your data validation projects.

Using the Exception Management Block

Now you have a couple of new DLLs. If you are paying attention and looking through the code, you will notice that you have a new user control called "exceptionManagementEventLogInstaller."

This set of classes provides a great deal of functionality for just a single line of code on your part. For instance, if you publish an error you will get the following information written to your log file:

- The computer name where the exception was created. This is great for client/server applications.

- The date and time when the exception occurred.

- Information on the thread where the exception was created.

- The application domain name where the exception occurred. This is helpful when you have several applications writing to the same log file, such as the Windows event log.

The following are several benefits to using this set of classes:

- You can publish exceptions with just one line of code in your Catch block.

- It gives you a consistent interface for handling errors.

- It lets you easily add new exception publishers.

- It lets you add publishers without changing your code. These new publishers can reside in a separate component.

- It gives you a way to easily redirect exceptions to different publishers via XML configuration files.

In their basic configuration, the exception classes publish errors in the Windows event log. I covered the event log back in Chapter 7. Of course, you can create your own publishers and redirect error-capturing text to any output you like.

As I mentioned in Chapter 7, it is best if you do not clog up the Windows event log file with all kinds of stuff. Besides this being wasteful, it makes it difficult to distinguish your log entries from entries of any other program running on your computer. You are better off defining your own publisher. The help file shows you how to do this easily enough. After reading this book, you certainly have enough knowledge to do so without too much trouble.

So, once you have included references to the new DLLs you created, you need just one line of code to set the exception ball rolling. Here it is—don't blink.

C#

```
catch(Exception e)
{
  ExceptionManager.Publish(e);
}
```

VB

```
Catch ex as Exception
  ExceptionManager.Publish(e);
```

That's it. Where it goes is defined by values in your *<application name>*.exe.config file. What gets published is defined by the default publisher or by you if you create a new publisher.

By the way, in keeping with the spirit of XML, you're able to publish exceptions in XML format as well. Pretty cool, isn't it?

The Ultimate Error Handler

How could you use this code to make your development life easier? Here is one idea: Develop a publisher for testing purposes.

It is not a stretch to include some custom information that can be sent to your publisher. Such useful information could be the class name, the method name, and the identifier for the code block where the error occurred. If you could gather this information, your publisher could e-mail you when the tester's machine crashed with all the relevant information to fix the problem in a hurry. You know how a tester can make software crash when it works fine on your machine. Now there would be no excuses or rejected bug reports because "it works on my machine."

This code and the other Application Blocks are free. The code is robust, well thought out, and consistent. It is also well documented. Using this and the Data Access Application Block will save you a great deal of time and headaches on all your projects.

Index

Symbols

A

B

C